AF674984

# ENCYCLOPEDIA OF INDIAN PHILOSOPHIES

ENCYCLOPEDIA OF INDIAN PHILOSOPHIES
General Editor: Karl H. Potter

VOLUMES ALREADY PUBLISHED

I. **Bibliography [Sections I and II] (1995)**—Ed. *Karl H. Potter*

II. **Indian Metaphysics and Epistemology**: The Tradition of Nyāya Vaiśeṣika up to Gaṅgeśa (1977)—Ed. *Karl H. Potter*

III. **Advaita Vedānta up to Śaṁkara and His Pupils (1981)** —Ed. *Karl H. Potter*

IV. **Sāṁkhya:** A Dualist Tradition in Indian Philosophy (1987) —Eds. *Gerald James Larson & Ram Shankar Bhattacharyya*

V. **The Philosophy of the Grammarians (1990)**—Eds. *H.G. Coward & K. Kunjunni Raja*

VI. **Indian Philosophical Analysis:** Nyāya-Vaiśeṣika from Gaṅgeśa to Raghunātha Śiromaṇi (1993)—Eds. *Karl H. Potter & Sibjiban Bhattacharyya*

VII. **Abhidharma Buddhism with to 150 A.D. (1996)**—Eds. *Karl H. Potter*, with *Robert E. Buswell Jr., Padmanabh S. Jaini & Noble Ross Reat*

VIII. **Buddhist Philosophy from 100 to 350 A.D. (1999)** —Ed. *Karl H. Potter*

IX. **Buddhist Philosophy from 350 to 600 A.D. (2003)** —Ed. *Karl H. Potter*

X. **Jain Philosophy [Part I] (2007)**—Eds. *Dalsukh Malvania & Jayendra Soni*

XI. **Advaita Vedānta from 800 to 1200 A.D. (2006)**—Ed. *Karl H. Potter*

XII. **Yoga: India's Philosophy of Meditation (2008)**—Eds. *Gerald J. Larson & Rama Shankar Bhattacharyya*

XIII. **Nyāya-Vaiśeṣika Philosophy from 1515 to 1660 A.D. (2010)** —Eds. *Sibjiban Bhattacharyya & Karl H. Potter*

XIV. **Jain Philosophy [Part II]**—Eds. *Karl H. Potter & Piotr Balcerowicz*

XV. **Bhedabheda and Dvaitādvaita Philosophy**—Eds. *M.M. Agrawal & Karl H. Potter*

VOLUMES UNDER PREPARATION

**Buddhist Philosophy from 600 to 750 A.D.**—Ed. *Eli Franco*

**Buddhist Philosophy from 750 to 1300 A.D.**—Ed. *Karl H. Potter*

**Kaśmīr Śaiva Philosophy**—Ed. *Navjivan Rastogi*

**Viśiṣṭādvaita Vedānta Philosophy**–Eds. *Stephen H. Phillips & M. Narasimhachary*

**Advaita Vedānta from 1200 A.D. to the present**—Ed. *Godavarisa Misra*

**Pūrvamīmāṁsā Philosophy**—Eds. *K.T. Pandurangi & Karl H. Potter*

**Acintyabhedābheda Philosophy**—Ed. *Srivatsa Goswami*

**Dvaita Vedānta Philosophy**—Ed. *Sarothaman*

**Cārvāka Philosophy**—Ed. *Eli Franco*

**Śuddhādvaita Vedānta Philosophy**—Eds. *Sharad Aniruddha Goswami & Shyam Manoharaji Goswami*

**Vīraśaiva Philosophy**—Eds. *N.G. Mahadevappa*

**Collective Glossary-Index**—Ed. *Karl H. Potter*

# ENCYCLOPEDIA OF INDIAN PHILOSOPHIES

## VOLUME VIII

### Buddhist Philosophy from 100 to 350 A.D.

EDITED BY
KARL H. POTTER

MOTILAL BANARSIDASS PUBLISHERS
PRIVATE LIMITED • DELHI

*2nd Reprint: Delhi, 2011*
*First Edition: Delhi, 1999*

© MOTILAL BANARSIDASS PUBLISHERS PRIVATE LIMITED
All Rights Reserved

ISBN: 978-81-208-1553-7

MOTILAL BANARSIDASS
41 U.A. Bungalow Road, Jawahar Nagar, Delhi 110 007
8 Mahalaxmi Chamber, 22 Bhulabhai Desai Road, Mumbai 400 026
203 Royapettah High Road, Mylapore, Chennai 600 004
236, 9th Main III Block, Jayanagar, Bangalore 560 011
Sanas Plaza, 1302 Baji Rao Road, Pune 411 002
8 Camac Street, Kolkata 700 017
Ashok Rajpath, Patna 800 004
Chowk, Varanasi 221 001

*Printed in India*

By Jainendra Prakash Jain at Shri Jainendra Press,
A-45 Naraina, Phase-I, New Delhi 110 028
and Published by Narendra Prakash Jain for
Motilal Banarsidass Publishers Private Limited,
Bungalow Road, Delhi 110 007

Contributors:

Stefan Anacker
Kamaleshwar Bhattacharya
Bhadanta Santi Bhiksu
Robert Buswell, Jr.
Edward Conze
Collett Cox
Peter Della Santina
Bart Dessein
Nalinaksha Dutt
Paul Griffiths
Paul Harrison
Megumu Honda
Charles W. Huntington, Jr.
Leslie S. Kawamura
John P. Keenan
Jan Hendrik Kern
Karen Lang
Christian Lindtner
Rajendralal Mitra
Robert F. Olson
Paul Pelliot
Karl H. Potter
Constantin Regamey
David Seyfort Ruegg
N. H. Samtani
Lambert Schmithausen
Nancy Schuster
George Teschner
K. Timura
A. K. Warder
Alex Wayman
Hideko Wayman

# CONTENTS

# PREFACE

The following Volume constitutes the second in a series devoted to Buddhist philosophy. It takes up more or less where its predecessor, Volume Seven of this Encyclopedia, leaves off, around the beginning of the second century A.D. This is a period still not well understood, with a good deal of scholarly disagreement remaining about many aspects of the history and thought of the period. As merely one example, it remains a debated point whether there were one or two Vasubandhus, with respected scholars taking both sides of the issue. The Editor of the present Volume makes no claim to expertise on such issues. Where reputable scholars disagree it is difficult to know which way to turn when attempting to summarize the history and beliefs of the period. We have tried to utilize the most up-to-date scholarship known to us at the time of writing, with full realization that tomorrow new evidence or better arguments may settle such issues definitively in the minds of scholars. When this happens, the treatment here will evidently become out of date. Since given the plan of the entire Encyclopedia we are more or less committed to presenting as consistent an account as possible of the history of Indian philosophical thought, citing experts known to us on points that seem debatable.

It will be evident to the reader of what follows that there remains a good deal to be done in bringing to light the thought of the Buddhists of the present period. A large number of texts are essentially unexplored by scholars in the Western world, at least. The Editor of the present Volume, being unable to read the languages of much excellent scholarship--Chinese, Japanese and Russian, e.g.-- and whose facility in European languages is halting, has been forced to rely on publications in English for the most part, although he has tried to become acquainted with some of the material available in French and German. Furthermore, he is not conversant with Tibetan, the language in which quite a bit of Buddhist literature is primarily and in some cases solely available. Fortunately others have conveyed to the English-reading public some of the most important findings of those writing in other languages. Nevertheless, these failings underline the point that our attempt here to deal with the scholarship on Indian philosophy has serious limitations, and that improvements on it by those whose linguistic abilities are greater, or who number more than the single person who has tried to put the present account together, are clearly called for.

Thanks are due to various sources of funding that helped make the present volume possible: in particular, grants from the Smithsonian Institution, the American Institute of Indian Studies, and the National Endowment for the Humanities contributed to the overall effort. We owe our gratitude to those scholars, living and dead, whose understanding of the contents of the works summarized here is utilized. In particular, I wish to thank Stefan Anacker and Christian Lindtner for their generous assistance and for helpful comments on sections of the manuscript, though they are in no way responsible for the mistakes that have inevitably crept into the results.

May 1997 KARL H. POTTER

# PART ONE

## INTRODUCTION

# 1

# INTRODUCTION

1.*The First Truth: Everything is Frustrating.* Here we are, in a world with others--people, animals, demons and deities. We eat, sleep, dream, work, play, laugh, cry, calculate, argue. If you are an Indian in the middle of the second century A.D., you probably grew up accepting the fundamental beliefs of your parents and teachers--that what we are and what we do is, at least in part, the result of who we were and what we did before this, in our present lifetime and an indefinite number of previous lives. Each life, whatever fleeting joys it may provide, is on balance frustrating. Life is frustrating because one is ever in danger of, if not actually experiencing, unhappiness, sorrow, torment and pain; life is frustrating because it is, to a greater or less degree, brutish and short. And the sources of this frustration, unhappiness and pain are in large part of our own making. It is our own deeds that breed the karmic traces which, stored up and activated later--perhaps much later--determine our place in the hierarchy of being and the frustrations we constantly experience there. If you are a Buddhist in the middle of the second century A.D. you are aware that your inherited faith purports to provide you with insights which promise to help you alleviate this frustrating existence. The Buddha taught many inspiring messages, notable among which are the four noble truths, the middle way, the twelve-fold chain of origination, the questions which tend not to edification, the basic beliefs in the transitoriness of all things and the lack of an essential self-nature. Gautama himself, after meditating at length and resisting any susceptibility to distraction and backsliding, awoke to his *nirvāṇa,* after which he spent several decades winning converts to pass along his insights and addressing the general public as well. If there is anyone to whom you may look for guidance, surely it is this Buddha. Yet, as we have seen and as is possibly inevitable, even the Tathāgata's teachings, no matter how clear and inspiring, are not entirely resistant to misinterpretation. Possibly within Gautama's own lifetime, certainly soon after, his followers came to disagree about the specifics, even possibly the substance, of his teachings. Sectarian splits haunted the several councils of elders that were held during the first few centuries after the Buddha's *parinirvāṇa*. From these splits arose in due course myriad Buddhist sects. Several times during the five or more centuries between the time of the Buddha and the second century A.D. meetings were convened at which attempts were made to canonize Buddhist philosophy. The *Mahāvibhāṣā* was the most recent of these attempts (summarized in Volume VII of this *Encyclopedia*) and it is from the time that mammoth text was generated that the period covered in the present volume begins.

Despite the proliferation of sects through the South Asian subcontinent there was apparently general agreement among Buddhists of the second century on the karmic account, together with belief in the Buddha's wisdom, insight and liberation. The Buddha's words hold promise of a way of assessing the human predicament, a way that recognized the seriousness of that predicament while providing the possibility of a way to escape it, as the Buddha himself had done. The human predicament--indeed, the predicament of all beings from the highest gods to the foulest denizens of hell--was this: that each being, having performed actions without beginning, carried residues laid down by past acts, residues which determined subsequent experiences and thus conditioned present and future actions. As long as we remain ignorant of and misunderstand our karmic situation we have no hope of being able to bring an end to the frustrations of the actions that karmic residues influence. And precisely this was the message Gautama delivered in his first sermon: that everything is frustrating.

II.*The Second Truth: Frustration Has a Cause*. The Buddha's second noble truth was that the situation of beings, so described, is itself causally conditioned. If it were not so, there would be no hope of gaining release from the karmic cycle through any activity of ours. If *saṃsāra*--the cycle of rebirths--were not causally regulated, there really *would* be no hope of eliminating karma, no way of assuring that the frustrations bred by action would ever cease. This second truth, then, begins the Buddha's message of relief, of hope. Since our bondage has a cause, there is at least the possibility that the cause (or causes) of bondage can be controlled and eventually eliminated.

But let's get down to specifics. What precisely is it that constitutes the conditions of our bondage? The Buddha is taken as pointing his finger at *two* fundamental sources of frustration: (1) the inexorable production of karmic residues by actions, and (2) our ignorance, wrong views about the actual nature of things. Just what is the proper way of seeing the relation between (1) and (2), and what does that insight tell us to do to bring about the elimination of frustration?

Ignorance is wrong views. What causes wrong views? If the answer is merely that the causes of wrong views are our past actions, our karma, this appears to land us in a circle. Karma--our actions--produce ignorance, and that ignorance is itself the cause of, determines those future acts we will engage in, our karma. That way of putting the puzzle provides no way out of bondage unless we can find something *else* on which both ignorance and action depend. The Buddha did not speak of any single root cause, yet he tells us that there is a cause of frustration and bondage, a cause that can be removed or neutralized, rendered unproductive. It would seem, then, that the supposition that ignorance and karma reciprocally and independently produce each other will lead us soon into precisely that despair the Buddha's message was intended to alleviate.

Let's take a different approach. What is an "action"? Arguably, it is something one *does*, not just anything that happens to one. It is a peculiarity of Sanskrit etymology that the root *kṛ*, from which the word "*karman*" is derived, functions to mean both what we mean in English by "to do" and "to make". Thus "*karman*" refers, and properly so, *both* to what is *done*--our actions--and what is *made*, i.e., produced by those actions--the residues that condition future doings. But what *is* done? Indian philosophy regularly counts three kinds of deeds: bodily, vocal and mental. Karma, then, can be understood both as our bodily, vocal and mental acts and what those acts make--i.e., the traces they lay down.

But is *everything* we make by our bodily, vocal and mental doings karma? It seems not. A well-known statement in the *Yogasūtras* tells us that there are three kinds of karmic results--that is, three aspects of life that are causally conditioned by karmic traces. These are (1) the kind of birth one has--whether in hell, as ghost, as animal, as human or as a god; (2) one's destined length of life in that birth; and (3) the kinds of experiences one has while living out that life--broadly, that the karma produced by good deeds causes satisfying experiences while the karma produced by bad deeds causes frustrating, dissatisfying, or just plain painful experiences.

This leads to the crux of the matter. Just what is it that causes us to do these kinds of things? Or even better, under what conditions does one *act* at all, that is, do something that makes karma? Behavior may or may not be intentional. If someone hits me and I reel from the blow my behavior is unintentional--it is not an action, though it is a movement. If I hit someone (and am not constrained to do so by forces beyond my control) I am acting--my behavior is intentional.

"Intention" is a difficult concept, open to alternative interpretations (which is very possibly why the decision as to whether a given bit of behavior is an act or not is not always easy to answer). But it is fairly clear that when we class a behavior as intentional we impute to its perpetrator at least an awareness of what he/she is trying to do, normally a decision to exercise or withhold one's bodily, vocal or mental powers to some purpose or other. If such intentionality is absent we are inclined to exonerate the doer from blame for the results of what transpires. We are even inclined to say that he/she didn't do it at all; it just happened.

If, then, actions proper are intentional doings, and it is actions proper that produce karmic traces, then it would appear that one way to escape karmic bondage would be to stop acting by stopping awareness altogether. And at first blush that seems quite feasible--one just commits suicide. But it's not that simple, given the pan-Indian assumption about karma causing rebirth. Suicide, on karmic assumptions, is just another act--a bad act, indeed, as it involves willful killing. One needs to find a way to stop acting that not only stops the actions of this life but also doesn't engender its own karmic residues and so avoids rebirth and all future action.

There are other reasons why one can't just stop acting. Remember that "action" includes mental acts as well as bodily and vocal ones. What is a mental act? If, for example, any seeing or hearing constitutes a mental act, one would seem to have to be blind and deaf to stop. And not only the senses--thinking itself is a mental action, so wouldn't one have to stop thinking too?

One can't just stop acting, then. It would seem that what is needed is not to stop action altogether, but to stop just those kinds of actions that breed bondage, those involving intentionality, the desire to gain or avoid things. Such desires and aversions, the Buddha taught, are bred by wrong views, views that lead us to act and without the having of which we wouldn't be acting at all. If the cause of bondage is ignorance, wrong views, the problem now is--which views are the wrong ones, the ones engendering desires and aversions? These, at least, must be stamped out and replaced by right views.

The Buddha himself identified a number of wrong views. For a start there are the views that are eradicated by the Buddhist understanding of the fundamental doctrines (1) that all is frustrating, (2) that everything is momentary, fleeting, (3) that there is no self. In the same basic vein is avoidance of the two extremes between which the Middle Way preached by Gautama led: eternalism and nihilism. Early texts (see Volume VII) provide myriad other lists and views.[1]

The diversity of Abhidharma systems can be seen as generated from differences in emphasis as to which views are the wrong ones. The doctrinal divisions among the sects that developed in Buddhist philosophy starting from the first schism invariably turned on differences in what sort of emphasis to place in classifying views. The *Kathāvatthu* gives an exhaustive review of the different views espoused in Buddhism of a fairly early period. These differences were extrapolated many times over in the succeeding centuries, and the record of who believed what provides the most confusing aspect of the records that survive from that period. Suffice it to say that on just about any point Buddhist philosophers provide divergent opinions amongst themselves. Even on the fundamental planks (a few of which were mentioned in the previous paragraph) there was no general agreement. For example, the Buddha taught that everything was noneternal (*anitya*): this was interpreted by some schools to mean that all factors are strictly momentary, by others that they last a few moments only, by still others that most, but not necessarily all, factors are evanescent, and even by some that factors are eternal, only their occurrences being momentary. Again, schools were constantly criticizing each other over the extent to which they hewed to the line of no-self (*anātman*)--some spoke of "persons" (*pudgala*), others of a "store-consciousness" (*ālayavijñāna*), both of which views were castigated by opponents as contradicting the basic

Buddhist standpoint by admitting a persisting self under an easily-identified subterfuge.

Given this diversity of opinions on the fundamental theses of the Buddha it was apparently going to be difficult to say just which views are the wrong ones. Abhidharma adepts fought the battle in just these trenches, attempting to identify and refute wrong views where they found them and for reasons relevant to each case in point. An important exception is found in the position taken by Nāgārjuna, who must have lived around the time of the *Mahāvibhāṣā*.

Nāgārjuna's position was neat and tidy. As he sees it *any* and *all* opinions constitute wrong views! After all, he suggests, a view implicitly or explicitly ascribes an essential, independent nature to something, whereas the truth is that nothing has an independent nature, that everything is "empty" (*śūnya*), by which the Buddha meant that everything is dependently originated, causally conditioned. Nāgārjuna therefore applies a negatively dialectical method to each and every kind of category propounded by Abhidharmists, showing that each one is empty in that precise sense. The argument is altogether general: it even applies against the very idea of the Buddha's liberation! It applies, that is, against any idea whatsoever. Everything is empty.

A position of Nāgārjuna's sort might have been expected to constitute the culmination--and perhaps the elimination--of Buddhism as a viable philosophy, since its negative message might seem to undermine any eagerness to pursue the Buddhist path. Madhyamakas do not accept this implication, though it remained for philosophers/commentators after our period to fully defend Nāgārjuna's position.

In the period we're reviewing in this Volume, a third alternative (to Abhidharma and Madhyamaka) was developed explicitly in the fourth century at the hands of Asaṅga and Vasubandhu. On this third account there is only one *basic* wrong view, and that derives from our natural but mistaken temptation to assume an external reality independent of our mental ideas and impressions. It is common-sense realism which generates all mistaken ideas about persisting things and persisting selves cognizing those persisting things. For the Yogācāra (or Vijñānavādin, as a member of this third school is alternatively called) the only existent entities are the momentary flashes of awareness that constitute the streams of experience we confusedly refer to as "you" or "I". The Yogācāra traces all the wrong views identified in the Buddha's teachings to this basic wrong view.

III.*The Third Truth: The Cause(s) of Frustration Can Be Removed.* The Buddha's third noble truth states that, since at least one of the necessary causal conditions which bring about bondage can be rendered inoperative, there must exist a sufficient condition for the annulment of bondage, i.e., for the attainment of liberation. Just what constitutes that sufficient condition depends, of course, on what is identified as the necessary causal condition(s) that can be rendered inoperative. In the previous section on the cause(s) of bondage we saw that different Buddhists, followed by their different schools, identify ignorance about various things as the conditions. Depending on what those conditions were thought to be there were different accounts of how one eliminates bondage and gains liberation.

The various Abhidharma schools taught that through a thorough understanding of which factors (*dharma*) constitute the universe one would by the same token understand which ideas constitute right view. Having gained such clarity of understanding (the path of vision) one still must internalize it through meditative practice (the path of cultivation), or perhaps one meditates first in order to gain that understanding. Meditation serves to train one to eschew all temptations to think, speak and act in ways that stem from wrong views.

The perfection of meditation does not often happen suddenly or even in forty days, as it did for the Buddha. It takes several lifetimes. Different texts report somewhat divergent accounts of the number of lives it takes one who has "entered the stream" to liberation to gain the final life of a perfected being, a Buddha. Perhaps the most common account distinguishes stream-enterers, those with only seven lives to live, those with only one more life to live, and the perfected nonreturners.

The 172.*Abhisamayālaṃkāra*, a work attributed to Asaṅga but showing little leaning toward specifically Yogācāra or Madhyamaka tenets, gives us a good account of the eight perfections of wisdom (*prajñāpāramitā*). These are not stages in a progression, but rather a bringing together under one rubric of what are presumably the most important notions involved in spelling out the path to liberation. All of these notions are drawn from Abhidharma traditions testified to in the literature, although the doctrine of the three bodies of a Buddha--the *dharmakāya* or physical body endowed with auspicious marks, the *sambhogakāya* or body of enjoyments, and the magical body (*nirmāṇakāya*) of a Bodhisattva--reflects the encroachment of specifically Mahāyāna emphases supposed to be enshrined in Prajñāpāramitā works.

The Abhidharma approach to removing ignorance stresses the step-wise treatment of many factors in many ways. Nāgārjuna's Madhyamaka, on the other hand, treats one thing in just one way, a dialectically-based rejection of belief in the actuality of anything. To be sure, this rejection, which takes place on the mundane or language-based plane (since distinctions can only apply there), is accomplished in full realization that empirical doings require such worldly distinctions. On the empirical level the world can be accepted as it is found to be, so that Abhidharma-like advice on how to improve oneself in the empirical world is by no means deprived of scope. As Nāgārjuna points out at the beginning of his rebuttal in the 34.*Vigrahavyāvarttanī*, it doesn't follow that because something is dependent on other things it cannot function. Indeed our experience attests quite the reverse: it is precisely things born of causes and conditions that themselves occasion their own particular results. It would seem to follow that the way to escape bondage is not to dig up more causes and conditions for old or new factors, but rather to desist from digging, to stop thinking in terms of causes and conditions.

The Yogācāra method in a sense combines the approach of Abhidharma and Madhyamaka. It uses the negatively dialectical approach to refute all claims of and beliefs in externally real objects. What remains is the stream of consciousness itself. What can be positively clarified is a perspicuous account of the flux of awarenesses, the different categories of mentality and their relationships. Distinguishing the different levels of mentality--e.g., the level of ordinary or constructed awarenesses, the level of causally dependent awarenesses that constitute the stream of consciousness itself, the level of perfected construction-free awareness meditationally achieved--is one way of classifying awarenesses. It is not the only one. Another angle is to distinguish

awarenesses. It is not the only one. Another angle is to distinguish three levels of (1) consciousness *per se*--the abode-consciousness (*ālayavijñāna*), in which the karmic seeds are stored, (2) the mental level, in which the stream constituting the abode-consciousness evolves into e.g. discriminations of mine vs. other's due to the defilements karmically conditioned, and (3) the full discrimination of objects sensorily apprehended as desirable or undesirable, good or bad, black or white, etc. When the dialectical critique of distinctions, which is equally the critique of identifications, is meditationally accomplished, all that is left is the stream of undifferentiated awareness, the abode-consciousness without any defilements to nurture the seeds, which are thus as if burnt and no longer potent. Once the life of such an enlightened Buddha ends there is nothing to cause any rearising of classifications or discriminations in that stream. This is liberation.

IV.*The Fourth Truth: The Path to Liberation.* The Buddha spelled out the way in terms of eight categories: right view, right conceptualizing, right speaking, right action, right living, right effort, right mindfulness and right concentration. And indeed these are the things that are treated at length in Buddhist texts; they continue to constitute the largest part of the Buddhist corpus in the period here under scrutiny. This introductory Chapter has taken its point of departure from the topic of "view," and we have seen that there are different conceptions of, or at least different emphases on, what constitutes right view. A similar treatment could be undertaken with respect to each of the other seven categories. The last five--action, living, effort, mindfulness, concentration--relate to the specifics of the path to be followed. Right conceptualizing and (understood in at least one way) right speaking pertain to more theoretical aspects of Buddhist thought, and it is with these that we shall be having the most to do in the remainder of this Introduction.

## NĀGĀRJUNA AND ĀRYADEVA

Nāgārjuna repudiated all views. We do not know exactly how he arrived at the list of views that needed repudiation, the list he gives in his master work, the 33.*Madhyamakakārikās*. His pupil Āryadeva wrote three works in which views are likewise catalogued and criticized. If we examine these four works we can get a pretty good idea which views were conceived to need rejection, and from this come to an improved understanding of what views Nāgārjuna and Āryadeva found to be particularly important to criticize.

The views that Nāgārjuna and Āryadeva discuss cover the entire spectrum of Buddhist thought, the entire Abhidharmic position as it was being propounded in the second-third century A.D. The Abhidharma systems took what the Buddha said entirely literally. Among the major lessons they assumed that the Buddha taught were the following:

(1) There are no persisting entities. What exist are factors (*dharma*), evanescent flashes of energy, which last only for a moment. Nothing persists, so nothing moves, nothing acts.

(2) So causality has to be understood as a relation among momentary factors. When we say A causes B what is really the case is that a momentary flash of a type we call A is followed by a flash of a type we call B, where we have experienced flashes of type A regularly accompanied or followed by those of type B.

(3) Our common sense beliefs in the existence of tables and chairs, bodies, organs and objects have to be rethought to accord with (1) and (2).

(4) In particular my natural belief that I am a persistent seat of consciousness, that there is an essentially identical self that underlies my fleeting varied experiences, has to be abandoned.

(5) It is belief in persisting entities, especially one's self, that breeds the karmic traces that occasion subsequent rebirths and frustrations. Even satisfactions--such as pleasant experiences--are karmically conditioned. As long as we operate under such beliefs our actions--mental as well as bodily and vocal--will lay down karmic traces that are subsequently worked off in the course of later actions.

(6) The factors that actually constitute our streams can be either defiled or pure. They are defiled as long as they result from actions performed under misguided beliefs in selves, persistence, objects. Purified factors occur when realization has taken place, the stream of factors no longer breeding karmic residues that require further lives to work them off.

(7) Purification is likely to be gradual. The series of truths that constitute (1)-(6) above dawns on one slowly, and full

understanding and appreciation of them requires serious meditative practice. When one meditates one gains the ability to internalize right views in a nondiscursive manner, so that one learns not to be the victim of conceptual categories of the sort that pervade ordinary discourse and thought.

(8) When one has corrected all wrong views and has internalized insight through meditation one becomes a perfected being. Without karmic traces, purified and liberated, such a Buddha teaches by his very example until "his body" drops off of natural causes, i.e., his stream ceases. This is Gautama's final liberation, a goal available to all beings though difficult to attain.

The views that are summarized in (1)-(8) above appear to be what Gautama the Buddha taught, and it is essentially those views that continue to be taught by Abhidharma schools. Yet it appears that Nāgārjuna, at the very beginning of our present period, produced a systematic critique of *all* views, specifically including the eight just outlined! Nagarjuna has become a celebrated Buddhist, classified as a skeptic by some, a nihilist by others, an absolutist by still others,[2] yet counted as one of the great Buddhists, perhaps second only to the Buddha himself in rank among Buddhist philosophers. Scholars have found this assessment puzzling, and a vast amount of scholarship has been directed his way. If he was such a skeptic, nihilist or absolutist, why isn't he seen by Buddhists as an enemy rather than a defender of the Buddha's teachings?

What Nāgārjuna is criticizing is the Abhidharmists' failure to carry the Buddha's logic through to conclusion. The Buddha himself often criticized views through a fourfold negation: as he might have put it, "I do not say that that view is true, I don't say it's false, I don't say it's both, and I don't say it's neither." Nāgārjuna simply applies this logic to what are taken to be Buddhist tenets. We have just identified a number of them, and these are among the most important Abhidharmic theses that Nāgārjuna and Āryadeva criticize.

The first thesis in our list is the thesis of momentariness. The Buddha taught that nothing persists for more than a moment. Thus "factors" are actually momentary flashes--but flashes of what? The Sarvāstivādins appear to have taught that that which flashes in the present is what might be called a "permanent possibility of sensation", so that in a sense a factor is a persistent, indeed eternal entity, like each of the pickets in a fence lit up by a motorcar's headlights passing by. Such a view might seem completely contrary to the Buddha's intent in teaching momentariness, but that leaves unanswered the question of what the flashes are flashes *of*.

Nāgārjuna's insight is that factors are not flashes of anything. To suppose that there is something that flashes is to return to precisely the viewpoint, so Nāgārjuna claims, that the Buddha was trying to avoid. When the Buddha taught that there are no eternal things he didn't mean to say that there are noneternal things. "Everything is noneternal" misses the point as much as "everything is eternal." In truth nothing originates at all, so the question whether things that arise are really eternal, momentary, both or neither can't properly be posed.

Since nothing is actually caused there are actually no causes at all. And since there are no causes there are no effects either. It's not just that though there aren't any tables or chairs there are factors constituting a stream we call "table" or "chair". There are no such factors. In particular, the same argument applies to oneself. It's not that though there is no self there is a stream of mental factors we call our "self". There is no such stream either.

One's beliefs in persisting things, especially in one's self, appear to breed karmic traces that have to be worked off later, but since nothing can actually be "bred" that appearance of traces cannot ultimately be defended. By the same token no factors can be defiled, and none pure, since nothing can cause them to be so. The whole gradual path to purification and enlightenment, postulated by Abhidharma Buddhists, must be only an appearance; nothing of the sort can actually be caused to happen.

So all views are wrong. In particular, the view that we are now bound and can be freed, that the Buddha was bound who is now freed, is a mistake. No one is bound, no one is liberated, no one frustrated, no one satisfied. It is not even that one is in some third state--a combination, say, or something else entirely. The whole set of categories--cause and effect, motion and rest, action and inaction, bondage and liberation, real and unreal, identity and difference, pure and defiled, self and other, frustration and satisfaction--the entire collection is empty, without actuality.

It is tempting to misconstrue Nāgārjuna as a nihilist. If all views are wrong Nāgārjuna's view itself must be wrong--or so it may be argued. In answer Nāgārjuna replies "I have no view!".[3] But if he has no view why should we heed what he says when he, for example, advises us to take heed of the Buddha's ethical advice? If liberation is empty, doesn't that undermine Buddhism?

One has to be quite clear what is being said when Nāgārjuna dubs all things "empty". "Empty" (*śūnya*) is a technical term for Nāgārjuna. When he calls something empty he is implying it doesn't really exist, but he is by no means suggesting that it doesn't seem to exist and that its functioning may well seem to occasion results such as misery and pain. After all, with misery and pain (with pleasure and satisfaction too) it is the seeming that is all important. For feelings seeming is being. So the fact that a thing is empty--that it is completely dependent on causes and conditions--doesn't at all render it nonfunctional. Indeed, functioning things are precisely those things that are involved in causal relations, that appear to arise when and only when certain kinds of other things appear to arise. Satisfaction and frustration seem to us to be effects of causes and conditions, and if that's what we want that's what we'll get. That both causes and effects are empty doesn't lessen the pain or pleasure we experience at their hand.

Someone who believes that everything is empty can thus perfectly well be one who counsels moral behavior. Whether Nāgārjuna did so is a question of which are his writings, not a matter of consistency. Even if one doubts that he wrote avowedly ethical works such as the letters of moral advice known as 38.*Ratnāvalī* and 40.*Suhṛllekha,* his surely authentic writings such as 34.*Vigrahavyāvarttanī* display a moral seriousness that should quash any reservations on that score.

Nāgārjuna's dialectic does not undermine Buddhist morality. But does it help it? What can we learn of a positive nature from Nāgārjuna's and Āryadeva's negative critique? Strangely enough, we can gain a renewed respect for the Buddha and his teaching by understanding what it is not. The Buddha in Nāgārjuna's eyes is seen not as a philosopher proposing arguments, not as a religionist propounding doctrines, not even as a spiritual advisor offering counsel. Instead the Buddha is someone who managed to expunge from his mentality all contentions, all views of how things really are, serving instead as a sounding-board from which we who are not yet uncontentious can hear how *we* sound as we contend. Nāgārjuna's Buddha does not teach views, but he helps save those who have them. That causes and effects are empty doesn't lessen the pain or pleasure we experience at their hand. But knowing them to be empty one no longer strains to gain or avoid them, nor to gain the pleasure nor avoid the pains that they seem to produce. The equanimity that the Buddha had and taught emanated from his knowledge of emptiness.

It will, I hope, be evident that nothing in Nāgārjuna's position undermines the account that Abhidharmists give of the path to liberation. That factors are unreal, dependently co-arising, doesn't lessen the necessity to purify them. And purification may well take time, since the truth of emptiness may well dawn on one gradually. That purification doesn't *really* cause liberation in no way lessens the need to purify, since the meditation one accomplishes in purifying constitutes or leads into nonconceptual insight, the abandonment of attachment to any views, and that *is* liberation. There is no difference, says Nāgārjuna, between *nirvāṇa* and *saṃsāra*, by which he means that no conceptualization of any such difference is correct, both of them being empty.

It is commonly believed that Nāgārjuna was a Mahāyānist.[4] There is not much evidence for that, however, and if the foregoing account of Nāgārjuna's teaching is correct the question of his affiliation with one or another school of Buddhism becomes moot. After all, if the method is to abandon all views it seems idle to worry about which views are correct. Rather, one concentrates on a method of abandoning views, a method Nāgārjuna found in dialectic.

Nāgārjuna's arguments appear to have been addressed exclusively against Abhidharma interpretations of the Buddha's teachings.[5] Āryadeva differs from his teacher by paying specific attention to other systems, notably Sāṃkhya and Vaiśeṣika. But the approach, indeed the list of topics criticized, is largely the same as Nāgārjuna's.

## THE PRAJÑĀPĀRAMITĀ AND THE RISE OF MAHĀYĀNA

By the middle of the second century A.D. a new type of text had begun to find its way around northern India (at least), and very shortly afterward it began being translated into Chinese and, later, into Tibetan. It became known eventually as the "Prajñāpāramitā" literature, and came to comprise the most popular and influential scriptures of Buddhism after the Buddha's words themselves.

Just who composed these texts and for what purpose initially is not entirely clear. Gregory Schopen, who has studied these materials in relation to inscriptional evidence pertaining to the period, has suggested that Buddhism may have constituted at the beginning of our period a group of disparate sects organized around a "cult of the book", i.e., around particular treatises, and spread unconnectedly around the subcontinent (or at least its northern portion). But Schopen notes that of "at least 159 separate image inscriptions from Mathurā that are dated in, or can be assigned to, the Kuṣān Period (78-280 A.D.) less than one third of the inscriptions are Buddhist",[6] which suggests that "Buddhism itself was there and then a minority movement".[7]

In another place Schopen addresses himself to the question how Mahāyāna Buddhism arose. Studying the idea, found in the *nikāyas*, of the memory of former births (*jātismara*), he notes that between the *nikāya* literature giving the Buddha's own words and the "medieval Mahāyāna *sūtra* literature...a distinct and fundamental shift has taken place".[8] "In the *Nikāya/Āgama* literature...*jātismara* usually occurs as only one item in at least three stereotyped lists--the *vidyās, abhijñās, balas* or, at least, in close association with one or more of the other items in these lists. Moreover, it was attributed almost exclusively to the religious virtuoso, and it appears to have been thought to have been attainable only by means of sophisticated form of meditational or yogic practice. In the Mahāyāna *sūtra* literature...the situation is different on all three counts. Here, *jātismara* has completely disassociated from the traditional lists of *abhijñās, balas,* etc., and occurs almost always as an independent item, without reference to its earlier associates. Moreover, these texts make it abundantly clear that, far from being restricted to the religious virtuoso, it is here within the reach of virtually everyone: monks, nuns, lay men and women--or simply men or women--*brāhmaṇas, kṣatriyas, vaiśyas, śūdras,* and those reborn in the hells or other unfortunate destinies. Perhaps the most significant shift, however, concerns the means by which *jātismara* was thought to be obtainable. First of all, it is clear from a number of texts that the authors or compilers of some Mahāyāna *sūtras* held that the obtainment of *jātismara* by the individual could be effected by agents external to him--by a Bodhisattva working for the sake of "maturing" beings (*Upāliparipṛcchā*), by other individuals undertaking specific ritual or merit-making activity on his behalf, etc. This, of course, marks a major transformation of the 'original' concept. But this is not all. Even in regard to the means by which the individual can obtain *jātismara* for himself there has been a clearly observable shift. Rather than by sophisticated meditational technique, the province in fact of the ascetic few, in Mahāyāna *sūtra* literature current in the medieval period *jātismara* was available by means of a variety of non-meditational activities: ritualized acts of worship, often directed towards sacred images; activity connected with sacred names--hearing, reciting, etc.; activity connected with sacred texts--reciting, copying, preserving, worshipping, etc.; and activity connected with *dhāraṇīs*--reciting, copying, preserving, and depositing in *stūpas*, etc."[9] In earlier sections of the same article Schopen gives details about these changes, and in the paragraph following the one just quoted he cites a number of other Buddhist ideas that underwent similar transformations, and suggests that it is these changes which should be thought of as heralding the appearance of Mahāyāna Buddhism.

If Schopen is right it will be a mistake to picture the appearance of Mahāyāna, as is commonly done, as a large-scale change of mind among Buddhists that coincides with the first Prajñāpāramitā *sūtras*. "That movement we now call 'the Mahāyāna'...was, and remained for several centuries, a very limited minority movement".[10] In fact, "the movement we now call 'the Mahāyāna' had not yet achieved complete independence even as late as the second quarter of the 5th century A.D."[11] "There was--as we know from Chinese translations--a large and early Mahāyāna literature, (but) there was no early organized...movement that it could have belonged to."[12]

Our attention is thus directed to that "large and early Mahāyāna literature," the Prajñāpāramitā literature. The texts thus referred to are of widely varying lengths, disparate dates, concern widely varying topics. They probably represent collections of materials from differing times and hands, even different countries. They are couched in a style that matches the canonical *sūtras*--discussions among Gautama and his cohorts. These texts are of fundamental importance for understanding the spread of Buddhism into East Asia. What is not clear is what they constituted in the minds and activities of those who wrote and disseminated them in India of the first couple of centuries A.D.

Because of their vast influence within Buddhist India as well as world Buddhism we shall, in this Volume, try to identify and briefly characterize those among the Prajñāpāramitā texts that appear to date from prior to 350 A.D. Some of them were commented on by Madhyamaka and Yogācāra philosophers, and where these commentaries have philosophical content and a summarizer is available they are summarized in this and the subsequent Buddhist volumes of the *Encyclopedia.* In some cases we give an outline or encapsulation with a guide to the literature for those who wish to delve further.

Buddhist texts began to be translated into Chinese in the middle of the second century A.D. We quote here from the most recently-published (at this time of writing) study on the matter by Emile Zürcher:[13] "Chinese Buddhism starts with a mysterious embryonic phase about which very little is known. There is a gap of about eight decades between the first unquestionable sign of Buddhism in China (65 A.D.) and the arrival of An Shigao in Luoyang (148 A.D.) that marks the beginning of regular translation activities. We do not know any literary product of that primeval period...

"The oldest and most primitive nucleus in our materials is formed by the sixteen short scriptures which may be regarded as genuine products of An Shigao and his collaborators." These sixteen texts are preserved in Chinese under the following entries in the Taisho listing: T.s 13, 14, 31, 32, 36, 48, 57, 98, 112, 150, 602, 603, 605, 607, 792, 1508. Zürcher gives brief descriptions of their contents. Some of them appear to relate to philosophical themes[14] and may be considered among the earliest Mahāyāna *sūtras.* "The language is erratic, crude, full of vulgarisms, often chaotic to the point of unintelligibility...The works of this type were produced roughly between 150 and 170 A.D."

"In the next phase (ca. 170-190 A.D.), the Indo-Scythian Lokakṣema and his collaborators produced a number of translations, seven of which have been preserved." These are #s 16-23 of our texts in this Volume. "These again form a distinct and very homogeneous type, very different from the products of An Shigao and his school. The language is more natural and intelligible than that of An Shigao; in certain narrative passages it may reach a high level of fluency and liveliness, with abundant use of vernacular elements. On the other hand, Lokakṣema's versions are characterized by a preference for transcriptions of both proper names and technical terms that frequently overburden the narrative with phonetic renderings of up to twelve syllables..."[15]

We thus have a suggestion as to what was going on in India among some Buddhists of the first few centuries A.D., perhaps even before, and what was being said and thought by them is beginning to become available through Chinese translations which were preserved, though much of the original Indic materials presumably were lost to the heat and humidity of the subcontinent. But we also can get some idea of what was transpiring by attending to the reports of a few named individuals and a larger number of names of the sects they belonged to.

## BUDDHIST SCHOOLS AND SECTS

In Volume VII of this Encyclopedia[16] it was indicated that many of the myriad schools of Abhidharma Buddhism were known to the author(s) of the *Kathāvatthu* in (presumably) the third to second centuries B.C. The names of schools crop up regularly in the works surveyed in the present Volume, and some of those works appear to represent the beliefs and insights peculiar to a specific school. A sizable literature[17] has grown up around the question of which were these schools, how important they were and what they represented, but despite the extensive attention given to the topic it remains a puzzling corner of history.

Buddhist thought, as was seen in Volume Seven, developed a variety of different interpretations of the Buddha's message starting as early as the first "schism", and by the time we are dealing with here writers were aware of the variety of Buddhist persuasions. Etienne Lamotte[18] points out that the "*nikāyas*", i.e., groups or schools, "do not necessarily originate as the result of a schism". Furthermore, Buddhist schools appear to have "developed spontaneously...throughout the whole of India". Lamotte believes, in contrast to Schopen, that the schools often emanated from "the religion of a particular monastery (which) tended to specialize in a specific branch of learning",[19] and it was resulting differences, together with differences in practical customs of a region, that he thinks distinguished the several sects from each other.

The names of these sects derived from the doctrine they professed, the assembly they represented, the region they stemmed from, or the name--usually fictitious--of a founding father. Lamotte suggests that "the old authors built history, even philosophy, with popular etymologies".[20] The "history" provided by such accounts is, he believes, largely spurious. Nevertheless, one can derive from the extant literature the beginnings of a picture for each such system of what it taught, despite the apparent infrequency of any such attempt on their part.

The sects, as noted, developed throughout South Asia. A list of inscriptional evidence drawn up by Lamotte locates fifteen such sects in places ranging from Central Asia to Sri Lanka and from modern Nepal to Nagarjunikonda on the Bay of Bengal. Different reports dating from different periods inform us about specific, rather randomly-organized beliefs ascribed to a number of these systems.

The most thorough review to date of evidence pertaining to the schools can be found in André Bareau, *Les Sectes Bouddhiques du Pétit Véhicule* (Publications de l'École Francaise d'Extrème-Orient 38, Paris 1955). What follows here is an encapsulation of what he provides concerning those schools which seem to have flourished during our period. After reviewing the specific lists of schools found in various literary sources, all of which date from after 300 A.D., Bareau provides the following tabular summary of the sects:

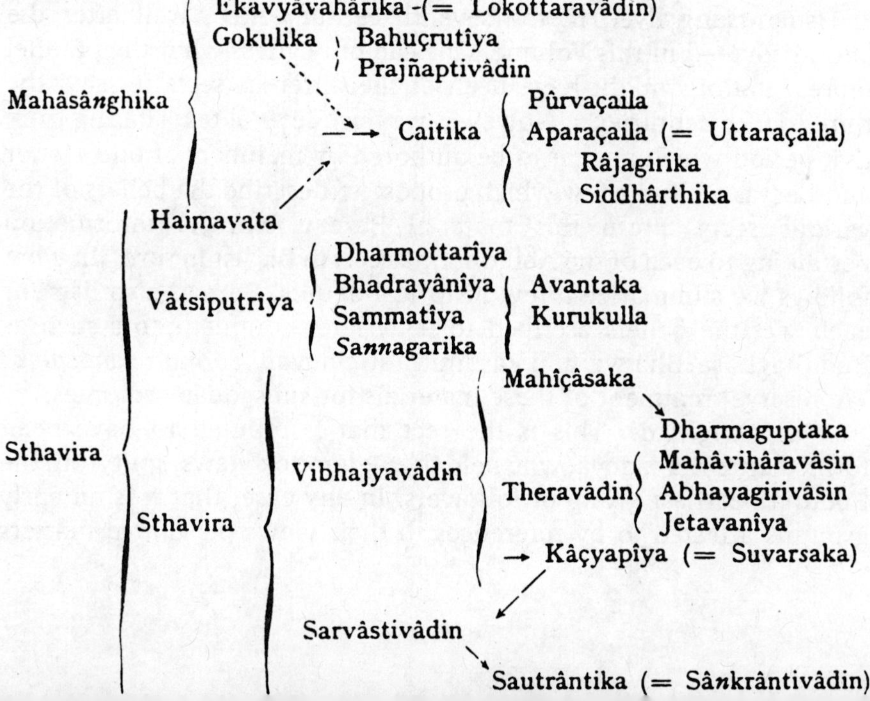

All of the sects listed in the above diagram probably flourished prior to the beginning of the Christian era, with the exceptions of the Rājagirikas, Siddhārthikas and Sautrāntikas (and possibly the Haimavatas, of whose history we know litttle). Inscriptions record the presence of the rest of these schools in various localities throughout India and present-day Sri Lanka, Pakistan and Afghanistan prior to the second century A.D., and Hsüan-tsang provides a precise-sounding account of the number of monks and of monasteries associated with a number of these sects dating from the 7th century.[21] Only the Sammitīyas, the Sarvāstivādins and the Sthaviras (Theravādins) are distinguished as such by Hsüan-tsang. The figures Hsüan-tsang gives suggest that the Sammitīyas consisted of 65,000 monks inhabiting 1,000 monasteries at the feet of the Indus and Ganges rivers, that 16,000 monks in 500 monasteries mainly in North-west India and Central Asia represented Sarvāstivāda, and 20,000 monks in 200 monasteries in Sri Lanka and South India, but also in Saurashtra, espoused Theravāda. The Mahāsāṃghikas count 1,000 monks in 20 monasteries in Kashmir and northeast Afghanistan. And followers of Mahāyāna count 70,000 monks in more than 1,000 monasteries spread widely around India as well as Afghanistan and Khotan. Though these numbers are surely merely conjecture, they suggest that there were thought to be a large number of Buddhists inhabiting or represented by South Asian monasteries.

Hsüan-tsang lived in the seventh century A.D., well after the period covered in this Volume. One can only guess what the parallel representations might have been of the different sects in, say, the third to fifth centuries.[22] However, we have several texts dating from that period which appear to be authored by members of one sect or another, as well as a few which propose to describe the beliefs of the various sects. From this material Bareau extracts information pertaining to each of the Abhidharma sects in his list in turn. In what follows we summarize a few historical details. Bareau also lists for each sect the beliefs ascribed to it by later commentators such as Buddhaghoṣa, Bhavya, and Vasumitra's *Samayabhedoparacanacakra*. We reserve treatment of these materials for subsequent volumes.

*Mahāsāṃghikas*. This is the sect that is reputed to have been formed after Mahādeva, who held five heterodox views, split from the Buddha's earliest group of followers. In any case, that it is an early group is attested to by references to their views on *vinaya* matters mentioned in the reports of the Councils at Rājagṛha and Vaiśālī. Their original center appears to have been in Magadha, but by the second century A.D. inscriptions referring to them are to be found in Mathurā, at Karli and Kabul. Information about their ethical tenets can be gained from consulting 140.*Ekottarāgama-* and 150.*Śāriputraparipṛcchā-sūtras*, possibly dating from the fourth century A.D., though by that time several subsects such as Lokottaravādins, etc. had come into being. Mahāsāṃghikas are attested to as late as the seventh century in Magadha and eastern India by I-tsing, and even migrated out of India.

*Lokottaravādins* and/or Ekavyavahāravādins seem to date from the end of the second century B.C. at the same time as the Gokulikas. Bareau thinks it likely that "Lokottaravāda" and "Ekavyavahārika" are two names for the same sect. It is an offshoot of the Mahāsāṃghika, and shares most of the same beliefs. Bareau, as well as various other scholars, have suggested that these sects may have constituted the original form of what became the Mahāyāna, given the supernormal properties it attributes to the Buddha.

*Gokulikas*. This sect is referred to in the *Kathāvatthu* as the Kukkuṭikas. Buddhaghoṣa says that section II.6 of the *Kathāvatthu* discusses one of their beliefs. Paramārtha, in the fifth century, reports that this school held that only the Abhidharma section of the canon is important, the other two sections only speaking to preparatory training, and placed their emphasis on logic, claiming that overattention to the *sūtras* interferes with the chance of gaining liberation.

*Bahuśrutīyas*. According to one tradition, maintained in the Northwest, this sect derived directly from the Mahāsāṃghika schism; according to the Theravāda tradition they are descendants of the Gokulikas. We have one major work representing their beliefs, the 126.*Tattvasiddhi(śāstra)* of Harivarman. Bareau suggests the Bahuśrutīyas represent a point midway between Hīnayāna and Mahāyāna. It is hard to say where they flourished.

*Prajñaptivādins*. Another sect that is said to derive from the same sources as the previous four, this sect is also known as "Vibhajyavāda" in some sources, though distin-guished from them by, e.g., Saṃghabhadra. They are said to emphasize the difference between the supreme (*lokottara, paramārtha*) and mundane (*laukika, saṃvṛti*). Saṃghabhadra represents them as saying that factors are pure fictions, in contrast to what he terms the Vibhajyavādins, who believe that present factors, as well as past factors that are still bearing fruit, really exist. But there is much disagreement among later authorities, each of whom attributes different beliefs to this sect. We know nothing of their whereabouts.

*Caitīyas* or Caitasikas. Vasumitra and Paramārtha trace the origin of this sect to a second Mahādeva who, with his disciples, retired to a sanctuary (*caitya*) and reexamined the five propositions of the earlier Mahādeva, and whose followers eventually divided into two (or three) sects called Caityaśaila and Uttaraśaila (and/or Aparaśaila). Inscriptions at Amaravati in present-day Andhra show the sect's presence there in the early part of the second century A.D.

*Andhakas*. Buddhaghoṣa speaks of four sects called Pūrvaśaila, Aparaśaila, Rājagṛhya and Siddhārthika, and some seventy-two of the views discussed in the *Kathāvatthu* are ascribed to them.[23] They seem also to have flourished in Andhra (thus are "Andhakas"), and Bareau thinks it likely that their theses were shared by the Caitīyas, which may have been the earlier name of the same sect.

*Sthaviravādins*. This name refers to the original group of monks from whom the Mahāsāṃghikas separated in the third century B.C. This group is in some sources (such as Vasumitra) identified with the Haimavatas, though other sources disagree. (The Haimavata is not viewed as a school until rather late--the fourth century A.D., says Bareau[24]--and the several authorities have quite divergent accounts of its affiliations, with evidence as to their beliefs largely lacking.)

*Vātsīputrīyas*. All sources agree that this is the first (other than the Haimavatas) to separate from the Sthaviravāda. The sect is named after its founder, Vātsīputra, but we have no evidence about its locale. It is especially known for its espousal of the theory that an individual self (*pudgala*) really exists, a position that is taken up for repudiation at some length by Vasubandhu in Chapter Nine of the 168.*Abhidharmakośa*, but referred to frequently in the *Kathāvatthu* and the *Vibhāṣā* literature.

*Sammitīyas*. They are generally said to have arisen from the Vātsīputrīyas, along with two or three others, in the second or third century B.C., though in fact there is no evidence of it before the second century A.D., when inscriptions locate them in Mathura and Sarnath. Later they become the preeminent branch of the Vātsīputrīyas. At least thirty different beliefs are attributed to them in the *Kathāvatthu*. I-tsing claims their Tripiṭaka was vast--some 200,000 *ślokas*. Among the works surveyed in this Volume 160.*Sammitīyanikāyaśāstra* stems from this school.

*Dharmottarīyas*. This is another school that is believed to have derived from the Vātsīputrīyas. Inscriptions signal their presence in Karli and Junnar in the second century A.D., leading them to be referred to alternatively as Mahāgiriyas. We know next to nothing of their doctrines.

*Bhadrayānīyas*. Yet another branch of Vātsīputrīyas. Again, we know little of their beliefs.

*Sannagarikas* or Sandagriyas. Still another branch of Vātsīputrīyas, about which we know next to nothing.

*Sarvāstivādins*. This school, about which we know more than any other Hīnayāna school save the Theravādins, probably separated from the Sthaviras in the reign of Aśoka, around 244 B.C. We know little of their history, but we have a sizable literature that represents their views, a number of which are summarized in Volume Seven and in this Volume of the Encyclopedia. In particular the *Mahāvibhāṣā* represents their views in great detail, and the author of #s205-206 Saṃghabhadra, the great critic of Vasubandhu, espoused the views of this school. Their ranks grew later on, so that by Hsüan-tsang's time many thousands of adherents are attested to as living throughout India, Pakistan and Central Asia. For an account of their special views see Volume Seven of this Encyclopedia, especially pp. 100-119. As was shown in Volume Seven the Sarvāstivādins had their own *Tripiṭaka*, with separate Abhidharma texts from those to be found in the Pāli canon of the Theravādins.

*Sautrāntikas*. This appears to have been a sect deriving from, but with sharply diverging views from, the Sarvāstivādins. They are said to recognize as authority only the *Sūtrapiṭaka*, hence the name "Sautrāntika". According to Bareau a chief, specific view of this school was that the five aggregates (*skandha*) transmigrate from birth to birth without pause. They denied the existence of a *pudgala*. Once again we know little to nothing of their whereabouts or history, and have no texts specifically representing them until Vasubandhu's *Abhidharmakośabhāṣya*.

*Dārṣṭāntikas*. Though this sect appears to hold the same views as the Sautrāntikas, the *Vibhāṣā* and (later) Vasubandhu agree that it is a separate school.

*Vibhajyavādins*. It is difficult to know whether this term refers to a distinct sect or a group of diverse schools. Both interpretations have their proponents. The *Vibhāṣā* appears to view the Vibhajyavādins as skeptics without any doctrine of their own. On the other hand Vasubandhu in his 173*Abhidharmakośa* identifies the Vibhajyavādins as "those who admit the existence of the present and of part of the past, who deny the existence of the future and the other part of the past". This is precisely the view held by the Kāśyapīyas. However, later treatments extend the term "Vibhajyavāda" to cover many more skeptical positions, unfortunately without giving any actual names of sects, and subsequently the term is used with great vagueness to cover a large number of schools, so that Bareau concludes that the Vibhajyavādins, as referred to latterly in Buddhism, include just about all the above schools excepting the Sarvāstivādins. That conclusion Bareau draws from a survey of documents representing the oldest traditions; reviewing the literature stemming from after the 6th century he finds an even more diverse and puzzling picture.

*Mahīśāsikas*. If one thinks of the Vibhajyavādins as being that group of Sthaviravādins who did not accept Sarvāstivāda, then the Mahīśāsakas are the most important sect of that group. One inscription from the third century at Nagarjunikonda makes reference to them; all other references stem from sources dating several hundred years later. We do not know which part of the subcontinent they occupied early on, and authorities differ on their later whereabouts. Of literature stemming from their persuasion we only know of material on *vinaya* available to us in Chinese translation.

*Dharmaguptakas*. As shown in the chart above, the Dharmaguptakas were a sect of the Vibhajyavādins distinct from the Mahīśāsakas. All sources cite their presence in North India around the first century B.C. They had their own canon, with a *Vinaya* section divided into four parts, different from, e.g., the Haimavatas, and this section has been preserved in Chinese translation from the first part of the fifth century A.D. We probably also have the first section of their *Sūtrapiṭaka* dating from the same period.

*Kāśyapīyas*. About a century before Christ, at about the same time as the previously discussed school, the Kāśyapīyas constitute another section of the Vibhajyavādins. They are evidenced by inscriptions at Taksasila dating from the third century A.D., as well as others of a later date. One or two works, presently available only in Chinese, appear to represent their views, which must not have differed greatly from those of the Haimavatas.

*Theravāda*. Given the myriad numbers of sects previously reviewed, it is not easy to say what exactly were taken to be the distinctions among sects in, say the second century B.C., after the various schisms that separated many of these persuasions from one another. Whether there was a Theravāda school that was consistently recognized and identified even by themselves throughout this period is problematic. Though we have seen above that there may have been a school called "Sthaviravāda" in the third century B.C., it is not entirely evident that this had any particular relationship to the peculiar point of view developed in Ceylon by the Theravādins of more recent times. Buddhism was introduced into Ceylon, according to Singhalese tradition, in the reign of Mahinda and Saṃghamittā, the son and daughter of Aśoka, but we have no datable evidence about Theravāda there before the third century A.D. Tradition says that Theravāda was in place there as a distinct sect by 109 B.C., under King Duṭṭhagāmani. Eventually the sect grew in numbers and even returned in some force to South India in the form of monks and monasteries during the time of Hsüan-tsang. It also spread into Southeast Asia as well, and has remained in force to the present day in both Sri Lanka and Southeast Asia.

*Abhayagirivāsins*. One of the two schools of Theravāda in Ceylon that broke away from the major Mahāvihāra school, the Abhayagiri *vihāra* was established at Anuradhapura in Ceylon, according to tradition, 217 years after the founding of the Mahāvihāra, which is traditionally dated to the year 24 A.D. From its inception this sect seems to have bred heretics, and it was at a Council called shortly thereafter by the King to deal with them that the (now lost) commentaries (*aṭṭhakathā*) on the basic seven works of the Pāli canon were written down. The monastery was razed in the fourth century but restored fifteen years later, and by the fifth century Fa-hsien found 5,000 Abhayagiri monks there, outnumbering the Mahāvihārins. It is not clear that any works stemming from this sect are preserved, although some scholars associate the 119.*Vimuttimagga* of Upatissa with it.

*Jetavanīyas*. Another schismatic school of Singhalese Theravāda. The Jetavanavihāra was built in the fourth century A.D. The sect that made its home there is also called the Sāgalikas after its founder. It seems not to have been well known in Ceylon, is not mentioned by many of those who visited there. We know nothing about their doctrines and works, although it is also possible that 124.*Vimuttimagga* should be associated with this school rather than the previous one.

There are a number of other schools referred to in the literature, but most of them appear to be alternative names of the above, or else flourished after the period we are dealing with in our Volume here.

## THERAVĀDA IN ŚRĪ LAṄKĀ

One sect in particular, the Theravāda, appears to have moved its center southwards to Ceylon, modern Śrī Laṅkā, some time during the period of our study. Specifically, there were apparently composed in North India a series of commentaries called *Aṭṭhakathās* on the three basket (Tripiṭaka) literature. These commentaries were initially composed in Māgadhī or other dialects of Middle Indo-Aryan, as were the three baskets themselves; they specifically state that Māgadhī was the language of the Buddha himself. K.R.Norman has pointed out that although we now refer regularly to the "Pāli canon", in fact there was no language called "Pāli" at that time--indeed, the term appears to have been based on a misunderstanding by Western scholars of the eighteenth and nineteenth century. The three baskets were originally composed in North Indian dialects, and only later turned into the version we now have.[25]

The only sources available for ascertaining how Theravāda migrated to Ceylon are two chronicles of the history of Ceylon dating from the fourth to fifth century A.D., the *Dīpavaṃsa* and *Mahāvaṃsa*. These accounts review the assembling of the various councils, the schisms that occurred, etc. It seems evident that these two chronicles were based on the afore-mentioned *Aṭṭhakathās*, which they state were brought from India to Ceylon by Mahinda in the middle of the third century B.C. and were kept in the Mahāvihāra at Anuradhapura. These early commentaries are no longer extant. However, Buddhaghoṣa in the fifth century based his classic commentaries on Pāli canonical works on these *Aṭṭhakathās*. In the next Volume of this Encyclopedia dealing with the subsequent history of Buddhist philosophy we shall summarize Buddhaghoṣa's works.[26]

The only sources available for ascertaining how Theravāda migrated tc Ceylon are two chronicles of the history of Ceylon dating from the fourth to fifth century A.D., the *Dīpavaṃsa* and *Mahāvaṃsa*. These accounts review the assembling of the various councils, the schisms that occurred, etc. It seems evident that these two chronicles were based on the afore-mentioned *Aṭṭhakathās*, which they state were brought from India to Ceylon by Mahinda in the middle of the third century B.C. and were kept in the Mahāvihāra at Anuradhapura. These early commentaries are no longer extant. However, Buddhaghoṣa in the fifth century based his classic commentaries on Pāli canonical works on these *Aṭṭhakathās*. In the next Volume of this Encyclopedia dealing with the subsequent history of Buddhist philosophy we shall summarize Buddhaghosa's works.[26]

## THE COMING OF YOGĀCĀRA

We have very little evidence of the philosophical stances of Buddhist thinkers in the period between Āryadeva's time and that of Asaṅga, apart from what may be guessed from the Prajñāpāramitā texts just considered, the dates of which are in any case problematic. One exception, available now only in Chinese, is a work known as 126.*Tattvasiddhi* or *Satyasiddhi*, whose author's name is given as Harivarman.

We know very little more about Harivarman than we do about any of the authors of Indian texts of this period. However, in this case there is extant a biography of Harivarman written by a Chinese monk, Hsüan-tsang, in the fifth century.[27] Some scholars estimate Harivarman's date to include 263 A.D., and a biography locates Harivarman's locale in Central India. He is said to have been a student of 72.Kumāralāta, though not everyone agrees on this.

Thus we are brought to the fourth century, very likely the period most central to the development of Yogācāra Buddhism, but also the time of many now-famous Mahāyāna *sūtras*. It is impossible, at least in our present state of knowledge, to date most Buddhist texts. As has been pointed out before, many of the *sūtras* are very likely texts whose present state consists of a now-indiscernible core buttressed by accretions added over a period of several centuries. One can make some guesses about which were the earlier elements--in many cases there are several Chinese and Tibetan translations dating from

what come to be the characteristic terms of Yogācāra.

As we come to the fourth century, then, we arrive at the time of Asaṅga and Vasubandhu. Tradition has it that these two were brothers, the younger Vasubandhu beginning his career as an Abhidharmist and becoming converted to Yogācāra by his elder brother later in life. The scholarly problem of the identity of Vasubandhu and his authorship of works attributed to him has occasioned much controversy. Some of the details of evidence on this point are reviewed in the introductions to the sections on the two authors, but it must be admitted that the jury is still out on the question both of date and of authorship of works attributed to authors under these names. Many scholars will find the dating followed here unlikely or just plain wrong, but others provide what they consider to be powerful evidence in favor of it. Here we only try to provide guidance to relevant published scholarship on the point. We also try to follow the latest authoritative scholarship on which are the works of each writer, without making any claims about the ultimate worth of the assessments presently being made about both dating and authorship. In any case it is clear that the works attributed to the two brothers include many of the most influential works of both Abhidharma and Yogācāra Buddhism. This Volume ends essentially with Vasubandhu's works, except that since one other personage of the period, Saṃghabhadra, seems to have lived at essentially the same time as Vasubandhu and wrote works which specifically controvert Vasubandhu's treatment of Abhidharma topics, a partial summary of his vast and major work constitutes the very last text summarized below.

# 2

# THE BUDDHIST PICTURE OF KARMA

How shall we picture the world as the Buddhist sees it? We have seen that for the Buddhist all things are empty: nothing persists in time for more than a moment. What we call a "thing" is actually a series of moments, and each moment comprises a vast array of factors flashing at the same moment but separately. A "person" is a certain kind of thing, and this same analysis applies to him or her. A person is only a series of momentarily flashing factors.

The factors that flash at a moment in the history of an individual person are of various sorts, or at any rate are experienced by us as being so. For one thing, what I take to be me is actually one series, among others, of apparently bodily physical factors, causing me to view myself as occupying a particular place at a particular time, to have a certain series of repeated visual experiences related in the way that causes me to speak of "my body", "my sense-organs", "my location in a world of physical objects and other bodies", and so on. In fact, there is no such spread-out physical world--the appearance of bodies, organs and objects is an interpretation, a construction made on the basis of moments of color, sound, smell, taste and touch. Even this last division of kinds of momentary flash-factors may or may not be independent of our conceptualizing abilities--Madhyamakas and Yogācāras say they are not, that they too are imaginary constructions. Besides physical-appearing factors, the flashes constituting our experience comprise myriad qualitative factors covering all the distinguishable sorts of data we experience in daily life--sensations, emotions, theories, interpretations, attitudes, ideas. Given the vast proliferation of factors that can be distinguished as comprising each moment of one's existence, it is not surprising that what we find in these texts is *not* an attempt to classify *all* the kinds of factors that there are (possibly a hopeless task), but rather a series of attempts to identify those particular factors which comprise our bondage, which breed karma and its resultant frustrating continuance of life from birth to death and around again. In the present Chapter we are not attempting to provide an exhaustive metaphysical account, but to summarily report what the texts under survey here pick out as those factors which cause bondage and whose "rooting out" promises liberation.

Let's rehearse the picture of man's place in the universe as it was seen by Buddhists in the period we are endeavoring to survey. Living beings occupy at any given time one or another of five courses (*gati*): hell, the animal realm, the world of ghosts, the human realm, or heaven as a god. Which course they occupy is determined by a portion of one's karma, part of the result of his actions in previous existences. It has always been thus, beginninglessly. Furthermore, differences among those occupying any one of these courses is also conditioned by one's karma, differences in appearance, health, wealth and influene, in the experiences a person has. The Pāli *sūtras* lay out a good deal of information specifying which sorts of acts breed which sorts of karma.[28]

But talk of acting seems to bring with it commitment to something acting, an agent. Since the Buddha taught that nothing lasts for more than a moment, karma would seem to be impossible, at least in the sense of something that is laid down in the agent and retained for a time, to be worked out in some subsequent action. One sect of Buddhists, the Vātsīputrīyas (also called Pudgalavādins), posited a personal agent (*pudgala*) who transmigrates from existence to existence. This notion of a person was roundly attacked by other Buddhist schools as contravening the Buddha's explicit words, but the problem remains for Buddhists in general to explain how the residues produced by actions at one point in time remain available to be worked out at a subsequent point. In particular, for example, and leaving aside the basic question of maintenance for a moment, when one dies how is it that "one's karma" is preserved so that it may become pertinent to "the same one" in the next birth? In answer to this, some schools (Sarvāstivādins, Vātsīputrīyas and Sammitīyas) posited an intermediate state (*antarābhava*), consisting of the series of five aggregates, which connects the place of death to the place of rebirth. Vasubandhu sets forth this account at length in the

173*Abhidharmakośa* (hereafter referred to merely as *Kośa* in this Introduction).[29] But the other Buddhist schools generally rejected the theory of an intermediate state.

Another way of facing up to this problem of the persistence of karmic residues was by making a distinction between manifest (*vijñapti*) and unmanifest *(avijñapti)* karma. Manifest karma is the immediate and evident result of a bodily or vocal act -- e.g., the pain experienced from a good swift kick. Unmanifest karma, on the other hand, is the disposition or potency laid down in the mind of someone performing a bodily or vocal action, a disposition which is not evident at that moment but will produce appropriate karmic results at a later time.[30]

But how can anything--e.g., unmanifest karma--be laid down and maintained, given the Buddhist commitment to momentariness? To answer this challenge the Sarvāstivādins or Vaibhāṣikas, who maintained a theory of time on which the past and future as well as the present exists, suggested a particular type of factor called *prāpti*, rendered here as "possession", which, though momentary like every factor, engenders another of its sort constituting a following moment, and so on until the karmic result of the originating act occurs. Sautrāntikas, who deny that the past or future of a moment exist at that moment's occurrence, rejected the foregoing theory, arguing instead that an action lays down a trace (*vāsanā*, literally a "perfume") or potency (*śakti*) that conditions each moment in the series following the action, this trace also being termed a "seed" (*bīja*). It is easy to imagine how the question of where these seeds exist while they are waiting to bear fruit in the form of karmic maturations led to the Yogācāra postulation of a storehouse-consciousness *(ālayavijñāna)*. Vasubandhu, in the fourth Chapter of the *Kośa*, develops an account of what a full-fledged action consists of. It has three parts, he says: first, the preparation (*prayoga*), the preparatory actions of collecting implements together along with one's intention to perform the action; second, the action itself together with the laying down of karma; third, what he terms the "back" (*pṛṣṭha*), the succeeding moments, such as the satisfaction of the actor and the string of unmanifest karma that follows on the action itself. This last element allows, e.g. for the reduction of karmic force of an act if the agent repents immediately after performing the action.

We have not as yet indicated how the Theravādins handled rebirth. Although the complete development of their theory on this is only available to us in sources dating from at least slightly after our period (in Buddhaghoṣa's works), the occurrence of some of the key technical terms in that theory occur in literature of our period if not in the earlier period covered in Volume Seven. It is also likely that the theory was developed in the lost commentaries on the Pāli *sūtras* which are said to have been composed in Sri Lanka around the second or third centuries. In the following paragraphs we summarize the theory, based on a thorough account by Shanta Ratnayaka.[31]

The theory analyzes the factors in the history of the stream of consciousness that comprises an arising of an awareness of an object. Having such a historical account in hand, we can then indicate what is occurring at the time between death and rebirth. The basic notion in this account is that of a *bhavaṅga*, which Ratnayaka translates as a momentary part of an "unconscious continuum", i.e., what we call a "self" when it is not conscious. Let us suppose an unconscious continuum is, as it were, disturbed by a sensory or mental stimulus. Then a series of awakening moments (vibrating, followed by awakening, followed by inquisitive *bhavaṅga*) will occur, culminating in a visual awareness. This is in turn followed by a receptive awareness, an investigative one (an awareness determining what response to make), and then a series of exercitive (*javana*) awarenesses during which the response is made, i.e., as we say, the act occurs. These acts are followed by a couple of moments of retentive awareness, after which a moment of unconscious continuum recurs, constituting the seventeenth moment in the account.

The process just reviewed describes the moments in the stream that occur during (what we term) performance of an action. The same sort of analysis is offered to explain the process of death and rebirth, that is, to specify the moments in the stream that comprise that process. Again, we start with a moment of unconsciousness, followed by vibrating, awakening and inquisitiveness. But now, since the dying person's energy is weak, this is immediately followed by five moments of exercitive awareness, two of retention, a moment of unconsciousness, and then a second unconscious moment called the death-awareness. This is immediately followed by an unconscious moment called the birth-awareness, which is followed by a series of moments of unconsciousness until a series of the first sort, of awakening moments arising from sensory or mental stimulation, occurs.

## THE PATH

We do not have any Buddhist text after the *Mahāvibhāṣā* and before the 173.*Abhidharmakośa* which provides a really complete account of the path to liberation. The closest any author of this period comes to that occurs in the *Śrāvakabhūmi* section of the 166.*Yogācārabhūmi*. Furthermore, Vasubandhu's work, the *Kośa*, appears to collect a great many different classifications of things and bind them together into a very rough order, which makes the actual tracing of a "path" to liberation based on that work rather difficult. Nevertheless, a rapid survey of the *Kośa*'s structure and summary of its contents may help to get an orientation to the Buddhist view of the path, even though Vasubandhu has imported so many lists from earlier sources that it is difficult to get a clear picture of the sequence of stages on the path he is describing.

The *Abhidharmakośa* is organized into nine chapters. The first two of these set forth the factors organized under categories such as aggregates, sense-bases and elements, factors which are classified by distinguishing, e.g., pure vs. impure factors and conditioned vs. unconditioned ones. Some seventy-five factors are thus generated, a list which because of the *Kośa*'s unchallenged position and availability has come to be thought of as the definitive Abhidharma account. We shall deal with this list in Chapter Three of this Introduction.

In his third chapter Vasubandhu gives a picture of the constitution of the universe as it may have been widely conceived in his time, organizing the various heavens and hells frequently alluded to in Abhidharma literature, discussing the eons of time constituting the stages of history within an age, and adding some material about the four kinds of states one may be reborn to, the intermediate state, and a discussion of dependent origination. And in the fourth chapter he reviews karma theory in a useful account to which we have already briefly referred in a previous section.

It is in Chapter Five of the *Kośa* that Vasubandhu takes up the stages of the path to liberation. This Chapter deals with the sources of bondage, variously termed proclivities (*anuśaya*), defilements (*kleśa*), contaminants (*āsrava*), floods (*ogha*), bonds (*yoga*), afflictions (*upakleśa*) and envelopers (*paryavasthāna*). These terms are inherited from earlier discussions, and provide differing classifications of the factors which must be expunged from one's stream when one is seeking liberation. In fact, it appears from the *Kośa*'s account that the expunging of these factors is all that it takes to insure liberation. What the Chapter goes on to do is to summarily outline the antidotes to these proclivities, analyze them in terms of, e.g., the four meditative stages, and relate these antidotes to the various stages called "stream-enterer", etc., indicating the way in which these proclivities are to be disconnected from the stream of factors we think of as a person.

Chapter Six of the *Kośa* provides further details on these stages and the methods of arriving at them, and discusses the stages near to liberation that the adept attains as he rids himself of the last of these proclivities. Chapters Seven and Eight turn to a characterization of the noble person who has achieved the status of a Buddha, reviewing again a vast list of classifications inherited from earlier traditions. Chapter Nine is a kind of appendix, in which Vasubandhu argues against the theory of a person (*pudgalavāda*) espoused by the Vātsīputrīya sect.

The attention of the disciple is thus fastened on the proclivities. The basic list comprehends six proclivities: attachment (*rāga*), repugnance or aversion (*pratigha, dveṣa*), pride (*māna*), ignorance (*avidyā*), wrong view (*dṛṣṭi*) and perplexity (*vicikitsā*). By relating these to the lists of defilements, contaminants, floods, bonds, afflictions and envelopers a highly complex analysis is generated in Chapter Five. Collet Cox characterizes the situation thus arrived at in the following terms: "Within post-*Vibhāṣā* Sarvāstivādin Abhidharma texts, categories of defilements come to be differentiated according to their functions, which in turn become the subject of heated sectarian controversy. This controversy reflects the further refinement of theories concerning the operation of both thought and proclivities, as well as the methods by which proclivities are to be abandoned. It is also interconnected with the development of more sophisticated ontological theories, which inevitably affected all aspects of Abhidharma doctrine. In particular, this controversy involves the possibility of a distinction between latent and active proclivities, and the relation between these proclivities (whether latent or active) and the thought processes of the individual life-stream that they characterize."

"At issue is the development of a model that could successfully explain the apparent, persistent activity of certain proclivities, the reemergence of their activity after an interruption, and the mechanism by which they are to be abandoned. For example, can unvirtuous proclivities arise conditioned by a morally dissimilar virtuous factor? If not, then what is the causal mechanism by which defilements arise immediately after a virtuous moment of thought? Further, if defilements are associated with thought, since two associated thought-concomitants of differing moral quality cannot occur simultaneously, how can the virtuous counteragent that obstructs a particular proclivity arise simultaneously with it? If, however, proclivities are not understood to be associated with thought, their very activity of defiling thought is meaningless, and no abandonment is necessary. Finally, if proclivities are understood to exist as real entities in the past and future as well as in the present, then they can never be destroyed in the sense that they become nonexistent, so in what sense can they be said to be abandoned?"[32]

Fourth-century Buddhists, notably Vasubandhu and Saṃghabhadra, attempted to deal with some of the problems Cox alludes to by invoking further distinctions. For example, Vasubandhu inherited a distinction between proclivities, which he took to be latent dispositions not necessarily present to consciousness (i.e., unassociated with awareness (*cittaviprayukta*)), and envelopers, which were in their nature active and present in awareness. Envelopers, then, he held to be produced from proclivities. This distinction was rejected by Kashmiri Sarvāstivāda-Vaibhāṣikas such as Saṃghabhadra.[33] Making the distinction allowed Vasubandhu to interpret these proclivities unassociated with awareness as seeds (*bīja*) constituting a series of dormant factors initiated by an action, a later member of which series can emerge at the proper time to fulfil its karmic function. Sarvāstivādins like Saṃghabhadra instead explained the connection between a given defilement and the subsequent moments of differing moral quality in a stream by appeal to the notion of the possession (*prāpti*) of a proclivity-moment by a factor in the stream of an individual existent. The notion of possession, discussed above, was rejected vehemently by Vasubandhu; the notion of seeds naturally leads one to the conception of a place where the seeds can be stored, and this appears to have helped occasion the notion that led to Vasubandhu's conversion to Yogācāra and its storehouse consciousness.

Since the central task for a Buddhist disciple is to eliminate the factors that bind us, let's take a moment to collect the kinds of things that are said about such factors.

1. Proclivities (*anuśaya*). There are six main proclivities: attachment, repugnance (or hatred), pride, ignorance, views and perplexity. This list becomes seven when one distinguishes attachment to desire from attachment to existence, the will to live. These proclivities are inherited karmically from past actions and are held by Yogācāra to be preserved sequentially as seeds in what they call the "storehouse consciousness" (*ālayavijñāna*). We may think of them as tendencies (thus, "proclivities") to think and act in the relevant ways; the thoughts and deeds that result are spoken of as defilements (*kleśa*), and classed under the same six or seven rubrics.

A list of ninety-eight proclivities, found alluded to by Harivarman, Dharmatrāta and Vasubandhu, is generated in the following way. There are in our world--the realm of desire--five attachments, five sorts of repugnances, five of pride, five of ignorance, twelve views and four perplexities, thus thirty-six proclivities in this realm. (The fives are said in the *Kośa* to consist of those to be abandoned by each of the four noble truths plus those to be abandoned by meditation.) In each of the next two higher realms--the material and immaterial realms--there are thirty-one proclivities (the five repugnances dropping out). Thus we get a total of 36+31+31=98 proclivities.

2. Defilements (*kleśa*) or contaminants (*āsrava*). As just seen, these are the same in name as the six or seven proclivities, but represent the actions actually performed as opposed to the proclivities, the tendencies to act that way. Consequently, where one is said to "abandon" or "root out" the proclivities, one actually "destroys" or "heads off" the defilements. Our texts are full of suggestions as to how to destroy them.

The defilements range from gross to subtle. One example offered (in 126.*Tattvasiddhi* 141) concerns our habit of classifying people as male and female with the well-known results of sexual desire and the resulting unhappinesses occasioned thereby. We are counselled to meet these urges by analyzing a member of the opposite sex into a congeries of bone, flesh, hair and other uninteresting parts, thereby meeting the tendency to desire the other sex; this process reaches its logical conclusion when we reflect that the male or female other is as empty as everything else.

Defilements are no more entities in a real world than are the proclivities which engender them. Since they are based on delusion one eliminates them by eliminating ignorance. This would seem to suggest a fundamentally epistemic answer to the problem. We can see that most defilements are eradicated by vision (some eighty-eight of the ninety-eight proclivities) while the remainder are to be eradicated by meditation.

Advanced meditators who have reached the fourth sphere of meditation--viz., Bodhisattvas--are said to be able to block the defilements of others by their endeavors, specifically through what is termed "diamond-like meditation". On the other hand, defilements can well breed other defilements--e.g., when a grasping attitude toward one kind of thing leads to hatred towards a rival.

3. Afflictions (*upakleśa*) or envelopers (*paryavasthāna*). A wide variety of tendencies are comprised under these headings. The lists vary a bit, but usually include sleepiness or lethargy, excitedness, craftiness, shamelessness, heedlessness, forgetfulness, etc.--all too human tendencies in pleasant, ordinary folk. We are told that beings are born afflicted with these; indeed, one's present body is formed from previous afflictions. On the other hand, the noble person is one who is free from afflictions, though he may still harbor proclivities that require further rooting out.

Afflictions are traced by Vasubandhu to our insistence on holding fast to illusions about entities that are actually nonexistent. They are the subtler causes of defilements. Vasubandhu terms some of them neutral in the realm of desire--viz., lethargy, excitedness, sleepiness; in higher realms all envelopers are bad forces to be reckoned with.

4. Fetters (*saṃyojana*) or obstructions (*āvaraṇa*). These classifications seemingly cut across some of the first three. The list of fetters tends to include some proclivities and some defilements, but numbers a few more than six or seven; one finds nine or ten fetters listed in various texts. Likewise for obstructions.

Just how are those factors that constitute proclivities, etc. to be abandoned? Both Vasubandhu and Saṃghabhadra in answering this basic question adopt a classification of four methods derived from Upaśānta's 52.*Abhidharmahṛdaya* and the 133.*Saṃyuktābhidharma-hṛdayasūtra* attributed to Dharmatrāta. Not all of these four methods can be used on every proclivity; it depends on whether the proclivity involves a supporting object. If it does, the method of abandonment includes (1) the ascertainment (*parijñāna*) of its supporting object, (2) the destruction of those other proclivities that have that supporting object as theirs too, and (3) the abandonment of that supporting object. If no supporting object is involved abandonment is to be obtained through (4) the arising of an antidote (*pratipakṣa*).[34]

Vasubandhu expounds at length toward the end of Chapter Five on the nature of these antidotes, classifying them into four varieties, and explains in which order and under what circumstances (stream-enterer, etc.) proclivities are separated from the factors constituting a stream and so disconnected from that stream. The distinction between the first three methods and the last is broached in terms of the distinction between the path of vision and the path of cultivation or spiritual practice, but in actuality the discussion in this connection becomes so complicated that a radical division between the two paths becomes lost. And indeed Cox argues that the very distinction, of which a good deal seems to be made in several texts, is hardly an exclusive classification, and that they do not in fact involve mutually exclusive patterns of abandonment of proclivities but only the different kinds of proclivities and the stage of advancement in practice of the aspirant in question.[35]

The Theravādin account of the path to liberation takes a number of forms. A recurrent exposition is the account in terms of purifications (*viśuddhi*). One account begins with (1) moral purification, observation of Buddhist ethical precepts. Next comes (2) mental purification, involving meditation leading to eight meditative attainments (the four trance states plus the four immaterial meditations described in Volume Seven, p. 66-67 on space, consciousness, nothingness and neither-perception-nor-nonperception). (3) Purification is purification of views, the mastering of the bases of Abhidharma metaphysics through categorizing and analyzing correctly the four great elements, five aggregates, and the other classifications of factors. In (4) purification by overcoming doubts, the disciple considers and resolves such questions as whether the self is persistent, whether there is a God, and whether there can be rebirth. In (5) knowledge of what does and does not constitute the path, there is further consideration and rejection of wrong theories about the path. (6) is knowledge of the path itself. Up to this point the disciple is still bound by fetters and has not yet attained knowledge. In the final stages of (6), however, one has obtained correct understanding of the four noble truths and this produces in him what is known as change of lineage (*gotrabhūmi*) leading to (7) purification through the vision of knowledge. One who arrives at this point is termed "noble" (*ārya*), and progresses through such stages as stream-enterer, once-returner, nonreturner and perfected being

Other accounts are found, e.g., in the 5.*Aṣṭasāhasrikāprajñāpāramitāsūtra*, which distinguishes worldlings (*pṛthagjana*), disciples (*śrāvaka*), those self-enlightened (*pratyekabuddha*), Bodhisattvas, and Buddhas. Hirakawa[36] shows how the list found in the 83.*Daśabhūmikasūtra*, dividing the path into ten stages, provides a chart collating the lists of the ten stages provided in four other texts. The Yogācāra provide a fivefold division of stages on the path into the stages of equipment (*sambhāra*), of preparation (*prayoga*), of vision (*darśana*), of practice (*bhāvanā*) and of completion or beyond instruction (*niṣṭha, aśaikṣa*)

## CULMINATING STAGES OF THE PATH

In accounts of the stages along the way that are found in virtually all Buddhist literature going back to the Pāli canon, we can find a significant distinction between the preparatory stages, during which the aspirant practices Buddhist moral virtues and meditates on the factors, and the later, higher stages of the path. As we have just seen, this difference is sometimes identified as "change of lineage". After this change, which one can find in each of the accounts of the path reviewed in preceding paragraphs, the adept becomes a stream-enterer (*srotāpanna*). In some accounts the stage of stream-entry is the second of eight such stages, the first being "stream-entry candidate", corresponding to the final stage of knowledge of the path (explained two paragraphs back). The four-fold classification of stream-enterer, once-returner, nonreturner and perfected being is expanded to eight by distinguishing candidates from achievers for each of the basic four, and in some texts (notably in the *Tattvasiddhi*, *Yogācārabhūmi* and *Abhidharmakośa*) the number of stages grows to as many as thirty-six.

A stream-enterer has overcome belief in a self, pursuance of a heavenly outcome through performance of rituals, and doubts about Buddhist doctrine. He cannot (unless he backslides) be reborn in a lower stage of existence than he is now, i.e., no lower than the human stage. He is also said to be destined to become liberated by the time he lives seven more lives. The once-returner has weakened the hold of the three "poisons" of desire, hatred and delusion, and will be reborn only once more. The nonreturner does no more bad karma and is reborn only among the gods.

Which brings us to the fourth and final stage, the term for which ("*arhat*") we translate as "perfected being". There is a good deal of confusion about the relationship between such a being and one who is a *buddha*, a *pratyekabuddha*, one who has reached *nirvāṇa*, one who has reached *parinirvāṇa*, a *bodhisattva*, enlightenment (*bodhi*) and whether the perfected being is a disciple (*śrāvaka*) and if not, what? While some of this is due to failure to hew to a consistent terminology in the texts, in fact the usage there is fairly standard. It is the interpretation placed on the terms which appears to have shifted a bit on the rise of what we now term the Mahāyāna. This shift is particularly evident only on hindsight, however; in the materials from the period of the present study, usage remains fairly consistent.

Who is a perfected being? Precisely, one who has destroyed all his contaminants, who is free from the various proclivities that were alluded to earlier. The *arhat* should be carefully distinguished from a "noble" (*ārya*), a term that as we saw applies to one who has just undergone the initial change of lineage. That confusion is made rather easier by the classification of all those at any stage of the path as disciples (*śrāvaka*); a perfected being is a disciple still, given the parlance of classical Buddhism.

The texts are full of references to *bodhisattvas*, *pratyekabuddhas*, *sammā-sambuddhas*, and the like. How do these terms relate to that of perfected being? And when do disciples arrive at these stages? Are there stages of perfected being? With some danger of being overprecise, since there is, as noted, some discrepancy in terminology apparent even in the texts of our period, we may try to answer these questions as briskly as possible. A disciple, one who achieves the fourth stage by destroying his proclivities, is termed a perfected being. He has attained a kind of enlightenment (*bodhi*), viz., the enlightenment of a disciple (*śrāvakabodhi*). Thus he is a (kind of) *buddha*. One might ask why he remains in an embodied state: the answer would seem to be the standard one that the karmic residues slated to work themselves out in his current lifetime need the remainder of time and opportunity to do so.

Are there stages of perfected being? Not if we are using the term in its specific meaning. Of course, a perfected being may arrive at his state of perfection in more than one way, and under more than one kind of circumstance, and those differences are made the basis for terminology that seems to indicate degrees of perfection. For example, does a perfected being have to master the four kinds of meditational trance (*dhyāna*), or can he attain perfection directly through insight? Although there is no unanimity on this, the use of a term such as "liberated both ways" (*ubhatobhāgavimukta*) in contrast to other kinds of liberations (*vimokṣa*) would seem to suggest he may or may not have to both master meditation and attain insight. Again, some perfected beings obtain enlightenment on their own and are termed *pratyekabuddhas* or "self-enlightened". Such a liberation occurs during a period or in a place where there is no Buddha to teach or order to join, though preparation for this state may cover many lives during such periods. The self-enlightened goes through the same kinds of ascetic, instructional and meditative practices as do other Buddhist disciples; he must understand the same truths and eliminate the same kinds of proclivities. It is suggested in the Pāli *sūtras* that one self-enlightened may not offer instruction to others; however, he teaches by example and through brief but cogent remarks, etc.[37]

Can a perfected being backslide? No, since he by definition has destroyed all the proclivities which could occasion backsliding. Well, how does one come to know that someone, or he himself, is a perfected being? The Buddha himself anticipated this question and at one point provides a list of questions that should be put to one who is claimed to be perfected.[38]

Is a perfected being a Bodhisattva? Yes he is. However, there are two kinds of Bodhisattvas, the Buddha himself and those who are disciple Bodhisattvas. Names of perfected disciple Bodhisattvas are frequent in Buddhist literature--Śāriputra, Maudgalyāyana, Mahākāśyapa, Anuruddha, etc. Is a perfected disciple Bodhisattva a *buddha*? Yes, in a sense, but no by his own choice, since he chooses to remain "in the world" to help other beings achieve enlightenment.

Has a perfected being attained *nirvāṇa*? Yes, since liberation is defined as the termination of the proclivities and the perfected being has attained that. How about *parinirvāṇa*? While it is commonly supposed that the term *parinirvāṇa* applies to the Buddha's last death E.J.Thomas[39] and, more recently, Peter Masefield[40] and K.R.Norman[41] have all argued for different reasons that such an interpretation may be mistaken at least if too broadly generalized, since in the Nikāyas one finds passages in which persons who have attained *parinirvāṇa* are depicted as very much alive. Masefield goes on to show that the other, later terminology (of *sopādhiśeṣa/nirupādhiśeṣadhātu*) for the distinction between liberation before death and liberation at death is confusedly interpreted by Buddhaghoṣa and thus by modern Buddhists as well. He suggests that the contrast between *nirvāṇa* and *parinirvāṇa* is rather the distinction between liberation achieved by a perfected being in the present lifetime and the liberation that will be attained by a perfected being in some future life when the karmic traces still in need of expiation will be fully lived out. However, Norman suggests that in fact there is no distinction, or rather, that the difference is merely grammatical of the process/product sort, "*nirvāṇa*" meaning the attaining of liberation, "*parinirvāṇa*" meaning the state attained.

The account of the perfected being just provided is the account apparently maintained in the Pāli canon and the Theravāda and Sarvāstivāda literature. With the coming of the beginnings of Mahāyāna that view of the perfected being changes. This very question of the attitude toward the perfected being in early Prajñāpāramitā literature has been addressed by Paul Harrison.[42] Specifically studying the eleven texts translated into Chinese by Lokakṣema in the middle of the second century A.D., Harrison provides a fascinating picture of how new atttitudes are displayed therein. These views are not yet frequently characterized as "Mahāyāna", and indeed at this stage, says Harrison ,"there was no rigid division of the Buddhist Saṅgha into two hostile camps". Nevertheless, "there was a new spirit abroad..."

There is no doubt, writes Harrison, "that the level these venerable figures represent, that of the *arhats* and the *pratyekabuddhas*...is one that is to be transcended by the *bodhisattvas*...A hierarchy of attainments is in fact envisaged, leading from the state of an ordinary person at the bottom, through those of a 'stream-winner', a 'once-returner', a 'non-returner', an *arhat* and a *pratyekabuddha* to the state of a *buddha* or a *tathāgata* at the top. In aiming for the top, *bodhisattvas*, aspirants to the full awakening of a *buddha*, are warned repeatedly not to fall back to the level of the *arhats/śrāvakas* and the *pratyekabuddhas* or to join their ranks, and such a regression is represented as a fearful misfortune...The *śrāvakayāna* is characterised by attachment and limitation, and those who opt for it do so primarily out of fear of *saṃsāra*, which renders them incapable of aspiring to buddhahood. Not only is their courage thus inferior to that of the *bodhisattvas*, but their wisdom is too."

Thus, "what the (Prajñāpāramitāsūtras) tell us is that the early adherents of the Bodhisattvayāna--who were probably very much in the minority--were prepared to go to great lengths to uphold their ideal against what they conceived to be the traditional goal of Buddhist practice, namely arhatship or *nirvāṇa* for oneself alone, but they were not prepared to write off the rest of the Buddhist *saṅgha* or sever their own connection with it by the wholesale use of such terms as 'Hīnayāna' and 'Mahāyāna' as sectarian categories."

Harrison's depiction stems from materials dating from the second century A.D. While such new attitudes are found in Abhidharma treatises throughout our period, it is in the literature beginning with certain later Prajñāpāramitā *sūtras* and on into the works ascribed to Asaṅga and Vasubandhu that one finds increased attention paid to precisely how one achieves liberation, how the factors that bind can be rendered like burnt seeds, unable to generate further karma and so nonexistent.

Although it is standard to equate the development of this new approach to liberation with the rise of the Yogācāra school, examination of the texts, at least, does not entirely bear this out. Most of the concepts crucial for the new ways of thinking on these matters can be traced terminologically to origins in such texts as the *Mahāvibhāṣā* and other Abhidharma literature. Indeed, some of the texts standardly ascribed to Asaṅga seem not to utilize such terms, although others certainly do so. Furthermore, there are different sets of "Yogācāra terms". It seems likely that the firming up of a Yogācāra school postdates our period, although without doubt the basic notions of Yogācāra are to be found in a number of our texts, including a few of the Prajñāpāramitā *sūtras*.

## REVOLUTION AT THE BASIS

One of the most wide-ranging and important concepts we now associate with Yogācāra is first heard of at least once in the *Mahāvibhāṣā* but comes to the forefront in the writings of Asaṅga and Vasubandhu. This is the notion of *āśrayaparāvṛtti*[43], which is translated here as "revolution at the basis". It is by no means a term unique to Yogācāra writings, as Davidson shows, having originated somewhere within the Abhidharma system.[44] But it finds its way into Yogācāra through the influence of the 136.*Saṃdhinirmocanasūtra* and works, such as the *Śrāvakabhūmi* section of the 166.*Yogācārabhūmi*, which preceded but are standardly ascribed to Asaṅga.

The central task for a Yogācāra aspirant is to get rid of his proclivities. If he tries to do this sequentially he is likely to face a never-ending task, for unless he is remarkably well-coached or inexplicably lucky he is going to breed further proclivities as he goes about his attempts to rid himself of older ones. Recognition of this must have led Buddhist philosophers of the period to reflect not only on the specific nature of seeds and what lays them down, but also on the general nature of seeds and of what can be hoped to eradicate them. One presumes that from this reflecting arose the idea of revolution at the basis, a transformation in approach which would render one no longer subject to the growth of seeds into actions of the sort that breeds proclivities and thus more seeds.

A natural enough way of thinking about this problem was to view the actions that lay down seeds as dependent on depravities (*dauṣṭhulya*), the kinds of physical and mental shortcomings that block the aspirant's way to his goal. An example of a physical depravity might be being overly exhausted, of mental depravity obsessively thinking on some real or imagined slight, or just being depressed. At one point in the *Viniścayasaṃgrahaṇī* of the 166.*Yogācārabhūmi* a classification of some eighteen sorts of such depravities is provided.[45] Now how should one deal with these depravities? The answer suggested is that he should replace these depravities by thoughts which are "clean" (*praśrabdhi*), that is, which cleanse one's mind by ridding his awareness of the factors that constitute and generate depravities. One does this by meditating. And what one gets by thoroughly cleansing one's mind of depravities is termed a revolution at the basis.

The *Śrāvakabhūmi*, for example, distinguishes four varieties of meditative attention (*manaskāra*), the directing of one's attention first towards factors which need attention, second towards the outflows of such factors, third towards that which generates defilementlessness, and fourth towards that which cleanses the vision of knowledge, that is, which produces the higher insight achieved by the enlightened Buddha. In another passage from the same text we are told that through proper meditation one purifies his body and mind of all depravities, purifies supporting objects through examining the actual nature of the objects we know, purifies one's mind through eliminating all desires, and purifies one's knowledge by eliminating ignorance.[46]

The notion of revolution at the basis is projected far wider in the *Viniścayasaṃgrahaṇī* section of the *Yogācārabhūmi*, where it is applied, for example, to the six senses and put to use in addressing distinctions within the penultimate stages on the path to liberation. The question arises whether the noble person still utilizes the six senses in the same way as before, and if so, how there can be any revolution at the basis by which one terminates the proclivities? Asaṅga avoids the trap by answering that it cannot be said whether or not revolution at the basis applies to the senses.

A standard distinction drawn between two kinds of liberation reflects this precise question. In the kind of state called liberation with residues (*sopadhiśeṣa)* one still has the sensory experiences requiring the six senses, whereas in liberation without residues (*nirupadhiśeṣa*) no sensory experiences arise--yet there is said to be revolution at the basis in the latter state. This state is regularly addressed in language bordering on the mystical: liberation without residues is said to be lacking in manifoldness (*niṣprapañca*) and to deal with the purification of the realm of factors (*dharmadhātuviśuddhi*), to involve unshakeableness and blissfulness. Special terminology to characterize this state is invoked: what one knows in liberation without residues is termed thusness (*tathatā*), a notion which grows in importance toward the end of our period.

But just what is this "basis" where the revolution occurs, which becomes transformed? As the Yogācāra literature develops toward the end of our period, it becomes increasingly evident that it is the storehouse-consciousness (*ālayavijñāna*) itself that is transformed through the meditative purification of all the proclivities. In fact, what happens at liberation is precisely that the storehouse-consciousness ceases to exist, so that there is no longer any place where the karmic seeds can be stored. All that is left at liberation is consciousness, but not consciousness of anything, merely pure consciousness.

# 3

# CATEGORIES OF FACTORS

As readers of Volume Seven of this Encyclopedia know, the basic metaphysical concept in Abhidharma Buddhism is that of a "factor" (*dharma*). For those philosophical varieties of Buddhism which admit the existence of entities of any sort, factors are what fundamentally exist. As Paul Griffiths puts it, "a dharma is that which possesses its own unique defining characteristic (*svalakṣaṇa*) and that which exists inherently (*svabhāva*). There are, naturally, many things which exist but which do not have their own inherent existence; for Vasubandhu, examples of such existents would be tables, chairs, persons and numbers. Such things are not factors, though they do exist in the somewhat limited sense of being possible objects of cognition and possible referents of propositions. A factor, therefore, is not the only kind of existent, simply one which possesses a special kind of existence, an existence which marks it off from all other possible existents by the possession of a unique defining characteristic and which is irreducible because inherent."

"Saṃghabhadra...made the distinction between different kinds and levels of existence very clear. Dharmas exist substantially or genuinely and possess the kind of inherent irreducible existence already mentioned: they cannot be reduced by observational or logical analysis into component parts, since they possess none, and the defining characteristic of any particular dharma is not shared by any other since this defining characteristic is unique. In contrast to this substantial existence (*dravyasat*)--the kind of existence properly predicated of dharmas--there is existence as a designation (*prajñaptisat*), the kind of existence belonging to things simply in virtue of there being linguistic conventions which refer to them. This secondary existence, the result of linguistic convention, belongs to complex compounded entities which are composed of those entities (*dharmas*) which possess primary or substantial existence."[47]

Lists of factors are the central business of Theravāda, Sarvāstivāda and Sautrāntika works (though not, of course, of Madhyamaka and Yogācāra works, since these systems deny the independent reality of the factors that constitute the lists of these Abhidharma schools). Readers are directed to Volume Seven of this Encyclopedia for an account of the factors that were accepted by the authors of Abhidharma works prior to our period. Of the Ābhidharmikas stemming from the period covered here, the most important lists we know of are to be found in Harivarman's 121.*Tattvasiddhi* and in Vasubandhu's 163.*Abhidharma-kośa* and his 174.*Bhāṣya* thereon, and in Saṃghabhadra's 206.*Nyāyānusāra*. Vasubandhu's list of seventy-five factors, because of the fame and availability of his works, has come to be taken to be the essential ontological account of Abhidharma Buddhism, and it is this list which organizes Saṃghabhadra's work as well. Harivarman's list, not well known at all, suffers in addition by virtue of being uncountable because innumerable. We shall, therefore, follow Vasubandhu's list, noting that it is by no means the only one available, and at least indicating briefly divergences in Harivarman's and Saṃghabhadra's accounts.

Vasubandhu divides his seventy-five kinds of factors into five categories. It is evident that his idea is that these seventy-five are the only kinds of factors that need be admitted, that they comprise all and only those actual factors. Of course there are legions of types of things that we think about and are referred to in our language, but only the seventy-five are actual entities (*dravyasat*), the others are our constructions (*saṃvṛtisat*), the kinds of things we find expedient to talk about in everyday language. Vasubandhu's five categories divide factors into (1) physical factors, (2) mental factors, (3) factors related to mind, (4) factors separate from both matter and mind, and (5) unconditioned factors, although as we shall see most of the seventy-five fall into the third category.

## PHYSICAL FACTORS

The term rendered here as "physical" is in fact *rūpa*, a term which itself breeds a problem. Since everything is momentary in Buddhism, it can easily be doubted that terms such as "physical" or "material" have any scope at all. Mustn't something, in order to be material or physical, persist in time, occupy space and provide resistance? But such things are ruled out from the start under Buddhist assumptions.

So what can possibly be the items brought under this rubric for Buddhists?

Although there are passing references to atoms in the *Mahāvibhāṣā* (see Volume Seven of this Encyclopedia, Index under "atom") the standard Theravāda atomic theory is first found developed in Buddhaghoṣa's *Visuddhimagga,* covered in a succeeding volume to this one. Atoms were doubtless part of Abhidharma theory as found in the various schools, and views about them are set forth and argued out in Vasubandhu's 174.*Abhidharmakośabhāṣya.*

Vaibhāṣikas apparently applied the word "*aṇu*" to two kinds of things: the unitary substantial atom (*dravyaparamāṇu*) and the aggregated atom or molecule (*saṃghāta-paramāṇu*). A substantial atom is without any parts, cannot be divided, has no spatial dimensions, is imperceptible. A single atom never occurs by itself, but only in combination with others to make up a molecule. Though a single atom is unresistant by itself, it makes up resistant molecules. A molecule comprises a number of atoms--at least eight, consisting of four elemental atoms--one each of earth, air, fire and water--and four qualitative atoms of color, smell, taste and tangibility. They are not necessarily of equal intensity--at least, Vasubandhu has the Vaibhāṣika explain that the reason we perceive color rather than smell, say, in a given aggregate-atom is because the color-atom is predominant.

Vasubandhu's own (Sautrāntika) idea seems to be that there are five kinds of atoms--of color, sound, smell, taste and touch--and that there are likewise five atoms constituting the stream that we in ordinary language mistakenly think of as sense-organs: eyes, ears, nose, tongue and the bodily source of touch sensations. An atom is impenetrable, indivisible, and exercises resistance as a matter of its nature. But note that this account omits the four "great elements" of earth, air, fire and water--these are viewed in Sautrāntika as mere designations.

The question arises: if an atom has no parts, how can it touch other atoms so as to constitute a molecule? Used by Nāgārjuna and Āryadeva (as well as Vasubandhu himself *qua* Yogācāra) as an argument to explode the entire notion of atoms and molecules, the issue clearly demanded attention, which it had received by the beginning of our period in the *Mahāvibhāṣā* and repeated by Vasubandhu *qua* Ābhidharmika and by Saṃghabhadra. We are asked to paint a picture in our minds of a number of atoms making up a molecule by impinging on each other at a number of different points. A conundrum is then posed: an atom is defined as an entity without any parts, but surely that part of atom A, say, that impinges on and so coincides with a part of atom B is a smaller part of atoms A and B. So A and B are not atoms after all! So either there are no atoms, to avoid infinite regress--which is what the Madhyamakas conclude--or atoms cannot combine and thus are of no use in explaining the makeup of larger-sized material things. This argument is utterly basic and can hardly be ignored by the Ābhidharmika.

The Ābhidharmika was not without an answer. Since the Vaibhāṣikas held that an atom had no parts, they held that between any two atoms there is necessarily a space, though it is so small that no light can enter and no atom can occupy it. When asked why, if there is space between two of the atoms constituting a molecule, the molecule doesn't fall apart, they answered that air (*vāyu*) keeps them together.

An eleventh kind of matter produces extensive discussion among Buddhists of Vasubandhu's time, although it is hardly known prior to that. Vasubandhu as Vaibhāṣika introduces a type of matter which does not cause anyone to be aware of it and is thus termed "*avijñaptirūpa*", "unmanifested matter". It is also classified as karma (thus is also "*avijñaptikarman*"), since it occasions a stream into the future in the way that actions do, and is laid down initially by an action. According to Vaibhāṣika understanding this unmanifested matter/karma is constituted by the four primary elements and, in the subsequent moments in the karmic stream occasioned by the initiating act the subsequent unmanifested matter conditioned by the originating matter is likewise supported by the elements. Unmanifested matter/karma is good or bad depending on the quality of the initiating act.

The Sautrāntikas, by contrast, do not accept such a kind of matter. For one thing, they say, the term "*avijñapti*" merely connotes inaction, an absence, and so involves no karmic result. Furthermore, since (*pace* Sarvāstivāda) past factors no longer exist, there is no way such a streaṃ can exist--only present momentary factors exist. Finally, such a kind of karma can't properly be termed "material" (*rūpa*), since matter is destroyed at the next moment and this supposed "unmanifested matter" is not allowed to be so.

The Vaibhāṣikas are given an extended rebuttal in the *Kośabhāṣya*, and are then in turn refuted. (Similar arguments are offered by Vasubandhu in his 197.*Karmasiddhiprakaraṇa*.) Some of the arguments involve scriptural references. The Vaibhāṣika cites scripture to show that it refers to a type of matter that is indestructible, pure matter. The Sautrāntika questions the interpretation placed on the relevant passages. Furthermore, the Vaibhāṣika cites scripture to prove that there can be increase of merit in a virtuous person and that that can only be explained if that person's good unmanifest karma increases. The Sautrāntika points out that any plausible explanation of how that could happen itself conflicts with scripture. Vasubandhu, then, eventually rejects entirely the distinction between manifested and unmanifested matter.

Nevertheless, there is clearly a need within Abhidharma to find a place for karma, and unmanifested matter/karma is that place for the Vaibhāṣikas. For the Sautrāntikas, karma is properly classified in a different place. For them, volition (*cetanā*) is the essence of karma, and the way it works is that the agent intentionally performing an action lays down a seed (*bīja*) which in turn breeds subsequent seeds until at some later time the appropriate occasion for the "growth" of that seed into a sprout occurs, that is, some experience takes place which constitutes the working out of that karmic residue. It will be appreciated that this interpretation makes karma less "objective" and more a matter of how one experiences things, and this coincides with the tendency that grows, as Buddhism progresses from Abhidharma to Yogācāra in response to Madhyamaka, to assign fewer and fewer factors to an objective world and more and more to internalize factors on the analogy of the growth in us of plants emanating from karmic seeds.

## MENTAL FACTORS

The second category of Vasubandhu's five consists of precisely one type of factor. We are told many times in the literature that this one type goes under several names, among which are prominently "awareness" (*jñāna*), "consciousness" (*vijñāna*) and "mind" (*manas*).

The Abhidharma assumption concerning consciousness is that it is one of the basic five aggregates of which the Buddha constantly spoke. These five aggregates are independent and real: therein lies the basic reason for classing Abhidharma as a system which promulgates epistemological realism. Specifically, since the first kind of aggregate, material factors, is on the Abhidharma assumption really distinct from the fifth kind, consciousness, we are forced to conclude that, e.g., there could still be matter if there were no mind and vice versa.

This basic difference, however, brought forth from Nāgārjuna and Āryadeva the criticism that if awareness and matter are so different it is inexplicable how there can be awareness of material objects. The Madhyamaka conclusion is that awareness is empty, that our assumption that we are seats of consciousness apprehending material things through our sense organs is mistaken, a mere manner of speaking and thinking. This argument is buttressed by supplementary considerations. E.g., on the Buddhist assumption of momentariness one awareness cannot grasp more than one content, and two or more awarenesses cannot have the same content; so that even if there were matter we couldn't perceive it, since the eye, e.g., is not conscious and consciousness is not a sense-organ. Again (versus Nyāya), an awareness has no cause to arise before sense-object contact, but can't arise afterward because it has no object to comprise a content. All in all, says the Madhyamaka, the notion of sensory awareness entirely belongs to the realm of illusion.

However, even the Madhyamaka finds it hard to deny consciousness at some level. Āryadeva at one point identifies consciousness as the seed of the cycle of existence, telling us that it will only cease when selflessness is appreciated by everyone. A Madhyamaka can deny a great deal, but unless he is (as he is charged to be) a nihilist he must admit at least one basic type of existent, and consciousness seems a likely candidate. Some such consideration seems to have helped lead to the development of the various ways of thinking that we call Yogācāra. Specifically, it became helpful to the Buddhist to distinguish between construction-filled (*savikalpaka*) and construction-free (*nirvikalpaka*) consciousness, a distinction which was also coming to the fore elsewhere in Indian thought.

As Charlene McDermott engagingly puts it: "The nerve of the Yogācāra 'ideation only' position seems to be the therapeutic reiteration and defense of what is scarcely more than a bare tautology, viz., 'What we mean by phenomenal world is merely the sum total of what is intended by consciousness'. (I.e., the world is a world for consciousness. The limits of the world are precisely the limits of cognizability.) and, since we obviously never have access to anything but our cognitions, the existence of a trans-cognitional correlate (and cause) for a given eidetic experience is at best a gratuitous hypothesis - at worst, perhaps a self-contradictory one...

"And, in support of the foregoing, the Yogācāra philosophers marshal the following considerations:

"(a) In the experiences of dreams, reveries and hallucinations, even opponents of the Yogācāras concede that there are no extra-mental 'objective' correlates accompanying and engendering the imagery. But since there is no foolproof criterion for universally distinguishing genuine sensory phenomena from the data of dreams, hallucinations, etc., it follows that veridical experiences are also not necessarily connected with any trans-mental sources.

"(b) Moreover, all perceptions can be shown to be relative to some percipient subject, whence phenomena can be seen to be unpackable as the modes of minding of some mind or other. Consciousness is thus the horizon of all things.

"(c) Finally, small wonder that the 'relation' between the phenomenal and the trans-phenomenal (or noumenal) turns out to be unintelligible. The very validity of the notion of relation is restricted to the domain of phenomena."

"What is warranted on the basis of (a), (b) and (c) is, strictly speaking a purely *agnostic* attitude towards the noumenal realm. However, Asaṅga goes one step further and *flatly rejects* the existence of such a realm. To arrive at a categorical assertion that there is *nothing but* mind, he has recourse to the evidence from meditational experiences and the testimony of Buddhas (as recorded in, for instance, the *Saṃdhinirmocanasūtra*). Furthermore, there is a pragmatic justification for going on to a dogmatic idealism - it is more expedient so to believe, the better to leave off grasping."[48]

Though not everyone has agreed with McDermott that Asaṅga did in fact go on to a dogmatic idealism, it seems that something not far short of that is what is taught in a number of the works attributed to Asaṅga and Vasubandhu. We find in those works structures that clearly suggest an idealist understanding. One of these is the reference in the 164.*Madhyāntavibhāga* (regularly attributed to Asaṅga but probably not by him) to the "construction of what was not" (*abhūtaparikalpa*) as the basis for all the content-filled experiences we normally are having. In a somewhat mysterious way, the author of that text refuses to say specifically whether this entity (or state) exists or does not exist, but it is clearly the source of our normal experiences of objects and bodies as well as of colors and shapes. The same notion is featured in the 138.*Laṅkāvatārasūtra*, probably at least in part prior to the 164.*Madhyāntavibhāga* and perhaps the source of this particular rubric.

The notion of a construction of what doesn't exist is filled out in Yogācāra into a basic triadic distinction between the constructed (*parikalpita*), dependent (*paratantra*) and perfected (*pariniṣpanna*) natures. What can this triad connote? Fortunately, the relevant terms have been studied with great insight and scholarship by Hugh B. Urban and Paul J. Griffiths, and in explaining this fundamental triad we lean heavily on their analysis.[49]

Urban and Griffiths are exploring the following question which on the basis of our discussion so far must seem extremely pertinent: When Yogācāra Buddhists speak of emptiness do they mean by that term the complete absence of anything and everything, or is there something left over? They cite Gadjin Nagao[50] as concluding "that, according to the views expressed in the texts of the classical Indian Yogācāra, 'emptiness' (*śūnyatā*) does not denote simple nonexistence (*abhāva*); rather, there is always something left over or remaining (*avaśiṣṭa*) in emptiness, something that is identified with the basis for or locus of all human activity, and that is otherwise called the 'dependent' (*paratantra*) aspect of experience. This remains even for the Buddha: the realization of emptiness, claims Nagao, does not entail the end of the flow of experience, of what the Yogācāra calls *abhūtaparikalpa*, the comprehensive construction of what is unreal. Rather, this constructive activity continues, though it is now radically different, and is called 'perfected' (*pariniṣpanna*)."[51]

After a careful survey of all the occurrences of the relevant terms, Urban and Griffiths sum up by remarking "A strong case can be made, then, for the conclusion that phenomenally rich mental images--designated by *vijñapti, pratibhāsa, nimitta,* or *abhūtaparikalpa*--do remain in emptiness but that these cannot have been subject to the constructive activity denoted by *vikalpa*."[52] That is, the liberated person, such as the Buddha, is not without experiences, nor even confined to "empty", i.e., contentless experiences, but is aware of "a flow of mental images (*nimitta*), appearances (*pratibhāsa*), and representations with phenomenal properties *(vijñapti)*. It [that liberated person] would not, however, experience any sort of conceptual construction (*vikalpa*), since this necessarily involves the reification of these illusory appearances, the separation of their phenomenal properties, the formation of names and categories, and their bifurcation into subject and object. In more standard Yogācāra terms, Buddha would still perceive the pure flow of phenomena which constitutes the *paratantrasvabhāva*, but without the dualities and distinctions which constitute the *parikalpitasvabhāva*."[53]

Thus constructed awarenesses are those whose contents do not exist at all--they are conceptual constructions, imaginary entities. Dependent awarenesses are described in the foregoing paragraph, the "flow of mental images, appearances and representations" which a Buddha has but which is obscured for the unliberated by constructions. The perfected awareness, finally, is the pure, contentless consciousness, equated also with emptiness, suchness, reality, what is signless and called by the honorific term "root of factors" (*dharmadhātu*). This perfected nature is the way things really are, their thusness (*tathatā*); it is liberation (*nirvāṇa*) and it is also the essentiality of the path (*mārga*).[54] Insofar as a Buddha is still having content-filled experiences those experiences belong to dependent awareness.

Now it needs to be emphasized that these three natures are not actually different entities.[55] Every dependent or constructed awareness is a perfected awareness improperly construed as content-filled in the fashion we are familiar with in daily life (in the case of constructions); it can be, as well, construed as contentless (at least sometimes) in advanced stages of meditation. In fact, in advanced stages of meditation one is said in Buddhist texts to attain remarkable states of progressively contentless concentration. These include the four meditations--on infinite space, infinite consciousness, nothingness, and neither-identification-nor-nonidentification--which were proposed in earlier Abhidharma texts as constituting altered states attained by the meditator. The general term for these states is *samāpatti*, translated in our Volumes as "absorption" or "trance". Paul Griffiths describes these four altered states as follows.

"In the first case, that of transcending the conceptualizations of physical form and attaining the sphere of infinite space, the practitioner achieves his goal, it seems by taking the sphere of infinite space as the object of contemplative exercise. It seems that the practitioner is intended to actively think--even to verbalize--that space is infinite and to contemplate this idea until the possibility of cognizing physical form in any way has completely vanished. The practitioner will then be established in a condition wherein the only object of cognition that occurs to him is that of featureless, formless undifferentiated space. Much of the same applies to the second and third formless spheres--those of the infinity of consciousness and of nothing at all. Here also progress is achieved by the use of active thought and verbalization--on the one hand that consciousness is infinite and on the other that nothing whatever exists."

"It is evident that the content of consciousness becomes increasingly attenuated as the practitioner progresses through the stages of formlessness. By the third stage, the practitioner has developed the ability to cognize nothingness or, more precisely, to empty the content of awareness of everything except the consciousness that nothing exists. But even this is not the highest state possible; in the third stage, the sphere of nothing at all, the ability to form concepts and the concomitant ability to verbalize them (if indeed the two can properly be distinguished) remains. In the fourth state--that of neither conceptualization nor non-conceptualization--even this vanishes, and the ability to form concepts exists in such an attenuated form that it is neither thought proper to say that it exists or that it does not." But the mastery of meditative abilities does not end here; it goes on to an even further state (or perhaps several such), the most important of which is termed *nirodhasamāpatti*, the attainment of cessation. "Finally, in the attainment of cessation, otherwise called the cessation of sensation and conceptualization, even this vanishes, and the practitioner enters a cataleptic trance..."[56] The ability to undergo this extreme stage of meditation is said to be limited to noble ones (*ārya*) and perfected beings (*arhat*). The (meditative) techniques (described in the previous two paragraphs) "are, therefore, essentially enstatic. That is, they are designed initially to progressively withdraw the practitioner from all sensory contact with the external world and then to progressively bring to a halt all inner mental activity. The process culminates in the attainment of cessation, wherein there are no mental events and no contacts with the external world. Actions are not initiated and stimuli are not responded to; the continuum of mental events which constitutes the psychological existence of the practitioner according to Buddhist theory runs out into silence. There is some evidence...that this kind of cessation was identified by some Buddhists at some periods with Nirvana and was thus thought of as the ultimately desirable goal for all Buddhists."[57]

Griffiths studies the attainment of cessation as it is treated in Theravāda, Vaibhāṣika, Sautrāntika and Yogācāra. The ultimate development of the Theravāda treatment of this topic is developed by Buddhaghoṣa and subsequently in a period, beyond our purview here, that we shall consider in the next Volume of this series devoted to Buddhist thought. But the positions of the other three treatments are developed, e.g., in Vasubandhu's *Kośa* and are properly dealt with in the present context following Griffiths' exposition.

The puzzle that Griffiths is concerned with in his book is this. If, as it is stated, a meditator in the extreme trance-states of attainment of cessation stops feeling and thinking altogether, since this would seem to suggest a hiatus in that stream of consciousness, why is it not the case that this trance-state constitutes liberation, and why and how can one come out of such a state and find himself still attached to all the traces, etc., which he was attached to before trance? If consciousnesses (*citta*) cease during this trance, what can cause them to start again? The Vaibhāṣika solution pertains to an exceptional view of causation. Since every event must have an immediately antecedent and similar causal condition, the problem arises: if there is no immediately antecedent condition prior to the awakening of the meditator from the attainment of cessation, how can it ever arise? According to the Vaibhāṣika, however, an immediately antecedent condition need not occur in a moment immediately preceding the effect--there may be a period of time separating cause and effect. If one asks a slightly different question--why *should* one in the attainment of cessation ever come out of the trance?--the answer is that the meditator explicitly decides, prior to beginning this kind of meditation, that he will terminate the trance after such-and-such a period of time.

It will be evident that, whatever other difficulties the above explanation may incur, it is hopeless unless time is understood in the common-sensical way we and the Vaibhāṣikas do, as comprising a real past, present and future. But the Sautrāntikas specifically do not share that understanding; indeed, they explicitly deny that the past and the future exist. Thus it is not possible for the Sautrāntika to accept the foregoing way out of the problem concerning the awakening from the attainment of cessation. His answer, instead, appeals to an analogy, the planting of seeds. "On this view...the last moments of consciousness before entry into the àttaiment of cessation plant seeds in the continuing stream of physical events--'the body with its senses'--and that in due time these seeds ripen and produce their fruit, the emergence of consciousness from the attainment of cessation...(Thus) The Sautrāntikas also wish to preserve the necessity of an immediately antecedent and similar condition for the emergent consciousness, but by allotting that function to the 'seeded' physical body they are forced to loosen, almost to the point of disregarding, the requirement that the relevant condition be 'similar'."[58]

Griffiths produces an elegant argument to illustrate the dilemma faced by both the Vaibhāṣika and the Sautrāntika viewpoints. It runs as follows:

"(1) For the occurrence of any given event, Y, there exists a necessary and sufficient condition, X.

(2) For the occurrence of any given event, Y, there exists a necessary condition, X, which is temporally contiguous with, and phenomenologically similar to, Y.

(3) There are two kinds of events: mental and physical.

(4) Every event is located in a continuum; every continuum can be (theoretically) individuated from every other continuum.

(5) It is possible that, in a given continuum, C, at a given time, T, there be a complete absence of mental events while physical events continue.

(6) It is possible that, in C at T-plus-n, mental events may begin again."[59]

This set of assumptions involves contradiction, is inconsistent. So one or another of the assumptions made must be modified. Vaibhāṣikas and Sautrāntikas solve the problem by modifying step (2) or rejecting step (5), the Vaibhāṣika by relaxing the requirement of temporal contiguity of X and Y, the Sautrāntika by abandoning the requirement of phenomenological similarity between X and Y. The Vaibhāṣikas save their argument by postulating the reality of past and future as well as present factors. The Sautrāntikas propose either "that: (i) there really are mental events in the attainment of cessation--and thus (5) is rejected; or (ii) the re-emergence of mind referred to in (6) is actually caused by purely physical events--and thus (2) is modified."[60] Neither of the two solutions appears satisfactory.

The Yogācāra solution to the problem in effect denies step (3) of the argument in the preceding paragraph by denying outright the existence of physical events, and as we have recently seen they adopt the theory of three natures (constructed, dependent, perfected). They also retain the agricultural analogy of seeds and sprouts, fleshing out talk of a "dependent" nature in terms of seeds laid down by our awarenesses; a seed, perfumed by the trace created in the awareness which caused it, conditions a subsequent act in the future. Misunderstood as involving the distinction between a real knowing subject and a real object as content, this dependent nature is (as was said before) interpreted through constructions; rightly understood as free from all differentiations, it is properly seen as perfected.

However, the thought sooner or later occurred to the Yogacāras that talk of seeds and sprouts is clearly an analogy. How does this analogy work without additional assumptions? What are these things metaphorically called "seeds" in actuality, and where do they reside, especially since they must apparently maintain their existence during such periods of almost complete stoppage that characterize the attainment of cessation? How shall we explain the continuity between the stream that apparently ends as the meditator enters trance, and the stream that seemingly begins again when, as we say, the meditator leaves such a state? What is maintained during the interval, given that cessation is clearly described as a stoppage of all thought, and that Yogācāras view the world as nothing but thought, i.e., as consciousness-only. Where are those "seeds" "stored"?

Well, naturally enough, where they are stored must be consciousness--since that's the only kind of thing there is--and so it seems completely understandable that these thinkers arrived in due course at the notion of a storehouse-consciousness (*ālayavijñāna*). What happens is that the seeds laid down by the events we construe as actions in the lifetime of a stream-of-consciousness are stored in the storehouse-consciousness; these seeds initiate their own streams until the occasion arises for the maturation of a seed in the form of an action. This store-house consciousness may superficially look like the much-denied self of non-Buddhist belief, but it is stoutly denied that it is a self: it is not a substantially existing or persisting thing, but merely a way of referring to the collection of the moments in those streams which comprise the momentary, karmically occasioned results of momentary actions.

A substantial Yogācāra literature is devoted to developing arguments to show the nature and existence of the store-consciousness. For one thing, since each of the six kinds of awareness (the five sensory awareness plus merely mental awareness) requires a sense-organ as locus and an immediately antecedent event as causal condition, it is evident that a distinct kind of consciousness needs to be presumed in order to account for, e.g., the karmic acquisition of an appropriate kind of rebirth at the beginning of each lifetime, accounting for such a rebirth in terms of the kinds of seeds that are slated to come to fruition during the ensuing lifetime in a certain kind of embodiment.

The assumption of a storehouse-consciousness also helps us understand how two or more sense-organs can function at once; how the first moment of consciousness in a given life can arise; what can explain our ability to cognize anything at all, given that a content of awareness only exists for a moment and, since gone by the next, can only be remembered; how action can occur at all; how there can be experience of a manifold of things at once; what it is that separates from the body at death; and what it is that still persists during cessation. The answer to all these questions turns on the existence of a storehouse-consciousness.[61] And the last-mentioned answer solves the question posed a few paragraphs back about making sense of the attainment of the cessation trance.

## CONCOMITANT AWARENESSES

By far the largest group of factors in Vasubandhu's *Abhidharmakośa* constitutes the list of derived or concomitant awarenesses (*caitta*). This whole separate category of concomitant awarenesses is denied by Harivarman, who treats at length an objection representing the point of view later adopted by Vasubandhu. In fact, Harivarman is generally antipathetic toward categories comprising large numbers of factors--he also rejects such divisions as are found in Abhidharma texts of factors into elements, senses, etc., and suggests that each aggregate comprises a variety of sorts and that these are what others (e.g., Vasubandhu, later) classify into separate groups or categories. Harivarman says they are all kinds of awareness, that the only relevant category is in fact awareness itself. Furthermore, since awareness causes, e.g., a feeling (the first sort of concomitant awareness listed by Vasubandhu), the feeling cannot be a separate kind of thing and occur simultaneously with the awareness.

For Vasubandhu, however, there are some forty-six kinds of concomitant awarenesses. He divides them into six varieties, and we shall follow his division below. The first category of generally permeating (*mahābhūmika*) factors comprises ten types. According to Vasubandhu, in opposition to Śrīlāta, every momentary slice of awareness includes one factor of each of these ten types. Secondly there are ten good permeating factors (*kuśalamahābhūmika*), with one of each of these kinds accompanying every good awareness. Defiling permeating factors number some eighteen sorts; they are divided by Vasubandhu into three categories: six types of factors which arise with every defilement (*kleśamahābhūmika*), though a given factor of this sort is not necessarily bad--it may be neutral; two types of factors which are always defiling and always bad (*akuśalabhūmika*); and ten afflicting factors (*upakleśabhūmika*) which may accompany the other defilements. Finally, there is a group of indeterminate or neutral factors, neither good nor bad (*aniyatabhūmika*).

### I.Generally permeating factors.

The forty-six kinds of awareness cover a large variety of kinds of mental state. If one understands meditation in a broad sense to include any level of concentration, including the minimal attention required of any intentional mental state above mere sensation, the list makes somewhat more sense than otherwise, and one can in fact suggest a kind of progress from the first of these generally permeating ten types to the last as indicating states of increased concentration as one becomes less and less distracted, more and more focussed in one's attention.

1.Feeling (*vedanā*). Feelings are classified into eighteen kinds at one point in the *Kośa*, into five at another, and into two at two further points in that work. Feelings arise as a result of karmic conditioning, and broadly speaking are either satisfying or frustrating, breeding contentment or irritation or equanimity. But as Buddhists mustn't we classify all feelings as frustrating? Certainly, but satisfaction still occurs from time to time, so that some feelings, while temporarily satisfying, are in the end frustrating. A feeling is the basic kind of mental response to a sensory stimulus.

2.Identification (*saṃjñā*). It is difficult to find a totally satisfying translation for this term. While we are rendering it as "identification", at least two other respected Buddhist scholars suggest "recognition".[62] Paul Williams, in a brilliant and extended discussion of this notion, suggests that it corresponds to one's thinking of a thing as being, e.g., colored ("x (is) blue"), and is closely connected with giving a name to a thing (in fact it is explicitly glossed as *nāman* by Saṃghabhadra, though described as "produced by name" by the Sarvāstivādins. It is identification that produces the grasping of signs (*nimitta*) and the breeding of conceptual construction (*vikalpa*), and it works selectively to pick out a supporting object (*ālambana*) or "sign".[63] An identification leads to a feeling and is the occasion for karmic maturation -- in fact, the Dārṣṭāntikas are reported to have made identifying the *only* cause of maturation, to which Theravādins and Mahāsāṃghikas demur. When one gets to a sufficiently advanced stage of meditation one of the states gained is classified as *asaṃjñīsamāpatti*, "nonrecognizing".

3.Volition (*cetanā*). Equated with the mind, with synonyms which suggest our thirst to make aggregates, it is rendered as "will" by Carolyn Rhys Davids. The Vaibhāṣikas held that all thoughts are the results of karma, but Vasubandhu disagrees, which is why he denies that a separate category of "unmanifest karma" is necessary.

4.Contact (*sparśa*). The Sanskrit term is decidedly ambiguous, appearing also as the term denoting the sense-organ of touch. In the presently relevant sense, it is for the Sarvāstivāda and Vaibhāṣika the relation between a sense-organ and a content grasped. Strictly speaking, of course, the organ does not literally touch the object, for it does not last long enough to do that. For this reason the Sautrāntikas came to view this factor as not a real distinct entity. But the Sarvāstivādins, as said, say it is a distinct entity. Vasubandhu in the *Kośa* carries on an extended debate with 158.Śrīlāta, the latter denying that it is necessarily accompanied by any awareness. The term also is used to describe the relation between a sense-organ and a content grasped---as we have seen, the organ does not strictly speaking touch any object, but the atoms comprising both are in close proximity. One should perhaps be careful to distinguish the physical object comprised of atoms from the epistemic content displayed in the cognizer's awareness.

5.Interest (*chanda*). This, we are told by e.g. Saṃghabhadra, is not to be confused with desire or thirst (*tṛṣṇā*), but is equated (by Harivarman) with covetousness. It is the first of a closely related series of states of mind occasioned by one's conceiving a content on the basis of identifying a feeling occasioned in thought by the connection of that content with an appropriate sense (including mental) organ.

6.Intellection (*mati*), that is, having an increasingly specific conception of a content as an object.

7.Memory or mindfulness (*smṛti*). In the present context the latter translation is perhaps more pertinent, suggesting as it does the bringing to mind of a content for the purpose of meditation. But memory is certainly also involved, since to meditate on an object, requiring attention to a content over a period of time, necessarily involves more than mere momentary sensory awareness.[64]

8.Attention (*manaskāra*). The zeroing in on a meditative or supporting object is a requisite stage in meditation and requires a distinct act, thus a distinct factor, for each resulting awareness. Attending can be right or wrong, and when indulged in carelessly results in the breeding of proclivites.

9.Resolve (*adhimokṣa*). As the term suggests, one with his wits about him and desirous of liberation resolutely enters into appropriate states of meditation or concentration, which comprises the tenth of these ten categories, viz.,

10.Concentration (*samādhi*) or meditation (*dhyāna*). The literature here studied and summarized is full of extended advice and descriptions of how to meditate, stages of meditation, what to meditate on, etc. The reader is invited to consult the Introduction to Volume Seven of this Encyclopedia for a description of some of the facets of meditation as understood in early Buddhism. In the period covered in the present Volume much of the same general structure is presumed, e.g., the four stages of meditation leading to advanced states of meditation on space, consciousness, etc. and culminating in the crowning type of meditation on cessation (*nirodhasamāpatti*) where one's body and organs cease functioning. This general, presupposed account of meditation is adumbrated at great length in the texts surveyed here; however, we shall not attempt to summarily analyze the accounts, which can be gleaned from the summaries below and fleshed out by consulting the texts referred to.

II.Good permeating factors.

These factors always breed good karmic results.

1.Faith (*śraddhā*). If one feels uncomfortable with a term which has such strong Christian overtones an alternative term is "confidence" (*prasāda*). The notion is defined variously, by Harivarman as concentration on a content, by Saṃghabhadra as affection not involving attachment (thus not defiled). Faith produces energy, the next in the present list. The term plays a role in two technical terms used in classifying stages on the path. "Faith-followers" are those about to become stream-enterers on the path of vision and who have "mild faculties", i.e., who are not of an intellectual bent. Those "resolved in faith" are faith-followers who have become perfected beings.

2.Energy (*vīrya*), produced by faith, is one of the four practices leading toward supernatural powers (*ṛddhipada*), the other practices being appropriate interest in gaining such powers, mental application toward that end, and careful examination of the powers themselves.

3.Equanimity (*upekṣā*). A state of mind free from conceptual construction, devoid of any feeling of superiority or inferiority, a culminating stage in meditation.

4.Shame (*hrī*), 5.Modesty (*anapatrāpya*), 6.Absence of greed (*alobha*), 7.Lack of hatred (*adveṣa*), 8.Nonviolence (*ahiṃsā*), 9.Tranquility (*praśrabdhi*),10.Heedfulness (*apramāda*). The English terms are suggestive; one hopes they are reasonably accurate!

III.Defiling[65] permeating factors (*kleśamahābhūmika)*.

As Anacker notes: "Afflicted states [i.e., what we are calling "defiling" states] are 'bad', being suffering, but are not necessarily unbeneficial (i.e., 'bad' in the sense of ethically reprehensible). There is an entire category of factors which are categorized as afflicted, but which are ethically beneficial (the *kuśalasāsravas*), and another of factors which are similarly afflicted but ethically indeterminate (the *nivṛtāvyākṛtas*, "obstructed but indeterminate events" [rendered in our Volume here as "obstructed-neutral"]. For instance, attachment may sometimes be beneficial, and doubts, remorse, and aversion, though afflicted, may have good results. Similarly, any afflicted state which has come about as a result of retribution is by necessity indeterminate..., since anything which is retribution itself carries no further retribution. (A very just credo which leaves everybody an opening for escape from suffering.)"

In fact, Vasubandhu's classifications here are somewhat vague, and his treatment of them differs in works other than the *Kośa*. Delusion (*moha*) or ignorance (*avidyā*) is, as we have seen, one of the six proclivities: it is listed as the first in the present group of defiling permeating factors, while the other five do not appear at all in Vasubandhu's classification though some are apparently to be found in the final group (below, VI.Neutral Factors). Likewise, the list of defilements (Anacker's "afflicted states") given in Vasubandhu's 200.*Madhyāntavibhāgabhāṣya* II.2-3a comprises nine types which overlap the six defilements proper. We seem to be working with several distinctions here, easily confused.[66]

The *Kośa* lists six types of factors under the present heading.

1.Delusion (*moha*) or ignorance (*avidyā*). One of the three bad roots that produce filthy awarenesses. It is always present in defiled minds, but (as the other five listed here) can be neutral (when it constitutes karmic retribution) as well as bad. It produces doubt and error; a residue in every feeling, it causes what is really frustrating to be viewed as satisfying.

2.Heedlessness (*pramāda*). Harivarman denies that either this or its opposite, heedfulness, are separate factors.

3.Sloth (*kauśīdya*), 4.Lack of confidence (*aśrabdhi*), 5.Lethargy (*styāna*), 6.Excitedness (*auddhatya*).

IV.Factors That Are Always Bad.

1.Shamelessness (*ahrīkya*) and 2.Disregard (*anapatrāpya*) concerning one's acts and their results.

V.Afflicting Factors (*upakleśa*).

Vasubandhu provides a list of these numbering ten; Harivarman's list comes to eighteen. By conditioning actions involving conceptual constructing they breed karma in everyone, even those on the path, up to the final stage of a noble person who has realized the truth of cessation--such a one has destroyed all his afflictions and will not breed any more. Vasubandhu's list is as follows: 1.Anger (*krodha*), 2.Hypocrisy (*mrakṣa*), 3.Selfishness (*mātsarya*), 4.Envy (*īrṣyā*), 5.Spite (*pradāsa*), 6.Violence (*vihiṃsā*), 7.Vengefulness (*upanāha*), 8.Deceit (*māyā*), 9.Craftiness (*śāṭhya*), and 10.Arrogance (*mada*).

It should not be assumed that the perfected being is entirely free from feelings. Neutrality (*upekṣā*) is a feeling, as are compassion (*karuṇā*), friendship (*maitrī*) and a kind of excitement (*saṃvega*): they are among the feelings the perfected being experiences.[67]

VI.Neutral Factors.

Vasubandhu mentions four of these--regret (*kaukṛtya*), sleepiness (*middha*), initial thought (*vitarka*) and sustained thought (*vicāra*)--but the tradition is that there are eight in all, with four of the six proclivities--attachment, repugnance, pride and perplexity--making up the remaining four. Vasubandhu does not actually name these, although it is regularly assumed he must have meant to put them here, and this is borne out in a way by another list of ten such factors, with the first two of Vasubandhu's *Kośa* list missing and the remaining items constituting four kinds of wrong view.

## DISSOCIATED FACTORS

Factors classified in the *Kośa* as contents of concomitant awarenesses are factors which arise at the same moment as an awareness (*citta*): thus they constitute conditioning factors associated with awareness (*cittasamprayuktasaṃskāra*). Vasubandhu in the *Kośa* also identifies some fourteen conditioning factors dissociated from awareness (*cittaviprayuktasaṃskāra*), so called because they are neither themselves material factors nor mental states complete with contents.

Lists of such dissociated factors can be found in the Buddhist literature as far back as the *Dharmaskandha* (summarized in Volume Seven of this Encyclopedia), which mentions some sixteen such factors. Indeed, that list, as well as lists found in such works as Ghoṣaka's *Abhidharmāmṛta* and the *Abhidharmahṛdayas* attributed to Dharmaśrī and Upaśānta, comprise the fourteen factors also found in Vasubandhu's 173.*Kośa* and in Saṃghabhadra's 206.*Nyāyānusāra*, although Saṃghabhadra argues for the incorporation of added types of factors into the list either as added kinds or as new varieties of kinds already in the list.

Not all schools admitted this kind of factor as actual existents. The Sarvāstivādins took them to be, like the other factors in their lists, real entities (*dravya*) having each its own essential nature. But other schools disagreed, and "the attribution of a specific activity to a particular factor and the existential status if that discrete factor continued to be subject of heated controversy in early northern Indian Abhidharma texts long after the dissociated forces were first isolated."[68]

1.Possession (*prāpti*). This category was mentioned briefly earlier in our exposition. Vasubandhu explains it as comprising either the occurrence ("acquisition") for the first time of the experience of a factor, or the occurrence ("accompaniment") of the experience of a type of factor in subsequent moments following the initial one. A lengthy discussion in the *Mahāvibhāṣā* concerns the difference between acquisition and accompaniment, which is taken up again in the differing interpretations of Vasubandhu and of Saṃghabhadra. Vasubandhu interprets the difference to relate to the difference between the first moment and subsequent moments in the experience (as we would put it) of a thing, remembering that, for Vasubandhu, a "thing" cannot persist through the three time periods of past, present and future. Saṃghabhadra, on the other hand, who thinks a factor can persist through past, present and future, interprets "acquisition" as the first time in a person's history that a factor has occurred, and "accompaniment" as describing the relation between that person's life-stream and subsequent moment of the same sort.

The postulation of possession is intended to answer the otherwise difficult question of how the factors or events making up "my" stream are mine in distinction to those that are "yours". In particular, the factors explaining our talk about "cessation", which lie outside of normal causal chains, are part of the life-stream of a particular person, and the problem is to account for the relation between these factors (referred to in our Volume as "calculated" and "uncalculated cessation") and the factors that constitute the stream we call the person undergoing these states. Furthermore, it is crucial to tie the karmic traces (i.e., the streams constituting such traces) into the stream corresponding to the agent of the acts that laid those traces down. To accomplish all these tasks the factor of possession was postulated.[69]

2.Nonpossession (*aprāpti*). When liberation approaches, the stream we call a person enters various states of cessation and loses the proclivities and other factors that occasion the breeding of karmic traces. As we saw earlier, the severance of a given type of factor from a given stream comes about through a process termed "revolution at the basis", whereby one acquires, as it were, counteragents (*pratipakṣa*) to specific proclivities. The proclivity then ceases to arise in that stream, i.e., becomes separated from the stream of the rest of the factors comprising what we consider to be the person. Why should that happen, and how can it happen, given that the ordinary causal process requires a factor to causally condition either another factor of the same or similar sort or at any rate some factor or other? The answer provided in these schools of Buddhism postulates an added factor of nonpossession to explain that separation.

3.Homogeneity (*sabhāgatā*). Why is it that those reborn on this earth comprise species whose bodies, organs, etc. are so similar? If karma determines one's rebirth, and each person's karmic store is different from the next one's, why aren't there as many different types of embodiments as there are streams of factors constituting what we take to be persons? To answer this question Buddhists posited a type of factor, the term for which (*sabhāgatā*) literally means "the character of having the same kinds of parts", translated here as "homogeneity". Indeed, Vasubandhu specifically refers to at least two kinds of homogeneity found in humans, one the general homogeneity common to all living beings, second the commonality which binds, e.g., humans and distinguishes them from other animals.

Vasubandhu and Saṃghabhadra in fact differ over whether homogeneity is a real factor or only a conceptual construction. Saṃghabhadra thinks it is a real factor, arguing that if it were not we would not be able to classify beings in the way we do. Vasubandhu, on the other hand, after presenting the Vaibhāṣika position, argues against it in the *Kośa*, offering as reasons that homogeneity is actually nothing but being what one is, and that in fact not only living beings have parts of the same sort as others of the same species but so do nonliving things as well; indeed things in general fall into classes in virtue of their similarities and differences, so that being homogeneous is a general property of everything, not a specific property of anything.

4.Non-ideation (*āsaṃjñika*), 5.Nonideation Trance (*asaṃjñīsamāpatti*) and 6.Cessation Trance (*nirodhasamāpatti*). We have seen before that Buddhism develops a fairly elaborate theory of advanced sorts of meditative states. Some of these--we have spoken of the cessation-trance--involve states where no ideas of any sort occur and yet the meditator is still living and breathing, will in due course return from his trance to a life of sensations and thoughts. For example, during the moment or moments between death and the beginning of the next life, without the relevant mental and bodily factors which make thought possible, the moments in the stream corresponding to a "person" are devoid of content, are as good as nonexistent, and yet the stream continues through such moments. How can that be? The topic was discussed extensively in texts such as the *Mahāvibhāṣā*, and it is from such sources that both Vasubandhu and Saṃghabhadra derive their views.

Harking back to such sources we find reference to a disagreement between the Sarvāstivādins or Vaibhāṣikas on the one hand, the Dārṣṭāntikas and Sautrāntikas on the other. Saṃghabhadra sides with the former, Vasubandhu with the latter. Saṃghabhadra assumes 4, 5, and 6 are real independent factors, arguing that they are required to explain why no awarenesses or mental concomitants occur during trance. Since such blocking factors are clearly not awarenesses, nor are they material entities, he classifies them among the dissociated factors. For Vasubandhu, on the other hand, it is the thought immediately preceding the first moment of nonideation or cessation that causes such a moment to arise and to produce a material location in the body to locate such a trance state. In each successive moment another similar empty location is caused to arise, for as long as the trance lasts. Thus for Vasubandhu it is not necessary to assume the existence as independent factors of these three kinds of meditative states; they are simply constructions, manners of speaking of the nonoperation of thought. We saw earlier how this account presents problems as to how the series of content-filled awarenesses begins afresh.[70]

7.Vitality or life-force (*jīvita*). Since on Buddhist assumptions each "person" is merely a series of momentary factors, what distinguishes a stream of factors constituting a person from a stream constituting, e.g., a chair, and in particular keeps a person "alive" during trance states, e.g., in contrast to inanimate objects which are never alive and thus pose no such problem? As early as the Buddhist *sūtras* one finds reference to a controlling faculty made responsible for this peculiarity, as well as to faculties of masculinity and femininity made responsible for gender differentiations. It is not surprising then that vitality finds itS way into Vasubandhu's list of dissociated factors. What is perhaps surprising is that masculinity and femininity did not find their way onto the same list.

The topic of vitality continues to be a problem much discussed by Vasubandhu and Saṃghabhadra and later. "There are three major issues in these later treatments of vitality: first, the possibility of states without thought--specifically, the state of non-conception and the two states of equipoise of non-conception and cessation--which would lack perceptual consciousness; second, the possibility of rebirth in the formless realm, which would lack warmth; and third, the discrimination of life from death within the stream of any given sentient being. Underlying these specific issues is a fundamental disagreement concerning the ontological status of vitality as a discrete factor. For Saṃghabhadra and the Sarvāstivāda-Vaibhāṣikas, the three factors of vitality, warmth, and perceptual consciousness are not in all cases inextricably linked; for if they were, states said to be without thought would have thought (i.e., perceptual consciousness), and rebirth states in the formless realm would have form (i.e., warmth). If life were distinguished from death only by the presence of perceptual consciousness, states without thought would be tantamount to death. Further, since beings in the formless realm lack a corporeal basis, and therefore, warmth, were it not for vitality, their thought would be without a support...Therefore, vitality must be admitted to exist as a discrete and real force capable of supporting both warmth and perceptual consciousness. What then would support vitality, especially given the fact that vitality remains when either warmth or perceptual consciousness is absent? Vitality is itself supported by previous action (*karman*) and homogeneous character (*sabhāgatā*) both of which are also, like vitality, characteristic only of sentient beings."[71]

Saṃghabhadra views these reasons as sufficient to warrant postulation of vitality as a distinct and real dissociated factor. Vasubandhu, however, does not, though without completely explaining his answers to the three "major issues" Cox refers to in the above-quoted passage. For Vasubandhu, vitality is one more conceptual construction.

8.Birth (*jāti*), 9.Duration (*sthiti*), 10.Aging (*jarā*) and 11.Termination (*anityatā*). These four states characterize all conditioned factors, providing each factor the time to perform the function appropriate to it. Again, where Saṃghabhadra accepts these four as actual factors, Vasubandhu disagrees. The issues mirror problems discussed in earlier periods among Dārṣṭāntikas and Sautrāntikas.

12.Collection of Words (*nāmakāya*), 13.Collection of Phrases (*padakāya*), 14.Collection of Phonemes (*vyañjanakāya*). In Abhidharma analysis the "phoneme" or syllable consists of either a vowel alone, or a consonant or consonant-cluster plus a vowel. (Thus, the term "Abhidharma" consists of the phonemes "*a*", "*bhi*", "*dha*" and "*rma*".) These phonemes then form the basis of words (e.g., "*dharma*") and of phrases (e.g., "*abhidharma*"). As before, names, phrases and phonemes constitute separate and real factors for the Sarvāstivādins, and are classed among the dissociated factors since they are related to both material items and to thought. Vasubandhu defines a word as a collection of identifications (*saṃjñāsamukṭi*).

In now-familiar fashion Vasubandhu and Saṃghabhadra differ in their interpretation of these three categories. Whereas Saṃghabhadra analyzes language as involving factors of these three categories in relation to one another, Vasubandhu claims that the three categories are unnecessary, that what must be postulated is language. A word, for him, is not a separate factor, and words and phrases are not collections of sounds indicating phonemes. Rather, it is speech, language itself, that constitutes language. Saṃghabhadra's objection to this is that "language itself" cannot be identified with either sound alone, with internal thoughts of objects, nor with what is conveyed in communication. Thus he prefers to classify the components of language as dissociated factors.

## UNCONDITIONED FACTORS

The final three factors in Vasubandhu's list of seventy-five are the unconditioned (*asaṃskṛta*) or uncompounded group consisting of empty space (*ākāśa*), calculated cessation (*pratisaṃkhyānirodha*) and uncalculated cessation (*apratisaṃkhyānirodha*). His list is austere in contrast to lists of other schools, which numbered nine or more, including such things as dependent origination and the four immaterial realms of infinite space, consciousness, nothingness and neither-consciousness-nor-nonconsciousness. Vasubandhu apparently did not consider these latter items factors themselves, but rather types or "locales" of factors.

Unconditioned factors are eternal and noncontaminating, which is to say, they do not produce karmic residues. However, according to Vasubandhu they do enter into causal series, at least in a limited fashion. Although Vasubandhu's list includes these three unconditioned factors, in fact he argues *qua* Sautrāntika that they are actually merely absences and thus not real. Saṃghabhadra, predictably now, disagrees. Calculated cessation is an effect, though it has no effect: it can enter into meditation as a supporting object, and is acquired by practice of the noble path. Thus it is not merely an absence.

Empty space is a clear enough notion, although one should be careful to distinguish this unconditioned space from the element space, which Saṃghabhadra (unlike Vasubandhu) takes to be a different actual factor. But what are we to understand by the second and third unconditioned factors, translated here as "calculated" and "uncalculated cessation"?

These translations are unhappy, but no helpful alternatives come to mind.The designation of our term "calculated cessation" is in fact liberation, *nirvāṇa,* the cessation of all factors, arrived at through the intentional attainment of the stage of perfected being. "Uncalculated cessation" refers to the cessation of a type of factor when the necessary conditions for its production are cut off for all future time. Thus, for example, if one meets a premature death those factors which would have conditioned the remainder of his life's experiences are unable to arise, and this inability is termed uncalculated cessation. As one proceeds along the path by rooting out proclivities the factors which would have instantiated those proclivities in future lives undergo this "uncalculated" cessation. (Clearly, the English term fails to convey the proper sense here. But alternatives suggested in the literature are no better. For example, Hirakawa suggests "analytical" for "*pratisaṃkhyā*", but again the translation seems to bear no relation to the sense involved. At least "calculated" seems etymologically appropriate, since "*saṃkhyā*" is a standard term for number, but if either of the two unconditioned factors being discussed is to be called "calculated" it seems it ought to be the *apratisaṃkhyā* sort, since it is that which is the actual result striven for in a given meditative practice.)

# PART TWO

## SUMMARIES OF WORKS
## (Arranged Chronologically

1. AUTHOR UNKNOWN (1st c. B.C.), *Ṣaṭpāramitā*.

According to Akira Hirakawa, "it probably consisted of a description of the six perfections" and was "probably compiled in the first century B.C.E., i.e. before the Christian era. Its title in Chinese is *Liu po-lo-mi ching*. It is quoted in 17.*Kāśyapaparivarta*.[72]

2. AUTHOR UNKNOWN (lst c. A.D.?), *Bodhisattvapiṭaka*

Chinese *P'u-sa tsang-ching*, also quoted in 17.*Kāśyapaparivarta*. Its contents are not known, though several later works appear to have been based on it.[73]

3. AUTHOR UNKNOWN (1st c.A.D.), *Triskandhadharmaparyāya*.

Chinese *San-p'in ching*. The work is related to 27.*Ugradattaparipṛcchā*,[74] and dealt with such topics as *stūpa*-worship, confession to the Buddha of one's wrongdoings, transference of merit, etc.[75]

4. AUTHOR UNKNOWN, *Kātyāyanāvadānasūtra* (1st c. A.D.?).

This *sūtra* is mentioned by Nāgārjuna in 33.*Madhyamakakārikā* 13.7. Jacques May says that "the antinomy between substantialism and nihilism...was formally expressed in the *Kātyāyana-avadāna-sūtra*".[76]

5. AUTHOR UNKNOWN (100 A.D.),
*Aṣṭasāhasrikā(prajñāpāramitāsūtra)*.[77]

"This work, which exists in several closely-related versions...seems to have attained its earliest version some time between 100 B.C.E. and 50 A.D.."[78] A.K.Warder (who also provides a brief summary) attempts to pick out themes that represent a departure from Abhidharma texts of a similar date. He speculates that the Sinhalese commentaries and this text "seem to be contemporary in origin and probably developed in deliberate opposition to one another", for "the writer of the (*Aṣṭa*-) wished to attack the conceptions of the *abhidharma* commentators".[79]

Indeed, the *Aṣṭa* regularly asserts that all factors are without essential nature (*asvabhāva*), and draws the conclusion we find in Nāgārjuna's works, such that no one is bound, no one freed, that all such contrasts fail to apply since all factors are empty. To understand this is to gain "perfection of understanding" (Conze's translation of *prajñāpāramitā*). The Bodhisattva who gains that perfection is called *tathāgata*, "thus-gone", for his "thusness" is gone just as each factor, properly understood, has been "gone" all along.

Summary by Robert F. Olson[80]

"The stated purpose of the *Perfection of Insight* as a teaching is essentially the same as that of Nāgārjuna--getting rid of attachment: 'This dharma is taught for the sake of not-taking-hold (*anudgraha*) of any dharma--yet the world carries on taking-hold...This perfection of insight is presented for a great purpose: for [bringing about] non-acquisition (*aparigraha*), for [bringing about] non-addiction (*anabhiniveśa*).'"

"Such a program aims at the elimination of a mode of experience, that is, experience qualified by attachment. The goal is a detached mode of knowing--perfect insight or enlightenment--which is described in negative terms: 'The Tathāgatas' non-attachment-knowing (*asaṅgajñāna*) is indeed perfect insight...Non-apprehension (*anupalambha*) of any dharma is the perfection of insight. Thus it is said that when there is no idea (*saṃjñā*), name (*nāman*), designation (*prajñapti*), or conventional language (*vyavahāra*)--then [there is] perfect insight...This is that perfection of insight--no supposition (*manyamānatā*) about any dharma at all.'"

"From this we gather that the unattached mode of knowing real things (*dharmas*) is a mode of knowing without conceptualization. Insofar, then, as any real thing is conceived or talked about, it is known in the attached mode and is thereby falsified. *Dharmas* or *dharmatā* (real-thing-hood, the nature of reality) as conceived, schematized (for example, in *abhidharma* thought), and talked about are fabrications (*kalpanā*)."

"For those dharmas are not there in the way that untaught, simple people are addicted to them...The way they are not there is the way they are there. Thus they are not-being-here (*avidyamāna*), so they are called ignorance (*avidyā*). Untaught, simple people are addicted to them. All dharmas, not being there, are fabricated (*kalpita*) by them. Having fabricated them they are attached to the two extremes (existence and non-existence, etc.) and neither know nor see those dharmas (as they really are)...Having fabricated them they become addicted to the two extremes. Having become addicted, and relying on that source as [a basis of] apprehension, they fabricate past dharmas, future dharmas, present dharmas. Having fabricated these they become addicted to name and form (the five bundles[1])...Fabricating all those dharmas which are not there they neither know nor see the Path as it really is...They do not go forth from the triple world. They do not wake up to the true end (*bhūtakoṭi*, i.e. ultimate reality)."

"'Attachment is by means of both name (*nāman*) and sign (*nimitta*)...[Thinking] 'form and the other aggregates are empty'--this is attachment. (If) one entertains the ideas 'past dharmas' with regard to past dharmas, 'future dharmas' with regard to future dharmas, 'present dharmas' with regard to present dharmas--this is attachment.'"

"The term '*dharmas*' here is necessarily ambiguous. Its basic function is to designate something real or valid. Thus *dharmatā* refers to the nature of all that is real, what constitutes actuality. But 'dharma' is itself a word, and when *dharmas* are named--form, consciousness, *bodhisattva, nirvāṇa,* or whatever--they are totally within the sphere of the attached mode. It is in this sense that 'all dharmas are made up by fabrication.' At the same time the terms 'dharma' and 'dharmatā' are used to refer to what is ultimately real, apart from fabrication: 'All dharmas are talked about only by means of names, only by means of [linguistic] transaction (*vyavahāra*). But the transaction is nowhere, is out of nowhere, is not a transaction at all: all dharmas are free of transaction, free of talk, not transacted, not talked about.'"

"The skill-in-means (*upāyakauśalya*) of the *bodhisattva* is both to perceive signs--the images, ideas, and names mentally abstractable from experience--and to develop his awareness of the signlessness of reality as it is ultimately. This is an expression of the doctrine of the two truths, conventional and ultimate, applied in a way which reveals the *bodhisattva* to be a being 'in this world but not of it.' It

---

1. Olson translates "*skandha*" as "bundle". In the present volume we are translating the term as "aggregate". To avoid confusion we replace Olson's translation by ours for the remainder of this section.

is this skill-in-means which enables him to operate in the two modes simultaneously. However, because he does remain in the unattached mode, he is not karmically bound to those experiences which are normally in the sphere of atachment: 'He cultivates, devotes himself to, and honors forms, sounds, odors, tastes, touches--but he does so because, in fact, he has 'overcome'. (*abhibhūya*) these, he has no attachment or objective supports (*ālambana*) and his acts thus arise out of skill-in-means."

"Conventional or transactional truth includes the entire realm of discourse, not only what is invalid in relation to Buddhist discourse but Buddhist discourse as well: 'In reality no distinction or difference between [any of] these dharmas can be apprehended (*na upalabhyate*). As talk they are described by the Tathāgata..."empty," or "signless,", or "wishless," or "without formation," or "non-arising," or "without birth," or "non-existence," or "dispassion," or "cessation," or "nirvāṇa"--these are [just] talked about...All dharmas whatever are beyond talk (*anabhilāpya*)."

"'Perfection of insight'--this is only name-giving. And [the possibility of validly asserting:] 'that name is this [actual thing]' cannot be apprehended. We say that the name has only speech as its object-of-reference, while that perfection of insight is neither found nor apprehended: just as it is a name, just so is it perfection of insight; just as perfection of insight is, just so is the name. A duality of dharmas here is neither found nor apprehended."

"The actual references of the word 'perfection-of-insight' is not to a real thing but to a speech-thing, verbalized reality--or as the commentary says, the term just reflects the discrimination (*vikalpapratibimbaka*) of the attached mode. The real thing which is being talked about, that is, the state of perfect insight, is not capable of comparison with the name or concept, since names can only be compared with names--and it is only when there are no names that the reality of perfect insight is found. Even the negative language associated with ultimate truth has finally to be seen in this light: 'Non-arising (*anutpāda*) appears to you to be talked about, but this same non-arising is [only] talk...Form is unthinkable and so are the other aggregates. [When a *bodhisattva* does not even entertain the idea "form is unthinkable," he proceeds in the perfection of insight."

"The nonattached mode of knowing is present when one

'proceeds but does not arrive at [the considerations] "I proceed" and "I will proceed" because all dharmas are neither arrived at nor depended upon [in reality]. This is the bodhisattvas' *samādhi* called 'non-dependency upon any dharma (*sarvadharma-anupādāna*)'. This mode is spoken of as 'standing in emptiness', which is where the Tathāgata stood and where all those who follow him should stand--precisely nowhere at all--because his mind was not fixated (*apratiṣṭhamānasa*) by any conceptualized *dharma* or consideration."

"The inevitable conclusion is that what is so for the unattached mode has nothing to do with understanding, hence the paradoxic rejoinder by Subhūti to those who find the teaching on the perfection of insight difficult to understand: 'It can't be understood, it can't be understood (*na vijñāyate*)...for in it nothing at all is pointed out, nothing at all is learned.' And as there is no *dharma* at all pointed out, illuminated, or communicated no one will ever gain the perfection of insight from Subhūti's teaching of it."

"Looked at from this paradoxic angle, that is, from the point of view of ultimate truth, all *doxa*--the points of view of transactional truth--are equally mere fabrications, none of which can be said to be even relatively adequate to express or describe perfect insight, since the latter is not "available" for comparison with its linguistic descriptions. We are apparently no closer to a possible link between conceptuality and enlightenment, intelligibility and *nirvāṇa*. But from the very discontinuity between the two, there emerges an interesting corollary: while on the one hand the real and the fictive, or fabricative, cannot be distinguished because distinguishing is itself conceptual, on the other hand what fabrication, discriminations, concepts *really are* is, in fact, the perfection of insight."

"This perfection of insight cannot be taught or learned or distinguished or considered or demonstrated or reflected upon by means of the aggregates or by means of the elements (*dhātu*) or by means of the sense-fields (*āyatana*). The reason for this is the isolation (*viviktatva*) of all dharmas, the absolute isolation of all dharmas...But the perfection of insight is not to be understood apart from the aggregates, etc. The reason for this is that it is just the very aggregates, etc., which are empty, isolated, quieted. For thus are the perfection of insight and the aggregates, etc.: a non-duality which is without division and cannot be apprehended because of its emptiness...its isolation...and hence its being quieted."

"This nondual nature is referred to in quasi-positive terms as 'suchness' (*tathatā*): 'The Tathāgata knows form (and each of the aggregates) as suchness...The suchness of the aggregates is the suchness of the world; the suchness of the world is the suchness of all dharmas...This is all just one suchness which has left behind the manifold [states] of existence and non-existence, because it is not one, not many, not disappearing, without modification, without duality, undivided...This one suchness of all real things is also identical with perfect insight, the state of enlightenment...Because of the boundlessness of objective supports (*ālambana*; intended object), this perfection of insight is a boundless perfection. Because of the boundlessness of sentient beings this perfection of insight is a boundless perfection. Because all dharmas are without a beginning, middle, or end this perfection of insight is a boundless perfection."

"This absence of own-being (*svabhāva*) in beings should be known as the nature of the perfection of insight. The absence of own-being (that is, independent self-existence) in beings demonstrates the absence of it in the perfection of insight. Similarly, their isolation, unthinkability, indestructible nature, and the fact that they are not in the process of becoming enlightened--all demonstrate the same for the perfection of insight."

"If then the nature of reality is not different from enlightenment, then the nature of reality must share the unattached, nondepending, nonapprehending character of enlightenment. A hint of this can be seen in two of the terms often associated (as above) with *śūnya* (empty), namely, *vivikta* (isolated), and *śānta* (quieted). Both of these seem to have their origin in the language of meditation proper: the isolation or separation of the meditator from his conceptual and emotional 'connectedness' with his normal social world, followed by his development of inner quiet or tranquillity (*śamatha, upaśama*, etc.). With the *Perfection of Insight* tradition these subjective aspects of disconnectedness and tranquillity are said to be the ultimate nature of all real things."

"The ultimate nature of reality shares in the disconnectedness which characterizes the perfection of insight. Since this insight is unattached knowing, the Tathāgatas 'demonstrate Dharma to beings for the sake of non-clinging (*aśleṣa*)...The non-connection (*asambandha*) of form (and the other aggregates) is the non-clinging of form...The non-connection of form is form's lack of origination and cessation...In this way non-clinging comes to be, as a result of knowing and seeing that all dharmas are not clinging, not connected.'"

"This common nature leads to further implications. Perfect insight is not different from the real nature of those characteristics of the attached mode which, conventionally, the perfection of insight is supposed to eliminate. 'This is the perfection of non-discipline (*avinaya*), because there is no apprehension of past, future, and present goals...This is the perfection of nonaffliction (*asaṃkleśa*), because there is no own-being to greed, anger, and delusion...This is the perfection of dispassion, because there is no falseness in any dharma...This is the perfection of non-arising, because there is no discrimination in any dharma...This is the perfection of non-discrimination, because of its identity with discrimination (*vikalpasamatā*)...This is the perfection of suffering, because the nature of dharmas is like space...Distracted thoughts are thoughts distracted from the nature of dharmas (*dharmatā*). But such thoughts when seen as they really are by insight are without [intrinsic] characteristics and are in reality not distracted. Indeed, those thoughts are by nature brightly clear (*prakṛtiprabhāsvara*).'"

"After all, if it is *all dharmas* which share the same nature, suchness, with the perfection of insight, then such unwholesome (*akuśala*) *dharmas* as anger, delusion, discrimination, distraction, suffering, etc. are not to be excluded."

"Finally, there is the clear implication that it is the *given* nature of things which is identical with the perfection of insight, and therefore this insight is not something which has yet to be attained by the striving *bodhisattva*. Enlightenment, in short, is what the *bodhisattva* already really is. 'The [meditative] actualization (*bhāvanā*) of the perfection of insight is an actualization of space. Homage should be paid to those bodhisattvas who put *this* armor on, for he who fastens on his armor for the sake of beings seeks to be armed with space...For the sake of beings who are [themselves] like space, like the dharma-realm, he seeks to be armed, he seeks to become fully enlightened. He seeks to liberate space, he seeks to get rid of space...He will make efforts about space, about wide-open space, who thinks of being trained in or of making efforts about the perfection of insight...Deep is the perfection of insight: it is not actualized by anything, for no one actualizes it...nor is there anything to be actualized...anywhere. The actualization of the perfection of insight is actualization of space, of all dharmas, of non-attachment, of the limitless, of non-existence, of non-acquiring."

"The nature of things is not something which requires actualization: space is empty without needing to develop that emptiness. In exactly the same way the perfection of insight is not in need of development. The implication is evident that the essential original nature of thought (*citta*), brightly clear, as well as the nature of things in general, is unattached knowing, the perfection of insight which constitutes buddhahood: 'The nature of all dharmas is complete purity...All dharmas have attained *nirvāṇa,* [and hence] are identical with suchness...All dharmas are noble arhats, completely purified by nature...All dharmas are enlightenment because they cause one to be aware of the buddha-knowing (*buddhajñāna*)."

### 6. AUTHOR UNKNOWN, *Ren ben yu sheng jing.*[81]

This and the following nine works were translated by An Shih-kao into Chinese between 150 and 170 A.D. The brief summaries given of works numbered 6-15 are provided by E. Zürcher. None of them have, so far as we know, been translated into Western languages; it is not even clear what an appropriate retranslation from the Chinese of the original Sanskrit titles might be. Zürcher elsewhere[82] characterizes An Shih-kao's translations thus: "As translations, they are generally of the poorest quality. It is somewhat surprising that later Chinese Buddhist bibliographers...have praised the products of An Shih-kao and his school as masterpieces and classical examples of the art of translating. It is hard to see on what criteria their appreciation was based...Most archaic versions are actually no more than free paraphrases or extracts of the original texts, teeming with obscure and not yet standardized technical expressions, and coated in a language which is chaotic to the extreme and not seldom quite unintelligible..."

Zürcher provides the following description of the gist of these and the other nine works: "To judge from the nature of the scriptures translated, the two main subjects of his teachings seem to have been (a) the system of mental exercises commonly called *dhyāna* (*ch'an*) in Chinese sources, but which is more adequately covered by the term 'Buddhist yoga', comprising such practices as the preparatory technique of counting the respirations leading to mental concentration (*ānāpānasmṛti*), the contemplation of the body as being perishable, composed of elements, impure and full of suffering; the visualization of internal and external images of various colours, etc.; (b) the explanation of numerical categories such as the six *āyatana*, the five *skandha*, the four *ṛddhipāda*, the five *bala*, the four *smṛtyupasthāna*, etc.; short sūtras devoted to such classifications form the bulk of the *oeuvre* attributed to him."[83]

7. AUTHOR UNKNOWN, *Yiqie liu she shou yin jing.*[84]

"Very short text explaining the way to extirpate the Impurities (*āsrava*)."

8. AUTHOR UNKNOWN, *Si di jing.*[85]

"Exposition of the Four Noble Truths."

9. AUTHOR UNKNOWN, *Ben xiang yi zhi jing.*[86]

"Causal series leading from 'bad company', viz. 'unbelief', 'wrong thoughts'...to 'desire', and the opposite series, leading from 'good company' to 'emancipation'."

10. AUTHOR UNKNOWN, *Lou fenbu jing.*[87]

"Scholastic enumeration of the Impurities, Sense-desires, Feelings, Perceptions, etc., together with their causal factors and their bad consequences."

11. AUTHOR UNKNOWN, *Pu fayi jing.*[88]

"Various series of 12, 20, 16...etc. factors, every series being either conducive or obstructive to Emancipation."

12. AUTHOR UNKNOWN, *Ba zheng dao jing.*[89]

"The eight bad ways of action and the eight good ways of action that constitute the Eightfold Path."

13. AUTHOR UNKNOWN, *Da anban shouyi jing.*[90]

"Treatise describing the practice of "Respiratory Concentration" (*ānāpāna-smṛti*), together with a commentary that has become inextricably mixed up with the text."

14. AUTHOR UNKNOWN, *Yin chi ru jing.*[91]

"Scholastic compendium dealing with sense-perception, the four bases of super-natural power, the five powers, etc."

15. AUTHOR UNKNOWN, *Chanxing faxiang jing.*[92]

"Very short text containing a list of themes for contemplation."

16. AUTHOR UNKNOWN (125), *Ajātaśatrukaukṛtyavinodanasūtra.*[93]

17. AUTHOR UNKNOWN (125), *Kāśyapaparivartasūtra.*[94]

In this *sūtra* the Buddha reviews for Mahākāśyapa the conditions that cause backsliding, that lead to wisdom and the growth of virtue, and that indicate the marks of a Bodhisattva. He describes the middle way between extremes, dependent origination, the emptiness of things, but warns one not to become attached to emptiness. The truth is indicated by a number of pithy illustrations. Notable are examples to show that there is no such thing as a "mind", and that supposing that there is breeds karma. A section, also found in several other texts, alludes to the defection of the "five hundred", presumably the Mahāsāṃghikas, and how they were wooed back into the fold by magical monks sent by the Buddha, monks who taught the defecters the correct understanding of emptiness.

18. AUTHOR UNKNOWN (125), *Akṣobhya(tathāgatasya)vyūhasūtra.*[95]

This work tells of a pupil of the Buddha who resolved to seek to avoid the way of a *śrāvaka* or *pratyekabuddha* and become the Bodhisattva Akṣobhya (meaning "Immovable"). Gautama confirms that Akṣobhya will indeed become a *tathāgata* and there is great rejoicing. The Buddha goes on to describe the pleasures of the heaven attained by Akṣobhya and the power of his vows.

## 19. AUTHOR UNKNOWN (125), *Drumakinnararājaparipṛcchāsūtra*.[96]

Summary by Paul Harrison

"(T)he DKP is a scripture which deals with the perfections or transcendent qualities (*pāramitā*) within a narrative framework in which a leading role is taken, not by a *bhikṣu* or *bodhisattva*, as is customary, but by a non-human being, a *kinnara* king whose name is Druma (which means "tree"). *Kinnaras*...are a class of mythical beings who are sometimes depicted as having the heads of horses and the bodies of human beings (or vice versa). They possess a special aptitude, which they share with *gandharvas*, for making music; and their celestial music-making is of great power and beauty. In fact, music and sound in general play an important part in this text...Music symbolises the syren call of the senses which only highly advanced *bodhisattvas* and Buddhas have transcended entirely, and at the same time, it stands as a metaphor for the elusive and ephemeral nature of all phenomena, which are in the final analysis as ungraspable as echoes; in short, it stands for "emptiness"...King Druma shows special understanding of the emptiness of sensory experience, and his eventual awakening to Buddhahood is predicted later in the work (Chap. 7). The doctrine of emptiness is alluded to or treated extensively at various points, and the perfections are also expounded systematically in Chap. 7, which, significantly, describes the six standard perfections in order, followed by *upāyakauśalya*, skill in the use of creative stratagems, which is presented more or less as a seventh perfection, although it is not designated as such. *Upāyakauśalya* is in fact one of the key doctrinal elements of the text. Other special features of the DKP are the dramatic richness of its narrative passages and its extensive section dealing with the way in which, and the reasons for which, women are to be reborn as men before they can achieve awakening (Chap. 9). One particularly interesting element is the protective *mantra* which appears in Chap. 15, possibly the first such formula to be transcribed and translated into Chinese. Another is the clear reference to the content of the 16. *Ajātaśatru-kaukṛtya-vinodana-sūtra* which appears in Chapter 12...It is in my experience very rare for one Mahāyāna sūtra to refer to another in this way--striking evidence, quite apart from their thematic links and the fact that they were both translated by Lokakṣema, that these two texts were produced or circulated in the same milieu."[97]

## 20. AUTHOR UNKNOWN (125), *Lokānuvartanasūtra.*[98]

### Summary by Paul Harrison

"The text falls, very roughly, into two halves. The first half deals with the Buddha's person, working item by item through the major events of his life (e.g. the birth of Rāhula) as well as its recurrent day-to-day activities (e.g., cleaning the teeth) to show that all these are part of a deliberately fostered illusion of humanity - that the true nature of the Buddha's being and his real attributes are quite different from those which he projects among men in order to further their salvations. Despite all appearances to the contrary, the Buddha remains above this world--he is 'supramundane' or 'transcendent' (*lokottara*). The second half of the sūtra addresses itself by and large to the Buddha's teaching, and once again, the truth about phenomena is contrasted with what the Buddha actually proclaimed during his ministry. The Buddha's teaching, like his person, is far more than it appears to be. It is in this 'ontological' section of the *LAn* that one finds expressed a doctrinal standpoint very similar to that of the early Prajñāpāramitā as set forth in the *Aṣṭasāhasrikā*, a standpoint which insists upon the 'emptiness' of all dharmas, their non-arising (the term *anutpattidharmakṣānti* occurs) and lack of own-being (*svabhāva*), the merely conventional validity of verbal distinctions as opposed to the true undifferentiated nature of the *dharmadhātu*, and so on."

## 21. AUTHOR UNKNOWN (125), *Pratyutpannabuddhasaṃmukhāvasthitasūtra*[99]

In Appendix A of his translation Paul Harrison reviews the textual history of various versions of this text. His conclusions are as follows: Lokakṣema and an Indian collaborator translated this work in 179 A.D. "In 208 the translation was completely revised, possibly by members of Lokakṣema's school..." It continued to be retranslated or abridged until by the beginning of the ninth century it had been translated into Tibetan "in a form...which differs considerably from that which the Chinese versions reveal." In the next few paragraphs we provide selections from Harrison's section on "The structure of the PraS", pp. xxvii-xxxiii of his book in which the translation appears.

## Summary by Paul Harrison

"The PraS opens with a long *nidāna* (1A-I) describing the assembling of the Buddha's audience in the Veṇuvana outside Rājagṛha; pride of place is given to eight *bodhisattvas*...each from one of the eight major cities of the Buddha's world. Bhadrapāla...asks the Buddha which *samādhi bodhisattvas* should practice in order to acquire them (1J-Y)..the Buddha states that the *samādhi* required is the *pratyutpanna-samādhi*..(2B-J)...the vividness and yet the ultimate unreality of that which is perceived during the *samādhi* are emphasized (3A-O). In Chap. 4 the Buddha outlines some of the practical and ethical prerequisites for the practice of the *samādhi*, while in Chap. 5 he stresses the need for reverence for the preacher of Dharma (5A), and describes the great efficacy of the *pratyutpanna-samādhi*...(5B-E). Chap. 6 deals with the considerable loss to be suffered by those future followers of the Buddha who will refuse to accept and practice the *samādhi*...Great is the merit to be derived from believing in this teaching, the Buddha solemnly avows to his audience (6A-J).

"The Buddha continues to praise in the most fulsome terms the excellence of those who take up the *samādhi* (7A-G), before returning in Chap. 8 to the practice of the *samādhi* itself. Some quite 'philosophical'...passages deal with various points of doctrine--relating mainly to the perception of phenomena--which *bodhisattvas* should attempt to internalise in their practice of the *samādhi* (8A-K). Following this the Buddha outlines the qualities--moral attitudinal, practical, social--required of *bodhisattvas* who have given up the household life...(9A-M). Subsequently the Buddha deals in turn with those things required of Mahāyāna *bhikṣuṇīs* (10A-C), householder *bodhisattvas*...(11A-D), and Mahāyāna *upāsikās* (12A-c).

"Bhadrapāla...asks if (the Buddha's teaching) will continue to circulate in Jambudvīpa after the Buddha's demise (13A). The

Buddha replies that the *samādhi* will disappear sometime after his Parinirvāṇa, but that it will re-appear in the 'last five hundred years' to be taken up and propagated by a few faithful souls (13B). Moved to tears of joy by this revelation, Bhadrapāla and his seven *bodhisattva* companions undertake to preach the *samādhi* in the terrible 'last five hundred years' (13C-F). They are joined by five hundred other followers, and beseech the Buddha to entrust the *samādhi* to the eight *bodhisattvas* (13G-H). The Buddha responds with one of his famous similes (13I), and Ānanda, on cue as ever, asks in verse what the reason is for this (13J). By way of reply the Buddha recapitulates in verse...(13K). The eight *bodhisattvas* rejoice over these revelations...(14A).

"Bhadrapāla then enquires after further prerequisites for correct practice, and the Buddha enumerates four (14B), after which he goes on to detail the many worldly advantages to be derived from the *samādhi*, including the capacity to acquire, even in one's dreams, hitherto unknown teachings (14C-J)....Further philosophical' passages follow, in which the correct practice of the four *smṛtyupasthāna* is related to that of the *samādhi*, and various statements are made concerning the nature of phenomena and the proper attitude to them (15J-N).

"Bhadrapāla next asks the Buddha what things will enable the *bodhisattva* to acquire the *samādhi* successfully (16K). The Buddha details another series of attributes, attitudes, practices, etc. (16L-V), and then recalls the prediction of his own awakening during the time of Dīpaṃkara...(17A-B)...

"Bhadrapāla again asks how *bodhisattvas* should cultivate the *samādhi*, and the Buddha in reply discusses the required understanding of 'all dharmas' and the proper attitude to them, with reference to the correct practice of the *smṛtyupasthānas* (18A-F)...

"Chap. 19 contains further instructions on correct practice (19A-B), and lists eight *dharmas* which *bodhisattvas* engaged in the *samādhi* will acquire (19C)...In addition to these eight *dharmas*, *bodhisattvas* will acquire the ten powers of a Tathāgata (20A-K), the four assurances (21A-E) and the eighteen dharmas exclusive to a Buddha (22A-B).

"At the beginning of Chap. 23 the Buddha propounds four acts of 'rejoicing' which *bodhisattvas* should formally rehearse with regard to the *samādhi* (23A-D). The merit from this, which is to be 'dedicated' to others for the sake of perfect awakening, is described as very great indeed (23E-F)...The Buddha then tells how the *samādhi* should be preserved for future believers by being copied out and stored away...(24A-B)...

"Finally, the Buddha addresses himself to Bhadrapāla and his seven companions, their five hundred followers, and the rest of his audience (26B)...He tells Bhadrapāla that the *samādhi* is to be mastered and taught to others so that it will endure (26D)..."

### 22. AUTHOR UNKNOWN, *Dousha jing.*[100]

### 23. AUTHOR UNKNOWN, *Wenshushili wen pusa shu jing.*[101]

### 24. AUTHOR UNKNOWN, *Śūraṅgama(samādhi)sūtra.*[102]

Pasadika translates the title of this work as "Contemplation Leading to Power", Lamotte as "Le Concentration de la Marche Héroique".

Rather than attempt a summary, we provide an excerpt from a discussion of the opening topic by George Teschner.[103]

"In the beginning of the *Śūraṅgama Sūtra,* the Buddha asks Ānanda where the perceptions of the eyes and the activities of the mind are. Ānanda replies that the eyes are on the face and the mind is within the body...Ānanda's reply has erroneously located mind within body and body within the external world, whereas, for the *Śūraṅgama,* both body and the world are phenomena of the mind. If the mind is within the body, the mind should see the inside of the body, the *Śūraṅgama Sūtra* reasons...Since the mind does not see the interior of the body, the relationship between mind and body cannot be conceived of as an observer within a room looking through a window at what is outside. Ānanda then argues that the mind may be like a lamp placed outside a house. What lies outside is illuminated whereas what lies within is hidden in darkness...The Buddha uses two arguments against this position...(I)f consciousness is placed outside the body, then there seems to be no way of explaining how each could be aware of the internal states of the other...Similarly, in placing consciousness outside the body, Ānanda then is unable to account for the perspectival character of each individual's perception...

"Ānanda...accounts for why there is not an awareness of the body by saying the body is like an almost perfectly transparent bowl placed over the eyes...The Buddha objects that although the eye is able to see through the bowl, it is, nevertheless, still able to see the bowl, whereas mind, in the same way, is not able to see the sense organs.

"If the mind cannot see the inside of the body and also cannot be outside it since it interacts with the body, then Ānanda concludes it must be in some sense between the body and external things. The Buddha asks where is this place between? If it is between external things and the body, in the sense that it is just beneath the surface of the body, then it is within the body and should see the inside. If it is between, in the sense of having a location among external things, then it should see things, including the body, from an unchanging perspective. If the mind is between...then the mind must consist of a duality of which one part is able to interact with the conscious perceiver and the other part with the insentient object. The question then becomes, how could these two opposing realities combine in the same being?

"The difficulty throughout the dialogue is that Ānanda is attempting to conceive of the relation between mind and body according to some spatial relation. To say that the mind is inside the body does not accord with the nature of perception as interpreted by Ānanda; to say it is outside the body cannot explain how the mind and body interact or have experiences in common; to say that it is in between would suffer from both the foregoing difficulties...

The entire polemic is a *reductio ad absurdum* argument. Ānanda is unable to consider a reality which is without location but which, nevertheless, enters into a relationship with the body and external objects. In order to do this, he must in the *Śūraṅgama* be brought to understand that the reality of spatial relationships is a phenomenon of the mind and that there are no spatial relationships in themselves..."

25. AUTHOR UNKNOWN (130), *Dharmacakrapravartanasūtra.*[104]

26. AUTHOR UNKNOWN (130), *Maitreyaparipṛcchāsūtra*[105]

27. AUTHOR UNKNOWN (150), *Ugra(datta)paripṛcchāsūtra.*[106]

Nancy Schuster believes that this is one of the earliest Mahāyāna *sūtras.*[107] It is one of a group of works about a householder named "Ugra", stories about whom probably go back to earliest Buddhist times. In the first part of this *sūtra* Ugra is counseled by the Buddha on how to live life properly as a "householder *bodhisattva*". The second part gives advice to *bodhisattvas* who have gone forth (*pravrajita*) from their homes to the forest to seek knowledge. "There, they realize that all fears arise from the sense of self, and in the forest they get rid of all sense of self. Then for them all *dharmas* become quiescent, they are attached to no *dharmas* whatsoever, sense perceptions do not deceive them, they are content in the *āryavaṃśa*" (the tradition of nobles), "contented through understanding (*prajñā*), and able to take on the 'heavy burden' of worldly existence. When the sense of self has disappeared because of understanding, the *pravrajita bodhisattva* can then fulfill the six perfections."

"Finally, when fear is destroyed and the sense of self is lost, the *pravrajita bodhisattva* is to go down to the towns and villages to teach *Dharma* to the people, and to study it further himself with teachers who are to be deeply revered forever for the sake of the precious gifts they have given. After all this, he can at last practice pure *śīla*, pure *samādhi* and pure *prajñā*."[108]

28. AUTHOR UNKNOWN, *Chengju guangming dingyi jing.*[109]

"Mahāyāna scripture treating two different subjects. The first part is devoted to the Six Perfections (*pāramitā*) and the "Mental Concentration of Integral Illumination". The second part contains a description of the moral and religious duties of various classes of lay devotees.[110]

29. AUTHOR UNKNOWN (150), Larger *Sukhāvatīvyūhasūtra.*[111]

This work can be briefly summarized thus:

1-4. The Buddha tells Ānanda the names of eighty-two previous Bodhisattvas, culminating in Lokeśvararāja and his pupil Dharmākara who are present at the gathering.

5-10. Dharmākara, after five eons of study, returns to the Buddha and makes forty-eight (or forty-six) vows of Bodhisattvahood, promising not to attain enlightenment until everyone else does. He follows this with a number of verses extolling the Buddha.

11-38. The Buddha tells Ānanda that Dharmākara now presides

over the country called Sukhāvatī as the Bodhisattva Amitābha, whose virtues he praises. He goes on to describe the wonders of Sukhāvatī in detail.

39-end. The Buddha provides Ānanda with a vision of Sukhāvatī. He then explains who goes to Sukhāvatī, viz., backsliding or doubting Bodhisattvas.

30. AUTHOR UNKNOWN (150), Smaller *Sukhāvatīvyūha*[112]

The Buddha teaches Śāriputra of the world of Sukhāvatī, where Amitāyus (whose name means "immeasurably long life") lives. Sukhāvatī's marvels are described, and the name of the Buddhas who dwell there are listed. They will not return again to the world, since they possess understanding.

31. AUTHOR UNKNOWN (150), *Ratnaguṇasaṃcayagāthā.*[113]

This is, at least in part, a summary in 302 verses of 5.*Aṣṭasāhasrikā.* Conze translated the title as "Verses on the Perfection of Wisdom Which is the Storehouse of Precious Virtues". It exists in five recensions, two in Sanskrit, two in Tibetan, and one in Chinese. Akira Yuyama, who has studied this text closely, remarks "The *Rgs*...appears to be the only extant Prajñāpāramitā text written in the so-called Buddhist Sanskrit language.

Edward Conze has made an English translation of the version ascribed to Haribhadra and translated into Chinese in 1001.[114] Conze believed the 41 verses of the first two chapters may date to 100 B.C. and "constitute the original Prajñāpāramitā..."[115] He has provided a survey of the contents.[116]

32. AUTHOR UNKNOWN (150), *Gaṇḍavyūha.*[117]

"The main theme of the *Gaṇḍavyūha* is the *bodhisattva*'s quest for enlightenment...Alternatively...it is the progress from seeing the universe as ordinary people see it, when filled with attachment and petty, selfish desires, to seeing it as the (true) *bodhisattva* sees it. In the former aspect it is known as the 'element of the world' (*lokadhātu*), in the latter as the 'element of phenomena' (*dharmadhātu*), i.e., the ultimate reality..."

"In the course of this description we learn more about the ultimate reality, the element of phenomena, and the main contribution of the *Gaṇḍavyūha* to philosophy: the conception of the perfect interpenetration of everything in the universe, in which everything is as if reflected in everything else, without any mutual obstruction. The phenomenal and transcendental universes are identical, with separateness of phenomena on the surface but perfect harmony and unity within..."[118]

## NĀGĀRJUNA

As with Śaṃkarācārya in the Hindu context, Nāgārjuna, sometimes called the "father" of Indian philosophy, has been identified as the author of a vast number of texts. Scholars have devoted a good deal of effort to the attempt to pick out which of these ascriptions of authorship applies to the Nāgārjuna who was resposible for the 33.*(Mūla)Madhyamakakārikās* (MK), clearly the fundamental work of Madhyamaka Buddhism. Discussion of his works can be found by a variety of scholars.[119] We follow the discussion of Christian Lindtner in picking out the relatively small number of texts summarized here as having been written by the author of MK. It seems likely that several different authors, living from the third to the eighth or ninth centuries, were responsible for the various works identified by tradition as being by Nāgārjuna; their dates are guessed at in the various works ascribed to "Nāgārjuna" subsequently in our coverage.

Little to nothing is known about the first Nāgārjuna, who he was and when and where he lived, even his date. He appears to have come from the Andhra district. Nalinaksha Dutt reports that he was born in Vidarbha (Berar), but lived his life in South India, passing his last days at Śrīparvata (modern Śrīśailam).[120] He is said to have also lived for a time at Nālandā. There are various works celebrating his life, but they provide no firm historical information. Given the difficulty of determining the authorship of works ascribed to him, it can be suspected that even the few meager facts just noted may apply to another Nāgārjuna than the one presently under discussion.

As for Nāgārjuna's date, it is variously estimated between the first century and 250 A.D. Since the encyclopedic *Mahāvibhāṣā* contributors do not seem to know or include him we may guess he lived after the meeting that spawned that great compendium. We have estimated 150 A.D. in this Volume, but with no great conviction. The most cogent reason for not placing him as much as a hundred years later has mainly to do with the apparently close relation of some of his putative opponents with positions and arguments appearing in the *Nyāyasūtras* of Gautama, but since the most cogent reason for dating Gautama at 150 A.D. is the very same relationship we are not provided with any certainty about dates.[121]

### 33. NĀGĀRJUNA, *(Mūla)Madhyamakakārikās*

In the following summary "E" refers to P.L.Vaidya's edition, Buddhist Sanskrit Texts No. 10. Darbhanga 1960. "T" references are to Frederick J. Streng's *Emptiness: A Study in Religious Meaning* (Nashville, N.Y.1967).[122]

Summary by Christian Lindtner

This is Nāgārjuna's philosophical masterpiece, as proved by the work's scope and character. It consists of 448 verses divided into 27 chapters (*prakaraṇa*). Some of the verses[123] are fundamental to the topic, or axiomatic, while the rest are mostly destructive argumentation. Chapters XVIII, XXVI and XXVII have a special role, as we see later.

The central position of this work is indirectly shown by the great influence it had in later times. In India alone at least ten commentaries and two subcommentaries are known to have been written, but several of these are no longer extant. Today we have only 137.*Akutobhayā*, incorrectly ascribed to Nāgārjuna, Buddhapālita's commentary and Bhavya's *Prajñāpradīpa*, to which Avalokitavrata wrote a mammoth subcommentary. These texts exist now only in Tibetan translation. The lone extant Sanskrit commentary is Candrakīrti's *Prasannapadā*, written with a knowledge of the first three, but earlier than Avalokitavrata's encyclopedic work. All these are indispensable for an assessment of the role of the MK, and I have combed them thoroughly. In Chinese there is Piṅgala's *Zhonglun* (T. 1564) and Sthiramati's *Dacheng zhongguan shilun* (T. 1567). Piṅgala's commentary is closely related to *Akutobhayā* [our #137], either a free translation or based on the same (now lost) source as the *Akutobhayā*. But I have only made occasional use of the Chinese translations, and never against the other authorities. This is principally because of the uncertainty inherent in the Chinese versions, especially when the subject is philosophical. One can get the general meaning and often guess the original Sanskrit term when one is familiar with the translator's technique, but many doubtful points always remain. Philologically this is not good enough, let alone for an abstract philosophical text. It is quite certain that there must have been many passages that were quite incomprehensible, even misleading, for the Chinese reader.

My summary of the MK is based on my edition of the Sanskrit text (Copenhagen 1982). I have, as said, consulted the commentaries carefully but, nevertheless, in a number of cases deliberately neglected them to follow instead the principle that an author is his own best commentator. In a few cases there can be no doubt that what the commentaries offer is no more than intelligent guesses.

Before going into the separate chapters, it would be profitable to consider the work as a whole. The overriding intention of the author is evident from the introductory paean (incorrectly considered spurious by some scholars) and the last verse of Chapter XXVII. Buddha has shown that the True Doctrine is conditioned co-origination (*pratītyasamutpāda*), which points beyond the multiplicity of the world of experience to an ineffable peace removed from all and every contradiction. MK sets out to prove that the correct understanding of *pratītyasamutpāda* is synonymous with the elimination of all the speculative views and dogmas (*dṛṣṭi*) championed by one or more Buddhist schools. It is important to note that the argumentation is throughout strictly methodical. Nāgārjuna can lead with a "negative" proposition, or the opponent can submit a "positive" view. Then the formal possibilities and alternatives are stated one by one, purely hypothetically. The inescapable conclusion is that neither the view that is being promoted, nor its opposite, can stand up to a critical scrutiny which, to be sure, avails itself of specific logical reasons for "nonorigination" as a means of forcing the opponent into absurdity.

The question of the topics and sequences of the chapters is

interesting, and not quite straightforward. The Indian commentators have not paid it any attention, taking the chapters as they come, and leaving it up to an imaginary opponent to decide the next issue on the agenda. Can one see a progression in the work, or could one envisage a change in the argument or the chapter sequence without too much disturbance? Serious matters like momentariness and the independent existence of consciousness, discussed in some of the author's other works, could for my part well have had a chapter in MK, but the fact remains, it did not happen. As far as I can see there are intimations of a progression, in MK as in most other works by Nāgārjuna, but nothing more. A theme is dealt with, you go on to a new one, and back to the old one again. On the other hand, one must not overlook the fact that topics dealt with only once are treated systematically and consistently. This is best seen in MK and 34.*Vigrahavyāvartanī*, and also in 36.*Vaidalya*, where the sixteen basic concepts of the Nyāya school are rejected step by step.

My view of all this is that we have eight loosely connected "groups" of chapters: Chapters I-II attack the two cornerstones of the ontology of the archenemy, the Sarvāstivāda, namely, causality and the movement of the *dharmas*, which are the natural prerequisites for any sort of causality. The next three chapters belong together in that they deal with "everything that exists," that is to say, the five *skandhas* (IV), the twelve/eighteen bases (III), and the six elements (V). The eighteen elements were indirectly disposed of in Chapter III. Chapter VI investigates the relation between desire and the desiring subject, but this is obviously an arbitrary choice, dictated by "rhetorical" motive. The real subject is coexistence (*sahabhāva*), a key concept in the Sarvāstivāda type of causal theory in which independent *dharmas* are assumed to enter just such a coexistence, whether, as in this instance, it is an action-agent relationship, or in any other way. Chapter VII disproves the three characteristics, origination, duration, and cessation, inseparable from anything causally created, that is, composite (*saṃskṛta*), and to that extent elaborates the discussion on causation. In addition Chapter VII has a long digression criticising an auxiliary hypothesis of the Vātsīputrīya (Sāmmitīya), a school that makes its first appearance here. One could say that VII. 34 is a sort of preliminary conclusion to I-VII: Objective multiplicity considered as a series of independent factors subjected to change according to a given causal pattern is illusory.

Chapters VIII-X have a strong thematic connection, attacking the thesis peculiar to the Vātsīputrīya of the existence of a personal substance (a "soul"), which is its own creative principle, and for which the physical and psychical components of the personality are merely instruments in *saṃsāra*. In Chapter X, as in Chapter VI, one concrete example is taken from the set to illustrate how an ontological entity is disproved.

Chapter XI brings us on to new ground, in my opinion connecting up with Chapters XII and XIII. Nāgārjuna discourses here on "things" in their widest generality. *Saṃsāra* is limitless in space and time (Chapter XI). Therefore everything bounded by *saṃsāra* is without a beginning and without limits. This is in fact the ontological *raison d'etre* behind Nāgārjuna's attack on all the distinctions and entities of discursive thought. Chapter XI, though brief, is a vital part of the work. In Chapter XII, with suffering as the particular case (as in Chapters VI and X), things in general are also shown to be indeterminate by the very fact that they are "nonoriginated." They cannot be created from themselves, from anything else, both, or neither. The purpose of Chapter XIII was evidently to forestall the objection that however Nāgārjuna may disprove things in general in Chapters XI and XII, is not the inconstancy of the empirical world a palpable fact that only a fool would deny? No, because alteration (*anyathābhāva*) is a logical impossibility.

In the next four chapters Nāgārjuna concentrates again on specifically Buddhist concepts. Chapter XIV resumes a theme from Chapter III, which is also found in Chapter VI: Even admitting that the twelve bases and the eighteen elements exist, they cannot possibly enter into combination. Chapter XIV establishes that the Sarvāstivādin's belief in an immutable *svabhāva* is both illogical and unorthodox. Whereas Chapter XI assumed that the reality of *saṃsāra* (i.e., on the level of relative truth), transmigration is rejected in Chapter XVI because neither the five *skandhas* nor the "soul" (the Vātsīputrīya concept) can in any way be said to migrate. Therefore there is no *nirvāṇa* either, the idea of absolute truth that can hold only in contrast to *saṃsāra*. (For the two truths see Chapter XXIV.) Chapter XVII is about karma, a central concept closely connected with that of *saṃsāra*. It begins (verses 1-20) with a very detailed account from the relative standpoint of karma's nature and aspects in relation to the various schools of Abhidharma. In the absolute sense there is nothing that is called karma (verses 21-33).

Chapter XVIII is not well-arranged, but it does, in a very condensed manner, give a better idea of the essence of the author's own philosophy than any other chapter in MK. The belief in "I" and "mine" (i.e., the five *skandhas*) is due to discursive thought (*vikalpa*), which, again, is due to ignorance. This *vikalpa* produces the defilements (*kleśa*), which again activate karma, which in turn leads to rebirth. Emptiness is the weapon that destroys the expanded world (*prapañca*) forming the basis of *vikalpa*. The absolute truth, liberation, is beyond *prapañca*, and therefore nothing can be said about it. So the Buddhas can preach one doctrine at one time, or its exact opposite at another time, depending on the needs and presuppositions of their audience. There are three groups of Buddhists, and it is depth of insight that distinguishes them from one another.

Chapter XIX leads rather abruptly back to a typical Sarvāstivāda problem: the three periods of the factors, in one word, time. The same goes for Chapters XX and XXI, the critical examination of causality and of existence-cessation. They give an added emphasis to the criticism in Chapter I, and together with Chapter XIX they can be considered as a sort of appendix to Chapter I.

Chapters XIX-XXI tolled the knell for the long-drawn-out refutation of the two major Buddhist dogmatic schools, Sarvāstivāda and Vātsīputrīya. All possible views were shown to be empty in the absolute sense. Chapters XXII-XXIV are coherent in the sense that they have no regard for the holiest of the holies for any Buddhist, the concept of Tathāgata, the Buddha himself (XXII); the four misconceptions, that is, the ignorance in which Buddha found the cause for the sufferings of existence (XXIII); the four noble truths, and even the highest goal for Buddhism, *nirvāṇa* (XXV); all so that Nāgārjuna could ram home his basic idea of the emptiness of things. These four chapters effectively conclude the author's rejection of all conceivable dogmas (*dṛṣṭi*).

The last two chapters in MK are not polemical. On first reading it is rather an anticlimax because Nāgārjuna has obviously deigned to come down to the relative plane, without the rhetorical *élan* of the Absolute. The role of these chapters is to show how important it was for the author to be considered a good Buddhist. According to tradition, it was during the night of his enlightenment that Buddha became aware of the twelve members from whose activity suffering stemmed. The interpretation of this formula of the twelve members has always been regarded as problematic and crucial. Therefore, in Chapter XXVI Nāgārjuna must emphasize that the realization of emptiness provides exactly the means desired to terminate the ignorance which, as the first member of the formula, is at the bottom of the occurrence of suffering. Moreover, in the oldest canonical texts we sometimes see that the Buddha warns against the acceptance of sixteen dogmas which presuppose that either the "soul" or the world should be finite or infinite with respect to time (eternal, etc.). As announced in the two introductory verses, and in the final verse of the work, it is precisely these two dogmatic extremes that Nāgārjuna has tried to avoid by enlisting emptiness. It is essential to embrace this doctrine if one wishes to understand the Buddha correctly. The purpose of the two final chapters, then, is immediately obvious once one remembers that MK is addressed to Buddhist monks, some of whom in the course of their study of this revolutionary manual of meditation may well have had their doubts about the orthodoxy of its author.

Basically Nāgārjuna only has one criterion of true reality, namely, that something, in order to be real, must exist in and by itself. All his arguments can be reduced to this presupposition. Experience and logic, however, amply show that nothing whatsoever meets this demand. Hence everything is unreal "ontologically" speaking. His arguments are by no means intended to add to our knowledge or even to correct any positive knowledge that we may already have. On the contrary, they presuppose that we already have a view of the world, as had his first readers, too much of it, according to Nāgārjuna. In the sense that Nāgārjuna's arguments start by presupposing what they end up discarding they are certainly of dubious "scientific" value. On the other hand, Nāgārjuna never really pretends that his arguments are more than means of getting rid of what we believe that we already know. As such they are obviously effective and "psychologically" valid. The real philosophical problem in Madhyamaka is the problem of two truths, two degrees or kinds of reality, depending on the eyes that see. But this is a problem that cannot be solved "scientifically", there being no relational bridge linking the two together. The acceptance of the distinction between two truths is based on an act of faith, not of reason. It may, of course, be supported by subsequent reasoning (*yukti*), but it is still based on faith in the value of Buddhist tradition (*āgama*). Philosophy is but the handmaid of religion. MK was never meant to be read isolated from its religious Mahāyāna background (*Ratnāvalī*, *Sūtrasamuccaya*, etc.)

The question of the value of Nāgārjuna's arguments, then, is a strictly "subjective" or personal matter. Nāgārjuna himself is perfectly aware that this is so. One must therefore assess his arguments in much the same way as one would assess rhetorical arguments, namely, on the basis of their powers of persuasion. Such arguments, as we know very well, are often, if not always, much more efficient than dry and rational ones. Nāgārjuna knew that too. So, in the study of MK the real problems that we are faced with are of a psychological rather than of a philosophical nature.

The fact that Nāgārjuna soon had to write two supplements to MK--for this is how we have to regard his *Vigrahavyāvartanī* and *Śūnyatāsaptati*--shows that MK did not meet with unconditioned approval in all quarters of Buddhism.

In the following analysis of each of the twenty-seven chapters I concentrate on pointing out the flow and structure of the arguments.

## CHAPTER I: Investigation of the Four Conditions[124]

(The target for the reasoned argument of the introductory chapter is the theory of causation in scholastic Buddhism (Sarvāstivāda) according to which four conditions (see verse two) determine how a given factor arises as a particular concept in the mind of a particular individual at a given time.)

3-4 of E; 1-2 of T (E4, 26; T183) Nāgārjuna bases himself on this encapsulation of the world-view of Mahāyāna in formulating his first and fundamental thesis: "There is no origination whatsoever", to which his opponent rejoins that a given factor does in fact arise when the four conditions (cause, supporting object, proximate condition and dominant factor) are present.

5-12 of E; 3-10 of T (E26-30; T183-184) Nāgārjuna denies that the four conditions could be the ground for any origination. It would be generally agreed that something dependent cannot be anything in its own right, and consequently not in virtue of anything else either. It is also impossible to define a relation between conditions and the process that produces the effect. Conditions can, hypothetically, only be restrictions on something existing or not existing, but both alternatives are absurd. Therefore the first of the four conditions, a cause producing the factor, is out of the question. The second condition, a supporting object of consciousness, is otiose in the light of the assertion that a given conceptual factor is sufficient in itself. As no concept has arisen, a "proximate" condition cannot be precedent to anything, and has even less claim to be a condition at all. Nor can the fourth, the dominant factor, allegedly a necessary concomitant for the production of a particular thing, be established, since it is proved that nothing independently exists.

13-16 of E; 11-14 of T (E30-31; T184) Having dismissed the four conditions, Nāgārjuna - just to be sure - attacks the complementary concept, effect. An effect cannot be produced by conditions because it is not contained in them. But if it could, all the same, be produced without ever having been in the conditions beforehand, then it could just as well have been produced by the wrong conditions. Moreover, the effect cannot possess the nature of the conditions, that is, be identical with them, for they are nothing in themselves. The conclusion is that there is no effect whatsoever, therefore no condition of any sort attached to it.[1]

---

1.In this chapter Nāgārjuna is pleading for the central concept of Mahāyāna, nonorigination, by showing that since both conditions (cause) and effect are empty notions, the concept of origination, which naturally presumes the reality of condition and effect, lacks a logical function.

It is not without good reason that Nāgārjuna, in the introduction to his principal work, directs his criticism against the elaboration of causation theory which is peculiar to the Sarvāstivāda school. The argument that follows will confirm that its dogmatic posture constituted in Nāgārjuna's eyes the most serious threat to the proper acquisition of the Budha's teaching.

## CHAPTER II: Investigation of Motion[125]

1-7 (E33-35; T184-185) Nāgārjuna's first thesis is that motion cannot be localized in any of the three aspects of time, to which the opponent replies that movement really occurs in a passing (*gati*) in the course of a place's being passed (*gata*). But, says Nāgārjuna, this implies that the place will be devoid of passing (which is unthinkable, but unavoidable), since by definition that which is passively passed is that which is being passed, while active passing passes. Otherwise, if the place was not devoid of passing, there would be two passings, one for the active member and one for the passive, which is absurd.

8-21 (E35-39; T185-186) Having thus dismissed the concept of a passing being passed, and implicitly a passing going on there, Nāgārjuna turns to the passing subject as such, with an analogous argument. Supposing there was movement after all, where and when should its motion begin? Motion is purely illogical. In the same way, the opposite concept, cessation, is shown to be illogical. Who should stop and when? Furthermore, the movement and its subject cannot be conceived either as identical or different and therefore, being indeterminate, cannot be established.

22-25 (E40; T186) Finally, motion cannot be established on the ground that the subject performs an action that makes it traverse a certain distance. In that case the subject must surely be separate from the action in order to avoid identity of agent and object. But it is not. Whether the subject existed or not, it would not be able to accomplish anything. The conclusion is that there is no movement, because it cannot be established in any of its three (grammatically, as we would add) conceivable aspects.[1]

---

1.Obviously, Nāgārjuna's argument against motion is applicable in principle to any realistic world-view, but it is the Sarvāstivāda school that figures most prominently for Nāgārjuna. The central concept for them was: Things are eternal in their essential nature (*svabhāva*), but in their passage through the three periods of time they appear as impermanent forms of existence (*bhāva*).

## CHAPTER III: Investigation of the Sense-Bases[126]

(Chapters III-V are closely connected, as all three examine the components that in one way or another can be said to make up an individual. The individual as a conscious being presupposes twelve senses, consisting of the six sense organs and the corresponding six sense objects. Each of these six sets form the ground for a corresponding awareness.)[1]

1-8 (in E43-47); 1-9 (in T186-187) The opponent defends the twelve sense-bases. Nāgārjuna argues that since sight cannot see itself, it cannot see other things either. It was customary in debate to justify such arguments by an example (*dṛṣṭānta*), but the example of fire (or a torch, see VII, 8-12) used here is invalid according to the argument of II.1. This means that the opponent has to give up his initial thesis, and therefore Nāgārjuna can conclude that neither sight nor nonsight, obviously, and far less the presumed seeing subject, can see anything at all. This subject could not in any case be determined as identical with or different from sight. Therefore neither sight as the organ of sense, nor anything else visible such as form (i.e., shape and color) have any existence. In the same way, neither consciousness, contact, feeling, desire nor appropriating have any existence. Similarly with the ten remaining senses.[2]

## CHAPTER IV: Investigation of the Five Aggregates[127]

---

1.These three chapters were later supplemented by 35.*Śūnyatāsaptati* 45-57.

2.This chapter has shown one of Nāgārjuna's philosophical presuppositions: An activity can only be considered real if it can be directed against itself, that is, if it is entirely independent. Moreover we see Nāgārjuna arguing on a relative level: An assertion (*pakṣa*) must be supported by a valid example to be acceptable (cf. 34.*Vigrahavyāvartanī* 21-27). Finally, one may note that the fact that he takes up sight (rather than one of the other bases) is inspired by *Bhavasaṃkrāntisūtra*, a canonical text to which he often alludes.

1-7 (E48-49; T187) Nāgārjuna begins by noting that physical form (*rūpa*) is neither the same as nor different from its component matter (*rūpakāraṇa*). If it were different, it would lack a cause, and if matter were different from form, it would not be a cause and thus form would not be its effect. Whether form is assumed to exist or not, it cannot possibly have a cause. Nor can form be different from matter, since it would then lack a cause. Thus it cannot be determined either as having a cause or as having no cause. This leads to the general statement that cause and effect are neither identical nor different. Similarly for the other four aggregates, and in general for any concept whatsoever.

8-9 (E49-50; T188) Nāgārjuna's next two verses are of fundamental import, though at first sight unrelated to the above. Whatever the champion of universal emptiness propounds or explains, his basic position is that whatever objection the opponent may make, every concept that his argument is based on can be refuted as being empty.

## CHAPTER V: Investigation of the Six Elements[128]

1-7 (E51-53; T188-189) The Buddha has said that an individual is composed of six elements: earth, water, fire, air, *ākāśa* and consciousness. Each has its distinguishing trait, to be firm, flowing, etc. Nāgārjuna comments that *ākāśa*, for example, distinguished as such, cannot exist in advance of its characteristic mark. There is in fact nothing which can do so. Therefore the mark itself cannot begin to operate, either in association with what is already distinguished or with what is not, and there is no third possibility. Consequently there can be nothing, no substance or subject, that is distinguished. Therefore a thing like *ākāśa* cannot be conceived as either unmarked or marked, nor can anything besides these two be said to exist. Therefore one cannot talk of the negation of a thing, its absence, and even less of a peculiar subject that is supposed to be different from existing or nonexistent things. The other elements likewise.

8 (E54; T189) It must be recognized that those who view things in positive-negative contradictions will never get behind the curtain

of empirical illusion.[1]

## CHAPTER VI: Investigation of Attachment and Attached[129]

1-10 (E55-58; T189-190) The three "vices", attachment, aversion and delusion, have their source in conceptual notions which form the basis for karma leading to rebirth in the circuit of existence. But, as Nāgārjuna explains, attachment cannot arise, whether the attached subject has come into existence or not. Likewise, the attached subject cannot begin to exist prior to his attachment. Nor can the two be simultaneous, as they would each have to have independent existence, but that is impossible, whether they are treated as identical, or different while simultaneous, and there is no third option. But supposing that they did exist as different side by side, that would not make sense, and it is out of the question that they could belong together. On the other hand, they would not be anything together unless they were different. That they can each separately have meaning must be excluded. The conclusion is that correlatives like attachment/attached cannot be described either as having independent existence or as having simultaneous relationship.[2]

---

1.Now Nāgārjuna has rejected the six elements on the ground that they cannot be defined as mark, marked, existing or nonexistent. As the sequel will show, this does not imply that Nāgārjuna cancels the practical validity of these concepts. On the contrary, for him speculation and dogmatic pronouncements on these concepts are the source of utter misery, because one tends to treat the concepts as entities with substance, and thereby fails to grasp the purpose of the Buddha's teaching.

2.Nāgārjuna shows here that vices, etc., are not precisely delimited concepts whether considered together or separately. Therefore they cannot be established as real. This analysis has confirmed the saying of the Buddha that the vices are due to conceptual notions.

## CHAPTER VII: Investigation of the Conditioned[130]

1-3 (E59-60; 190) Everything in the empirical world is composite, associated with the three marks origination, duration and destruction. But what of origination, for instance, itself? Is it, Nāgārjuna asks, composite like everything else, and thus itself subject to duration, etc.? He remarks parenthetically that none of the three marks, separately or as a unit, could mark the composite, and adds that the three marks cannot possibly be themselves composite because that would mean recursion to infinity.

4 (E60; T190) To avoid the unspoken absurdity that the three are alternatively noncomposite, the opponent (Vātsīputrīya) puts forward an ancillary hypothesis that the ordinary or initial "radical" (*mūla*) origination", being composite, must also be subject to an origination, the "origination of origination," which is in turn brought into existence by the radical origination which it has itself brought about. In this ingenious way, the opponent thinks, the proposition that *everything*, origination included, is composite is thus upheld and recursion to infinity is avoided.

5-13 (E61-64; T190-191) All right, answers Nāgārjuna, but how can the radical origination be brought about the very first time? It cannot be brought about by the origination of the origination which the radical origination itself still has to bring about without help. Obviously, the radical origination cannot be produced at the very moment of birth, since the origination of the origination must by that time already be real. Now the opponent could say that the radical origination produces itself, simultaneously with the origination of the origination, on the analogy of a torch, which operates on itself and on other things, in particular the dark. Nāgārjuna explains that on the one hand this analogy does not fit, so that the thesis of an activity directed towards itself and other things is untenable, and on the other hand, it would be nonsensical if the radical origination, once it has properly arisen, begins to produce the origination of the origination.

14-21 (E64-67; T191) The concept of origination is criticized now from a different point of view. It cannot take place in any division of time. As for the "thing that arises", it cannot be allowed to be prior to or simultaneous with "origination". The two concepts are properly speaking correlative (*pratītya*). Only if the thing existed before its origination could it arise, but it does not. The thing that arises cannot be due to the origination either, since that could not be established either on the basis of another origination (which would imply the absurdity of recursion) or without a cause. Moreover, neither the existing nor the nonexistence can undergo a process of origination, and certainly not something that is decaying. The alternative to this last, that something once arose, never to decay, is unthinkable.

22-25 (E68; T191-192) Having rejected arising from several perspectives, the second characteristic of the composite, duration, is rejected analogously. There is neither anything that endures nor any duration as such.

26-32 (E69-71; T192) The conclusion is that since these characteristics, origination, etc., are, on closer scrutiny, unsubstantiated, they cannot distinguish anything composite. Therefore the logical antithesis to anything composite, the uncomposite, is also excluded. The three concepts are, in other words, purely and simply illusory.[1]

## CHAPTER VIII: Investigation of Agent/Action[131]

(Chapters VIII-X form a thematic group, because they disprove the concept of a person from three points of view. From the first angle, the person is considered as an agent, who realizes existence by means of appropriating assuming the five aggregates.)

1-13 (E75-80; T192-193) Nāgārjuna's thesis is that the agent, whether existent or not, does not perform any action. This is justified in detail as follows: The concept "existent" excludes the concept of empirical activity. If agent and action exist, they could, of course, exist without each other. If they do not exist, it would be purely arbitrary whether a nonexistent agent did anything. It would

---

1.Although Nāgārjuna would be the last person to deny origination, etc., in the empirical, conventional sense, he has shown, as foreshadowed in the introductory verse, that they cannot be established in the ultimate sense. These concepts are definitively empty.

unleash a string of consequences absurd for a Buddhist if strict causality were denied. The next five verses, with less logical content than usual, reject all possible agent-action relationships. The two concepts are correlative, nothing in themselves. This line of argument can also be used to dismiss agent-action concepts other than the "person" and appropriating. By adducing that the existence must be invariably inactive and that the nonexistent cannot possibly be active, Nāgārjuna has disproved agent over against action.

CHAPTER IX: Investigation of a Grasper and His Support.[132]

1-2 (E81; 193) Now one could maintain, along with one of the schools (Vātsīputrīya), that there really does exist a person or self prior to or after any kind of sense-perception or internal emotion, since these phenomena must surely belong to someone, that is, to a person.

3-12 (E81-84; T194) But, Nāgārjuna replies, if the person should exist prior to sight, e.g., and then take possession of sight, sight should also be able to exist beforehand independently of the person. But this makes no sense. Thus they are indissolubly linked. The opponent thinks he can save his case by admitting that there is no person prior to sensations, but different ones bobbing up all the time. But, answers Nāgārjuna, whether it is the same person that shows up like that, or a different one, with no third possibility, it would in either case be absurd. Moreover, the person is not to be found in the basic elements. The conclusion is that a pre-empirical person does not exist, and consequently his sight, etc., do not exist either. It cannot be said to exist, or, by that very fact, not to exist.[1]

---

1.Thus Nāgārjuna has denied the existence of a person, without confirming his nonexistence. Nāgārjuna is convinced, as we shall see, that this posture, neither affirming nor denying, is the most faithful transmission of the Buddha's attitude toward all speculations that lead away from liberation or spiritual freedom.

## CHAPTER X: Investigation of Fire-Fuel[133]

1-16 (E86-92; T194-196) We see in the canon that the relationship between the "person" and the appropriating (i.e., the five aggregates) is modelled on the analogy of fire and fuel. This could be taken to imply that the person and the appropriating actually exist independently of each other. But, replies Nāgārjuna, person and appropriating cannot really be considered as either identical or different, and so cannot be constituted as real. It would be absurd if the first existed independently. If the opponent points out that something can actually be burning, that is, fuel, he must explain what sets it on fire. It is absurd that a tongue of fire should independently come from nowhere and set it on fire. Fire and fuel (as fuel) occur only in interdependence (*āpekṣya*). Moreover it would involve the mistake of establishing an already established fire. Next come two verses on interdependence in general. In interdependence one member is not given beforehand, and even if it could be so, why should it enter into correlation? This rule is of course valid for fire-fuel as well. The conclusion is that the relation fire-fuel cannot be established, not even from other possible viewpoints. To postulate an independent person in relation to appropriating or its cognizer is thus the enunciation of a conceptual fiction.

## CHAPTER XI: Investigation of the Round of Rebirth[134]

1-8 (E95-98; T196) The Buddha has asserted, as is well known, that the circuit of *saṃsāra* is unlimited. This implies, according to Nāgārjuna, that the temporal concepts "before", "after" and "contemporaneous" have no definite (independent) meaning. It would lead to a long series of palpable absurdities if they had. Consequently there is no actual subject that experiences rebirth in the course or circuit of time. That goes for other dogmatic concepts, too; they cannot be pinned down as relatively before, after or contemporaneous.[1]

## CHAPTER XII: Investigation of Frustration[135]

1-10 (E100-102; T197) Is not believing that there exists no actual subject, no person in the circuit of transmigration, to admit that frustration, viz., the five aggregates,, etc. is a fact? No, answers Nāgārjuna, for as the Buddha has declared, it cannot have arisen in any way, to wit, not out of its own aggregates, nor aggregates from elsewhere, nor from the same person, nor any other person. Obviously the notion of other-created presupposes that the self-created is established, which is not the case. Frustration is thus neither self-created nor created by others, so it cannot be created by both or be without a cause (implicit in verse 1). Everything else can be shown not to be able to arise, neither from itself, from another, from both or neither.[2]

## CHAPTER XIII: Investigation of Reality[136]

1-8 (E204-208; T198) The Buddha has stated that everything is false (unreal) because it is *moṣa* (which can either mean elusive, thus the opponent, or delusive, thus Nāgārjuna). This implies, so Nāgārjuna says, that by the very fact of being false nothing can in

---

1.The brevity of the chapter should not lead one to believe that its subject is unimportant. Nāgārjuna, by accepting the idea that the circuit of existence is endless and therefore indeterminate, provides the best ontological foundation for his thesis that everything is correlative even to the extreme that *saṃsāra* and *nirvāṇa* cannot be separated (cf. XXV, 20, to be read in this light)..

2.Nāgārjuna has now proved that frustration or suffering, the basic empirical fact of existence, the presence of which is the driving force for all serious Buddhists, has not properly speaking come into actual existence.

fact be elusive. In other words, everything is empty, meaning that it cannot even be elusive. No, replies the opponent, the concept of emptiness is on the contrary synonymous with variability or change. Change is the true nature of things, and the true meaning of emptiness. No, replies Nāgārjuna, if things, hypothetically speaking, had a fixed nature they would by that token be unchangeable. But in fact there is nothing that can change, neither the same (unchanged) thing nor any other (which has already changed). Thus there is nothing nonempty (i.e., permanent and substantial), and one cannot talk of an alternative called empty. The teaching of the Buddha, when he talks about emptiness, points beyond any diametrical opposition.[1]

## CHAPTER XIV: Investigation of Combination[137]

1-8 (E110-113; T198-199) Now what if someone claimed reality for empirical things by referring to the fact that they enter into combination? But the concept "combination" is not possible, says Nāgārjuna. The premise for combination is that things are different and that they have independent existence. If they are absolutely different, these criteria cannot be fulfilled. The premise for combination is thereby annulled.[2]

## CHAPTER XV: Investigation of Being and Nonbeing[138]

1-9 (E114-119; T199-200) This chapter is not directed against a

---

1.According to Mahāyāna emptiness (an old Canonical term) means nonorigination. According to other Buddhist schools it means impermanence. Cf. *Ratnāvalī* IV. 86.

2.This chapter should be read in the light of Chapter XXVI. 3 ff.: "Now that sensation has been shown to be out of the question, the feelings, desire, appropriating and so on are prevented from further development. If with insight just one of the twelve members is brought to a standstill, the remainder can be prevented from further development."

particular concept in the opponent's dogmas, but against the fundamental idea that a given conceptual phenomenon exists substantially and immutably, and that it possesses being in and by itself. Nāgārjuna replies that the concept of "own-being" excludes, of course, any suggestion of composition or dependence, ideally speaking. But obviously the existence of any such thing is logically and empirically impossible. The derived or secondary modes of being, other-existence, a particular existence, and absence are included in the refutation. The proponent of the substantiality of things simply fails to see the purpose of the Buddha's teaching. It should be obvious that the very concept of "substance" or fixed nature (and of course the complete absence of it) excludes the concept of alteration. The wise Buddhist will therefore distance himself from both dogmatic extremes, agreeing to the existence of anything permanent, and denying it, that is, believing in impermanence.[1]

CHAPTER XVI: Investigation of Bondage and Liberation[139]

1-10 (E123-130; T200-201) Surely there is someone who is forced to go through *saṃsāra*? No, answers Nāgārjuna. On the one hand the components cannot travel in *saṃsāra*, whether they (or the "person") are thought of as eternally immutable or repeatedly momentary. On the other hand, the person cannot go into orbit, whether he is thought of as being one with the aggregates or quite different from them. And when there is no one in *saṃsāra*, who will then go into *nirvāṇa*? From another point of view the concepts of bondage and liberation are empty, because they are not compatible with the common understanding that things are momentary. Where and when should the binding take place? No

---

1.This chapter is so basic that one wonders why it does not come much earlier. Nāgārjuna does not dispute that there is empirical impermanence, but shows that, in reality, on a higher plane, as it were, nothing can be declared to be permanent, and nothing can be declared to be the opposite of permanent. Truth, or reality, is beyond contradictions, and can be realized as such by our faculty of *buddhi* or *prajñā*, i.e. in yoga.

one can be liberated from a bond that does not bind. The whole trouble comes from dissociating *saṃsāra* and *nirvāṇa* as being two independent opposites.[1]

CHAPTER XVII: Investigation of Karma and Its Fruits[140]

1-11 (E132-136; T201-202) The belief in the law of karma, that sound and healthy actions lead to happiness and that bad actions lead to the opposite, is the basis on which Buddhists conduct their daily lives. The immense practical significance of this is the reason why Nāgārjuna makes such free use of common sense notions about karma's nature. Karma is will and action. Action is mental, bodily, or linguistic. These three each admit of seven divisions. From intention to the final ripening of the fruit of karma there runs a continuous series, designed to avoid the two extremes of permanence and destruction.

12-20 (E136-139; T202-203) Another Buddhist school prefers, instead of the karma-continuum, the commercial analogy of a debt coming due for payment on a certain date. It can only be annulled by death or by the debtor (or creditor) becoming an *arhat* or Buddhist saint.

21-33 (E139-143; T203) Nāgārjuna brushes aside all speculation.[2] It would be absurd if karma were substantial. Karma is directed by the defilements and therefore empty. The body it belongs to is therefore also empty. There is no agent, or creator of karma, consequently no karma and no fruit of karma. Agent and karma are illusory.[3]

---

1.In this chapter Nāgārjuna touches on a theme that will be treated again in Chapter XXV, that in reality there is no difference between *saṃsāra* and *nirvāṇa*. It goes without saying that he is well aware of the rhetorical force of his argument.

2.His own opinion can be gleaned from 38.*Ratnāvalī*, etc.

3.This chapter shows clearly that the law of karma is sovereign in practice, and sovereign in definitive truth is the emptiness and unreality of karma, and everything else. More about karma in 35.*Śūnyatāsaptati* 39-44, q.v.

## CHAPTER XVIII: Investigation of the Self and Factors[141]

1-12 (E145-161; T204-205) The idea of a personal substance has already been refuted in Chapters VIII-XII, and indirectly in III-VI, so Nāgārjuna has only to recall that the self is neither one with the aggregates nor different from them. When there is no ego, no "I", there is no "mine" (the aggregates). Appropriating (of the aggregates) is thus unsubstantiated. It comes from karma and the defilements, which themselves are due to the formation of a conceptually expanded world of manifoldness (*prapañca*). Liberation is obtained by the recognition of its emptiness, that is, by getting rid of ignorance. It is now clear that even the many-faceted teaching of the Buddhas only operates on the conventional plane without really referring to anything. They speak "psychological", not "ontological" truths. The fading out of contradictions must be experienced personally. According to their depth of insight there are three groups of Buddhists.[1]

## CHAPTER XIX: Investigation of the Periods of Time[142]

1-3 (E163; T205) The opponent's idea is that time is real. It is what things, in various guises, traverse from the future, over the present, and down into the past. But, answers Nāgārjuna, these periods must be present at least two by two (simultaneous) before they can be put into relationshp with each other. That is of course absurd and excluded. On the other hand, the three periods cannot be established without such a relation. Therefore they are all unreal.

4 (E164; T205) All other corresponding sets of concepts can be dealt with in the same way.

5-6 (E165-166; T205) Furthermore, time cannot be established, whether one takes it as momentaneous or static. Finally, one cannot establish the reality of time because things exist in it, i.e., by

---

1.This verse has been misunderstood by all the commentators, ancient and modern.

inference. They do not, as has often been shown.[1]

## CHAPTER XX: Investigation of Cause and Effect[143]

1-4 (E168-169; T205) The effect does not arise in the complex where it is supposed already to exist, nor in a complex where it is not found to exist.

5-6 (E170; T206) The cause does not cease to act, either after it was supposed to be in operation, or before it has effects.

7-9 (E170-171; T206) The effect does not exist simultaneously with, before, or after its sufficient condition.

10-11 (E171-172; T206) An actual effect is not brought about by a cause that is absent, or present, whether it is supposed to be coupled with the effect or not.

12-15 (E172-173; T206) A previous, contemporaneous, or future effect is not linked to a cause, whether it is past, future, or present. These three verses prove that effect and cause do not meet each other, or even if they did, it would be absurd if the cause should produce yet another effect.

16 (E173; T206) The effect is not brought about by a cause that is devoid of effect, or by one that is not.

17-18 (E174; T206) No effect can get established, neither the nonempty (substantial) nor the empty (totally absent).

19-24 (E174-176; 206-207) Cause and effect are neither identical nor different. The cause does not produce existence or nonexistence, and consequently cannot be the cause of any effect. The effect cannot be brought about by its set of sufficient conditions, for it would then have to be self-productive, nor can it be brought about by any other set, which would be the wrong set. Therefore the sufficient condition cannot lead to any effect.

---

1.This chapter, which comes rather abruptly as a new topic, must be taken together with what follows as Nāgārjuna's final attack on the realistic categories of time and causality. Its arguments are recapitulated in 35.*Śūnyatāsaptati* 29.

## CHAPTER XXI: Investigation of Integration and Disintegration[144]

1-5 (E178-179; T207) Disintegration can neither be simultaneous with, nor (quite) without integration, and vice versa. Each point is proved separately.

6 (E180: T207) In general, two things that are neither together nor separate cannot be established.

7-21 (E180-185; T207-209) Integration and disintegration do not apply to what has ceased. They can be associated with a specific thing, which is bound to keep on changing, so that they cannot be predicated of the same thing. They do not apply to what is empty (total absence) or nonempty (substantial). They are not identical or different. That they are perceived at all is because of pure ignorance. Being does not arise from nonbeing, etc. Any one of these ideas would imply the heresy of "something permanent". The opponent thinks, though, that the theory of a continuum or a series overcomes this fatal implication. No, answers Nāgārjuna, whether the cause is assumed to come to an end or not, this would involve many absurdities. And *when* should this new existence (the aggregates) begin? Not after, during, and obviously not before the old existence. The conclusion is that a continuum cannot be established chronologically and its existence is therefore not proved.

## CHAPTER XXII: Investigation of the Buddha (*tathāgata*)[145]

1-11 (E187-193; T209-210) Nāgārjuna begins by examining the Buddha-figure. Buddha is neither identical with nor different from the aggregates, and so unreal. If the Buddha existed only on the basis of the aggregates or quite independently of them, that would be absurd. Both cases would imply an existence prior to appropriating. Therefore the Buddha cannot be established on the basis of grasping. Consequently there can be no appropriating associated with anyone at all. Both concepts are equally empty. All forms of expression can therefore only be suggestions, indications, nominal designations (*prajñapti*).

12-16 (E194-195; T210) This is the only way to avoid the many misconceptions about the Buddha, the world, and *nirvāṇa*. The Buddha is in fact as empty and incomprehensible as the world around us.[1]

## CHAPTER XXIII: Investigation of Misconceptions[146]

1 (E197; T210) In Buddhism a fundamental article of faith is that the defilements attachment, aversion and delusion, which cease only with *nirvāṇa*, have their source in conceptualizings, which confuse good with bad, fair with foul, solid with hollow, and permanent with transitory. These are the four misconceptions.

2-25 (E197-207; T210-212) But, Nāgārjuna reminds his opponent, since the defilements arise dependently, they are nothing in their own right. Further, they cannot belong to the self or be in any way related to it. In addition to this, the grounds for the defilements, the four misconceptions, do not exist. This is because their objects are empty. Fair and foul (and the other three pairs) give no meaning when taken separately (and can consequently not establish each other). Can the defilements be established on such a basis? Again, there cannot be a correct or a mistaken conception, since there is in fact nothing permanent or impermanent to be mistaken about. Therefore all possible aspects of a given conception come to nothing. There is no subject which can possess the misconceptions. Whether anything permanent can be taken to exist or not, it cannot be the source for misconceptions. By thus eliminating misconceptions, ignorance, etc., are also abolished, even though, properly speaking, there is no question of abolishing any

---

1.As Chapters III-V and VIII-XI were closely connected, so these Chapters XXII-XXV have the common theme that even Buddhism's most sacred concepts cannot escape the verdict that they are in the final analysis empty. By proving that the Buddha and appropriation cannot be used to establish each other, which means that they are both empty, Nāgārjuna has removed any possible basis for the growth of misconceptions. The dogmas fade away, only suggestions point the way.

defilements, whether existing or nonexistent.[1]

## CHAPTER XXIV: Investigation of the Noble Truths[147]

1-40 (E208-225; T212-215) First a colleague upbraids Nāgārjuna for posing as an iconoclast or nihilist with his doctrine of total vacuity. This gives Nāgārjuna the opportunity to define "emptiness", its significance and purpose. Difficult as it may be to take in, the proponent of emptiness is in the closest agreement with Buddhist practice. Conversely, to recognize anything nonempty (substantial) is a desecration of the Buddha's teaching about the correlativity (emptiness) of all things. All the accusations are turned back on the prosecutor. To admit the substantial existence of things is the same as denying the possibility of any change or development at all. It would be impossible to practise Buddhism.

## CHAPTER XXV: Investigation of *Nirvāṇa*[148]

1 (E227; T215) The opponent still thinks that the concept of emptiness excludes the abolition of the defilements, that is to say, of achieving liberation first with, later without aggregates remaining.

2-24 (E225-236; T215-217) On the contrary, replies Nāgārjuna, it is only when emptiness is accepted that liberation is at all possible. *Nirvāṇa* is free from all contradictions. Developed in more detail, *nirvāṇa* can neither be a positive form of existence, i.e., a thing, nor a negative form of existence, i.e., an absence. Nor can it be both, or neither. Thus it is impossible to assert anything about the Buddha in connection with *nirvāṇa*. Nor is it possible to assert anything about the world. Since *nirvāṇa* is undifferentiated there is no Buddha who has preached anything to anyone (cf. XVIII).

---

1.It is easy to see why it is important to dispose of the four misconceptions. Then ignorance, the first constituent of existence, ceases, and with it all suffering. The theme is further developed in 35.*Śūnyatāsaptati* 9-16 and 58-66, q.v.

## CHAPTER XXVI: Investigation of the Twelve Members[149]

1-12 (E238-244; T217-218) Nāgārjuna begins with a resumé of the emanation formula, which the Buddhist tradition takes as the expression of the Buddha's realization, in retrospect, of the genesis of frustration. It is a sort of "fall from grace." If the individual suffers from ignorance, and we all do, the personal karma begins to function. Our karma, or will, arouses consciousness. Step by step one awakens to "self-consciousness" and generates a personal existence. In so doing one becomes subject to the frustrations of the circuit of existence. This calamity can be treated only in one place, at the root, by the abolition of ignorance. The process operates all over the twelve members, i.e., ignorance is omnipresent.[1]

## CHAPTER XXVII: Investigation of Dogmatic View[150]

1-14 (E248-254; T218-219) Dogmatic views, sixteen in all, grow out of two (false) assumptions, that something (the self or the world) is either limited (impermanent) or infinite (permanent). The first to be rejected is that the self, in one of four ways, has always existed in the past. It cannot be asserted to be identical with appropriating or different from it, without incurring numerous absurdities. The four ways in which the self could hypothetically be thought to cease some time in the future are rejected analogously.

15-28 (E254-259; T219-220) Second, the remaining eight views about the world. If the world were eternal everything would remain in its own fixed place. All actual change in connection with rebirth (god to man, for example) would be excluded. If the world were on the other hand limited, and in one way or another could come to a stop, that would also lead to absurdities.

---

1.What is it that Nāgārjuna wishes to convey in his reference to one of the most vital and obscure passages in the Canon? He wants to reassure his Buddhist readers or students of his orthodoxy. Suffering is due to all-pervasive ignorance. This is what Nāgārjuna has striven, chapter by chapter, to overcome. Cf. 48.*Catuḥśataka* XVI.1. The theme is further developed in 35.*Śūnyatāsaptati*.

29-30 (E258; T220) The conclusion is that no one can establish any dogma.The premisses are false. We should merely praise the Buddha for having abolished all dogmas.

## 34. NĀGĀRJUNA, *Vigrahavyāvartanī*

Summary by Kamaleshwar Bhattacharya

This treatise consists of seventy verses in *āryā* meter, with a commentary in prose. Both the *kārikās* and the *vṛtti* are ascribed by tradition to Nāgārjuna himself.[151] It was written after the 33.*Mūlamadhyamakakārikās*.

The text is extant in Sanskrit, Tibetan and Chinese, and has often been translated into modern Western languages.[152] Unfortunately, the Sanskrit material, discovered by Rahula Sankrtyayana and edited by him, is far from satisfactory; it is to the labors of E.H. Johnston and Arnold Kunst[153] that we owe "the nearest approximation of Nāgārjuna's original text." One can see, however, even from this imperfect material, that the prose of the commentary, like that of other commentaries of Nāgārjuna,[154] is modelled on that of Patañjali's *Mahābhāṣya.*[155]

The purpose of the text is to defend--in accordance with the prevailing rules of debate[156]--Nāgārjuna's thesis that all things are empty (*śūnya*) because devoid of an essential nature (*niḥsvabhāva*). It is divided into two parts, the first twenty verses setting forth the opponent's (or opponents') objections, and the remainder Nāgārjuna's own replies, a searching critique of the opponent's logical and epistemological assumptions, and a demonstration of the validity of the Madhyamaka theory and method.

Opinions vary as to the identity of the opponent (or opponents): a Naiyāyika and a Buddhist, according to Johnston and Kunst[157] and Tucci[158]; a Naiyāyika, who occasionally assumes the standpoint of the Buddhist realists[159]; "an Ābhidharmika following, of course, the rules of debate prescribed in some Buddhist work on logic such as **Upāyahṛdaya*, etc."[160]. At any rate, it was very much related to the *Nyāyasūtras*.

"E" and "T" references are to pages of Kamaleshwar Bhattacharya's (47.13.10), separately paginated.

## OBJECTIONS

1-2 (E10-11; T5-7) If, as Nāgārjuna says, "All things lack an essential nature" (or "Things have no essential nature" or "All things are empty"), saying so must be equally "lacking in essential nature" or "empty". But then, how can an empty statement deny other empty things? If this denial is valid, saying so is not empty. But, in that case, not all things are empty, since the saying of it, which is included in "all things", is not empty. Nāgārjuna's thesis (*pratijñā*) "All things are empty" is thus destroyed. There arises a discrepancy, namely that some things are empty while some others are not, and he should state the special reason for that difference.

3 (E13; T7-8) It cannot be said that just as the sound "Do not make a sound" prevents another sound, even so the empty statement "All things are empty" prevents things from having an essential nature. For, in the example, a sound that exists prevents a (not-yet-existent) future sound; but it is not an existent statement that prevents things having an essential nature.

4 (E13-14; T8-9) Nor can Nāgārjuna contend that, according to the same line of argument, the opponent's denial of the statement denying the essential nature of all things is also impossible. For the latter does not hold that all things are empty; his statement, therefore, is not empty.

5-6 (E14-15; T9-10) Nāgārjuna cannot say that he denies all things after having apprehended them through any of the four instruments of knowledge, viz., perception, inference, comparison and verbal testimony. For these instruments of knowledge, being included in "all things", are equally empty. The objects to be apprehended through these means, as well as the person who apprehends them, are also empty. Thus there is no apprehension of things, and a denial of that which is not apprehended is a logical impossibility.[1]

7-8 (E15-17; T10-11) People conversant with the state of things hold that the essential nature of things is of different kinds: good things have a good intrinsic nature, bad things a bad intrinsic

1.For a denial is not possible without a thing being denied. See 11-12 below.

nature, and so on. Therefore, the statement that all things lack an essential nature and hence are empty is not valid. (The *vṛtti* gives a long list of *dharmas*. The "people conversant with the state of things" are clearly Buddhists, but the school they belonged to has not yet been identified.)

9 (E17; T11) If things were to lack an essential nature, then even the term "lacking an essential nature" would not be possible; for this term must refer to something which is absent.

10 (E18; T11-12) Nāgārjuna cannot counter this objection by saying that there is an essential nature but that it does not belong to things. For there would be, then, an essential nature not belonging to things, and he should explain what it is the nature of!

11-12 (E18-19; T12-13) It is something existing somewhere (or in some point of time) that is denied to be somewhere else (or in some other point of time), as, for instance, when one says: "There is no pot in the house." Likewise, Nāgārjuna's negation "Things have no essential nature" is not the denial of an absolutely nonexistent essential nature. By the very fact that a denial is possible is established the essential nature of all things. A significant denial is of a real entity, not of a fictitious one. The denial of a nonentity is established even without words. What, then, does Nāgārjuna deny by his statement, if the essential nature he denies does not exist at all?

13-16 (E19-20; T13-14) Nāgārjuna may say that, just as ignorant people wrongly perceive a mirage as water and that wrong perception is removed by some person who knows, saying "But that mirage is without water", even so his statement "All things lack an essential nature" is meant for removing people's wrong perception of an essential nature in things which are lacking an essential nature. But then, the aggregate of the following six things exists: a perception, the object to be perceived, the perceiver of the object, the denial of the wrong perception, the object denied, and the denier. And these things being established, the statement that all things are empty is not valid. Nor can Nāgārjuna argue that there is no perception, no object to be perceived, and no perceiver, for in that case there would be no denial, no object denied, and no denier. And, if these absences do not exist, then not all things are denied, and some have an essential nature.

17-19 (E21; T14-15) To establish his thesis that all things lack an essential nature Nāgārjuna needs a reason (*hetu*); but how can there be a reason for him, when everything lacks an essential nature and hence is empty? If he holds that the lack of essential nature is established without any reason, then the opponent's affirmation of the essential nature will be equally established without any reason. Nor can he hold that the things' lacking an essential nature is the existence of the reason; for there is nothing in the world which lacks an essential nature and is at the same time existent.

20 (E22; T16) Finally, denial is not possible in any of the three times (before, during and after). The denial cannot come first and then the thing to be denied; for if the thing to be denied does not exist, what is it that is denied? Nor can the denial come after the thing to be denied; for if the thing to be denied is already established, what purpose is served by denying it? Nor even is it possible to hold that the denial and the thing denied are simultaneous; for then, the denial is not the cause of thing denied, nor is the thing denied the cause of the denial--just as of two horns simultaneously grown, the right horn is not the cause of the left, nor is the left horn the cause of the right. The essential nature of all things is, therefore, established.

## REPLIES

21-24 responding to 1 (E2326; T19) The statement "All things are empty" is itself as empty as any other thing. Only the opponent has not understood the meaning of emptiness. It does not mean nonexistence, even from the empirical standpoint, but rather dependent origination. Those things which are dependently originated are not, indeed, endowed with an essential nature, because they are dependent on causes and conditions. But things thus dependently originated, and hence empty, perform actions nevertheless. An empty statement can, therefore, establish the lack of essential nature, i.e., emptiness, of things. And since the statement, being dependently originated, lacks an essential nature as do all other things, there is no abandonment of position on the part of Nāgārjuna. There is no discrepancy, and hence there is no special reason to be stated.

25-28 responding to 2-3 (E7-29; T20-22) The example "Do not make a sound" has been badly chosen by the opponent. There a sound is prevented by another sound, but that a statement lacks an essential nature does not prevent other things from lacking an intrinsic nature. If it did, from the cessation of things' lacking an essential nature it would be established that they are possessed of an essential nature! Or--Nāgārjuna uses his favorite concept of *sādhyasama*--the example is acceptable to him; for all things, lacking an essential nature, are alike, and that sound, which is dependently originated, has no more existence by its own nature than any other thing--contrary to the opponent's assumption that "a sound that is existent prevents the other sound that will be". It proves, therefore, his thesis. However, adds Nāgārjuna, the empty statement "All things are empty" has an empirical reality like all other things; and it is surely not possible to teach the absolute Truth (*paramārtha*) without having recourse to the conventional truth (*vyavahāra*) (here 33.*Madhyamakakārikā* is quoted).

29 responding to 4 (E29; T23)[161] To the opponent's objection that the defect mentioned by him affects only Nāgārjuna's thesis, not his own, Nāgārjuna's answer is simple: he has no thesis at all!

30 (30-51 responding to 5-6) (E30; T24-25) To the objection that a denial of the essential nature of things that are not apprehended through any of the instruments of knowledge is a logical impossibility, Nāgārjuna's answer is equally simple: he does not apprehend anything at all with the help of the four instruments of knowledge; he, therefore, neither affirms nor denies.

31 (E31; T25) If such and such objects are established through the instruments of knowledge, how are the instruments themselves established?

32 (E31-32; T25-26) If they are established through other instruments of knowledge then there is an infinite regress.

33-39 (E32-35; T26-29)[162] Nor can the opponent say that the instruments of knowledge are established without instruments of knowledge while objects known are established through the instruments; for, then, he abandons his position that all objects are established through instruments of knowledge. There is, further, a discrepancy, namely that some objects are established through instruments of knowledge while some others are not, and he should state the special reason for that.

The opponent replies: The instruments of knowedge establish themselves as well as other things, just as fire illuminates itself as well as other things.[163] But Nāgārjuna demonstrates at length (34-39) that the assumption that fire illuminates itself is wrong, by questioning how fire can get to darkness to illuminate it (i.e., cause it to be lighted up) without getting into contact with it somehow, which is absurd.

40-41 (E35-36; T30) Furthermore, if the instruments of knowledge are self-established, then the instruments are established independently of their objects, for self-establishment does not require another thing. Thus the instruments of knowedge are instruments of nothing!

42 (E36; T30-31) Nor can the instruments be established in relation to their objects; for that would be proving what is already proved (*siddhasādhana*). Something that is not established does not require something else to establish it!

43 (E37; T31) Besides, if the instruments are established in relation to the objects, then the objects are not established in relation to the instruments. The object to be established (*sādhya*) does not, indeed, establish the instrument (*sādhana*) by which it is established.

44 (E37; T31) And if the objects are established independently of the instruments, what is gained by establishing the instruments? That whose purpose they are supposedly needed to serve is already served!

45 (E37-38; T31) Further, if the instruments are established in relation to the objects, then there is an interchange of instruments and objects; the instruments become objects because they are established (by the objects), and the objects become instruments because they establish (the instruments).

46-48 (E38-39; T32-33) It may be thought that the instruments and the objects establish themselves mutually. But then, neither the objects nor the instruments are established. If the objects are established by the instruments, and if those instruments are to be established by those very objects, then the objects not having been established, the instruments are not established, because their established, i.e., the objects, are not established. Thus they cannot establish the objects. Similarly, if the instruments are established by the objects, and if those objects are to be established by those very instruments, then the instruments not having been established, the objects are not established.

49-50 (E39-40; T33) It is as if the son were to be produced by the father, and that father were to be produced by that very son. Which of these is the father, and which other the son?

51 (E40; T34) Nāgārjuna concludes: "The instruments are not established by themselves or by one another or by other instruments. Nor are they established by the objects, or accidentally."

52-56 in answer to 7-8 (E41-44; T35-38) The theory of the people conversant with the nature of things is thus refuted by Nāgārjuna: If the so-called good essential nature, and so on, originate in dependence upon the cause-condition complex, they are only dependent natures, not essential natures of the good things, etc. The opponent may think that they do not originate dependently. But then, there is no practice of religious life (*brahmacarya*). By rejecting dependent origination, one rejects the vision of dependent origination. But if there is no vision of dependent origination there can be no vision of *dharma*, for the Buddha has said "He who sees dependent origination sees the *dharma*". And if one does not see the *dharma*, there can be no practice of religious life. Or, rejecting dependent origination, one rejects the four noble truths. There is no merit (*dharma*), no demerit (*adharma*), no worldly conventions; and all things, being endowed with an essential nature, become permanent. There follows the nonpractice of religious life, and the opponent contradicts his own tenet, namely that all conditioned things are impermanent.[1]

---

1.This part of the text has to be read along with 33.*Madhyamakakārikā* XXIV, where Nāgārjuna shows how his doctrine of emptiness, far from jeopardizing our activities, religious or not, in the world actually makes them possible. Emptiness is dependent origination. Now, if there is no dependent origination, there is no sorrow, no origination of sorrow, and for that reason, no cessation of sorrow and no way leading to the cessation of sorrow. Everything is immutable, free from the vicissitudes of the empirical world. Thus, if emptiness is denied, the four noble truths, which constitute the foundation of all religious practice of Buddhism, cannot be understood. The four noble truths, it may be recalled, have for Nāgārjuna only an empirical validity.

57 in answer to 9 (E44-45; T38-40) To the objection that if things were to lack an essential nature then even the term "lacking an essential nature" would not be possible, Nāgārjuna replies saying that there is no term which is really existent. Lacking an intrinsic nature, terms are as empty as all other things.

58 (E45; T39) Furthermore, does the term "nonexistent", which the opponent considers to be existent, designate something existent or something nonexistent? Either alternative involves a self-contradiction. If the thing named is existent, then it has to be replied: the same thing cannot be both nonexistent and existent. If, on the other hand, the thing named is nonexistent, then it has to be replied: that which is nonexistent has no name.

59 (E45-46; T39-40) The objection, after all, is quite irrelevant, since the Madhyamaka has established the emptiness of all things, including terms.

60 in answer to 10 (E46; T40) Also irrelevant is the opponent's assumption that there is an essential nature which does not belong to the things (10 above); for Nāgārjuna neither denies the essential nature of things (see 64 below) nor affirms the essential nature of an object apart from the object.

61-63 in answer to 11 (E46-48; T40-41) As for the denial in 11 above, Nāgārjuna can easily use the opponent's own logic against him: If denial is of an existent and not of a nonexistent, and if the opponent denies emptiness, then this emptiness is established! Or, if the opponent denies emptiness and that emptiness does not exist, then he abandons his own thesis. It is, moreover, absurd to say that Nāgārjuna denies anything since, all things being empty, there is for him neither a thing to be denied nor a denial.

64 in answer to 12 (E48-49; T42) Concerning the opponent's objection that denial of a nonexistent is established even without words, what purpose is served by Nāgārjuna's statement negating the essential nature of all things, if that essential nature does not exist at all? Nāgārjuna observes that his statement does not create things' lacking essential nature, but merely makes known the absence of an essential nature where people wrongly see an

essential nature.[1]

65-67 in answer to 13-16 (E49-50; T43-44) The example of the mirage, cited by the opponent for refutation (13-16) above, is welcome to Nāgārjuna. With this example he shows how all the six things mentioned by the opponent are dependently originated, and hence empty.

68 in answer to 17-19 (E51; T45) With this Nāgārjuna also answers the objection of the absence of a reason (17-19 above). His "reason" (*hetu*) for establishing the emptiness of all things is none other than the fact that they are dependently originated.[2]

69 (E51-52; T45-46) To refute the objection that a denial is not possible in any of the three points of time (20 above), Nāgārjuna

---

1.Nāgārjuna admits the cogency of the Naiyāyika's arguments. In 33.*Madhyamakakārikās* he often even bases his own argumentation on the latter's principle that a negation is not possible if the object to be negated is not real. Candrakīrti makes it clear in his *Prasannapadā*. Only, Nāgārjuna does not negate anything, for there is nothing to be negated. The function of the statement "All things are devoid of an intrinsic nature" or "Things have no intrinsic nature" is to "make known" the absence of an intrinsic nature in all things, because they are naturally "devoid of an intrinsic nature" (*svabhāvaśūnya*), being "dependently originated". Nāgārjuna's negation of the intrinsic nature is thus designed for dissipating the error of people who see an intrinsic nature in things where there is none. In other words, it has merely a therapeutic value--as Candrakīrti makes clear in his comment on MK XV.11. It is possible that in 64 of the present text Nāgārjuna drew his inspiration from Patañjali's *Mahābhāṣya* on Pāṇini's *Aṣṭādhyāyī* II.2.6, where the grammarian discusses the question whether the negative particle *na* creates absence or simply makes an absence known. See also Vātsyāyana's *Bhāṣya* on *Nyāyasūtra* II.1.11 and Uddyotakara's *Vārttika* thereon.

2.As a *prāsaṅgika*, Nāgārjuna shows no predilection for "independent inference" (*svātantrikānumāna*). Nevertheless, he cannot be accused of not vindicating his position from the standpoint of formal logic.

once more appeals to his concept of *sādhyasama* (cf. 28 above). The three times are as empty as all other things. The up-holders of the doctrine of emptiness can therefore deny in all the three times, whereas the Naiyāyika cannot. Of course, Nāgārjuna also points out that, in accordance with the latter's own doctrine, a denial of the Mādhyamika's denial is not possible either.

70 (E52-53; T47-48) Nāgārjuna concludes his work by vindicating empirical reality from the standpoint of the doctrine of emptiness, i.e. dependent origination (cf. 52-56 above), and pays homage to the "incomparable Buddha", who taught emptiness, dependent origination and the middle way as equivalent.

## 35. NĀGĀRJUNA, *Śūnyatāsaptati*

Summarized by Peter Della Santina

Nāgārjuna's *Śūnyatāsaptati* comprises one of the important works of the Madhyamaka system. Along with the 33.*Mūlamadhyamakakārikās*, 37.*Yuktiśaṣṭikā* and others, it is one of the six works of Nāgārjuna the study of which is required by the Tibetan Buddhist tradition for a proper comprehension of the Madhyamaka philosophy which is an indispensable part of the Mahāyāna. As its name indicates, the *Śūnyatāsaptati* is devoted to an exposition of emptiness by means of the refutation of the independent reality of factors. Like the *Mūlamadhyamakakārikās*, the *Śūnyatāsaptati* treats a number of concepts from the Madhyamaka standpoint. However, because of its brevity, consisting of only seventy stanzas along with their autocommentary, the ideas presented in the *Śūnyatāsaptati* are more easily assimilated than those found in the *Mūlamadhyamakakārikās*.

The method of argument employed by Nāgārjuna in the *Śūnyatāsaptati* is the same as is to be found in the *Mūlamadhyamakakārikās* and other fundamental works of the Madhyamaka school. It may briefly be described as a method of argument which employs the tenets of the opponent of the system in order to demonstrate the ultimate inconsistency of the doctrines advocated by the opponent. Thus, on the basis of facts the reality of which is accepted by the opponent, Nāgārjuna establishes the impossibility and relativity of the concepts which make up his universe of discourse, thereby revealing the nature of the ultimately real which is empty and devoid of conceptualisation.

In the *Mūlamadhyamakakārikās*, *Śūnyatāsaptati* and other works, Nāgārjuna was principally concerned to establish the Madhyamaka philosophy within the Buddhist fold. It was left to his disciples like Āryadeva and others to show that the Madhyamaka critique was equally applicable to non-Buddhist doctrines. Therefore, with few if any exceptions, it is the doctrines advocated by Ābhidharmika schools of Buddhism, or in other words, the Buddhist realists, that are refuted in the *Śūnyatāsaptati*. The reality of the factors (*dharma*), aggregates (*skandha*), senses (*āyatana*) as well as that of causality, karma and impermanence is systematically refuted. Yet, it must not be thought that Nāgārjuna set forth a doctrine fundamentally at variance with the teaching of the Buddha. On the contrary, it is argued that the philosophy of the Madhyamaka in fact represents a more faithful interpretation of the essential teaching of the Buddha Śākyamuni. The key to this understanding lies in the doctrine of interdependent origination which has remained the central tenet of Buddhist thought throughout centuries of interpretation and reinterpretation. Nāgārjuna's philosophy essentially springs from a reinterpretation of the meaning of dependent origination. It may be said that the very interdependently originated nature of phenomena constitutes their ultimate lack of independent existence and therefore their emptiness. Thus, interdependent origination and emptiness, far from being contradictory, are in reality identical in import.

The work is available only in Tibetan (Toh. 3827, 3831, 3867) in translations made in the ninth through the eleventh century. However, Bhavya, Candrakīrti and other later Madhyamaka writers take Nāgārjuna's authorship for granted, and *kārikās* are quoted, though without identification, in the 133.*Akutobhayā* and later texts. The present summary is based on an English translation by L. Jamspal and Peter della Santina made for the Sakya Institute of Tibetan Philosophy in Missouri in 1978, as well as a translation of the *kārikās* by Christian Lindtner (*Nagarjuniana*, pp. 35-69). We have also consulted the translation by Tola and Dragonetti, Journal of Indian Philosophy 15, 1987, pp. 1-55 (who question the ascription of the *Svavṛtti* to this Nāgārjuna). "E" and "T" references are to Tola and Dragonetti just referred to. [164]

1 (E10; T24) Existence and nonexistence, beginning and end, better and worse are not actual (*tattva*), but only practical ways of speaking (*lokavyavahāra*).

2 (E11; T24) Everything--self, not-self, both self and not-self--being nameable things, are, like *nirvāṇa,* devoid of essential nature.

3 (E11; T24) Since there is no essential nature in things' causes and conditions, whether taken separately or collectively, everything is empty.

4 (E11; T24-25) What exists doesn't begin since it already exists. What doesn't exist doesn't begin since it doesn't exist. To both exist and not to exist is contradictory. Since nothing begins, there is no duration and no destruction.

Objection: The beginning, duration and end of things is known to us, as well as the beginning of beginning, duration of duration and end of end.

5 (E11; T25) Answer: What has already been born cannot begin, what is unborn cannot be born. What is being born cannot rightly be called a "beginning", since it is partly born and partly unborn. Moreover, there is no beginning because a cause is not justified. Why? Because

6 (E11; T25) If the effect exists a "cause" that possesses it as effect is not its cause. If the effect is nonexistent, its "cause" is no cause. If the effect neither exists nor doesn't exist it is contradictory. A cause cannot be consistently assigned to any of the three times.

Objection: Things are not empty, for their number is justified. The numbers one (*eka*), two and many (*aneka*) exist, but number is justified only if things exist. Therefore, things are not empty.

7 (E12; T25) Answer: Without one, many does not occur; without many one does not occur; therefore, dependently originated entities are signless.

Objection: Dependent origination, involving frustration, has been set forth in the scriptures. It has also been demonstrated by the masters as involving either one awareness or several awarenesses. So, all things are empty.

8 (E12; T25-26) The twelve members (of the chain of dependent origination) cannot arise, since they cannot constitute a single awareness or a series of awarenesses. If they arise in a single awareness the effect would originate simultaneously with its cause, while if they occur in a series of awarenesses the preceding

members, having been destroyed, cannot be the cause of the succeeding ones. So dependent origination cannot arise.

Dependent origination is wrongly thought to arise from ignorance, and ignorance in turn from erroneous views. These erroneous views are also in their own nature empty.

9 (E12; T26) Nothing is permanent, nothing impermanent; nothing is selfless, nothing has a self; nothing is pure, nothing impure; nothing satisfying, nothing frustrating. So there can be no erroneous views.

10 (E12; T26) Without erroneous views there is no ignorance, and without ignorance conditioning factors don't originate, nor do any of the rest of the members of the chain of dependent origination.

11 (E12; T26) Without conditioning factors ignorance does not arise, and without ignorance the conditioning factors don't arise. Since they also are mutually caused, they are not established as having an essential nature.

12 (E12-13; T26) How can what is not established as having an essential nature produce other things? Conditions established by others cannot cause the origination of others.

13 (E13; T26) The father is not his son nor is the son his father, nor can they exist without each other. Likewise for the twelve members (of the chain of dependent origination).

14 (E13; T26-27) Just as the satisfaction or frustration experienced in a dream do not have an actual thing as content, likewise neither do what originates dependently nor that upon which it depends exist.

15 (E13; T27) Objection: If things are without an essential nature they can't be proved to be of differing natures from one another.

16 (E13; T27) Answer: If an essential nature for things were established the origination of things cannot be dependent on anything else. If something essentially exists it can't cease to exist, since what is essential to a thing cannot disappear.

Objection: But whether things have an intrinsic nature, a dependent nature, or a lack of nature those natures are not nonexistent, and so things are not empty.

17 (E13; T27) Answer: Those--intrinsic nature, dependent nature, lack of nature--are perverted views, and cannot abide in what doesn't exist at all.

18 (E14; T27) Objection: If things are empty they can't begin or end. So how can an empty thing begin or end?

19 (E14; T27-28) Answer: An existent and an absence cannot exist simultaneously. Without an absence there is no being. An entity will always be something and not be something else. Without nonbeing there is no being.

A presence and an absence cannot exist at one time in the same place. Here someone says "only positive entities exist". The text answers "Without an absence there is no being", because no being lacks impermanence, so every being is a presence (of something) and an absence (of something else), i.e., impermanent.

Here someone may object "although a thing is always bound up with impermanence, still, at the time of origination and duration, impermanence is latent, while at the time of destruction, impermanence destroys the thing." The text answers "Without nonbeing there is no being", which is to say that a thing is not existent without an absence, since without destruction nothing can be impermanent. So (again) everything is a presence (of something) and an absence (of something else).

20 (E14; T28) Without existence there is no absence. An existent can come from neither itself nor from another. Thus there are no existents, and therefore no absences either.

21 (E14; T28) If there are only positive things that is eternalism; if there are only absences that is nihilism. If a positive entity exists these two views follow. Therefore no positive being should be accepted.

22 (E14; T28) Objection: There is a series of causes and effects, so neither (eternalism nor nihilism) apply. When a thing causes it ceases to exist.

Answer: As was shown, this is not acceptable, and also, the causal sequence will be interrupted.

A presence and an absence cannot be identical. That is why the sequence you propose cannot be accepted.

23 (E14-15; T28) Objection: The Buddha's teaching of the path to liberation involves origination and destruction, not emptiness.

Answer: These two (origination and destruction) are contradictory to each other.

24 (E15; T28) Objection: If neither origination nor destruction exist, the cessation of what constitutes liberation?

Answer: Isn"t liberation precisely that which neither originates nor ceases?

25 (E15; T29) If liberation were destruction that would be nihilism; if not, that would be eternalism. So, liberation is neither a positive entity nor an absence. It neither originates nor ceases.

26 (E15; T29) If some cessation could persist it would be devoid of any positive entity. But it can't occur without a positive entity occurring, and without an absence cessation cannot occur.

27 (E15; T29) A marked thing is so in virtue of a characteristic mark other than that marked thing. It is not proved by itself, nor can mark and marked prove each other, since what is not proved cannot prove.

28 (E15; T29) In this way cause and effect, feeling and feeler, seer and seen, etc. are all explained.

29 (E16; T29) The three times do not exist and are merely conceptual constructions, since they are not fixed (*asthita*), are reciprocally established, are changing, are not established independently, and because a positive being doesn't exist.

Why is time not established? Because it is not fixed, and what is not fixed cannot be apprehended, since to apprehend is to classify and one cannot classify what is not fixed. So time does not exist. Furthermore, the three times each depend on the others for their proof. Also, the three times change--what is present is past, and what is future is present. Finally, since positive entities don't exist (as shown before) time is not established as a positive entity.

Objection: It was taught that all conditioned factors have three marks--origination, duration and destruction. Opposed to these are the unconditioned factors. So conditioned and unconditioned factors exist.

30 (E16; T30) Answer: Those three marks of origination, duration and destruction don't exist, so no factor, conditioned or unconditioned, exists.

Even if conditioned factors are accepted, still they should be deemed nonexistent since, when analyzed, they are not justified. Why?

31 (E16; T30) The undestroyed is not destroyed, nor is the destroyed; the enduring does not endure, nor does the nonenduring endure; the originated does not originate, nor does the nonoriginated.

32 (E16; T30) Conditioned factors and unconditioned factors are neither many nor one, neither existent nor nonexistent, nor both existent and nonexistent. Within this perimeter, all possibilities are included.

33 (E16; T30) Objection: The Buddha proclaimed the enduring of karma, proclaimed karma and its fruit, proclaimed that the sentient being is the doer of karma and that karma is not lost.

34 (E16-17; T30-31) Answer: It has been demonstrated that karma has no essential nature. Karma does not originate, hence it cannot be destroyed. Egoism (*ahaṃkāra*) arises from karma. And that appropriating which produces karma originates from conceptual construction.

35 (E17; T31) If karma had an essential nature, then the body originated from it would be permanent; it would not result in frustration. Therefore, karma would be substantial.

36 (E17; T31) Karma is not born of conditions, nor does it arise without conditions, for conditions are like an illusion, a fairy city or a mirage.

37 (E17; T31) Karma has defilements as its cause; conditioning factors are substantiated by karma and defilements. The body has karma as its cause; so all three are essentially empty.

38 (E17; T31) Without karma there is no agent; without these two, nothing results from action, and without any of them there is no experiencer. Hence all are empty.

39 (E17; T31) If one understands that karma is empty, because of that insight karma will not originate. Without karma, that which originated from karma will not arise.

40 (E18; T31-32) Where the Lord Tathāgata creates a magical being, and that magical being creates another,

41 (E18; T32) there, the magical being created by the Lord and the second magical being are both empty, mere names, conceptual constructions.

42 (E18; T32) Similarly, the agent is like the magical being; karma is like what is created by the magical being. They are essentially empty, conceptual constructions.

43 (E18; T32) If karma had an essential nature, there would be no *nirvāṇa*. If karma did not exist, there would be no satisfying or frustrating results originated from karma.

Question: Since it is extensively proclaimed in the canonical discourses that karma exists, how can it be called nonexistent?

44 (E18; T32) What Buddhas say exists exists, what they don't say exists also exists, and what both exists and doesn't exist exists. It is not easy to understand.

45 (E18-19; T32) If matter is itself derived it is not derived from matter. It can't be derived from itself, nor from anything else. So it doesn't exist.

46 (E19; T33) The four great elements are not existent in any one of them, nor is one existent in all four. So how can matter be established as depending on the four nonexistent great elements as its cause?

47 (E19; T33) Since subtle matter is never apprehended, gross matter, it seems, doesn't exist. If you say there is a reason for thinking it does exist, that reason itself doesn't exist, since it too is born from causes and conditions. And to suppose that matter exists without any reason for thinking so is contrary to reason.

48 (E19; T33) If awareness could appropriate matter it could appropriate its own essential nature. How could an awareness which doesn't essentially exist, being born from conditions, actually understand the nonexistence of matter?

49 (E19; T33) Since a moment of awareness can't apprehend the matter born at that very moment, how can it comprehend past and future matter?

50 (E19; T33) Since color and shape never exist separately, they cannot be conceived to be separate. Isn't matter generally understood as single?

51 (E20; T33-34) Visual awareness is not inside the eye; it is not inside matter; nor is it somewhere in between. That conceptual construction is dependent on the eye and matter is erroneous.

52 (E20; T34) If the eye does not see itself, how can it see matter? Therefore, the eye and matter are insubstantial. Likewise for the remaining (sense-)bases.

53 (E20; T34) The eye is empty of its own self; it is empty of any other's self. Matter is similarly empty. The remaining (sense-)bases are similar to it.

Moreover, matter is empty because it is dependently originated. In this case, what is established from the great elements of matter having functioned as a cause is originated dependently. Hence, what is originated dependently is not originated in its own actuality.

Thus, matter is empty of its own self. And since matter is the object to the eye and its awareness which are the subject, and since the subject is not that subject's object, matter is also empty of another's self.

Alternatively, awareness is internal, while matter is external. So matter is again empty of another's self.

Question: From what is visual awareness dependently originated, and how is it dependently originated?

Answer: Awareness is established dependent upon the object comprehended, etc. What is dependently originated is not established in its own self. Thus that awareness is empty. Therefore, to say that awareness apprehends objects is not appropriate.

54 (E20; T34) When one sense(-organ) is in contact (with an object), at that time the other senses are empty (of contact). The empty does not depend upon the nonempty; the nonempty also does not depend on the empty.

55 (E20; T34) The three (organ, object and awareness), being without an independent nature, cannot come into contact. Since there is no contact of this sort feelings do not exist.

56 (E20-21; T34) Awareness arises dependent on inner and outer senses. So awareness is empty, like a mirage or a magical creation.

57 (E21; T35) Since awareness arises only as dependent on an object it doesn't exist. Since there is no awareness and no content of awareness, there is no cognizer.

58 (E21; T35) "All things are noneternal" really indicates that neither eternality nor noneternal things ever exist. If entities existed, they would be either eternal or not eternal, but how can anything exist?

59 (E21; T35) Desire, aversion and delusion arise from perverted views about what is clean or foul. Therefore, those three are essentially nonexistent.

60 (E21; T35) Since one may desire, hate or be deluded by the same thing, these passions are produced by conceptual constructions, which don't really exist.

61 (E21; T35) What is constructed doesn't exist. Without a constructed object how can construction itself exist? Therefore, since they are originated from conditions, constructed objects as well as constructions are empty.

62 (E22; T36) When the truth is understood, there is no ignorance deriving from the four perverted views. Since (then) ignorance is nonexistent, conditioning factors do not arise, and the remaining elements of ignorance don't arise either.

63 (E22; T36) What originates dependent upon something originates from that. Without that it does not originate. Entities and nonentities, as well as conditioned elements and unconditioned ones, are calm and extinguished.

64 (E22; T36) That entities originated from causes and conditions are real is called ignorance by the Buddha. From that, the twelve members of (the chain of) dependent origination arise.

65 (E22; T36) When one understands that things are empty one is not deluded. Just that is the cessation of ignorance. Thereupon the twelve members (of the chain of dependent origination) cease.

66 (E22; T36) Conditioning factors are like the city of the Gandharvas, *māyā*, a mirage, nets of hair, foam, bubbles, magical fire, dreams and the whirling firebrand.

67 (E23; T37) No entity whatsoever is existent in its essential nature, nor does any absence exist either. Entities and absences, originating from causes and conditions, are empty.

68 (E23; T37) Since all entities are empty of essential nature, the dependent origination of entities is particularly demonstrated by the incomparable Tathāgata.

69 (E23; T37) The highest truth is no other than this emptiness. The blessed Buddha, the Lord, relying upon worldly convention, imagined all possibilities.

70 (E23; T37) Worldly *dharma* is not destroyed. In reality no norms are taught. It is by not comprehending the proclamation of the Tathāgata that one becomes afraid of the spotless teaching.

71 (E23; T37) The worldly principle that the arising of a thing is dependent on another is not denied. What is dependently originated is lacking intrinsic nature: how can it be existent? This is ultimate certitude.

72 (E23; T37-38) One who diligently seeks the truth, who considers each aspect logically and relies on *dharma,* abandons positive being and absences and attains peace.

73 (E24; T38) Having comprehended phenomenal conditionality, the net of false views is swept aside. Consequently, abandoning attachment, delusion and anger, without stain, one surely reaches

liberation.

## 36. NĀGĀRJUNA, *Vaidalyaprakaraṇa*

Summary by Christian Lindtner

This work, extant in Tibetan only, consists of seventy-four brief *sūtras.* With Nāgārjuna's own commentary, together they form a *prakaraṇa.* Unlike the 34.*Vigrahavyāvartanī,* to which it forms a pendant, this work is solely addressed to non-Buddhist logicians, more specifically, to the adherents of "the subtle Nyāya". This fact accounts for its *sūtra* style, unusual with Buddhists (cf. 50.*Akṣaraśataka,* against Sāṃkhya and Vaiśeṣika), as well as the unusual polemical fervor compared to the author's other works. The title of the work, "The Pulverization", alludes to the epithet "subtle" used in those days for the followers of Akṣapāda. Nāgārjuna's work is written in order to grind their sixteen categories to fine little pieces, Sanskrit *sūkṣma* meaning subtle as well as fine.

The edition of the *Nyāyasūtra* known to Nāgārjuna was definitely an earlier recension than our *textus receptus.* For details see Lindtner, *Nagarjuniana,* pp. 87-93.[165]

The work is organized so as to deal successively with each of the sixteen categories we find set forth in *Nyāyasūtra* I.1. Section headings correspond to those categories.

### 1. Instrument and Object of Knowledge

1-19. Nāgārjuna's initial hypothesis is that the instrument of knowledge and the object known are indissolubly joined and therefore they cannot be established independently.

The opponent allows that they are correlates, but thinks all the same that they can establish each other. Therefore Nāgārjuna must refute the three ways in which this could, hypothetically, come about. Neither what exists, what does not exist, nor what exists and does not exist can enter into relation. This argument is of general application, including, of course, instrument and object of knowledge.

If the objector insists that everything is established by instruments of knowledge, then this must include the instruments as well, which leads to infinite regress. Alternatively, the instruments of knowledge may be denied altogether, but this means giving up the hypothesis.

But the objector persists in maintaining that instruments of knowledge are self-established because they "illuminate" themselves, like a lamp. Nāgārjuna rejoins that this example is most unhappy, since a lamp cannot possibly illuminate anything, itself or anything else, whether it is in contact with its object or not. Besides, the relationship between instrument and object cannot be established in any of the three periods of time.

The objector's reply, that the same, then, goes for Nāgārjuna's denial, makes Nāgārjuna triumph: If the objector thinks that Nāgārjuna then instead maintains his denial, and the objector accepts this, he by that very fact accepts that the instrument and object must be denied; then, in a flash, all disputes are settled. But actually Nāgārjuna neither accepts a denial nor something to be denied, he merely tries to indicate the absence of essential being.

The objector still insists that the *pramāṇas* exist because they provide correct understanding, and when Nāgārjuna asks how one can be sure that an object exists independently of awareness, the objector claims that the awareness of a jar is the instrument, whereas the jar as such is the object.

But, replies Nāgārjuna, the objector recognizes that awareness arises from the contact of organ and object of sense, and since the jar must be a specific condition of awareness beforehand, awareness cannot be the instrument of it, and the jar is not the object. Besides, the objector himself categorizes awareness as an instrument, not as an object of knowledge.

## 3-4. Doubt and Purpose

20-23. Could Nāgārjuna's treatment of instrument and object of knowledge not give rise to some doubt? No, there is nothing to be in doubt about, neither that which is comprehended, which exists, nor that which is not comprehended, which doesn't exist.

Even if the objector finds lack of decisive characteristic in something to be the cause of doubt about it, the same argument applies here.

But may one not be uncertain about a purpose? No, for the objector himself maintains that the object one is concerned about is the object he purposefully seeks, and the object that one is concerned about can only either exist or not exist, hence not be an object of doubt.

## 5. Example

24-30. If the objector objects that there are examples of things that serve a purpose, like sand, Nāgārjuna's refutation remains the same as above. Besides, there is no example because there is no beginning and no middle.[1] Still the objector maintains the possibility of an example that may be either of the same or of a different kind--but Nāgārjuna rejoins that neither that which is of the same kind as that it is supposed to examplify (e.g., fire of fire) nor that which is of another kind--whether it be so entirely or only to some extent--can serve as an example.

## 6. Tenets

31. When Nāgārjuna claims that everything is unestablished mustn't he himself accept something as established, namely his own tenets? No, not at all, for without something established at the beginning, how can he accept something established at the end?

## 7. Members of an Inference

32-48. First the five members of an inference are refuted in general. Since they are not subject to a whole or parts of an independent group, and since they would be identical if they were one with the whole--for if they were different there would be six, and also because they are unestablished in any of the three times--therefore the members are not established.

Objection: The five members can operate together, like cotton

1.To understand this argument one must recall that Sanskrit "*dṛṣṭānta*" ("example") = *dṛṣṭa* + *anta,* lit. "seen" + "end". So: no end, therefore no beginning and no middle.

threads. A single thread accomplishes nothing, but many combined into one can tether an elephant.

Answer: No, the individual threads are no better off. What cannot be achieved by a single son of a barren woman cannot be achieved by any number of them, and even if it be granted that they might do so by working simultaneously, the five members never occur simultaneously as a single whole. Besides, before the members can prove anything they themselves must be proved, namely by other members, and so on *ad infinitum*.

Next, the five members are refuted one by one. A hypothesis is impossible since it is neither identical with nor different from its reason. A reason is impossible since it either must have another reason and so forth *ad infinitum*, or else a reason is present without a reason. But that is absurd and would lead to a total confusion. So since there is no hypothesis, no reason, and no example, the remaining two members of an inference, application and conclusion, simply lapse. Even if a hypothesis could be established without a reason, that would mean that the other three members were established without a reason.

Again, if proof were due to a reason, then an example would be quite superfluous, and if not, then the reason would be otiose, but in that case example, etc., would be superfluous.

The objector's specific hypothesis, that the self is eternal because it is without body, like space, is refuted. Further, since hypothesis and reason can only be denominated successively, a hypothesis cannot be a hypothesis to its (coexisting) reason, and vice versa.

Objection: But when Nāgārjuna denies all the members it would seem that he implicitly accepts a hypothesis, and, *eo ipso*, the four remaining members of inference. Answer: No, since there is no hypothesis (*pratijñā*), for *prati* and *jñā* must be enunciated separately one after the other.

## 8. *Tarka*

49. This category cannot be sanctioned either, since neither the *artha* that is already known nor the *artha* that is unknown can be an object of deliberation (*tarka*). So what remains to be deliberated?

### 9. Ascertainment

50. This is also impossible since substance, being, one, etc., which could serve to fix something definitely, are neither identical nor different nor both. (Without any means of ascertainment, there is nothing to ascertain, and, therefore, no ascertainment.)

### 10. Discussion

51-55. Objection: Nāgārjuna must, obviously, accept the category of discussion (since we're having one now)!

Answer: No, because talk (*abhidhāna*) and the issue under debate (*abhidheya*) cannot be established, as they are neither single nor many. Nor can they alternatively be connected by definite conventional relations of names to things, which would, incidentally, imply that the things/meaning/object (*artha*) of the objector's sixteen categories should not be taken more seriously than the significance of names such as Devadatta or Indragupta, because the very fact that any word can function as a synonym or homonym of well-nigh anything excludes any definite and indissoluble relationship between names and things/meanings. Finally, they cannot belong to one another. Thus the preconditions of debate are absent.

### 11-12. Sophistry and Cavil

56. These two categories are refuted in the same way as debate was.

### 13. Fallacies of the Reason

57-66. Objection: Everything that you say is fallacious reasoning (*hetvābhā*sa) and incapable of refuting anything!

Answer: No. Neither by being the same kind as nor by being of a different kind from the actual *h* can a fallacious *h* come into question. If a fallacious *h* is qualified as an *h* that is deviating, this is wrong, since neither the *h* which is valid (*sādhyasādhaka*) nor the one which is not can be classified as deviating.

The objector insists that an *h* may be deviating in the sense of equivocal (*anaikāntika*). Thus immateriality can serve as an *h*, now for *ākāśa*, now for karma. No, says Nāgārjuna, these are two different types of immateriality, as one may prove the permanence of one thing, the impermanence of another. Consequently the *h* adduced during proof and refutation is not itself deviating. Again, there can be no *h* which is deviating in relation to the *s*, for as things occur instantaneously, proof and refutation are not concurrent with what has to be proved or refuted.

The objector now suggests that every *h* discarded by Nāgārjuna is, if not deviating, at least contradictory (*viruddha*). No, replies Nāgārjuna, for how can two utterances be conflicting since it is obvious that when the first statement is being formulated, the second has not yet occurred. They can only be conflicting if they are simultaneous. And yet simultaneous statements cannot be conflicting either, since it is impossible for proponent and antagonist to put forward charge and rebuttal at the same time.

The objector then proposes that an *h* which is "mistimed" (*kālātīta*) does in fact constitute a fallacy. Nāgārjuna disagrees, for a previous basis for something present cannot, by reason of being past, be a basis for anything present which does not occur yet. One had better not play fast and loose with past, present and future for all normal intercourse will then be suspended. Besides, since what is previous is past and gone, an *h* localized there cannot form the basis for anything in the present time.

### 14. Quibble

67. Objection: All Nāgārjuna's statements are simply conscious distortions of the meanings of my words.

Nāgārjuna: O no, then any attempt at critical aloofness or disagreement would be distortion or quibble.

### 15. Futile Rejoinder

68. The concept of *jāti*, futile rejoinder, is impossible. Without what is rejoined to, not rejoined to, or to be rejoined to, futile

rejoinder is precluded.[1]

## 16. Ways of Losing an Argument

68-71. Nāgārjuna is now blamed for having incriminated himself on account of repetition, one of the ways of losing an argument. But Nāgārjuna does not plead guilty, as what is supposed to have been repeated is neither identical with nor different from what it repeats. In any case, a way of losing an argument does not exist either when the charge has been made or when it has not yet been made. As for the third possibility, one is not convicted on any count as long as one is still being prosecuted, any more than one is trussed before the final knot is tied.

## Conclusion

72-73. Now that the sixteen topics or "categories" have been made the objects of denial, denial is also rendered impossible. Hence there is no talk and nothing to talk about, and therefore one cannot distinguish the Buddhist idea of liberation (*nirvāṇa*) from the Nyāya idea of liberation (*apavarga*).[1]

---

[1]Note that the refutation of futile rejoinder is a nice example of quibble. Again, there is a play on words in the original Sanskrit.

[1]Herewith Nāgārjuna has, as announced at the outset, crushed the arrogance of the heretics. It all proceeded according to the principles that are known from his other works (viz. that ultimately nothing can be conceived as one or many), but with a wit and virtuosity not met with elsewhere.

It is important to note that, for Nāgārjuna, the Nyāya *apavarga*--and the Vaiśeṣika *niḥśreyasa* (see *Ratnāvali* 5)--are more or less synonyms for the Buddhist *nirvāṇa*. This "inclusivistic" attitude suggests the orthodox Brahminical background of Nāgārjuna.

## 37. NĀGĀRJUNA, *Yuktiṣaṣṭikā*

The following summary is based on the translation by Christian Lindtner in *Nagarjuniana*, pp. 103-119. Use has also been made of the reconstruction of the first twelve stanzas into Sanskrit by Tola/Dragonetti, Journal of the International Association of Buddhist Studies 6.2, 1983, 94-123, the work referred to as "S" in the following summary. "E" and "T" references are to Lindtner's Tibetan edition and translation cited above. A full review of materials on this work can be found in S pp. 94-97.

Homage to the Buddha, who taught dependent origination, by which teaching arising and destruction are eliminated.

1-3 (E102; T103; S97) Those whose awareness (*buddhi* = wisdom, *prajñā*) goes beyond becoming and nonbecoming know the real meaning of "conditions". First, things' actually coming to be, the source of all defects, must be obstructed. But here is a logical argument for rejecting the coming to be of things: If things come to be why isn't liberation viewed as nonbecoming?

4-8 (E102,104; T103,105; S98) Neither coming to be nor nonbecoming yield liberation; only through comprehension of both are the great ones who have *bodhi* liberated. Those who do not really understand believe in bondage and liberation; those who really understand believe in neither. Coming to be and liberation do not *both* occur, since liberation just *is* knowledge of both. Just as it is supposed that there is the destruction of what has come to be when it is destroyed, likewise the cessation of what has come to be should be thought of as magical. How can anything be dissolved?

9-12 (E104,106; T105,107; S98) Objection: If the aggregates are not destroyed then one will not reach liberation even when one's defilements are terminated--but the cessation of them *is* liberation.

Answer: When one correctly understands that things are conditioned by ignorance one realizes there is no origination and no cessation. This is liberation through understanding *dharma*; it completes one's task. However, if after knowing *dharma* one still thinks there are distinctions, believes in the eternality of even the most subtle thing, such a person does not understand the meaning of dependent origination.

13-17 (E106; T107) Objection: If a monk whose defilements are terminated no longer transmigrates (so transmigration has an end), why does the Buddha deny that transmigration has any beginning?

Answer: The idea that there is a beginning for transmigration is a wrong view. How can something dependently originated have a beginning or an end? Things appear illusorily like a mirage, without any start or finish.

18-21 (E106,108; T107,109) One who thinks that a conditioned thing has beginning or end doesn't understand dependent origination. A thing dependently arisen has not actually arisen. A thing that has ceased because its causes are terminated is considered terminated itself, but how can something that has not naturally ceased be called "terminated"? So there is no arising and no cessation. The paths of arising and cessation are spoken of by the Buddha for practical purposes.

22-23 (E108; T109) Understanding arising one understands cessation. By understanding cessation one understands impermanence, and by understanding impermanence one understands the correct *dharma*. Those who know that dependent origination does not arise nor cease have transcended views.

24-27 (E108,110; T109,111) Ordinary people who believe in existent things are dominated by defilements; they are deceived by their own awareness. Those who understand existent things see them as impermanent, confusing, empty, without self, disconnected, without a resting-place, nonobject, rootless, unfixed and caused by ignorance throughout.

28-32 (E110; T111) Brahmā, etc., which are accepted ordinarily, are said by the Noble One to be false--what of everything else? One shouldn't expect the views of what is good held by the ignorant and the wise to be the same. The truth-seeker should first be told "everything exists" so that when he understands he will attain discrimination without attachment. People who don't understand discrimination, who merely hear the words without doing good, are lost. Karma and rebirth have been fully explained by the Buddha.

33-38 (E110,112; T111,113) The Buddhas have spoken of "I" and "mine", "aggregates", "senses" and "elements" for practical purposes. The great elements, etc. exist only in consciousness; when understood they dissolve--so they are imaginary. Since the Buddha has told us *nirvāṇa* is true, how could one not conclude the rest is false? Since he has told us the world is caused by ignorance, why not admit that it is a conceptual construction? When ignorance stops it must be clear that what stops was constructed from ignorance.

39-42 (E112; T113) How can what is conditioned by causes be supposed to exist? That eternalists behave the way they do is not surprising; what is surprising is that Buddhists who believe in impermanence remain attached to things. The wise man, hearing an argument about what is true of X, does not agree or disagree when he knows X doesn't exist!

43-45 (E114; T115) People who think there is an underived self or world are captivated by views about permanence and impermanence, etc. Those who think that positive things are established as real, they too are subject to the same mistakes. But those who think things are neither real nor unreal, like the moon reflected in the water, are not carried away by theories.

46-48 (E114; T115) When one believes in positive things he is gripped by excessive and offensive views. It is from attachment and aversion that disagreements arise; they are the cause of all dogma. Without those beliefs defilements do not occur. So when this is understood dogma and defilements disappear. And it is understood by realizing the truth of dependent origination. The Buddha said that that which is dependently born is unborn.

49-54 (E114,116; T115,117) Those with false awareness take what is not true as true; for them a series of appropriating and contention arises. The great ones have neither thesis nor contention; for them there can be no contrary thesis. Taking a position breeds defilements, but one who takes no stand is not caught. When a fool sees reflections he thinks they are true, but when a great soul sees that things are reflections he is not misled.

55-60 (E116,118; T117,119) Fools are attached to matter, ordinary folk gain dispassion, but the enlightened are liberated by knowing the essential nature of matter. Pleasure breeds attachment, giving it up one escapes attachment, but by seeing it to be empty like a magical man one gets liberated. Those who understand being and nonbeing are not subject to defilements stemming from error. If a thing existed the great ones might be attached to or detached from it; since they have no standpoint they have neither attachment nor nonattachment. The one whose mind is not concerned even at the thought of emptiness has crossed the ocean of existence that is agitated by the passions.

May everyone, having through this work attained merit and insight, gain the benefits that accrue from those two (namely, the two bodies of a Buddha).

## 38. NĀGĀRJUNA, *Ratnāvalī*

Summary by Christian Lindtner and K.H. Potter

The current state of scholarship on this work is thoroughly reviewed by Hahn[166]. The relation of this work's style to the question of its attribution to this Nāgārjuna is discussed by Vetter[167]. The edition that appears in Hahn constitutes "E" in the summary that appears below. Hahn's own proposed translation, announced as a second volume, had not appeared as of the time of the present work's preparation.

In the summary that follows, we make use of Lindtner, *Nagarjuniana*, pp. 163-166 (="L"). Giuseppe Tucci's partial edition and translation is referred to as "T".[168] The fifth book has been edited in Sanskrit and Tibetan in Sieglinde Dietz, "The fifth chapter of Nāgārjuna's Ratnāvalī", Journal of the Nepal Research Centre 4, 1980, 189-220 (=D).

### CHAPTER ONE

1-5 (E2; T308-309) Paying my respects to the Buddha, I offer the King an account of *dharma* for his profit.

When *dharma* rises the satisfaction of liberation eventually appears. From faith comes *dharma,* from wisdom comes truth. Of these, wisdom is the chief, but faith comes first.

6-24 (E4-10; T309-313) A man of faith does not violate *dharma* out of interest, hatred, fear or delusion. One who knows whether his bodily, mental and verbal acts are good for him or not is truly wise. One does not get at *dharma* through ascetic practices alone--one cannot that way help or avoid harming others. The results of violation of *dharma* through evil actions, false speech and concupiscence are detailed: these are all bad acts. All frustrations, every woeful course, arises from bad actions, while from good acts arises satisfaction. Avoidance of what is bad and performance of what is good in body, speech and mind makes one a person of twofold mindfulness. By its practice one avoids bad rebirths and gains good ones through meditations, boundless states and the immeasurables. This is the *dharma* of the good life and its results.

25-38 (E10-16; T313-316) In contrast, the *dharma* of liberation is subtle and deep vision. When the childish person hears "I don't exist, nor will I exist; nothing belongs to or ever will belong to me" he is fearful where the wise man is reconciled. The Buddha, who says only what is helpful to men, said that it is false to suppose an ego or something that is mine, since neither belief visits one who knows how things really are. Aggregates arise from egoity, and egoity is not an actual entity. If the seed is unreal how can the sprout exist? If the aggregates are seen to be unreal egoity is defeated, and on the defeat of egoity there is no possibility of the aggregates' reality.

The ego is like the reflection of a face in a mirror; without the mirror no face will appear--just so, without the imputation of aggregates no ego will appear. Life is like a circle of fire: it whirls without beginning or end, its three stages (ego, karma, birth) causing each other. The ego cannot be proved to be produced by itself, by another, or both. It can't be shown to exist in past, present or future. When this is realized the ego is destroyed along with karma and rebirth. Having realized this a person finds it difficult to believe that the world is any one way and not another, existent or nonexistent.

39-42 (E16-18; T316-317) The unwise man, hearing this *dharma* that terminates all frustrations, fears a condition that is unterrifying. You do not fear the nonexistence of all this in *nirvāṇa*; why do you fear the nonexistence of it here? If you savor the absence of aggregates and self at liberation, why aren't you pleased to know they are absent in this very life? Though *nirvāṇa* is not even an absence--it is the destruction of the idea of both presence and absence.

43-51 (E18-22; T317-319) The denial of karma's operation is nihilism; it breeds bad lower realms of rebirth and is a false view. The positive view that effects of karma do arise is a right view and leads to good rebirths. But when these negative and positive views are both avoided one has surmounted vice *and* virtue; this is said to be liberation. Realizing that the arising of anything is caused, one avoids nihilism. Realizing the cessation of everything with their causes avoids eternalism. A cause cannot precede nor accompany its effect; thus the production of a thing cannot be real even conventionally.

When one appreciates the truth of mutual dependence, e.g., of short with long, of light with lamp, and learns that causality is like this he is no longer subject to nihilism, since he allows that things really are displayed in different ways to us. Still, that very display breeds the cessation of things, which precludes their independent reality. Thus one is liberated from both views.

52-56 (E22-24; T319-320) If a mirage were really water one would find it so when one gets closer to it. Since one doesn't it's a mirage. Likewise, this world, which appears differently when one gets closer to the truth about it, must be like the mirage. A mirage looks like real water but is neither water nor real, just as the aggregates look like a real self but are actually neither a self nor real. If someone, seeing a mirage, goes up to it and, finding no water, says water doesn't exist at all, he is a fool. Likewise, if a man takes this world either to exist or to be nonexistent, *he* is a fool. And there is no liberation for a fool.

57-61 (E24-26; T320-321) The nihilist gets bad courses, the realist good courses of existence. But those who know how things actually are, accepting neither view, attain liberation. For us there is no thesis to be proved, no rules of conduct, no awareness even; but since we depend on enlightenment, ours is the *real* nihilism; so why should we be called (ordinary) nihilists?! Ask anyone--Sāṃkhyas, Vaiśeṣikas, Jains, Pudgalavādins--whether they share our view that is beyond both realism and nihilism.

62-66 (E26-28; T321-322) The Buddha taught this deep doctrine: How can the world be real? It is not born, it does not disappear, it doesn't persist even for a moment--it is beyond time. Neither the world nor *nirvāṇa* exists at any time--so how can they be really different? Since nothing persists, nothing arises or is destroyed. If things are naturally changing they are momentary; if there is no change how can you explain the differences between things?

67-72 (E28--30; T322-324) Momentariness implies that something persists partially or totally. But no difference between those two cases can be seen--so both theories are wrong. If things are momentary how can they exist? How can one be older than another? If things are not momentary one thing cannot be older than another either.

If a moment ends it must begin and persist--but then, having three parts, it can't be a moment. And if the three parts are themselves moments divided into three parts, being with beginning, middle and end is incapable of an explanation either as natural or as induced.

Nothing can be single, since it has many parts; but nothing can be without parts either. But without singleness plurality doesn't exist and vice-versa.

Existence can only fail to exist if it is destroyed or countered. But if existence is impossible how can it be destroyed or countered?

73-77 (E30-32; T323-325) So liberation doesn't involve the cessation of anything. That's why the Buddha refused to answer whether the world has an end or not. He did not try to convey his *dharma* to those unable to understand it. Those liberated ones who know the truth say that the *dharma* involves commitment to no thesis, indicating there is nothing one can depend on. Ordinary people want something they can depend on; they fear this *dharma* that refuses to give them any such thing, and so are lost. And being lost they want to ruin others who also fear what need not be feared. Take care, O King, that you not be ruined by them as well.

76-100. L165 "...The author finally lays down a method according to *āgama* of how one can argue that there is neither a *pudgala* nor any *dharma*, such as the *skandhas*, *mahābhūtas*, *dhātus*, etc., and thus personally realize the *nairātmyadvaya* of Mahāyāna, or *mokṣa*."

## CHAPTER TWO

1-6 (E40-42; T240-241) Just as a tree when split along with its parts is nothing, so the self (*puruṣa*) when split along with its elements is nothing. Thus the Buddhas say that all factors are without self; they understand the nature of the elements and their unreality. Thus actually neither self nor nonself is acceptable. So the Buddha denied both views. He said that what is seen or heard, etc., is neither true nor false. From any hypothesis its denial comes; neither are actual. So really speaking the world is beyond both truth and falsity; it admits neither existence nor nonexistence. How then could the omniscient one say that all this that cannot be sensibly spoken of has an end or is endless, is dual or nondual?

7-15 (E42-44; T241-242) Objection: Many Buddhas have come and gone and many exist now. This implies the existence of time. Since there's no reason to suppose new beings replacing those who are gone, how could the beginning and end of things be left unexplained by the Buddha?

Answer: That is the depth of the *dharma*, which keeps it secret from ordinary folk. Buddhas teach that the universe is *māyā*. A magical elephant appears by *māyā* to be born and die, though really there is no birth or death; likewise the world appears to begin and end, though actually there is neither beginning nor ending. The world, like the magical elephant, comes from and goes nowhere--it is merely due to delusion, it doesn't exist anywhere. So what is this world in reality, this world which, transcending the threefold temporal relation, neither exists nor fails to exist except in ordinary usage?

16-23 (E46-48; T242-243) We do not recognize the impurity of the body even though the body is gross and perceptible--why should you expect this subtle, deep doctrine to be easily understood? That's why the Buddha, when he learned this *dharma*, didn't at first explain it; he realized it was difficult for ordinary folk to understand. If wrongly understood this doctrine causes destruction by leading to nihilism. Others who criticize it, thinking themselves wise, go to hell, ruined by their criticism. Just as undigested food destroys one but that same food when well digested produces long life, health and strength, so misunderstood truth destroys one, but when rightly understood produces satisfaction and enlightenment. So, abandoning criticism and nihilism, seek right understanding in order to gain all your purposes.

24-27 (E48-50; T243-244) Egoism derives from wrong understanding of *dharma*, and from that good as well as bad karma arises, which in turn gives rise to good and bad rebirths. As long as this *dharma*, which dispels egoism, is not understood, you should apply yourself carefully to the *dharma* consisting of giving, morality and patience. One who acts according to *dharma* does not sink in this world or the next. From *dharma* one gets satisfaction and has no cause to fear during life or at the time of death; he experiences satisfaction in another world, and always practices the *dharma*.

28-32 (E50-52; T244-245) *Dharma* alone is the highest policy;

the world is fond of *dharma*, and when that fondness is secured one does not stray in this life or the next. What is anti-*dharma* displeases the world, and when the world is displeased one is not glad, in this life or the next. How can those who cheat others suppose evil awareness, deceptive and leading to bad rebirths, to be a purposeful science? How can cheating others be deemed good policy when on the contrary he deceives himself for thousands of rebirths? If you want to displease your enemy, give up sin and adopt good qualities; thus you will get what benefits you *and* your enemy will be displeased!

33-46 (E52-58; T245-246) The virtues of giving, kind speech, and helping others are extolled, and a number of wise and inspirational stanzas follow.

51-100 (E (Tibetan) 61-71) L165: "Devices for abandoning the defilements are given (41-74). By following the *dharma* the king will succeed in obtaining the thirty-two *lakṣaṇas* and the 80 *anuvyañjanas* specific to a *mahāpuruṣa*."

## CHAPTER THREE

1-100 (E72-91) (in Tibetan) L, p. 165: "The third chapter, **Bodhisaṃbhāraka*... resumes (1-10) the traditional doctrine of the *mahāpuruṣalakṣaṇa*. Now (12-13) a couple of significant verses succinctly summarize the entire purpose of Mahāyāna in theory and practice, ,viz. the attainment of Buddhahood. It has two aspects, a *rūpakāya* which is the outcome of an immense mass of merit (*puṇyasaṃbhāra*), and a *dharmakāya*, the result of an unlimited *jñānasaṃbhāra*. After this culmination the remaining 86 verses depict some of the endless forms a *bodhisattvacaryā*...intent upon *puṇyasaṃbhāra* may take motivated by *karuṇā*. It is a life of mental and physical happiness (*sukha*, cf. I, 4). In another cardinal stanza (30) the notion of *saṃbhāra* is linked to that of *abhyudaya* and *niḥśreyasa* (cf. I, 3-4). With a wealth of casuistic details, often of great cultural interest, the king is advised to benefit himself as well as others by developing the *pāramitās*."[1]

## CHAPTER FOUR

1-45 (E92-108; T423-427) Advice is offered to the King on how to conduct himself properly in his role.

46-55 (E110-112; T427-429) Even if you, as king, obtain the world with its four continents, still you can only enjoy two kinds of satisfaction--physical and mental. Physical satisfaction is merely the feeling of the nonexperiencing of frustration. Mental satisfaction is just conceptual identification through conceptual constructions. In this world all satisfaction is really useless. Only when we are aware of something can satisfaction arise; everything else is irrelevant inasmuch as one is not aware of it. When one's sense-organs--say his eyes--are fixed on a content but there is no conceptual construction one will not feel satisfaction.

Only one content of one sense-organ can be appreciated at a time, since when one's awareness is taking place nothing else is a content of awareness. The internal organ, making its object something that has been apprehended by a sense-organ and is past, constructing it, believes it to be satisfying. In this world, since one sense can only know one thing at a time, an organ without a content is purposeless and an object without that sense is likewise purposeless. Just as the birth of a son requires parents, so the birth of an awareness requires a sense-organ like the eye.

56-61 (E114-116; T429-430) Past and future objects and awarenesses are useless, and the present ones also, since they can't be distinguished from those past and future ones. Perception is no more of useful objects than is a "wheel of fire" seen when a torch is whipped around. Organs and objects can't be useful, since the five aggregates are themselves useless. If the aggregates operated alone fire could burn without fuel; if their combination is required the aggregates lack characteristics of their own. Since in either case the

---

1."Note that while the theme of this chapter is the same as that of **Bodhisaṃbhāra*ka...the treatment of this 'endless subject'...differs so much that the author hardly ever has to repeat himself." (L, 165)

aggregates are useless, their combination is as well. The same argument shows the uselessness of consciousness, feelings, identifications and conditionings. Really there is nothing real!

62-64 (E116; T430) Satisfaction is only the lack of frustration; frustration derives from lack of satisfaction. By seeing that everything lacks an essential nature one precludes the desire that follows satisfaction and so attains the stopping of frustration; thence stems liberation.

Objection: How can that be seen?

Answer: Practically, it is awareness that sees, but awareness can't occur without accompanying mental factors, nor need it occur without those factors, since it is rendered functionless thereby.

65-85 (E116-124; T430-433) Finding the world useless and thus seeing it as it is, lacking any appropriating, one becomes released, like fire when the fuel has run out.

The Bodhisattva who sees this is sure to be enlightened, but out of compassion continues to be reborn. The Buddha has explained this in the Mahāyāna. One who abuses the Mahāyāna knowingly cannot tell the difference between merits and faults, thinks merits defects, or hates them. He knows that evil harms others and merits benefit them, and he still abuses the Mahāyāna. One who hates the Mahāyāna is burnt, even if he possesses faith, should he hate through confusion or anger. Even if it is frustrating a man must destroy what is not good for him.

86-89 (E126; T433) In Mahāyāna emptiness is the absence of rebirth; for other systems it is destruction. In fact, destruction and absence of rebirth are identical. How then can the rest of the Mahāyāna be unacceptable to the wise?

It is not easy to understand what Buddhas mean. So guard yourself with equanimity on issues of doctrine.

90-93 (E126-128; T433-434) Question: In the vehicle of the disciples the vows and virtues of Bodhisattvas are not mentioned. How, then, can one become a Bodhisattva by following that teaching?

Answer: The Buddha didn't happen to speak of that. But what other authority is there? It is taught in the Mahāyāna and so should be accepted by wise persons.

94-100 (E128-130; T434) The Buddha taught the *dharma* to different pupils for different purposes. To some he preached conversion, to others morals, to others escape from duality, to others the terrifying principle beyond duality, to still others emptiness and compassion. Thus one should outgrow repugnance towards Mahāyāna and make peace with it if one desires true realization. Having faith and following it one will attain liberation.

## CHAPTER FIVE

1-100 (D193-199) L166: "As we saw the *dharma* has a *nivṛtti*- and a *pravṛtti*-aspect (I,22). It was thus shown how a *gṛhastha* should abstain from the ten *akuśaladharmapatha* and instead collect *puṇya* by engaging himself in the perfection of *dāna, śīla, kṣānti,* etc. Now the author focuses on the duties of a *pravrajita.* Disciplining himself in the (three) *śikṣās...,* the code of *prātimokṣa* and studying the *sūtras,* etc., he should abandon the fifty-seven *doṣas...*"

"Having thus abandoned these and other *doṣas,* a bodhisattva performs the six *pāramitās* in a spirit of *karuṇā* (35-39). Doing so he will gradually advance through the ten *bodhisattvabhūmis*...and accomplish his task by finally becoming a buddha (40-64). While still a Bodhisattva he must not forget to perform the *saptavidhānuttarapūjā* regularly (65-87). A final exhortation to practise Buddhism so as to attain *bodhi* for the benefit of all living beings (88-101)."

## 39. NĀGĀRJUNA, *Pratītyasamutpādahṛdaya*

The text adopted for the preparation of this summary is one of several Tibetan translations which appears in the gTen-gyur. The Tibetan translation followed here was made in the first quarter of the ninth century by Jinamitra, Dānaśīla, Śīlendrabodhi and Ye-śes-sde under the auspices of Khri-srong-lde-btsan. "E" references are to the Sanskrit restoration from this text by L. Jamspal and Peter Della Santina published in the Journal of the Department of Buddhist Studies, University of Delhi 2.1, 1974, 29-32. "T" references are to the translation in the same article, pp. 20-24. We have replaced the translations of technical terms in the original by those used in the present Volume.

Summary by Peter Della Santina

The *kārikās* are widely attributed to Nāgārjuna. In this case the traditional attribution has been largely accepted by modern scholars, not least on the strength of the fact that Candrakīrti cites a *kārikā* and a half from the work in his *Prasannapadā.*[169]

It seems reasonable to assume that only the first five of the seven verses found in the Tibetan actually belong to the original period of composition. This assumption follows from the fact that the commentary *Vyākhyāna*, by one Śuddhamati, covers only the first five stanzas.

The *Pratītyasamutpādahṛdayakārikā,* although short, is undoubtedly an important work because of the axiological nature of the topic which it treats. The value of declamatory and didactic statement on the part of Nāgārjuna with regard to the central doctrine of the Buddhist tradition, the doctrine of dependent origination, can scarcely be questioned given the polemical orientation of works such as 33.*Mūlamadhyamakakārikā* and 35.*Śūnyatāsaptati*. The treatment accorded to the doctrine of dependent origination by Nāgārjuna in the present work has to be seen as having a formative function for the whole of the Mahāyāna tradition.

1-3 (E29-31; T20-22) 1. The twelve discrete constituents of dependent origination which were taught by the Sage are wholly included in three: defilements, actions and frustrations.

2. The first (ignorance), eighth (desire) and ninth (attachment) are defilements, the second (traces) and tenth (existence) are actions, while the remaining seven are frustrations. Thus the twelve elements are included in three.

3. From the three two originate, from the two originate seven, and from these seven, in turn, originate the three; thus the wheel of existence revolves again and again.

An analogous definition of the term "discrete" (*bheda*) suggests the twelve factors are separate in a manner analogous to the parts of a chariot.

The term "Sage" (*muni*) which occurs in the first verse is defined as "mighty of body, voice and mind."

A number of purported causes extraneous to the twelve factors of dependent origination are discarded. God, nature, time and the like are cited as examples of noncauses.[1]

The twelve factors are interdependently originated, i.e., they are dependent upon one another as the roof-beams of a house depend on one another.

An important qualification of the metaphor of the wheel, expressive of cyclical existence, is offered. While the rotation of a wheel is characterized by the regular succession of points on the circumference following upon one another in order, this regular movement is not characteristic of cyclical existence, in which the points on the circumference of the wheel, i.e., the six sensory realms, arise in irregular succession for an experiencing subject.

4 (E31-32; T20,22) Cause and effect are declared to exclusively constitute the world. Apart from cause and effect, no sentient being, no self exists. The factors are declared to be empty, but this does not contradict the causal dependence of factors, because from factors which are empty empty factors originate.

## 40.NĀGĀRJUNA, *Suhṛllekha*

Summary by Peter Della Santina

Nāgārjuna's *Suhṛllekha* is most highly regarded as the precursor of an entire class of Buddhist literature. The class in question includes all those expositions of the Buddhist path to perfection which aspire to be both practical and comprehensive. Hsüan-tsang affirms that the *Suhṛllekha* had achieved great popularity in India as a didactic poem. The form, however, was to achieve its greatest diffusion in Tibet, where almost all the great teachers of the various traditions composed expositions of the Buddhist path more or less

1. A similar list appears in the 40.*Suhṛllekha*. See its summary below, verse 50.

closely modelled on Nāgārjuna's letter.[1] Such compositions, however, never totally supplanted Nāgārjuna's own work, which continued to be used very widely as an introductory manual. The letter enjoyed great popularity in China too, as is shown by the several translations of it in Chinese.

No Sanskrit fragment of this work remains. It is available in three Chinese translations (T.1672-1674), the earliest of which, by Guṇavarman, stems from 431 A.D., and two Tibetan translations. There are no references to it prior to one in a work of Candrakīrti. These dates lead Sieglinde Dietz[170] to doubt the ascription of this work to our present Nāgārjuna. Christian Lindtner[171], on the other hand, is inclined to support that ascription, finding a number of parallels with Nāgārjuna's other works. Bharat Singh Upadhyaya[172] writes that Nāgārjuna "was a friend and contemporary of the Sātavāhana king, Yajñaśrī Gautamīputra (166-196 A.D.)", to whom the *Suhṛllekha* was written. Other scholars provide differing identifications for this king, however.

"T" references are to the translation from the Tibetan in Lobzang Jamspal, Ngawang Samten Chophel and Peter della Santina, *Nāgārjuna's Letter to King Gautamīputra*, Delhi 1983. The Tibetan text is available as an Appendix to that volume. Several other translations are available; see Bibliography, Third Edition, #47.8.

1-3 (T1-2) The text commences with a few words of encouragement addressed to the reader. The contents of the letter are worthy of study, because merit arises from hearing the Sugata's words upon which the letter is based. The aesthetic merits of the composition are of no relevance. It ought to be taken seriously, because it contains an exposition of the Buddha's teaching. In the same way, an image of the Buddha is worshipped by the wise regardless of its material or aesthetic value. Finally, although the text may not contain anything actually new, the teachings it contains may be brought into clearer relief by a fresh presentation.

4 (T2-3) Six items worthy of being borne in mind are mentioned,

---

1.Such expositions include: *The Jewel Ornament of Liberation* of sGam-po-pa and *The Great and Small Graduated Path* treatises of Tson-kha-pa, to name only a couple.

viz., the Buddha, the *dharma*, the *saṅgha*, giving, morality and the gods.[1]

5 (T5) One is asked to practice the ten precepts,[2] to abstain from alcohol and to sustain oneself by means of a right livelihood.

6 (T5) Wealth is said to be unreliable and insubstantial. Therefore one is encouraged to give to monks, Brahmins, to poor and friends. Giving is said to be like a kinsman for the future life.

7 (T6) Morality is said to be the foundation of all virtues.

8 (T6-7) Nāgārjuna refers to attaining Buddhahood by means of the practice of the six perfections, viz., giving, morality, patience, energy, concentration and wisdom.

9 (T7) The text encourages one to revere one's parents. It is said that such reverence will bring renown in the present life and rebirth in the fortunate realms in the future.

10-11 (T8) The text refers to the eight precepts.[3] It likens them to the morality practised by the Arhats. It goes on to assert that their practice can be the cause of achieving the form of a god of the

---

[1]The advice, like much of the contents of the letter, is clearly largely intended for laymen. The reference to the gods may be explained in terms of the exemplary function. In other words, by bearing in mind the gods, the practitioner may be encouraged to liken his own practice of giving and morality to the practice of these virtues by the gods in the past.

[2]They are: avoidance of killing, stealing, sexual misconduct, lying, slander, malicious speech, idle speech, covetousness, malevolence and erroneous views.

[3]They are the five precepts, viz., the avoidance of killing, of stealing,of sexual misconduct, of lying and of alcohol, and the three additional special precepts, viz., avoidance of food after midday, of high and luxurious seats and beds and of entertainments and adornments.

realm of desire in the future life.[1]

12 (T8) Thirteen bad factors which Nāgārjuna terms enemies are enumerated. The list commences with avarice and ends with the pride of race, appearance, learning, youth and power.

13-14 (T9) Nāgārjuna extols the value of being heedful. Heedfulness is said to be the cause of deathlessness, that is, *nirvāṇa*, while heedlessness is said to be the cause of death, that is to say, *saṃsāra*. Four examples of persons who have changed their destiny by means of developing heedfulness are cited. They are Nanda, Aṅgulimāla, Ajātaśatru and Udayana.[2]

15 (T9-100 The practice of patience is extolled in counter-distinction to the common practice of austerities. One who avoids anger and practices patience, it is said, attains the irreversible stage.

16 (T10) Nāgārjuna admonishes one to cast off resentment. Harboring the notions that one has been abused, constrained, defeated or robbed by others produces quarrels, but one who does not harbor such notions sleeps peacefully.

17 (T10) Nāgārjuna offers a threefold classification of mental states determined by their relative persistence. Relatively persistent states are likened to letters engraved upon stone. Those of lesser persistence are likened to letters scrawled upon earth, while those of the least persistence are likened to letters written upon water. Nāgārjuna says that one should seek to develop persistent good states, but should seek to make bad states as ephemeral as letters written upon water.

18 (T11) Speech may be pleasant, truthful or wrong. Avoiding the last category, one should seek to speak what is pleasant and what is true.

---

[1]The realm of desire, the lowest of the three *dhātus*, includes, in addition to hell beings, hungry ghosts, animals and men, and a number of gods

[2]Nanda was the relative of the Buddha who was obsessed by sensual desire. Aṅgulimāla was the infamous bandit who was converted by the Buddha. Ajātaśatru murdered his father, Bimbisāra, then King of Magadha. Udayana murdered his mother.

19 (T11) A fourfold classification of migration conditioned by karma is given. The metaphor of light and darkness is employed. The migration of sentient beings is therefore either from light to light or from darkness to darkness. Again, the migration of sentient beings may also be from light to darkness or from darkness to light. Among these, the first is to be preferred.

20 (T12) A fourfold classification of the motivations and overt behavior of individuals is presented. The simile of mangoes is used to carry the message. Mangoes are said to be of four kinds: those which are green, but appear to be ripened; those which are ripened, but appear to be green; those which are green and also appear to be green; and lastly, those which are ripened and also appear to be ripened.

21 (T12) Nāgārjuna enjoins one to overcome desire for the wives of others by regarding them in accord with their age as either mother, sister or daughter. If desire still persists, however, one should meditate upon impurity.

22 (T13) The special and precious nature of the mind is indicated by means of the similes of a son, a treasure and of life itself. The mind, which is fickle, should be protected and withdrawn from sense desires, which are likened to a snake, poison, a weapon, an enemy and fire.

23 (T13) Sense desires are likened to a fruit which, although it has a pleasant appearance and may even be enjoyable to eat, produces disastrous consequences when ingested. Because sense desires bind one to *saṃsāra*, they should be renounced.

24 (T14) One who is able to conquer the momentary objects of the senses is worthy of the name of a hero far more than one who may win victory in worldly battle.

25 (T14) Meditation upon the impurity of the female body is offered as a remedy for sensual desire. Specific reference is made to the impurities issuing from the nine bodily orifices.

26 (T15) Sense desires can never be satisfied. The example of a leper who is supposed to have sought relief by immersing his leprous insect-ridden limbs in fire is offered.

27 (T15) Nāgārjuna refers to seeing phenomena in accord with the ultimate truth (*paramārthasatya*). He affirms that no other practice has similar quality.

28 (T16-17) Morality and wisdom elevate one who possesses

them above the average run of men, even though one may lack other common qualities.

29 (T17-18) The verse refers to the eight worldly factors: profit, loss, happiness, pain, fame, notoriety, praise and blame. One is asked to regard the eight with equanimity.

30-31 (T18-19) In these verses Nāgārjuna commences a discussion of karma. He admonishes one not to commit bad actions even for the sake of others, because although such actions may have been done for other's sake, their effects will be borne by one alone. Although the effects of bad actions may not appear at once, they will appear at the time of death. Therefore bad actions should be avoided.

32 (T19) Nāgārjuna refers to the seven treasures of the nobles: faith, morality, giving, study, modesty, humility and wisdom.[1]

33 (T20) Nāgārjuna again draws directly upon the words of the Buddha when he refers to six activities which are the cause of the loss of wealth and good name.[2] They are: gambling, lavish entertainment, unwholesome friends, laziness, drink and aimless wandering at night.

34-35 (T21) Satisfaction, says Nāgārjuna, is the best of all riches. One who is content with what he has, though he may have little, is really the happiest of men. The advantages of renunciation are elaborated. Possessions only bring suffering. The case of the many-headed Nāga[3] whose sufferings were as many as his many heads is cited in support of the statement.

36-37 (T22) Nāgārjuna again draws upon the words of the Buddha in order to give the reader some advice regarding the choice

---

[1]The seven treasures of the holy were given to Rāhula by the Buddha when the former approached him to request his inheritance.

[2]See the *Sigālovāda-sutta* of the Pāli canon.

[3]Nāgas are creatures which have bodies half human and half serpent. They are believed to dwell in the earth and in bodies of water.

of wives.[1] There are seven kinds of wives, three to be avoided and four to be accepted. The three to be avoided are those who are: associated with enemies of the husband, disrespectful toward the husband, or of a thieving nature. The four to be accepted are those who are kind, affectionate, beneficial or submissive.

38 (T22) One is encouraged to regard food with indifference, that is, with neither attachment nor aversion. Food is simply required for sustaining the body. It is likened to medicine.

39 (T23) Nāgārjuna encourages the reader to minimize the time allocated to sleep. He advises sleeping mindfully only during the middle watch of the night in order to dedicate more time to practice.

40 (T23) Nāgārjuna prescribes the practice of the four immeasurables: loving kindness, compassion, sympathy and equanimity. He says that even if the ultimate goal, that is, *nirvāṇa*, is not reached, still through the practice of the four, the happiness of the world of Brahmā will be achieved.

41 (T24) Next, the four trances are treated. The practice of the four trances frees the practitioner from the vicissitudes of the sphere of desire and he can achieve rebirth among the gods of the material sphere. The names of the four gods of the material sphere are mentioned. They are: Brahmā, Ābhāsvara, Śubhakṛtsna and Bṛhatphala.

42-43 (T24-25) Nāgārjuna returns to the theme of karma in two verses. A scheme for assessing the weight of karmic actions is indicated. The scheme includes five subjective and objective components whose presence or absence determines the weight of a given karmic deed. The subjective components are: persistence, that is, the repetition of an act; intentionality; and the act's unmitigatedness. The objective components have reference to the indebtedness of the subject to the object of an act, and the worth of the object toward which an act is directed.

A small measure of bad karma may be dissipated by a large measure of good karma, just as a small measure of salt is dissipated

---

[1]The scheme is taken from the Buddha's discourse to the daughter-in-law of Anāthapiṇḍika, the famous lay disciple of the Buddha.

by the waters of the Ganges, but a small measure of good karma cannot dissipate a small measure of bad karma. Therefore one should seek to acquire a large measure of good karma.

44 (T25) The five obstructions well-known to Ābhidharmic literature are mentioned. They are: desire, doubt, sloth and torpor, ill will, and restlessness and worry. Nāgārjuna calls them thieves which steal one's good karma.

45 (T26) The five faculties are listed. They are: faith, energy, mindfulness, concentration and wisdom. They are termed strength, power and the most excellent.[1]

46 (T27) One is reminded that one's own actions are the cause of one's failure to escape from old age, sickness and death. The recollection of this fact, it is said, functions as an antidote to arrogance.

47 (T28) The importance of cultivating right understanding in order to gain heaven and liberation is emphasized. Even persons who perform meritorious actions without right understanding are liable to evil consequences.

48 (T28) Mindfulness with regard to the antidotes to the four perverted views is advocated. One should recall frustration, impermanence, not-self and impurity.

49 (T29) An analysis of the self and the aggregates in relation to each other is presented. Matter is not the self, the self does not possess matter, the self is not found within matter, nor is matter found within the self. The remaining aggregates should be examined in a similar manner in order to comprehend that they are empty.

50 (T29) A number of spurious causes of the aggregates are rejected. They include: change, time, nature, God and the like. The aggregates, it is said, originate from ignorance, karma and craving.

51 (T30) The three fetters: attachment to the self, doubt, and belief in the sufficiency of moral observances and austerities are

---

[1]The verse refers to strength, power and the most excellent, which are related by the commentaries, both Indian and Tibetan, to the four degrees of the path of application (*prayogamārga*).

obstacles to liberation.[1]

52 (T31) The importance of self-reliance is emphasized. Liberation depends upon oneself alone, therefore one is encouraged to cultivate the four noble truths through the devices of morality, study and concentration.

53 (T32) Reference is made to the three disciplines: morality, meditation and wisdom. More than one hundred and fifty precepts are said to be included in these three.[2]

54 (T33) Mindfulness regarding the body, Nāgārjuna says, was taught by the Buddha to be the only path to liberation. Therefore one should cultivate mindfulness regarding the body.

55-57 (T33-35) Human life is impermanent like a bubble of water. It is a matter of wonder that one continues to live for any length of time at all, given the many obstacles to life. At the time of death the body, which is in any case insubstantial, will be disposed of in a variety of ways. Its elements will be separated and dispersed. Inasmuch as even large and apparently solid objects like the earth, etc. are subject to destruction at the end of an eon, surely human beings too cannot be expected to endure for long.

58 (T35) *Saṃsāra* is in general like a banana tree. It is impermanent, without substance or refuge. Therefore one should seek to achieve detachment from *saṃsāra*.

59 (T36) Next, the unique and precious nature of human life, endowed with the conditions conducive to the practice of religion, is treated. The canonical analogy of the tortoise inhabiting the ocean is cited by way of illustration of the difficulty of achieving a human birth endowed with the right conditions.[3]

60 (T37) Human life is likened to a golden vase ornamented with jewels. One who would use such a vessel for containing filth would surely be considered foolish. Therefore human life should be used

---

[1]The three fetters referred to in the letter are the three broken by a stream-winner on the Arhat path.

[2]The reference to the figure of one hundred and fifty is said by the commentaries to indicate the monastic codes.

[3]See *Majjhima Nikāya* III, 169.

for the practice of religion.

61 (T37) Nāgārjuna refers to four special conditions which the reader of this letter possesses that make the practice of religion even easier for him. They are: dwelling in a particularly suitable place, relying upon holy teachers, religious application in former lives, and the accumulation of merit.[1]

62 (T38) Nāgārjuna specially indicates the importance of good company. The path to freedom, he says, is accomplished by consulting a good friend.

63-64 (T38) The importance of freedom from the eight unfavorable situations is indicated. When one has achieved freedom from birth among heretics, animals, hungry ghosts, hell beings, barbarians, fools, gods and a locality where no teaching of *dharma* exists, one should strive to put an end to birth.

65 (T38-39) *Saṃsāra* is full of frustration, disease and death. It is therefore fit to be lamented over.

66 (T39) There are no certainties in regard to relations among sentient beings in the universe of *saṃsāra*. Fathers become sons, mothers become wives and friends become enemies, and vice versa.

67 (T39) Moreover, one has experienced countless instances of birth in the universe of cyclical existence. If the mother's milk one has drunk in the course of countless existences were measured, it would equal the water in the four great oceans.

68 (T40) Not only has one experienced countless instances of birth, but one has also experienced countless instances of death and rebirth as well. If the skeletons one has had in the course of countless existences were to be heaped up one upon another, the pile would exceed the legendary Mount Sumeru in height. Again, if the entire earth were to be made into bits the size of juniper seeds, it would still not suffice to equal the number of mothers one has had.

69 (T40) There is no certainty of position either in *saṃsāra*. Even Indra, the king of the gods and the universal monarch fall from their lofty positions and become the servants of servants in *saṃsāra*.

70 (T41) The theme of the uncertainty of position in *saṃsāra* is

---

1.The four special conditions are termed *cakras*. They also occur, according to Chr. Lindtner, in *Aṅguttara Nikāya* II.

elaborated further. Even though one may enjoy the company of heavenly nymphs in the paradises of the sphere of desire, one can again find oneself in the hells where one's organs are tortured by the instruments of infernal torment.

71 (T41) Even though one may experience the pleasure of dwelling upon the summit of Mount Sumeru where the surface of the earth accommodates one's footsteps, one may again find oneself in one of the hells where the suffering of treading upon burning embers and decomposing corpses is experienced.

72-73 (T41-42) The theme in hand is further developed in two verses. The pleasure of heavenly gardens and rivers where celestial nymphs play may soon be replaced by the gardens and rivers to be found in the hells. There the trees are armed with leaves like swords and the rivers are hot and difficult to bear.

74-75 (T42) Even having attained the station of the gods of the sphere of desire or even that of those of the material sphere, one can still become fuel for the hottest of the hells (*avīci*). Even having attained the station of the sun or the moon, one can still find oneself engulfed in endless darkness.

76 (T43) Death can occur at any time and precipitate one into unknown situations. Therefore, while the opportunity is at hand, one should practise good actions of body, speech and mind, because only good actions are of any use at the time of death.

77-88 (T44-47) Nāgārjuna commences a review of the suffering in the hells. Those who have committed many unwholesome actions, he says, will be born in the hells, like Reviving Hell (*saṃjīva*), Black Thread Hell (*kālasūtra*), Crushing Hell (*saṃghāṭa*), Howling Hell (*raurava*), Great Howling Hell (*mahāraurava*), Heating Hell (*tapana*), Intense Heating Hell (*pratāpana*) and Uninterrupted Hell (*avīci*). A few examples of the suffering in the hells are given. There the inmates are pressed like sesamum, ground into flour and the like. Molten bronze is poured into the mouths of some, while others are impaled upon barbed iron stakes. There the inmates are attacked by dogs with iron fangs and by birds with iron claws and the like. They are also beset by countless insects. In yet another of the hells, the inmates are charred in heaps of embers and cooked in cauldrons like rice.

Hardened criminals, habituated to committing many bad actions, are not moved by accounts of the hells. When merely hearing of the suffering of the hells produces fear, the actual experience must be awful indeed. Freedom from desire is the most excellent of happinesses, while the suffering of *avīci* is the greatest of all sufferings. The suffering experienced in the present life cannot be likened even to a fraction of the suffering experienced in the hells. The inmates of the hells will continue to suffer in the ways described until such time as the effects of the bad actions they have committed are exhausted. Bad actions of body, speech and mind are the cause of the suffering of the hells; therefore one should seek to avoid such actions by means of intelligence.

89-90 (T48) The suffering of animals is considered in two verses. Those who stray from the path of action leading to peace are liable to be born as animals. Animals suffer from the pain of eating one another. Moreover, they are bound and beaten by man, as well as being killed by him for food, pearls, fur and so on.

91-97 (T48-50) Nāgārjuna devotes several verses to a consideration of the suffering of hungry ghosts. The hungry ghosts suffer continuously because of the deprivation of objects they desire. The suffering of the hungry ghosts engendered by their constitutions and situations are described in graphic detail. Even should they come upon a little coarse sustenance, it is said, their mouths are the size of the eye of needles and their throats as thin as hairs. Consequently, they are able to ingest such sustenance only with great difficulty, and all to no avail for their stomachs are as large as mountains. Flames are said to issue from the mouths of some hungry ghosts. Others vie with their fellows for even the foulest of food.

The hungry ghosts are said to have so little merit that even the sun is felt by them to be cold, while the moon is felt to be hot. Rivers dry up when gazed upon by hungry ghosts, and trees bearing fruit become withered and dry. Inasmuch as they are bound by the force of the bad actions they have committed, the hungry ghosts have to suffer in this way for a very long time. While the sufferings of the hungry ghosts are various, they are of one taste. Their cause is avarice, miserliness and ignobility.

98-101 (T51-52) Even existence in the higher realms is beset with frustration. Nāgārjuna dedicates four verses to the frustrations of the gods. Because of the pleasures experienced by the gods in the heavens the pain they experience on the occasion of their death and fall from heaven is all the greater. Nāgārjuna refers to five signs which are said to appear presaging the death of a god and his fall from heaven: loss of beauty, boredom, the withering of flower adornments, the soiling of garments and appearance of bodily dirt and sweat. If no merit remains upon the death of a god, then, helpless, he is liable to be reborn even in the three lower realms of animals, hungry ghosts or denizens of hell. Consequently, existence in the heavens is not desirable.

102 (T53) Existence among the demigods too is beset with frustrations. The existence of the demigods is troubled by jealousy and strife.

103 (T53) As has been shown in the foregoing verses, *saṃsāra* is full of frustration no matter where within its confines one is born.

104 (T54) One should lose no time in striving to put an end to rebirth by means of transcending action, as one would not hesitate to extinguish a fire that had taken hold of one's head or dress.

105 (T54) Once again the means of achieving *nirvāṇa* is the three disciplines: morality, meditation and wisdom. *Nirvāṇa* is described as ageless, deathless, inexhaustible and devoid of earth, water, fire, air, sun and moon.

106 (T55) Practise the seven limbs of enlightenment: mindfulness, energy, investigation, interest, tranquillity, concentration and equanimity.

107 (T56) The importance of concentration and wisdom and their mutually implicit character is stressed. By means of the union of concentration and wisdom, the ocean of cyclical existence can be exhausted by one who possesses them.

108 (T57) Avoid speculation in regard to the fourteen inexpressibles (*avyākṛta*)[1] inasmuch as such speculation does not conduce to peace.

---

[1]Viz., whether the universe is: eternal, not eternal, both eternal and not eternal, and neither eternal nor not eternal; whether the universe is finite, infinite, both finite and infinite, and neither finite nor infinite; whether the Tathāgata exists after death, does not exist after death, both exists after death and does not exist after death, and neither exists after death nor does not exist after death; whether the soul is identical with the body or different from it.

conduce to peace.

109-112 (T58-59) The twelve consituents of dependent origination are listed. The doctrine of dependent origination is the profound treasure of the conqueror's teaching. He who sees dependent origination sees the Buddha.

113 (T62) The steps of the noble eightfold path are listed.

114-115 (T62) The four noble truths are stated. Nāgārjuna says that even the layman living in the lap of prosperity can cross the river of afflictions by means of the knowledge of the truths.

116 (T64) The enlightened ones did not fall from the sky or spring up from the earth. They were formerly persons who were subject to the afflictions, but who achieved perfection through practice.

117 (T64) The fundamental importance of disciplining the mind is indicated. Nāgārjuna says: the Buddha said the mind is the root of all good factors.

118 (T65) The reader is encouraged to make his life meaningful through the correct practice of any of the injunctions contained in this letter. It is admitted that it would be difficult to practise all of them, even for a monk living in isolation.

119-120a (T65-66) The reader is asked to rejoice in the good actions of others and to dedicate his own merit to the attainment of Buddhahood. Through the mastery of yoga, it is said, he can attain countless births among gods and men.

120b-121 (T66) The verses contain specific references to Avalokiteśvara and Amitābha and his Buddha field. The reader is encouraged to become like the former.[1]

122-123 (T167) The practices of giving, morality and wisdom are again cited. The reader is encouraged to allay the suffering of others and to achieve *nirvāṇa*, which is faultless, ageless, fearless, peaceful, only an idea and supramundane.

---

[1]The verses supply the clearest evidence of the author's commitment to the Mahāyāna.

## 41.NĀGĀRJUNA, *Bodhisambhāraka*

Christian Lindtner has reviewed the evidence for ascribing this text to this Nāgārjuna. It is only available in a Chinese translation (T.1660) made by Dharmagupta between 605-616 A.D. The following reasons are given by Lindtner for assenting to Nāgārjuna's authorship: "The external evidence is provided by two quotations from (this text) in Candrakīrti's *Catuḥśatakaṭīkā*...I have also come across a quotation...in Asvabhāva's *Mahāyānasaṃgrahopanibandhana*...Moreover an early date of *Bodhisambhāra* is ensured by the fact that it is quoted in the *Daśabhūmikavibhāṣā* of which a Chinese version from ca. 408 still exists, where an earlier one (by Dharmarakṣa) from ca. 265 is lost. In both cases Nāgārjuna was held to be the author."[173]

"T" reference are to the translation by Christian Lindtner in *Nagarjuniana.*

1-4 (T228) The preparations for enlightenment (*bodhisambhāra*) will be explained here. Question: How can they be explained, since they are infinite?

Answer: True; the Buddha body has infinite qualities of which these preparations are the basis, and so the preparations have no limit. But I shall only explain a small portion of them.

5-9 (T228-229) Perfect wisdom (*prajñāpāramitā*) is the chief preparation for enlightenment. Its father is skill in the means to it, its mother is compassion. It includes as chief elements giving, moral precepts, patience, energy and trance, all due to wisdom and involving perfection.

10-16 (T229-230) A *bodhisattva* must take care of living beings by trying to convert as many of them as possible. Some who gain instruction as disciples (*śrāvakayāna*) or singly enlightened (*pratyekabuddhayāna*) are too weak to become Mahāyānists. Those who can't achieve any of these should do good deeds. If someone cannot hope for heaven or liberation he should be brought to the fold by the advantages in this world that accrue thereby. The *bodhisattva* should have great compassion for those who cannot be induced to conversion.

17-18 (T230) Skilful means (*upāyakauśalya*) of conversion include gifts, teaching them the dharma, doing good to them. By benefitting others the *bodhisattva* benefits himself.

19-27 (T230-231) By understanding the deepest element of factors beyond conceptual constructions attachment to everything is spontaneously abandoned. Unattached to profit, reputation, honors and satisfaction, etc., and not committed to their opposites--this is renunciation. The *bodhisattva* should pursue these actions energetically as long as he has not reached the irreversible state; if he reaches it without pursuing them he will become a mortal through his carelessness and reenter the path of disciple or enlightened for oneself, the roots of his knowledge being cut off. This fate, unlike even going to hell, is an absolute hindrance to enlightenment, and ought to be feared.

28-30 (T231-232) The patience of nonorigination (*anutpādakṣānti*) involves seeing all as not arisen, not destroyed, not both, not neither, neither empty nor nonempty. When one cleaves to the middle path about every factor this patience of nonorigination is gained because all constructions are eliminated. Such a one will certainly become an enlightened one (*buddha*).

31-33 (T232) Until one attains readiness (*abhimukha*) he should steadily practise concentration and not be careless.

34-47 (T232-233) Enlightenment can't be gained by only a little merit, but even a small task must be conducive to the help of living beings by involving meritorious intentions. Examples of meritorious intentions are provided. Their value is immeasurable and leads to Bodhisattvahood.

48-54 (T233-234) Buddhas are extolled and their assistance is sought.

55-65 (T234-235) How the aspirant should behave is explained.

66-76 (T235-237) Liberation is not attained directly; the perfection of wisdom must be ripened. Just as an archer supports an arrow in the target by shooting another directly through it, so one should aim his awareness at the goal called empty--the arrows of the method support it so that it does not fall into *nirvāṇa*! Thus others are not abandoned. Even a *bodhisattva* who is destined for Buddhahood should practise the method. Despite distaste for *saṃsāra* he still turns toward it and abandons *nirvāṇa*.

77-89 (T237-238) A *bodhisattva*'s nature is passionate; the passions must be burned off to produce the seed of enlightenment. A *bodhisattva* teaches all *śāstras*, visits all stages and castes, does not flatter, deceive or boast, cultivates moral rules, contemplates in solitude with mindfulness, abandons bad thoughts and cultivates good ones, pursues his end energetically.

90-133 (T234-244) Further description of the *bodhisattva*'s methods. The descriptions gradually become advice about how to act under various circumstances. One should cultivate the thirty-seven aids to enlightenment, the five spheres of liberation, the ten notions of impurity, the eight thoughts of a great soul, the five higher faculties, the four supernatural powers, the four boundless states.

134-148 (T244-246) It is wrong for a *bodhisattva* to teach the Mahāyāna to those who believe in the *śrāvaka*- or *pratyekabuddha*-vehicles. Those two sorts of persons, along with those who believe in worldly sciences and are after worldly goods, are bad friends of a *bodhisattva*. Good friends are teachers, the Buddha, ascetics and monks.

149-165 (T246-248) A wise man does not treat emptiness as the nature of things and base his action on it--that would be the fault of believing in a self-nature. One should view all factors as unborn, not present and not future. One should not be elated at being worthy through merit, nor should one be downcast if one is in need. When ascetics and householders have collected these things for as many eons as the sands of the Ganges they will attain enlightenment.

## 42. NĀGĀRJUNA, *Vyavahārasiddhi*

Translation by Christian Lindtner

This is only a fragment comprising six verses. It is quoted by Śāntarakṣita in his *Madhyamakālaṃkāra* and ascribed to Nāgārjuna in Kamalaśīla's commentary. The style and doctrine of the text is quite similar to the authentic works of Nāgārjuna. The text is edited, translated and discussed in Lindtner, *Nagarjuniana*, pp. 94-99. The translation is brief enough to be provided here in full:

(1) One syllable does not make a *mantra*. On the other hand many syllables do not make a *mantra* either. Dependent upon syllables that are (therefore) unoriginated this (*mantra* neither

exists) nor does not exist.

(2) Likewise no medicine appears independently of its specific ingredients. It appears (like) an illusory elephant, i.e., it is not identical (with its causes), nor is it (absolutely) different from them.

(3) It arises in dependent co-origination (*pratītyasamutpāda*). Who would (be so ignorant as to) maintain that it exists or does not exist! Actually visual consciousness arises (similarly) when it is based upon (eye and form).

(4) Projected by the power of (his) karma and passions (*kleśa*), the appropriator arises out of existence. Form also arises in the same manner. Who would (be so ignorant as to) maintain that it exists or does not exist?!

(5) Similarly *all* the (twelve) members of existence (*bhavāṅga*) are simply conventional designations (*vyavahārataḥ prajñapti*). Consequently all phenomena such as extinction have only been advocated (by the Buddhas) with the purpose (of explaining the emptiness of the soul and the factors).

(6) As it (appears to be) a *mantra* without (really being) a *mantra*, and as it (appears to be) a medicine without (really in itself being) a medicine, thus (all phenomena) are stated to be dependent (*pratītya*). Neither of the two (cause or effect) can be established (as existing independently).

## 43. NĀGĀRJUNA, *Mahāyānaviṃśikā*

Summary by Christian Lindtner

Though this brief verse-summary of Mahāyāna has always enjoyed considerable popularity--it is often quoted as Nāgārjuna's and there is one Chinese and two Tibetan translations--its authenticity is nevertheless dubious. On the other hand its style and doctrine show considerable similarity to some of Nāgārjuna's authentic works. The summary below is based on the Sanskrit text edited by G. Tucci.[174] compared with the Tibetan and Chinese versions edited by V. Bhattacharya, Calcutta 1931. These all differ considerably from the Sanskrit and from one another.

1-3. First, the Buddha is praised for, out of compassion, having preached the *dharma* that is, strictly speaking, beyond words. In reality, i.e., from the absolute point of view, the Buddhas, all living beings and all karmic creations, in other words, the entire world, is unoriginated and empty like an illusion.

4-11. Nevertheless, due to sheer ignorance, people imagine that the world of *saṃsāra* exists. Hence they experience suffering, happiness, etc. The manifold world is a creation of their own mind, and they can be compared to a painter who becomes afraid of a monster painted by himself.

12-20. Had it not been for the Buddhas' compassion we would all have been utterly lost. The Buddhas guide living beings out of their illusions, and finally, when mankind has accumulated sufficient merit and insight, it too becomes enlightened and understands that everything was created by ignorance. There is only rebirth as long as there is ignorance.

Only by means of Mahāyāna can one ever hope to cross the terrible ocean of *saṃsāra*.

## 44. NĀGĀRJUNA, *Catuḥstava*

Summary by Christian Lindtner

If we define Buddhism as *bhakti* to the Bhagavat Buddha as a compassionate preacher of an eternal *dharma* that points the way to *svarga* and to *mokṣa* (by means of good karma and *tattvajñāna* respectively) it is only to be expected that his grateful devotees would compose hymns in praise of their Leader. The collection of four hymns ascribed to Nāgārjuna, titled *Lokātīta-*, *Niraupamya-*, *Acintya-* and *Paramārtha-stavas*, are the only ones (among several others) still available in Sanskrit. (The *Dharmadhātustava* is also available in a Sanskrit manuscript from Tibet/China but has not yet been edited.) The first and third were first edited by Christian Lindtner in *Nagarjuniana* and reproduced, along with the less important second and fourth, by F. Tola and C. Dragonetti.[175] (47.2.13) This Tola/Dragonetti version constitutes our "E" and "T".

The following sums up the gist of the work: Due to ignorance there seem to be two worlds, one unreal, ruled by karmic laws, and one real, profound, and empty like space, only accessible by waking up as a Buddha. Out of compassion the Buddha plays along by trying to awaken all beings from their ignorance. For this he deserves our *bhakti* and endless hymns of praise. Through the yoga of emptiness one should remove the unreal barrier of ignorance that separates microcosm from macrocosm[176]--an old Aryan ideal.

### I. *Lokātītastava*

1-4 (E10; T20) The Buddha is extolled for his supreme insight and compassion. There is no soul, only the five aggregates, and yet, in the ultimate sense, these aggregates are also empty, illusions. This is because they arise from causes.

5-10 (E10-11; T20-21) Each of the five aggregates is shown to be dependent upon something else, i.e. nothing in and by itself.

11-18 (E11; T21-22) In general, things and their characteristic marks are neither identical nor different. So how can one appropriate them and so speak of them? Nothing arises, neither from itself nor from anything else. A thing is not different from its destruction. An effect cannot arise from a cause. Phenomena are like illusions.

19 (E11; T22) As such they are the products of imagination (*parikalpa*).

20-27 (E12; T23) Again, nothing (be it permanent or not) can be created, neither from itself or from anything else. Everything, again, is dependent, i.e. empty. This eternal doctrine which has been preached repeatedly in the *sūtras* of Mahāyāna is intended to liberate one from all conceptualizing. The spirit (*vijñāna*) should become "free from marks", i.e. free from appropriating, in order to attain liberation. Everything is to be found in Mahāyāna.

28 (E12; T24) Final transfer of merit.

### 2. *Niraupamyastava*

1-6 (E12-13; T24) The Buddha experiences emptiness but

mankind at large suffers from dogmatic views (*dṛṣṭi*).[1] But, in the ultimate sense, there is nothing to "see" or know. All opposites are the same if only one does not hang onto them.

7-10 (E13; 25) The Buddha has not really preached anything, his mind (*citta*) is empty like space. He has compassion, but his mind (*buddhi*) does not cling to anything.

11-24 (E13-14; T25-27) The Buddha, in fact, has or seems to have two bodies. The spiritual body is permanent and full of bliss (*śiva*, cf. *Madhyamakakārikā* 25.24). It cannot really be seen. It is not at all like his beautiful physical body which can be seen and which he compassionatly displays in order to guide the three kinds of Buddhists (cf. *Madhyamakakārikā* 18.12). Without his doing anything, as it were, he accomplishes his liberating duty as a Buddha.

25 (E14; T27) Final transfer of merit.

### 3. *Acintyastava*

1-4 (E14-15; T27) Out of pure compassion the inconceivable Buddha has, in Mahāyāna, preached what he himself has experienced, that all factors are empty. This means that they are dependently originated, i.e. unborn, empty like an echo, etc.

5-7 (E15; T28) All conditioned things are relative and unreal,

8-9 (E15; T28) and so they cannot really be born.

10-16 (E15-16; T28-29) Nothing really exists in and by itself, and therefore also not by means of something else. Even relativity (*paratantra*) itself does not exist.

17-18 (E16; T29) All factors, as said, are unborn, without an essential nature, like illusions.

19-20 (E16; T29-30) The senses and their objects are unreal,

21 (E16; T30) and it is due to ignorance that people do not know reality.

---

[1]"Psychologically" a *dṛṣṭi* is formed by the manifold activity of *kalpanā*, viz., *saṇkalpa, parikalpa*, etc. This expanding activity, *prapañca*, can be stopped by seeing, with the help of *buddhi, citta* and *vijñāna*, that there is nothing--i.e. only emptiness--to be seen. This is but simple yoga, but in specific Mahāyāna terminology.

22-24 (E16; T30) Since things are really unborn, like illusions, one cannot really distinguish them and say that they exist or do not exist.

25-30 (E16-17; T30-31) All things, including liberation, appear as dreams and so they are not really dual. They are, in fact, unborn.

31-34 (E17; T31) The Buddhas have liberated numerous beings, or so it seems. In reality not one has been liberated; the agent and his works are empty.

35-41 (E17; T32) The entire world (the five aggregates) is but "names" and opinions; there is no object or subject in and by itself. Emptiness is an inconceivable reality that cannot be grasped. It is the same as the Buddha and his *dharma*.

42-43 (E18'; T32-33) Indeed, the Buddha, living beings, everything is simply emptiness.

44-50 (E18; T33) A distinction is to be made between the relative truth of affirmations and negations (as opposed to absolute non-reality, *parikalpitasvabhāva*), and the absolute truth beyond duality.[177]

51-58 (E18-19; T33-35) The purpose of teaching the ultimate truth, emptiness, is simply to heal people from their wrong belief in relative reality. This is appropriating. The Buddha's teaching is always based on two truths (*satyadvaya*). By means of *prajñāpāramitā* one eventually becomes a Buddha.

59 (E19; T35) Final transfer of merit.

## 4. *Paramārthastava*

1-10 (E19-20; T35-36) The Buddha is really unborn, so he can only be praised--out of *bhakti* and based on relative *lokaprajñapti*[178]--in negative terms as neither this nor that. He is, e.g., neither permanent nor impermanent, he has no color, no size, no location etc. He has, however, attained "profundity" (*gambhīratā*, cf. *Ṛgveda* 10.129). Everything being empty, who has praised whom, and for what?

11 (E20; T36) Nevertheless: a final transfer of merit, no matter how unreal, ultimately speaking.

## 45. AUTHOR UNKNOWN, *Samādhirājasūtra*[179]

This work exists in one Tibetan and three Chinese translations, only one of which is complete. One of the incomplete translations, by An Shih Kao of the later Han dynasty, is estimated by Constantin Regamey[180] to have been made in 148 A.D. The complete text was translated into Chinese by Nārendrayaśas in the sixth century, and the Tibetan translation dates from the ninth century. Nalinaksha Dutt infers "that the *sūtra* in its original form was much shorter than the one translated by Nārendrayaśas..."[181]

Complete editions of the work are found in Dutt and Vaidya.[182] There is no complete translation into any Western language at this point. In footnotes accompanying the summary of each chapter below we indicate the availability of editions and translations of particular chapters. The summary provided here is a combination of several sources: titles taken from Gomez/Silk[183], summaries of chapters taken from a combination of R.L. Mitra[184] = "M" and Dutt = "D".

### Chapter I. The Setting[185]

"Prince Candraprabha takes leave of the Buddha to ask a question...How would a person attain the inconceivable truth and realise the real nature of constituted things and...perfect himself in *śīla, dhyāna* and *prajñā*?..."(D, 2.1,xiii). "The Lord replied that a Bodhisattva can easily attain all these by practising..." (M, 203) "such concentration of mind in which one realises that all things of the world remain in the same state for ever."(D, 2.1,xiv).

### Chapter II. Previous Life of the Buddha as Sālendrarāja[186]

### Chapter III. The Virtues of a Buddha[187]

"The merits of a Tathāgata are that he is perfectly enlightened, learned, well-conducted, well-bestowed; that he is perfectly conversant with the ways of men; he is without a superior; he has complete control over the senses." (M, 203)

Chapter IV. Different Aspects of *Samādhi* and Meditation on the Buddha's Virtues[188]

"The real nature of the Samādhi is that the mind, unclouded by ignorance, should be fixed on one point. The knowledge of restraint put upon by ignorance, removal of the burdens of the world, the control of passions, and the correction of faults,--these also are essential to the Samādhi." (M, 203)

Chapter V. Story of the Former Buddha Ghoṣadatta

Chapter VI. Prerequisites for *Samādhi*[189]

"...Preparatory exercises for perfecting oneself in the highest meditation...are (1) development of a compassionate mind, (2) acquisition of merits, and (3) worship of the *dharmakāya* and not the *rūpakāya* of the Tathāgata." (D, 2.1,xvii.

Chapter VII. Three Patiences (*kṣānti*)

"By the first *kṣānti*, a person avoids quarrels, realises the illusory nature of things, acquires knowledge of the scriptures...develops faith and takes the vow to attain the highest knowledge. By the second..a person becomes steadfast like the mountain, develops concentration of thoughts, acquires the five *abhijñās*, ultimately extends his thoughts beyond limitation. By the third...a person visualizes the innumerable Buddhas preaching to beings, comprehends the ways and manners of Buddhas, and remains unmoved by worldly gains or fame...He now possesses not only *kṣānti*, but also *maitrī* and *karuṇā*". (D, 2.1, xvii-xviii)

Chapter VIII. Story of the Former Buddha Abhāvasamudgata[190]

The stanzas accompanying this story contain valuable philosophical material reinforcing the connection between the doctrine of emptiness and the practice of *samādhi*.

## Chapter IX. Receptivity to the Profound *Dharma*[191]

"This chapter...offers in charming similes and sonorous verses an excellent exposition of the *śūnyatā* doctrine, i.e., non-existence of the things of the world. It shows that things have no more existence than a mirage...The things of the world are compared to sky, fleeting clouds, sea-foam...objects seen in a dream. It tells us to avoid the extreme assertions like "is" or "is not", and criticises those Hīnayānists who regard themselves as...seers of the four truths as in reality such acquisitions also do not exist." (D, 2.1, xviiii-xix).

## Chapter X. The Buddha Visits Candraprabha

"When Buddha placed his footsteps on the threshold of Candraprabha's palace, the earth quaked and many miracles happened, and all beings in hells and elsewhere felt happy." (D 2.1, xix-xx)

## Chapter XI. Preserving the *Sūtra*[192]

"Candraprabha...put the following questions...: By what practices can a Bodhisattva realise the real nature of worldly objects, be a performer of proper deeds, be able to remember his former births, possess a *saṅgha* without any dissension...The only answer given by Buddha...was that a Bodhisattva could obtain all knowledge if he would understand only that 'all dharmas are devoid of any appellation or description, and are without origin or decay'." (D 2.1, xx)

## Chapter XII. Recounting the Virtues of the Buddha through the Practice of *Samādhi*

The Buddha's virtues and the state of mind that is the liberating *samādhi* are the same insofar as they are both unappropriatable and empty. The Chapter further addresses a Bodhisattva's detachment.

## Chapter XIII. Explanation of the True Meaning of *Samādhi*

The true meaning of the king of *Samādhis* is the experience of emptiness.

Chapter XIV. The Reasons for the Buddha's Smile[193]

The Budha smiled "because he foresaw that Candraprabha's merits and aspirations were such that he would ultimately become a Buddha." (D 2.1, xxii)

Chapter XVI. Previous Existence of the Buddha as the Son of Matirāja[194]

"On listening to the (Buddha's) discourse, the nature of dharma became apparent to him (the prince, who had fallen ill,) and his disease at once disappeared." (D 2.1, xxiii)

Chapter XVII. Approaches to the *Samādhi* that Manifests Multiple Buddhas[195]

"A Bodhisattva should equip himself with the following four acquisitions: (1) Tolerance...(2) Perfection in morality...(3) Aversion for worldly existence...(4) Strong faith (in himself). (D 2.2, i)

Chapter XVIII. Transmission of the *Samādhi* to Candraprabha

"Bhagavān now tells Prince Candraprabha that a Bodhisattva who wishes to learn and propagate this Samādhi (leading to the realisation of the sameness of all objects) should take to meditational exercises by which he will be (1) unwearied in acquisition of merits, (ii) unassailable by enemies, (iii) immeasurable in knowledge, and (iv) extremely powerful in eloquence..." (D 2.2, p. iv)

Chapter XIX. Explanation of the Inconceivable *Dharma* of the Buddha[196]

This Chapter deals with the impossibility of conceiving the full nature of Buddhas or their teachings.

Chapter XX. Teachings of the Former Buddha Indraketu

This is an exposition of the teachings of emptiness and the

paradox of teaching and preserving the *dharma* in words.

Chapter XXI. A Previous Existence

"...(A Bodhisattva) should believe firmly in the identity of the Tathāgata with feelings, perception, passions and impressions. So that he should believe that pentaform matter is nothing but the Tathāgata." (M 208)

Chapter XXII. Description of the Body of a *Tathāgata*[197]

This Chapter discusses the Bodhisattva's detachment and the two bodies of a *buddha, rūpakāya* and *dharmakāya.*

Chapter XXIII. The Inconceivability of the *Tathāgata*

This is an exposition on the four kinds of "penetrating understanding" (*pratisaṃvid*) as a key to the nature of reality and Buddhahood, and a discussion of their inconceivability.

Chapter XXIV. Approaches to Penetrating Understanding

"The material elements (*rūpa*) are in *bodhi* and *bodhi* is in the material elements, the two are identical. By means of words *Nirvāṇa* is described but in fact neither *Nirvā*ṇa nor the words are to be found in reality. The *dharmas* never actually come into being in this world; hence they remain the same whether before or after their so called appearance..." (D 2.2, xi)

Chapter XXV. Rejoicing at the Merit of Others

This Chapter concerns (1) the transfer to other beings of the merit of aspiration toward Buddhahood and (2) the merit of taking pleasure in the merit of others

Chapter XXVI. The Value of Generosity

Chapter XXVII. Explanation of the Virtue of Morality

"In this Chapter are enumerated the fruits of hearing and of practising the great Samādhi". (M 210)

Chapter XXVIII. Ten Advantages

A series of sets of ten fruits that accrue to the Bodhisattva who perfects himself in various ways is listed.

Chapter XXIX. Explanation of the Three Hundred Terms

"Not to perceive the purity of character, not to practice the Samādhi, not to inculcate knowledge, to scrutinize the doctrine of mukti, and to know it as the doctrine of the soul's salvation is called *aparigraha* or non-acceptance of all qualities." (M, 210)

Chapter XXX. Merits of the *Samādhi*

Chapter XXXI. Explanation of the Absence of an Essence in All *Dharmas*

Chapter XXXII. The Value of Preserving the *Sūtra*

"Ānanda asked the Lord why Bodhisattvas feel no pain even when their limbs are torn asunder. The Lord replies, as a worldly-minded man, every part of whose body is burning under the fire of sin, can feel pleasure without the fire being extinguished...so does a Bodhisattva who is desirous of escaping from the burning fires of grief, birth and decrepitude and longs to obtain nirvāṇa, feel no pain from such trifling matters as the amputation of a hand or a foot." (M, 212)

Chapter XXXIII. The Story of Buddha as Kṣemadatta[198]

"When a Bodhisattva wishes to attain the excellent Bodhi knowledge he should listen to, practise, and preach the great Samādhi." (M, 212)

Chapter XXXIV. The Story of Jñānavatī[199]

Chapter XXXV. The Story of Supuṣpacandra

"The three delights of *mokṣa* are--the delight afforded by the knowledge of Nihility, the delight afforded by the knowledge that things are produced without a cause, and the delight that he has to perform no samādhis any more." (M, 213)

Chapter XXXVI. Explanation of the Element of Morality in the Path

"The next step to be taken by a Bodhisattva is to aim at the purity of physical actions, and at the restraints of speech...The latter shows the inactivity of existence in Nihility, the illusive nature of all things created, and that annihilation is the only truth.

Chapter XXXVII. Previous Life of Śākyamuni as Yaśaḥprabha

"The restraint of mind...shows that the mind is unreal like a dream, an illusion, a mirage. From it men become fearless, worship Buddha, and learn a samādhi named Jvālāntarābha." (M, 214)

Chapter XXXVIII. The True Meaning of Restraint of Body, Speech and Mind

"Let those who seek perfection quickly listen to Buddha's instructions on mental restraint. By perfection in mental restraint a person obtains the inconceivable *dharmas* attainable by the Jinas, mental emancipation, and other attainments...He gets rid of wrong views, deceitfulness towards the elders, attachment, delusion and all other evils. He easily comprehends impermanence, non-substantiality, soullessness, causal origin of objects, which, in fact, neither appear nor disappear. The real mental restraint consists in not forming any conception about phenomenal objects and even about the highest truth or Nirvāṇa." (D 3, xxvi)

Chapter XXXIX. Explanation of the Three Hundred Terms

"This chapter deals with the concepts enumerated...in a catechetical method in the style of the Pāli Abhidhammapiṭaka. It opens, e.g., with the question 'what is purity in deeds?' The answer given is that 'it produces non-attachment to the three worlds, which have no more existence than that of a dream.'" (D 3, xxvi)

Chapter XL. Transmission

"This is the concluding chapter eulogizing the present text and adducing reasons for describing it as a *Vaipulyasūtra*." (D 3, xxvii)

## 46. AUTHOR UNKNOWN, *Vimalakīrtinirdeśasūtra*.[200]
Summary by A. K. Warder

[201]"The hero of the present *Sūtra*, the *bodhisattva* Vimalakīrti...is a Licchavi householder in Vaiśālī in the time of the Buddha, living very much in the world, even to the extent of visiting the geisha girls, taverns and casinos and indulging in all the pleasures of life. However, he is in reality a model *bodhisattva*, even a *śramaṇa* (ascetic-philosopher), and mixes with worldly people in order to show them the disadvantages of pursuing pleasure. He is universally respected and his conversation is in conformity with his doctrine as well as skilful, so that his activities in the world serve to ripen people's understanding and draw them away from attachment to pleasures."

"One day Vimalakīrti gives out that he is ill, though this is only another expedient. According to Indian custom many people go to visit him and inquire whether he is feeling better, to which inquiry he replies with discourses on the impermanence, unhappiness, etc., of the elements of which the body is composed and the diseases to which it is subject. Naturally, when the Buddha...knows of Vimalakīrti's illness he wishes to send a monk to visit the sick man...In turn he asks Śāriputra, Maudgalyāyana, Subhūti, Ānanda and many others to go. All refuse, on the ground that they are incapable of holding conversation with Vimalakīrti, having been humiliated by him on some previous occasion, when they were each reduced to silence. For example the *bodhisattva* Maitreya had been told by the Buddha that he will be the next *buddha*, after one more birth. Vimalakīrti found him discussing the stage he had reached with the Tuṣita gods and took him up on this question of 'birth': it is only by non-birth that one can reach this stage, Maitreya's thusness is only the thusness of all phenomena, there is no duality between him and all other living beings, so that when he becomes enlightened all beings will become enlightened; anyway, all beings are extinct already, this is their thusness, so Maitreya ought not to deceive the gods with this talk about his going to attain enlightenment. Maitreya could think of nothing to say to this on that occasion and declares himself now incapable of asking Vimalakīrti about his illness."

"At last the *bodhisattva* Mañjuśrī agrees to go, though the task is difficult. Many monks, *bodhisattvas* and gods go with him to hear what promises to be a remarkable conversation. They find the house appropriately empty and Vimalakīrti tells Mañjuśrī he is well-come, especially as he has not come...As to his illness, it will last as long as living beings are ignorant and desire existence. Starting thus, the conversation and the episodes which follow express in narrative and dramatic form the main teaching of the Madhyamaka. Śāriputra plays the part of the clown who asks foolish questions (i.e., at the concealing level), complaining that there are no seats for the visitors, not enough food for them, etc. The house-goddess of Vimalakīrti's house makes game of him with displays of magic. Seeing that she has made such progress on the way Śāriputra is foolish enough to ask her why she does not change her female sex (traditionally regarded as a disadvantage, at least by monks), evidently having the power to do so. The goddess replies that so far she has not been able to discover what this 'female sex' is: like all phenomena it is only an artifice or illusion (*māyā*), it is not real (is nothing in itself), so there isn't anything to change. However she punishes Śāriputra for his suggestion, making a woman of him by her magic: he finds he has the body of the goddess whilst she appears like the elder Śāriputra and asks him why he does not change his 'female sex.' She restores him after a sufficient lecture, adding that ultimately no changes take place."

"Vimalakīrti explains to Mañjuśrī how a *bodhisattva* lives in the world without being attached to it, conforming to passion and aversion, though being free from these, and to delusion though he has understanding. He asks Mañjuśrī to tell him what the 'clan of the thus-gone' is--a new concept...This 'clan', says Mañjuśrī, is that of ignorance, desire for existence, passion, averson, delusion, error, the obstacles, etc., in other words of all bad phenomena which lead to transmigration. Asked what this signifies he explains that the thought of enlightenment can occur only in transmigration (among synthesized phenomena), as lotuses grow only in the mud."

## 47. AUTHOR UNKNOWN, *Śālistambasūtra*

Summary by Karl H. Potter

Noble Ross Reat,[202] who has made a life's work out of the study of this text, believes it may be the earliest Mahāyāna *sūtra*. However, its earliest known translation dates from the fourth century, though a closely related work was translated by Ji Zhan in 220-252 (T.708). Although commentaries ascribed to "Nāgārjuna" are available in three Tibetan versions (P.5466, 5485-5486) it is fairly clear none are by the Nāgārjuna we just finished reviewing. Nevertheless, it cannot be doubted that the work is a rather early one. Reat ascribes to it Mahāyāna leanings on the grounds that the text argues "that enlightenment represents a realization of *Dharmakāya* Buddha"[203], but admits that the language and style is reminiscent of Theravāda.

Reat's text is necessarily a combination of several sources, but he manages to reconstruct about 90% of the Sanskrit text on the basis of quotations found elsewhere in the literature. He also provides a Tibetan text and an English translation, referred to below as "ET".[204]

In addition to ET Jeffrey D. Schoening has recently edited and translated this work with its commentaries in two volumes as Wiener Studien zur Tibetologie und Buddhismuskunde, Heft 35.1, Wien 1995.

1-6 (ET26-31) Maitreya advises Śāriputra on dependent origination, the nature of *dharma,* and why it is that on seeing dependent origination one sees *dharma* and sees the Buddha.

The twelve-fold chain of dependent origination is stated. Each member is the cause of the next, and the cessation of a member is the cause of the cessation of its preceding member.

*Dharma* is defined as the noble eight-fold path (its members listed). And the Buddha is one who understands all factors, who has the wisdom-eye and whose body is all factors, who sees the factors of both the disciple and the adept.

7-14 (ET32-39) Understanding dependent origination is to understand *dharma*, and one understanding *dharma* sees the unsurpassable body of factors of the Buddha. Why is it called "dependent origination"? Because it arises from causes and conditions. Whether or not Tathāgatas arise, or questions are asked, etc., the nature of factors (*dharmatā*), suchness, reality, truth are constant. (This theme is echoed throughout the remainder of the text.)

What are the causes? As, e.g., a sprout only arises when there is a seed, and a seed only from a sprout, but neither seed nor sprout are aware of their connection.

What are the conditions? They are six: earth, water, fire, wind, space and season (*ṛtu*). Each has its specific function--earth to support, water to moisten, heat to mature, wind to bring out, space to provide room, and season to transform the seed. When all function a sprout is developed.

15-20 (ET40-42) External dependent origination can be understood as five ways of being a cause: as nonpersisting, as not nonpersisting, as nontransmigratory, as producing a large result from a small cause, and being bound by similarity. The seed is not the sprout, and when one ceases the other arises. Thus the cause is nonpersisting. But the seed does not arise from the cessation of the sprout, nor vice versa; rather, the sprout arises just as the seed ceases; thus the cause is not nonpersisting. Since seed and sprout are dissimilar, the cause is not transmigratory. A sprout is many times larger than a seed. And the effect is of a similar kind to its cause.

21-26 (ET43-49) Internal dependent origination can be understood as two ways of being causal: causal *qua* cause and causal *qua* condition. Each member of the twelvefold chain is a condition for the arising of the next: this is being causal *qua* cause. But all of the six conditioning elements mentioned above must come together if a result is to occur: this is being causal *qua* condition.

Thus, the earth element produces a body's solidity, the water element its cohesion, the fire element its ability to consume, the wind element its ability to breathe, the space element the hollowness inside its body. That which causes the psychophysical complex to develop is called its "consciousness-element" (*vijñānadhātu*) associated with the contaminating combination of five consciousnesses plus mental consciousness. Without these conditions there is no embodiment. None of these elements constitute a self, person or ego, nor is what is spoken of male or female or neuter.

27-30 (ET49-57) That ignorance which consists in perceiving these six conditioning elements as one self spawns the traces of greed, hatred and delusion concerning sense-contents. Consciousness consists in the manifestation of objects. The four appropriating, nonmaterial aggregates that arise with consciousness are termed "name", and this, together with the four great elements and derived matter ("form"), constitutes the psychophysical complex. The sense-organs connected with the psychophysical complex comprise the six sense-bases. Contact is the connection of three (viz., organ, object and visual awareness). Experiencing contact is feeling. Clinging to feeling is appropriating. Action (*karman*) deriving from appropriating and producing rebirth is existing. The manifestation of the aggregates caused by existing is birth, the maturing of the aggregates one is born with is decay, the destruction of worn out aggregates is death. A dying person's internal burning is sorrow, and expressing sorrow is lamentation. Experiencing unpleasantness associated with the five consciousness-bodies is frustration. Mental frustration is depression. And the afflictions associated with these constitute irritation. (The twelvefold chain is rehearsed twice more in different terminology in 28-29).

31-38 (ET58-66 ) In this flowing stream of dependent origination four limbs (*aṅga*) are responsible for assembling things in appropriate order. These four are ignorance, craving, karma and consciousness. Consciousness causes by being a seed; karmic defilements cause the seed to be born and function as the field of consciousness; cravings water the consciousness-seed, and ignorance scatters it. Without them the development of the consciousness-seed doesn't occur. Here and there a consciousness-seed causes a sprout, a psychophysical complex, to arise through rebirth in a mother's womb.

Here visual consciousness arises from five causal factors: the eye, the object (color/shape: *rūpa*), light, space and attention.

But nothing transmigrates from this world to another world. There is only the appearance of karmic fruits. It is like the reflection of a face in a mirror: no face transmigrates into the mirror, but because of causes and conditions there is the appearance of a face, as there is only the appearance of the results of karmic actions. So nothing departs from this world or is reborn in another.

39-44 (ET67-70) Internal dependent origination can be understood in five ways: as nonpersisting, as persisting, as nontransmigratory, as producing a large result from a small cause, as being bound by similarity. It is nonpersisting, since the aggregates at death are one thing, the aggregates at arising another. It is not nonpersisting, since the new aggregates arise just as the old ones cease. It is nontransmigratory, since beings of heterogeneous forces within one lifetime arise with homogeneous forces in the next. Because a small deed may bear a large fruit, a large result can come from a small cause. And because the results of an action are similar in feeling to their causes, the effect is similar to its cause.

45-48 (ET70-74) One who correctly (spelled out at length) understands dependent origination, who cuts off at their roots all dogmatic views concerning self, person, etc., it is said by the Buddha that he will attain superior enlightenment.

## ĀRYADEVA

Tom Tillemans has given the most recent assessment of the life and works of this author.[205] Summarizing briefly, it seems likely that Āryadeva was born in Lanka, which appears to have meant modern Sri Lanka, although this has been questioned.[206] It is clear he studied with Nāgārjuna. He is to be distinguished from another Āryadeva who wrote commentaries on the *Guhyasamājatantra* and the *Cittaviśuddhiprakaraṇa*. That author, who must have lived several centuries later, may have also authored two other works attributed to an Āryadeva by the Tibetan sources, viz. the *Skhalitapramathanayuktihetusiddhi* and the *Madhyamakabhramaghāta*.

## 48. ĀRYADEVA, *Catuḥśataka*.[207]

### Summarized by Karen Lang

"ET" references are to the Lang edition and translation just cited.

### Chapter One: Rejecting Belief in Permanence

1-9 (ET26-29) Āryadeva first attacks the perverted view of noneternal things as eternal. In this chapter he uses human beings to illustrate the thesis that whatever comes into being must cease. There is no one who is born who does not proceed inevitably towards death. One should fear death because, unlike the symptoms of illness and old age, it cannot be treated. Though the time of death is uncertain, it will come. He suggests ironically that someone who engages in evil actions without fear of the consequences must have abandoned all attachment to himself.

10 (ET28-29) What is called "life" is nothing but a moment of consciousness; since ordinary people do not understand this fact, self-knowledge is rare.

12-22 (E28-31) It is wrong to grieve over others' deaths and ignore one's own impending death. Attachment to others makes even rebirth in heaven unlikely. If the bonds of affection were permanent, the pain of separation from loved ones should never be alleviated, which is contrary to experience. Compliance with society's customs for mourning the dead is hypocritical and ineffective in relieving pain.

23-25 (ET32-33) Householders are advised not to delay leaving home, since death makes separation inevitable. Someone who forsakes all attachment to others and reflects on his own death will no longer fear death.

### Chapter Two: Rejecting Belief in Pleasure

1-18 (ET32-37) Āryadeva examines the second erroneous conception, namely, that things actually characterized by frustration are satisfying in regard to the human body. Although the body should be taken care of so that merit may accumulate over a long life, it is wrong to value it, because it is a source of frustration.

Frustration is the essential nature of the body. Two types of frustrations--mental and physical--daily afflict people. Satisfaction depends upon one's own conceptual constructions, and since frustration easily overcomes these conceptions of satisfaction, frustration has superior power. Various external causes and internal conditions establish the body as a source of frustration. The body experiences the physical pain of exertion, cold, hunger, disease, and dying. Frustration, moreover, is inherent in the very nature of the body since even the four elements which compose it cause frustration because they are constantly in a state of conflict.

19 (ET36-37) One should avoid evil in this world and the next because it is wrong to think that a bad rebirth is pleasurable.

20-24 (ET36-39) The body experiences frustration when initially pleasurable sensations change and become frustrating. Ordinary people mistakenly believe that relieving pain is satisfying, but no pleasure can overcome frustration.

25 (ET38-39) Everything that is impermanent must also be considered frustrating.

## Chapter Three: Rejecting Belief in Purity

1-16 (ET38-43) The human body illustrates also the third erroneous conception of impure things being pure. The insatiable craving for sense pleasures is the basis for attachment to women. This attachment which others--even dogs--share is impermanent and productive of frustration, not satisfaction. Rational people turn their minds away from sensual pleasures; fools suffer jealousy and endure abuse from women because of their blind passion.

17-25 (ET42-45) The human body is impure since it harbors filth, and no one should be proud of it or attached to it. Neither bathing nor wearing flower garlands can remedy this impurity. But meditation on the body's impurity can produce non-attachment. Impermanence, impurity, pain, and the absence of a self are all seen in the human body.

## Chapter Four: Rejecting Egotism[208]

1-17 (ET46-51) Āryadeva analyzes the last of the four erroneous conceptions, the mistaken belief in a real and substantial self when there is no such self, in relation to ordinary people's concepts of "I" and "mine" His remarks addressed to an unnamed Indian king criticize his pride in thinking "I am a generous donor" and "I am the protector of my people". Āryadeva points out that the wealth the king donates comes from the labor of his subjects and is not really his. The people also must protect him by their support if his reign is to continue. Moreover, in protecting them he engages in merciless and evil actions, e.g., the punishment of criminals and war.

18-25 (ET50-53) The king's position as a sovereign is useless in achieving liberation. Past merit accounts for his present birth in a high position but his future birth is in danger because of his merciless actions.

Chapter Five: The Acts of a Bodhisattva

1-3 (ET52-55) In this chapter on the Bodhisattva's career, Āryadeva emphasizes that Buddhas and Bodhisattvas work actively for the benefit of all beings. Buddhas direct all their actions towards benefitting others; their power over actions indicates omniscience.

4-7 (ET54-57) The intention behind an action determines its merit. Because of the Bodhisattvas' intentions (*saṃkalpa*) and their control over mind, all their actions are good, even those considered foul when undertaken by others. The merit of a Bodhisattva's intention far exceeds the merit that would make all people on earth universal monarchs (*cakravartin*). The merit of training someone to produce the intention of enlightenment even exceeds that of building a *stūpa*.

8-16 (ET56-59) Bodhisattvas must use both skillful methods and compassion in diagnosing and treating their students' defilements. Others blame them if uninstructed beings go to a bad rebirth. People indifferent or hostile to the Bodhisattvas' teachings will incur bad rebirths.

17-23 (ET58-63) Bodhisattvas may be reborn voluntarily in inferior births, although their control over mind enables them to be reborn continuously as kings. Because of their control over mind, no harm comes to them even in this world; consequently there is no difference to them between *saṃsāra* and *nirvāṇa*. Bodhisattvas practise generosity without regard to any reward. The merit they derive from skillful methods is immeasurable; this vast quantity of accumulated good karma renders negligible any past nonvirtuous action and makes their actions in benefitting others successful.

24-25 (ET62-63) The *tathāgata*'s power is inconceivable, but some people fear the teaching of marvels (*adbhutadharma*), just as fools fear the profound teaching.

## Chapter Six: Rejecting the Defilements

1-7 (ET62-65) Each of the three defilements--delusion, attachment and hatred--causes frustration and harms people. A skillful teacher identifies which defilement most affects a student and then applies the proper antidote: harsh treatment to counteract attachment and kind treatment to counteract hatred.

8-9 (ET64-65) The defilements arise either from internal causes, e.g., habitual inclinations or proclivities (*anuśaya*), or from external conditions, e.g., a bad friend. Defilements that arise from external conditions are easy to suppress; the others are not.

10-11 (ET66-67) The elimination of delusion eliminates attachment and hatred since it is their basis. Understanding dependent origination eliminates delusion.

12-24 (ET66-69) The characteristics of people afflicted by attachment and hatred and the appropriate countermeasures for these defilements are discussed.

25 (ET68-69) The defilements will cease once the duration, etc., of consciousness is understood.

## Chapter Seven: Rejecting Attachment to Sensual Pleasures[209]

1-8 (ET70-73) Rebirth in *saṃsāra* is never voluntary; bondage in this ocean of suffering should be feared. Most people hold the wrong views and proceed to a bad rebirth. Because the maturation of evil is harmful, an intelligent person directs his mind towards the exhaustion of all karma.

10-12 (ET72-73) The initial cause of an effect is never seen. Not every effect is necessarily attained, but every completed result is destroyed effortlessly.

13-23 (ET72-77) The wise fear rebirth in heaven--which is rare--as much as hell. It is wrong to turn away from mundane objects in the expectation of enjoying divine objects. Even though they are acquired through merit, the most desirable sense objects and sovereign power are best repudiated since they are impermanent.

24 (ET78-79) People who see the world as being composed of collections of machines (*yantra*) and illusory beings (*māyāpuruṣa*) attain the highest state.

Chapter Eight: The Conduct of a Student[210]

1-3 (ET78-79) The arising of attachment and the other defilements is not based upon a real object, for a real object would produce the same response in all observers. The existence of attachment, etc., depends upon conceptual constructions.

5-7 (ET80-81) Skeptical analysis (*saṃdeha*), by focussing attention on this teaching (of emptiness), can lead to the destruction of *saṃsāra*. But *nirvāṇa* cannot be attained through the wrong apprehension of emptiness. It is wrong to regard something that is not empty as empty because of a selfish desire to attain *nirvāṇa*.

8-11 (ET80-83) Worldly teaching involves activity: the ultimate teaching involves a withdrawal from activity; *nirvāṇa* is for those who are inactive and rebirth is for those who are active. People partial to their own theses who criticize others will not attain *nirvāṇa*, since tranquillity does not result from divisive quarrels.

12-13 (ET82-83) The desire for continued existence in this world and the desire for death because of overwhelming pain are both criticized as not leading to *nirvāṇa*.

14-15 (ET82-83) *Tathāgatas* proclaim a gradual teaching: giving is recommended to people of low ability; moral behavior to people of middling ability; and the cultivation of tranquillity to people of the highest ability. First the rejection of demeritorious actions must be understood; next, the rejection of the self; and finally the rejection of all things, e.g., the aggregates, the sense bases, and the elements.

16 (ET82-83) The emptiness of one thing is precisely the emptiness of all.

17 (ET84-85) Attachment to *dharma* is only for those who seek heaven, not for those who seek liberation.

18-20 (ET84-85) Instruction should conform to the students' abilities, just as a physician prescribes medicine in accordance with the illness. Emptiness should not be taught to everyone, since unsuitable medicine becomes poison. The medicine, viz., the *catuṣkoṭi* method of analysis, should be applied in accordance with the illness. It is impossible to teach worldly people the truth without referring first to the existence of worldly things.

21-22 (ET84-87) A good rebirth is acquired through a partial understanding of the truth; the highest state through a complete understanding. Intelligent people, therefore, constantly direct their minds towards inner contemplation (*adhyātmacintā*). If someone who understands the truth does not attain *nirvāṇa* in this life, he will attain it in the next life, in accordance with his karma.

23-25 (ET86-87) *Nirvāṇa* is not absent in this world, but people who are suitably disciplined and liberated are rare. Contemplation of the body's lack of virtuous qualities stops desire. Rebirth ceases after its cause, the afflictions and karma, cease.

## Chapter Nine: The Refutation of Permanent Things[211]

1-4 (ET88-89) Experience indicates that no existent things arise independently of causes; all are effects. If created things are not permanent and uncreated things are permanent, it should follow that if created things exist, permanent things do not exist.

5 (ET88-89) Even ordinary people do not conceive of *ākāśa* as a permanent thing.

6 (ET88-89) One spatial part does not cover the whole space; therefore it must have other spatial parts. Whatever has parts is created and not permanent.

7 (ET90-91) Time undergoes change because we see both activity and inactivity in relation to it. Because it depends on something else, it must be an effect and not permanent.

8-9 (ET90-91) Cause and effect are mutually established, for without the existence of an effect nothing can be called a cause. A cause undergoes change in becoming a cause, and nothing that undergoes change can be permanent.

10 (ET90-91) A thing whose cause is something permanent produces itself after having been nonexistent. A cause of a thing that has been produced by itself serves no purpose.

11 (ET90-91) Since cause and effect never have dissimilar characteristics, a permanent cause should never result in an

impermanent effect.

12 (ET90-91) An atom that has one part that is a cause and another that is not is a composite thing, and it is not possible for a composite thing to be permanent.

13-17 (ET90-93) Because the "atomic" size (*pārimaṇḍalya*) of the cause is not present in the effect, it is impossible that atoms are in contact in their entirety. Moreover, because the locus of one atom cannot be that of another, the cause and the effect cannot be equal in dimension. But if there were partial contact, e.g., the eastern side of one atom touching the western side of another, atoms would have parts. Moreover, if an atom has no parts, it cannot move, since no front part will move forward. No one can see it if it has no front, middle, and rear parts.

18 (ET92-93) Either the effect destroys its cause and its cause, e.g., the atom, is not permanent or the cause remains and its effect is not found.

19 (ET92-93) No permanent thing has resistance.

20-23 (ET92-95)[212] Āryadeva criticizes Buddhists who believe in a permanent state of liberation. Liberation is not something different from bondage, the thing bound and the method of liberation; nor is it something permanent in which the aggregates or the personality (*pudgala*) exist. He rejects also the Sāṃkhya belief that a conscious or potentially conscious self exists in liberation.

24-25 (ET94-95) Belief in a self may have some value on a worldly level, but those who seek liberation should reject it, since it does not exist on an ultimate level.

## Chapter Ten: Refutation of the Self[213]

1-2 (ET94-95) The conviction "I am male" is based on ignorance, since neither the inner self (*antarātman*) nor the elements are male, female, or neuter.

3-4 (ET94-95) The concept of a self is based on impermanent things. The self, like the body, changes from one birth to another. Consequently, the opponent should not claim that the self is different from the body and permanent.

5 (ET96-97) The self is not the agent of the body's actions, because motion does not arise from something that is intangible.

6 (ET96-97) Since no harm should come to a permanent self, there should be on that view no need to protect oneself by doing virtuous actions!

7 (ET96-97) The opponent assumes that the self is the substratum for the memory of past lives and that the self bears the impressions of past births from one life to the next. Āryadeva replies that one might assume also that the body bears the impressions of past scars from one life to the next and reach the absurd conclusion that the body is permanent!

8-9 (ET96-97) If the self (*jīva*), as the Nyāya-Vaiśeṣikas claim, becomes connected with such qualities as awareness and satisfaction, it undergoes change and is not permanent.

10-12 (ET98-99) If consciousness (*caitanya*) is a permanent attribute of the self, as the Sāṃkhya opponent claims, the sense organ (*karaṇa*) serves no purpose. If the self is potentially conscious at one moment and actually conscious at another, it undergoes change and is not permanent.

13-14 (ET98-99) If consciousness were minute and the self vast in size, this disparity would make it difficult for such a small amount of consciousness to make the self conscious and unconsciousness would characterize the self's essential nature. Moreover, if the self were all-pervasive, the term "I" should designate both oneself and somebody else!

15-16 (ET98-101) The Sāṃkhya thesis that the three unconscious *guṇas* construct the world but that the conscious self experiences the results is irrational.

17 (ET100-101) The connection between the self and action is criticized: something that is permanent and all-pervasive does not possess action, and without the ability to instigate action one may as well say that the self does not exist.

18 (ET100-101) Some speculate that the self is vast, some that it is the size of a person's body, and others that it is minute; but the wise know that it doesn't exist.

19-21 (ET100-101) Since a permanent self cannot experience the pain that motivates people to seek liberation, belief in the existence of a self is incompatible with *nirvāṇa*.

22-25 (ET102-103) Impermanent things are never annihilated, since impermanent seeds produce impermanent sprouts. There is no annihilation because things continue, and there is no permanence because things cease.

## Chapter Eleven: Refutation of Time[214]

1 (ET102-103) Āryadeva argues against the concept of time as permanent through an examination of the existence of past, present and future. He first considers various Ābhidharmika theses.

Buddhadeva's objection: The past and the present are called "past" and "present" in relation to the future.

Answer: If past and present pots are related to the future pot, they should exist in the future. But if past and present are also the future, there is no distinguishable future.

4-8 (ET102-105) The Sarvāstivāda claim that past, present and future exist is said to imply that a thing exists at all times, which contradicts the tenet that things are impermanent. Past, present and future time are conceived in relation to things which arise, endure and cease. The change that these things undergo indicates that they are not permanent; similarly, time is not permanent.

9-13 (ET104-107) The existence of a thing before it is produced supports the eternalist thesis that things have a predetermined and unalterable nature. Against the Sāṃkhya thesis of a pre-existent effect (*satkārya*), Āryadeva argues that it is illogical that something should already exist and yet be referred to as something whose coming into existence is produced. For example, if virtuous behavior were innate, self-restraint would be unnecessary. But if any action is required, a pre-existent effect is not possible. Moreover, a thing that exists both before and after its production must be permanent, and experience shows that things begin and end. He criticizes the Nyāya-Vaiśeṣika thesis that the effect is nonexistent before its production (*asatkārya*) because then cause and effect would be unrelated.

16 (ET106-107) The Sāṃkhya conception of time based on the transformation of things is rejected because the mind (*manas*) cannot perceive this transformation.

18 (ET108-109) One awareness cannot apprehend two objects; two awarenesses cannot apprehend one object.

19-24 (ET108-109) Impermanence and duration cannot at the same time mark a thing nor is it possible to establish how they succeed one another.

25 (ET108-109) Memory is false because both the object cognized and the cognition are past and will not arise again.

## Chapter Twelve: The Refutation of Speculative Views[215]

1-4 (ET110-111) Most people lack the impartiality, intelligence, and industriousness needed to understand the Buddhist view of *saṃsāra* and *nirvāṇa*. The Buddha taught about the cycle of existence and the means of renouncing it, as well as tranquillity and the means of cultivating it. Hypocritical philosophers (*pāṣaṇḍa*) advocate renunciation but reject Buddhist teachings; these teachings alone proclaim the right method of renunciation, which leads to tranquillity.

5 (ET110-111) People confident of the Buddha's teaching on emptiness will gain confidence in his teaching on things that are not directly perceptible.

6-10 (ET112-113) People fear the profound teaching because they are unintelligent, unaccustomed to it, or misled by other teachers.

11 (ET112-113) One loses less by rejecting moral behavior than by rejecting the right view of selflessness since moral conduct leads to rebirth in heaven but the right view leads to *nirvāṇa*.

12 (ET114-115) For some less intelligent people, teaching about the ego is better than teaching about selflessness, since motivated by concern for themselves they will avoid bad rebirths. But intelligent people who understand the teaching of selflessness proceed to the tranquility of *nirvāṇa*.

13-17 (ET114-115) Selflessness is the sole gateway to tranquillity, the sphere (*viṣaya*) of all the Buddhas, and terrifying to those who hold wrong views. Even though the Buddhas did not proclaim this teaching for the sake of argumentation, it terrifies opponents because it destroys their teachings just like fire destroys fuel. For those partial to other teachings, it becomes the door to their destruction.

18-22 (ET116-117) The Buddha's teachings are more subtle than those of the brahmins and naked ascetics, because ears apprehend the brahmins' recitation of scriptures, eyes apprehend how the ascetics torment their bodies, but mind apprehends Buddhist teachings. Moreover, the brahmins' religious practices are just an outward show and the ascetics' practices are mere stupidity! Though one might respect the brahmins' knowledge and pity the ascetics' pain, neither religious practice constitutes a valid norm (*dharma*) because both brahmin birth and the pain ascetics experience is the result of past karma.

23 (ET116-117) The Buddha's teaching is twofold: nonviolence constitutes *dharma*, and *nirvāṇa* is emptiness.

24-25 (ET116-117) People's partiality to their theses and their distress at defeat is criticized; an opponent's good arguments should be accepted.

## Chapter Thireen: Refutation of Sense Faculties and Their Objects[216]

1-4 (ET118-119) Āryadeva denies that the pot is directly perceptible because the entire pot is not perceived when just a part of the pot, e.g., its color, is perceived. The entire color also cannot be perceived because it has inner, outer, and middle parts.

5 (ET118-119) Matter can be broken down into its constituent parts but atoms also have parts. Since the atom itself still needs to be established, it cannot establish anything else without incurring the logical fallacy of question-begging (*sādhyasama*).

6 (ET118-119) If a thing can be both a part and a whole, it would follow that the syllable (*akṣara*), which makes up part of a statement, should convey the entire sense of that statement.

7 (ET120-121) Matter is twofold: shape (*saṃsthāna*) and color (*varṇa*). If shape and color are different, the visual organ, which apprehends the color, will be unable to perceive the shape. But if shape and color are not different, the tactile organ should be able to apprehend both shape and color.

8-9 (ET120-121) Earth and the other three elements cannot be apprehended apart from the matter derived from them, yet the visual sense faculty cannot perceive both the earth element and matter. Since the tactile organ apprehends earth's hardness, earth is just an object of touch.

10 (ET120-121) Since the quality color as a condition for the pot's perceptibility hasn't been established, the universal "perceptibility" doesn't exist.

11 (ET120-121) The eye and the ear are both derived matter but

they have separate functions. The eye sees; the ear doesn't.

12 (ET120-121) When the conditions that produce an awareness are incomplete, the awareness cannot precede perception. But if the awareness comes after the perception, it has no object. The awareness and perception are not simultaneous either.

13 (ET120-121) If the eye moves towards its object, it would take longer to perceive things at a distance than up close.

14 (ET122-123) If the eye moved after the visible object had been perceived, there would be no point in its having moved.

15 (ET122-123) If the eye perceives its object without moving towards it, nothing should be beyond its range; and there would be no reason to distinguish between things that are close by and things at a distance.

16 (ET122-123) Objection: The essential nature of things must be seen first in the things themselves.

Answer: Why doesn't the eye see itself?

17 (ET122-123) The perception of color/form/matter is questioned because the eye does not possess consciousness, consciousness does not possess perception, and color/form/matter does not possess either one.

18 (ET122-123) If the sound which makes the noise reaches the ear, why shouldn't it be considered the speaker? But if the sound, without making a noise, reaches the ear, why should confidence be placed in it?

19 (ET122-123) If the entire sound is heard after it reaches the ear, the beginning of the sound cannot be heard. But if the entire sound does not reach the ear, the entire sound cannot be heard.

20 (ET124-125) Sound cannot be called sound until it is heard; nor can something that is not sound be called sound.

21 (ET124-125) Perception does not result from contact between mind and object. After mind has come into contact with an object, it cannot act, since it has been separated from the other five sense faculties. Moreover, every time mind goes out to contact an object, the self must be left without a mind.

22-23 (ET124-125) Because the visual sense faculty first perceives the object which mind apprehends, this object, which is no longer present, seems like a mirage. Because the mental faculty arises in dependence on the five sense faculties and their objects, it has no real existence of its own and is like an illusion.

25 (ET124-125) The cycle of existence is compared to such insubstantial things as a firebrand's circle, a magical creation, a dream, an illusion, the moon reflected in water, vapor, an echo, a mirage, and a cloud.

## Chapter Fourteen: Refutation of Belief in Extreme Views[217]

1 (ET126-127) A thing that is not dependent upon something else does not exist anywhere.

2 (ET126-127) The pot and its color are neither identical nor different; nor is the color located in the pot or vice versa.

3 (ET126-127) Nyāya-Vaiśeṣika objection: Because of a difference in mark, the (substance) pot is different from (the universal) existence (*bhāva*).

Answer: No. It would follow that existence is different from the pot and the pot would be nonexistent.

4 (ET126-1270) If the pot is not one in number naturally, it cannot become one. Since there is no connection between dissimilar things, the (substance) pot is not connected with (the quality, viz. number)) one.

5 (ET126-127) When the substance possesses large size, its color should possess it also. But this contradicts the Nyāya-Vaiśeṣika tenet that qualities cannot possess other qualities. One's own doctrine can be asserted only if the opponent is not from a different school.

6 (ET128-129) The mark cannot establish the marked thing, and the marked thing cannot exist independently of its marks.

7 (ET128-129) It is impossible to predicate unity for the pot because it cannot be separated from its multiple marks; nor can there be multiple pots since pot is absent in each mark..

8 (ET128-129) The pot cannot be a combination of its constituent material qualities. There can be no connection between the tangible pot and the intangible color.

9 (ET128-129) Since the color is a part of the pot, it cannot be the pot as a whole. Since there is no whole, there is no part either.

10 (ET128-129) If all material qualities have the same indistinguishable property of being material, why should the pot-status apply only to one and not the others?

11 (ET128-129) Objection: Color is different from other material qualities such as taste but not from the pot.

Answer: Since the pot cannot exist independently of these material qualities, it also must be different from the color.

12 (ET130-131) Objection: The pot has no cause.

Answer: An effect cannot produce itself; for this reason, the pot does not exist independently of its material qualities.

13 (ET130-131) Objection: The pot is established by a cause.

Answer: That cause must be established by another cause. If the cause can't produce itself, it shouldn't be able to produce something else either.

14 (ET130-131) Even if the opponent assumes that qualities inhere in things, color cannot smell; the unity of such composite things (*samūha*) as the pot is impossible.

15 (ET130-131) The pot is dependent upon its material qualities in the same way as this material quality is dependent upon air and the other three elements of which it is comprised.

16-18 (ET130-133) Fire and fuel (=the other three elements) are interdependent. Fire is defined as something that is hot and fuel as something that is not hot. Because something that is not hot cannot burn, there is no so-called fuel. Without fuel, there is no fire either. If fuel becomes hot, it should become fire. But if it does not become hot, there is nothing else inside fire that is not hot. If the atom of fire does not possess fuel, fire will exist without fuel. But if the fire atom did possess fuel, it would not be one in nature.

19 (ET132-133) Unity and plurality are interdependent concepts. Since there are no things that are one in nature, there are no things that are plural in nature either.

20 (ET132-133) Āryadeva criticizes the Sāṃkhya thesis that material nature is one since there are three *guṇas* which comprise it.

21 (ET132-133) Intelligent people should analyze such theses as unity by applying the method of the *catuṣkoṭi*.

22 (ET132-133) People might say that permanent things exist if they perceive the series of factors in the wrong way, or say that a thing exists if they perceive the collection of causes and conditions in the wrong way.

23 (ET134-135) All things that have arisen in dependence, e.g., the aggregates, lack independent reality. Consequently, there is no essential nature.

24 (ET134-135) A thing cannot be a union without at the same

time being an effect. According to the noble ones, this kind of union is not a real union.

25 (ET134-135) Consciousness is the seed of the cycle of existence; sense objects are the sphere of its activity. When selflessness is perceived in all sense objects, this seed will cease.

Chapter Fifteen: The Refutation of Conditioned Things[218]

1-3 (ET134-137) Āryadeva criticizes the *asatkāryavāda* thesis since there can be no relation between the cause and its previously nonexistent effect if that effect, at the time of its origination, destroys the cause. He criticizes the *satkāryavāda* thesis since there is no need for the origination of something that already exists.

4 (ET136-137) Something that has its own nature, e.g., milk, cannot change and become something different, e.g., curds.

5 (ET136-137) Each mark--origination, duration, and cessation--depends on the other two.

6 (ET136-137) The essential nature or identity of a thing is determined in relation to something else that has a different nature. Because of the interdependence of one nature with another, nothing can be said to arise solely from itself or from something different.

7 (ET136-137) The mark does not arise before, after, or simultaneously with the marked thing.

8 (ET136-137) Something that has newly arisen in the past cannot change its nature and become old, nor can something that will newly arise in the future change its nature and become old.

9 (ET136-137) The present thing does not come into existence by itself, since cause and effect do not exist simultaneously, nor does it come into existence from a nonexistent cause, e.g., past or future.

10-13 (ET138-139) The marks of origination, duration, and cessation have no real existence and are like illusions. They cannot occur simultaneously because of their mutually incompatible natures, nor can they occur sequentially because each arises in dependence upon the other two. To suggest that each mark also contains within itself the secondary marks (*anulakṣaṇa*) of origination, duration, and cessation leads to difficulties in distinguishing one from another.

14-15 (ET138-139) Existent things and nonexistent things do not originate from causes like themselves or different from themselves.

16-24 (ET140-143) There is no origination of a thing in relation to the completed past, the uncompleted future, or a third intermediate state presently in the process of completion. A thing does not arise when it is presently in the process of arising because at that time it is only half-arisen. Alternatively, if past and future also are in the process of arising, it would follow that everything would be in the process of arising. The cessation of the process of arising does not produce a thing that has arisen because once something that has arisen exists, there is no further occurrence of the process of arising. The process of arising, moreover, is not the unarisen having arisen, for that is like saying that something which is nonexistent arises.

25 (ET142-143) Since cause and effect have no independent existence, both activity and inactivity have no substratum.

## Chapter Sixteen: The Discussion between Teacher and Student[219]

1 (ET142-143) All the preceding chapters refute the views of those who perceive empty things as if they were not empty.

2 (ET142-143) Objection: Since the disputant, his subject, and his assertions exist, it is wrong to say that everything is empty.

Answer: There is no intrinsic nature in any of these three things that could be the basis for their arising.

3-5 (ET142-145) The opponent (or the student assuming his role as the title suggests) claims that by discovering an error (*doṣa*) which refutes his adversary's thesis that things are empty, his own thesis that things are not empty is affirmed. Āryadeva responds in kind that the refutation of his opponent's thesis should establish his thesis of emptiness. But the opponents' theses of identity, difference, or indeterminability are not real theses because they cannot withstand critical analysis.

6 (ET144-145) Objection: In our system, which holds that a pot is directly perceptible, the thesis that it is empty is rejected.

Answer: Any reason (in argument) based upon beliefs held in the opponent's system is not valid when applied to other systems.

7-8 (ET144-145) Objection: How can something empty occur without something nonempty? A counterthesis must have a thesis opposed to it.

Answer: If anything could be a thesis, even what is not a thesis (i.e., emptiness) would have the appearance of a thesis. But since there is no nonthesis, there is no counterthesis either.

9 (ET144-145) To the opponent's contention that if things are nonexistent fire should not be hot, Āryadeva responds that the refutation of the relation between fire and heat is given above (at 14.16-17).

10 (ET144-145) If the thesis that a thing is nonexistent can refute the thesis that it is existent, once the error in all four positions (of the *catuṣkoṭi*) is rejected, what thesis will there be then?

11 (ET146-147) Even atoms cannot be characterized as having real existence.

12-13 (ET146-147) If all things are characterized as nondual nothing could have real existence because this distinction is based upon duality. Moreover, when all things are characterized as nonexistent, it is impossible to distinguish one from another, since a property that all possess cannot be the basis for discriminating among different substances.

14 (ET146-147) The opponent claims that the Madhyamakas cannot refute their opponent's theses because they deny the existence of real theses. Āryadeva responds that his opponent cannot prove his thesis either (the opponent's "own thesis" = the "Madhyamaka's opponent's thesis").

15 (ET146-147) Why, if Madhyamakas find it easy to refute others' theses, can't their opponents point out the error in Madhyamaka theses?

16 (ET148-149) If something exists simply because an opponent affirms its existence, why isn't it nonexistent simply because the Madhyamakas deny its existence?

17 (ET148-149) Objection: Since we employ the term "existing" there must be some existent thing to which this term refers.

Answer: The term itself is artificially created and thus not really existent.

18 (ET148-149) The claim that things referred to by ordinary language exist in a conventional sense cannot prove that these things really exist.

19-20 (ET148-149) The opponent suggests that the Madhyamakas' refutation of all things is nihilism. Āryadeva's reply stresses the interdependent establishMent of existent and nonexistent things.

21-22 (ET148-151) The opponent contends that the Madhyamakas' use of arguments and examples in debate implies that not all things are empty. Āryadeva replies that both the thesis and the argument are similarly empty and the argument, being the same as the thesis, cannot prove anything. Some examples, however, are more appropriate than others.

23 (ET150-151) The benefit of perceiving the emptiness of things lies in the destruction of the bondage caused by conceptual constructions.

24 (ET150-151) The ascription of existence to one thing and nonexistence to another is not in accord with either ultimate truth or the conventions of ordinary language.

25 (ET150-151) No criticism can be leveled against an opponent who does not hold any thesis, e.g., existence, nonexistence, both or neither.

## 49. ĀRYADEVA, **Śataka*

Summary by Karen C. Lang

The **Śata(ka)śāstra* (*Pai-lun*) exists only in Kumārajīva's Chinese translation. This translation includes a commentary by Vasu which closely resembles certain passages in the *Ta chih tu lun*.[220] Both the preface of Seng-chao and Chi-tsang's commentary indicate that Kumārajīva translated (in 404 C.E.) only 50 of Āryadeva's original 100 *sūtras*.[221] The authenticity of the **Śataka* has been questioned. But the *T'i p'o p'u sa chuan* states that Āryadeva wrote two works: the **Śataka* in twenty chapters and *Catuḥśataka*; and the 1Dan dkar ma catalog lists a text in 100 verses by Āryadeva extant in Tibet in the eighth century C.E. Although the **Śataka* and the *Catuḥśataka* discuss many of the same topics, the arrangement of the topics, the arguments used against the opponents' theses, and the length and style of these two texts differ.[222]

The work has been translated by G. Tucci (50.4.3)(our "T") in *Pre-Diṅnāga Texts on Buddhist Logic* (Gaekwad's Oriental Series XLIX, Baroda 1929.

## Chapter One: Renunciation of Demerit and Merit

1 (T3-9) Only the Buddha's teaching, summarized as the elimination of evil and cultivation of merit, is the right view. Against criticism of the Buddhist position on pleasure, Āryadeva replies that there is no satisfaction because experience shows that no object will invariably produce a satisfying response in all people. The mark of satisfaction is not inherently produced, like the taste of salt; neither is it produced by some other cause nor by itself and something else. He rejects the argument that something inherently satisfying can cause something frustrating by using the analogy of a lamp, which cannot illuminate itself and something else, viz., darkness, since marks like light and darkness (or satisfaction and frustration) cannot exist simultaneously. Further, the great power of frustration overcomes anything that is initially satisfying.

2 (T10-18) Objection: One should cultivate merit because it brings good results.

Answer: Giving is meritorious but it is taught to people of low ability; moral conduct is taught to people of middling ability, and knowledge to people of the highest ability. Giving or moral conduct undertaken for reward (e.g., wealth, a better rebirth) is inferior; inferior knowledge concerns worldly activities. The cultivation of merit and the rejection of evil is the teaching that involves activity but the renunciation of both merit and demerit is the teaching that involves withdrawal from activity. Merit should be rejected since it has a double nature and is not permanent; the merit from sacrifice especially should be rejected since it involves taking life.

3. (T19) When mind no longer focusses on the marks of past, present, or future *dharmas*, since none have a nature of their own--this is what is meant by knowledge of the signless.

## Chapter Two: Refutation of the Self

1 (T19-22) Sāṃkhya: Not all phenomena are empty and signless because the self exists and consciousness is its mark.

Answer: If consciousness is its mark, the self cannot be permanent because consciousness is caused and caused phenomena are impermanent. Consciousness cannot characterize the self since it is limited and the self is all-pervasive and should have the marks of consciousness and unconsciousness. If the opponent then claims that the power to become conscious is a latent force which the self possesses, brought about by a combination of causes, the response is the same: if the power and its possessor are not different, both will be caused and impermanent.

2 (T23-26) Nyāya-Vaiśeṣika: The self and awareness are different phenomena which become united.

Answer: The ability to know characterizes consciousness.

3 (T27-28) The self cannot be described as one if it is marked by consciousness since our conscious experiences are multiple and diverse.

4 (T28-31) Inference cannot prove the self. The opponent's example of fire existing in the ashes when there is no smoke does not prove his claim that the self exists when there is no conscious experience.

5 (T31-34) The claim that the self exists because color is perceived is challenged: If the self can see why doesn't it use ears instead of eyes? When the opponent replies that the relation between sense faculty and object is fixed, Āryadeva counters: The self doesn't have eyes and without eyes it must be blind!

Objection: The internal organ aids the self in perception.

Answer: What use is the self if the internal organ knows objects?

6 (T34-37) Objection: A permanent self is the basis for the memory of past experiences.

Answer: If the self is all-pervasive, everything must be remembered simultaneously.

## Chapter Three: Refutation of Identity

1 (T37-39) Objection: The substance pot and its marks *existence* and *unity* are one.

Answer: If the two are identical, it is impossible to determine that existence is located only in the pot. The pot and its mark *existence* are two things and the mark *two* should characterize the pot, not *one*.

2 (T40) The opponent objects that the pot exists because people see it and believe that it exists. Āryadeva responds that if existence is not somehow different from the thing that exists, things would not exist.

3 (T40-41) Objection: The pot is related to existence in the same way that parts (e.g., feet, head) are related to the whole (e.g., the body).

Answer: If the foot and the body are not different, the foot should not be different from the head either! If the parts were entirely different, no whole could be comprised of these unrelated parts.

4 (T41-42) Objection: The multiple material forms color, taste, etc. produce the pot as their one effect.

Answer: The pot is multiple and not one because the material forms that comprise it are multiple. Since the opponent has failed to prove that a single pot exists, the "forms" said to be the causes of this nonexistent effect also do not exist.

5 (T43) The claim that cause and effect are proven since they are mutually dependent like long and short is rejected because there is no real mark *long* that is present in something long, for some other cause is required to prove the mark *long*. Nor can the mark *long* be present in something short because this would be contradictory.

## Chapter Four: Refutation of Difference

1 (T430-46) If the pot and its marks *existence* and *unity* are different, then the pot is neither one nor existent.

2 (T47) If the mark *existence* establishes the marked thing then duality, not unity, is assumed.

3 (T47-49) The whole/part relationship is rejected on the same grounds as in Chapter III, except that there the opponent claims that atoms are the parts that make up a whole and that each atom has this creative power.

## Chapter Five: Refutation of Sense Perception

1 (T50-51) Āryadeva argues against the Nyāya-Vaiśeṣika thesis that awareness arises from the contact of the visual sense faculty, color and the mental faculty by analyzing the relation between knowledge and perception and between the sense faculty and its object. Awareness cannot arise prior to vision because it will have no cause; it cannot arise afterwards because it will have no function.

2 (E52-54) If the mental faculty moves out to contact the object,

the body will be left unconscious. Alternatively, if the mental faculty remains in the body, there will be no contact between the sense faculty and the object. Because the mental faculty cannot see, the visual sense faculty cannot know, and the object cannot do either one, how can perception occur?

## Chapter Six: Refutation of Sense Objects

1 (T54-57) The direct perception of the entire pot is not possible by perceiving one part, e.g., color. Direct perception of partless atoms is not possible either. Touch apprehends some parts of the pot, but Āryadeva questions how the tangible parts of the pot can unite with nontangible parts. Further, if the pot is something different from its tangible parts, how can it unite with them?

2 (T57-58) The four great elements are not directly perceptible.

3 (T58-59) Objection: Present objects are perceptible and present time must exist because the marks *old* and *new* are admitted.

Answer: Present time is not involved in calling something "old" or "new". When something arises it is called "new"; otherwise it is "old".

## Chapter Seven: Refutation of *Satkāryavāda*

1 (T59-63) Sāṃkhya: The effect pre-exists in its cause and is a transformation of its cause: cause and effect are one in substance.

Reply: This position is a form of eternalism. When nothing is impermanent, merit cannot replace evil and the future cannot replace the present. Āryadeva denies that the effect pre-exists in its cause even in subtle form.

2 (T64-65) An opponent objects that the effect pre-exists in its cause because specific causes produce specific effects. In reply, Āryadeva attacks the underlying premise of identity between cause and effect: if the effect and its cause exist together, both will perish together.

3 (T64) The Sarvāstivādin acceptance of a series of marks--origination, duration, cessation--supports the opposite view that the effect is nonexistent prior to its production because an effect which has an origin cannot pre-exist. To the charge that rejection of a pre-existent effect leads to nihilism, Āryadeva replies that because

continuity is admitted, the nihilist thesis is rejected, and because cessation is admitted, the eternalist thesis is rejected.

## Chapter Eight: Refutation of *Asatkāryavāda*

1 (T65-68) Āryadeva rejects the origination of an arisen or an unarisen effect, as well as one in the process of arising. Things do not originate either in a series or simultaneously.

2 (T69-72) Things do not originate from themselves, from something else, or from both. Because there is no relation between something which is the object of origination and the mark *origination* (*utpāda*), neither can be used to prove that the other exists, nor can they together be used to prove that any factor exists. Existent things do not originate from existent things, and nonexistent things do not originate from nonexistent things.

## Chapter Nine: Refutation of Permanence

1 (T72-74) Objection: Uncaused and permanent things--*ākāśa*, time, spatial direction, atoms, and *nirvāṇa*--must exist, since they have not been refuted. Because there are created things which are impermanent, there must be uncreated things which are permanent.

Answer: By the same logic, if created things are existent, uncreated things must be nonexistent!

2 (T74-76) Objection: *Ākāśa* is permanent, all-pervasive, partless, and the substratum of motion.

Answer: Space is not partless, an all-pervasive substratum, or permanent because it is divisible into parts.

3 (T76-78) Objection: Time is a permanent thing; it is not directly perceived but rather inferred from the seasons, etc.

Answer: Time is not a permanent thing with its own mark because each of its divisions--past, present, and future--depends on the others.

4 (T78-79) Nyāya-Vaiśeṣika: Spatial direction is a permanent thing.

Answer: It is not permanent because it has parts, e.g., the eastern direction.

5 (ET79-80) Nyāya-Vaiśeṣika: Atoms are permanent things.

Answer: Atoms are not entirely in contact with one another because the atomic size of a single atom, the cause, is not seen in the double atom, the effect. This partial contact indicates that atoms have parts separated by space and therefore atoms are not partless and not permanent.

6 (T80-81) Objection: *Nirvāṇa* is the permanent absence of the defilements.

Answer: *Nirvāṇa* would then be a condition.

7 (T81) The opponent claims that *nirvāṇa* is the efficient cause of the cessation of the defilements.

Answer: The cause of the defilements' cessation is not the same as the result of their cessation. On the other hand, if the opponent claims that *nirvāṇa* is the result of the nonexistence of the defilements, Āryadeva replies: If *nirvāṇa* were something different from the bond (= the defilements), the one bound, and the means of liberation, it could not arise from them. Further, *nirvāṇa* is not a place which a self or the aggregates can reach.

## Chapter Ten: Refutation of Wrong Views of Emptiness

1 (T82) The opponent argues that since Madhyamakas use negation some things, e.g., negations, etc., must exist. On the other hand, if the Madhyamakas deny that their negation is real, the things which it is supposed to negate must exist. Āryadeva replies that the negation is the same as the things negated, i.e., empty.

2 (T83-85) Objection: The refutation of an opponent's thesis proves one's own.

Answer: A thesis that affirms and one that refutes are not the same. The opponent objects that Madhyamaka tenets are contrary to world opinion. Āryadeva denies that this is so.

3 (T85) The opponent objects that the Madhyamakas' denial that they hold a thesis is in fact a thesis. Āryadeva replies that what is not a thesis should not be called a thesis, just as nonexistence is not called existence.

4 (T86) Objection: Things exist because they are mutually established.

Answer: How is mutual establishment possible when one of the related things doesn't exist? The opponent argues that, like *long* and *short*, things establish one another.

5 (T86-87) Objection: Your negation is not valid because it is empty.

Answer: Although empty of any essential nature, things bind.

6 (T87-88) The opponent claims that if emptiness exists, all speech, including Buddhist teachings, should also be empty. Āryadeva responds that Buddhist teachings are effective because they are expressed in ordinary language. When the opponent objects that worldly truth is not real, Āryadeva replies that both truths are real because each depends on the other.

7 (T88-89) Objection: What benefit is there in knowing this?

Answer: Liberation results from repudiating factors, as well as from repudiating the self.

## 50. ĀRYADEVA, *Akṣaraśataka* and *Ṭīkā* thereon

Summary by Karen C. Lang

The Chinese tradition attributes the verses to Āryadeva and the commentary to an unnamed student of Āryadeva's; the Tibetan tradition attributes both text and commentary to Nāgārjuna. The *Akṣaraśataka* examines in much the same manner material treated in the **Śataka* and the *Catuḥśataka*, and Āryadeva is likely its author. The commentary's organization of the material follows an order similar to the commentary on the **Śataka* II-X.

"T" references are to Gokhale (50.1.1).[223]

### 1. Things Are Not Identical

(T4) A Sāṃkhya opponent claims that because all things have an identical mark, the nature of such things as pot and cloth is identical.

Answer: A reason (*hetu)* must support the thesis. If the opponent contends that singularity constitutes the mark, this claim cannot serve as a reason because it is the same as what is to be proved (*sādhyasama*); and if duality exists it defeats the thesis of identity.

## 2. Things Are Not Different

(T4-5) A Vaiśeṣika opponent claims that things are different because they have different marks.

Answer: Differences in mark cannot serve as the reason for the thesis of difference because it is the same as what is to be proved. Even if the marks are different, the thesis is not proved, for if the opponent says that this and that mark are not the same, each mark is specific (*viśeṣa*) and individual things so marked are themselves one in nature.

## 3. Existence Must Be Proved

(T5-6) Objection: Things exist because we see that they have the mark *existence* and flowers in the sky do not.

Answer: Either the reason has the mark of existence or the mark of nonexistence. If it has the mark of existence, this is the same as what is to be proved, since both the mark of direct perception and the mark of existence must be proved. The alternative defeats the thesis.

## 4. There Is No Cause

(T6-7) Objection: Things exist because they have causes.

Answer: If the effect pre-exists in the cause, clay is not the cause of the pot's existence because it already exists. But if the effect is nonexistent in the cause, there is still no cause for the pot since it does not exist. The example, viz., sand is not the cause of oil, implies that cause and effect are not random relations. The claim that the effect both exists and does not exist in its cause incurs the fallacies of both theses. Further, if a thing is produced without a cause, the cause has no function; this last alternative defeats the thesis.

## 5. Things are Dependent

(T7) The opponent claims that because of causal efficacy (*śakti*) both cause and effect should be admitted.

Answer: Both cause and effect depend on each other. Causality applies to a cause because it has an effect. Because of this interdependence of cause and effect, it follows that causality applies also to the effect. Since the effect has causality, it is a cause and not an effect. Without effects, there are no causes. Such causes as primal nature (*prakṛti*), God, atoms, space, and time are interdependent causes and are not permanent.

### 6. A Thesis Is Not Proved by Tenets Which The Opponent Accepts

(T7-8) The opponent cannot use arguments based on tenets of his own school to prove his theses.

### 7. The Reason Is Ineffective

(T8-9) The opponent argues that no causes produce nonexistent things, e.g., a barren woman's son. But causes regularly produce certain effects, e.g., sesame produces oil.

Answer: The opponent must state the *hetu*, *sapakṣa* and *vipakṣa* to prove the thesis of causality. Yet when the thesis is stated, the reason is not present because it has not yet been stated; when the reason is stated, the thesis has ceased being stated. The simultaneity of the thesis and the reason is not possible, for when one says "*pra*", the "*ti*" and "*jñā*" are not uttered. Thus reasons are ineffective in establishing the thesis of causality, just as causes are ineffective in producing a eunuch's son.

### 8. The Nature Of A "Self" Must Be Explained

(T9) The opponent claims that the self exists and is challenged to state its nature. If the essential nature of the self is consciousness, the self is not permanent because consciousness is not permanent. If the essential nature of the self is unconsciousness, the unconscious self cannot experience pleasure or pain. The opponent now argues that the self becomes conscious when it is connected with consciousness. The Buddhist replies that because consciousness is then connected with this unconscious self it should become unconscious.

9. There Is Error In Identity

(T9) The opponent argues for identity because the pot is not different from the marks *existence* and *one*.

Answer: If the pot without its marks is not the pot, the marks *existence* and *one* must be the pot and the pot must be multiple in nature and not one. Furthermore, if one, existence, and the pot are identical, existence and one should be destroyed when the pot is destroyed, just as the *kara* (a word meaning hand) is destroyed when the *hasta* (another word meaning hand) is destroyed.

10. If There Is Difference, The Thing is Nonexistent

(T9-10) The Vaiśeṣika opponent argues for difference because the pot and its marks are different. The pot, the number one, and existence are not confused because substances, qualities, motions, universals, individuators, and inherence are different things; e.g., the pot is a substance, the number one is a quality, and existence is a universal.

Answer: If the pot is separate from existence, it doesn't exist. We see that the sword and its sheath are different things, but because we cannot see the pot and its marks separately their difference is not proved.

11. The Five Senses Do Not Apprehend Their Objects

(T10) The opponent claims that through direct perception the pot is seen, whereas nonexistent things, e.g., flowers in the sky, are never seen. The Buddhist denies that the pot is seen by mounting an attack on the sense faculties' ability to perceive an object. Either the eye or the internal organ/mind (*manas*) must see the pot. If the eye sees it, the eyes of a dead man should see it also! If the mind sees it, a blind man should see it!

12. Color Is A Name; The Colored Thing Also Is Not Perceived

(T10-11) The opponent now argues that the pot is seen because its color is seen.

Answer: The pot and the color must be identical or different. If they are identical, the pot should be seen when that color is seen. Furthermore, if the pot and its color are identical, when the pot is destroyed, the color would be destroyed also. But if they are different, the pot cannot be visible. In response to the opponent's claim that the pot exists because it is visible, the Buddhist argues that when the pot is located in a place obstructed from vision it is invisible and then it should not exist.

## 13. What Exists Is Not The Object of Action

(T11) The opponent claims that the cause pre-exists in subtle and imperceptible form in its cause. After it arises, it becomes gross and can be perceived.

Answer: If it already exists there is no need for an agent to bring it into existence. Further, if the effect pre-exists in the cause it is not a future thing. If there is no future thing there is no origination and destruction. Without origination and destruction there is no good and evil. Without good and evil there is no agent, action, demerit, merit, fruit and maturation. Moreover, if the effect which pre-exists in the cause is subtle, it is not gross. It is this gross effect, which does not pre-exist in the cause, that arises; the origination of a previously nonexistent effect contradicts your explanation of causality.

## 14. Things Do Not Have Origination

(T11-12) The opponent claims that his thesis, that the effect which is nonexistent in the cause arises, avoids the error of denying origination and cessation.

Answer: If the pot is nonexistent in the clay, it is like tortoise hair, which cannot be woven. Neither a pre-existent effect nor a previously nonexistent effect arises. The already arisen doesn't arise because it has already arisen; the unarisen doesn't arise because it has not yet arisen. Moreover, it is wrong that a body originates by itself or from something else. If it is self-originated, what's the point of origination? If it's not self-originated, how can it originate from something else? The claim that it originates by itself and from something else is also wrong. Consequently, all things lack origination.

## 15. Conditioned Things Do Not Exist

(T12-13) Objection: If there is no origination, conditioned things do not exist, since the three marks origination, duration and cessation characterize conditioned things.

Answer: Neither conditioned things nor their marks exist. The three marks do not exist sequentially because it is wrong that when one exists, the other two do not. They cannot be simultaneous either, for if there is cessation where there is origination, origination is not origination. Since the marks *origination* and *cessation* are mutually incompatible, they cannot exist at the same time. Nor is it possible that origination, being a conditioned thing itself, has these three marks, because this would lead to an infinite regress of marks.

## 16. Unconditioned Things Do Not Exist

(T13-14) The opponent argues that the negation of conditioned things establishes the existence of unconditioned things; and if unconditioned things exist, their opposites, conditioned things, must also exist. He cites space (*ākāśa)* as an example of an unconditioned thing, and describes it as all-pervasive and partless.

Answer: Space either has parts or it doesn't. If it has parts, the space must remain confined within the limits of the body that contains it. If it doesn't have parts, either the body pervades space or vice versa. In either case, space has limits, and like other limited things, e.g., pot, space is impermanent. Moreover, permanent causes should produce permanent effects; if the effect is impermanent, its cause should be impermanent.

Objection: There are two kinds of causes: instrumental causes (*kāraṇahetu*) and manifesting causes (*vyañjakahetu*). Instrumental causes produce impermanent things, e.g., a pot. Manifesting causes reveal things already present, e.g., a lamp's light reveals the pot. Because these revealed things are not created, they are permanent.

Answer: We see that created things exist but not uncreated things. Since they do not exist, uncreated things are not permanent.

### 17. Things Are Like Dreams

(T14-15) The comparison of things to dreams means that they exist on a conventional level. A dream is not substantially existent, it is not nonexistent, and it is not uncaused; the same description applies to such things as houses constructed from beams.

### 18. The Name (Or Mark) Doesn't Exist

Answer: The name is not the thing. If names were the thing, the name "pot" should contain milk, etc. Just by saying the name a pot should appear without any effort by the potter! The name is just conventional, not real.

### 19. It Is The Same As What Is To Be Proved

(T15) Objection: Does what you refute have an essential nature or not? If it has, your thesis is negated. But if it hasn't, it cannot be refuted because it has no essential nature.

Answer: The refutation, the thing refuted, and the person making the refutation are interdependent. We refute your thesis that essential nature is the mark of things. If there is no nature that exists by virtue of itself, there is nothing for us to refute.

## 51.AUTHOR UNKNOWN, *Tathāgatotpattisambhavanirdeśasūtra*[224]

## 52. UPAŚĀNTA, *Abhidharmahṛdaya*[225]

Charles Willemen says that this author "must have lived between the time of the five hundred arhats in Kaśmīr (second century A.D.)" (which are mentioned more than once) "and the time of Dharmatrāta, author of the *Saṃyuktābhidharmahṛdaya* (fourth century)", who mentions Upaśānta. He was a master of Gāndhāra.[226] Willemen reports that the stanzas of Upaśānta's text are the same as those of Dharmatrāta's work by the same name (#21 of Volume Seven of this Encyclopedia), but that the commentary is more detailed.[227]

53. AUTHOR UNKNOWN, *Śatasāhasrikāprajñāpāramitā*[228]

This text, along with 54 and 55 below, "are really one and the same book. They only differ in the extent to which the 'repetitions' are copied out."[229] The *Śatasāhasrikā*--meaning 100,000 lines--is extant in Sanskrit, Chinese and Tibetan manuscripts. It consists of three parts: the first part is "an expansion of Chapter I of the *Aṣṭasāhasrikāprajñāpāramitā*"[230] with new items added; the second "follows *Aṣṭa* chapters 2 to 18 fairly closely";[231] and the third "is an independent treatise...throughout concerned with the obvious conflict that exists between an ontology which proclaims the emptiness of everything, and the practical needs of the struggle for enlightenment."[232]

54. AUTHOR UNKNOWN, *Pañcaviṃśatiprajñāpāramitā*

A portion of this work--25,000 lines--has been discovered among the Gilgit mss., and some other passages are preserved in Sanskrit. The work is available in Chinese and Tibetan. The Chinese translations date from the third to the seventh century A.D.[233]

55.AUTHOR UNKNOWN, *Aṣṭādaśasāhasrikāprajñāpāramitā*[234]

There remains no complete Sanskrit manuscript of this work--18,000 lines. Gilgit manuscripts of portions have been edited.

56. AUTHOR UNKNOWN, *Ṣaṇmukhidhāraṇī*[235]

Summary by Stefan Anacker

This small text which includes a *dhāraṇī* (*mantra*) consisting of feminine vocatives, is termed by later Tibetan classification a text of the Sautrāntikas. There is, however, not much to support this view. It seems a fully Mahāyāna text with a focus on the path of *bodhisattvas*.

The Six Doors

(1) The sufferings which I have felt in *saṃsāra* are felt by all sentient beings indiscriminately.

(2) The worldly success and happiness which I have experienced

should be experienced by all sentient beings.

(3) My bad actions and the roots of the badness within me should be confessed in an ultimate confession.

(4) The acts of Māra against me should be known by an ultimate comprehension.

(5) My roots of goodness, joined with the perfections whether worldly or supramundane, should be experienced by all sentient beings.

(6) My liberation should serve that of all sentient beings. May I be established in neither *saṃsāra* nor *nirvāṇa*.

### 57. AUTHOR UNKNOWN, *Jinaputrārthasiddhisūtra*[236]

### 58. AUTHOR UNKNOWN, *Kṣemaṃkaraparipṛcchāsūtra*[237]

### 59. AUTHOR UNKNOWN, *Mahālālikaparipṛcchāsūtra*[238]

### 60. AUTHOR UNKNOWN, *Nāgaropamāsūtra*[239]

### 61. AUTHOR UNKNOWN, *Nandopanandanāgarājasūtra*[240]

### 62. AUTHOR UNKNOWN, *Puṣpakūṭadhāraṇīsūtra*[241]

### 63. AUTHOR UNKNOWN, *Tathāgatajñānamudrā(samādhi)sūtra*[242]

### 64. AUTHOR UNKNOWN, *Vatsasūtra*[243]

### 65. AUTHOR UNKNOWN, *Tathāgatapratibimbapratiṣṭhānasūtra*[244]

### 66. AUTHOR UNKNOWN, *Surataparipṛcchāsūtra*[245]

## MĀTṚCEṬA

Summaries by Christian Lindtner

Mātṛceṭa, a pupil of Āryadeva, Nāgārjuna's personal student, was a contemporary of a certain Kuṣāṇa king Kaniṣka (there are at least three known *mahārājas* of that name). Besides the works treated below, one should mention *Praṇidhānasaptati*[246] and *Caturviparyayakathā*, which, like several passages in the works of Nāgārjuna and Āryadeva, deals, in thirty-one stanzas, with the four misconceptions, i.e., the fundamental evil of ignorance. Mātṛceṭa is often mentioned or quoted in later literature, e.g., in the *Mahāprajñāpāramitopadeśa*, the Chinese translation of which, by Kumārajīva, was completed in 406 A.D.

### 67. *Mahārājakaniṣkalekha*

(The work is edited by M. Hahn, Bern 1992. It is composed of 85 verses. )

The king, addressed as "god" (*deva*), is encouraged to practise virtues (*guṇa*), like a god, and to avoid immoral vices (*doṣa*). The common people will remain loyal to him when they also accumulate good karma in this way. Rebirth (*saṃsāra*) is suffering, and the only thing that counts is one's good or bad actions. One must never cause harm to other living beings, but rather show compassion towards them.

### 68.*Varṇārhavarṇa* or *Catuḥśataka*

(This hymn has been edited by Jens-Uwe Hartmann, Gottingen 1987, and is addressed to the Buddha. It is probably earlier than 69.*Śatapañcāśatka*, and consists of twelve chapters totalling 386 stanzas. )

The virtues of the Buddha are so numerous and so profound that it is impossible to praise him adequately. He is simply incomparable. Nevertheless, it is a matter of great virtue to spend one's time praising what cannot really be praised! And so the Buddha is praised with devotion (*bhakti*) for being omniscient, compassionate, an *arhat*, the most precious of all jewels, the most beautiful of all beings, the greatest ascetic, the knower of the Vedas and Vedāṅgas, the teacher of the world, a lion among men, a man of racial purity (*ājāneya*), the best among physicians, the originator of gain and security (i.e., happiness, *yogakṣema*, cf. *Bhagavadgītā* 9.22), the most perfectly pure, the one whose soul has developed into emptiness, who is absolutely free, the most beautiful sight to be seen, the one who has two bodies, the one whose actions are absolutely pure, who is silent, the master of the world, the best among bipeds, the eye and the light of the world, the guru of gurus without a guru, the one to be praised by all, etc. etc. What, in short, is more reasonable to do than to bow down in adoration of the Buddha? Furthermore, the Buddha has the thirty-two major and the eighty minor marks of a true superman. He belongs to the pure Aryan race like all the other Buddhas.[247] His beautiful body shines upon the world like the sun, and he has a complete knowledge of all *dharmas*. He is the best among living beings, just as freedom is the best kind of purity, emptiness the best among truths, and patience the best kind of austerity. He, of course, has the ten cognitive powers (*bala*) and the four convictions (*vaiśāradya*) so characteristic of all Buddhas.

Chapters 5-7 provide us, as it were, with a small compendium of the Buddhist "art of speech", i.e. rhetoric or religious oratory. The words of the Buddha are pure, i.e. they are clear, persuasive and consistent, they are not repetitious, ambiguous or contradictory. Avoiding disputes (*avivāda*) he refutes his opponents by good arguments (*nyāya*) and proofs (*upapatti*). Moreover, his speech is in accordance with the two truths. It is neither too sweet nor rude. It is not partial and not intemperate. It is encouraging, not contemptuous. It is to the point, sometimes brief, sometimes detailed. It is harmonious, free, rich, never vain. Without confusing the issues it is full of marvels, captivating, not colored but bright and unresistable, penetrating and incomprehensible for ordinary folk. For a good man, however, it is like nectar. In the relative sense, karmic purity and impurity are simple facts. In the ultimate sense, however, in emptiness, there is no "soul" or agent responsible for karma.

That all factors are empty, that things are momentary, that *nirvāṇa* is peace, are dharmic facts beyond dispute. Why should the Buddha who knows the truth engage himself in a dispute with the world which does not know the truth? The difference between the Buddha's *dharma* and that of others is simply enormous! His is true and pure, that of others false and impure. However, if we choose to allegorise (*anuvāda*) the Veda we can say that the Buddha corresponds to Brahmā, his Dharma to Brahman, and a Buddhist to a true Brāhmaṇa, priest or theologian. The three main Vedic metres are even expressed in the Buddhist *pratītyasamutpāda*!

The Buddha has made the path to *nirvāṇa* into a royal highway that even children and women can follow. In *saṃsāra* he makes a distinction between good and bad factors. Good karma brings about happiness in life. After enlightenment, in *nirvāṇa*, however, when one is a Buddha, there is, in a sense, neither good nor bad karma. Still the Buddha, through his great compassion, does everything he can to help all suffering beings out of *saṃsāra* by opening the glorious road that leads to immortality. Some follow the path of Śrāvakas, others that of Pratyekabuddhas, others that of Mahāyāna. With his great compassion he embraces the entire world, as it were. He is the leader and good friend of all living beings. His generosity towards all is in fact so great that one can only praise him as one who can never be repaid for all the good he has done.

In two chapters (10 and 11) Mātṛceṭa praises the beauty of the Buddha's physical body: his deep blue eyes, his lips, his teeth, his hair, etc. No less than thirty-three verses are composed in praise of the "great tongue" of the Buddha. In it Mātṛceṭa saw the personification or rather *embodiment* of Sarasvatī, the Indian goddess of speech. After all, no tongue, no teaching!

To conclude: There is no "field" of merit in the three worlds as pure as that of the Buddha, whose compassion has brought him from his peace in *nirvāṇa* into the impermanence and suffering of *saṃsāra*. Buddhism is not what it used to be when the Lord was still here. Turning away in defeat from this life one should carefully keep in mind the *parinirvāṇa* of the Buddhas (all thirty-five). (A final chapter 13, only in Tibetan, may well be authentic, but hardly contains anything new.)

### 69. *Śatapañcāśatka* or *Prasādapratibhodbhava*

(This work has been edited by D.R. Shackleton Bailey, Cambridge 1951.)

The theme is the same as in the previously summarized work (68). The Buddha has no faults at all in thought, word or deed, and his virtues simply range beyond calculation. Still, it brings merit to praise them! He has the six perfections leading to enlightenment, he is incomparable, his wonders are worthy of praise, and so is the beauty of his body, his great compassion, his speech, and his teaching. One should praise his previous vows: to listen to him brings satisfaction, to see him brings tranquillity, his speech refreshes, and his teaching liberates. Likewise, he deserves praise for compassionately offering all living beings guidance. His arduous deed should be praised, and so should his skill in expedients. One can never hope to make recompense to the Buddha for all the good things he has done by means of his spiritual and physical body. Still, it is, as said, a very good thing for oneself and perhaps also for others to celebrate "not even a part of a fraction" of his virtues.[248]

## 70. UDBHAṬASIDDHASVĀMIN, *Viśeṣastava*

Summary by Christian Lindtner

(One of the earliest hymns of Mahāyāna to extol the virtues of the Bhagavat Buddha and, at the same time, to condemn the vices of rival religious teachers is the rather neglected *Viśeṣa-* or *Viśiṣṭa-stava* of Udbhaṭasiddhasvāmin. His date is uncertain: according to Tāranātha he lived shortly after Kaniṣka, which would mean that he roughly belongs to the same milieu as Nāgārjuna and Mātṛceṭa. The contents of this hymn, in seventy-six (or seventy-seven) verses, in praise of the virtues of the Buddha that distinguish him from others (hence the title), point in the same direction. There is an excellent edition of the Tibetan with a German translation by Johannes Schneider: *Der Lobpreis der Vorzüglichkeit des Buddha. Udbhaṭasiddhasvāmins Viśeṣastava mit Prajñāvarmans Kommentar*, Bonn 1993.)

1-3. It is because most people do not recognize faults as faults that they, instead of recognizing the virtues of the Bhagavat (Buddha), naively believe in Kṛṣṇa (Viṣṇu), Īśvara etc.

4-12. But, as many well-known legends show, Mahādeva (Śiva) was full of anger and desire, he was vulnerable to harm and deception--as opposed to the Buddha.

13-16. Brahman and the other gods imagine that they have created the world, not being aware that it is in fact created by karma.

17-18. As opposed to others the Buddha has only sacrificed himself, not other living creatures.

19-22. He never curses other people, only their ignorance and desire; and he does not contradict himself, or merely repeat what others have said, like Vyāsa.

23-27. As opposed to Vedic words those of the Buddha's lion's roar are not at all secret! Followers of Sāṃkhya, Vaiśeṣika and Jainism are often lustful, exclusive or too much devoted to external *tapas*, respectively, and as opposed to the Buddhists. The *tārkikas* have not realized the doctrine of emptiness of substances.

28-29. Śuka, as opposed to his teacher Janaka, was liberated by going through the disc of the sun. The Buddhists follow *their* teacher, and are liberated where they are.

30-41. Further examples of gods and heroes who were dominated by their wives, or who caused harm to or deceived others, or have otherwise, again as opposed to *the* Bhagavat, behaved inappropriately.

42. The priests think that good and bad karma can be transferred to others, but the Buddha knows that only oneself is responsible for one's own karma.

43-45. The followers of Sāṃkhya, Vaiśeṣika and Jainism respectively think that the soul has consciousness, lacks consciousness, or that it has the same size as the body; but the Buddha has refuted all these notions.

46. Nor does he, like the priests, accept a permanent soul.

47-49. Kapila has no compassion, he did not understand that people are reborn due to their vices and karma, and he (and others) believed that even the liberated soul could be the cause of existence (rebirth).

50-53. Other misunderstandings not shared by the Buddha: that liberation is related to movement, that building gardens, etc. is evil, that life moves from one body to another, that one gets a good rebirth if killed by a furious enemy in battle.

54-56. The Buddha condemns incest (*agamyāgamana*), he is never armed, he is no terrorist.

57-60. He is omniscient, his words are never contradictory, he preaches to all who wish to listen, he is free from passion.

61. The sensual cognition of Kapila cannot bring about liberation.

62. The idea that one can transfer one's good karma to other living beings is *only* to be found in Mahāyāna.

63-64. Again, the Buddha strongly condemns bloody sacrifices.

65. His good *dharma* is one of truth, honesty, *brahmacarya*,

discipline and love.

66-70. The Buddha treats his enemies with compassion, as opposed to Kṛṣṇa, etc.

71-76. The more one contemplates the folly of the opponents the stronger one's faith. It corresponds to Mātṛceṭa's *prasāda* in the omniscient Buddha. To proclaim his virtues is good not merely for oneself but, hopefully, also for all others!

## 71. RĀHULABHADRA, *Prajñāpāramitāstotra*

David Seyfort Ruegg[249] provides a thorough account of what is known or can be conjectured about this writer. He is cited in various places as a teacher of Nāgārjuna, in various other places as a disciple of Nāgārjuna.[250] He is credited with a commentary on Nāgārjuna's 33.*Mūlamadhyamakakārikās*, which is said to have been translated into Chinese by Paramārtha, but is not available now. He also composed a hymn in twenty verses to the 103.*Saddharmapuṇḍarīka*. The text has been edited by R. Hikata and translated by Edward Conze.[251]

### Summary by David Seyfort Ruegg[252]

"In the *Prajñāpāramitāstotra* the *prajñāpāramitā* is described as beyond dichotomizing conceptualization (*nirvikalpa*) and discursive development (*niṣprapañca*). Rāhulabhadra writes: He who sees thee as thou really art (or: devotedly)[253] sees the *tathāgata*. The Buddhas are thy beloved sons, and thou art thus the tender progenetrix of all Heroes devoted to the weal of others. Though one, thou are praised under various appellations by the *tathāgatas*, who thus make thee accessible to their disciples. Also when thou are reached, faults and disputes raised by polemicists vanish. Thus thou terrifiest the foolish whilst thou comfortest the wise. Not coming from anywhere and not going anywhere, thou are not made into an object of perception (*anupalabhyase*) by the wise; however, those who see thee not but do truly (or devotedly, *bhavatas*) take recourse to thee are released as soon as they have done so: this is a great marvel! By the protectors of the world (*lokanātha*) who, for the sake of conventional communication (*prajñaptyartha*) with incarnate beings, adopt transactional linguistic usage (*vyavahāra*), thou are expressed out of compassion--without being (really thus) expressed. Indeed, who is able to praise thee who art without phenomenal mark (*nirnimitta*) and pure (*nirañjana*), who transcendest the entire realm of words, and who art not fixed anywhere? However, we who have praised thee who art not to be praised according to convention (*saṃvṛti*) are fulfilled through verbal expressions."

## 72. KUMĀRALĀTA

Kumāralāta is an important teacher prior to Asaṅga and Vasubandhu to whom they both refer but whose works have not been found. According to Jean Przyluski[254] Kumāralāta was the founder of the Dārṣṭāntika sect, and his followers included 126.Harivarman and 158.Śrīlāta. Junsho Kato[255] has collected references to Kumāralāta found in various places. He is said to have written two works, one titled *Kie man louen,* translated as *Dṛṣṭāntapaṅkti,* the other *Koueng chouo p'i yu* or *Dṛṣṭāntamālya,*[256] apparently lost. The former work may be the same as a work titled *Kalpanāmaṇḍatikā,* which is ascribed to Kumāralāta in the colophon found in a fragment, and is the same work as the *Sūtrālaṃkāra* ascribed to Aśvaghoṣa.[257] Kato and others believe Kumāralāta was Śrīlāta's teacher, but this is not absolutely clear. Przyluski thinks Kumāralāta composed the *Sūtrālaṃkāra* regularly attributed to Aśvaghoṣa. Given this multitude of conflicting opinion we place Kumāralāta here chronologically as Harivarman's teacher, but with little conviction.

## 73. AUTHOR UNKNOWN, *Akṣayamatinirdeśa*sūtra[258]

Summary by Leslie S. Kawamura

Akṣayamati's discourse concerns eighty inexhaustible topics. 1. The first occurrence of an enlightenment mind.[259] 2. Earnest intention. 3. The linking-up phase. 4. Aspiration. 5. Perfection of giving. 6. Perfection of ethical behavior. 7. Perfection of endurance. 8. Perfection of endeavour. 9. Perfection of meditation. 10. Perfection of discriminating awareness. 11. Friendliness. 12. Loving-kindness. 13. Sympathetic joy. 14. Equanimity. 15-19. Five supersensible cognitions. 20-23. Four factors of attracting (people). 24-27. Four detailed and accurate knowledges. 28-31. Four supports of confidence. 32-33. The two preparations of merit and knowledge. 34-37. Four sustained attentivenesses. 38-41. Four correct exertions. 42-45. Four footholds for higher cognition. 46-50. Five powers. 51-55. Five strengths. 56-62. Seven adjuncts to enlightenment. 63-70. The noble eightfold path. 71-72. Calm and extraordinary seeing. 73-74. Unfailing memory and eloquent speech. 75-78. Four axioms of the teaching. 79. The only path to walk. 80. Expertise concerning appropriate action.

## 74. AUTHOR UNKNOWN, *Aṅgulimālikāsūtra*[260]

## 75. AUTHOR UNKNOWN *Aśokadattavyākaraṇasūtra*[261]

## 76. AUTHOR UNKNOWN, *Aśokarājāvadānasūtra*[262]

## 77. AUTHOR UNKNOWN, *Aṣṭabuddhakasūtra*[263]

## 78. AUTHOR UNKNOWN, *Bhadrakalpikasamādhisūtra*[264]

It "extolls the thousand Buddhas in the present age (Bhadrakalpa), and enjoins the practice of 84,000 Perfections (*pāramitās*)."[265]

## 79. AUTHOR UNKNOWN, *Bhadramāyākāravyākaraṇasūtra*[266]

Summary by Constantin Regamey

"The anecdotal contents of the sūtra are constituted by the story of the juggler Bhadra who wanted to deceive the Buddha with magical tricks in order to prove that the claim of the Tathāgata to omniscience was false. He created a magical feast in a rubbish hole and invited the Buddha with his monks. The Buddha saw through this stratagem, but performed such a magic that Bhadra could not revoke his charms, was obliged to acknowledge the superiority of the Buddha and was converted..."

"Sections 79-121 are unconnected with the principal subject of the sūtra. They contain the enumeration of the *dharmas* which characterize a Bodhisattva,...belong mostly to the category of practical features or duties of the Bodhisattvas."[267]

### 80. AUTHOR UNKNOWN, *Buddhasaṃgītisūtra*[268]

### 81. AUTHOR UNKNOWN, *Candraprabhākumārasūtra.*[269]

### 82. AUTHOR UNKNOWN, *Caturdārakasamādhisūtra*[270]

### 83. AUTHOR UNKNOWN, *Daśabhūmikāsūtra*[271]

The work describes in detail the ten stages (*daśabhūmi*) of a Bodhisattva. A Bodhisattva is possessed of (1) delight (*pramudita*) arising from committing himself to ten vows under ten fundamental descriptions while renouncing all worldly wealth and pleasures and tisatyanirdeitaspractising ten virtues, (2) purity (*vimala*) in virtue of his morality of speech and conduct, (3) being a maker of light (*prabhākari*) through his realization of fundamental Buddhist truths about impermanence and non-egoity, and by his commitment to saving others from afflictions which he attains by mastering the four meditative stages and mystic trances. The Bodhisattva is (4) brilliant (*arciṣmati*) through his practice of the thirty-seven allies of enlightenment, (5) very difficult to conquer (*sudurjaya*), having mastered the ten purifications of awareness; he realizes that all factors are empty, yet studies carefully all sorts of subject-matters in order to gain the truth, (6) facing forward (*abhimukhi*) in virtue of his wisdom, (7) hard to measure (*dūraṅgama*), ceaselessly contemplating emptiness, signlessness and aimlessness, (8) immovable (*acala*) since nonretrogressing, he helps all by endowing them with visions of his wondrousness and does not enter *nirvāṇa* but remains to help all others, (9) possessing goodness (*sādhumati*), he has the knowledge of disciples, those self-enlightened, the Bodhisattvas and the Tathāgata himself, (10) the cloud of *dharma*. Having arrived at the summit he "puts out the flame of the afflictions produced by ignorance...His knowledge *qua* virtue of perfection becomes predominant..."[272]

Hirakawa points out that "in this text, the last of the six perfections, the perfection of wisdom, was expanded by adding four new aspects to it--skill in means (*upāya*), vows (*praṇidhāna*), strength (*bala*), and knowledge (*jñāna*), making a new total of ten perfections."[273]

### 84. AUTHOR UNKNOWN, *Daśādigandhakāravidhvaṃsaṇasūtra*[274]

### 85. AUTHOR UNKNOWN, *Garbhāvakrāntinirdeśasūtra*[275]

### 86. AUTHOR UNKNOWN, *Hastikākṣayasūtra*[276]

According to Nakamura this is a "Meditation Sūtra...Meditation was regarded as endowed with some miraculous power. For example, the *Hastikākṣaya-sūtra* says that one who observes this *sūtra* becomes as powerful as an elephant."[277]

### 87. AUTHOR UNKNOWN, *(Upāyakauśalya)Jñānottarabodhisattvaparipṛcchāsūtra*[278]

### 88. AUTHOR UNKNOWN, *Kāruṇikarājasūtra*[279]

### 89. AUTHOR UNKNOWN, *Lokanāthavyākaraṇasūtra*[280]

### 90. AUTHOR UNKNOWN, *Mahāvaipulyamūrdharājasūtra*[281]

### 91. AUTHOR UNKNOWN, *Mahāyānopadeśasūtra*[282]

### 92. AUTHOR UNKNOWN, *Maitreyaparipṛcchāparivartasūtra*[283]

### 93. AUTHOR UNKNOWN, *Mañjuśrībuddhakṣetraguṇavyūhasūtra*[284]

The usual collection of Bodhisattvas listens to a discussion between Mañjuśrī, the Buddha and others. Some knotty philosophical puzzles are posed. E.g., what is the *dharma* of a Buddha? Is it a factor or not? What can be said about it? Mañjuśrī's answer is "nothing can be said about it, any more than one can say whether empty space is or is not a factor".

Or again, someone asks Mañjuśrī "since you have attained the ten stages of Bodhisattvahood why don't you attain enlightenment?" Answer: "I already have!" Or, "why don't you urge all sentient beings to attain enlightenment?" Answer: "Because there are no sentient beings".

## 94. AUTHOR UNKNOWN, *Mañjuśrīvikrīḍitasūtra*[285]

## 95. AUTHOR UNKNOWN, *Mañjuśrīvikurvaṇaparivartasūtra*[286]

## 96. AUTHOR UNKNOWN, *Nandapravrajyāsūtra*[287]

## 97. AUTHOR UNKNOWN, *Paramārthasaṃvṛtisatyanirdeśasūtra*[288]

## 98. AUTHOR UNKNOWN, *Pravaraṇasūtra*[289]

## 99. AUTHOR UNKNOWN, *Ratnacandraparipṛcchāsūtra*[290]

## 100. AUTHOR UNKNOWN, *Ratnacūḍaparipṛcchāsūtra*[291]

## 101. AUTHOR UNKNOWN, *Ratnajaliparipṛcchāsūtra*[292]

## 102. SAMANTABHADRA, *Ratnakaraṇḍasūtra*[293]

## 103. AUTHOR UNKNOWN, *Saddharmapuṇḍarīkasūtra*[294]

### Summary by Jan Hendrik Kern

This is the famous "Lotus Sūtra", much studied, recited and revered throughout Asia. Jan Hendrik Kern's translation (103.1.4) is preceded by the following summary of the work's chapters:

"1. Prologue

2. Awakening of the Lord from his mystic trance; display of his transcendent skilfulness, proved by the apparent trinity of vehicles, whereas in reality there is but one vehicle.

3. Prophecy of the Lord regarding the future destiny of Śāriputra, his eldest son...Parable of the burning house...

4. Another parable.

5. Parable of the plants and the rain, to exemplify the impartiality and equal care of the Lord for all creatures. Parable of the blind man, to intimate that the phenomena have but an apparent reality, and that the ultimate goal of all endeavors must be to reach all-

knowingness, which in fact is identical with complete nescience.

6. Sundry predictions as proofs of the power of the Sugata to look into the future.

7. He has an equal knowledge of the remotest past; his remembrance of the turning of the wheel by the Tathāgata.

8. Prophecy regarding five hundred Arhats.

9. Prophecy concerning Ānanda, Rāhula, and the two thousand monks.

10. The Lord teaches how pious preachers of the law, who will come in after-times, ought to be duly honored, and promises that he will always protect the ministers of religion.

11. Display of the miraculous power of Śākyamuni...How Śākyamuni in a former birth strove to acquire the Lotus of the True Law.

12. Prediction to Gautamī, Yaśodharā, and the nuns in their train. Promise of the host of disciples and Bodhisattvas to take up the difficult task of preaching the holy word in days to come, after the Lord's *nirvāṇa*.

13. Vocation of the ministers of religion, and practical rules for their conduct in and out of society.

14. Splendid phantasmagory of innumerable Bodhisattvas.

15. The Buddha...reveal(s) the immense duration of his lifetime, in the past and the future.

16. Meritoriousness of the belief in the immense duration of the Tathāgatas and all those who have once become Buddhas.

17. The Lord details the great merit attending a ready acceptance of the preaching of the law.

18. Exposition of the advantages, worldly and spiritual, enjoyed by the ministers of religion.

19. Story of Sadāparibhūta...

20. Grand show exhibited by the two Tathāgatas Śākyamuni and Prabhuratna con-jointly.

21. Efficacy of talismanic spells (*dhāraṇ*īs).

22. Self-sacrifice of the Bodhisattva Sarvasattvapriyadarśana, otherwise called Bhaiṣajyaguru.

23. Visit of the Bodhisattva Gadgadāśvara to the Saha-world...

24. Grandeur and ubiquitousness of Avalokiteśvara.

25. Wonderful and edifying story of the conversion of the king Śubhavyūha through the instrumentality of his two sons.

26. The Bodhisattva Samantabhadra charges himself with the task of being a protector to the preachers of religion in after-times after the Lord's *nirvāṇa*."

## 104. AUTHOR UNKNOWN, *Sāharanāgaraparipṛcchāsūtra*[295]

## 105. AUTHOR UNKNOWN, *Samantamukhaparivartasūtra*[296]

## 106. AUTHOR UNKNOWN, *Sarvapuṇyasamuccayasamādhisūtra*[297]

## 107. AUTHOR UNKNOWN, *Sarvavaipulyavidyāsiddhasūtra*[298]

## 108. AUTHOR UNKNOWN, *Siṃhaparipṛcchāsūtra*[299]

## 109. AUTHOR UNKNOWN, *Śrīmālādevīsiṃhanādasūtra*[300]

Summary by Alex and Hideko Wayman

"The scripture opens in Śrāvasti. King Prasenajit and his Queen Mallikā move to interest their daughter Queen Śrīmālā in the Buddha's doctrine."

"Chapter One. Eliminating All Doubts. 1. Śrīmālā evokes the Buddha, who approaches in his inconceivable body. She praises his two bodies which are bodily form and the knowledge body. The Lord prophesies that Queen Śrīmālā will attain the incomparable right perfected enlightenment. 2. Queen Śrīmālā takes ten great vows, the first five constituting Hīnayāna ethics, the second five, Mahāyāna ethics..."

"Chapter Two. Deciding the Cause. 3. Queen Śrīmālā forms three great aspirations: to always comprehend the Illustrious Doctrine; to teach unweariedly the Illustrious Doctrine; and to protect and uphold the Illustrious Doctrine without regard to body, life force, or possessions. These three comprise all Bodhisattva aspirations. 4. She prays for the Tathāgata's power to make her eloquent when teaching in the scope of the great aspirations;..."

"Chapter Three. Clarifying the Final Meaning. 5. The queen eloquently preaches the embrace of the Illustrious Doctrine that was held by all the Buddhas. The "Illustrious Doctrine" is a term for the

Great Vehicle...The Arhats and the Pratyekabuddhas with fear take refuge in the Lord. What they call "*nirvāṇa*" is a means belonging to the Tathāgatas, because the Arhats and the Pratyekabuddhas do not have all merits, have measurable and conceivable merit, have a remainder of faults, and so are far away from the *nirvāṇa*-realm. Concerning the liberation of Arhats and Pratyekabuddhas, there are two kinds of passing away--discontinuous passing away of ordinary sentient beings, and the inconceivable transference of the Arhats, Pratyekabuddhas, and Bodhisattvas who have attained power. The Arhats and the Pratyekabuddhas have neither eliminated all defilements nor avoided all rebirth...The vehicles of the Disciples and the Self-Enlightened are included in the Great Vehicle. "Great Vehicle" is an expression for the Buddha vehicle, and so the three vehicles are counted as one vehicle (*ekayāna*)...6. The four Noble Truths do not belong to the Disciples and the Self-Enlightened, for these persons do not have the supramundane knowledge of the non-progressive Noble Truths. The four Truths belong to the Tathāgatas, who eliminate the store of all defilements by inconceivable voidness knowledge. 7. The Tathāgatagarbha is covered by the defilements' store; when liberated from this store it is the Dharmakāya of the Tathāgata...8-9. The cessation of suffering is the Tathāgata's Dharmakāya, or Tathāgatagarbha freed from defilement by the two kinds of voidness knowledge of the Tathāgatas, namely, the Tathāgatagarbha is void of the stores of defilement, and the Tathāgatagarbha is not void of the Buddha natures. 10. The Noble Truth "Cessation of Suffering" is the true refuge. The other three Noble Truths...are not the true refuge. 11-12. Immature ordinary persons have the wayward views of the two extremes. When they think "The constructions are impermanent" it is their eternalistic view. This is because they have four wayward ideas that the impermanent is permanent, suffering is pleasure, nonself is self, the impure is pure...13. The Tathāgatagarbha is the base either of non-discrete constructed Buddha natures or of discrete constructed defilements. The Tathāgatagarbha experiences suffering, is the reason for aspiration towards *nirvāṇa,* and the reason for "cyclical flow" (*saṃsāra*); it is not a "self". There are two difficult doctrines: that consciousness is intrinsically pure, and that intrinsically pure consciousness can be defiled."

"Chapter Four. Entering the One Vehicle Path. 14. By two

discipleship levels, a third with a knowledge in the precincts of the Dharma involving five visions, and a fourth reaching certainty in the two difficult doctrines, the Disciples can then enroll others in the Great Vehicle. 15. The queen gains eloquence for further explanations of the faultless meaning...As queen she converts the women in the capital, and as king he converts the men."

### 110. AUTHOR UNKNOWN, *Śrīmatībrāhmaṇiparipṛcchāsūtra*[301]

### 111. AUTHOR UNKNOWN, *Strīvivartyavyākaraṇasūtra*[302]

### 112. AUTHOR UNKNOWN, *Sumatidārikaparipṛcchāsūtra*[303]

Advice issued by the Buddha to an eight-year-old girl named Sumati.

### 113. AUTHOR UNKNOWN, *Susthitamatidevaputraparipṛcchāsūtra*[304]

### 114. AUTHOR UNKNOWN, *Svapnanirdeśasūtra*[305]

### 115. AUTHOR UNKNOWN, *Tathāgatacintyaguhyanirdeśasūtra*[306]

### 116. AUTHOR UNKNOWN, *Tathāgatagarbhasūtra*[307]

### 117. AUTHOR UNKNOWN, *Udayanavatsarājaparipṛcchāsūtra*[308]

### 118. AUTHOR UNKNOWN, *Upāyakauśalyasūtra*[309]

### 119. AUTHOR UNKNOWN, *Vaiduryarājasūtra*[310]

### 120. AUTHOR UNKNOWN, *Vidyutprāptaparipṛcchāsūtra*[311]

### 121. AUTHOR UNKNOWN, *Vīradatta(gṛhapati)paripṛcchāsūtra*[312]

### 122. AUTHOR UNKNOWN, *Vimaladattaparipṛcchāsūtra*[313]

### 123. AUTHOR UNKNOWN, *Viśeṣacintā(brahma)paripṛcchāsūtra*[314]

## 124. UPATISSA, *Vimuttimagga*

Summary by Karl H. Potter

We list this work here, although the evidence is not determinative as to this author's date. P.V. Bapat, who has published several articles on the topic, thinks it likely that Buddhaghoṣa knew of Upatissa's work and refers to it a number of times in his *Visuddhimagga*.[315] However, he admits that Buddhaghoṣa's references may be to someone else. And of course we may be once again confronting an amalgam of several different works from different periods. There was an Upatissa Thera who apparently lived in the first-second century A.D., and there is a tradition that this work was brought to Ceylon from India. On the other hand it is also said that the work was composed in the Abhayagiri monastery in Sri Lanka, which would suggest a date in the fifth century or so. We place this work at the present date merely to find a way between all these opinions.

The summary is based entirely on the English translation ("T") from the Chinese texts by N.R.M. Ehara, S. Thera and K. Thera, *The Path of Freedom* (Kandy, 1977). Since there is no text to provide checks for Pāli equivalents, our summary necessarily depends on the published translation together with the footnotes suggesting equivalent Pāli terms in some places.

### CHAPTER ONE: Introduction

(T1-5) One who wishes to achieve *nirvāṇa* should be versed in the *sūtra*, *vinaya* and *abhidharma*. This is the path of freedom. "Freedom" has five kinds: (1) freedom of restraint, suppression of the passions through the practice of the first meditation; (2) freedom of parts, from views through meditation; (3) freedom of eradication, the destruction of the fetters through the path of the other world; (4) freedom of tranquillity, the satisfaction of one who obtains results; (5) freedom of escape, *nirvāṇa* without residue.

A man who acknowledges this path of freedom fulfils three branches (*skandha*): (1) of precepts, viz., right speech, right action, etc.; (2) of concentration, viz., right effort, right mindfulness, etc.; (3) of wisdom, viz., right understanding, right thought, etc. He should be triply trained in (1) higher virtue, (2) higher awareness, (3) higher wisdom. The first comes through virtue, the second through concentration, the third through wisdom. Through these one obtains purity of virtue, thought and views respectively, three kinds of good, and three kinds of satisfaction correspondingly. Having acknowledged the path of freedom a man attains the perfection of the middle way between the two extremes. Through virtue he transcends backsliding to lower realms, through concentration he transcends the plane of desire, through wisdom he transcends all becoming. If he practises virtue fully but little of the other two he becomes a stream-enterer and a once-returner. If he practices virtue and concentration but little of wisdom he becomes a nonreturner. If he practises all three to the full he becomes a perfected being.

## CHAPTER TWO: On Distinguishing Virtue

(T6-38) There are three kinds of virtue--of volition, of abstention, of nontransgression. A long list of examples is provided. "Virtue" involves removal of transgressions of virtue by dignity. The three transgressions are transgressing the rules of the community of monks, transgressing of the virtues pertaining to the conditions, and transgressing the virtues pertaining to the senses. The former involves loss of faith in the Buddha through shamelessness and indecorum, the second involves e.g. concern with adornment of the body, the third involves distraction of the senses, i.e., nonattentiveness.

The benefits of virtue are delineated, as well as its causes. Virtue may be good, bad, or indeterminate. The first is meritorious behavior that gives satisfaction, the second demeritorious behavior that gives frustration, the third is defilement-free activity that gives neither satisfaction nor frustration.

There are thirty-four factors which are obstacles to virtue.

Now virtues are classified in Abhidharma fashion into groups of pairs, triplets, etc. E.g., pairs of classifications include prescriptions and prohibitions, abandoning what is nonvirtuous and undertaking what is virtuous, worldly vs. other-worldly virtue, measurable vs. immeasurable, limitful and limitless, dependent and nondependent, etc. Triplets include tarnished, nontarnished, and tranquillized virtue; virtue swayed by the world, swayed by the body, swayed by *dharma*, fearful, anxious, fatuous. Quadruples include disadvantageous, maintenance-conducive, advantageous, and penetration-aiding; precepts for monks, nuns, the not-yet-ordained, and for householders; natural virtue, virtue that is good manners, virtue that is law (*dharma*), and virtue that is the result of previous births; virtue of the restraints through the rules of the monastic order, through purity of living, through restraint of faculties, through conditions.

Good behavior and misbehavior are exemplified, and these various virtues are clarified at length, with special attention to the last mentioned of the quadruples. There is a lot of specific information about how a monk should behave.

## CHAPTER THREE: On Distinguishing Concentration

(T39-47) Concentration is defined and its features identified. Four beneficial results are listed: (1) satisfying existence in this life, (2) enjoyment of the objects one concentrates on, (3) acquisition of knowledge, and (4) attainment of perfection.

The obstacles to concentration are: lust, hatred, indolence, rigidity, agitation, uncertainty, delusion, absence of joy, and bliss. There are eight causes of concentration: renunciation, nonhatred, brightness, nondisturbedness, all skilful *dharmas*, sustained application of thought, gladness, and those *dharmas* that arouse knowledge. Seven prerequisites for concentration are virtue, contentment, shielding of the faculties, moderation in drink and food, not sleeping in the first, middle and last watches of the night, being intent on wisdom , and a calm and quiet dwelling-place.

Now concentration is analyzed into pairs--e.g., mundane and otherworldly; triplets--e.g., involving both initial and sustained thought, involving sustained but not initial thought, and involving neither; quadruples--e.g., the four realms of sensual pleasure, matter, immateriality and the unincluded; and quintuples--e.g., five kinds of concentration characterized respectively by initial thought, sustained thought, joy, bliss, and unification of mind.

## CHAPTER FOUR: On Approaching a Good Friend

(T48-53) Concentration requires advice from others; so one who intends to practise concentration should seek out a good friend who can teach him or at any rate act so as to help him meditate. The duties of a pupil toward his teacher are set forth in detail.

## CHAPTER FIVE: Distinguishing Marks of Behavior

(T54-62) Fourteen kinds of behavior are listed, and fourteen kinds of persons correspondingly. These are (1) passionate, (2) hating, (3) deluded, (4) faithful, (5) intelligent, (6) involving initial thought, (7) passionate-hating, (8) passionate-infatuated, (9) hate-infatuated, (10) passionate-hating-infatuated, (11) faithfully intelligent, (12) faithfully excogitative, (13) intelligently excogitative, and (14) faithfullly intelligently excogitative. These may be reduced to seven according to the following pairs of kinds of behavior becoming one: (1)-(4), (2)-(5), (3)-(6), (7)-(11), (8)-(12), (9)-(13) and (10)-(14). These in turn can be reduced to three kinds, (1), (2) and (3).

The causes of these three kinds of behavior are, respectively, good karma, bad karma resulting from violence, and bad karma resulting from low stupid practices. Behavior has seven aspects: (1) related to objects, (2) related to the defilements, (3) related to walking, (4) related to dress, (5) related to food, (6) related to work, and (7) related to sleep.

## CHAPTER SIX: The Subjects of Meditation

(T63-70) There are thirty-eight kinds of things to meditate upon. These include the ten symbolic meditative devices; ten meditations on revolting aspects of the body; ten recollections (of the Buddha, the *dharma*, the *saṅgha*, of virtue, liberality, deities, death, body, respiration and peace); four boundless thoughts: loving-kindness, compassion, sympathy, equanimity; determining of the four elements; perceiving the foulness of food; the sphere of nothingness; and the sphere of neither identification nor nonidentification. These thirty-eight are studied from the standpoint of meditation, of how each does or does not transcend form, of which ones should and can be increased, of which are causes of supernormal powers, of which ones have which kinds of objects, of the special or outstanding features of each, of which realms each arises in, of how each is grasped, and of who can and should practise each one.

## CHAPTER SEVEN: Entering the Subject of Meditation

(T71-98) Now each of the thirty-eight subjects are explained in detail, beginning with the meditative devices. The ten devices are earth, water, fire, air, dark color, yellow, red, white, *ākāśa* and consciousness. The nature of meditation on each, its cause and results and the appropriate *maṇḍala* to be constructed is explained. For example, meditation on the first or earth device involves considering the tribulations of sensual desires and the benefits of renouncing them. The beneficial results of this meditation include separation from the defilements, freedom, enjoyment of renunciation, the ability to endure frustration, wisdom. Then there follows a detailed description of just how the meditator should reflect, construct his *maṇḍala,* gaze upon it, the afterimage that arises, and the sign or conditioning cause that the yogi acquires. A preparatory stage (access-meditation) and a concluding or fixed stage are distinguished. In meditating the *yogin* should increase gradually the extent of the area over which the topic (say, earth) extends. Various aids to skilfulness in meditation are described.

Joy and bliss are both results of meditation. Joy is ease of mind arising from satisfaction of desires, from faith, from nonrigidity, from meditative solitude, from concentration (in the second stage), and from enlightenment. Bliss is contact with lovable and ease-giving things and persons. The difference between joy and bliss is that between coarse and fine. Joy belongs to the aggregate of conditioning factors, bliss to the aggregate of feelings. Joy is always accompanied by bliss, but not necessarily vice-versa.

There are five factors that hinder and which are rooted out by meditation. These five are: (1) sensual interests, (2) malice, (3) rigidity and sleepiness, (4) agitation and regret, and (5) perplexity. They are rooted out by meditations of the first stage involving initial and sustained thought, joy, bliss and unification of mind.

A yogi who attains the lower first meditation will be reborn into Brahmā's retinue (*brahmaparisajja*) and remain there for one-third of an eon. If he practises the middle-range first meditation he will be reborn as a chief Brahmā (*brahmapurohita*) and will remain there for half an eon. If he practises the higher first meditation he will be reborn as a great Brahmā (*mahābrahmā*) and will live as such for a whole eon. The possibility of backsliding is admitted, and several opinions about that matter are briefly reviewed.

(T99-104) But the first meditation also still contains the seeds of distraction by the hindrances, so that one's meditation may become coarse. This leads the yogi on to practise the second meditation. This has four factors: (1) it involves the stilling of both initial and sustained thought, (2) involves internal tranquillity and mind-predominance, (3) is born of concentration, (4) is full of joy and bliss. One who practises the lower second meditation will be reborn in the abode of lesser light and live there for two eons. One who practises the middling second meditation will be reborn in the abode of measureless light and stay for four eons. And if he practises the higher second meditation he will be reborn in the abode of resplendence and live for eight eons there.

(T104-109) But the yogi may well find even the second meditation coarse and strive for the third meditation. The second meditation still contains the seeds of distraction through initial and sustained thought, and may involve attachment to joy; it does not yet provide supernormal powers. So one seeks the third meditative stage where one becomes free from joy and dwells instead in equanimity. Eight varieties of equanimity are distinguished. These are then reclassified into six and again into three--equanimity as a vehicle of concentration, as a state of little activity, as inactivity. In this third meditation one abides in equanimity, mindful and completely conscious. Mindfulness is remembering everything; complete consciousness is being rightly aware of one's distinctive marks and of worldly conditions. Of course, mindfulness and consciousness are required in the previous meditations also, but in this third one joy, bliss and other meditative factors are stilled and only mindful complete consciousness persists.

(T109-113) Still, joy and bliss remain tempting even in the third meditation which has so recently overcome them. Thus the yogi may strive for the fourth meditation, where one's mindfulness is clarified and purified by equanimity, so that there is no receiving or rejecting of inputs that ordinarily occasion thought and result in satisfaction or frustration. Such a meditator is reborn in heaven.

(T113-116) Up to this point the meditator has been concentrating on earth and others of the meditative devices up to *ākāśa*. Now, wishing to transcend the material realm, he may concentrate on *ākāśa* and become freed from any awareness of diversity, so that no perceptions take place, and thus accordingly no feelings, no traces, no (finite) consciousness. One who meditates thus will be reborn in the sphere of *ākāśa* and remain there for 2,000 eons.

(T116-117) Now the yogin wishes to transcend even the sphere of *ākāśa* and to attain the sphere of infinite consciousness. So he meditates on consciousness, and is reborn in that sphere and remains there for 4,000 eons.

(T117-118) Next he wishes to transcend even the sphere of infinite consciousness and achieve the sphere of nothingness. So he goes beyond consciousness altogether to the sphere of nothingness, which is empty. He is reborn there and his life there will be 6,000 eons.

(T118-120) Finally, he wishes to transcend even the sphere of nothingness and achieve the concentration of neither perception nor nonperception. This final concentration achieves all the merits of the previous ones and none of their defects. He is reborn there and remains for 84,000 eons. But even by this remarkable meditation he is not able to destroy the defilements (and so is not liberated even thus). Why are the defilements not destroyed? Because one who separates himself from perception is not able to see the path, and one in this state of neither perception nor nonperception is not able to discern the nature of that state, which discernment is required for the path.

(T121-132) The foregoing review of various stages of meditation has been predicated on the assumption that the meditator started meditating on earth. But he can also meditate on the other seven meditative devices. The particular marks, benefits and results of meditating on each are distinguished. Meditation on space and on consciousness were alluded to above.

(T132-140) The ten meditations on revolting aspects of the body are now explained. These include (1) the bloatedness of a corpse, (2) its discoloration, (3) its festering, (4) its being cracked, (5) gnawed, (6) dismembered, (7) cut and dismembered, (8) bloodstained, (9) full of worms, and (10) its practically skeletal condition. The marks, benefits and results of meditating on each are distinguished.

(T140-148) Now recollection of the Buddha is explained. Eighteen benefits of this meditation are distinguished, including such things as increase of confidence, mindfulness, wisdom, reverence, merit, joy, fearlessness, etc. How such epithets as "perfected", "sublime", "omniscient" (i.e., "knower of the world"), etc., apply to the Buddha are carefully explained. The Buddha's ten powers, fourteen kinds of knowledge, and eighteen virtues are laid out.

(T149-180) Similarly, the other nine recollections are discussed. The recollection of virtue conduces to morality on the part of the meditator; the recollection of liberality leads to his giving; the recollection of deities leads to the acquisition of the merits of the gods and earns a life in heaven like theirs. Recollection of respiration is the breath-control of the yogi; it is explained in generous detail, showing how control of each kind of breath contributes to enlightenment. Recollection of death involves full awareness of the ways of dying and the psychological states that may accompany thought of death. Various ways of summarizing the pertinent features of the body are outlined for the one who recollects the body, including a lengthy section on the 80,000 worms that gnaw on the body.

(T181-197) Continuing the detailed description of the thirty-eight subjects of meditation, the discussion turns now to the four immeasurable thoughts.

(T197-208) This section discusses each of the four elements--earth, fire, water and air--as well as the meditation on foulness of food.

## CHAPTER EIGHT: The Higher Knowledge

(T209-228) Having gotten to this point, the meditator in the fourth meditative stage has gained the five forms of higher knowledge: supernatural power, divine ear, knowledge of others' thoughts, recollection of former lives, divine vision. Supernatural powers are divided into three, and then into seven. The former classification is used in what follows: it divides supernatural powers into (1) that of resolve, which enables the yogi to become many or one at will, to become invisible, to fly or walk on water, to handle the sun and the moon; (2) that of transformation, by which he can make his body light and pliant and less of a load on his mind, by which he can change his body into another form--e.g., that of a boy, or a lion, or an army; (3) that caused by mind, by which he can create things, e.g., other bodies to occupy when visiting the world of Brahmā. By divine hearing he can hear sounds far away or beyond human capacity to hear. Knowing others' thoughts is self-explanatory, but the yogi practises it by first entering the light device, discovering his own heart's color through divine sight, learning thereby to know his own states of consciousness, and then using these methods to understand others. The memory of past lives enables the yogi to recall the order of his previous lives, the kinds of bodies they were in, and thus to condition his future births. Divine sight operates through the light *kasina* and enables the yogi to see objects far away, beyond normal human ability to see, for example, mental objects, as well as past and future things, things like karma which aren't normally seen. All five of these powers are gradually developed by the yogi, and the greatest powers are achieved by the most enlightened ones, culminating in the Buddha himself.

## CHAPTER NINE: Wisdom

(T229-236) Wisdom is seeing things as they are. It is here classified into a pair (worldly and otherworldly), several triplets, and goodly number of quadruples, mostly distinguished according to the subject-matter over which the knowledge ranges.

## CHAPTER TEN: Five Methods

(T237-282) The five methods of acquiring wisdom are these: (1) the method of the aggregates, (2) the method of the senses, (3) the method of the elements, (4) the method of dependent origination, (5) the method of truth. The aspects of material aggregates, viz., the senses and elements, āre identified, as well as the thirty kinds of matter derived from the elements. These last are classified briefly according to their origin, their groups (*kalāpa*), whether they arise at the moment of birth, and then by twos, threes and fours.

Following this, the other four aggregates are explained. This is followed in turn by an explanation of dependent origination and of the four noble truths.

## CHAPTER ELEVEN: On Discerning Truth

(T283-326) The progressive methods of the yogi who practises the method of truth are set forth, illustrated by a number of similes. Since he has understood the four truths he realizes the rise and fall of the aggregates, which leads him on to appreciating how the aggregates break up, that they are impermanent, and this in turn leads him to fear birth. A result of that fear is the desire for liberation, which leads the yogi to adaptive knowledge, i.e., enlightenment, which sows the seeds of *nirvāṇa*. After this he practises the path, enters the stream and cuts off the three fetters of wrongly viewing the body as the self, doubt, and addiction to rites and ceremonies, along with the proclivities resulting therefrom. During this stage he gradually achieves the status of once-returner, nonreturner, and *arhat*.

The work concludes with a brief review of an assortment of traditional classifications such as three liberations, one hundred and thirty four defilements, four contaminants, four floods, four knots, five obstructions, nine kinds of pride, ten defilements, ten fetters, and a description of the result of this path, viz., the dissolution of perception and feeling that is neither identification nor nonidentification.

# 125.AUTHOR UNKNOWN, *Atānātikasūtra*[316]

# 126.HARIVARMAN, *Tattvasiddhi*[317]

Summary by Karl H. Potter

The work is also known as "*Satyasiddhi*", but that is no longer the preferred translation. The date of its composition is estimated by Étienne Lamotte as 253 A.D., which has been accepted by other scholars. It appears to present the persuasions of the Bahuśrutīya school.

"E" references are to the edition by N. Aiyaswami Sastri and "T" references are to Sastri's translation.[318] This summary has been prepared on the basis of T, but with the help of the unpublished doctoral dissertation of Shoryu Katsura, which is referred to as "K".

## BOOK ONE

### CHAPTER ONE: The Three Jewels

#### Section A: The Buddha

1.(E1-6; T1-4) After a salutation, the author indicates that, having studied the opinions of others, he will in this work clarify the actual meaing of the *Tripiṭaka*. The Buddha is worthy of salutation because, though a human being, he is omniscient concerning the essential natures of all the factors, he is free from all bad features and has all the good ones, and he seeks the good of all beings. Though others have the five aggregates of factors listed below, the Buddha's are purer. These five aggregates of factors are (1) moral precepts, (2) concentration, (3) wisdom, (4) liberation, and (5) knowledge. (1) Morality is good conduct. (2) The Buddha's concentration is superior to that of others, for it is firm, does not depend on causal conditions and so is continuous, undistracted, such that he can possess the supernatural powers, has full understanding of the meditations so that he can enter and leave any of them. (3) His insight has destroyed the twofold ignorance which hides meditation and produces defilements. (4) Thus, he is liberated from that twofold ignorance. (5) He has knowledge and vision of that liberation, and can teach anyone according to his needs.

2.(E7-10; T5-7) Ten powers that the Buddha has in accordance with his insight are: (1) knows what exists and what doesn't, through understanding the causal, directly antecedent and dominant conditions of every single thing; (2) discerns all attitudes produced by factors--(a) frustrating now but causing satisfying results, (b) satisfying now but producing frustrating results, (c) satisfying here and producing satisfying results, (d) frustrating here and producing frustrating results; (3) discerns the effects of all meditations, liberations, concentrations and trances; (4) can distinguish people with keen faculties from those with dull ones; (5) understands the variety of resolves; (6) understands the variety of realms; (7) understands all modes of progress; (8) knows which are the results of which previous actions; (9) sees the future with his divine eye; (10) understands the stoppage of the contaminants.

3.(E11-15; T7-11) The four confidences are (1) omniscience, (2) destruction of all contaminants, (3) prophecy of the obstructions to the path, and (4) knowledge of the path that destroys frustrations. These are "fearlessnesses" because they result from the powers detailed in the previous section.

Objection: Why should we believe in the Buddha's omniscience? After all, he says various things suggesting he seeks understanding, such as "where do you come from?", and there are passages which suggest the Buddha was sometimes greedy and proud. Finally, the Buddha says that sex is an obstruction to the path, but some people who practise the path enjoy sex.

Answer: The Buddha talks in worldly fashion in order to teach. As for sex, one who is on the path is not necessarily free from obstructions.

4.(E15-17; T11-13) Ten names of the Buddha.

5.(E17-19; T13-15) The Buddha does not guard any actions of body, speech or mind, since he has no misdeeds to guard from others.

### Section B. The *Dharma*

6.(E20-22; T15-17) The virtues in the Buddha's *dharma*.

7.(E22-25; T17-20) More virtues.

8.(E25-27; T20-23) Twelve branches of the discourse.

### Section C.The Order

9.(E27-29; T23-24) Primary purity of the order.

10.(E29-34; T24-28) The four main kinds of noble ones are (1) progressing, (2) stream-enterer, (3) once-returner, (4) nonreturner. (1) is divided into (a) faith-followers, (b) followers of the *dharma*, and (c) signless followers, i.e., faith-followers and *dharma*-followers that have entered the path and understood the third noble truth.

There are eight kinds of nonreturner: (a) he who will obtain liberation immediately after death, (b) the one who turns away from the world and enters liberation, (c) he who spontaneously enters liberation, (d) he who does so with effort, (e) those in higher streams, (f) those in the immaterial realm, (g) one who enter neither the material nor immaterial realms, (h) the one who enters liberation in this very body. This last, (h), has two kinds: (1) liberated by faith and (2) having attained vision.

There is a classification of nine kinds of noble ones.

11.(E35-37; T28-29) The Field of Merit.

12.(E37; T29-30) *Maṅgala*

CHAPTER TWO: Justification of the Composition of This Text

13.(E38-40; T30-32) The Buddha's *dharma* is now going to be made known.

Objecton: If the Buddha has already made it known no elucidation is needed. If he hasn't, since his meaning is obscure, no elucidation is possible. And the obscurity of his meaning is evident from the variety of opinions about it; even he himself said that no one understood it (in *Parapravādasūtra*).

Answer: There are both noble and ordinary ways of discerning the meaning of others. Even in the *Paraṃpravādasūtra* the Buddha implies that Kātyāyana and others have understood his subtlest meaning, and endorsed what others preached in his name. And the Buddha also advised the monks to compose a Buddhist system.

14.(E40-45; T32-35) The following are principles on which our system is based: (1) the distinction between the worldly and the highest, e.g., that there is a self from the worldly standpoint, but no self from the highest standpoint; (2) distinction between a principle of the teaching and ordinary usage; (3) matter exists in all the three times; (4) not all the senses are causal conditions in the awareness of every factor; (5) rules have exceptions; (6) the distinction between matters that are unconditionally the case versus those which are only conditionally the case; (7) the distinction between artifical and natural; (8) reference to X is to be understood as including what is proximate to X; (9) reference to X is to be understood as including what is similar to X; (10) generalizations can be made in accordance with a majority of cases; (11) reference to causes through mentioning their effect; (12) reference to effects through mentioning their causes.

15.(E45-49; T35-37) Commendation of *Śāstra*

16.(E49-52; T37-39) Fourfold *Dharma*

17.(E52-57;T39-44)[319] Various standard Buddhist classifica-tions (*mātṛkā*) of the four truths are summarized. Under the first truth, for example, we have: three realms, four stations of consciousness, four kinds of birth, four foods, six paths, six elements, six contacts, seven stations of consciousness, eight worldly factors, nine abodes of beings, and a fivefold classification into five aggregates, twelve senses, eighteen elements, twenty-two parts of the chain of dependent origination and twenty-five faculties. Similar lists are provided for the other three truths. Explanations of constituent terms are brief.

18.(E58-64; T45-48) A series of classifications of things into pairs, triples, quadruples, etc.[320]

## CHAPTER THREE: Ten Points of Controversy

19.(E67-69; T48-51)[321] Some say that past and future factors exist, and define "existence" as being a content of awareness. But we are aware of all sorts of things that don't exist--the contents of false judgments, the double-moon.

Objection: No. Consciousness arises only in dependence on an existent locus and an existent supporting object, never without them. Because, e.g., if consciousness could lack an object it might arise at any time and there would be no liberation; too, doubt could never arise about such a consciousness, since there would be no content of the awareness to doubt. Scripture attests that factors are objects; if it is knowledge its claim of the existence of its object must be correct; if it's correct, it's not knowledge.

Answer: The response is mistaken. Awarenesses and their accompanying factors may arise without supporting objects, for they do not grasp the highest reality, and because factors are not ultimately real. Of course any awareness arises supported by causal conditions, but it doesn't follow that it arises from the content of the awareness as presented. To say so would be to court the view that the effect preexists in the cause. And if the yogi understands one thing (an existent) as another (a nonexistent) his awareness is erroneous. As for the double moon, this supports our contention. Thus your definition of existence as a content of awareness is mistaken.

20.(E69-71; T52-53) Objection: Factors are grouped as aggregates, elements and senses, so they must exist.

Answer: That follows from ordinary usage, but not from the point of view of the *dharma*. If what you say were true, unconditioned things should exist, but they do not. Therefore the aggregates, etc., may be nonexistent.

Objection: To be is to be perceived, i.e., to be believed in on the basis of perceptual awareness.

Answer: It is a conceptual construction and not what is experienced. The *sūtra* tells us to resort to *jñāna*, not to *vijñāna*. Things such as matter, etc., which have essential natures are not the contents of experience.

Objection: A thing exists if it is connected with existence.

Answer: Nothing is connected with another thing. Everything comes from causes and conditions, so their existence is constructed, not experienced, worldly, not ultimately real.

There are ten points of controversy to be considered:

(1) Do the past and future exist? We say no, because past and future factors have no function and so do not exist. If a thing has no function, it has no self-nature. All factors arise from causes and conditions; since past and future factors have no causes and conditions, they can't exist. If future factors did exist they would be eternal, and thus wouldn't be created. And only present and conditioned factors have the three characteristics of arising, ending and change.

21.(E71-72; T53-54) Objection: Past and future factors do exist, because factors exist if awarenesses arise about them, as you admit is the case with present factors and unconditioned ones. Too, the Buddha taught that there are past and future factors. Past karma has results, so must exist. Again, mental consciousness (*manovijñāna*) depends on the mind, which is past; if there were neither past nor future factors, what could be the object of mental consciousness?

22.(E72-74; T54-56) Answer: We've already answered your first point. The Buddha was speaking to ordinary folk, not the ultimate truth. Even though they have results, past deeds (karma) do not now exist. And mental consciousness does not really depend on the mind in the way visual awareness depends on the eye; mental consciousness is merely occasioned by the previous awareness. So past and future factors are only believed in by ignorant men.

23.(E74-75; T56-57) (2) Some say that everything exists, e.g., (the Sarvāstivādins, who say) that the twelve senses are taught by the Buddha and include everything, or (the Vaiśeṣikas, who say) that there are six categories--substance, quality, motion, universal, individuator, inherence, or (the Sāṃkhyas, who say) that there is *prakṛti*. But all these things are nonexistent. And anyway, existence is defined in different ways by different schools. That all exists, or that nothing exists, are taught only as an expedient, in order to preach the middle way between those extremes of eternalism and nihilism.

24.(E75-76; T57-58) (3) Some say there is an intermediate existence between death and rebirth.

25.(E76-78; T58-59) Others deny such an existence, interpreting the Buddha's words differently. The Buddha was speaking about the existence of another world, not of an intermediate state. And anyway, the intermediate state is a kind of rebirth itself.

Objection: The intermediate state is the entering of consciousness into the embryo.

Answer: But since it is karma which occasions this entering as well as the rebirth in the body, postulation of two rebirths (one in the intermediate state, the other in the body) is unnecessarily complex.[322]

26.(E78-79; T59-60) (4) Some say that understanding of the four noble truths is gradual, citing the Buddha.[323]

27.(E79-80; T60-61) Others[324] say that understanding is sudden, reinterpreting some of the passages cited and questioning others. But for the yogi there is only one truth (not four), and the gaining of the path is the result of visualizing that one truth, namely, the truth of the cessation of frustration.

28.(E80-81; T61) (5) Some say that a perfected being may relapse out of that state, citing *sūtras*.[325]

29.(E81-83; T51-63) Others[326] say that a perfected being cannot fall from that state, though he may regress from a higher state of meditation to a lower one.

Objection: Godhika is said to have fallen six times from liberation and to have committed suicide. If he merely fell from meditation he would not have committed suicide.

Answer: A perfected being achieves purity by meditation, and once having achieved it, he cannot lose it.

30.(E84; T63-64) (6) Some[327] say that awareness is naturally pure and becomes sullied by accidental impurities. This is wrong,[328] for the defilements are in awareness and do not intrude from elsewhere. Awareness exists only for a moment, so nothing can intrude into it. When the Buddha says awareness is pure he is warning men against supposing that it persists, because if they supposed that a persisting awareness were naturally impure they would not attempt to purify it.

31.(E85; T64-65) (7) Some[329] say that the proclivities are associated with awareness, since attachments to interests, etc., are expressions of the defilements which are associated with the proclivities. The view that the proclivities are dissociated from awareness and form the cause of the arising of the fetters which are associated with awareness[330] is wrong. A *sūtra* says that the fetters arise from ignorance, etc., not from concomitants. And proclivities are not the cause of the arising of the fetters, since bodily and vocal actions satisfy your definition of "proclivity" and yet are not considered to be proclivities. If they are so considered, the result would arise not from previous deeds but from present acts alone.

32.(E86; T65) (8) Kāśyapīya: The only deeds that exist in the past are those which have not yet come to fruition.

Answer: Everything past, including karma, disappears after performing its causal function.

33.(E86-87; T65-66) (9) The view that the Buddha is included in the order is wrong.[331]

34.(E87-90; T67-69) (10) The Vātsīputrīyas say there is a person (*pudgala*); others rightly deny it on grounds of scriptural authority, here reviewed.

35.(E90-95; T69-74) Objection: A person exists, because it is a wrong view to deny that he who acts gets the fruit of his actions. Further, the Buddha had many previous lives. That the person is a mere name is wrong. The person is the five aggregates collectively, and it is this that reaps the reward of its actions in the past. Otherwise many factors mentioned in Buddhism, such as the foundations, the liberations, wouldn't exist.

Answer: The person has nominal existence only. The Buddha expressly denied that there is anything which underlies the changing aggregates. It is awareness which has the defilements, not a person; there is no persisting thing that has them. The five aggregates are spoken of as persisting, but that is only a manner of speaking. When we say the person is nominal we do not mean that it doesn't exist, but rather that there is no such actual entity.

Vātsīputrīya: The person cannot be said to be either the same as or different from the aggregates, any more than fire and fuel can be said to be the same as or different from each other.

Answer: This is doubtful, since the analogy itself is dubious. What is fire, and what fuel? Depending on how these terms are defined, they will be the same or different.

## BOOK TWO: The Frustration Truth

### CHAPTER ONE: Matter

36.(E96-97; T75-76) This entire work explicates the nature of the "truths", i.e., the four noble truths of frustration, its origin, its cessation and the path to that. Frustration is the five appropriating aggregates. Its origin is from defilements and karma. Its cessation is its destruction, and the path has eight members.

What are termed the four great elements--earth, water, fire and wind--depend on what are really the four great elements, namely color, smell, taste and touch. And the five sense-organs are produced from the contact of the (so-called) great elements (earth, water, fire and wind).

The aggregate of color, etc., when dominated by hardness, is called "earth". When dominated by moisture it is "water", when dominated by heat "fire", and when dominated by lightness and movement, "air".

37.(E98-99; T76) There is no other matter than these four. They are nominal existents. A great element is called "great" because it is pervasive and gross. It is without shape, not spatially located. Awarenesses and accompanying mental factors are not "great" because they are invisible.

38.(E99-101; T76-78) The Sāṃkhyas say that color, etc., are themselves the great elements, whereas the Vaiśeṣikas say the great elements exist independently of color, etc. The correct view is that they are nominal, being derived from color, etc. All things which are derived are nominal.

39.(E101-103; T78-79) Objection: In Abhidharma it is said that since earth has the property of hardness, water of moisture, etc., these great elements must be substantial, not nominal, for what is only nominally existent cannot produce a factor. In the *sūtras* each great element is said to have two properties--e.g., earth has solidity and what is related to solidity, water viscidity and what is related to viscidity, etc. The suggestion is that solidity and viscidity are properties of actual entities, what is related to solidity or to viscidity are nominal entities. Indeed, it is stated in the Abhidharma that each is the sense of configuration whereas the earth element has the mark solidity. The Buddha said that solidity and what is related to solidity in the eyeball is earth, viscidity and what is related to viscidity there is water, etc. The Buddha does not speak of the locus of air; therefore, air must be a substance. Furthermore, if the great elements were nominal, anything that is hard would be earth, anything moist water, etc. But water is sometimes hard, clay is moist, and so forth. So those elements are not merely nominal entities. Finally, the great elements are produced simultaneously and are inseparable. A *sūtra* says that matter is made of all four great elements. But this is inconsistent with the theory that the great elements are merely nominal.

40-41.(E103-111; T79-87) Answer: The previous Abhidharma arguments are wrong. The first argument, that solidity, etc. are properties arising from the great elements, is wrong since those items arise from other causes, viz., actions and defilements.

Objection: Even so, the great elements form part of the causes of the arising of color and solidity, along with karma.

Answer: Some things arise without any causes, e.g., the great deluge at the beginning or end of a *kalpa*. A god can bring something about just by thinking of it. So sometimes added causal factors to karma are needed, and sometimes not. And since both color and solidity arise simultaneously, why do you think the color arises on the basis of the solidity and not vice versa?

Opponent: A lamp and its light arise simultaneously; nevertheless the light is based in the lamp and not vice versa.

Answer: They are the same thing. A lamp is composed of color (light) and touch faculties. So the example is inappropriate.

Opponent: But the light is found outside the lamp.

Answer: If so, it would be experienced independently of the lamp. And anyway, the causal factors which give rise to a thing must be of the same form as the effect. Therefore color comes from matter, which is of the same form as it, rather than from the great elements, which are of a different form.

Opponent: Scorpions arise from dungheaps, a cause of a different form.

Answer: Some of the causal conditions may be of a different form: what we are saying is that among those conditions there must be some of the same form.

You said that the four "great elements are produced simultaneously and are inseparable." But it is not so. There is only color and hot touch in sunbeams; some things are without taste, e.g., a diamond; gold and silver do not smell; the moon lacks heat, etc.

Objection: These qualities of the elements you list are specifically activated by external conditions. E.g., gold possesses fluidity which may be activated when fire is present, grass possesses mobility which may be activated by wind. So the essential natures of things are activated by conditions, and if they lack such natures how could they be activated?

Answer: If that were so, air would have smell. If the great elements were inseparable the effect would be in its cause, which is contrary to Buddhist belief.

Your argument that solidity is a property of an actual entity while what is derived from solidity is of a nominal entity is wrong. Arguments from ordinary usage cannot be cited as authority, or else many Buddhist theses (e.g., the twelve senses) would turn out to be false. Anyway, why do you assume that "element" indicates substantiality and not a nominal nature?

The passage you cited, in which the Buddha speaks of the hardness in the eyeball, is intended to show that the eyeball is a product of the four great elements and thus nonexistent because merely nominal, generated by conceptual construction.

The reason the Buddha does not speak of a locus for air

corresponding to solidity for earth, moisture for water, etc., is because lightness is not really comparable to those but is indeed a property of air.

Moisture is water, and solidity earth, so nothing else than earth can be solid, nothing else but water moist. And it is not the case that all four great elements are produced simultaneously--e.g., in sunlight there is only color and ḥeat. Otherwise the unwanted theory that the effect preexists in the cause will follow, since every entity will have within it all properties and there will be no point to a classification into four elements.

41-43.(E111-113; T86-87) Objection: You say that the collection of color, etc., dominated by solidity is earth, and therefore earth is a nominal entity. But that is wrong, for solidity is not a factor, since (1) something may be now hard, later soft; (2) solidity is a notion derived from atoms being more or less closely packed.

Answer: (1) We do not accept that an actual something--say, a lump of clay--may be now hard, later soft, because we don't accept a lump of clay as substantially existent, only as nominally so. (2) Granted it derives from closeness or looseness, still solidity exists, and since it is experienced (3) doesn't cut any ice. (4) Sweetness, though relative, exists, as does shortness, etc. (5) We don't see solidity, rather we infer it, from prior associations between touch and sight.

Solidity, etc., are substantial existents because they produce constructive awarenesses. If solidity didn't exist, what could be constructed? Furthermore, it is experienced conceptually.

44.(E113-117; T87-91) Question: Is hail solid water or fluid earth? Is gold fluid earth or solid water?

Answer: Solidity is the specific characteristic of earth, fluidity of water.

Objection: But solid gold loses its solidity when heated, and water loses its fluidity when frozen; so those can't be their specific characteristics.

Answer: No solid thing becomes fluid, no fluid thing becomes solid. Rather, what is solid causes fluidity, and what is fluid causes solidity. Solidity is another name of earth, fluidity of water.

Objection: But fluidity is a visible quality of water, so it is not another name for the water itself.

Answer: True, fluidity is water's functioning, while moisture is a mark of water. Likewise, light weight is a mark of air, while movement (*samudīraṇa*) is its function.

Objection: Since everything is momentary there can be no movement.

Answer: Ours is a worldly classification, not ultimately true. Indeed, really what is called motion is the arising of something different in a contiguous place.

Objection: Lightness is not a fixed thing (i.e., it is relative).

Answer: But it exists in dependence on awareness, as does heaviness. If one cited relativity as a reason against existence lots of evidently existent things would have to be denied existence. And in any case, light weight is not a relative notion; rather, air is unweighable. (Further discussion about relative weight.)

45.(E117-120; T91-94)[332] Question: Are the sense-organs the same as the four great elements or not?

Answer: The sense-organs are formed from karma out of the great elements, so they are also nominal entities. For the Buddha said that a thing formed on the basis of a nominal entity is itself nominal.

46.(E120-121; T94-95) Question: If the five sense-organs each have the same amount of each great element, why does one grasp visual data, another gustatory, etc.?

Answer: Because of different karma being manifest through them.

Question: Then why are five sense-organs needed? Consciousness alone produced by karma should be able to grasp any object.

Answer: Well, we just find in the world that visual cognition doesn't arise without eyes, etc.

Question: Then why isn't that true also of awareness, i.e., mental awareness? Awareness does not require any organ--it depends on the immediately preceding awareness only.

Answer: Well, that's the way it is.

Question: But if mental consciousness is not based in any organ, where is it located?

Answer: It depends on embodiment, but it isn't located at any particular location.

47.(E121-123; T95-97) The Tīrthikas say that the five sense-organs are produced from five great elements. But that is not ultimately correct, since there is no such element as *ākāśadhātu*. They also say that the reason why the eye grasps visual data is because it is helped by the presence of external light, say, from a lamp, or the sun. That is also incorrect. Sometimes external light is required, other times not--e.g., owls and cats don't require external light to see.

There is also the (Nyāya-Vaiśeṣika) notion that the visual organ contacts an object through its ray going out to the surface of the object. But there is no such ray. The sense-organs are impermanent and cannot travel. And *ākāśa*, having no form, cannot be contacted in this way.

Some teachers hold that each sense-organ has a single essential nature grasping just one quality, so that in earth there is only smell, which is grasped by the olfactory organ, in water there is only taste grasped by the gustatory organ, etc. But this is incorrect, since other things smell besides earth, and because the great elements intermingle. Otherwise, e.g., one could only taste cool sensations (of water) and not hot ones (which arise from fire), etc.

48.(E124-128; T97-101)[333] Only consciousness cognizes, not the sense-organs.

Objection: The organ illuminates a thing, and consciousness makes it known.

Answer: No. The ear doesn't illuminate anything. Even if we suppose it does, there will be an infinite regress problem: for the organ to illuminate something will require another (external) illuminator, which will require another one, etc. *ad infinitum*. When it is said that the eye sees (i.e., cognizes) what is meant is that it supports consciousness.

Objection: A *sūtra* says that the internal organ (*manas*) is the gate for cognizing *dharma*, so it must cognize objects.

Answer: That internal organ is, in fact, an awareness (*citta*) which, having disappeared in the previous moment, cannot cognize anything. But the Buddha frequently followed ordinary usage when he spoke, and spoke of the eyes seeing, etc.

Anyway, on your own (apparently, Sāṃkhya) view the sense-organ does not think, and cognition does not depend on the senses, since awareness, ego, etc. are produced before the sense-organs are. Though, since there isn't any primordial materiality, those things don't exist either.

49.(E128-1340 T101-106) Nyāya-Vaiśeṣika: There must be contact between organ and object; otherwise, why shouldn't there be visual awareness of everything? It is because the organ doesn't go everywhere. Your *sūtra* also speaks of the impingement (*pratigha*) of organ on object. As for the other senses, it is likewise there too. A sound is only heard when it reaches the auditory organ. Even the internal organ goes to its object according to your own *sūtra*. Thus, all organs function through contacting their objects.

Answer: Your theory involves the assumption of a ray for visual sensation, but that assumption is wrong. If there were such a ray which issued forth when one doubts whether a distant object is a man or a post, then the doubt couldn't be explained. Again, things too close are not seen. And why does the ray grasp gross things but not subtle ones? And anyway, we don't see any such ray.

Objection: During the day the ray is rendered invisible by being covered by the sun's rays, and during the night there is no external light so it is not seen.

Answer: You asked why there shouldn't be visual awareness of everything. It is because what is seen is within the scope of awareness. And when is that so? When there is contiguity between the visual organ and color.

Objection: If the organ does not go to the object, what is this contiguity?

Answer: Here there is nothing to choose between our views. On your view the organ goes to the object and sometimes sees it and sometimes doesn't. On our view the organ stays, where it sees what is in its scope and doesn't see what is not. Factors are listed which preclude an object from falling within the scope of visual awareness--(1) being past or future, (2) being overcome by a more powerful light (the stars in the daytime), (3) being appropriate to another meditational stage, (4) lack of external light, (5) supernatural powers, the body of a ghost (*bhūta*), (6) thick covering, such as the color of the mountain's surface, (6) too far away, (8) too near, (9) the object's not being reached, e.g., the atoms outside the sun's rays, (10) being too subtle, (11) homogeneity, e.g., one crow in a flock of crows, (12) defects in the sense organs.

Visual defects include: when affected by wind one sees colors, when by heat one sees flames, by cold one sees cold colors and water, when going without sleep one sees things blurred, when the mind is tired one fails to discern an object, seeing a double moon, seeing things occasioned by ghosts, ugliness occasioned by demerit, beautiful things occasioned by merit, when affected by bile one sees flames, when veiled by darkness one does not see at all. Similar defects can be found affecting the other senses.

There is also a list given of things which do not fall within the range of awareness, as well as a list of defects of awareness such as distraction, perversion, pride, drunkenness, anger, etc.

You said our *sūtra* speaks of impingement. But there is no such impingement. What explains "impingement" is contiguity.

50.(E134-138; T106-110) You argued (at the beginning of the previous Chapter) that a sound reaches the auditory organ. But there are alternative explanations for one's. not hearing a softly spoken word other than sound reaching or failing to reach his auditory organ. There are also difficulties in the notion of sound-waves, notably that no appropriate example of analogous sorts of waves can be found. Furthermore, being momentary it cannot produce another sound(-wave). Rather, like motions (in your Nyāya-Vaiśeṣika system) it produces a trace which produces a subsequent motion which in turn produces another trace, etc. But there is no substance sound (or *ākāśa*) in all this.

Objection: A sound-wave destroys its predecessor.

Answer: Why so? A sound is produced by something striking something. The subsequent sound is not thus produced. Is it a reflection, like the color mirrored in the water, say? If so, the *Vaiśeṣikasūtra* will be undermined. Also, you hold that sound can be produced from disjunction, but that is not right, for no sound issues when one removes his hand from the wall (say).

51.(E138-141; T110-113) Odor does not travel to the nose to get smelt, any more than sound goes to the ear to get heard. What happens is that the flower's smell scents a portion of the air, which then scents another portion until the series arrives at the nose. Likewise, the heat in air, or the cold there, are not carried by hot or cold particles of fire or water, but the air is tinged. If it were not so we would see fiery color or watery colors in the hot or cold air. And if neither explanation is accepted air will be without touch, which is contrary to experience.

Objection: But in an airtight room a smell arises, so that it can't be passed through the air; it must be that there is a series of smells.

Answer: We admit that in such a case that must be, but where there is air it is as we said.

52.(E141; T113) The same kind of explanation is offered for touch, i.e., that it does not travel nor does its locus (a particle) do so, but a series of touches is passed through the air, e.g., from the sun. So, after the sun has set and we can't see its color we still feel its heat--thus some fire has color and some not.

53.(E141-143; T113-115) You said that the internal organ travels, but that is wrong. It arises and is destroyed at each moment, so cannot move. Various unwanted results accrue from the notion that the internal organ travels--e.g., that doubt will not be possible; if the internal organ goes to another world when it recollects a former life there the body will die.

Objection: In dreams the internal organ travels to other places.

Answer: Not so; people talk like that, but in fact the activities in dreams are false, though some activities (like wet dreams) take place in the body then.

54.(E143-148; T115-119) The sense-organs are formed of the great elements, but they are not limited spatially to the places in the body which support them (viz., the eye-socket, the nasal passages, the auditory cavity, etc.). Those (Sāṃkhyas) who say that they are produced from ego and are thus without form are wrong, since they are material and impinge on their objects, as we have seen. But it is evident that they are not limited by their loci in or on the body, as we can see that the visual organ can grasp big and small things at the same time, have different tactile sensations at once, etc. So the organ is not confined to the body; if it were, we would have two visual organs, two olfactory organs (one for each eye and for each nostril), etc. (The Nyāya-Vaiśeṣika account in terms of a ray for vision is taken up again and refuted.)

Objection: The sense-organs are limited. They each grasp certain kinds of objects, not others, and they only contact the limited natures of the appropriate kinds of objects.

Answer: Although all matter is derived from the great elements, only some of it makes up the sense-organs. Likewise only some of it is limited; the rest is not. And we have already discussed the question of sense-object contact.

55.(E148-149; T119) It is blue, yellow, etc., which are termed bases of color.

Objection: The *sūtra* says that karma and size are also bases of color.

Answer: Configurations are varieties of colors.

Objection: But we cognize colors first, then configurations.

Answer: The cognition of short, long, etc. (i.e., of shape and size) arises in mental awareness supported by the experience of colors, not in the sense-organ. And karma is past (and so not part of the senses).

Objection: You hold that the past doesn't exist. So, since karma is past, it doesn't exist, and thus there is no merit or demerit, and no karmic result.

Answer: Merit and demerit are achieved when something arises in a different place and time from its karmic occasion.

56.(E149-151; T120-121) Sounds, which do not produce great elements, are unlike color and the other qualities that do so in several ways. A sound does not reproduce its kind over and over in its locus as color does. And it isn't produced in the same way as a color is. Colors grow along with the growth of the colored things, but sounds don't. Nobody speaks of the sound on the drum as one does of the color on the table.

Objection: When things strike each other they sound.

Answer: Not always. Anyway, the relationship is different. It is a matter of perception that sounds arise from the great elements, as well as in accord with usage--we say "the sound of the bell" or "of the drum", etc., where the kind of sound is identified through the matter causing it (unlike color, whose kinds may occur in any locus). *Ākāśa* is not the cause of sound, since it is not regularly accompanied by a sound.

57.(E149-153; T121-123) The characteristics of smell.

58.(E153; T123) The characteristics of taste.

59.(E153-155; T123-125) The kinds of touch are listed. The Vaiśeṣika position that there are only three kinds--hot, cold and neither--is criticized. They say that water has only cold touch, but surely a watery gruel in order to have the beneficial results that medical doctor ascribes to it must be hot.

## CHAPTER TWO: Awareness

60.(E156-157; T125-126)[334] There is only awareness (*citta*);

there are no mental associates (*caitasika*). It is the same thing that is called variously "awareness", "mind", "consciousness". Likewise, feelings, identifications and traces are particular bits of awareness.

Objection:[335] So why aren't feelings, identifications and traces called "awarenesses", since they too have contents.

Answer: Lots of things have more than one name.

61.(E157-159; T126-128) Objection: Since there is connection between them there must be both awareness and mental associates. An awareness cannot be associated with another awareness. Furthermore, awareness falls under seven elements, one sense and one aggregate, while mental associates come under one element, one sense and three aggregates. Awareness is the locus; the associates are located there. A *sūtra* says that there will be no aggregates if there are no mental associates. And they arise from different factors--awareness from two (sense-organ and object), mental associates from three (those two plus awareness). The Buddha says that mental associates are born from and are supported by awareness, not that there is only awareness. Furthermore, if only one of the two exist, why shouldn't it be the mental associates?

62.(E159-160; T128-129) Objection continued: Furthermore, there must be mental associates, since awareness and the associates have different marks. Consciousness is what cognizes, feeling experiences satisfaction and frustration, identification grasps things as blue, yellow, etc., and traces condition the cognitions of things. The things cognized, felt, identified and made are different from consciousness, feeling, identification and trace. Also, you say that awareness is what is liberated. But in fact the *sūtra* says that wisdom is liberated because of separation from ignorance, but that mere awareness is not liberated. The Buddha also says that what is "internal" is the body of consciousness, i.e., consciousness together with the sense-organs, and what is "external" is the content of that consciousness. Later in the same *sūtra* the external is precisely the mental associates.

63.(E160-161; T129-131) Answer: There are no such separate things as mental associates. And the Buddha didn't classify awareness under elements, senses, etc.--that is the work of the compilers of the *sūtras.* As for the argument about awareness being the locus and the associates the located, you believe that mental consciousness is located in awareness but you don't call it a mental associate, so in fairness you shouldn't make this argument here. The aggregates, in my view, are several distinct kinds of awareness, just as for you they are several distinct kinds of mental associates. Since awareness and its purported associates come into existence simultaneously there is no reason to attribute the one to two factors, the other to three. And you argue that the Buddha didn't deny mental associates, nor do I do so--rather, I view them as kinds of awareness. In fact, the necessity for admitting mental associates other than awareness only arises if those associates are thought of as objects, and that argument is unacceptable here. It is just awareness that arises from awareness.

64.(E163-167; T131-132) You further argued (in 62 above) that the mental associates have different distinguishing marks from awareness. But that is incorrect. It is just awareness which is grasped as feelings, identifications and traces as well as cognitions. The *sūtra* on which you base your next argument--that mere awareness is not liberated--is improperly understood. In fact the *sūtra* says that awareness gets liberated from the threefold contaminants.

65.(E163-167; T132-136)[336] No simultaneity is possible between a cause and its effect, so feeling, etc., cannot be associated simultaneously with awareness. The supporting object cannot arise at the same time as the awareness, for then there would be two awarenesses at the same time, which is impossible. The development of the several kinds of awareness is gradual, not simultaneous, since the *sūtra* clearly implies that one can be aware without identification or feeling, etc. Again, initial thought is absent from the five kinds of sensory awareness, since you admit that sensation is devoid of conceptual construction inasmuch as there is no desire to communicate to another at that point. And it is likewise evident that initial and sustained thought do not occur simultaneously.

Again, how can memory and the joy of having remembered, or desire and lack of desire, or knowledge and ignorance, doubt and decision, belief and disbelief occur in the same (act of) awareness? If you say that satisfaction and frustration reside in different awarenesses, then knowledge and ignorance should also be attributed to different awarenesses. The Buddha explains the successiveness of awarenesses corresponding to the different "mental associates" in the *Bodhyāṅgasūtra* and *Aṣṭāṅgamārgasūtra* as well as the *Anukramasūtra*, the *Nidānasūtra* and the *Srotāpannasūtra*.

66.(E167-168; T137-138) Objection: There is association. Awareness resides in the self, as do the other aggregates. If awareness and the mental associates develop gradually a person will depend on two aggregates, not five, since you say the five aggregates do not exist in the present. Furthermore, association is spoken of in the *sūtras* (passages quoted). And the Ābhidharmika says: The elements of enlightenment are not dissociated from one who is yoked in spiritual practice. So, they must be associated.

67.(E168-171; T138-141) Answer: The self doctrine is a wrong view. As for what we say about the aggregates: what we say is that four factors gradually appear in the contentfilled acts of understanding of individuals: identification arises after consciousness, feeling after identification, volition after feeling, and joy or depression, etc., after volition. The *sūtras* that speak of association are in some cases of questionable authenticity, in others are misinterpreted by you. (The passages are interpreted properly.) The passage about the elements of enlightenment is likewise misinterpreted by you; it does not mean that one should meditate on all the elements simultaneously, but that they should be meditated on on suitable occasions.

68.(E171-173; T141-143)[337] *Vijñāna* and *citta* are the same thing, viz., awareness, and there are many kinds of it. For awareness of color is different from awareness of smell, etc., and visual awareness depends on light while auditory awareness depends on other things. Right awareness is different from wrong awareness, good from bad awareness. So, awarenesses differ on account of their causal conditions, as well as on their purity or impurity and the feelings involved therein.

69.(E173-174; T143-144) Objection: There is just one awareness. A single awareness operates through the five sense-organs. Furthermore, since a self is unacceptable, it is awareness that performs actions and reaps their results. It is awareness that dies, is born, gets bound and released, that remembers and accumulates traces.

70.(E174-175; T144-145) Objection continued: It is wrong to say that awareness of color is different from awareness of smell, etc. Just as one person inside his house watches different events through different windows, so the one awareness experiences different data through different organs. Furthermore, wrong awareness becomes right awareness, bad becomes good, one does past and future acts and is thus pure or impure, etc. So there is only one awareness.

71.(E175-176; T145-146) Answer: Awareness does not cognize itself. Memory is of previously experienced things, not of itself. This talk of awareness acting, experiencing, dying, getting born, etc., is conventional only. You mention the accumulation of traces--but if awareness were permanent it would need no traces. The postulation of traces is required to explain how one awareness affects another, and is not required if there is only one awareness.

72.(E176-177; T146-148) You are wrong to say that one awareness can perform several cognitive acts. Just as the hand holds the pot and cannot hold another actual object, so the awareness that grasps color cannot also grasp sound, etc. Since both the visual organ and the visible object are momentary, visual awareness must also be momentary. And what is momentary does not move. In your example of a person in his house watching different events the person is treated in the conventional manner as a single individual, but in a scientific treatise such as this the true nature of things is being investigated, and so everything should be treated in terms of its true nature. A person is five aggregates, not a single individual. The argument about karma and fruition has been replied to elsewhere.

73.(E178; T148-149)[338] Objection: If awareness is momentary it cannot give rise to a thought of color, etc. Even though a flash of lightning remains for a short time it doesn't provide identification--how much less a momentary awareness! You say that it is the stream of consciousness that reflectively discerns, but that is not right. For if a single awareness does not discern, a stream of them cannot do so. It is not like the strength in a cloth made of threads lacking that strength, for a single awareness has no capacity to arouse thought, and so a whole stream of them doesn't either.

74.(E179-180; T149-151) Answer: Awareness produces thought through the force of the signs formed in awareness, not because it remains for a short time. If it were not so we would not experience momentary sounds arousing thoughts. The awareness that arouses the thought of blue does not arouse the thought of yellow, so even if awareness were to last for a time it wouldn't help to explain the production of thoughts. Again, there are two kinds of grasping, discerning and nondiscerning. If awareness were not momentary it would discern every graspable thing in its entirety. In our view, however, the grasping of a stream of several awarenesses is what discerns an object, while a practically momentary awareness or set of awarenesses is nondiscerning.

Awarenesses, minds and consciousnesses are momentary, because when an aggregate of blue, say, is presented in front of one, consciousness is immediately produced. A person may think he is experiencing all objects at a single time; if awareness continued for a time he could not have had that erroneous thought. Again, if one believes that awareness is not momentary he must admit that the same awareness is both true and false, and that a doubting awareness is the same as a belief.

75.(E180-181; T151)[339] Objection: Some Ābhidharmikas say that awarenesses can occur simultaneously, since a person can grasp various sense-contents at the same time--can see a pot, hear music, smell fragrance, taste food, and feel a breeze all at the same time. Now if it is one consciousness that grasps all these things this will conflict with the Buddha's denial of wholes distinct from collections of parts; so we conclude that this experience (of grasping various sense-contents at once) requires simultaneous awarenesses for its explanation.

76.(E181-182; T151-153) Answer: Your explanation fails to note that awareness depends on attention. Visual, etc. awareness depends on attention to visual contents, etc. Things come to be depending on their karmic causes, and since awarenesses arise one by one no maturation is experienced simultaneously either on earth or in hell. Awareness grasps its object very quickly; sometime, as in the circle of fire, the intervals between awarenesses are not noticed. If awarenesses were simultaneous, everything could be produced at once, and a man could be liberated without effort. That awarenesses occur gradually is attested by experience.

Question: Because of what are the awarenesses necessarily gradual in occurrence?

Answer: Because of their directly antecedent conditions. Just as for you one self has one internal organ, so for us one awareness has one directly antecedent condition, just as the sprout springs up following the seed and not otherwise.

## CHAPTER THREE: Identification

77.(E183-186; T153-157) Identification is the grasping of the signs of empirical factors. It involves perverted views, such as that the noneternal is eternal, frustration is satisfying, what is without self is with self, etc. There are three kinds of identifications--pleasing, hateful and neutral, and three kinds of feelings that arise from them productive of three kinds of poison. So the Buddha says that identifications should be abandoned.

Objection: This cannot be right, since one rejects the defilements through identification following the *sūtras* which speak of identification as eradicating greed, ignorance, etc.

Answer: In those passages "identification" refers to wisdom. (Other passages are cited to support this.)

Identifications grasp signs, it was said. What are "signs"? Some say that they are five--past, future, convention, contact and person, but that is wrong since a person is based in the five aggregates. Rather, these "signs" are the supporting objects corresponding to the empirical factors that signify the presence of those factors, and which are different from those factors themselves.

Objection: The signs cannot be supporting objects, for there is a type of concentration which has as its supporting object a state called "signless".

Answer: There are two kinds of signs, blameworthy and not blameworthy. In order to preclude the first kind the adept is advised to experience directly without registering the signs of empirical things, but it is not a defect to experience blameless supporting objects through their signs, objects such as liberation, concentration and the like.

## CHAPTER FOUR: Feelings

78.(E186-188; T157-158) There are three kinds of feelings: satisfying, frustrating, and neither. The satisfying kind occurs when body and mind are expanded, the frustrating kind when they are contracted. The third kind is contrary to both the other two.

Feelings are either one or another of these three kinds, but the objects of feelings are not, since under different circumstances a thing may occasion one or another kind of feeling. When frustration is caused to stop a satisfying feeling arises. There the satisfying feeling is conventional, not absolutely real.

Objection: That cannot be right, for satisfaction is the result of meritorious behavior and frustration the result of demeritorious behavior. Furthermore the material and immaterial realms must be the abodes of satisfaction, not to speak of the presence of satisfactions in the realm of desire.

Answer: If anything were really satisfying that would contradict the (Buddhist) tenet that all is frustrating. Satisfaction is only a lessening of frustration.

79.(E188-189; T158-161) Extended arguments are reviewed showing that only frustration is real, not satisfaction. Furthermore, the body is the source of all frustrations. Thus the functioning of the body is frustrating.

80.(E190-192; T161-163) Since the feeling of satisfaction is the root cause of karmic activities the wise man abandons that feeling.

81.(E192-196; T163-168) Objection: There is no such thing as (the third alleged kind of feeling, viz.,) a feeling that is neither satisfying nor frustrating. No such thing is ever felt.

Answer: Surely there is such a feeling; it arises from objects to which one is indifferent. There are eight worldly factors: lust, nonlust, blame, praise, fame, ill-fame, satisfaction and frustration. Four are favorable, four are unfavorable to ordinary persons. But the noble ones, who are free from desire, are indifferent to such things. And that indifference is itself a feeling.

All accompaniments of mind are feelings. And all conditioning factors are frustrating, since they cause frustration.

Question: How about pure feelings?

Answer: Even they are productive of frustration, since they involve the view of self. But pure feelings are superior to impure ones since they are propadeutic to liberation, involving the realization that all is frustration. If a pure feeling were satisfying the wise man would not direct his mind on *nirvāṇa*.

Question: In each feeling three residues of the afflictions arise. But how can attraction arise as a residue in a satisfying feeling?

Answer: No attraction arises as residue in a frustrating feeling. Delusion is a residue in every feeling. It is because of delusion that frustration is misidentified as satisfying. When an entity is not properly identified and taken to be frustrating, aversion arises. And in the third kind of feeling (neither frustrating nor satisfying) only delusion, and not attraction nor aversion, are experienced. Because of this people call the supporting object of such a feeling superior, but the Buddha tells us that the object is not superior, for an object is merely an occasion which may trigger any kind of feeling. In fact, satisfaction and frustration are present in the third kind of feeling but are not noticed since their respective objects are not experienced.

There follows an extended discussion of the proper interpretation of scriptural passages bearing on this question.

82.(E196-199; T168-170) Question: Who feels--the person or the feeling?

Answer: The person. Though the *sūtra* says it is the feeling that feels, what is meant is the awarenesses which experience the feelings, being qualified by those feelings as signs.

The Buddha speaks of bodily as well as mental feelings in order to quiet the Tīrthikas who locate feelings in a self. The "bodily" feelings are those arising from the external sense-organs. Such feelings are only satisfying or frustrating, not indifferent.

Question: Which of the three kinds of feelings produces the heaviest afflictions?

Answer: One can find among Ābhidharmikas those who contend for each of the three (satisfying, frustrating, neither) involving the heaviest afflictions. Some of their arguments are reviewed.

83.(E199-203; T171-173) This section explores which feelings are experienced in the higher meditative stages.

## CHAPTER FIVE: Conditioning Factors

84.(E203-206; T174-176) Synonyms for *cetanā* ("volition") are *prārthana* and *praṇidhāna*. Conditioning factors are things which make things. *Prārthana* is that which has a thirst for making aggregates.

Objection: *Prārthana* is then thirst, not volition.

Answer: No, since volition is the result of thirst, not its cause. Furthermore, volition is the same thing as the mind. Otherwise there would be no mental action.

85.(E206-208; T176-178) Contact (*sparśa*) is consciousness relating to a supporting object. The commonly proclaimed definition of contact, that it is the meeting of three (elements), is not the correct definition, for no sense-organ reaches to the supporting object.

Objection: Contact is a distinct accompanying factor. A *sūtra* speaks of a twofold contact--one the contact between three elements, and second the result of such contact.

Answer: This view, though regularly cited, runs counter to the factor's definition. If contact were a distinct accompanying factor it would differ from other such factors, since it is itself the condition of accompanying factors. It cannot be its own condition.

Objection: A particular contact conditions the accompanying factors which cause (other) contacts, just as thirst conditions feeling but that feeling does not condition that thirst.

Answer: In the first moment there is thirst, in the next, feeling; there is nothing found in between, and so no cause to postulate any contact.

86.(E208-210; T178-180) Each act of attention (*manaskāra*) determines a distinct awareness. Attention is of two kinds: right and wrong. Right attention is that involving correct reasoning and directed toward the nature of things; it is also generated at an appropriate time and place. The reverse of this is wrong attention.

87.(E210-211; T180-181) Interest is covetousness.

88.(E211-212; T181-182) Joy is delight

89.(E212-213; T182-183) Faith is concentration on a content. It is the purity of mind gotten from listening to others speaking of *dharma*. Since those who speak of *dharma* may not themselves have faith, or be good teachers, one can divide faith into delusive and nondelusive, or into three--good, bad and neutral--on the grounds of distinctions among those toward whom the faith is directed.

90.(E213; T183) Energy is venturing (*abhyutsāha*). It accompanies attention and concentration. It has three kinds: good, bad and neutral. Good energy is what is included in the four right efforts. Good effort is also known as good belief, and assists attention and concentration gaining everything.

91.(E213-214; T183-185) Memory is awareness of what was previously experienced.

Objection: Since awareness is momentary, how can what is experienced by one awareness be remembered by another?

Answer: That's how memory works. For example, what was grasped by a visual awareness is subsequently grasped by a mental awareness. Likewise, a noble person can cognize what was experienced in another body in some previous life through memory.

92.(E215-216; T185-186) Initial and sustained thought are respectively gross and subtle stages of unconcentrated awareness.

93.(E216-217; T186-187) Heedlessness is wrongly performing or failing to perform meritorious acts. Neither it nor its opposite, heedfulness, is a separate factor.

Tranquillity is when while the mind is working the body and mind become free from depravity.

94.(E218-221; T187-190) The dissociated mental factors are said to be possession, nonpossession, nonconceptual identification, cessation-trance, life-faculty, birth, disappearance, duration, change, old age, death, collection of words, collection of terms, collection of syllables, ordinariness, etc.

Possession is only the coming together of factors in an existent being. One who has all five aggregates is termed "(having) possessed (*prāpta*) karma", i.e., one who experiences the results of previous good and bad acts. But neither possession nor the lack of it nor nonpossession are separate factors dissociated from awareness.

Nor is there a factor called "nonconceptual identification" for there is no stage where all awarenesses and associated factors disappear for ordinary people They still operate, but very subtly, so the state is called "nonidentifying". Likewise, cessation-trance is not a separate factor, any more than *nirvāṇa* is. The life-faculty is the stream of the five aggregates born of karma. Birth is the arising of the aggregates. Disappearance is their cessation from the present moment. Duration is their continuity in a modified form through change. None of these are separate factors. Phonemes, words and sentences are not separate factors, but are to be brought under the sense-organs.

Some say there is a distinct factor called ordinariness (*pṛthagjanatva*) distinct from the ordinary man, but this is a heretical view and would let in all sorts of abstract entities of the sort Vaiśeṣikas speak of. Ābhidharmikas have studied the books of these heretics and have as a result composed works such as the *Abhidharmasūtras* in which entities such as ordinariness are postulated. Other Ābhidharmikas say there are factors like suchness (*tathatā*), the highest point (*bhūtakoṭi*), and dependent origination. So analysis is required, not merely quoting the Buddha.

## BOOK THREE: Origin

### CHAPTER ONE: Karma

95.(E222-223; T191-192) The second truth, the truth of origin, consists of karma and defilements. There are three kinds of karma: bodily, vocal and mental. Mental karma is of two kinds: mind and what arises from mind. The mental act is mind, consisting of a belief such as "I shall kill this being"; this act *qua* accumulated demerit exceeds bodily and vocal karma. When there is no belief the mind is different from karma. From manifest karma there arises unmanifest karma. It pertains to mind as well as body and speech.

96.(E223-225; T192-194) Unmanifest karma is the merit and demerit that arise dependent on awarenesses and which continues to operate even in deep sleep or faint, etc.

Some say that we perceive manifest karma, and since we do not perceive unmanifest karma it doesn't exist. But if it didn't exist then the merit accruing from, e.g., abstention from killing wouldn't exist.

Objection: Abstention is negative, thus not an entity. The results--e.g., of going to heaven--which are said to accrue from abstention from killing, actually arise from good awareness.

Answer: No, for then the increase in morality couldn't be explained. For that matter manifest karma is not merely the act of killing, but rather a factor arising immediately following killing, immediately after which one gets the demerit of killing. E.g., if someone orders another person to kill someone, the first one (who gave the order) gets demerit immediately upon the act. This proves there is unmanifest karma. Mind and moral restraint are not the same thing, for one may have a bad or indeterminate mind, or even be without awareness, and still be said to be moral--or, for that matter, immoral.

Question: Is unmanifest karma material or a dissociated factor?

Answer: Since it is a "manufacturer" (*abhisaṃskāra*) and not a "modifier" (*rūpaka*) it is brought under conditioning factors and not under matter.

Question: But it is not one of the six "bodies of volition" (*cetanakāya*) which are said in the *sūtra* to comprise the conditioning aggregates. Nor is it mentioned as a dissociated factor.

Answer: We have previously said that there are merit and demerit apart from awareness.

Question: What is wrong with saying unmanifest karma is material?

Answer: Color, sound, smell, taste and touch are not in themselves meritorious or demeritorious; so unmanifest karma is not material.

Unmanifest karma arises from good and bad actions, not from indeterminate ones. It arises at the moment of the second awareness. And it lasts for a longer or shorter time depending on its strength.

97.(E226-228; T194-197) An act that is preceded by awareness is done with a cause; the opposite is what is not done with a cause.

Question: Isn't this something "not done with a cause" an act?

Answer: It is an act. However, an act done with a cause has maturation. It is done with conviction. The act "not done with a cause" is one done without conviction. Talk (about killing) by soldiers is without a cause; such talk by others is with a cause. When, e.g., one kills small creatures by walking on them, the act is without a cause. Such acts do not produce maturations.

There are four classes of acts: (1) done but without preparation, e.g., when one repents of an act, or forgets to carry it out after planning it; (2) not done but with preparation, e.g., one who incites another to kill or to give a donation comes to be of pleasant disposition but earns demerit or merit for later; (3) done with preparation, e.g., one himself killing or donating comes to be of pleasant disposition but earns demerit or merit for later; (4) not done and without accumulating karma.

Objection: Since the maturations will go on indefinitely there can be no liberation.

Answer: A knower of the truth, though he performs acts with a cause, does not accumulate (merit or demerit). The seed that is burnt cannot germinate.

Acts can be distinguished into those that have regular maturation and those that have irregular maturation. The former comprise not only the five producers of early retribution, but many other acts where the objects or the awarenesses involved are heavy.

98.(E228-229; T197-198) Heavy evil is that whose results will be experienced in hell. They include acts that cause schisms in the order or splits in the *dharma*. Such acts are performed by those with extreme wrong views, with intense ill-will toward the Buddha. Pūraṇa is mentioned as such a one. Generally, more serious evil is counted as heavy.

99.(E229-231; T198-201) The greatest purpose is immediate enlightenment. A scale of actions slightly inferior to each other leads from the path to enlightenment for oneself, through the path of being a disciple, to that earning life in *bhavāgra* for eighty thousand *mahākalpas* (the highest purpose achievable in *saṃsāra*), through that by which one obtains existence in the realm of nothingness for 60,000 eons and the *brahmaloka* for half an eon, through that which gets one life among the *paranirmita* gods for 60,000 years, etc.

Enlightenment consists in that type of factor called extreme emptiness. It is higher even than abandonment. Omniscience has as its purpose abandonment. Staying in the Bodhisattva state for a long time has for its purpose right abandonment, which is the same as shedding the fetters and the notion of self gradually through enlightenment.

The stream-enterer, even though enjoying objects of desire, is said to be "the field of merit" because of his wisdom, but not the ordinary person who has abandoned passions and who is destined for *bhavāgra*. The former has knowledge, the latter not so much. Maitreya is given due respect by perfected beings because of his awareness of enlightenment .causing emptiness; likewise for any monk who awakens the highest awareness of enlightenment. This has been clearly expounded in the "*Dṛṣṭānta*" (perhaps 72.Kumāralāta's?).

100.(E231-242; T201-215) Acts are: good, bad or neutral. A good act is one done for another's welfare, i.e., causing satisfaction in others. What causes frustration in others is called bad. Medical treatments and operations, though causing temporary frustration, eventually produce satisfaction, so they are not bad actions.

Adultery, on the other hand, though producing temporary satisfaction, yields eventual frustration and so is bad. One who unknowingly provides poisonous food or drink with good intentions does a good act.

Question: What about an act that serves others by killing living beings, for example?

Answer: It causes both merit and demerit.

Objection: But since the killing is done with good intentions, it should be good in accordance with the previous analysis. And we know that the good warrior goes to heaven.

Answer: No. One necessarily earns demerit as a result of impure actions. The warrior, like the butcher, earns demerit by killing, though if he has a compassionate heart towards his victim he obtains merit thereby. (This discussion is quite extensive.)

Objection: Your claim that good is an act done for another's welfare and bad what is intended to cause another's frustration is mistaken since, e.g., feeding oneself is meritorious, or sprinkling water on a shrine. Likewise, on your account one would accrue no demerit from violating the shrine, since no one is harmed, or from speaking ill of one who does not hear it.

Answer: Feeding oneself is not in itself meritorious, but if done for the purpose of preparing the body to help others, it is. Sprinkling the shrine is symbolic to others and so does relate to others' welfare. And speaking ill of someone to others develops frustration for the person slandered, and so is demeritorious.

Satisfaction comes as maturation of good acts, frustration of bad acts. Neutral acts earn no maturation at all.

101.(E242-243; T214-215) Bad conduct.

102.(E244-245; T215-217) Good conduct.

103.(E245-248; T217-221) There are three sorts of acts: (1) that act related to the realm of desire from the hells to the *paranirmitavaśavartin* gods; (2) relating to the material realm, from the *brahmaloka* to the *akaniṣṭha* heaven; (3) relating to the immaterial realm, from the realm of nothingness to that of neither-identification-nor- nonidentification. Indeterminate action and acts with irregular maturations relate to realm of desire. All actions in the realm of desire have their maturations in that realm.

Objection: If so this is the system of the heretics. All actions, whether meritorious or not, having maturation or not, are the results of previous actions. Then there will be no purpose in trying to gain merit, and no liberation is possible, for the maturations cannot be completely exhausted.

Answer: This heretical view is not correct. It holds that satisfactions and frustrations, whether higher or lower, are all maturations of previous acts. Our view, however, is that the actual entities in the world are produced from causes and conditions operating at the present moment like the sprout and the seed. It is not correct to think that everything is conditioned by previous karma.

Objection: If every maturation produces another one there will be an infinite regress.

Answer: No. There are three kinds of maturations--good, bad and neutral. The first two produce maturations, but the third doesn't. There is purpose in trying to gain merit, for only by good actions now will the seeds of satisfying maturations in the future be sown. And liberation is possible, for karma is destroyed through attaining knowledge.

Furthermore, every factor that arises has its root in some act, since it is regulated as arising from this person's body and from that one's. The regularity requires explanation through karma.

Question: Why not hold that factors come from their material causes only? For example, black gram comes from black gram.

Answer: Yes, that also has its root in action. Black gram comes from black gram on condition that some appropriate action arises. We infer this from the fact that in ancient times when people performed only good acts their rice supplies flowed spontaneously.

Objection: Yes, right things are not born earlier.

Answer: No, both right and wrong things are rooted in karma, being the maturations of general activity. E.g., the earth, etc. comes to be from obtaining the conditions for the activity of walking around; the moon and the sun come into being from obtaining the conditions of the activity of illuminating. So every entity that is born has action (*karman*) as its root. Even the pure conditioned things are rooted in karma. In this case the power of the knowledge conditioned by good conduct in previous births is responsible.

104.(E248-251; T221-223) The Buddha says in a *sūtra* that there are three kinds of maturations of karma--(1) in this life, (2) in the next birth, and (3) in some subsequent life. Maturations of actions in the intermediate state immediately following this life will be experienced in the next life; those of other intermediate states will be experienced in future lives.

Question: Are these actions of regulated maturation and at a regulated time?

Answer: Some say that all three kinds of act have regulated maturations. But that is not right, since then the five producers of early retribution will not be of regulated maturation, but in the *Ṣaṭpādābhidharma* it is said that they are. However, in the *Lavaṇopamasūtra* they are said to be of unregulated maturation. In any case, all actions mature at a regulated time. An act need not mature, but if it does mature at all, it will do so at a specific one of the three times mentioned.

Others say that a medical treatment is experienced in this world, as is good or bad action done relating to the Buddha, to noble persons or parents. Heavier actions which do not relate to these things, e.g., the five producers of early retribution, mature in the next life. Actions of Cakravartins and Bodhisattvas, being heavier still, mature in future births.

Others say that all three kinds of acts mature in accordance with one's vow.

Someone in the womb, asleep, or insane, etc., cannot accumulate karma, since (s)he does not think. All who have the idea of self accumulate karma, even if they are free from passion. A noble person, who is free of the idea of self, does not accumulate karma.

105.(E251-253; T223-226) In the realm of desire good acts produce satisfying maturations, bad acts frustrating maturations. Neutral acts may produce no feeling, or if they do they will be satisfying only.

Some say that depression is not a maturation because it is a result of conceptual construction and so is very light and can be set aside. But this is wrong, since depression is worse than mere frustration; it produces more severe unhappiness. The ignorant are always in a state of depression, which is produced both from (previous) depression and from contentedness. E.g., when one loses someone one loves depression is born from joy, whereas when it is born from jealousy it is born from depression. Furthermore, that a maturation can be set aside is no argument, for a stream-enterer, for example, sets aside the maturations of hell, etc. (Āryadeva's

48.*Catuḥśataka* is quoted in this passage.)

106.(E253-255; T226-229) The three obstructions are acting, defilement, and maturation. Actions, by producing maturations, obstruct the path to liberation. Defilements, by distracting one, obstruct liberation. And maturations of an intense sort likewise make it difficult or impossible for one to contemplate the path.

107.(E256-257; T229-231) There are four kinds of acts: (1) black with black maturation, an action because of which one is reborn in the *avaivartika* hell or as an animal or a ghost; (2) white with white maturation, an act through which one is born into one of the three realms as man or god; (3) black-white with black-white maturation, an act that is the mixture of the previous two; and (4) neither black nor white with neither black nor white maturation, a pure act that destroys the other three sorts of karma.

108.(E259-259; T231-232) Five things are called "producers of early retribution" because their maturation is experienced immediately following this life. They are heavy because of the importance of the fields over which they range. They are (1) splitting the order, (2) causing bleeding in the body of a *tathāgata*, (3) killing a noble person, (4) killing one's father or (5) killing one's mother.

109.(E259; T233) Five morals.

110.(E259-265; T233-238) Acts may be classified as to which world they mature in--hell, animal, ghosts, humans, gods, and nonconcentration. The first has been explained in the *Ṣaṭpādābhidharme Lokaprajñapti*. Killing brings rebirth in hell or for a very short span among animals, ghosts or humans, depending on the heaviness of the act. The animal rebirths involve specific retributions--e.g., intense hatred brings rebirth as a snake or scorpion, intense delusion as a pig, intense brutality as a lion or tiger, etc. Jealousy and greed bring rebirth respectively as ghosts with jealous or miserly dispositions. Similarly with other rebirths.

111.(E266-267; T238-239) The seven kinds of bad behavior are killing, stealing, adultery, slander, harsh words, lying, and speaking senselessly.

112.(E267-269; T239-242) The seven kinds of good behavior are the oppposite of the foregoing seven. There are three classes of these: moral behavior, meditation and concentration. Pure behavior is included in the second and third of these.

113.(E270-271; T243-244) Eight-limbed fasting.

114.(E271; T244-245) There are four impure positions: (1) someone who sees and denies that he does; (2) someone who does not see and affirms that he does; (3) someone who does not see affirming it but then denying it later (e.g., in court), (4) someone who sees denying it but later affirming it. There are four pure positions, the reverse of the above.

Question: What is the difference between *dṛṣṭi*, *śruti*, *buddhi* and *jñāna*?

Answer: The first three are varieties of belief. *Dṛṣṭi* is belief in arising things. *Śruti* is belief in what an adept says. *Jñāna* is inferential awareness. *Buddhi* is the wisdom by which one discriminates the foregoing three.

115.(E271-273; T245-247) In the realm of desire there is manifest karma, unmanifest karma, and what is neither manifest nor unmanifest. Likewise in the material realm. In the immaterial realm there is manifest, unmanifest, and pure karma.

Manifest karma is what is done by body or speech. The accumulation of merit and demerit arising in dependence on manifest karma is unmanifest karma, the factors dissociated from awareness. There is also unmanifest karma that is born of awareness alone. What is neither manifest nor unmanifest is mind itself, the volition that is called action. How much unmanifest karma is obtained depends on how much mental effort is made. E.g., making a vow necessarily obtains unmanifest karma.

Some say that in the *brahmaloka* there can be no manifest action productive of unmanifest karma because there are neither initial nor sustained thought there and those two are what produce karma. This opinion is wrong; there are both initial and sustained thought in the *brahmaloka*.

116.(E273-279; T247-254) There are seven bad restraints plus the three intense kinds of mental acts, viz., passion, hatred and delusion.

117.(E279; T254) Ten good action-paths.

118.(E279-280; T255-256) The outcomes of bad actions are delineated.

119.(E281-285; T256-261) Question: Which are most essential (lit., heavier)--bodily, vocal or mental acts? Some say that the first two are essential, since the producers of early retribution fall into those classes. Furthermore, one cannot kill a person through mere volition. Indeed, mere mental action has no maturation. One cannot get merit by merely wishing to be charitable; he's got to give something away.

Answer: You are wrong. Mental action is more essential than the others, for without it the others do not exist. The maturation of mental acts can result in a life of 80,000 *mahākalpas*. Again, a person of good conduct who at the end of his life adopts a wrong view goes to hell. The reason why the producers of early retribution are essential is because the volition there is heavier. Actions of the relevant sorts--e.g., patricide--are not sinful if the mind is not aware of what is being done. And one certainly can gain merit by taking a vow, for example.

120.(E285-287; T261-264) Various opinions are held about the body--that it is formed from *prakṛti*, from God, from *mahāpuruṣa*, or naturally. Different things have different sorts of causes. Since these things--*prakṛti*, God, etc.--are not of varying sorts, they cannot be the causes in question. In fact, bodies are made from karma, for actions are of varying sorts. So a body is the result of karma of a given kind, not God's work.

## CHAPTER TWO

121.(E288-290; T264-266) A defilement is an activity of filthy awareness. Awareness is called filthy when it is led by attachment, hatred and/or delusion. The accumulations produced by a filthy mind are called proclivities, of which there are ninety-eight varieties. But the defilements themselves are ten, viz., (1) attachment, (2) hatred, (3) delusion, (4) doubt, (5) pride, and (6-10) the five wrong views. (1) Attachment, called devotion to satisfaction, is of three kinds--sexual desire, the desire to come to be, and the desire not to come to be, i.e., to cease.

Objection: Devotion to satisfaction is a feeling, not a desire.

Answer: The desire is caused by the expectation of satisfaction.

122.(E290-291; T266-268) Classifications of attachment into several kinds.

123.(E291-293; T269-270) The causes of desire.

124.(E293-297; T270-274) The frustrating outcome of desire is illustrated at length.

125.(E297-298; T274-275) One checks and eventually abandons attachment by meditating on it as impure and on the impermanence of everything.

126.(E298-301; T275-279) (2) Hatred is malice. Its varieties are illustrated. It is likewise eradicated by meditating on its impurity and on impermanence.

127.(E302-307; T279-285) (3) Delusion or ignorance is adverting to conventional designations, e.g., speaking as if there were a self. It is not mere lack of knowledge, but false, perverse awareness. It is the cause of all the conditioning factors. The noble one, having destroyed ignorance, has no such factors. All the other defilements are limbs of ignorance, since they all involve bad conduct which depends on wrong notions.

Ignorance arises from thinking about what one has heard that is not properly conveyed. This occurs whenever one or another of bad causal factors, viz., bad friends, hearing wrong *dharma*, attending to the wrong things, or wrong activities, etc.

One abandons ignorance by cultivating knowledge.

Question: Knowledge is correct awareness about aggregates, elements and senses. So why does a *sūtra* say that dependent origination and the meditation on it are the cure for ignorance?

Answer: To avoid being taken in by the opinions of heretics. E.g., heretics say that God is the cause of the world, that there is substance, that there is a whole, etc. By meditating on dependent origination one avoids these views. Knowledge of aggregates, elements and senses is included within such meditation.

128.(E307-310; T285-288) Elevating oneself through a false notion is (5) pride. It is the elevation of a lower self. Any notion of relative worth with respect to others is a case of pride, even that of being equal among equals. It has many varieties, some of which are illustrated. It arises for those who do not understand the actual nature of the aggregates, who take material and other constituents for their self. Thus to remove pride one should meditate on impermanence, etc.

129.(E320-321; T288-291) (4) Doubt is uncertainty about whether there is liberation or not, whether there are merit and demerit or not, whether there are three jewels or not.

Question: What about empirical doubts about whether it is a tree or a post, etc.? Are they to be classified under the category of defilements also?

Answer: No. Those doubts are not defilements, for they do not occasion rebirth and can arise in persons free from contaminants. Doubt arises when cognizing two opposing features of a thing. It also arises from conditions such as excessive distance, etc., causing one not to comprehend the demarcating feature of a thing. So it is removed as soon as one does comprehend that feature.

130.(E313-317; T291-297) (6) It is a wrong view to take there to be a self among the five aggregates.

Objection: What is the harm in calling the five aggregates a self, any more than there is in classifying pots, etc., according to their specific marks?

Answer: One is misled thereby into thinking the aggregates are permanent and that the self is single. One is unable to comprehend the emptiness of things, and as a result defilements arise. The self-concept is a result of conceptual construction occasioned by listening to people speaking of "man", "god", etc.

Conceptions of the self are mentioned, including a Vedic view (quoted from the *Puruṣasūkta*), the materialist view, the idealist view (that conceptual identification is the self), the view that conditions are the self or that consciousness is.

Though it is a wrong view to hold that the self exists ultimately, it is also a wrong view to hold that the self does not exist relatively. To make the latter mistake is to fall into an extreme of nihilism, to make the former is to espouse eternalism. Both are wrong. Passages are quoted from works called *Paramārthaśūnyatāsūtra* and *Mahāśūnyatāsūtra* which say that the various things, such as the visual organ, old age and death, etc., though they do not exist ultimately, do exist relatively.[340]

131.(E318-320; T297-299) The view of (7) eternalism and the view of (8) nihilism are the extreme views. They are abandoned when one meditates on emptiness.

132.(E320-325; T299-305) (9) To say that something exists when it doesn't, or (10) to deny that it exists when it does, is to express a false view. False views arise from delusion, through what is not a cause or what is only an apparent cause. Various false views are considered.

133.(E326-327; T305-307) A perverse view is, e.g., asserting that what is false is true. Again, it is rating something or someone superior that (or who) is inferior. Perverse morals is indifference toward enlightenment and attempting to become pure through mere ritual.

134..(E327-328; T307-308) The afflictions are listed as sleepiness, excitedness, regret, *māyā*, craftiness, shamelessness, disregard, heedlessness, cheating propaganda, insincere praise, praising one person in order to censure another, desire for gaining a gift by offering a small one, discontent, yawning, immoderation in eating, not making a sufficient effort, insufficient respect for one's leader, preferring evil to good.

135.(E328-330; T308-310) The bad roots are lust, hate and delusion.

Question: Do these roots reside in factors or in the beings affected by them?

Answer: The idea of a living being arises from factors, and feelings arise in turn from the idea of a living being. From those feelings these three bad roots come forth. So these proclivities reside in living beings. Otherwise they would not cease when a given person loses them.

136.(E330-339; T311-318) Three proclivities: desire, becoming, and ignorance. Four floods: desire, becoming, (wrong) views, ignorance. Four appropriatings: desire, (wrong) view, moral precepts and vows, and self-doctrine. Four knots: bodily covetousness, bodily malevolence, merely following rules concerning the body, attachment to the bodily *status-quo*. Five obstructions: sensual desire, malice, lethargy, excitedness, and perplexity. Five fetters relating to lower things: sensual desire, malice, attachment to mere rules, doubt, and self-view. Five fetters relating to higher things: excitedness, pride, ignorance, material desires, immaterial desires. Five kinds of selfishness: of abode, of family, of gain, of praise, of *dharma*. Five gaps (*khila*): doubting the teacher, doubting the Buddha, doubting the scripture, doubting the practice, doubting good people. These are "gaps" because one afflicted by them does not maintain goodness. Doubt of the Buddha comes from being unlearned, from being confused as a result of studying Veda and grammar, etc. Five (?) attachments: attachment to body, to sensual desires, failure to appreciate noble speech, pride in a small triumph. (It is not clear whether these are the five, or what is the fifth.)

Proclivities are associated with awareness.

Objection: They are dissociated from awareness, since children, who do not think on sensual desire, are nevertheless caught in the grip of sensory proclivities.

Answer: No, there is no residue of sensual desire in children. If they are said to be subject to it it is only in the sense that they have not got the means to avoid it.

Eight wrong paths explained.

137.(E339-340; T319-320) Nine fetters.

138.(E340-344; T320-324) Question: Are the ten generally permeating defilements--viz., lack of confidence, sloth, forgetfulness, distraction, ignorance, lack of comprehension, unreasoning attention, bad resolve, excitedness and heedlessness--associated with every defiled awareness?

Answer: No; for example, excitedness is not present in every defiled awareness.

Question: Some Ābhidharmikas say that the self-doctrine is neutral, since if it were bad everyone who holds that doctrine would go to hell.

Answer: It is not neutral; it is bad. One who asserts the self-doctrine to others goes to hell.

Question: Suppose one mentions a false view and occasions doubt in someone's mind?

Answer: That is not bad if he doesn't occasion a wrong view but merely occasions doubt.

139.(E344-347; T324-328) An opinion regarding the systematic ordering of thoughts leading to the cessation of faults is rejected. The author thinks that the afflictions are gotten rid of through a variety of awarenesses.

Question: Through which contemplations are the defilements destroyed?

Answer: As supported by seven restorers, even including concentration in the realm of desire.

The aspirant for liberation must understand that the defilements involve innumerable constructions; so the faults pertaining to the defilements must be consciously understood.

140.(E347-353; T328-333) One whose thoughts are on nominal designations accumulates karma. A noble person does not do so. In fact, there is no pure action; it is the one who dwells on nominal designations that performs actions. All actions arise from the defilements.

Question: Are living beings born defiled or undefiled?

Answer: With defilements, since their birth is determined by previous karma born of defilements.

Objection: Then a noble person shouldn't have a body, since the body is formed from the defilements and he doesn't have those.

Answer: But his body is formed from previous defilements. However, the noble person does not suffer any more defilements, and so is eventually not reborn.

Question: Isn't food a cause of the body as well as the defilements?

Answer: Food produces matter, etc., through conscious designations, but the defilements are not produced through conscious designations. See 110 above.

Question: If the body is caused by defilements then there can be no change in subsequent lives and so no possibility of liberation.

Answer: Even though one is in a low life a good thought may arise, just as even when one is in a high life a bad thought may arise. Thus one's future maturations are changed.

## BOOK FOUR: The Truth of Cessation[341]

### CHAPTER ONE

141.(E354-357; T334-337)[342] The *śāstra* says that the cessation-truth is the cessation of three awarenesses, viz., the awarenesses of designations, of factors and of emptiness. The first of these is caused to cease by awareness based on much learning or through thought. The second is caused to cease by becoming aware of emptiness. And the last ceases on entering the cessation trance, or at the time the stream of factors is completely destroyed by entering liberation without residue.

[343]A nominal designation is a conceptual construction of a person that arises in dependence on the five aggregates, or of a pot on the basis of color, taste, smell, etc. Such things (as person or pot) are mere names; the reality of factors is denied in the *sūtras*.

The Buddha says there are two truths, highest and conventional. The highest truths are matter, etc. and liberation. The conventional truth is what is mere designation, e.g., the pot or the person.

The conventional truth is useful not only for daily life but also so that the Buddhist message and discipline can be conveyed. One controls the mind through conventional truth, then destroys it by the highest truth. A *sūtra* says that *nirvāṇa* is to be understood by investigating the factors. The yogi having understood previously which factors are nominal designations and which are realities comes eventually to directly realize the truth of cessation. It is a gradual progress: first the defilements cease in order from gross toward subtle. E.g., the notions of male and female are caused to cease by analyzing them into various sorts of hair, etc., and then those notions in turn are caused to cease through analysis into emptiness. The middle way is accomplished through worldly truth between extremes in this progression. The Buddha even affirms that from the worldly point of view it is right to say that the self exists and wrong to deny it.

142.(E358-361; T337-341)[344] Pots, etc., are nominal existents, not actual ones. The marks of nominal existence are: (1) that signs are available--e.g., color is a sign of the pot, but not of matter; feeling has no color; (2) where something operates in dependence on association with something else--e.g., a lamp illuminates in dependence on the colors of the things illuminated, and burns in dependence on the touch associated with it in the things; (3) what is nominal depends on another factor, e.g., the pot depends on color, but feeling doesn't; (4) nominal designations possess various factors, e.g., a lamp can both illuminate and burn, but a feeling only feels; (5) the term corresponding to a designation applies to a thing with constituents--e.g., "chariot"--but a term for an actual entity such as "matter" does not so apply; (6) color, etc., when spoken of by that term are obtained, but pot, etc., when spoken of as "pot", etc., are not obtained; (7) awareness of nominally designated things wanders, is not concentrated. E.g., one says he sees a horse, another that he sees the skin of a horse. Or there is difference of opinion as to whether a pot is visible or not, etc. There is no such indecision about actual entities. I can see color but I cannot see sounds. (8) Nominally designated is what is knowable and speakable, but what is knowable but inexpressible is highest truth. E.g., matter, etc., is expressible through its own mark, but pot, etc. is not expressible through its own mark. So the latter are nominal designations. (9) Nominally designated is what has no mark of its own, what is real does. (10) The marks of the nominal are not single. Whereas feeling is marked as that which feels, a person is marked by good, bad and neutral acts. (11) Nominally designated factors cause proclivities, while real ones do not. (12) Awareness arises not from nominally designated things but from actual ones, e.g., the matter that is in front of one. At the next moment there is constructed by mental awareness "I see the pot", etc. This talk of "pot" depends on color, etc. What is real is such that awareness of it doesn't depend on any other thing. (13) Doubts arise about nominally designated things--e.g., whether one is a post or a man. But no doubt as to whether a color is a color or a sound can arise. Doubt can arise as to whether there is color or no color, e.g., when one is told that color is empty.

Objection: Then the cessation-truth must itself be a nominal designation, since doubt as to whether it exists or not may arise.

Answer: This happens to one who has not realized the cessation-truth, not when one has.

(14) One can have awareness of a pot's color, touch, etc., but not of color's different qualities. (15) What is grasped by many senses is nominal; not so the real. (16) A nominal thing is without essential nature and yet capable of action. (17) All actions such as coming or going, destroying, burning, etc., are nominal, not real. (18) What is relative is nominal; the real is not dependent. E.g., heavy, light, long, short, etc., are nominal designations, but color, which does not depend on anything, isn't. (19) Pursuing the conduct of emptiness is nominal; pursuing the conduct of no-self is real. (20) There are four opinions which involve ignorance--identity, multiplicity, indescribability and negation. Therefore pots, etc., are nominal designations. The doctrine of identity is that the pot is just its color, taste, smell and touch. The doctrine of multiplicity is that the pot is different from those qualities. The doctrine of indescribability is that one cannot say that the pot is identical with or different from those qualities. And the doctrine of negation is that the pot doesn't exist. All four doctrines are wrong.

143.(E361-363; T341-343) Each of the qualities color, taste, etc., are different and separate. If the pot were identical with one it could not be identical with the others.

Objection: One seed does not constitute a bundle, but that which seeds comprise does; likewise each of color, taste, etc. are not a piece of earth, but what they comprise is.

Answer: The example is inappropriate, since a bundle is only a nominal designation. We are criticizing the identity doctrine in its application to real factors.

Question: When one speaks of the color of the pot, etc., it is not like speaking of the house of Śīlapuruṣa (where the house and Śīlapuruṣa have distinct marks), but like speaking of Śīlapuruṣa's hand and foot, which are not separate from Śīlapuruṣa. The pot cannot exist separate from its color, but what harm is there in speaking as if it had its own nature?

Answer: This example too is not correct. For to speak of Śīlapuruṣa's hand is to indicate its distinction from his body. But there is no such distinction in reality, no Śīlapuruṣa exists to be identified or distinguished.

144.(E363-365; T343-345) If the piece of earth were different from its qualities we should have an awareness of it independently of those qualities. But we don't. We don't have sense-organs that grasp a piece of earth as a distinct factor. The five sense-organs each grasp their respective sense-contents. They do not grasp nominal things. The sixth organ does, of course, generate cognition of nominal things, for mental awareness has the capacity of ranging over everything. If, e.g., the visual organ could grasp both color and noncolored things all sorts of incongruities would arise. For example, if the visual organ could grasp what is not colored we should be able, e.g., to see sound. Again, if the post is visually perceptible just because its color is, then each organ should cognize its own substantial basis--not only the auditory organ should grasp *ākāśa*, but the visual organ should grasp its own fire, etc. But this is contrary to your own tenets.

Objection: Only color occasions perception, not the other factors.

Answer: But you have said previously that the perception of the pot is possible because it is constituted of several substances as well as through its color, which conflicts with what you now say. Furthermore, you hold that number and size, etc., can be visually perceived though they have no color.

Objection: If color is not the cause of perception, number and size, etc., would be invisible as well as air.

Answer: On our view only color is visibly perceptible; no other factors are. The visual organ sees when color is present, not otherwise. The idea of pot arises only when a color has been seen.

So it is impossible that the notion of a pot arises in the absence of seeing a color.

145.(E366; T345-346) Real factors are not inexpressible; they each have their respective nature. They are ordered and can be numbered, which they could not be if they were inexpressible.

146.(E366-367; T146-147) If everything is nonexistent merit and demerit and liberation will be nonexistent too. Furthermore, even the existence of the notion that nothing exists won't exist, since there is no thinker to think it and no hearer to hear it. If nothing really exists everything should be the same--why do we judge them different from each other, since on this doctrine they can have no demarcating marks?

147.(E367-369; T347-349) The nihilist says: Even though you criticize emptiness verbally, factors are really nonexistent, because they cannot be the contents of sense-organs. Pots cannot be seen; nor can their parts, which are conceived by abstraction from the whole pot. Even if they could be seen, since they would be analyzable indefinitely the process would culminate in emptiness. So parts are nonexistent from the point of view of reality. And for one who believes in parts the outcome would be that there cannot be two truths. Colors and other qualities are also nonexistent, since no visual organ can see subtle color, and the mind does not cognize present color. I.e., visual awareness does not conceptualize "this is color", and the mental awareness does not relate to present color. So there is nothing to conceptualize color, and so color is not cognizable.

Objection: First, visual awareness grasps the color and then mental awareness remembers it. So the latter is the conceptualizer.

Answer: How can it remember it since it never saw it?

148.(E370; T349) Since sounds are momentary, there can be no language, as there is no single consciousness which can hear more than one syllable. Linguistic sounds do not exist.

Some say that the auditory organ is ether in nature, and since ether is not a category the auditory organ doesn't exist either, and so language cannot be heard.

149.(E370; T350) The same type of argument is applied to show the nonexistence of the other three sense-organs.

150.(E371; T350-351) Mental awareness does not grasp factors, since it does not grasp colors, tastes, etc., occurring in the present, and what is past and future don't exist, as was already stated.

Objection: Mental awareness cognizes itself.

Answer: No factor can cognize itself, since no self-cognition is present at the present moment.

Question: If one can know the awareness of another, then mental awareness must be able to cognize the mental states of that other.

Answer: This is just a manner of speaking, as self-knowledge also is.

151.(E371-373; T351-352) Nihilist: If the result exists, it is either already there in its cause or else it arises as a quality which was nonexistent earlier. But both views are faulty. The sound produced by clapping one's hands wasn't there before, nor were the curds in the milk before their production. On the other hand, experience shows that the result is determined by the character of its cause, which contradicts the second hypothesis. So, since neither of these two hypotheses is correct, there is no result. If the effect exists in the cause, the result that exists will not arise. But if the effect does not exist in the cause, it couldn't arise either, since it doesn't exist.

Either the cause is before, after or simultaneous with its effect. But if it is before, since it has gone how can the effect appear? If it is after, it cannot produce an effect, not existing yet. And if it is simultaneous, neither one is cause or effect. Again, either the cause and its effect are different or the same. But if they are different the effect should be able to exist without its cause, and if they are the same, one cannot produce the other.

If an effect exists it must be either self-made, made by another, made by both or unmade. But none of these are correct. Nothing makes itself. Nor is it made by another, since, e.g., in the production of awareness none of the causative elements--the visual organ, the color, etc.--has any idea of agency, nothing is made. The third possibility involves the defects in both the first two. And if it is unmade then it doesn't exist.

152.(E373-374; T353-354) Reply to the nihilist: What you have been saying, viz., that all factors are empty, is not correct. If everything is nonexistent, this teaching is nonexistent also. And the Buddha himself says that some things are actual but unthinkable. I.e., ordinary persons cannot understand them; only *tathāgatas* can analyze the factors fully. Disciples and those self-enlightened have understood the factors to the extent necessary for coming to know *nirvāṇa.* But only Tathāgatas are capable of understanding the original naturelessness of all things in all their particular and general aspects. Awareness of emptiness is easy, but analytical understanding of the factors is hard.

Objection: What the Buddha teaches about the factors must be the way it is.

Answer: The Buddha only teaches those aspects of things that are conducive to liberation. E.g., he has taught dependent origination in general but has not said precisely what is the cause of each and every thing. It doesn't follow that those things he doesn't speak of don't exist. One doesn't say that because the blind don't see colors, colors are nonexistent; likewise, one shouldn't say things don't exist because they are dependently originated.

The omniscient Tathāgatas declare the existence of the aggregates. Therefore, we must understand that all factors--color, etc.--exist just as the pot etc. do, viz. conventionally.

## CHAPTER TWO

153.(E375-379; T354-359) It was said that the cessation-truth is the cessation of three awarenesses. The first has now been explained. As for the second, the cessation of awareness of factors, the awareness of factors is actually the awareness of the five aggregates. When the yogi meditates on the five aggregates as empty he gains cessation-awareness of factors.

Objection: The yogi in meditating on them comes to see them as impermanent, noneternal, destructible, etc., i.e., he comes to see them as empty. It is not that he does not see them at all.

Answer: He does not see them at all. He abandons all awareness of conditioned things, and sees only unconditioned things.

Spiritual practice is of two kinds, meditation on emptiness and meditation on selflessness. Meditation on emptiness is appreciating the nominal nature of the factors. But the meditation on selflessness is not seeing the factors at all. Through it one gets completely liberated. The cessation of all the five aggregates is selflessness.

Question: If so, are there any aggregates at all?

Answer: Not actually, but they exist conventionally.

Question: If so, why was it said that color, etc., are real (cf. section 141)?

Answer: For the good of living beings. Numerous passages are quoted to show that the ultimate message is that factors do not exist really though they do conventionally.

The yogi should suppress all signs. If signs were really existent, he would remember them. This is not to endorse the view of the Tīrthikas that at the time matter is suppressed it actually exists but is not recollected. Rather, the yogi necessarily sees the aggregates, but because of the vision of cessation he enters into the signless (state).

## CHAPTER THREE

154.(E379-381; T359-360)[345] That which has *nirvāṇa* as supporting object is called empty awareness. The awareness takes as supporting object the nonexistence of anything whatever. This awareness is finally suppressed in two states: (1) when one gains concentration without awareness, and (2) when one enters *nirvāṇa* without any limitations left over. Then, the stream of factors being cut off through the destruction of karma, the awareness ceases.

# BOOK FIVE

## CHAPTER ONE: Concentration

155.(E382-383; T361-362) The path is the noble eightfold path consisting of right view, etc., or in brief consisting of two--(1) concentration and (2) knowledge.

Concentration is awareness' resting on one (thing) only by meditating on it many times. A sign of it is mental ease, pleasure and calm. It is the cause of knowledge of things as they are, which is knowledge of emptiness.

156.(E383-385; T362-364) Question: Is concentration anything different from awareness?

Answer: No. Concentration is awareness that is fixed for a long time. It has two sorts: with contaminants and without contaminants. Concentration without contaminants is also called wisdom. Some Ābhidharmikas call it the cause of liberation, but that is not a proper way of speaking, since concentration with contaminants may also contribute toward liberation.

Again, one may divide concentration into three kinds: (1) limited, (2) wide, and (3) boundless, depending on the range of what is contemplated. It can also be divided into another three: (1) determination, (2) rising up (3) renunciation.

There are three kinds of method for concentration: (1) the means of entering it, viz., through *dharma*, (2) the means of remaining in it, stability, and (3) the means of leaving it, through *dharma*.

There are four conditions for gaining concentration: (1) present practice, (2) the condition of the front parts of the body, (3) understanding the marks of concentration, (4) following the *dharma* of concentration as taught.

157.(E385-387; T364-367) Several sets of three are considered, drawn from *sūtra* passages. Concentration may be (1) one-limbed, when one concentrates without wisdom, (2) two-limbed, when one practises with wisdom in the world, and (3) noble right concentration, when one fixed on *dharma* directly realizes the truth of cessation. Or, (1) emptiness-concentration, when the yogi does not see beings or factors, (2) signless concentration, when he has no concepts of these things, and (3) aimless concentration. Again, (1) the emptiness of the empty , when the yogi sees the five aggregates which are empty as empty, (2) the aimlessness of the aimless, when one becomes disinterested in aimlessness, and (3) the signlessness of the signless, when one loses the concept of conceptlessness.

158.(E387-389; T367-369) (1) There is the cultivation of concentration leading to worldly satisfaction in the second trance. (2) There is the cultivation of concentration leading to knowledge, viz., the eight liberations and the vision of the ten *kṛtsnāyatana*s (see 172 below). (3) There is the cultivation of concentration leading to the understanding of the aggregates. (4) And there is the cultivation of concentration leading to the destruction of contaminants.

159.(E389-395; T369-374) The four unlimited concentrations are loving kindness, compassion, sympathy, and equanimity.

160.(E395-396; T374-375) The five limbs of noble concentration are joy, satisfaction, purity of awareness, illumination, and cultivation.

161.(E396-398; T375-378) The six concentrations are (1)

cultivation (of one-pointedness) which is repeated), (2) the same when it arouses knowledge and vision (see above), (3) the same when both results follow, (4) cultivation of knowledge and vision in discerning the different natures of the factors that leads to one-pointed concentration; (5) the same leading to more knowledge-vision, (6) the same leading to both. Alternative interpretations attributed to "Ābhidharmikas" are considered and rejected.

162.(E399-400; T378-379)[346] Seven concentrations.

163.(E400-405; T379-384) Eight liberations.

164.(E405; T385) Eight overcoming senses.

165.(E405-408; T385-388) There are the four trance states and the four immaterial ones plus the cessation-trance. The first trance involves the pleasure of seclusion, being free from sensual desires and from bad factors but with initial and sustained thought still operating. The concentrator is subject to distractions and contaminants.

166.(E409-412; T388-3920 The second trance is like the first, but now free from initial and sustained thought, featuring one-pointedness of mind and inward serenity. Here the concentrator is not distracted. The pleasure of this state comes from concentration, not from seclusion. The concentrator is still subject to contaminants, being subject to the self-notion.

167.(E412-413; T392-394) In the third trance the yogi is nonattached to pleasure; he is mindful, experiences satisfaction in his body from praise of his accomplishments, though neutral with regard to it.

168.(E413-415; T394-396) The fourth trance involves the purity of neutrality, where neither satisfaction nor frustration are felt since there are no feelings. Here breathing stops since it is based on a stable body and mind. There is still a subtle residue of desire.

169.(E415-418; T396-399) Having passed beyond all material designations all designations of obstacles are put down as well as all kinds of designations about plurality. The yogi concentrates on space and enters the realm of endless space. Here "material designations" means the designations of color, taste, smell and touch; "designations of obstacles" means the obstacles created by the material designations; and "designations about plurality" covers all sorts of ideas about bells, drums, etc. These three kinds of designations cause various afflictions, actions and frustrations. The yogi passes beyond them all, realizing that matter, etc., are really empty like space, that the body was previously with space.

Objection: Space is by nature a material sense, so how can the yogi, taking that as his supporting object, pass beyond material designation?

Answer: Since space is unconditioned, it does not exist as an entity.

Objection: When color arises space is destroyed; so it is an entity.

Answer: No, nothing is destroyed when color arises, since the absence of color is space. And an absence cannot be made into another absence. We don't see space or any other absence. And it is not situated anywhere, as the elements, e.g., are.

170.(E419-421; T399-402) The yogi in turn then attains the sense of endless consciousness, the sense of nothingness, and the sense of neither-identification--nor- nonidentification. In the first he concentrates on limitless consciousness, in the second on nothing, and finally, realizing that he is taking nothing as something and that he gets no respite from identifications by concentrating on something or nothing, he stops thinking altogether.

171.(E421-428; T402-409) There are two kinds of cessation-trance: destructive of afflictions and not destructive of them. In the latter, though volition has ceased, there are other fetters; the former is the eighth liberation that is the same as the noble result, where all afflictions have been destroyed.

Objection: This trance cannot be free from awareness, since no one exists without awareness. One without awareness is dead. Rather, it must be that the one who enters liberation with residues has his afflicted awareness cease, while the one who achieves liberation without residues is one whose unafflicted awareness ceases also.

Answer: This state is different from death: breath and temperature persist, though awareness ceases, whereas in death all three cease. When the *sūtra* says that the three (breath, temperature and consciousness) are inseparable it means in the realms of desire and in the material realm. But in the immaterial realm there is breath and consciousness without temperature.

The yogi who leaves the cessation-trance does so gradually, coming to have three contacts: unchangeable, contact with empty awareness of conditioned elements; signless, not taking them as objects; and thus aimless, having no desire for those elements. This state of having woken up from *nirvāṇa* is not tainted with contaminants and involves no self-awareness.

172.(E428-430; T409-410) The power of awareness that is strong enough to shift attention from an old object is an all-inclusive sense. The yogi takes a limited sign for his meditation and then deepens it by resolve. This resolve has ten sorts--that concentrated on the four basic colors, on the four great elements, on space and on consciousness. The point is that these resolves artificially create signs of those kinds.

173-180.(E430-445; T411-421) The ten identifications are: noneternality, frustration, non-self, antipathy toward food, disgust with the world, unpleasantness, death, abandonment, nonattachment, and cessation. The advantages of each are set forth.

181-184.(E445-465; T421-438) There are eleven preliminaries to concentration: pure conduct, right-knowledge-gain, protection of the sense doors, taking limited food, being awake at the first and last parts of the night, possessing good initial thought, possessing good resolve, effort, possession of the liberation-sense, nonobscuration, nonattachment.

185.(E465-470; T438-442) Breathing.

186.(E471-475; T442-448) Pollutions of concentration.

187.(E476-479; T448-451) Calmness and insight.

188.(E480-485; T452-458) Cultivation of concentration.

## CHAPTER TWO: Knowledge

189.(E485-494; T458-467) Knowledge is wisdom about the nature of things. The nature of things is empty non-self. In the sphere of nominal designation it is wisdom, but conceptual identification is not knowledge since it grasps only conventional things.

Objection: But the *sūtras* tell us that consciousness cognizes the aggregates, elements and senses; these are not conventional things. Conventional things are those that arise in connection with impure awareness. The Buddha says there are two right views, worldly and otherworldly. The former comprises knowledge of factors, inferential knowledge and knowledge of others, and that identifications of previous births and of birth and death are impure.

So there must be impure wisdom.

Answer: If there is impure wisdom you will have to explain the distinction between impure and pure knowledge, and you can't do so. You think there is worldly knowledge about things that are not nominal designations (i.e., conventional things). But the Buddha teaches that worldly wisdom is awareness which involves the I-notion. You say the Buddha speaks of two kinds of worldly wisdom, two right views. I say there are two kinds of awareness, confused awareness and knowledge. The former has nominal factors as its objects, the latter has empty non-self as its object.

Objection: If you are right, then the noble person will be ignorant, since he has awarenesses of pots, etc.

Answer: The noble person has destroyed all nominal designations at his enlightenment. Though he talks of pots he does not have awarenesses having pots, etc., as supporting objects. There are three kinds of talk: (1) born of (wrong) views, (2) born of pride, (3) born of purposive action. Ordinary folk who talk of pots talk the first way. Learners, though they have learned the no-self doctrine, still in forgetfulness speak of the five aggregates, etc., as self, pot, etc. The noble person's talk is of the third kind.

As for the *sūtra* about the two right views, both kinds are identifications and merely spoken of as "knowledge" by the Buddha for the edification of certain levels of aspirants.

190.(E494-499; T467-474) Objection: One does not reach liberation merely by seeing the truth of cessation, as you claim. The Buddha says all four truths must be seen, and that these come to be seen gradually.

Answer: The seeing of the truth of cessation is the path, the seeing of the other three is the investigation leading to it. Why do you think the path involves seeing all four truths?

Objection: Because the time of gaining the path is the point at which knowledge of the abandonment of the afflictions occurs.

Answer: But the knowledge of the aggregates, etc., arises for the abandoning of the afflictions also.

The yogi may start, e.g., by realizing that there is no such thing as "woman" or "man", that such talk is deluded and perverse. Then meditating on matter as empty, he gradually comes to the realization that all the aggregates are empty and without a self. Until he comes to the full realization his vision of awareness is not pure. Finally, when he fully realizes the truth of cessation his afflictions are destroyed. It is only at this point that his identification of frustrations is completed. At that precise moment desire and the other fetters are abandoned.

191.(E499-505; T474-480) The knowledge of all things as supporting object ranges over all the elements and senses, etc., and includes everything, even the associated factors. So this knowledge has itself as supporting object.

Objection: The *sūtra* says that consciousness arises from two causal conditions. So knowledge cannot have itself as its supporting object.

Answer: There is no such rule that consciousness must arise from causal conditions. Knowledge may even be without supporting object, e.g., mental awareness, as well as awarenesses of past and future. The *sūtra* says this only to deny that four conditions are required in certain cases.

Objection: Past and future objects must exist. Otherwise how could they be known? There is no awareness of nonexistents such as hare's horn, etc.

Answer: Knowledge arises with regard to a thing's function. Past and future things have no function, and so knowledge cannot arise with regard to them. When the time of seeing a person is past, one remembers the pastness of that. There is no factor of memory. The hare's horn is not remembered, since it never occurred. So no knowledge is possible of it. But there must be consciousness of hare's horn; if not, how can we be talking of it?

Objection: A hare's horn is not something we can be conscious of, since we are not aware of any qualities that would be qualities of it, like shortness or length or color. Likewise, there is no consciousness of past things and future things.

Answer: The power of the knowledge of a noble person can make known something as yet nonexistent, just as we have the power of remembering something nonexistent. Just as visual consciousness does not cause the conceptual constructions of woman and man but mental consciousness nevertheless produces such constructions, so likewise the noble persons produce the knowledge of nonexistent things.

Objection: The Buddha says that all factors are without self. So the knowledge we are talking about ranges over everything, conditioned and unconditioned, and not just the aggregates.

Answer: "All" has two senses, one including the entire universe, the other only a part of that. When the Buddha says, e.g., "I am all-knowing" he is utilizing the first sense. In the present case, however, the second sense is in use, as also in "all is ablaze", which does not mean that the unconditioned and pure things are ablaze.

192.(E505-507; T480-481) Noble dwelling.

193.(E507-510; T481-485) What is the difference between right knowledge and right vision or view? There is no difference.

Objection: The marks of each that you have mentioned are not the same. E.g., patience is a mark of vision, not of knowledge, since if the patience of *dharma* toward frustration is knowledge, it is already known and would so constitute the faculty of understanding, not the sense that I am going to know.

Answer: Patience is itself knowledge, since "patience" is a synonym for "interest".

Objection: The fivefold sensuous consciousness which constitutes wisdom is knowledge, not view. These five are nonconceptual, because they go to their object for the first time, whereas a view is a thought that relies on the presentation of an object.

Answer: Your assumption is that the visual consciousness has as its object the stream of factors just like the mental consciousness, so neither should be view, which is absurd. Actually, the fivefold sensuous consciousness, being without understanding, not true, and adverting only to the nominal, is neither knowledge, wisdom nor view.

Some say that the visual organ is the viewer. But it is not, because (we hold) the visual consciousness takes an object. So the opinion mentioned is only a worldly notion.

194.(E510-517; T485-492).[347] The three kinds of wisdom are the wisdom born of hearing, of thinking, and of contemplation. All are obtained in the realm of desire.

195.(E517-519; T493-494) The four discriminations are (1) with reference to syllables, (2) with reference to speech, (3) with reference to both, (4) with reference to neither. They are obtained through the actions in previous births.

196.(E519-522; T494-497) The five knowledges are (1) knowledge of the origination of factors, (2) knowledge of the cessation of factors, (3) awareness of nonpassion, by which knowledge one does not quarrel with others, (4) unobstructed knowledge of everything, which only the Buddha has, (5) when the yogi secures complete mastery over the continuation or ending of his life.

There is a discussion over whether *nirvāṇa* is a factor. The question is how there can be knowledge of *nirvāṇa* if there is no factor answering to what is known by it. Harivarman replies that there is no such factor, that the concentration on *nirvāṇa* is signless, without concept. If *nirvāṇa* were a factor then one could never have the vision that it has no essential nature, since the (alleged) factor would never cease.

197.(E522-528; T497-505) The six higher faculties are (1) the yogi's powers of moving his body long distances and appearing and disappearing through his power of concentration, (2) the divine eye, the yogi's power of seeing all parts of the universe, which is not to be confused with wisdom, (3) the divine ear, (4) knowledge of the awarenesses of others, (5) recollection of former births, and (6) knowledge of the cessation of contaminants. Some opinions about (4)--that it only grasps awarenesses of others that are similar (either impure or pure) to one's own, or that it cannot grasp the truths about the path, are dismissed as being unnecessary restrictions. (4) has three varieties, (a) that obtained from signs, when one knows the thoughts of others through bodily signs and *mantras*, (b) that obtained from the maturation of karma, which belongs to *asuras*, (c) that obtained through cultivation, which arises from meditation and concentration.

(5) Recollection of former births is the recollection of one's own past aggregates as well as those of others. It too has three varieties: (a) obtained from cultivation, (b) obtained as maturation by *asuras*, and (c) productive of memory of oneself among humans, obtained by noninjury to living things.

(6) The sixth higher faculty, knowledge of the cessation of contaminants, is the diamond-like concentration gained upon completion of the path when the contaminants and obstruction to the path have ceased. Tīrthikas can only have the first five faculties--the sixth is unavailable to them, since they cannot grasp the truth.

Question: Since the knowledge of no-self destroys all concepts and thus causes the afflictions to cease, what is the need for a subsequent knowledge of this sort?

Answer: Because though the afflictions and concepts cease they arise again.

Question: If so they may rise up again endlessly and there is no possibility of the path of a perfected being.

Answer: No, there is a final limit. And in any case the noble person is not altogether free of concepts, since when he is not in concentration concepts are there for him, though they do not pollute him.

198.(E528-529; T504-505) Perseverance of knowledge.
199.(E529-531; T505-509) Nine knowledges.
200.(E532-536; T509-515) Ten knowledges.
201.(E536-538; T515-516) Fourty-four knowledges.
202.(E538-540; T516-518). Seventy-seven knowledges.

## 127. AUTHOR UNKNOWN, *Subāhuparipṛcchāsūtra*[348]

## 128. AUTHOR UNKNOWN, *Śukasūtra*[349]

## 129. AUTHOR UNKNOWN, *Samantabhadrabodhisattvadhayañcayādharmasūtra*[350]

## 130. AUTHOR UNKNOWN, *Bhaiṣajyaguruvaidūryaprabhasyapūrvapraṇidhānaviśeṣa-vistarasūtra*[351]

Summary from Nalinaksha Dutt's translation of Paul Pelliot's French rendition

"The Buddha arrives at Vaiśālī; he is surrounded by all the beings of the worlds. Mañjuśrīkumāra stands up and requests the Tathāgata to give an exposition of the vows made formerly by the past Buddhas for rescuing the living beings from the miseries of existence. Bhagavān grants the request and explains the twelve vows taken formerly, when he was a bodhisattva, by a Buddha whose world is separated from ours by Buddhakṣetras, the number of which is ten times the number of the sands of the Ganges; that

Buddha is Yao-che-lieou-li-kouang-jou-lai (Bhaiṣajyaguruvaidūryaprabha); he lives in the world Tsing-lieou-li. He wished that he himself might attain *bodhi*, be pure and resplendent as the *vaidūrya* (*maṇi*), and illumine the world immersed in darkness; he wished that his name if uttered might cure maladies, release the prisoners, change into men those women who are sick of their miserable condition, procure food for the famished, or clothes for the destitute. In short, in that world, for innumerable *kalpas* there would be neither suffering nor poverty; there would be no more feminine beings, nor beings in inferior states of existence; the soil would be of *vaidūrya*, ropes of gold would line the routes; the walls and the houses would be made of seven jewels and one would believe it to be the western Sukhāvatī...It will suffice only to think of his name for deliverance from all evils...If one makes an image of this Buddha, or if one recites the text of the sūtra, he will escape from the nine ways of death..."

## 131. AUTHOR UNKNOWN, *Mahāyānābhidharmasūtra*[352]

## 132. AUTHOR UNKNOWN, *Buddhabhūmisūtra*[353]

Summary by John P. Keenan

"The text opens with an introduction which describes the Buddha, the Pure Land in which he preaches this scripture, and the gathered assembly of *bodhisattvas*, *mahāśrāvakas*, and *mahāsattvas*. The body of the work treats the five factors which constitute the Buddha land: the pure Dharma realm, Mirror wisdom, Equality wisdom, Discernment wisdom, and Duty-fulfillment wisdom. Each of these factors is described by a series of ten descriptions or similes. The Pure Dharma realm is compared to empty space, which pervades all places without itself being in any way delimited. Mirror wisdom is likened to a round mirror which reflects all images without discrimination. Equality wisdom is simply described in ten statements on the equality of all things. Discernment wisdom is described by drawing comparisons from the world and its contents. Duty-fulfillment wisdom is understood through analogy with the actions of sentient beings in the world. In effect, the first two wisdoms correspond to the Yogācāra notion of Nondiscriminative wisdom (*nirvikalpajñāna*) and the last two to subsequently attained wisdom (*pṛṣṭhalabdhajñāna*). Both focus on the pure Dharma realm as the space of emptiness and the sphere of compassion."

"The concluding section of this scripture offers two similes to illustrate the nature of the wisdom described, now identified as a phenomenal wisdom all of one unified taste. The first simile depicts the luxurious grove of the gods wherein they lose any sense of their individual identities, drawing the analogy that entry into the Dharma realm of emptiness leads to the wisdom insight into the equality of all beings. The second simile notes the same point by describing the flow of all rivers and streams to the oneness of the great ocean."

"Four verses then summarize the meaning of the entire text."

## 133. DHARMATRĀTA, *Saṃyuktābhidharmahṛdayaśāstra*

Summary by Bart Dessein

This work is also known as *Kṣudrakābhidharmahṛdayaśāstra*, *Abhidharmasāraprakīrṇakaśāstra*, *Saṃyuktābhidharmasāra*, or *Miśrakābhidharmahṛdayaśāstra*. It is available in Chinese (T. 1552). The Chinese translation of the work was made by Saṃghavarman in Ch'ang-kan monastery in Chien-k'ang, capital of the Former Sung in 434 A.D. [354] The author Dharmatrāta is the second of three persons so named, the first of which is Bhadanta Dharmatrāta, a Dārṣṭāntika and one of the four masters mentioned in the *Mahāvibhāṣāśāstra*. Our present author lived in the beginning of the fourth century.

The present work takes the *Abhidharmahṛdayaśāstra* of Dharmaśreṣṭhin, #21 of Volume 7 of this Encyclopedia, as its fundament. All doctrinal deviations in our work are adaptations of the *Mahāvibhāṣā*, which makes the present work posterior to the *Mahāvibhāṣā*.

### CHAPTER ONE: Elements

1-2. Salutations to the Buddha.
3-6. Discussion on impure and pure factors
7-14. and on the five aggregates.

15-19. The twelve senses are explained. Ten are said to be material. Also, the specific characteristic marks of a thing (*dravyasvalakṣaṇa*) and of the sense-organ are discussed. *Dharma* is said to be four kinds of unmanifest matter. Because of the difference between basis, supporting object and specific characteristic there are in all eleven senses in one body.

20-22. The eighteen elements.

23-26. The difference between aggregates, senses and elements is discussed. All factors are said to be elements, the elements senses and, except for the three unconditioned ones, aggregates. However, the three kinds are spoken of because of the difference in delusion of beings, liberation of desire and unequalness of their faculties.

27-50. The different categories of eighteen elements in respect of which are blameworthy or not; good, bad or neutral; with or without retribution; atomic or formed; etc.

51-52. The characteristic marks of the factors.

## CHAPTER TWO: Conditioning Factors

53-54. Introduction.

55-60. Factors that are accompanying mental factors and dissociated factors are spoken of: factors arising with every awareness, arising with every good awareness, with every defiled awareness, with every bad awareness, with every awareness of minor defilement.

61-63. In the discussion concerning the simultaneous appearance of factors that accompany thought we are told that there are eighteen such factors in the obscure-neutral class and twenty-two of the good sort.

64-67. The simultaneous appearance of material factors. The four characteristic marks. Four forms of remoteness (*dūratā*): of mark, in nature, in place and in time.

68-76. The six causes.

77-82. The meaning of the different causes and the simultaneous appearance of factors.

83-88. Four conditions.

89. Limitation in name as one syllable, in matter as one atom, in time as one instant.

90-93. Increase of matter and the measure of the body of beings in the different realms.

94-95. Increase of time and duration of life of beings in the different realms.

96. Many factors, each formed by many conditioning factors, conspire to produce one single factor.

## CHAPTER THREE: Karma

97-99. Five kinds of birth result from bodily, verbal and mental karma.

100-101. Classification of types of karma.

102-124. Three unmanifest kinds of action: restraint of the code, the act of entering the order; restraint through trance, when one acquires good awarenesses in the material realm; pure restraint, when one has awarenesses of the four trances. The first of the three is abandoned at death, the second abandoned when proceeding to a higher or lower trance state, and the third in backsliding or when acquiring a noble result with growing faculties.

125-141. Ten paths of action.

142-152. Further differences among actions.

153-163. Five fruits of action: natural (=what is similar), the fruit of retribution (=what is dissimilar), the fruit of liberation (=abandonment), the fruit of human effort (=what is acquired through effort), the dominant fruit (=the single result of many factors). In the pure path there are only four fruits (minus the fruit of retribution).

164-171. The three obstructions: action, defilement and retribution. Breaking up the order, false views.

## CHAPTER FOUR: Proclivities

172-180. Seven proclivities are differentiated as to realm, aspect and mode of proceeding (thus making ninety-eight).

181-197. The objects of the ninety-eight proclivities.

198-206. Ten proclivities. From them come

207-213. ten envelopers: shamelessness, disregard, lethargy, regret, selfishness, envy, excitedness, sleepiness, anger and hypocrisy.

214-219. The relation between defilements and secondary afflictions.

220-229. Abandonment of defilements

230-231. There are three kinds of objects--good, bad and neither, and two ways of generating craving.

CHAPTER FIVE: Nobility

232-234. Spiritual practice distinguished.

235-237. Four establishments of mindfulness.

238-240. Four roots of merit: warmth, summit, patience, and the highest worldly factor.

241-265. The noble person in the path of vision. The stages of being on the path--stream-enterer, etc.--discussed.

266-273. The noble person in the path of the adept.

274-285. The merit of the noble person.

CHAPTER SIX: Knowledge

286-290. The ten knowledges as to realm and truths, antidote, preparation, etc.

291-298. Different categories of the ten knowledges.

299-303. Sixteen aspects of the four truths in relation to the ten knowledges.

304-313. Acquisition of the ten knowledges.

314-318. The knowledges as to vision or non-vision, wisdom, antidote, and as to supporting objects.

319. Higher faculties.

320-330. Eighteen unique factors: the ten knowledges plus four confidences plus three unique establishments of mindfulness plus great compassion.

331-336. Simultaneous factors

CHAPTER SEVEN: Concentration

337-346. The kinds of concentration.

347-362. Merit produced by concentration.

363-377. Relationship between concentration and merit.

378-379. Magical awareness.

## CHAPTER EIGHT: *Sūtra*

380. The meaning of "*sūtra*".

381-399. Four kinds of giving, four kinds of morality, two kinds of spiritual practice. Four kinds of restraint.

400-402. Forty abodes in the three realms: twenty in the realm of desire (eight great hells, animal birth, hungry ghosts, four continents, six gods of the realm of sexual passion); sixteen in the material realm; four in the immaterial realm. Seven abodes of consciousness: the good courses of the realm of passion, the three lower stages of the material realm, and three lower stages of the immaterial realm.

403-409. Dependent origination.

410. Birth and the courses of rebirth.

411. Six elements.

412-413. Four truths.

414. Four fruits of monkhood.

415-416. Characteristic marks of the path.

417. Four forms of perfect faith.

418-419. The marks of the development of concentration.

420-421. Good and conditioned factors produced by effort are the footing of supernatural powers.

422-425. The thirty-seven factors of enlightenment.

426. Four kinds of nutriment.

427. Three concentrations in respect to the sixteen aspects.

428. Four perverted views.

429-431. Five views.

432-441. Twenty-two faculties.

442-445. The object of consciousness and of knowledge.

446-448. Development of proclivities.

## CHAPTER NINE: Miscellaneous

453-457. The factors dissociated from awareness.

465. Acquisition of twelve awarenesses.

475. The perfected being abides in awarenesses through retribution and relating to deportment for *parinirvāṇa*.

CHAPTER TEN: Investigation

521. The fours kinds of antidote.

CHAPTER ELEVEN: Discussion

Twenty puzzles answered.

## 134. DHARMATRĀTA, *Pañcavastukavibhāṣā*[355]

Summary by Christian Lindtner

Dharmatrāta's commentary (ca. fourth century A.D.) on the *Pañcavastuka* (the first chapter of the *Prakaraṇapāda*; cf. Volume 7 of this Encyclopedia, #17) is only extant in Chinese apart from a brief Sanskrit fragment. The Chinese version abruptly breaks off in the section dealing with the first of the mental phenomena, viz., feeling (*vedanā*). On the whole it is a rather independent and instructive commentary full of interesting digressions and discussions. Among the sources and authorities referred to by Dharmatrāta are Pārśva, Ghoṣaka, the *Vijñānakāya, Jñānaprasthāna*, and *Mahāvibhāṣā* as well as a considerable number of *sūtras* and some unidentified individuals.

Vasumitra's *Pañcavastuka* itself is brief and often not explicit. Hence the purpose of Dharmatrāta's commentary is to make it more intelligible by offering a more detailed account of the particular and common features of all factors.

The factors may be classified in various ways. Basically, however, the classification into five basic factors called "actual entities" (*vastu*) comprises all of them. Hence the title *Pañcavastuka.*

"E" refers to N. Aiyaswami Sastri's text as in Visvabharati Annals 10, 1961, 1-54

### I. Matter

(E13-17) A lengthy discussion of the concept of matter. It is the first of the five actual entities to be dealt with because it is the "most gross" and because meditation on it is the "door" to the

Buddha's teaching. It is called "matter" not only because it sooner or later inevitably breaks up or changes, but also because it, as a physical body, indicates one's internal mental states and the character of one's previous karma. Some kinds of matter are visible and resistant, others, nonmaterial (i.e., the senses), are invisible and nonresistant, whereas unmanifest karma is neither.

(E17-23) (i) There are only four great elements; space is "great", but not to be included within matter. A discussion of the etymology and function of the four great elements; they are the cause of the derived elements. Each of the four elements can operate on its own independently of the three others. After this general account of the great elements their specific characteristics and their particular functions are discussed. It is impossible for a single factor to have several characteristics. In fact the elements can never be absolutely separated *in concreto* though their characters are in mutual conflict (water with fire, etc.).

(E23-31) (ii) On the material derivatives, i.e., the senses and their objects. Etymology of the term "sense" (*indriya*): it is the "master" of its object. A description of the five senses, their quality, specific nature and function. There are three kinds called *sabhāga*, i.e., the eye serving as basis of consciousness, and four kinds called *tatsabhāga*, i.e., the eye as subtle matter. The eye can only perceive a visible object when associated with consciousness. Various alternate opinions about perception are discussed. With regard to the object of the senses: matter consists of color and shape and is cognized first by perceptual consciousness and then by mental consciousness. The other objects are sound, smell, taste and part of the tangible.

(E32-35) (iii) Finally there is unmanifest karma. This is material and unmanifest. It may either be good or bad. In a long discussion the commentary follows the traditional Sarvāstivāda notions (see *Mahāvibhāṣā*, etc.) about the division and status of this third and final kind of matter.

## II. Awareness

(E36-40) The second actual entity is awareness (*citta*). There is no real difference between *citta*, *jñāna* and *vijñāna*. Nevertheless the different synonyms may be used with different connotations and specific meanings. Consciousness is classified according to the sense-organ that produces it when in contact with an object.

III. Mental Concomitants

(E40-48) In general, accompanying mental factors or concomitants must be distinguished from mind awareness. Various absurdities following from not distinguishing accompanying mental factors from awareness--the Dārṣṭāntika view--are pointed out. The first mental concomitant is feeling, the awareness of a content. There are three kinds of feeling--satisfying, frustrating and one that is neither. It is wrong, as some Buddhists do, only to assume the existence of frustrating feelings. The commentary ends in the midst of a long discussion of other aspects of feeling.

## 135. AUTHOR UNKNOWN, *Arthaviniścayasūtra*[356]

Summary by N.H. Samtani

This work has been edited several times, and partially translated into Italian (by A. Ferrari, unavailable to the editor of this Volume). "E" references below are to the edition by N.H.Samtani in Tibetan Sanskrit Works Series 13, Patna 1971. This summary has been prepared by the editor on the basis of Samtani's summary of the contents of the work. Numbered sections below refer to *sūtras*.

(E1-3) Introduction. The *sūtra* is addressed to 2500 monks by the Buddha when he was staying in Mṛgamata's palace.

1.(E3) Five aggregates.

2.(E3) Five aggregates involving appropriating.

3.(E4) Eighteen elements.

4.(E4) Twelve sense-bases.

5.(E5-14) Twelvefold chain of dependent origination.

Ignorance is subdivided into about thirty varieties. Conditioning factors have three varieties: bodily, vocal and mental. The consciousness-bodies (*vijñānakāya*) are six, corresponding to the six organs including mind. As for name-and-form (the psycho-physical complex), there are four names--feeling, identification, trace and consciousness--and one form--matter. Matter is further subdivided into four great elements (earth, water, light and wind elements). Each is defined. The sense-bases and contacts are counted as six each, as are the feelings and desires. As for appropriating, it is subdivided into four: appropriating from desire, from (wrong) views, from moral precepts and vows, and from view of self. The realms of existence (*bhava*) are three: sensual, material and immaterial. These are further subdivided. The sensual realm is divided into eight hot hells, eight cool hells. This realm includes ghosts, animals, men and six kinds of sensual realm gods termed *caturmahārājikas*, *trayastiṃśas*, *yamas*, *tuṣitas*, *nirmāṇaratis* and *paranirmitavasāvatirṇas*. The material realm includes sixteen kinds of gods: *brahmakāyikas*, *brahmapurohitas*, *mahābhramaṇas*, *parittābhas*, *apramāṇas*, *ābhāsvaras*, *parittaśubhas*, *śubhakṛtsnas*, *anabhrakas*, *puṇyaprasavas*, *bṛhatphalas*, *avṛhas*, *ātapas*, *śudras*, *sudarśanas*, and *akaniṣṭhas*. The immaterial realm includes the bases of endless space, endless consciousness, nothingness and neither-identification-nor-nonidentification. These four kinds of immaterial gods are termed "immersed in consciousness only" (*cittamātrādhyayana*).

6. (E14-16) Four noble truths.

7. (E16) Twenty-two faculties.

8. (E17) Four meditative states, described but not named.

9. (E18) Four formless meditative attainments.

10. (E18-19) Four sublime states--kindness, compassion, sympathy, equanimity.

11. (E19-22) Four modes of progress, two frustrating, two satisfying.

12. (E22-28) Four meditative practices: that which is undertaken to destroy desire, that undertaken to obtain the satisfaction of the *dharma*, that undertaken to achieve knowledge and correct view, and that undertaken to achieve wisdom.

13. (E28) Four establishments of mindfulness.

14. (E29) Four right efforts.

15. (E30-31) Four supernatural powers.

16. (E31-33) Five faculties.

17. (E33) Five powers--faith, energy, mindfulness, concentration, wisdom.

18. (E33-34) Seven constituents of enlightenment--of mindfulness,

discrimination of the factors, energy, joy, tranquillity, concentration and equanimity.

19.(E34-42 The eightfold path.

20.(E42-45) Sixteen kinds of mindfulness about breathing.

21.(E45-47) Four constituents of attaining the stream.

22.(E48-49) Ten powers of the Tathāgata.

23.(E49-51) Four grounds of confidence (or of fearlessness) of a Buddha.

24.(E51-52) Four discriminations of the Tathāgata--of things, of *dharma*, of usage, and of perspicuity.

25.(E52-53) Eighteen special characteristics of the Buddha.

26.(E53-62) Thirty-two marks of a great person.

27.(E63-68) Eighty minor marks of a Buddha.

## 136. AUTHOR UNKNOWN, *Saṃdhinirmocanasūtra*

"T" references are to the French translation by Étienne Lamotte (Louvain 1935, 1962).[357] An English translation and extensive discussion of sizable sections of the work are found in John Powers, *Hermeneutics and Tradition in the Saṃdhinirmocana-Sūtra* (Leiden, 1993). "P" references are to the pages of Powers' book.

One passage (T206-207) in Chapter Seven of this work is of such importance that we have ventured to provide a complete translation of it. It explicitly addresses the relationship between Abhidharma, Madhyamaka and Yogācāra in a remarkable fashion.

This work is "wholly incorporated in the *Viniścayasaṃgrahaṇī* section of 166.*Yogācārabhūmi*"[358]

### CHAPTER ONE

1-6.(T169-172; P42-45) "Conditioned" and "unconditioned" are explained as metaphorical terms whose meaning is a conventional or nominal designation. The noble ones understand it but it is actually ineffable. Why then are these terms "conditioned" and "unconditioned" invented? It is as when a magician explains his trick to a pupil: likewise, the noble ones have invented these terms "conditioned" and "unconditioned" to describe the indescribable nature of things.

## CHAPTER TWO

1-4.(T172-174; P47-53) The ultimate truth (*paramārtha*) is intuitively known to the nobles, but is a matter of speculative tradition for (some?) ordinary folk, who fall to quarrelling over it. The ultimate belongs to the signless realm beyond argumentation; it is ineffable and free from conventions of language.

## CHAPTER THREE

1-7.(T175-178; P54-60) Question: Some say that the conventional and the ultimate (truths) are the same, others that they are different. Which is right? If they're the same ordinary folk would see the truth and be liberated. If they are different, even seers of truth would not attain liberation.

Answer: The conventional and the ultimate are neither the same nor different in nature. But the obstacles of images and impotence can be overcome by attaining insight (*vipaśyanā*) and achieving peace (*śamatha*).

## CHAPTER FOUR

1-12.(T178-182; P61-64) Subhūti reviews a number of Abhidharma notions--aggregates, signs, origination, destruction, cessation, dependent origination, four truths, eighteen elements, four establishments of mindfulness, four supernatural powers, five faculties, five powers, seven or eight limbs of enlightenment. The ones who teach the differences among these ignore the highest truth, he says.

Buddha: You are right. The highest, the pure object, is not heterogeneous in character; it is understood by mystics. It cannot be caused or conditioned. If it were, one would have to seek something even more basic. But whether Tathāgatas arise or not, the element of factors (*dharmadhātu*) is necessarily established.

## CHAPTER FIVE

1-3.(T183-185) In the material world there are six courses. But at the beginning of each life in any of these courses two things are furnished from the seeds (*bīja*) which appropriate (*ādāna*) two things: the material organs for the body and the traces (*vāsanā*) of signs, words and conceptual constructions. The consciousness that results is called the "appropriating consciousness" (*ādānavijñāna*); it is also called the "storehouse consciousness" (*ālayavijñāna*), because in it the seeds are stored.

4.(T185) With this appropriating consciousness as base six groups of awarenesses are born: visual, auditory, olfactory, linguistic, bodily and mental. Visual awareness has as its base the eye together with consciousness and shape. Simultaneously with it functions a mental awareness (*manovijñāna*) which has the same base. Even if several kinds of awareness function at the same time, only one mental awareness, having a single content, occurs.

## CHAPTER SIX

1-7.(T188-189) Things are of three natures: constructed (*parikalpita*), dependent (*paratantra*) and perfected (*parinispanna*). The constructed nature involves specification of the things known by conventional names, couched in current language. The dependent nature is things involved in dependent origination, following the causal principle derived from traces conditioned by ignorance and causing the arising of frustrations. The perfected nature is the true nature of things known to Bodhisattvas through their energy and attention derived from spiritual practice; it arises based on superior enlightenment.

The constructed is the illusion of one affected with a diseased eye (*timira*); the dependent is the signs--hair, color, jewel--conditioning the one with the disease; and the perfected is the actual object, the proper domain of clear vision.

8-12.(189-191) A transparent crystal will be seen as having fantasized properties born from linguistic associations (the constructed); the colors with which these properties are associated is the dependent; the perpetual nonexistence of any such properties or color is the perfected.

The constructed is cognized as a qualitative form dependent on names attached to signs. The dependent is cognized depending on the insistence on the constructed nature as belonging to the perfected nature. The perfected is cognized depending on the insistence on the constructed nature as not belonging to the dependent. Bodhisattvas understand precisely the imaginary character attributed to the dependent: they know accurately that things are without characteristics, are "stainless". And thus they know their purity.

## CHAPTER SEVEN

1-9.(T192-195; P85-122) Question: Since the Buddha spoke of five aggregates, four truths, eighteen bases, etc. and also has affirmed that everything is without a specific characteristic, is unborn, undestroyed, calm from the outset, liberation--why do you lay all this (above) on us?

Answer: Good question! Listen. There are three ways of being unreal, without a specific characteristic (*niḥsvabhāva*): relating to character, to birth and to the highest. The unreality of character is the constructed nature; things arise from language and not by themselves. The unreality of birth is the dependent nature; things are born from conditions, not by or from themselves. The highest unreality is the perfected nature, the pure supporting object devoid of character like a sky-flower or like space. This triple unreality shows that everything is without an essential nature, that nothing is born or destroyed; all is calm, essentially liberated, cannot be born or die.

10-13.(T196-198) To those who have not planted good roots or purified the obstacles etc. this *dharma* of unreality is preached. To understand this is to undertand that the traces are causally conditioned, impermanent, unstable, changing; thus one will grow to detest these traces.

But even those who plant good roots and accumulate merit do not cognize exactly in the unreality of birth either the unreality of character or the double unreality of the highest unreality. It is to them that the Buddha teaches the *dharma* of these two sorts of unreality. Following that *dharma* they will no longer cling to the characteristics of the dependent nature, will examine and penetrate them exactly.

14-16.(T198-199) It is by this single vehicle (*ekayāna*) that disciples, self-enlightened ones and Bodhisattvas attain to liberation. There is no other path, though not every one is astute enough to appreciate that. E.g., a disciple whose compassion is mediocre and whose fear of frustration is extreme will not thus achieve liberation, but when he turns toward illumination I deem him a Bodhisattva, though given his nature at the outset he is still referred to as "disciple".

18-23.(T199-202) Some who have planted good roots, purified the obstacles, ripened their series, etc., honest by nature, because they are nonintellectual, do not precisely comprehend my teaching, though they adhere to it, speak the Buddha's word and praise him. Incapable of meditation they still by their store of merit and understanding grow to fullness and arrive at the goal.

Others who lack some of these features will fail. Some of these remain complacent in their error. Others, not complacent, explicitly reject the correct interpretation and fall into great misery, attaining covering by karma (*karmāvaraṇa*). These include intellectual types who deny that the correct teaching is that of the Buddha: while this is easy to say it will take millions of eons for the karma it produces to disappear.

(T206-207)[359] "The bodhisattva Paramārthasamudgata said to the Buddha: 'In Benares, at Ṛṣipatana in the Deer Park, the Blessed One first turned the wheel of doctrine, demonstrating the four noble truths for the followers of the hearers' vehicle. This turning of the wheel was marvellous and wonderful; it was such as nobody in the world, neither gods nor men, has turned before. Nevertheless, there were superior doctrines. This [first turning] gave rise to criticism, needed interpretation, and became an object of controversy. So then the Blessed One, with an implicit intention, turned the wheel for the second time for the sake of the followers of the great vehicle, explaining that all things are without essence, do not arise, are not destroyed, are quiescent from the beginning, and are originally in cessation. Nevertheless, there were teachings superior to this, for this also gave rise to criticism, needed interpretation, and became an object of controversy. So the Blessed One, with an explicit intention, turned the wheel a third time for the sake of the followers of all vehicles, explaining that all things are without essence, do not arise, are not destroyed, are quiescent from the beginning, and are originally in cessation. This turning of the wheel is absolutely marvellous and wonderful. It is unsurpassed, and does not give rise to criticism: it is explicit and does not become an object of controversy."

## CHAPTER EIGHT

1-8.(T209-213) The Buddha speaks of peace and insight. A series of questions exploring these two notions receive appropriate answers. Peace has construction not involving (conceptual) reflecting, whereas insight deals with constructions involving reflection.

Question: Are peace and insight distinct paths? Answer: Yes and no. Peace involves thoughts understood through insight, but minus the images that are found in insight.

Question: Are these images different from those of ordinary thought. Answer: No, they are only ideas. Indeed, I have said that every object is ideation-only (*vijñaptimātratā*).

Question: Can one have an idea of an idea. Answer: Sure, an idea can be of anything, but not be different from its content. E.g., a reflection in a mirror isn't really different from the awareness of it--it's not really "out there".

9-39.(T213-235) Peaceful awareness grasps fetterless contents, while insight grasps ideas of objects. In one-pointed concentration one practises peace and insight at the same time, recognizing its content to be only an idea.

Varieties of peace and insight are compared. They can be mixed, when one collects factors into a group and thinks of them as truth, illuminating, liberation, revolution at the basis (*āśrayaparāvṛtti*), good factors, etc. Such a meditation is analyzed as (1) demolishing the depravity (*dauṣṭhulya*) in each factor contemplated, (2) suppressing their differences and enjoying the happiness of *dharma*, (3) perfectly understanding their brilliance, (4) producing appropriate notions reflecting one's accomplishment of duty, purification and nonreflection, (5) attaining perfection and realizing the *dharmakāya*.

This procedure is re-analyzed by other methods. For example, knowing the *dharma* by knowing names, phrases, phonemes, knowing them separately and in tandem. Or again, knowing them under ten aspects of extension, essence, grasper, grasped, residence, enjoyment, error, nonerror, pollution and purification. (These are only two of a number of such methods.) The discussion covers a whole series of relations to other Buddhist notions such as thusness, calculation, emptiness, distractions, obstructions, antidotes, etc. assigned to ten stages (*daśabhūmi*), concluding with an explanation that in liberation all feelings are destroyed and a classification of feelings.

## CHAPTER NINE

1-5.(T236-242) The ten stages. Four purifications, eleven aspects, twenty-two delusions and eleven depravities are assigned to appropriate stages among the ten.

6-8.(T242-243) Eight purifications (*viśuddhi*): of intention, awareness, compassion, virtue, of the view of and service to the Buddha, of maturation, birth and ability. The Bodhisattva is extolled for his pure roots, clairvoyance, compassion for all beings, and unsulliedness.

9-31.(T243-255) Ten perfections: the usual six--giving, morality, patience, energy, ecstasy and wisdom--plus four more: helping others, energetic helping, attention, and ecstatic practices. Their features, applications, good and bad ways of assisting, karmic results, source, causes and defilements.

32-34.(T255-256) Reversion to the single-path theme.

## CHAPTER TEN

1-4.(T257-258) The three bodies of the Buddha. The *dharmakāya* is the revolution at the basis, inconceivable, indescribable, and alike for disciple and those self-enlightened.

5-8.(T258-267) *Sūtra, vinaya, mātṛkā* and *dhāraṇī* explained.

9.(T267-268) The effortless awareness of the Tathāgata.

12.(T269-270) The easy and the difficult path distinguished.

# 137. PIṄGALA, *Akutobhayā* on Nāgārjuna's *Madhyamakakārikās*[360]

Remarks by C. W. Huntington, Jr.

The *Akutobhayā* survives only in a Tibetan translation done some time during the first half of the ninth century. Our earliest known reference to the text is found in the Chinese biography of Nāgārjuna translated (or perhaps composed) by Kumārajīva in 405 A.D. Regardless of whether or not the biography actually dates back to the first half of the fourth century, as internal evidence suggests, we can be certain that along with the most ancient Madhyamaka texts the Chinese inherited from India a tradition that Nāgārjuna was the author of an autocommentary (*svávṛtti*) on the *Mūlamadhyamakakārikās* entitled *Akutobhayā,* or simply *Abhayaśāstra* (*wu wei lun*). Tibetan translators of the Madhyamaka literature also preserved this tradition in their catalogues and in the colophon to the *Akutobhayā,* as well as at the close of every chapter, where the text is specifically attributed to Nāgārjuna. Despite this undeniable evidence of what must have been a very old Indian tradition, aside from the testimony provided in the *Akutobhayā* itself we presently know of only two Indian texts which explicitly refer to an autocommentary on the *kārikās*.[361] Obviously there was some awareness of this tradition, and just as certainly the original texts of the *Akutobhayā* was circulated, in some form, within the most ancient Indian Madhyamaka community. Yet not one of the principal Indian Mādhyamikas mentions such a treatise. Even Buddhapālita fails to acknowledge his debt to this earlier work, although his own very famous commentary is identical to the *Akutobhayā* in many places. It remains a tantalizing mystery as to why later Indian Mādhyamikas almost totally neglected both this particular commentary and the tradition surrounding it. Largely because of this neglect, and also on account of a citation in the *Akutobhayā* lifted directly from the work of Nāgārjuna's disciple Āryadeva, most Tibetan scholars strongly contested any internal evidence that the text had been written by Nāgārjuna himself.

The situation becomes even more mysterious when we examine the relationship between the *Akutobhayā* and the Chinese *Chung-lun*, a commentary on the *Mūlamadhyamakakārikās* variously attributed to more than one otherwise unknown author. A close comparison of the Tibetan text of the *Akutobhayā* with the *Chung-lun* reveals that the two commentaries most definitely stem from a single, original Indian (probably Sanskrit) source that may have undergone more or less radical alterations even before it was used as a crib for either of these later works. As is the case with

Buddhapālita, once again we find that the author of the *Chung-lun* incorporated lengthy passages from this original source into his own commentary. There is also convincing evidence that the Chinese translator Kumārajīva went on to perform even more extensive editorial revisions before the text of the *Chung-lun* reached its final form.

On the basis of present knowledge, then, we may quite reasonably postulate the existence of an original exegetical tradition that circulated through the earliest Indian Madhyamaka community along with the *Mūlamadhyamakakārikās*. This traditional exegesis must necessarily have existed prior to Buddhapālita. The date of the Chinese translation of the *Chung-lun* would provide us with a *terminus ad quem* of 409 A.D. for the first redaction of what may have previously been an oral commentary on Nāgārjuna's stanzas. It seems likely that the *Akutobhayā* represents an actual recension of this first written text, while Buddhapālita composed a considerably enlarged version. The *Chung-lun* would certainly be farthest removed from the original. It is not possible to determine the earliest form of this commentary, but it may well have contained material common to the *Akutobhayā*, Buddhapālita's *vṛtti*, and the *Chung-lun*. We may also speculate as to what it might have excluded.

Careful analysis of these texts indicates that the Tibetan *Akutobhayā*, like the *Chung-lun*, is itself the end product of a series of editorial redactions. Both Buddhapālita and the *Chung-lun* consistently omit the brief illustrations often included at the close of sections of the *Akutobhayā* that are otherwise taken over verbatim. This fact suggests that such illustrations were appended at some point after the text had been incorporated into Buddhapālita's *vṛtti* and the *Chung-lun*, or else that these later commentaries made use of a different recension of the Indian source. One cannot entirely dismiss the possibility that the controversial stanza of Āryadeva quoted in Chapter 27 of the *Akutobhayā* was also added to the body of an earlier commentary. In any case, it is unlikely that we will ever be able to prove that the Tibetan *Akutobhayā* actually represents Nāgārjuna's own work, but nevertheless the text is still immensely valuable as a translation of the oldest extant version of this most ancient commentary on Nāgārjuna's *kārikās*.

The *Akutobhayā* is a rather brief, straightforward commentary. Except for the citation from Āryadeva, it incorporates only a very few quotations--all from the *sūtras*. Many explanations confine themselves to a restatement of the grammar and syntax of a particular *kārikā*. The *Akutobhayā* apparently differs from Buddhapālita in its interpretation of a *kārikā* in only five instances,[362] and none of these differences could be taken as a philosophical or doctrinal disagreement. Buddhapālita's *vṛtti* is in virtually every respect simply an amplification of the methodology and themes of the *Akutobhayā*, and is in fact to be preferred for its more detailed explanations.

Due to the nature of its close relationship with Buddhapālita's *vṛtti*, the *Akutobhayā* is primarily significant from a text-critical rather than a philosophical point of view. It is worth noting, however, that the commentary depends exclusively upon very simple, *reductio ad absurdum* argumentation (*prasaṅgavākya*)--a strong indication of the historical priority of this particular methodology within the Madhyamaka tradition.

## 138. AUTHOR UNKNOWN, *Laṅkāvatārasūtra*[363]

The literature abounds in a great deal of speculation about the date and nature of growth of this large work. Some estimate its date as preceding Nāgārjuna's, and for other reasons (see below) one might be inclined to date it quite a bit later. It is probable that the work grew in the same manner that many others covered here did, and that it is now impossible to disentangle the various sections, much less to date their composition. Lindtner[364] speaks of an "Ur-LS" which he believes was known to Nāgārjuna and Āryadeva, offering analyses of passages in support. Schmithausen[365], following a suggestion of Jikido Takasaki's, suggests that this text quotes Vasubandhu's 202.*Triṃśikā* and so must postdate that work, but Lindtner argues that Vasubandhu knew the *Laṅkāvatārasūtra* as well as the 136.*Saṃdhinirmocanasūtra*.

A thorough review of earlier thoughts about the dating and other information about the Chinese and Tibetan versions of this work are provided by Daiset Teitaro Suzuki.[366] The earliest of these, by Dharmarakṣa, Suzuki estimates as having been composed around

420-430. It is now lost, but a slightly later translation by Guṇabhadra in 435 is extant. Two other Chinese translations appear to date from 513 and 700-704. One of the Tibetan translations is in fact a translation from Guṇabhadra's Chinese version. Suzuki[367] compares these several translations.

Jikido Takasaki has also studied the likely origins of this work. He writes that "the Sūtra consists of two parts, one in mixed prose and verse and forming the main body of the Sūtra, and the other, a section exclusively in verse which was named *Sagāthakam* by Nanjio, the editor of the Sanskrit text...Development (of the two parts) took place in both independently until finally they were combined into one volume...The original form of the *Laṅkāvatāra* was in verses akin to the *Sagāthakam*."[368] As a leading scholar on the theory of *tathāgatagarbha* in Buddhism, and noting the references to it in this text, perhaps the earliest such references to be found, Takasaki is naturally interested in the relative chronology of this work and the *Ratnagotravibhāga*, the basic text for *tathāgatagarbha* theory. He writes: "Both the LV and the RGB share the Tathāgatagarbha theory, especially that of the *Śrīmālādevī-(sūtra)*, and both are proximate to the Yogācāra, but do not belong to the orthodox Vijñānavāda. Nevertheless they do not show any awareness of each other's existence, or at least we can say that the latter did not use the former as an authority. This would not mean that the RGB is of an earlier date than the LV, or *vice versa*, but rather it would show the distance between them both being on the peripheries of the Yogācāra but at opposite poles from each other. Due to their peculiar situation with regards to the Yogācāra, Vasubandhu never referred to either text even though he was acquainted with both of them to some extent. It was only after Vasubandhu, probably by the end of the fifth century, that both texts come to be 'enrolled' among the works of the Yogācāra as authorities of a sort, and this fact is shown by their having been translated by the team of Bodhiruci and Ratnamati around 510 along with other works of the Vijñānavāda."[369]

In any case it is evident that a number of the typical technical terms of Yogācāra surface in the *Laṅkāvatāra*, but that, depite a sizable literature on this text, its position among the schools of Buddhist thought is still somewhat unclear.

"E" references are to the edition in Vaidya[370]. "T" references are to D.T. Suzuki's translation[371]. Numbering of sections within chapters correspond to those in T. Various sections are translated by Edward Hamlin[372], indicated by "H". Some passages are also translated in D.T. Suzuki[373], referred to as "S".

## CHAPTER ONE

(E1-9; T3-21; S120-121)[374] "The *Laṅkāvatāra-sūtra* opens with a spectacle, a play of illusions which serves to introduce one of the central themes of the text: the doctrine of *māyā*, the dream-like quality of the phenomenal world."[375] This spectacle occurs in Laṅkā, i.e. modern Sri Lanka; thus the name of the work.

There is a reference to the problem of time.[376]

## CHAPTER TWO

1-2.(E10-16; T23-31) The Bodhisattva Mahāmati asks the Buddha one hundred and eight questions.

3.(E16-17; T31-33) One hundred and one negative assertions.

4.(E18; T33-35) Consciousness is classified in several ways.[377]

5.(E18; T35) Seven kinds of essential nature: origin, existence, characteristic mark, great element, cause, condition and fulfillment.

6.(E18; T18-19) Seven highest things (*paramārtha*): the realms of awareness (*cittagocara*), of knowledge (*jñānagocara*), of wisdom, of views, the world beyond views, the world beyond the earth, and the world of the path of a *tathāgata*.

The correct view is not to be confused with that of heretics (*tīrthakara)* who do not understand that views concern the conceptual constructions that are (actually) one's own awareness (*svacittaviṣayavikalpadṛṣṭyanavabodhana*).

7.(E19; T36-39; S96-98) Views of other systems about causation are here refuted: eternalists, nihilists, all who believe in the reality of cause and effect, of aggregates, elements and senses. But those who understand that awareness has nothing to do with causation, that differences are as in a dream, will soon appreciate the identity of *nirvāna* and *saṃsāra* and enter a state beyond mental awareness.

9.(E20-23; T39-44; T171-174, 188-189)[378] Why does visual

awareness occur? For four reasons: one's clinging to an external world, clinging to matter and traces bred by wrong views, the very nature of consciousness, and our wish for multiplicity. For these reasons the waves of consciousness stir on the abode-consciousness (*ālayavijñāna*). And this applies to all five kinds of sensory awareness together with mental awareness (*manovijñāna*).

Now yogis think they can stop this functioning of awareness by entering trance states, but since the seeds of karma are still operative they do not escape. But the Bodhisattvas who understand that the world is mind-only succeed where they fail.

11.(E23; T44-46) Three aspects of wisdom: freedom from appearances, when one has mastered the vehicles of disciples, the self-enlightened, and followers of other schools; the particular abilities obtained by Buddhas through their vows; and the stage of *dharmakāya* obtained by wisdom, by which is attained the status of *tathāgata*.

12.(E23-24; T46-49) The twin errors of asserting or denying that a rabbit has horns. Some philosophers believe that form (*rūpa*) is different from space (*ākāśa*). But they are the same thing.[379]

13.(E24; T49; S175) Five verses, the middle one of which relates to extension.[380]

14.(E25; T49-51; S208-208) Is purification of outflows instantaneous or gradual? It is both.

15.(E25; T51-52; S320-321) The Buddha that flows out of *dharmatā* and the Buddha who produces magical appearances distinguished.

16-17.(E25-26; T52-55) Two aspects of the way of the disciple: self-realization and adherence to the notion of self-nature. The eternal-unthinkable (*nityācintya*) that is wrongly taken to be a creator, since he would require a further creator, would not be eternal, would be only a verbal designation. By contrast our eternal-unthinkable is the highest reality, having nothing to do with being or nonbeing.

18.(E27; T55) The storehouse-consciousness *is* liberation, and *saṃsāra* as well.

19.(E27; T55-56; S190-191) Nothing is born.

20.(E27; T56-58; S148) Five kinds of people with insight: those with disciples' insight, those with the insight of the self-enlightened, those with the insight of a *tathāgata*, those of indeterminate lineage and those of no lineage at all. The *tathāgata*'s insight is itself of three sorts: seeing that the nature of things is not a self-nature, attainment through realization, and attainment of insight into all the lands of Buddhas. Those who attain these heights lack fear.

22.(E28-29; T58-59) There are two kinds of those who do not desire liberation (*icchāntika*)--those completely without *dharma* through having abandoned the teaching, and those who have vowed to remain after all are liberated--a Bodhisattva.

23.(E29; T59-60) Three kinds of essential nature: constructed (*parikalpita*), dependent (*paratantra*), and perfected (*parinispanna*). The first arises from attachment to names and to objects, the second from distinguishing loci and supporting objects. The third comes when one is free from signs, names, objects, marks and constructions.

24.(E29; T60-62) Twofold egolessness (*nairātmya*)--of persons, of the idea that there is "I" of a person--and of factors, the realization that the aggregates, elements and senses are the result of construction.

25.(E30; T62-64) Asserting (*samāropaṇa*) and refuting (*apavāda*) are to be avoided.

26.(E31; T64--65) Bodhisattvas assume different forms to assist others.

27.(E31-33; T65-68; S287-291) Seven kinds of emptiness: of marks; of essential nature; of the impossibility of action since all the aggregates are empty; of the necessity of action since things go on as long as cause and karma operate; of the unspeakableness of all things, being empty; of the great emptiness of everything from the standpoint of highest knowledge; and the emptiness of the notion of mutual absence. The last is the least profound.

Explanations of non-birth and nonduality.

28.(E33; T68-70; S138-139) Objection: Is not the *tathāgatagarbha* another name for a self?

Answer: No, for it is taught that *tathāgatagarbha* is emptiness, liberation; that theory is intended to show people that they should not cling to an ego.

30.(E34; T70-72) Four things that make a Bodhisattva a great yogi: seeing that everything is only awareness; abandoning the idea that things are born, remain and disappear; realizing that there is no external world; and attainment of realization through wisdom.

31.(E35-36; T72-75) Six causes: (1) becoming-cause (*bhaviṣyahetu*), (2) relation-cause (*sambandhahetu*), (3) mark-cause (*lakṣaṇahetu*), (4) causal cause (*kāraṇahetu*), (5) manifesting cause (*vyañjanahetu*), (6) dependent cause (*apekṣāhetu*). But though these are here discriminated they neither occur together nor separately.

32-34.(E36-37; T75-78) Four sorts of verbal constructions (*vāgvikalpa*): those indicating distinguishing marks, those indicating dream-objects, those arising from depravity and construction, and those arising from beginningless constructions, i.e., from karma.

Mahāmati: Are words the same as or different from conceptual constructions?

Answer: Neither. Language comes from constructions, so they cannot be the same, but if they are different they cannot have the meaning they do have.

Mahāmati: Is language real or what expresses reality?

Answer: Neither. Reality is a pleasurable state not gained by mere words, but rather by wisdom. And words are born and die and are conditioned; they are only indications, not reality.

35.(E37-40; T78-84) The world is illusory, like a dream, or a painting, or water-bubbles, etc. There is no external reality; it is like reflections, like a mirage.

36.(E40; T84-85) What the Buddha does not teach.

37.(E40-41; T85-86; S367) Four kinds of meditative trance: that of the ignorant, that which analyzes meanings, that which has suchness (*tathatā*) as its content, and the trance of the *tathāgatas*.

38.(E41; T86-87) *Nirvāṇa* explained. When all three types of consciousness--the storehouse-consciousness, the mind and the mental consciousness--undergo a revolution (*parāvṛtti*), that is liberation.

39.(E42; T87) Two kinds of attachment--to words and to objects as having an essential nature.

40.(E42-43; T87-90; S203-205) Two kinds of power (*adhiṣṭhitā*) possessed by noble and fully enlightened beings. One is that by which they undergo extensive concentration and trance; the other is that by which they are favored with a visitation by the Buddhas themselves. Without these powers they would backslide.

41.(E43; T90-91) Clearing up of confusion about dependent origination.

42.(E43-44; T91-92) Since there are words without things, words are unreal, and existence does not depend on words.

43.(E44-45; T92-95) The wise are still subject to the appearance of error (*bhrānti*), but they know it as error. The ignorant are taken in by it. Indeed, there are three kinds of wise people: the disciples, who preserve the notions of particular and general; the liberated for themselves, who retire from society; and the Buddhas, who know that there is nothing but awareness.

Mahāmati: Does error occur or not?

Answer: It is like *māyā*; it has no characteristic mark.

Mahāmati: If so, *māyā* will be the cause of further errors, etc.

Answer: No, *māyā* causes no error; it has no such capacity.

44.(E45-46; T95-96) It is not that *māyā* doesn't exist. Everything is *māyā*, being unreal and disappearing immediately upon occurring, but being classified as particular or general depending on how it is classified.

45.(E46; T96-97) Mahāmati: The Buddha says both that everything is unborn and that it all resembles *māyā*. This is a contradiction.

Answer: When one recognizes that the world is merely mind one will recognize that all is unborn. Still, I teach differently to different pupils depending on their needs.

46.(E46-47; T97-98) The name-body (*nāmakāya*) is the object or substance that constitutes the letter of the alphabet involved; the term-body (*padakāya*) completes the context of reference; the syllable-body (*vyañjanakāya*) is the verbal entity which is short or long.

47.(E47; T98-99) On the inexplicables (*avyākṛta*), such as:

48.(E47-48; T99-100; S304) Everything is without essential nature, unborn, without death, not eternal, not noneternal.

49.(E48-50; T100-105) Stream-enterers, once-returners, nonreturners and perfected beings distinguished.

50.(E50; T105-106) Two kinds of discriminatory awareness (*buddhi*)--the one that considers the inexplicables, etc. as inapplicable, and the one which distinguishes objects and breeds attachment.

51.(E50-51; T106-107; S368) Both the great elements and the substances derived from them are unreal, are only mind.

52.(E51; T107-108) On the five aggregates.

53.(E51-52; T108-110; S192-193) Four kinds of liberation: when essential natures are seen as nonexistent, when things are realized to be without characteristic marks, when things are seen to be without specific characteristics, when attachment to distinguishing particular and general characteristics is ended. On my view, liberation occurs when mental consciousness (*manovijñāna*) ceases.

Mahāmati: But there are eight consciousnesses, of which mental consciousness is only one.

Answer: The other seven arise when mental consciousness operates.

54.(E52-53; T110-112) When one can tell constructed things from others one will be able to terminate conceptual constructions. There are twelve sorts of constructions: constructions of (1) repeated words, attachment to nice sounds, (2) denotations, supposing there are distinct verbal entities corresponding to the things they name, (3) characteristic marks, classification into categories, (4) things, such as gold, etc. that are found desirable, (5) essential nature, classification according to philosophical system, (6) cause, (7) views, such as nihilistic, etc.; (8) reasoning (*yukti*), (9) origination, (10) nonorigination, (11) relation, (12) bondage and nonbondage, supposing there is something bound as if it were tied up.

55.(E53-54; T112-114; S160-162) Awareness involves relation to contents. In nonappearance (*nirābhāsa*) wisdom operates. Constructed things occur, but as dependent they do not; due to error constructed things appear, but construction does not (actually) occur. The appearance of different things is a mistake, causing bondage. What is constructed is just dependent, the appearance of many constructed. Construction belongs to the conventional (*saṃvṛti*) realm, and when it is cut the wise find highest truth (*paramārtha*). What is constructed cannot be perfected (*niṣpanna*)

56.(E54-55; T114-117; S360-361) The one-vehicle (*ekayāna*) way involves the non-operation of conceptual constructions such as grasper and grasped, constructed and true, etc., and has only been practised by the Buddha himself. The triple-vehicle (*triyāna*) way is intended for disciples and self-enlightened who have not yet destroyed karmic traces and whose knowledge is hidden, who cannot understand the selflessness of things; when, destroying bad karmic traces, they realize the selflessness of factors, they will not be full of arrogance over their concentration; going to the higher world of pure elements they will obtain the inconceivable *dharmakāya.*

## CHAPTER THREE

57.(E56; T118-119) Three kinds of mind-body (*manomayakāya*): (1) that gained in the third to fifth stages of meditation by the attainment of the satisfaction when one realizes that there is no external world; (2) that gained in the eighth stage through experiencing the essential nature of *dharma*, when one gains in meditation an unusual body capable like that in dream of remarkable accomplishments; (3) that gained in keeping with one's group by one who understands fully all the teachings of the Buddha.

58.(E56-57; T120-121; S363-364) The five producers of early retribution: murdering one's mother, murdering one's father, murdering a noble person, breaking up the Order, causing a Buddha's body to bleed. One committing any of these goes to Avīci hell. This is the external meaning. There is also a hidden meaning of each of the five: on that understanding (viz., the mother of all beings is desire, the father ignorance, the noble person is the subtle passions, the "Order" is the aggregates, the destruction of the eight bodies of consciousness is the bleeding of the Buddha's body) to experience these five is to gain full understanding.

60.(E57-58; T122-123; S351-352) Explanation of the Buddha's former births.

61.(E58-59; T123-125; S275) The Buddha said that silence is the Buddha's speech. What does he mean by that? That one's own *dharmatā* is beyond language, and it is established forever as truth, suchness, reality.[381]

62.(E59-60; T125-127) The faults of nihilism and eternalism.

63.(E60-61; T127-129; S350) Two features of the realization that provides liberation: that the realization itself is beyond language, it is an inner experience; but that the teaching about it fends off dualistic thoughts which otherwise block realization.

64.(E61-63; T129-133; S241-243) Construction of what was not (*abhūtaparikalpa*) explained. It involves the conceptual construction of things, distinctions among them, appropriating them and becoming attached to them.

Mahāmati: But isn't it attachment also when one conceives highest reality as distinct from what it is not, thus breeding conceptual constructions, etc.?

Answer: Conceptual constructions are not actually bred, nor are they actually gotten rid of. They are not real, since everything is consciousness-only (*cittamātra*). I talk as if it were real only in order to begin instruction.

65.(E63-64; T133-135) Question: The Buddha says that one should not grasp things according to language. But what is language? Why shouldn't one grasp its meaning?

Answer: Words and meanings are neither the same nor different from each other. But the fault is to become attached to them and develop views.

66.(E64-65; T135-137) On the differences between knowledge (*jñāṇa*) and mere awareness (*vijñāna*). There are three kinds of knowledge: worldly (*laukika*), other-worldly (*lokottara*) and beyond other-worldly (*lokottaratama*). Mere awareness is born and ends. Knowledge is without birth or death.[382] Worldly knowledge belongs to philosophers (*tīrthika*) and ordinary folks, other-worldly knowledge to disciples and those self-enlightened, and knowledge beyond other-worldly to Bodhisattvas. Knowledge is free from attachment; mere awareness concerns manifold contents. Awareness is the product of three features; knowledge is not; it is unattainable, the inner state of realization.

67.(E65; T137-138) Nine kinds of transformation: of configuration, of characteristic mark, of cause, of reasoning, of view, of arising, of being; of the manifestation of conditions, of the manifestation of action. (Only the first is explained here.)

68.(E65-66; T138-141) The variety of attachments.

69.(E66-67; T141-143) Mahāmati: You say that what is constructed cannot be real, yet both the wise and the ignorant continue to construct; it is only that what is constructed by the ignorant isn't real, while that constructed by the wise is. Thus in order to avoid the extremes of nihilism and eternalism you advise us to maintain realism, whereas since realism breeds clinging shouldn't you be teaching the doctrine of separateness (*viviktadharma*)?

Answer: I do not deny separateness, nor do I teach realism as a final truth, though each may be taught where appropriate.

70.(E67-69; T144-146) Furthermore I don't preach that everything is unborn as a thesis, for to do so would be paradoxical, since what I preach is born. Likewise with "everything is empty" or "everything is without an independent nature". There is no independent nature, no construction, no actual entities, no store-consciousness. But these denials are not made in some higher arena of truth; all this is like mirages in the air.

71.(E69-70; T146-148) Mahāmati: So, you are saying that whatever one says about things is mere manifestation (*vijñaptimātra*), that knowledge is unobtainable. But why is knowledge unobtainable? If a piece of awareness is unobtainable it is called a case of ignorance, not knowledge.

Answer: We know that awareness can arise without any supporting object. We see that thinking about things is mere manifestation. To see that knowledge is unobtainable is to see that what is seen is only mind, that no objects of the sort seen exist. But logicians (*tārkika*) cannot understand this; they speak of consciousness-only but cannot really understand it.

72.(E70; T148-149) One gains understanding either by study of texts or by turning away from constructing what is seen by one's own consciousness.

73.(E70-74; T149-157) Mahāmati: The materialist (*lokāyatika*), who is very skilled and knowledgeable in speaking, can provide, we are told, advice only about worldly things, not *dharma*. Why is that?

Answer: He does not understand *dharma*, confusing himself and others by the multitude of views and arguments he is master of.

Mahāmati: But doesn't the Buddha himself teach materialism?

Answer: No, I teach the unborn. Nothing exists externally, there is nothing to be attached to.

Stories about materialists are told.

74.(E74-76; T157-161; S74-76) Various alternative theories about liberation are reviewed. But all of them view liberation in a causal way--something arises, something disappears. But actually nothing arises, nothing disappears. *Nirvāṇa* is just the realization that there is nothing but consciousness.

75.(E76-77; T161-164; S134) The *tathāgata*--or noble, fully-enlightened being--is neither made nor nonmade, neither effect nor cause; he is outside worldly usage. When I say all things are without a self, I mean that each and every factor is to be understood in its own nature and not that of another. A cow's nature is not a horse's nature. That is what is meant by saying all things are empty. Everything is completely different from every other thing.

76.(E77-80; T164-169; S137, 347-348) The unborn, the *tathāgata*, goes by many names. People do not realize this, and think there are many different beings corresponding to those various names. One should not be tied to the letters of the words; truths are not dependent on letters or words, though without the words how would the truth be taught? So one should conform to the meaning, not the letter of the word.

77-78.(E80-83; T170-176; S353-354) Mahāmati: Your theory is really not different from other (Buddhist) philosophical theories. You all assume causation; you affirm unborn things--e.g., space, uncalculated cessation, liberation.

Answer: No, my no-self and no-cessation theories are unlike others who speak that way. They view no-self and no-cessation as the very nature of things. I do not say that objects are not existent essentially, nor do I say they are existent essentially. And it is this no-birth and no-cessation that I call *nirvāṇa*.

Verses set forth these ideas further.

79.(E83-85; T176-181) Eight[383] theories about noneternality: (1) things are born and die; (2) things change in shape; (3) matter itself comes to an end; (4) things change their form--milk goes sour, etc.; (5) there is something called "noneternality"; (6) the presence and absence of things is noneternality; (7) noneternality is nonarising. Noneternality actually means that things are naturally destructible and nonexperiencable. But noneternality is not to be taken as an entity that brings about the destruction of things. Views (1) - (7) are refuted.

## CHAPTER FOUR

80.(E86-89; T182-16; S292-299, 220-221) Mahāmati: What is cessation (*nirodha*) and how can it be gained?

Answer: In the sixth stage Bodhisattvas, as well as disciples and those self-enlightened, achieve the cessation trance. In the seventh stage the Bodhisattvas, but not the other two, attain permanent cessation. At the eighth stage all three stop entertaining any thoughts arising from awareness, mind and mental awareness. All three attain *nirvāṇa*, but a Bodhisattva does not enter into it out of choice. However, the disciples and self-enlightened are so caught up in what they have achieved that they are unable to abandon all views; they merely have the view of liberation and do not attain *parinirvāṇa*. The Bodhisattvas, though, while having achieved liberation, are not extinguished.

## CHAPTER FIVE

81.(E88-89; T187-189) The liberated, the *tathāgata*, is neither eternal nor noneternal, for a number of reasons.

## CHAPTER SIX

82.(E90-91; T190-193; S193-195) Mahāmati: Please explain how aggregates, elements and senses come to be and cease?

Answer: The *tathāgatagarbha* or storehouse-consciousness comprises the cause of both good and bad, and everything comes from it. It is without a self and therefore it is not a cause; it is the karmic influences which produce the other seven consciousnesses, which in turn produce ignorance.

This was made clear to me in the 105.*Śrīmālādevīsūtra*, a text meant for advanced thinkers rather than disciples, self-enlightened, and other philosophers.

83-84.(E91-93; T193-198) Mahāmati: Which are the five factors, the three essential natures, the consciousnesses and the twofold selflessness?

Answer: The five factors[384] are name, sign, conceptual construction, knowledge, and suchness. A *tathāgata* alone understands them and the other matters you asked about. He sees that the ignorant are confined to names and signs or appearances, whereas by conceptual construction, knowledge and suchness one overcomes that confinement to distinctions and gains the Bodhisattva stage of joy. From there he enters the higher-worldly path and eventually reaches the cloud of *dharma* (*dharmamegha*), from whence he reaches the stage of the thus-gone and achieves final liberation.

The three essential natures, eight consciousnesses and two

selflessnesses are all included within the five factors. Of those five, the first two--name and sign--are included in the constructed realm, relating to the idea of a self; construction is included in the dependent realm, relating to the manyness of objects; knowledge and suchness are included in the perfected realm, relating to the indestructible, viz., perfection.

85.(E93-95; T198-202; S149-153) Mahāmati: The Buddha says that *tathāgatas* are like the sands on the river Ganges. Is this to be taken literally?

Answer: No. This is an extended metaphor. Those sands are like the *tathāgatas* in being free from constructions, never destroyed, of immeasurable number, nontransmigrating, without a body, unconcerned.

86.(E95-96; T202-204; S198-199) Everything is momentary, even the *tathāgatagarbha*, except for the pure proclivities, gold, light, the relics of the Buddha and enlightenment.

87.(E96; T204-205) The six perfections are of three kinds: worldly, other-worldly, and above other-worldly.

## CHAPTER SEVEN

89.(E98-99; T207-210) A number of questions posed by Mahāmati and answered:

Why were disciples assured by the Buddha of their eventual enlightenment? So that they would seek Bodhisattvahood. It is nevertheless true that all three kinds of noble ones overcome the obstructions of the defilements, but only when selflessness is understood by a Bodhisattva do the obstructions of awareness cease.

How can one become a *tathāgata* without achieving *parinirvāṇa*? Since he does not deliberate or contemplate he has no more karma, is thus free from death, is beyond defilements and awareness.

Other questions of a similar sort are answered.

## CHAPTER EIGHT

(E200-205; T211-222) Why the Bodhisattva in particular, and the rest of men in general, should not eat meat.

## CHAPTER NINE

(E206; T223-225) Recitations which will guard one against misfortune.

## SAGĀTHAKAM

(E108-165; T226-295) This section consists of 884 verses of which 208 are repetitions of verses found in the verse Chapters above. T indicates which these 208 verses are.[385]

### 139. AUTHOR UNKNOWN, *Nirayasūtra*[386]

### 140. AUTHOR UNKNOWN, *Ekottarāgamasūtra*[387].

### 141. AUTHOR UNKNOWN, *Bodhisattvapūrvasūtra*[388]

### 142. AUTHOR UNKNOWN, *Buddhapiṭakaduḥśīlanirgrahasūtra*[389]

### 143. AUTHOR UNKNOWN, *Candragarbhasūtra*[390]

### 144. AUTHOR UNKNOWN, *Dhāraṇī(śvara)rājasūtra*

### 145. AUTHOR UNKNOWN, *Gayāśīrṣasūtra*[391]

### 146. AUTHOR UNKNOWN, *Kuśalamūlasamparigṛhasūtra*[392]

### 147. AUTHOR UNKNOWN, *Mahāmayūri(vidyārājñi)sūtra*[393]

### 148. AUTHOR UNKNOWN, *Maitreyavyākaraṇasūtra*[394]

### 149. AUTHOR UNKNOWN, *Pūrṇaparipṛcchāsūtra* or *Bodhisattvapiṭakasūtra*[395]

### 150. AUTHOR UNKNOWN, *Śāriputraparipṛcchāsūtra*[396]

### 151. AUTHOR UNKNOWN, *Saddharmapravṛttinirdeśasūtra*[397]

### 152. AUTHOR UNKNOWN, *Sumukha(dhāraṇī)sūtra*[398]

153. AUTHOR UNKNOWN, *Upāliparipṛcchāsūtra*[399]

154. AUTHOR UNKNOWN, *Vikurvanarājaparipṛcchāsūtra*[400]

155. NĀGĀRJUNA, *Daśabhūmikavibhāṣāśāstra*[401]

Hajime Nakamura writes: "This work is especially important because of a passage in which the way of Easy Practice by Faith is set forth. In this work the belief in Amitābha is set forth as the Easy Practice. If the aspirant, having heard the Name of Amitābha, thinks on Him and utters the Name with a faithful mind, he will attain the stage of Non-retrogression (*avinivartanīya*) toward perfect Enlightenment very quickly. Because of this idea, this work came to be highly esteemed by later Pure Land Buddhists in China and Japan."[402]

This text often quotes the 41.*Bodhisambhārasūtra*.

156. AUTHOR UNKNOWN, *Prajñāpāramitāhṛdayasūtra*[403]

There are two versions of this, the "Heart" Sūtra--one shorter, one longer. The shorter is presumably earlier, translated into Chinese by Kumārajīva around 400. This brief *sūtra*, together with 157.*Vajracchedikā*, are perhaps the most popular *sūtras* in Mahāyāna Buddhism as it finds its way into China and Japan. Since the *sūtra* is short, we provide in its entirety Edward Conze's translation.[404]

Translation by Edward Conze

"Homage to the Perfection of Wisdom, the Lovely, the Holy. Avalokita, the Holy Lord and Bodhisattva, was moving in the deep course of the wisdom which has gone beyond. He looked down from on high, he beheld but five heaps, and he saw that in their own-being they were empty.

Here, O Śāriputra, form is emptiness, and the very emptiness is form, emptiness does not differ from form, nor does form differ from emptiness; whatever is form, that is emptiness, whatever is emptiness, that is form. The same is true of feelings, perceptions, impulses and consciousness.

Here, O Śāriputra, all *dharmas* are marked with emptiness, there is neither form, nor feeling, nor perception, nor impulse, nor consciousness, no eye, or ear, or nose, or tongue, or body, or mind, no form nor sound, nor smell, nor taste, nor touchable, nor object of mind, no sight organ element, etc. until we come to no mind-consciousness element; there is no ignorance, no extinction of ignorance, etc., until we come to there is no decay and death, nor extinction of decay and death; there is no suffering, no origination, nor stopping, nor path; there is no cognition, no attainment and no nonattainment.

Therefore, O Śāriputra, owing to a Bodhisattva's indifference to any kind of personal attainment, and through his having relied on the perfection of wisdom, he dwells without thought-coverings. In the absence of thought-coverings he has not been made to tremble, he has overcome what can upset, in the end sustained by Nirvāṇa.

All those Buddhas who appear in the three periods of time, through having relied on the perfection of wisdom they fully awake to the utmost, right and perfect enlightenment.

Therefore one should know the Prajñāpāramitā as the great spell, the spell of great knowledge, the utmost spell, the inequalled spell, allayer of all suffering, in truth--for what could go wrong? By the Prajñāpāramitā has this spell been delivered. It runs like this: 'Gone, gone, gone beyond, gone altogether beyond, O what an awakening, all hail!"

## 157. AUTHOR UNKNOWN, *Vajracchedikāprajñāpāramitāsūtra*[405]

Edward Conze[406] sums up "the message of the Sūtra under five headings:

"I. One should not perceive a 'self', a being, a living soul, or a person.

II. One should not perceive a *dharma*, or separate entity, anywhere, because there is none.

III. Everything is not itself.

IV. One should not establish one's thoughts anywhere.

V. The Buddha and his enlightenment are strictly transcendental."

## 158. ŚRĪLĀTA

We know of this Buddhist scholar from references to him by Vasubandhu in the *Abhidharmakośabhāṣya*. Prabal Kumar Sen[407] has studied seven references to Śrīlāta in that work which range over various matters of Abhidharma theory, agreeing with Poussin and A.K. Bhattacharya (also with Warder) that Śrīlāta was in all likelihood a Sautrāntika. See also the comments on 72.Kumāralāta above, where it was suggested that Śrīlāta may have been Kumāralāta's pupil.

According to Jean Przyluski, following H. Lüders, Śrīlāta wrote a work titled *Sautrāntika-Vibhāṣā*.[408]

## 159. VASUBHADRA, *Caturāgamavibhāga* or *Tridharmaskandha*

We know nothing about this author, but since his work was translated in 381 we can suppose the work existed by about 350. The following summary is based on Eric Grinstead's unpublished manuscript.[409]

### PART ONE: On *Dharma*

(1-28). We here preach the triple *dharma*, consisting of merit, bad things and bases. One gets liberation by awareness of these three. Such liberation is sought by all who seek liberation, even insects.

Question: How can awareness of merit, bad things and bases bring liberation? You don't get well just by looking at the medicine!

Answer: But light destroys darkness directly. Knowledge and realization are the same thing.

Question: What is the good of talking of "knowledge" and "realization"? Language involves rebirths and sense-experiences.

Answer: If one has some virtue there are three kinds of good identification--(1) merit, (2) faculties and (3) virtue. Merit is giving, morality and discrimination. Giving consists of preaching the *dharma*, fearlessness in preferring the eight kinds of good conduct and the three refuges, and gifts. Morality is meritorious manifestation in body and speech. Discrimination is correct meditative practice, boundless and immaterial, involving meditation on the abandonment of desire, differentiation, satisfaction and frustration. It is boundless, involving loving kindness, compassion, sympathy and equanimity, and it involves the four immaterial states of the infinity of emptiness, of knowledge, of nothingness and of neither-identification-nor-nonidentification.

(29-65). Which are (2) the faculties? The "roots" of nonenvy, nonhatred, nondelusion. These are not the same as the roots of merit; they are supervenient on those roots--e.g., nonenvy is supervenient on giving, nonhatred on morality, nondelusion on discrimination. This supervenience is applied to the other two good identifications of the previous section.

Patience, learning and penetration breed certainty (*niṣkāṃkṣā*) in the conventional world, as in the realm of sexual passion. "Learning" means the *sūtras*, the *Abhidharma* and the *Vinaya piṭakas*. It is ridding oneself of all envy, hatred and delusion. Each of these three baskets has its own purpose--the *sūtras* to preach, the *Abhidharma* to explain, the *Vinaya* to counsel action. The limbs of the enlightenment one gets by learning involve good friends, thinking and acquisition. Learning is assisted by teachers, disciples and others in the assembly who possess compassion. It involves mindfulness of breathing, energy and restraint. Acquisition involves comprehension, method and result.

Comprehension is tantamount to liberation, and involves the higher life, cutting the roots, and adjacence to meditation. The higher life is achieved by taking the five vows, meditation and practising monkhood. These are explained, along with various requirements as to food, dress and behavior.

Cutting the roots requires meditation, patience and conceptual identification. It is the borderline concentration leading to release.

(65-90). The spiritual method consists of (1) morality, (2) resolution and (3) knowledge. There are two kinds of (1) morality, the everyday kind and the superior kind, which involves right speech, virtuous action and a beneficial type of rebirth as a devout layman or a monk. (2) Resolution involves energy, mindfulness and concentration. Energy is faith, renunciation and serenity; they lead to good actions. These are explained with examples. Mindfulness involves bodily, sensory and mental attentiveness. Concentration is emptiness, dispositionlessness and nonidentifyingness. "Emptiness" means "without any concept of self or anything belonging to self."

"Dispositionless" is to be without action, thus not wishing to be present at any time. "Nonidentifyingness" is to be without concepts; another term for it is "abandonment". Knowledge is initial and sustained awareness of all the first three stages, involving views, spiritual practice and the adept. It comprises knowledge of *dharma*, investigative knowledge, and the knowledge that one knows, which proceed in that order.

(91-103). Discriminative knowledge is of three kinds: (1) of characteristic marks, (2) of conditioning factors, and (3) of seeds. (1) The knowledge of the defining features of things is passing and subject to destruction. (2) Conditioning factors are noneternal, frustrating, involving the notion of self. (3) These seeds are the seeds of sensations, disaster and nonattachment.

The knowledge of a realized one is also of three kinds: (1) penetration, (2) knowledge of higher faculties, (3) perspicuity. (1) Penetration comprises knowledge of previous births and deaths and of the destruction of contaminants. (2) Knowledge of higher faculties includes extraordinary travel in space and time, entering the awarenesses of others, and the divine ear. (T. 506 appears to have a different list.) (3) Perspicuity is understanding of *dharma*, meanings, of grammar and the connections of things.

(104-128). In 29-65 above we analyzed acquisition as comprehension, method and result, but we haven't yet explained "result". The results are (1) a Buddha, (2) one self-enlightened, (3) the disciple. A Buddha "has no more" (*aśeṣa*), the self-enlightened is not dependent on others for enlightenment, the disciple is dependent on others for enlightenment.

Getting rid of bondage involves faith, resolve, conviction of right view, and internalized insight. When bondage is not gotten rid of the state is called "the eighth" or "stream-enterer", involving belief, insight and knowledge of *dharma*. Such a one has only seven more rebirths to go in good families or other worlds.

The perfected being may have dull, sharp or middling faculties, which are explained. Liberation is from desire, from unpleasantness, and clean. Or, it is of two kinds: by mindfulness and by knowledge. When final liberation or cessation occurs all awarenesses and accompanying mental factors are extinguished.

## PART TWO: Bad Things

(129-186). Actions involving frustration, desire and ignorance are bad. They are of bodily, vocal and mental varieties. Bodily bad actions include murder, stealing and treating others badly, whether by explicit intent, collusion or overt behavior. Bad vocal actions include lying, duplicity and frivolous speech. Bad mental actions involve desire, hatred and wrong views. One who is without wrong views means being without opinions concerning actions, results and human affairs generally.

What is desire? It is sensual attachment, anger, and pride. Attachments are to things desired, to existence, to the religious life. Anger (or repugnance) can be against oneself, one's family, one's enemy. Pride can be of oneself as better than, equivalent to or inferior to others.

How about ignorance? It is lack of knowledge, false opinion and doubt. Lack of knowledge can be internally or externally conditioned, unconditioned (at liberation) or indeterminate, i.e., without awareness of feeling of the past or of liberation. False opinions include the view that the self is real, extreme views, and adherence to particular views. Doubts include uncertainty about the three jewels (the Buddha, the *dharma*, the order), about the truth, and about concentration.

## PART THREE: On the Bases (*āśraya*)

(186-260). The bases are the aggregates, elements and senses. An aggregate is known as matter, conditions, awareness. A single material aggregate is a bundle of factors into material form--the four great elements and their sensations. Conditions are bodily, vocal and mental, and include feelings, identifications and consciousness. Feelings are satisfying, frustrating, neither--their supports and sources are identified. All feelings derive from action (karma), either one's own or that of others or both, and are determined by the time, disadvantageous occurrences (wind, bile, phlegm) and/or natural disasters.

There is an interesting but obscure discussion here of identifications.

What about elements? There are three realms of elements--the realm of sensual pleasure, the material and the immaterial realms. The realm of sensual pleasure involves birth as a god or a human being, or in a lower birth. Humans occupy four countries--Jambudvīpa, Videha, Godanīya and Uttarakuru. The gods occupy several heavens involving or not involving sexual activity, conversation, visual contact, etc. Lower births include hell, animal and ghostly existences, and are characterized as cold or hot (many examples given) or in between, explained as existing alone in caves and marshes. Animals and ghostly existences are classified and characterized.

The material realm comprises the part involving contentedness, that involving the absence of satisfaction, and that of equanimity. The second meditative trance state occurs in this material realm and involves mindfulness and contentedness; it results in rebirth as a teacher, a good body, or as part of a worthy group.

The immaterial realm involving absence of satisfaction arises in the higher trances, involves limited purity, unlimited purity or universal purity, and, when one's mindfulness is gone, leads to rebirth in various heavens. Restraint results in even higher rebirths as gods, nonidentifying beings and in pure abodes.

What about the senses? They are essentially those of the disciple, the adept and the liberated one. They are described in standard manner.

## 160. AUTHOR UNKNOWN, *Sammitīyanikāyaśāstra*

Summary by Robert Buswell, Jr.

The *Sammitīyanikāyaśāstra* provides a synopsis of some of the major doctrines of the Sammitīya school, a subsect of the Vatsīyaputrīyas, who are well known for their view that the person (*pudgala*) in some sense exists--the worst of heresies for the other Buddhists who rejected any conception of egoism. Little is known about the school from Sanskrit sources apart from indirect references in the polemical attacks of rival Buddhist sects. The only extant treatise by the Sammitīyas themselves is the Chinese translation of **Sammitīyanikāyaśāstra*, which gives an extensive defense of the *pudgalavāda* of the school, responding to challenges to that doctrine and providing a variety of proofs to support it.[410] The discussion on the person is in the context of a treatment of the process of rebirth, which also provides important information on the Sammitīya theory of an intermediate state between existences, which was accepted by other Buddhist schools as well, including the Sarvāstivādins and the later Mahīśāsakas.

No information is available as to the author, date of composition, or translator of the treatise. The text appears to be complete; K.Venkataramanan's suggestion that the treatise's reference to a "previous chapter" (*ch'ien-chang*) might have been an allusion to a lost chapter is clearly wrong; the reference is instead to the "preceding section of the extant texts".[411] The Chinese translation is in three fascicles (*chuan*), an arbitrary division based on length, not content; for this summary, I have adopted instead a topical divison. The original title of the treatise, as given at the conclusion of the translation, was probably *Āśrayaprajñaptinirdeśa*, which has more bearing on the actual content of the text, i.e., the view of the Sammitīyas that the individual was to be viewed as having conventional validity. As will be seen, the Sammitīyas did not claim that the self existed in reality--the heresy attributed to them by other Buddhist schools--but that the existence of a self in a conventional, nonultimate sense could not be denied.

"E" references are to the Chinese translation titled *Sam-mi-ti pu lun*, Taisho 1649.32.462a-473a, in three fascicles. The translator is unknown; the translation is included in the Chinese bibliographical catalogues among the anonymous translations from the period of the Western Chin dynasty (385-431 A.D.). "T" references are to K. Venkataramanan's translation (169.1.1).[412]

## I. The Process of Rebirth (E462a.2-b.5; T165-166)

The treatise opens with a discussion of the process of rebirth via the intermediate state. At the moment of death, the individual to be reborn assumes a neutral state of awareness that frees him from attachment to the present state of existence. The inertia of his compounded action then directs his awareness toward a state of existence consonant with the predominant orientation of his conduct (i.e., as either skillful or unskillful).

The author then clarifies that rebirth from one state of existence to another, whether exclusively within the sensual realm or between the sensual and the material realms, requires that the person arise first in the intermediate state. In the case of the Buddhas and disciples, however, the individual can progress from one intermediate state to another, without the necessity of taking rebirth in one of the three realms of existence. For example, the stream-enterer may have all of his required seven rebirths within the intermediate state, until he finally attains final liberation. This topic will be taken up again in the final section of the text.

II. Seven Theories about the Self (E462.6-466a.27; T166-182)[413]

(The treatment of the process of rebirth leads into a discussion of the nature of the self or person who so transmigrates. Seven conflicting views given by various Buddhist teachers are then presented (462b.7-464a.22), to each of which the Sammitīyas later respond (464a.28-466a.27). To make the argument and rebuttal easier to follow, I combine these two subsections.)

(1) In reality there is no self; there are only the aggregates and senses. Various scriptural citations are given which uphold the position that there is no "I" or "mine".

Sammitīya rebuttal: "Although there is a self, it is a conventional name. The self is not spoken of as being real. The self is dependent upon the aggregates, which are associated with the outflows." Similarly, the use of the words "I" and "mine" by the Buddha was also purely conventional and was not intended to convey any ultimate reality; thus the rejection of "I" and "mine" does not prove that there is no self. Finally, just because the Buddha did not say definitively that the self exists does not prove that the self does not exist.

(2) It cannot be said that the self either exists or does not exist. This is because the characteristics of the self are also indescribable. This view is justified because, of the four types of answers to questions allowed by the Buddha, queries about the self were included in the fourth type--questions that were dismissed without giving any answer. Hence, the Buddha never stated definitively either that the self did or did not exist. In addition, if the self either did or did not exist, the relationship between the aggregates and the self should have been clear: i.e., the self should be either identical

to, or different from, the aggregates. This relationship is, however, uncertain. Finally, the self cannot be called either eternal or impermanent and, consequently, its true nature cannot be said to be either existent or nonexistent.

Sammitīya rebuttal: While "it cannot be said that the characteristics of the self are either permanent or impermanent, it can be said that the self does exist." The fact that questions about the self were dismissed does not prove that the self either does or does not exist, but merely that the question was wrongly framed. Similarly, while some advocates may be unclear about the relationship between the aggregates and the self, this does not prove that the self does not exist; it merely shows that those people have not realized the self. One who experiences the self should be able to explain definitively the relationship between the aggregates and the self. Finally, if the self were explicated in terms of its being either eternal or impermanent, this would result in the wrong views of either nihilism or eternalism, both of which the Buddha rejected. If it were said that the person does not exist in any way whatsoever, this would be the wrong view of nihilism. But the Sammitīyas say that the *pudgala* does exist (presumably from the standpoint of conventional usage, though this is not specified in the text), and this is right view. "This is because the self takes its stand between existence and nonexistence. Thus we now advocate that if there were no self whatsoever, the Buddha would not have said that 'it takes its stand'. Since the Buddha did state that it 'takes its stand', there consequently is an existent self that can be discussed." (This statement clarifies the basic Sammitīya position that advocating a role for the self in Buddhism is not itself a heresy: the belief in a self only becomes wrong view if either that self is clung to as being absolutely real, thus resulting in eternalism, or the inability to locate anything permanent in objects leads one to reject the self entirely, resulting in nihilism. The self does have a conventional validity,[414] and is a valuable concept for explicating problematic areas of Buddhist doctrine, such as the relationship between action and its maturation, etc.).

(3) The self exists in reality. This is proven because of the statements in the *sūtra* that the individual is bound by the five aggregates, producing transmigration of the self. Furthermore, the admonition to cultivate the four foundations of mindfulness implies

that there actually is someone who should perform those contemplations. The Buddha also referred in several places to the person who burns his own body, or the person who attains contentment. Hence, the Buddha clearly states that there is a person, justifying the view that the self exists.

Sammitīya rebuttal: There is no person who is actually bound, even though there is said to be bondage. The existence of a self based on the admonition to cultivate the four foundations of mindfulness is also rejected. "The Buddha told Kātyāyana that there was nothing else but awareness because he wanted to reveal that (the nature of) body, feeling, awareness and factors (the four foundations of mindfulness) was just awareness. He said that there was nothing else but awareness that became all factors." Hence, the reference to cultivation did not pertain to a self but to awareness. (This statement seems to be the precursor of much that became characteristic of later Vijñānavāda thought.[415]) Finally, the statements in which the Buddha referred to a person were merely conventional, not definitive, statements. This is not, however, to say that the opposite view--that there is absolutely no self from any standpoint--is correct; for if that were the case, then there would be no murderer or victim, etc., and the law of moral action and retribution would become meaningless. This would lead inexorably to the rejection of causal relationships on a soteriological level as well: if there were no cause of *saṃsāra* (the second noble truth) or its extinction (the third noble truth), the Buddhist path (the fourth noble truth) would also be meaningless. If the four noble truths (the essence of the *dharma*) were meaningless, then there would be no Buddha and consequently no Order. Thus the rejection of the *pudgala* leads to the rejection of the truth of Buddhism. Only if the *pudgala* and the *ātman* are accepted does the Buddhist perspective remain viable.[1]

(4) The five aggregates are what the *pudgala* or the *ātman* is. This is justified because of scriptural passages in which the Buddha

---

1.We see here once again that the acceptance of a self by the Sammitīyas was not meant to be an ontological statement, but was instead an expedient teaching that they considered essential if the doctrinal indefeasability of Buddhism was to be maintained.

states that the six senses and the six types of sense-contact are the person, etc.

Sammitīya rebuttal: Were the five aggregates the same as the self, then if the body were cut up there would then be many separate selves. By the same token, the life-force and the physical body would also have to be coterminous, so that if this body still existed (as it would for some time after death) the life-force also would continue, which is absurd. Hence, the proposal that the aggregates are identical with the self should be rejected.[416]

(5) The self is different from the five aggregates. This view is justified because of the famous *sūtra* differentiating the burden (the five aggregates) from the bearer (the person). Other scriptures also describe the person as being the one who receives the fruition of past action; hence, while the aggregates perish in the transition from one life to the next, the person does not. Therefore the person is different from the aggregates. The Buddha also talked about his self, as when he said that in his previous birth he was named Mahādeva. Hence, while the Lord may have received a fresh set of aggregates in this present life, his self remains the same and is thus different from the aggregated. Finally, the Buddha placed the self among the neutral things, while he instead called the aggregates sometimes impermanent, sometimes permanent. For all these reasons, the self is different from the aggregates.

Sammitīya rebuttal: The distinction between action and maturation, for example, proves instead that there is a continuity between the actions done in the present life and the maturation that takes place in a future life. The Buddha's references to his different lifetimes shows similarly that there has been a transition between his lives, not that those lives are separate and distinct. The final justification is also rejected, because, like the self, the aggregates too should not be described as either permanent or impermanent. The Sammitīyas continue on to show the absurdities created by this position. If the self were different from the body, the self should be able to move at will from one body to another, or take birth in completely different realms. If the self were so able to move freely, responsibility for action would be obviated and bondage and liberation would become meaningless. Therefore, this proposition is to be dismissed.

(6) The self is eternal. This is because the self has no origin. The

Buddha specifically stated that an origin for the cycle of birth-and-death is indiscernible. But if something has no origin, it also cannot have an end, and thus the self must be eternal. A person is also able to remember his previous rebirths; thus, despite the fact that the aggregates perish from birth to birth, the *pudgala* does not. So the self is eternal. The Buddha has also explicitly stated that "he who crosses over to the other shore and abides in that land is called a *brāhmaṇa*." Hence, there is a person who is able to achieve liberation from *saṃsāra* and abide permanently in *nirvāṇa*. Elsewhere, the Buddha also refers to one who reaches the imperturbable bliss of true liberation. Therefore, the self is a real thing that abides in various permanent states and thus must itself be eternal.

Sammitīya rebuttal: To attempt to prove the eternality of the self because of its lack of origin would imply that *saṃsāra* is also eternal, since it too has no origin. This cannot be accepted, presumably because it would then imply that liberation would be impossible. The proof on the basis of past lives is also inadequate, since the sequence of lives pertaining to an independent, eternal self would become as if permanent itself, and thus the round of birth-and-death would actually remain eternal, which is not necessarily true. Statements by the Buddha that there is a person who achieves or attains certain exalted states have nothing to do with the existence of a self; if that were the meaning of such remarks, it would actually imply that there was no achievement or attainment, since the self, being eternal, would be unchanging.

(7) The self is impermanent. This is because the self has an origin, as in various *sūtras* where the Buddha states that "a person takes birth"; and since something that has a beginning must also have an end, the self is impermanent. The Buddha also remarks that beings are born and then die, and something that thus changes is impermanent, unlike *nirvāṇa*, which is eternal and therefore has no beginning or end.

Sammitīya rebuttal: The continuity of moral cause and effect refutes this claim. If the self were impermanent, deeds previously performed would perish without bringing about their effect, and effects could take place without a previous cause. In this wise, the whole soteriology of Buddhism would be undermined.

After completing his account of the seven wrong views of self, the author returns to consider the process by which a person is able to give up one life and take up another. Here the main premise of the Sammitīya school is given: "The person composed of the five aggregates is the real person. As the person composed of the five aggregates is the real person, it cannot be said that the *pudgala* is either permanent or impermanent."

III. Three Conceptions of the Person (E466a.28-c.27; T182-184)

A new section then begins, dealing with the three different explanations of the *pudgala* in Buddhism: (1) the person with reference to a locus (*i-shuo-jen*; **āśrayaprajñaptapudgala*), (2) the person with reference to transmigration (*tu-shuo-jen*; **saṅkramaprajñaptapudgala*), and (3) the person with reference to extinction (*mieh-shuo-jen*; **nirodhaprajñaptapudgala*). (This threefold sense of the person is otherwise unknown in Buddhist texts, and is another unique contribution of this treatise.)

(1) The person with reference to a locus. The *sūtra* explains that *āśrayaprajñapti* refers to the fact that the names for things are derived from something else that serves as their point of reference, just as fire is spoken of with reference to fuel or ghee is spoken of with reference to milk. Similarly, that which is produced from the four material elements is called the self, because the person who depends upon material form for his existence is spoken about with reference to that form. This is not to say that the person is identical to or different from the aggregates, which would lead either to nihilism or eternalism, as mentioned previously; rather it means that the person and the five aggregates have a derivative existence, in which the presence of one perforce allows the presence of the other to be derived.

(2) The person with reference to transmigration. Persons who cross from one state to another are said to transmigrate. This transition between states can thus refer to past, present, or future lifetimes. For example, where the Buddha says "In a past life, I was the highest of kings," he is referring to his person in a past "transmigration."

(3) The person with reference to extinction. Every sense of the person that is not covered by the previous two types is covered by this last type. This involves such usages of the word "person" as

when the Buddha says "when that past body perishes," or "when aggregates of a *bhikṣu* whose outflows are extinct will soon perish."

IV.Issues Concerning Transmigration (E466c.28-469a.28; T185 195)

Next, the interlocutor asks whether there is something remaining after the five aggregates perish, which is equivalent to asking what it is that leaves this existence to be reborn elsewhere. Three views are given as to what transmigrates: (1) the five aggregates, (2) the person, or (3) no person. The first view is rejected by the Sammitīyas on the grounds that if the aggregates were totally abandoned at the time of transmigration, there would be nothing remaining that would be able to move from this life to the next. "It is awareness that is pervaded by morality and concentration which relies upon these wholesome actions and takes rebirth in a higher plane." Therefore, at the time of transmigration, the five aggregates might perish, but something remains (apparently the awareness) and moves on to the next rebirth, depending on the direction of one's previous karma. Hence, the claim that it is the five aggregates which transmigrate should be rejected. If instead it were the person who transmigrates, this would imply that there exists a real entity which would have to be described either as eternal or mortal. But either way leads to wrong view, as discussed above, and denies the possibility of transmigration from one state to another. (This reply is apparently meant to cover the third view as well.) Hence, the *pudgala* is always associated with the aggregates, and cannot be said to exist in reality.

Next, the process of origin in the intermediate state is taken up. When moving from one state of existence to another, the person must first pass through the intermediate state. Abandoning the five aggregates of his present existence, he concurrently takes up the five aggregates of the intermediate state and, simultaneous with the final moment of the present existence, there is the arising of the awareness of one's intermediate state. If this exchange did not take place simultaneously, it would lead to two fallacies: either one person would have two existences (i.e., if the person first accepted the five aggregates of the intermediate state and then abandoned his present existence), or a gap would be present between lifetimes (i.e., if the aggregates of the present existence were abandoned before taking up the aggregates of the intermediate state).

The treatise then begins a lengthy discussion on the question of whether there can be any beginning to the cycle of birth and death. The Sammitīya position is that regardless of whether there is or is not a beginning, it cannot be known. Various similes are given and scriptural passages cited in support of their view that no such beginning can be posited.

V. The Nature of the Intermediate State (E469b.2-471c.3; T195-205)

Ten objections to the existence of an intermediate state are raised, and then rebutted by the Sammitīyas. (These two sections are also combined for clarity's sake.)

(1) There is no intermediate state because it is not mentioned as one of the five courses (viz., hell-beings, animals, ghosts, men, gods).

Sammitīya rebuttal: The intermediate state is the vehicle that conveys the being from one course to another; it is not itself a course. It is as when it is said that one goes from one city to another, only the cities are mentioned, not the vehicle by which one is conveyed. Hence, just because the Buddha did not mention the intermediate state in the context of the courses does not prove that it does not exist.

(2) The Buddha never predicted that anyone would be born in the intermediate state, as he did for the five courses.

Sammitīya rebuttal: The intermediate state is not an abiding place; it is merely a place where the life-force, joy and frustration, and merit and demerit are transferred. Therefore it was not mentioned as a place where one would be born.

(3) No actions were mentioned that led to the intermediate state, as was done for the five courses.

Samitīya rebuttal: The intermediate state conveys the actions done in the previous life to the next life; it is not a place where new actions are performed. Therefore the Buddha did not mention any actions that led to the intermediate state.

(4) The Buddha said definitively that there were five courses, but this was never said for the intermediate state.

Sammitīya rebuttal: Just because the Buddha did not speak of an intermediate state does not mean that there isn't one, because the

Buddha himself has said that there are many things he knows that he chooses not to mention.

(5) There is no intermediate state, because rebirth is instantaneous (*ānantarya*).

Sammitīya rebuttal: This was said only to deny that there are other states of existence that intervene between one life and the next. This does not however deny an intermediate state, which is not a true state of existence, but simply a transitional stage.

(6) If an intermediate state is posited between the previous life and the next, then there should also be another state intermediate between that intermediate state and the rebirth, and so on *ad infinitum*.

Sammitīya rebuttal: Between the first and second meditational trances, the Buddha has also taught there is a single intermediate trance, not an infinite series of such intermediate states. So too should the intermediate state between existences be understood.

(7) The intermediate state has no function, for it involves no duration of life, no action, and no sensation; therefore it should not be posited to exist.

Sammitīya rebuttal: The function of the intermediate state is to convey the being from one life to the next; therefore it has a function.

(8) If the intermediate state and rebirth are the same factor, then there would be no need to posit the separate existence of the intermediate state. But if they are different, then the intermediate state should be called a separate course.

Sammitīya rebuttal: The process of rebirth involves arising in both of those states: after arising in the intermediate state, the being then proceeds to be reborn. Hence, intermediate state and rebirth are the same in that they involve the same realm, but they are different in that the conveyance and the destination are not identical.

(9) The characteristics of the intermediate state are not mentioned, and anything that truly exists, like the five courses, has characteristics. Therefore the intermediate state must not exist.

Sammitīya rebuttal: This would only become an issue if the Buddha had said that there was an intermediate state. Since this was never stated categorically, there is no reason for him to have mentioned its characteristics.

(10) Rebirth takes place instantaneously from one's own body without requiring an intermediate state.

Sammitīya rebuttal: If this were the case, it would lead to the absurdity that, as that new existence has not yet arisen, that very body would have to take rebirth. Hence, the being arises first in the intermediate state from whence he passes into the next life. Leaving his present sphere of existence, he moves into the intermediate state, which seems as if empty. There, he sees an exact replica of his new body, which is however much subtler and more delicate. As this body is a product of his craving, he delights in it and thus looks forward to his rebirth. Hence, this point also does not prove that there is no intermediate state.

After responding to these criticisms of the doctrine of an intermediate state, the Sammitīyas then proceed to give their own reasons for accepting the existence of the intermediate state. Several similes are given and scriptural passages cited in support of the reality of the intermediate state, as for example where the Buddha states that there is a type of person who enters *nirvāṇa* via the intermediate state. These proofs are then rebutted by the opponent. The Sammitīyas have the last word, however, and restate two of their reasons: the Buddha sees with his divine eye that there are beings moving between different realms of existence, implying that there is an intermediate state; and without such a state there could be no continuity between existences, since it is logically impossible that death in the present life could take place at the precise same moment as birth in the next.

## VII. The Different Spheres of Existence (E471.c-473a.13; T205-211)

In this rather obscure section the Sammitīyas take up the various types of permutations that can take place in rebirth between different states of existence as, for example, from the realm of desire to the realm of the nonidentifying gods (*asaṃjñīsattva*). The number of rebirths required to achieve *nirvāṇa* for each of the persons in the four stages of sainthood is discussed. Thirteen types of persons are then listed: (1) an ordinary man who has not yet developed disgust for the realm of desire; (2) an ordinary person who has such disgust; (3) an ordinary person who is disgusted with the material realm; (4) a stream-enterer who has seven rebirths remaining; (5)

a once-returner; (6) a *kulaṃkula* once-returner; (7) an *ekavīcika* once-returner; (8) a nonreturner who is disgusted with material things and is thus born in a higher sphere; (9) three types of persons are delineated at this state: a person who enters *nirvāṇa* in this very life, a person who enters *nirvāṇa* through practice, and a person who enters *nirvāṇa* without practising it; (10) a person who enters *nirvāṇa* from the intermediate state; (11) a person who has disgust for material things and is reborn in a higher sphere; (12) a person who enters *nirvāṇa* through practice at the time of rebirth; (13) a noble person. The differences in the number of aggregates, elements and senses at the time of rebirth of each of these levels are then delineated. The treatise ends with an exhortation to strive according to the *dharma* in order to destroy the causes that produce the constant revolution of the aggregates between different existences.

### 161. AUTHOR UNKNOWN, *Dharmatārādhyānasūtra*[417]

### 162. AUTHOR UNKNOWN, *Ratnarāśisūtra*[418]

### 163. NĀGĀRJUNA, *Dvādaśa(dvārā)mukhaśāstra*

The Sanskrit title of the Chinese Taisho 1568 may be reconstructed as **Dvādaśamukhaśāstra*. It is regularly referred to in English as the "Twelve-Gate Treatise". It consists of 26 verses with commentary, of which 21 are identical to verses in the 33. *Madhyamakakārikās*, and one identical with a verse in 35.*Śūnyatāsaptati*, and it quotes the former text.[419] It was translated into Chinese by Kumārajīva (=T.1568); the Chinese title is *Shih-erh-men-lun*. David Ruegg informs us that it is "one of the three basic treatises of the Chinese Madhyamaka school" and that "The commentary on this work, also available in Chinese only, is ascribed sometimes to Nāgārjuna himself and sometimes to Ch'ing-mu."[420] Christian Lindtner remarks "While there can be no doubt that (nearly) all the verses were originally composed by Nāgārjuna...there are in my opinion several good reasons for maintaining that the author of the commentary (most probably identical with the compiler of the verses) is *not* Nāgārjuna but rather *Piṅgala." He suggests he will explain why "on a later occasion".[421]

The work is available only in Chinese. It has been translated by Hsueh-li Cheng,[422] our "T" here, and has been restored to Sanskrit (our "E") and summarized in English by N. Aiyasvami Sastri[423]. The Introduction to the commentary is translated in Robinson.[424] The summary below is composed by the Editor on the basis of these various sources.

1. Dependent Origination (E185-189; T53-58)

Mahāyāna is explained here out of compassion for people of modern times who are of less merit and ability to understand. A number of reasons are offered as to why the Mahāyāna is so called.

> "Factors are dependently originated; they are without essential nature. How can such things exist."[425]

Dependently originated factors are of two kinds: internal, that is, mental, and external, that is, material, and their conditions are also of those two kinds. Since they are dependently originated they are without essential natures.

If something lacks an essential nature it cannot have the nature of another nor have both self- and other-natures, since what is termed the nature of another has no essential nature either, being dependently originated. Otherwise everything would be the same and one couldn't sensibly speak of something being "other" than something else. Now if nothing has an essential nature, nothing--whether internal or external--can actually be produced, whether from material factors or from the twelve items in the chain of dependent origination.

Since everything is empty, aggregates, elements and senses, which constitute a "self", are empty--there is no self. And that being so, even *nirvāṇa* itself must be empty.

2. Does the Effect Exist in the Cause or Not? (E190-198;T59-69)

Factors cannot be produced.

> If the effect exists in its cause it is not produced; if it doesn't it can't be produced; if it both exists and doesn't exist it can't be produced either. So how can there be any production?[426]

If the effect exists already in its cause and then has to be produced again there will be infinite regress. If it does not exist already in its cause and yet constitutes a product, then what comes to be will constitute another production, and that too leads to infinite regress; the first product cannot come to be without the second.

Again, if the produced X is real and the X that is not produced is also real, then there shouldn't be any difference between them. But if the effect is not different from the cause nothing will get produced.

Objection: Though the effect pre-exists it has not yet manifested itself, and that's why it is not seen.

Answer: Then how do you know it's there in the cause? There is no evidence of its presence.

Objection: A thing may exist but not be manifested as distinct, because of any one of eight kinds of reasons: because it is too close, too far away, because the senses are deficient, because of inattention, because it is obstructed by something else, because it is merged with other things, because its manifestation is overpowered by others, because it is too small.

Answer: But things would have been manifested if these deficiencies were not operating. So these cases provide no analogies proving the nonmanifestation of existing things.

If the effect is present in the cause its features should be observable there. But on the *satkāryavāda* view no features of the effect are observable in its cause, which is unreasonable. Likewise, if the cause has the effect in it before the effect gets produced, nothing can produce it. But if an effect is not produced by anything it must be eternal, like *nirvāṇa*. Then everything will be eternal. But if everything is eternal nothing is, since the two contrasting terms require each other's possibility. But that's a contradiction!

Now suppose you say that the effect does *not* pre-exist in the cause. In that case something could be produced from nothing, which is untenable. Furthermore, anything could be produced from anything at all.

Objection: But we know from experience that, e.g., oil does not come from sand but does come from sesame seeds.

Answer: We don't know that from experience--we don't know *where* the oil came from--it just comes! Your argument begs the question by assuming that the effect "comes from" somewhere, that is, is caused by something.

I say that cause, effect and causation are all empty. But it is the logic of your own position that established what I say; it is not that I hold any position myself.

The effect cannot exist earlier and then both exist and not exist in the cause, because it is a contradiction to both exist and not exist.

Since these three positions exhaust the possibilities and since they all are now refuted, it must be that all conditioned things are empty, as well as all unconditioned things. That being so, it is especially true that the notion of self is empty.

### 3. Conditions (E197-198; T70-71)

That factors have causal conditions cannot be established.

> Effects are not present in their conditions; if effects are not there in the conditions how could they come from those conditions?

These "conditions" are four only: causal, proximate, supporting object and dominant. The causal condition is that from which something arises. The proximate condition is the factor that occurs just prior to the effect. The supporting object is that which determines the sort of factor it is--bodily, mental, etc. And the dominant factor is that which dominates.

These four conditions show that an effect does not arise in its cause, since otherwise the cause could not occur without its effect occurring.

Now if an effect, being nonexistent, can still arise from conditions, what stops it from arising from what are not conditions? So conditions do not produce effects either.

### 4. Characteristic Marks (E199-205; T174-176)

Why is everything empty?

> Both conditioned and unconditioned factors are empty,

because they have no defining marks.

What are "conditioned factors"? The distinguishing features of things. Shouldn't characteristic marks, such as the origin, maintenance and destruction of any created thing, be counted as conditioned factors of those things? No; if the origin (say) of things is conditioned then *it* (the origin of things) will itself have an origin, etc. If that origin is not conditioned how can it be a conditioned factor? There will be infinite regress. And likewise for maintenance, destruction and the rest of the conditioned factors. So all of them are empty.

Objection (by a Sammitīya, according to the *Madhyamakavṛtti*): Seven factors flash simultaneously: a factor (call it X), the origin of X, X's maintenance, X's destruction, the origin of X's origin, the maintenance of X's maintenance, the destruction of X's destruction. The origin of X produces the other six, and the origin of X's origin produces the origin of X.

Answer: How can the origin of X's origin produce the origin of X, since it requires it to be produced in the first place?

A possible response: It is like the lamp, which can light up the darkness at the precise moment of its arising.

Answer: Then lamplight in one place should light up the whole world even without reaching there!

Since conditioned things are empty, unconditioned ones are too. *Nirvāṇa* is the unconditioned cessation of conditioned things; so it is empty too.

Objection: Surely the characteristic feature of *nirvāṇa* is its lack of characteristic features!

Answer: We shall answer this in the next Chapter.

5. Having and Lacking Characteristic Marks (E205-208; T79-80)

Everything is empty, because

> A "characteristic mark" characterizes neither a thing with such marks nor one without them. So what can such a mark characterize?

If a thing already has a characteristic mark it doesn't need another one. And if the thing exists without characteristic marks, having them is of no use--it already exists! That is why both conditioned and unconditioned things are empty.

6. Unity and Diversity (E207-209; T81-84)

Everything is empty, because

> The thing characterized and its characteristic are neither the same nor different; so how can they be proved?

Objection: Obviously there is a difference between a characteristic and the thing it characterizes. Some marks define things--a conscious person is defined by consciousness. But the mark and thing marked don't have to share every feature. Though destruction of desire constitutes liberation, desire is conditioned but liberation is not. And some conditions are parts of the things they condition, e.g., origination is a part of the three marks of created things and also characterizes them.

Answer: If a conscious person is defined by consciousness he would know himself. But nothing can know itself. An eye cannot see itself, a finger cannot touch itself. As for liberation and the destruction of desire, desire is conditioned and thus different from liberation, but the destruction of desire isn't. As for the three marks of created things, since a thing is not a created thing unless it possesses all three marks it isn't really the case that one of the marks is a "part" of the thing.

7. Being and Nonbeing (E310-312; T85-88)

Everything is empty because presence (positive being) and absence (negative being, viz., nonbeing) cannot occur simultaneously.

> Presence and absence cannot occur at the same time. Too, presence cannot occur without absence; if it could, presence should always accompany absence.[427]

Presence and absence are essentially incompatible. Nothing can be both present and absent. In the Abhidharma it is said that presence is always accompanied by impermanence. Without absence presence cannot occur. If presence could occur without absence it would always be eternal; but then nothing could originate.

Objection: When something arises it is momentary but not yet active. When a thing is destroyed action occurs. Thus arising, persistence, decay and destruction take place at their appropriately different times, and although every factor is impermanent, a presence is not an absence.

Answer: You say that impermanence is the mark of destruction and that it occurs with the presence of something that is arising. So, at the same time presence is produced it is destroyed. So production must occur at the same time as destruction. But they are opposite, contradictory, and cannot occur together. So what you say is impossible.

You say that momentariness naturally accompanies birth, maintenance, decay and destruction. But that's nonsense. Suppose that being present accompanies impermanence. Now impermanence is the mark of decay. But the time when a thing is produced is not the time of its decay, nor is the time of its maintenance the time of its decay.

So presence cannot accompany absence, nor can either occur apart from the other. Thus they are empty, as indeed all things are empty.

### 8. Essential Nature (E213-216; T89-91)

Every factor is empty, because factors have no essential nature.

> Because factors have changing characteristics
> They are without essential natures.
> What is without essential nature is empty,
> So all factors are empty.[428]

Objection: If every factor is empty then there can be no arising or cessation, and so no truth of frustration, of frustration's origin, of frustration's cessation or of the path thereto. If the four truths don't apply there can be no such things as monks, Buddhas, *dharma*, the order or factors in the world. But that can't be right. So it's not that all factors are empty.

Answer: There are two truths--worldly and highest. Without practising the worldly truth the highest truth is not attainable. Without attaining the highest truth *nirvāṇa* is unattainable. Now you, having heard of worldly truth, take it to be the highest truth, and fall to your destruction. The Buddha's law of dependent origination is the ultimately highest truth. Factors dependently originated are without essential nature, thus empty.

## 9. Cause and Effect (E217-218; T982)

Factors lack essential nature, and their nature doesn't come from elsewhere either.

> No results are actually experienced in their conditions, and they do not come from elsewhere. So how can any result occur?

Argument as before.

## 10. Agents (E219-224; T93-100)

> All factors are empty, since frustrations do not make themselves. Nor are they made by something else. Nor both. Nor are they made from no cause at all. So there is no frustration![429]

A thing cannot make itself.

Objection: But frustrations can be made by something else.

Answer: If what is meant by "something else" is the collection of conditions then frustration is indeed made by "something else". But if a factor *is* just that collection of conditions those conditions aren't something else.

The refutations of the first two possibilities refute the third *a fortiori*. And the fourth--that things arise from no cause at all--involves various faults.

The Buddha did not reply positively to the question "who or what makes frustrations?" because the various answers proposed (that oneself, another, or God made them) are incorrect; but all alternatives are incorrect also.

Objection: All beings emanate from God. Frustration and satisfaction also come from God. He awards frustration to those who don't know (Him).

Answer: If beings are sons of God He should use satisfaction to eliminate frustration, not saddle beings with frustrations. This is especially true of those who worship Him. But in truth beings act for themselves and experience appropriate maturations. These are not made by God.

If there is a God He does not need anything. But if God doesn't need anything why did He bother to create? If God created beings, who created Him? Nothing can create itself, and if someone else created God He isn't God. Again, why did He create according to karmic conditions and not all at once--since He could have? Why did He create at all? Who created the place where He created beings? Another God? There can't be two Gods.

Objection: So you've shown that the Buddha refuted four wrong views about frustrations, but you haven't shown that frustrations are empty.

Answer: To refute the four views the Buddha shows that frustration arises through dependent origination. But that *is* just to show that frustrations are empty, since what is dependently originated lacks an essential nature, and what lacks an essential nature is empty.

### 11. The Three Times (E224-226; T101-103)

All factors are empty, since a cause can neither precede, succeed, nor occur at the same time as its effect.

> A factor cannot be proved to be earlier than, later than, or simultaneous with its causal factor(s). So how can factors constitute causes?[430]

A causal factor cannot precede what is thought to be its effect. If it could, it would already exist before the moment of causation--so what could occasion the effect? If the effect precedes the cause the cause is unnecessary. And if cause and effect are simultaneous they cannot cause each other any more than one of a cow's horns causes the other.

Objection: By parallel argument you can't refute the three times: if your refutation is prior to what it refutes it doesn't refute; if after, it is unnecessary; and if simultaneous no refutation occurs. So you haven't refuted the three times.

Answer: Your refutation and what it refutes share the same feature--both are empty. Your empty argument shows that my argument is empty too--this proves what I say! If I claimed that refutation and/or refuted exist I would be wrong--but I don't claim that, so there is no such problem.

Objection: But a potter who makes a pot *is* earlier than the pot, the pupils become pupils *after* being taught, and the lamp is the cause of its light though they occur simultaneously.

Answer: At the time there is no pot what can the potter do to make it? Without a pupil how can anyone teach? Since the lamp and its light are cotemporaneous why should one be the cause and the other the effect?

### 12. Birth (E227-228; T104-107)

All factors are empty, since

> What is already produced can't be produced.
> What is not yet produced can't be produced.
> Because of these facts nothing can be produced.[431]

If what is already produced needed to be produced again there would be infinite regress. And what is not yet produced can have no relation to a producer--otherwise products could occur without being produced. And since producing can't occur before or after the product, nothing can be a product. So, since nothing gets produced, everything should be understood to be empty.

## 164. AUTHOR UNKNOWN, *Madhyāntavibhāga*

This work is usually ascribed to Asaṅga, or we are told it was given to Asaṅga by Maitreya while Asaṅga was studying with him in the Tuṣita heaven. It seems unlikely that it is by the same author as the other works said to be Asaṅga's. Ronald Davidson writes: "I find it difficult to assume that the authors of the *Mahāyānasūtrālaṃkāra* and the *Madhyāntavibhāga* were one and the same person. The MSA is a compilation of material, and it shows, in its final form, the use of multiple verse forms and literary devices (*upamā*, etc.). The MAV is a relatively straightforward versified *śāstra*, obsessed with the doctrines surrounding *abhūtaparikalpa*, the *trisvabhāva*, and the path, with similes occurring in only three verses. Conversely, for the MSA, the cardinal system is that of the *gotra*, a term occurring once in an insignificant context in MAV I.19a. The longest chapter of the MAV is the final one, concerned with the *anuttarayāna*, a term which does not occur in the MSA. Furthermore, the relative discussions of path structure are ordered quite differently. Examples could, of course, be extended *ad infinitum*, but this should be sufficient."[432] We are on safer ground, then, if we assume that the work is by an unknown author who preceded Asaṅga by a few years at least.

This work has been edited a number of times (see Bibliography, #174.6). To the translations listed there add those contained among the references to translations of Vasubandhu's commentary in the Bibliography of Indian Philosophies under SWV and BDE in the Abbreviation List.

"ET" references are to the edition and translation by Stefan Anacker[433].

Summary by Stefan Anacker

## CHAPTER ONE

Introduction (E424; T211) The following should be calculated: the characteristic mark, its obstruction, its nature, its antidote, spiritual practice, its states, the acquisition of its result, and the superiority of the path.

1.(E424; T211) Construction of what was not (*abhūtaparikalpa*) exists. There is no duality in it. However, emptiness does exist there, and it (construction) is found there (in emptiness) also.

2.(E424; T212) Nothing is empty or nonempty; therefore everything is accounted for because of existence, because of nonexistence, and again because of existence. This is the middle way (*madhyamā pratipad).*

3.(E425; T212) Consciousness puts itself forward as the appearance of objects, beings, selves, and manifestations. These do not exist.

4.(E425; T213) The mental construction of what was not is established, since it does not exist as such. But it is not altogether absent either.

5.(E425; T213) There are just constructed, dependent and perfected ways of being, distinguished as objects, constructed things, and the absence of both.

6.(E426; T214) Apprehending this, nonapprehension arises; based on this non-apprehension, nonapprehension arises.

7.(E426; T214) So the essential nature of apprehension is nonapprehension, and so what should be understood is the apprehension of nonapprehension.

8.(E426; T214-215) The construction of what was not involves awareness and accompanying mental factors comprising the three realms. Consciousness perceives things, mental factors their specific qualities.

9.(E426; T215) On the one hand there is the conditioning consciousness, on the other experiencing. In the latter are the accompanying factors of experiencing, discrimination and motivation.

10-11.(E427; T215-216) Covering, establishing, leading, embracing, completing, triple determination, experiencing, drawing out, binding, turning toward, frustration. The world is afflicted in three, or two, or seven ways.

12.(E427; T217) These topics need to be understood: the defining characteristic of emptiness, the synonymous expressions for "emptiness", its purpose, its distinctions and its proof.

13.(E427-428; T217) The absence of two things, and the existence of this absence, is the defining characteristic of emptiness. It is not existent nor is it nonexistent, neither different nor the same--that is its mark.

14.(E428; T218) "Suchness", "the reality-limit", "signless", "the highest", "the ground of all factors"--these are the synonyms of "emptiness".

15.(E428-429; T218) Nondifference, nonerroneous cessation, having to do with the noble realm--these are the meanings of the synonyms for those of good *dharma*.

16.(E428; T218-219) Emptiness can be defiled or clear, impure or pure, like elementary water, gold or space.

17.(E429; T219) The experiencer, his experiencing, his body, the world around him, are actually empty, are the ways they are apprehended and their purpose.

18.(E429-430; T220) Emptiness' purpose is attaining two good ends, assisting living beings, not forsaking those in *saṃsāra*, the nondestruction of what is good.

19.(E430; T220) The Bodhisattva cognizes so as to clear the lineage and the Buddha's factors and to receive the marks of a great person.

20.(E430; T220) The absence of persons and factors is one emptiness, and the existence of this absence is another emptiness.

21.(E430; T221) If emptiness were not afflicted, everyone would be liberated; if it were clear all effort would be fruitless.

22.(E431; T221) But it is neither afflicted nor unafflicted, neither clear nor unclear, since awareness is luminous and the afflictions of it are adventitious.

## CHAPTER TWO

1-3.(E432-433; T222-223) The pervading and the limited, the excessive and the equal, accepting and abandoning--these are called obstructions of the two. Their defining marks are ninefold, being the fetters that obstruct commitment, equanimity and the vision of reality by encouraging belief in a self, obstructing insights about the self and about objects, about frustration, about the path, the jewels, and the attainments of others, and by leading to one's being satisfied with little. Still other things obstruct goodness, etc. in ten ways.

4-10.(E433-435; T224-227) These obstructions include lack of ability to rouse oneself from inactivity, nonuse of one's senses, carelessness, not doing good, not being ready, etc. (a long list). Obstructions arise for each of goodness, enlightenment, good attitude, insight, lack of confusion, nonobstruction, ability to develop, fearlessness, unselfishness and power. Ten corresponding kinds of causes of good results are listed. In addition there are obstructions to the limbs of enlightenment, to the perfections and to the sages.

11.(E435; T228) The obstructions to the limbs of enlightenment include lack of skill, sloth, two destructors of concentration, distractedness, weakness, fixed views and susceptibility to harm.

12-13.(E435; T228) Obstructions to the perfections include obstructions to lordliness, to happy states, to nonforsaking of beings, to the elimination of faults and the growth of virtues, to liberation, to inexhaustibility, to remaining well, to ascertainment, to enjoyment and to maturation of *dharma*.

14-16.(E436; T229) The stages are themselves the antidotes to their obstructions, which are listed.

17.(E437; T231) Obstructions may be divided into those that are defilements and those that obstruct what we can know.

## CHAPTER THREE

1-2.(E438; T231) The aspects of reality (*tattva*) to be discussed here include basic reality (*mūlatattva*), the reality of characteristic marks, the reality that is nonerroneous, the reality that is result and cause, subtler and grosser realities, the accepted, the aspect of clearing, the aspect of difference, and the tenfold aspect of skill, antidotes to belief in a self.

3.(E438; T232) The threefold essential nature is nonexistent, yet it always exists, but not really.

4-5a.(E438-439; T232-233) The reality of characteristic marks includes the superimposition and denial of factors and persons, things grasped and their graspers, being and nonbeing.

5b-6.(E439; T233) Objects are nonexistent, impermanent, arising and ceasing, are in basic reality with or without impurities.

7a.(E439; T234) Emptiness as nonbeing, as the absence of this or that, and as nature.

7b-8a.(E439-440; T234) Selflessness means being without a characteristic mark, having a different characteristic, or having itself as characteristic.

8b.(E440; T235) The truth of frustration is said to arise from proclivities, from increase and from lack of separation.

9a.(E440; T235) Nonarising of the double essential nature is considered as two kinds: impurity and peace.

9b-10a.(E440; T236) The truth of the path involves comprehension, abandoning, attainment and immediate awareness.

10b.(E441; T236) Nominal designation, progress and spiritual practice--but the highest pertains only to one.

11.(E441; T237) This highest is thought of in three ways--as regards object, attainment and practice. It is of two sorts as changeless and errorfree.

12.(E441; T237-238) What is commonly accepted is due to one, while what is right involves three. The twofold field of purity is only attained through one of them.

13.(E441-442; T238) There are two ways of comprising--that of the sign and its constructions, and that of naming.

14.(E442; T239) The aspects of positive activity are two--as intent and as disturbed. One is correct devotion to purity in the awareness of defining marks.

15-16.(E442; T239-240) There is self-view when there is the idea of single cause, a single enjoyer or agent persisting through time, a single locus of defilement and of purification, of yogihood, of being bound or free. The aggregates are among the three natures as constructed, as conceptions, as objects of *dharma*-ness.

17.(E443; T240-241) In regard to the first subject discussed (the aggregates), they can be viewed as compressed, as heaped up, or as distinct. Others are the seeds of the grasper, things grasped and their grasping.

18.(E443; T241) Still others are doors to feelings and distinguishing of objects, in order to have nonsuperimposition and nondenial of causes, effects and effort.

19.(E443; T242) Interdependence of what is and isn't desired, concerning simultaneous arising, supremacy, attainment and proper practice is still another topic.

20.(E444; T242-243) Grasping, standing, remaining, experiencing and the two kinds of purity. The use of effect and cause, past or future, is still another.

21.(E444; T243) Still others are feelings, their factors, their arising and removal.

22.(E444-445; T244) Deliverance relying on oneself or others through awareness of merits and faults, and through knowledge free from conceptual constructions, should be understood. The final stage operates through nominal designations, through causes, signs, quietude and through its objects.

## CHAPTER FOUR

1.(E446; T246) Cultivation of the establishment of mindfulness comes about through susceptibility to depravity, through the causes of desire, through the actual scope of what is termed "I", and through lack of confusion in relation to the four truths.

2.(E446; T246) When one fully comprehends the problems and their antidotes a fourfold energy arises for their removal.

3.(E446; T247) Skill is steadiness to the satisfaction of all purposes, following the eight motivating factors for the abandonment of the five faults.

4.(E447; T247) These five faults are sloth, forgetting instructions, slackness, excitedness, lack of motivation, and motivation.

5-7.(E447-448; T247-249) The locus, what is located in it, its marks, and its results; nonloss of the object of meditation, recognition of slackness and excitedness, motivation for their removal, and maintenance of tranquillity: when these factors conducive to liberation have been planted through energetic application, nonwavering attention, and investigation, the adverse factors are diminished.

8-9.(E448; T249-250) Two each of the factors conducive to penetration are faculties and powers. The limbs of enlightenment are the basis limb, the essential nature limb, the limb of deliverance, the limb of praising others, and the threefold limb of lack of defilements. It is called "threefold" because of its initial cause, support and essential nature.

10.(E448; T250) The limbs of the path are eightfold, comprising distinguishing accurately, attaining, three kinds of cultivation, and antidotes to adverse factors. Understanding by others comes through moral practice and satisfaction with little.

11-12.(E448-449; T251) The antidotes to defilements, afflictions and factors opposing one's power are favorable when reversed, supportive when unreversed, unsupportive of reversals when unreversed. There are differences between supporting objects, mental attention, and attainment.

13-14.(E449; T252) The stages on the way involve descending, preparation, fruition, the stage where there is something left to do, and the one where there isn't, the distinctive situation, what is higher and what is highest, entry, confidence, certainty, prediction, working toward attaining power, having good effects, and completion of all undertakings.

15-16.(E450; T253) There are three kinds of ground of all factors: impure, impure and pure, and pure. From this the stage of advancement of persons is known as fitting.

17.(E450; T253) Results include maturation, the power that comes through it, delight, growing, becoming clear.

18.(E451; T254) The order in which these results occur is described.

## CHAPTER FIVE

1-2.(E452; T256-257) The supremacy of this method lies in its practice, its support and its full realization. Its practice involves six things--the highest, attending, after-*dharma*, the avoidance of extremes, distinct and indistinct practice. Its highest is twelve-fold.

3-6.(E452-453; T257) The method involves generosity, persistence, development, inexhaustibility, continuity, lack of trouble, encompassing, undertaking, obtaining merit, outcome and fulfilment. The ten perfections correspond to these. They are giving, moral precepts, patience, energy, meditation, wisdom, skilful means, resolve, power and knowledge.

7-10.(E453-454; T259-260) Attention comes about through three kinds of insight in the Bodhisattva--through nurturing sensory domains, through entry and through success in aims. It is connected with ten good acts of writing, reverencing, giving, hearing, saying, taking up, explaining, studying by oneself, reflecting and meditating. These ten acts involve an immeasurable heap of merit.

11.(E455; T260) Practice after *dharma* is actions which may have to be taken immediately after emerging from meditation. Distraction may arise then.

12.(E455; T261) Distractedness involves emergence, sensory experience, relishing, slackness and excitedness, deliberate intentions toward experience, a sense of ego in mental attention, and defective awareness.

13-14.(E455-456; T261) Development of lack of reversals. In connection with a so-called object it may be thought "such and such is its name". Such a statement has meaning only because of its past familiarity, but is meaningless because of being a reversal.

15.(E456; T261) There is irreversibility in regard to a thing when it is observed that the thing does not exist as it appears, since it appears with the subject-object duality.

16-17a.(E456; T261-262) It is mental attention towards talk which is the only basis for the discrimination between object apprehended and the subject-apprehender.

17b-18.(E456-457; T262-263) An object exists and does not exist like *māyā*, etc. Everything is merely names.

19.(E457; T263) Being freed from the ground of all factors because no factor is found, a universal characteristic arises: this is a further lack of reversal.

20.(E457; T2630 The knowledge that the nonclarity of this ground consists only in the nonabandonment of reversed mental attention, and that clarity is its abandonment, is non-reversal in regard to nonclarity and clarity respectively.

21.(E457; T264) The ground is clear like the sky. There is total adventitiousness of duality and this is an additional lack of reversal.

22.(E457-458; T264) There is no affliction or thorough clearing either for factors or persons, and because of this nonexistence there can be neither fear nor pride, and this is an additional lack of reversal.

23-26.(E459; T266) The practice of avoidance of extremes is explained.

27-28.(E461; T2700) The similarities and differences among the ten stages is to be studied. Determination, the ground, what is to be brought about, bringing it about, sustenance, reflection, perseverance, penetration, extensiveness, going forth to meet others, remaining in a tranquil state, and pre-eminence.

29-30.(E462; T271) Nondeficiency, non-turning-away, nondistractedness, fulfilment, arising, nurturing, skill, the state of no-basis, the state of no obstructions, and not remaining tranquil in that state of no obstructions: that is full realization.

31.(E463; T272) This work is called *Madhyāntavibhāga* because it separates the Middle Path from extremes and explains them.

## 165.VYAVADĀTASAMAYA (standardly ascribed to ASAṄGA), *Mahāyānasūtrālaṃkāra*[434]

"ET" references are to the edition and translation by Dr. (Mrs.) Surekha Vijay Limaye in Bibliotheca Indo-Buddhica Series No. 94, Delhi 1992. Mrs. Limaye assumes without question that the same author also wrote the commentary often ascribed to Vasubandhu (which we place below under the works ascribed to Vasubandhu), and her book covers both works.

Summary by Stefan Anacker

In the Tibetan traditions this work is counted as the first of the five "treatises of Maitreya." This may possibly reflect a chronological fact, inasmuch as this work contains certain ideas which are more fully developed in works such as the *Madhyāntavibhāga* and the *Abhisamayālaṃkāra*. But it may also be that this feature is due to the form of this treatise, which is really an "ornament" (*alaṃkāra*) to the Mahāyāna *sūtras*; it is in verse of varied meters which is highly poetic. It is thus not a tightly-organized book such as the two works just referred to, perhaps also for this reason. This text is, however, an extremely important résumé of Mahāyāna ethics.[1]

## CHAPTER ONE

1.(ET1-2) The Buddha could not avoid using words (in spite of their erroneousness), because of compassion for all sentient beings.

2.(ET2-3) The *dharma* gives ultimate joy.

3.(ET3-4) The words of the *dharma*, when put in pleasing form, give delight just like a reflection in a mirror.[435]

8.(ET7) The Buddhas saw the *dharma* with their eyes of direct perception.

9.(ET8) The way of the disciple, in comparison to the Mahāyāna, is deficient because of its contradictoriness, lack of means, and lack of teaching things as they are.

10.(ET9-10) Its contradictoriness relates to five: goal, teaching, use, support and time.

11.(ET10) The *dharmatā* arises of itself, develops by itself, and is uncontradicted because of its strength and its profundity.

12.(ET11) The *dharma* is not a subject of *tarka*.

13.(ET12) There are two aspects to *dharma*: its strength and its profundity. Its strength relates to the maturing of sentient beings; its profundity is its nonconceptual nature.

14.(ET12-13) The great heap of lack of merit in the world is a

---

1.The text is composed of 797 verses in all. Ronald M. Davidson, in his 1985 U. of California dissertation, suggests that 472 of these verses are in *anuṣṭubh* metre, and that "for the most part, these 472 verses of the MSA give a clean reading all to themselves and are certainly more homogeneous than the verses taken as a whole", thus that they may constitute the original text.

source of dismay,

15.(ET14) to which the antidote is the Mahāyāna.

16.(ET15) The Mahāyāna is based on (careful) mental attention.

19.(ET18) Some disregard *sūtras* they have never heard before because they follow only those which they have already heard. Such people are unperceptive.

20.(ET18-19) And some, by constructing on received literature, while being based only on their own individual opinions, do harm to the *dharma*.

21.(ET19-20) The mind itself is flawed by nature; thus there is an incorrect form to any statements of *dharma*. When the *dharma* itself becomes doubted, equanimity, the best of all, the unflawed, arises.

## CHAPTER TWO

1-2.(ET24-25) The reason why the three gems (the Buddha, the *dharma*, the order) are taken as a refuge is because they all three deal with the saving of sentient beings.

3.(ET25-26) Engaged in saving all sentient beings, joined with skills in a knowledge path, with the same delight in going forth and staying calm, the Mahāyāna sage goes everywhere.

## CHAPTER THREE

5.(ET36) Of the three Buddhist lineages, the Mahāyāna is characterized by its compassion, its resolution, its patience and its practice of the perfections.

7.(ET37) Chief obstacles to Mahāyāna: becoming used to defilements, association with bad friends, lack of aiding others and dependence.

8.(ET37) The Mahāyānist is interested in saving all sentient beings, both from their dangers and for their liberation. He is ever full of concern for maturing sentient beings.

## CHAPTER FOUR

1.(ET42) The arising of the awareness of enlightenment is characterized by great enthusiasm, fervent taking up of both one's own and others' aims, and by the great arising of the first glimpses of complete enlightenment.

2.(ET43) The arising of the awareness of enlightenment gives the impetus for entering the Bodhisattva states.

3.(ET43-44) The root of all Mahāyāna is compassion.

7.(ET45-46) All the following are instrumental in the arising of the awareness of enlightenment: the friends one has, the previous good roots one has planted, the religious literature one has already heard, and being accustomed to aiding others.

8-9.(ET46-47) The awareness of enlightenment arises only with a state of sameness of awareness towards all phenomena, which comes from a knowledge of the absence of self in all events, and a knowledge of the sameness of all sentient beings.

10.(ET46-47) Liberation can be known as a skill in saving both "self" and "others".

11.(ET46-47) The practice of the perfections is possible through resolve on *dharma*: its mother is compassion, the womb of this mother is meditation.

12,(E46; T48) The enthusiasm which comes from taking the Bodhisattva's vows is due to an absence of fatigue in doing difficult things for a long time.

14.(ET47-48) And nonconceptual knowledge comes in liberation.

15-20.(ET49-50) Explanations of various metaphors used in Mahāyāna *sūtras* for the arising of the awareness of enlightenment.

21.(ET53) Without the arising of the awareness of enlightenment, sentient beings cannot obtain any of the following satisfactions: (1) the pleasure that comes from thinking of the aims of others, (2) the pleasure which comes from getting the skill in means to help others, (3) the pleasure of realizing the intentions in the deep Mahāyāna teachings, (4) the pleasure of seeing the ultimate truth, i.e., the selflessness of all factors.

22.(ET53-54) Even placed in a bad destiny the Mahāyānist rejoices at both satisfaction and frustration, always mindful of the welfare of others and filled with compassion.

23.(ET54) No continuation in bad action is possible if one is unmindful of one's own body, and engaged for the welfare of others.

24-25.(ET55) Knowing that all events are like a magical creation helps the Mahāyānist have no fear of defilements or frustrations.

The preoccupation with compassion becomes finally for them like child's play.

26.(ET56) If, for the sake of others, the Bodhisattva can go even to *avīci* hell, how can he be negatively affected by the harm others may wish to do him?

27.(ET56-57) The Mahāyānist becomes affected by the frustrations of others, and is incited by the good deeds of others, too.

28.(ET57) Warning against sloth or slackness in continuing efforts.

## CHAPTER FIVE

2.(ET60) The Mahāyāna path is both for oneself and others, because one makes no distinction between one's own and others' aims.

3.(ET60-61) The world does not evolve so pitilessly so as to cause incessant frustration, for the compassionate feel the frustrations of others as their own.

4-5.(ET61-62) On the divisions of practice for others' sake.

6.(ET62-63) The path is: favoring sentient beings, unreversed teaching, without egoism, skillful, patient, restrained, going far, and indestructible.

7.(ET63) People full of desire do themselves much harm, but those who love calm are always in the fundamental calm of all.

8.(ET64) Foolish people running after their own desires always suffer when they don't get them; but the steadfast is engaged for others, and based both on his own and others' aims, always enters into complete rest.

9.(ET64-65) As far as the eye can see, there are countless Bodhisattvas, motivating sentient beings with right and easily accessible words.

11.(ET66) The path of the one based on compassion goes everywhere with ultimate peace.

## CHAPTER SIX

1.(ET68) The characteristic of the highest is that it is neither existent nor nonexistent, neither like this nor different, it neither arises nor ceases, nor diminishes, nor increases, nor is purified, nor is not purified.

2.(ET69) No view of self possible.

3-4.(ET70) It is the absence of knowledge of dependent origination which makes the idea of "self" arise.

7.(ET72) Once it is understood that all objects are only talk[436] one is situated in awareness only, and so one realizes the *dharmadhātu* by direct perception, freed from any dualities.

8.(ET72) Having realized that there is nothing beyond awareness, he realizes by this the nonexistence of awareness itself, and by realizing the nonexistence of any duality, he is situated in the *dharmadhātu*.

9.(ET73) And for the steadfast, by the power of conceptualizing knowledge, everything is equal, and so even an amassment of the most dense flaws is nullified like poison in a great fever.

10.(ET74-75) Importance of mindfulness.

## CHAPTER SEVEN

1.(ET77) Strength in Mahāyāna practice includes knowledge of the birth of sentient beings, their awarenesses, their former good and bad actions, the location of sentient beings to be helped, and the means of liberating them.

2.(ET78) Meditation is the way to arrive at these strengths.

4.(ET79) All the world-realms and all sentient beings are like a magical creation.

## CHAPTER EIGHT

1.(ET85) Maturation in *dharma* is characterized by: taking delight in *dharma*, serenity, peace, compassion, patience, intelligence and strength.

2-8.(ET86-91) Description of each of these.

## CHAPTER NINE

1-3.(ET103-104) Description of knowledge of everything in all aspects, which is unlimited and freed from all obstructions.

4.(ET104) Though this knowledge knows all factors, it knows not a single one (since in ultimate truth there are no factors).

8-9.(ET107-108) The Hīnayāna is inferior because it has no means for the removal of injuries,

10.(ET108) and because the Mahāyāna leads to complete enlightenment.

12.(ET109-110)[437] Mentions briefly the idea of "seeds" deposited in the consciousness-stream by each obstruction of a defilement or limitation on awareness, and that revolution at the basis is their obtainment in a different manner, which makes them no longer efficacious. It is constructionfree knowledge and is linked with many excellent qualities.

22.(ET115) Suchness, Buddhahood is unclear because it does not distinguish the anterior and the succeeding; it is clear because it is freed from all obstructions.

23.(ET115) Buddhahood is neither being nor nonbeing.

26.(ET117) It is neither one nor many.

37.(ET122) Since suchness is in all sentient beings without any differentiation, all living beings are the *tathāgatagarbha*.

45.(ET126)[438] *Nirvāṇa* without a basis (*apratiṣṭhitanirvāṇa*) is achieved.

46.(ET126-127) In its aspect of reversion from sex, one stays in Buddha-bliss and looks upon all women as undefiled.

60.(ET135) Revolution at the basis = *dharmakāya*.

71-72.(ET140-141)[439] Compassion, loving kindness, and meditation emphasized.

77.(ET143) Because of the different kinds of enlightenment sought by the three different vehicles, there is not one Buddha-state, but many.

78.(ET144) The state of nonexisting = the state of existing. When one does not apprehend anything in any way, this is the ultimate apprehension.

81.(ET145-146) Seeing that all mental conceptions and all sensory perceptions are only constructions leads to a state of no mental constructions.

## CHAPTER TEN

(ET150-158) On sustaining interest in Mahāyāna. In this chapter is the surprising statement that limitless beings obtain enlightenment in every moment (11). This is said as an encouragement against slackness in practice.

## CHAPTER ELEVEN

1.(ET159-160) Praise of the *Tripiṭaka.*

2.(ET161) In considering the *Tripiṭaka,* the knowledge of everything in all modes can be reached.

5.(ET164) Though framed in dualities, the state of the nonapprehension of any dualities can be reached.

14.(ET172-173) It is an idiotic opinion that there's nothing in this world, and that only another world can be flawless.

15.(T173)[440] The construction of what was not is like a magic show, and the confusion of duality is like that which is produced in a magic show.

16.(ET174) When there is no being of duality, there is the highest truth. When there is grasping of things it is conventional truth.

17.(ET174-175) Revolution at the basis = absence of perception of any duality.

18.(ET175) One should go at will, as unconfused as the world is confused by special signs and marks; going at will, one's going forth is unreversed, because of revolution at the basis.

19.(ET175) The reason why the image of a magic show is used is because an appearance arises, the being of which doesn't exist. Thus it has both existence and nonexistence.

20.(ET176) It is neither being, nor nonbeing, nor both nonbeing and being.

24.(ET178) In an illusion, a material form is seen where there is only a nonmaterial perception.

27.(ET179) All phenomena have the character of illusion, because of being, nonbeing, and the nondifference between being and nonbeing.

28.(ET180) All phenomena are antidotal because of being, nonbeing, and being.

29.(ET181) One magically created king may be defeated by another magically created king.

30.(ET181-182) Image of a magical creation, dreams, mirages, reflections, an echo, the moon in the water.

31.(ET183) The construction of what was not neither was nor was not, and is neither construction nor nonconstruction.

32.(ET183-184) Defilements arise because of the semblance of duality.

35.(ET186) Awareness is the painter: it colors all experience.

36.(ET186-187) The only reason the Buddha spoke of characteristics, things having characteristics and secondary characteristics was to favor sentient beings.

37.(ET187) Something having characteristics exists only because an awareness linked with a view arises, and consequently it can be divided immeasurably.

38.(ET187-188) Its proclivities are special signs linked with the cognition of an "object", which is conditioned by linguistic habits--this kind of appearance of an "object" is (the) characteristic of the constructed.

39.(ET188)[441] The constructed is based on words only.

40.(ET189 The dependent has the characteristic of both object and subject: it is the construction of what was not.

41.(ET189-190) Since it can be said to be neither being nor nonbeing, the sameness of being and nonbeing is seen. Since it is neither noncalmed nor calmed, the sameness of noncalmed and calmed is seen. This is the characteristic of the perfected.

42.(ET190-191) It arises with careful mental attention.

43.(ET191-192) It has no differentiations.

47.(ET1940) Liberation is having realized the selflessness of "persons" and "factors", where sameness is known.

48.(ET195) All dharmic preparation is only words. Once it is seen that all this is only words, there is nothing further to be realized.

50.(ET196) The act of apprehension is itself without a nature.

51.(ET197) Through the selflessness of all, one can realize the lack of arising and lack of cessation of everything, and that everything is calm.

52.(ET198) *Saṃsāra* has always existed, hence there is no arising of it. In truth, there is no previous or subsequent: there is no arising of factors which didn't exist before. The constructed doesn't arise by nature, the dependent can't arise by itself, and the perfected has no evolvement into another mode, thus it also can't arise. Once defilements are removed, they can't arise; the excellent qualities of Buddhas don't arise either. When all this is known, the patience reached through the nonarising of factors is realized.

53.(ET199) Because of the selflessness of events, and the equality of all, there can be no divisions of Mahāyāna, Hīnayāna, etc.

## CHAPTER TWELVE

(ET224-243) On the teaching of the Buddha being pure expedient, for the true yogi's contemplation is without object.

## CHAPTER THIRTEEN

2.(ET245) Image of the *dharma* being a raft.

5-6.(ET246-247) In the path of vision there is the destruction of all afflictions; in the spiritual path there is the destruction of all obstructions of the knowable. The first is also called *dharma,* the second *anudharma*.

11.(ET250) There is not a single event separate from the *dharmadhātu,* thus passion, etc. are considered deliverance by the Buddha.

13.(ET251) If one has recourse to the passions, one can be liberated from them.

14-15.(ET251-252) There are no hell-states, and the quest for good qualities and calm is proper to Hīnayāna only.

16-19.(ET252-253) Everything which is constructed by the construction of that which was not is like a magical creation, and all the differentiations seen there don't really exist. Awareness which is luminous by nature becomes flawed by adventitious flaws.

20-23.(ET254-255) Compassion is a passion, and overcomes all repugnance.

24-28.(ET256-257) The Bodhisattva has recourse to nonexistent conceptions for healing sentient beings.

## CHAPTER FOURTEEN

(ET259-280) Further emphasis on the contrast between

nondiscriminatory basis (or nonbasis) of the Bodhisattva and the discriminations used by him to help others.

## CHAPTER SIXTEEN

2-3.(ET285-286) Giving is a perfection of enjoyment, ethics is a perfection in one's being, forbearance is the perfection of service to others, energy is the perfection of undertaking, meditation is the state of rendering the afflictions powerless, and insight is being always unreversed in one's actions.

One is careful to uphold an absence of hostility for the sake of all beings, and goes everywhere for one's own sake.

4.(ET287) Absence of trouble and fatigue emphasized.

6-13.(ET288-292) Enumeration of different advantages following from the perfections.

14-15.(ET292-294) The reason the *pāramitās* are enumerated in the manner they are is because one obtains the next by being based on the first.

17.(ET300) Volition is the basis of giving, etc.

21-22.(ET302-303) Forbearance is both for the sake of others and oneself, since finally one's own calm is possible through it.

23-24.(ET304-305) Energy = enthusiasm for the beneficial.

25-26.(ET305-306) Meditation is based on mindfulness and energy, and makes one able to stay in a higher faculty.

30.(ET308-309) The giving of a Bodhisattva is neither attached, nor nonattached, nor both attached and nonattached, nor neither attached nor nonattached.

31-35.(ET309-310) Same for ethics, patience, energy, meditation and insight.

## CHAPTER SEVENTEEN

(ET339-377) On the worship of the Buddhas and enlightenment, on service to others, where compassion and affection are emphasized.

## CHAPTER EIGHTEEN

1-3.(ET379-380) The importance of shame at offenses committed for the maturing of others. It is shame that motivates the Bodhisattva to overcome adverse factors. Even in meditation, shame may be a factor, since a weaker meditation is made into a stronger often through its agency.

5-7.(ET381-383) And of course regret at one's own bad actions stands at the basis of ethics.

9.(ET383-384) It is even through a type of shame that the Bodhisattva fulfills all preparations and that the Bodhisattva does not become depressed by the unbeneficial acts serving as the maturing of sentient beings.

10-15.(ET384-387) Further verses on importance of shame.

16-21.(ET387-389) Importance of steadfastness for energy, meditational concentration, and insight. Role of steadfastness in the arising of the awareness of enlightenment.

23-24.(ET390) Importance of lack of becoming fatigued or troubled.

25-26.(ET391-392) Importance of knowing the *śāstras*.

27.(ET392) The Bodhisattva distinguishes himself from others by his body, voice, and knowledge of truth.

29-30.(ET393-394) The knowledge of the world also includes knowledge of meditation, since Bodhisattvas wish to join all sentient beings to calm.

31-33.(ET394-395) On the refuges: one takes recourse to the meaning of the *dharma* and not to words, one takes recourse to the *dharma* and not to the idea of a person, one takes recourse to the *śāstras* of complete meaning and not to those that require further interpretation.

34-37.(ET396-398) Bodhisattvas may be unequal in their mastery of the discriminations, i.e., their knowledge of *dharma,* knowledge of meanings, knowledge of languages, presence of mind.

38-39.(ET398-399) On the preparations: all perfections serve as preparations.

42-44.(ET400-402) On the establishment of mindfulness.

45.(ET403) On the right efforts.

50-53.(ET406-407) On the supernatural powers, which are based on perfection of meditation.

55.(ET409) On the faculties (faith, etc.).

56.(ET409) On the powers.

57-68.(ET410-417) On limbs of enlightenment, including the statement (61) that equanimity is made possible by the nondiscrimination subsequently achieved. On the limbs of the path, on insight and peace.

69-70.(ET417-418) On skill in means.

74-76.(ET420-421) On the Bodhisattva's vows.

77-83.(ET421-427) On emptiness, wishlessness, and signlessness.

84-88.(ET430-433) On inner psychic accomplishment.

89-91.(ET436-437) All phenomena are momentary, and always divided into different sorts: colors, smells, etc. The transformations of consciousness are all momentary too.

92-103.(ET441-443) On absence of a self in all "persons", which includes the knowledge of the aggregates (93), the metaphor of the nondifference of fire and fuel (95), and the emptiness of all phenomena (101).

104.(ET452) Fitted out with all the qualities enumerated in this Chapter, the Bodhisattva achieves both his own and others' aims.

## CHAPTER NINETEEN

1-3.(ET455-456) Among the surprises of enlightenment are the ability to abandon one's own body, forbearance, equanimity, energy, pleasure in meditation, the nondiscriminatory state, and insight.

4.(ET456) The "nonsurprises" are nonattachment, compassion, and the cultivation of antidotes.

5.(ET457) Affection toward sentient beings emphasized.

6.(ET457) Patience seen as the root of the highest and most important ethics.

7.(ET457-458) Importance of meditation.

8-9.(ET458-459) On giving, ethics, assiduousness in teachings, removing doubts regarding them, and on helping sentient beings.

10-11.(ET459) On compassion and patience.

12-17.(ET460-462) Faith gets sentient beings interested in *dharma*; highest ethics leads to their liberation, and highest practice to their impulsion.

18-19.(ET462-463) On teaching the *dharma* correctly.

20.(ET463) On patience achieved in realizing the nonarising of factors.

28-29.(ET467) On giving, ethics, patience, energy, meditation, insight.

32-33.(ET468) Obstacles: fraud, hypocrisy, narcissism, greed, turning away from calm in body and voice, going counter to good speech and action.

34.(ET469) Giving very important for getting others interested in *dharma*.

35-37.(ET469-470) On prediction to full enlightenment.

47.(ET476-477) There are four kinds of investigation into *dharmas*: investigations of names, investigations of things, investigations using the conception of essential nature, and investigations according to conceptions of specific characteristics.

48.(ET477) On the nonapprehension of everything.

49-80.(ET478-495)[442] On various qualities arising at various moments on the Bodhisattva path.

## CHAPTERS TWENTY AND TWENTY-ONE

3.(ET498) Specifically mentions that a Bodhisattva may remain a householder.

6.(ET499) Divisions in the stages: unclear, clear, completely clear.

7-8.(ET500-501) On vows, sameness of awareness, control, and being able to attract the crowd.

10.(ET502) Emptiness of the "highest self".

11.(ET502) Through the limbs of enlightenment there is a transformation of sentient beings; when these allies do not arise, afflictions of awareness serve to mature sentient beings.

12.(ET502) There is only one path, and it is signless.

15.(ET504) Enlightenment may be attained in one moment.

17-21.(ET506-507) Highest ethics, highest awareness, highest insight, mental attention without signs, lack of motivating dispositions, and holding to *samādhis* all are the results of practice.

22.(ET508) On ethics, meditation, and insight.

23.(ET508) On the knowledge of liberation, and making this clear to others.

25.(ET509) All the stages are unfulfilled, fulfilled, fulfilled and unfulfilled, and fulfilled.

27.(ET510) The mark of interest in Mahāyāna is that one looks everywhere without slackness and without depression, and without relying on another.

28.(ET510-511) Penetration is everywhere, the sameness of awareness is everywhere. Importance of skill in means to attract the noninitiated.

29.(ET511-512) The Bodhisattva is neither without interest nor avid, neither small-hearted nor angry, based on loving kindness and compassion, not confused by constructions and discriminations, not distracted, not affected by satisfactions or frustrations, relying on good friends, based on religious literature and worship of the Teacher.

30.(ET512-513) When enough merit has been amassed, there is the transformation to complete enlightenment.

31.(ET513-514) Higher vision and calm exist in each stage.

32-40.(ET514-519) Reasons for the names of the stages.

41.(ET519-520) Acquisition of sustaining interest in Mahāyāna, acquisition of action, acquisition of penetration due to ultimate truth, and acquisition of fulfilment take place on different stages.

43.(ET521) On compassion on one hand, rejoicing at the joy of others on the other hand.

44-45.(ET521-522) On the removal of defilements.

46.(ET523) Not enslaved by pleasures, unattached, unaffected negatively, meditationally concentrated.

52.(ET527-528) Again the emphasis on fulfilling both one's own and others' aims.

53.(ET528) Honesty in dealing with students, and ability to attract a crowd.

54.(ET529) On all-knowledge.

55.(ET529-530) Activity for the sake of others isn't to be done only sometimes.

58.(ET532) On cutting off the desire of all sentient beings through the three Buddha-bodies.

60.(ET533 The deliverance of all sentient beings is the aim.

61.(ET533-534) Fitted out with all these qualities, one is seen in the world, but yet has entered the *maṇḍalas* unseen by gods and human beings.

# ASAṄGA

While there has been a large amount of scholarly speculation about the dates of Asaṅga and his brother Vasubandhu, the only accounts that have the authority born of antiquity appear to agree that the brothers were born in Puruṣapura, that is, modern Peshawar in Gāndhāra (modern-day Pakistan). Some accounts make them half-brothers, one having a Brahmin, the other a Kṣatriya mother. There is said to have been a third brother who is referred to as Viriñcivatsa; he apparently was not a philosopher.

Most accounts refer to some or all of the brothers entering a Sarvāstivādin school. Hsüan-tsang specifically identifies Asaṅga as belonging to the school of the Mahīśāsikas.[443] A famous story has Asaṅga studying with the god Maitreya in the Tuṣita heaven, but returning to earth to teach in Ayodhyā after receiving enlightenment from Maitreya. Some of the works by Asaṅga are said to have been given to him in the Tuṣita heaven by Maitreya, their real author. Tradition goes on to credit Asaṅga with having converted his brother Vasubandhu from Hīnayāna to Mahāyāna persuasion.

While the two previously-cited works have regularly been ascribed to Asaṅga, it seems likely they preceded him, given the fact that he comments on them. (This is not of course conclusive; authors frequently comment on their own works. And there is also the distinct possibility that it is a bit of both--parts of both earlier and later texts being written by different hands.)

Despite the rather fulsome account of Vasubandhu's life one finds in the texts of Hsüan-tsang and others, what we can glean of Asaṅga's is rather shallow.

Asaṅga is regularly credited with being, along with his brother, the founder of a school of Buddhism called "Yogācāra" or "Vijñānavāda". While there doubtless grew in due course a tradition known by these names, it seems premature to speak at this point of a school; there is no particular evidence of an attempt to gather converts, and the teachings as they can be gleaned from the texts summarized below were not immediately promulgated in classes or lectures, so far as we can be aware. It is quite possible that Asaṅga wrote from more than one viewpoint as his brother Vasubandhu did. It seems likely that at least some portions of the *Yogācārabhūmi* were collected or written in the mid-fourth century. It is the author of this material that we are identifying here as Asaṅga.

## 166. ASAṄGA, *Yogācārabhūmi*

It is highly likely that one would be seriously mistaken to suppose this vast work to be written by a single hand, or even entirely written within a few years time. The complexity of the situation is brought out by Lambert Schmithausen.[444] Schmithausen argues that what he considers to be the oldest sections of this work preceded the 136.*Saṃdhinirmocanasūtra*: these sections include the first two sections of Book One, together with sections 13 and 15 (the *Śrāvakabhūmi* and *Bodhisattvabhūmi*), along with third Book (*Vastusaṃgrahaṇī)*. His reasoning is based on the nonoccurrence of the term "*ālayavijñāna*" in those places. Schmithausen is convinced that the whole *Yogācārabhūmi* is a compilation, and that the various sections which comprise that compilation are themselves compilations. Under the circumstances, trying to date or order the sections is a highly complex problem, which Schmithausen addresses but which we cannot hope to recapitulate here. (E.g., Schmithausen believes the second book of the *Yogācārabhūmi*, titled *Viniścayasaṃgrahaṇī*, was written by someone else than Asaṅga, presumably at some time after Asaṅga's lifetime.) Thus the summary we provide follows the organization of sections as they are found in the work as known to us today, but one should be careful not to draw any conclusions based on chronology from the appearance of any terms or doctrines in this summary without careful consultation of the sources.[445]

### VOLUME ONE: *Bahubhūmikavastu*

### CHAPTER ONE (*pañcavijñānakāyasamprayuktābhūmi*)

"E" references in the summary of Chapters 1-5 are to the edition by Vidhusekhara Bhattacharya, Calcutta 1957.

(E4-6) The five bodies of consciousness are auditory, gustatory, olfactory, tangible and visual awareness. Each has its loci: e.g., the locus of visual awareness occurs together with the vision of it, whereas the locus of mental awareness immediately precedes it.

The locus of all seeds is the storehouse consciousness.[446] Loci are of two sorts: material and immaterial. Visual loci are material; the others are immaterial.

The modes (*paryāya*) of visual awareness are colors, shapes, and the awarenesses of them.

There are mental factors associated with the senses: attention, touch, feeling, identification and thought.

Karma is of six varieties: (1) awareness of the supporting object of an action, (2) awareness of an object's specific characteristic, (3) awareness of present time, (4) awareness of a single moment, (5) mental awareness of the object's double aspect (as implying grasped and grasper), and (6) awareness of the arising of karma following good defilements.

(E6-10) Specific definitions of auditory, olfactory, gustatory, tactual and visual awarenesses.

## CHAPTER TWO (*manobhūmi*)

(E11-13) A mental state may be considered (1) in itself, (2) as locus, (3) as supporting obect, (4) as a combination of factors, and (5) as karma. In themselves mental states are just mind. As loci they contain the seeds, they are the storehouse consciousness. As supporting objects they may be any factor, but only feelings, identifications and conditioning factors are seeds of various sorts of conditions. As a combination of factors they include a large variety of types of factors (which are listed). As karma they involve (1) the awareness of an action's impact on something else, (2) awareness of something of the same kind as the action's content, (3) awareness of something that happened in the past, is happening, or will happen, (4) momentary awareness, (5) awareness of factors and actions whether desired or not, pure or impure, (6) awareness of something breeding desired or undesired results, (7) outflows of awareness.

How are supporting objects constructed? In seven ways: construction of (1) an object previously experienced, (2) a future object, (3) an object occurring only through the force of the essence of its content, (4) an object arising in the path of *dharma*, (5) an object that is stopped when the path is followed, (6) a past or future object arising from desire, hatred, violence, etc., (7) of constructions good or neutral, such as renunciation, absence of malice, kindness, etc. which occur conjoined with good factors like faith, etc.

(E13-15) A supporting object may be determined through discipline, not so determined, or neither. It is determined through discipline when one takes what is fleeting as persisting, what is frustrating as satisfying, what is impure as pure, what lacks self as having a self. It is not determined through discipline when an existent thing is undermined by the false awareness that it is merely apparent, or when the awareness of a factor is thought to be about an actual object, or when correctness is imputed to a factor by a higher pure awareness.

A variety of mental states are now distinguished, including arrogance, infatuation, sleepiness, fainting, nonattachment, etc.

(E18-21) The intermediate state. Stream-enterers and once-returners are reborn with self-affection. But nonreturners are reborn without self-affection. They quickly experience the fruits of their good or bad karma in heaven or hell. There are two sorts: excessive and weak. The karma of an excessive person is difficult; the karma of the weak is easy. But in the upper realms everyone's karma is weak. In the material realm there is temporally spaced out action among all the senses, while in the realm of desire all the senses operate atemporally without the senses. The pure are said to have a quiet death, the impure an unquiet one.

All the senses persist in the intermediate state. The intermediate state of those who did bad things is hard--e.g., they are blind; the doers of good have "bright nights", pure divine eyes. But since there is a desire to continue self-existence there is no accomplishment of the blocking of consciousness; their desire for the manifoldness of awareness arises again, and they enter the bodies of men or gods once more.

(E21-23) Conception described. Faulty seeds arising from mother and/or father analyzed.

(E23-27) Life in the womb described.[447]

(E27-30) Birth.[448]

(E30-36) The wheel of rebirth.

(36-72) The cycle of existence. Geography; review of the meditative states; different kinds of beings; the six receptacles, seven embracing objects, ten requisites, eight states, various other such sets.

## CHAPTERS THREE TO FIVE (*savitarkādibhūmi*)

(73-76) The three states are the realm of desire, the material and the immaterial realms.

(76-77) The different sizes of the various kinds of beings from insects to gods.

(E77-79) Length of life discussed.

(E79-90) Sexual aspects of the lives of the various kinds of beings, from those in various hells to the gods.

(E90-99) Sustained thought in the material and immaterial realms.

(E100) Sexual enjoyment.

(E101-102) Range of beings where sexuality applies.

(E102-103) Range of beings where satisfaction applies.

(E103) Three longings--for love, for existence, for a religious life.

(E103-104) The kinds of rebirth.

(E105-106) The ways of identifying a causal effect are four: by its characteristic mark, by its support, by its species, by its conditions. A cause precedes its effect. The effect that is dependent upon, collocated with, and involves either the attainment, the establishment, the fulfilment or the action of a factor--of *those* that factor is its cause. Examples.

(E106-107) Fifteen kinds of results of causes are listed: speech, experiences, traces, natural results, seeds, liberation, contents of awareness, sense-organs, actions, human doings, sights of the truth, conforming effects, various causal efficacies, sufficient conditions, impediments, nonimpediments.

Ten kinds of causes. Four kinds of conditions. Five kinds of results.

(E107-114) Fifteen kinds of results are explained, compared and contrasted.

(E114-117) The basic aspects of attention are classified as seven; with respect to attention's abode, to its actual object, to its investigation, to its experience, to its right understanding, to the accumulation of it on the disciple's path, to its accumulation on the Buddha's path, and to the setting aside of it by attaining the perfections.

(E118) Sixteen mistaken views are now discussed: (1) That causes and effects exist. Specifically, the argument attacks Sāṃkhya (Vārṣagaṇya is mentioned by name) and Mīmāṃsakas.

(E120-122)[449] (2) Refutation of the view that there is manifestation of the cause in the effect (*satkāryavāda*). Several ways of understanding the theory that the effect exists in the cause are considered. E.g., does the effect exist while the obstruction which precluded its production still exists, or not? Is it the effect's existing which constitutes the obstruction, or the effect's nature? Is the cause different from the effect or not? None of the possible answers to these questions satisfy. So it must be concluded that if something exists it is perceived, and if it doesn't, it isn't perceived. However, under certain conditions an existent thing may not be perceived--if it's too far away, too subtle, if one isn't paying attention, if the senses are temporarily deranged, etc.

(E122-129) (3) That past and future factors exist is refuted.

(E129-137) (4) That selves exist is refuted.[450]

(E137-139) (5) Eternalism refuted.

(E139-140) (6) That previous causes still exist refuted.

(E140-142) (8) That things are produced by previous deeds refuted.

(E144-145)[451] (9) That God exists refuted. God cannot be the creator of the universe. Either He is in the universe or outside it. If He's in it He can't create it; if He's outside it He has no relation to it. Again, if He created the universe He must have done it either purposefully or accidentally. If purposefully, He is not the Lord, since He is at the mercy of His purpose, and if accidentally, He does not *create* the universe. Does He create by Himself alone or with help? If by Himself alone He is *both* cause *and* effect and no creation occurs. If He creates with help who provides the help? If God alone creates the help He cannot do it *seriatim*, and if someone else creates the help God is not the Lord, someone else is!

(E145-147) (9) That killing is right is refuted.

(E148) (10) That there is either an end or no end to things is refuted.

(E149-150) (11) That death need not be avoided is refuted.

(E150) (12) That there are no causes is refuted.

(E150-155) (13) Nihilism is refuted.

(E155-156) (14) Pride is criticized.

(E156-159) (15) The view that one is pure is refuted.

(E159-160) (16) The view that one is auspicious is refuted.

(E160-166) On the defilements.

(E166) Seven erroneous views about identification, view, awareness, persistence of things, about satisfaction and frustration, about purity and impurity, and about self.

(E166-170) Of synonyms for the defilements.

(E170-181) Of afflictions.

(E181-188) Distinguishing marks of factors.

(E188-193)[452] Perverted karmic views about action, appropriating, pleasure.

(E194) Seven kinds of disadvantage.

(E195-196) Lack of self-restraint.

(E198-203) Dependent origination.

(E204-232) The twelve members of dependent origination discriminated. The order of their occurrence. The etymology of the term "*pratītyasamutpāda*". The twelve conditions distinguished. Supporting passages cited.

## CHAPTERS SIX AND SEVEN (*samāhita-* and *asamāhita-bhūmis*)

These Chapters are not available in Sanskrit. According to Alex Wayman[453] these two Chapters "discuss the psychological states that were discussed extensively in the first five *bhūmis*...from another standpoint." Lambert Schmithausen has translated one passage from Chapter 6,[454] a passage he takes to "represent the starting-point of *ālayavijñāna* theory", that is, a theory of the storehouse-consciousness, as follows:

"When a person has entered (absorption into) the concentration trance, his awareness and mental concomitants have ceased; how, then, is it that (his) consciousness has not withdrawn from his body? - (Answer:) No problem, for in his case *ālayavijñāna* has not ceased (to be present) in the material senses, which are unimpaired: *ālayavijñāna* embraces the seeds of activated consciousness (*pravṛttivijñāna*), so that they are bound to re-arise in future (i.e., after emerging from concentration)."[455]

## CHAPTERS EIGHT AND NINE: (*sacittaka-* and *acittaka-bhūmis*)

These two brief chapters are edited by Alex Wayman[456] and Lambert Schmithausen[457]

## CHAPTER TEN: *Śrutamayī*

The latter part of this Chapter is presently available in Sanskrit in the *Śrāvakabhūmi* manuscript photographed by Rahul Sankrtyayana in the 1930s in Tibet. These photographs are held by the Bihar Research Society, Patna. This section has not been published. Some passages are referred to by Schmithausen.[458]

## CHAPTER ELEVEN: *Cintamayī*

About three-fourths of this Chapter is known to us in Sanskrit through the manuscript of the *Śrāvakabhūmi* procured by Rahula Sankrtyayana from Tibet in the 1930s. According to Alex Wayman three sets of *gāthās*--verses--with Asaṅga's commentary are included in this manuscript, two of which sets he has edited and translated. He suggests that the three, titled *Abhiprāyikārthagāthā*, *Paramārthagāthā* and *Śarīrārthagāthā*, deal respectively with three "instructions of morality, higher awareness and higher virtue...promulgated for the monks, not for laymen."[459]

Alex Wayman's edition and translation is referred to here as "ETW". Lambert Schmithausen has edited and translated verses 28-41 of the *Paramārthagāthā* with their commentary.[460] His translation is referred to below as "ETS".

### 1. *Abhiprāyikārthagāthā*

1. (ETW 354, 357) Brahmā Sahampati asked the Buddha: You have completed spiritual training and resolved all doubts. Tell me what that training is!

2-5. (ETW 354, 357-358) Answer: Morality, higher virtue and higher awareness are the three parts of spiritual training. One should be moral and follow the code of discipline with steady awareness in four ways through the four meditative states. The four ways involve good roots, inner peace, adoption of right views and avoidance of wrong ones.

6-13. (ETW354-355, 358-360) Ridding oneself of the sensual realm one should attain the upper realms and liberation. Morality brings higher virtue and awareness, while higher virtue brings on higher awareness and the morality of meditation. Higher awareness brings on liberation. One should cultivate them both independently and as combined.

14-23. (E355, 360-361) The three parts of spiritual training have respectively three aspects: giving up possessions, eliminating depravity, and perception of the four truths. The first aspect does not require a meditative object but the last two do. The practitioner is encouraged to be diligent in his practice and to avoid a variety of wrong or distracting tendencies, avoiding the extremes of sensual indulgence and asceticism.

24-38. (ETW355-356; 362-363) Specific advice to the adept as to how to behave, including what to wear, posture, attitudes to self and others, how to beg, avoidance of wrong thoughts such as the theory of the Lokāyatas, right friends and associates, maintenance of faith.

39-51. (ETW356-357, 363-366) Specific advice as to how to practise higher awareness by avoiding the five hindrances, eliminating eight attitudes involved in sensual desire, listening to the *dharma* and eliminating the depravity of the defilements.

## 2. *Paramārthagāthā*

1. (ETW167, 174, 178) No one owns, does or feels anything. All factors are inactive, yet actions occur. That is, there is no self relating to factors: still, ownership, action and feeling take place.

2. (ETW168, 174, 178) The twelve aspects of the life-continuum comprise aggregates, senses and elements; no person *(pudgala)* is found among them.

3. (ETW168, 174, 178) All is empty, both personal and external, and there is no one who cognizes emptiness.

4. (ETW 168, 175, 179) The "self" is no self. It is only something erroneously constructed. Factors are causally conditioned.

5-9. (ETW168, 175, 180) All conditioned factors are momentary. How can they act? Sensory "activity" is just the occurrence of the factors, and it is that occurrence that is called "agent". The senses don't *do* anything. Rather, things arise dependently and are naturally destroyed.

10-12. (ETW169, 175, 180-181) There are two ways of being--deluded and desirous. The twelve members (of dependent origination) can be divided between the two--ignorance and feeling arising from delusion, desire through old age and death arising from desire.

13-18. (ETW169-170, 175-176, 181-182) Actions are not done by a self, or by another, or by previous karma; still, they occur. Conditioning factors can't be known as present, past or future. Matter is like foam, feeling like a bubble, identification like a mirage, conditioning factors like plantains and consciousness like *māyā*.

19-20. (ETW170, 176, 182) No one really deludes anyone, yet there is delusion, which is unreasoned attention.

21. (ETW170, 176, 182) Conditioning factors breed good or bad perceptions. Though changeless they are thought to breed bodily, vocal and mental karma.

22-26. (ETW170-171, 176, 183) If conditioning factors are changeless how is it that awareness is said to change as a result of changes in factors? It doesn't really; saying so is conventional, just as speaking of the self as exhibiting similarities and dissimilarities within its stream is merely conventional. No one really does or feels anything; no one experiences the fruits of karma.

28-31. (ETS228-229, 234-236) The cause is delight in manifoldness, along with satisfying and frustrating karma. The result is maturation of all seeds with what is and what is not desired. This result comes to be viewed as the self, known only to one's own experience, being immaterial and shapeless. This belief in self spawns many other false views through taking things to be solid, through tracing it to its own seed, through habit, through bad companions, through listening to mistaken doctrines.

32-38. (ETS229-233, 236-241) From this in turn there arises attachment to oneself, and from wanting benefits to oneself comes coveting of outside things. What people fear they attract through their delusion. Having stuck to them before, they experience manifold things.[461] Ceaseless frustrations arise from these experiences, leading to the ideas of ego, of satisfaction and frustration. Frustration is like a mire in which one is stuck like an elephant, or a lake comprising all streams there are in this world, which cannot be dried up by fire, wind nor sun, but only by dharmic conduct. By thinking "I am frustrated" or "I am satisfied" one conceives frustrations as one's self, a false view.[462]

39-44. (ETS232-233, 241; ETW172-174, 177-178, 185) Each defiled awareness arises with defilement and ceases with it; one cannot gain release from them. It is not this same awareness that arises later as purified, but another awareness that is called "liberated from defilements." So any defiled awareness is absolutely defiled, any pure one altogether pure. So no one, nothing is purified from anything.

Liberation is of two kinds; from defilements and from actual objects. Liberation from defilements comes from destroying all seeds by ending defilements. It brings in turn liberation from actual objects, an end to manifoldness. Nothing transmigrates, no person, no factors--nothing, indeed, arrives at final liberation.

### 3. *Śarīrārthagāthā*[463]

## CHAPTER TWELVE: *Bhāvanāmayī*[464]

## CHAPTER THIRTEEN: *Śrāvakabhūmi*

There is only one, partial Sanskrit manuscript of this Chapter known to exist: it is held in the K.P. Jayaswal Research Institute in Patna. Chinese, Tibetan and Japanese versions are in addition available. Alex Wayman published in 1961 the text and a translation of those sections in the Patna manuscript;[465] this is our "T". More recently Karunesha Shukla has edited those sections together with a reconstruction from Tibetan into Sanskrit of the sections missing from the Patna manuscript.[466] This is our "E".

### Section One

#### Part I: On Lineage (*gotra*)

(T58-60) A person's lineage is his seeds. One stays in his lineage and does not obtain final liberation for four reasons: (1) because he is born in unfavorable circumstances, (2) out of carelessness, (3) because he follows wrong paths, or (4) because of conversion to a wrong faith.

(E5-6; T60-63) Favorable conditions for one's lineage are primary or secondary. The primary conditions are being made aware of correct *dharma* and by methodical attention to it. The secondary conditions are as follows: (1) Blessings of nature, such as (a) being born as a human being, (b) being born in a noble family, (c) having all one's organs in proper working order, (d) faith in Buddhism, (e) a proper occupation.

(E6-16; T61-63) (2) Blessings of good association with others, e.g., with Buddhas, with the Buddhist teaching; maintenance of *dharma*, the sympathy of others. (3) Good interest in *dharma*, involving commitment to *dharma*, moral restraint, restraint of the senses, eating proper amounts of food.[467] (4) Staying awake. (5) Alert conduct. (6) Seclusion. (7) Removal of obstructions--comprising sensual interests, malice, lethargy and sleepiness, excitedness and regret, and perplexity. (8) Remaining concentrated in the four trance states.

(E16-22; T63-64) The marks of a person belonging to a lineage are explained. The varieties of such persons are set forth.

## Part 2: On Entry Onto the Path

(E25-32; T65-66) Entry has four aspects: (1) its nature, (2) its establishment, (3) its marks, and (4) the one entering. (1) The nature of entry involves faithful practice of *dharma.* (2) The stages of entry differ depending on whether the one entering is merely potentially entered, is of weak, middling or strong merit, is of firm application, or is one who has "gone to liberation" (i.e., a noble person). (3) How these stages are related to each other is explained. (4) The marks of a person's entry and who those marks characterize.

## Part 3: On deliverance (*naiṣkramya*)

(E35-37; T66-67) The way to deliverance includes the worldly and supramundane paths and the preparation for them. One on the worldly path views the lower meditative trances as gross and seeks the tranquility of the higher trance states, thus attaining nonattachment and arriving at the stage of neither-identification-nor-nonidentification. The supramundane path involves both vision and meditative practice, and ends in detachment from both. These paths require the "secondary conditions" of Part 1 above, along with other similar practices.

(E37-63; T68-71) Moral restraint includes practice of the *prātimokṣa* vows, orderly conduct, proper posture, proper speech, the five practices of a monk, spiritual training, etc. These can be summarized into three requirements: continuation of proper practice, its essential nature, and its naturally good character. Ten causes that undermine morality are explained. The Buddha used various terms to characterize morality, such as "root", "ornament", "ointment", "good practice", "restraint", etc. These are each explained. The ten benefits accruing from moral practice are explained.

(E63-73; T68, 71) Explanation of restraint of the senses, involving their mindful and intelligent guarding. Bad factors--attachment, delusion--flow in all awareness; restraining the senses cuts off these factors.

(E73-97; T150-162) Explanation of what and how one should eat.

(E97-111; T71-73) Explanation of staying awake and alert conduct: how one should conduct meditation without being distracted by the five obstructions; how one should rest without falling asleep.

(E111-127; T74) Explanation of seclusion--the sorts of places one should choose for meditation.

(E127-140; T74-78) Who is a "good friend"? One who is moral, learned, wise, compassionate, not depressed, forbearing, confident and speaks well. Such a person can be trusted as he encourages, reminds one about things that need to be understood, gives good advice, teaches the *dharma*. That *dharma* was explained by the Buddhas and their disciples, and comprises twelve sorts of things: passages from the *sūtras*, verses from the *sūtras*, predictions of deaths and rebirths, other verses, teachings, the foundations of morality (e.g., in the *prātimokṣa*), instructive examples, tales of former lives, Jātaka stories, other instructive stories, specification of the features of *dharma*, of Buddhas and others, and the Abhidharma.

(E140-143; T78-80) Reasoning is called for in respect to six matters: self, beings, the world, karma, the shared and the specific features of things. Reasoning is of two kinds: counting and examining. Examining in turn has four kinds: consideration of what things depend on for their origination and for their designation; consideration of things' causal relations; consideration of the proofs of things; and consideration of their nature as factors--how factors arise and what their nature is.

(E144-149; T80-81) Renunciation is analyzed. What one should give, to whom, with what attitude.

(E155-166; T81-83) A monk is characterized as having faith, guileless, rarely ill, energetic, wise, desiring little, observing a dozen or so ways of living (prescribed in the *dharma* literature) starting with giving alms, begging, controlling what one eats, where one dwells, how one sits.

## Section Two

(E169-183; T83-85) Twenty-eight kinds of persons on their way to deliverance are described: they are (1) of lazy senses, (2) of keen senses, (3) strongly attached, (4) strongly hating, (5) largely confused, (6) basically proud, (7) thoughtful, (8) equally attached, hating and deluded, (9) weakly attached, (10) stream-enterers, (11) satisfied with results, (12) faith-followers, (13) followers of *dharma*, (14) resolved in faith, (15) view-attainers, (16) eye-witnesses, (17) with only seven rebirths ahead, (18) reborn in the same kind of family, (19) single-seekers, (20) liberated in the intermediate state, (21) liberated in this birth, (22) conditionally liberated, (23) unconditionally liberated, (24) going upward in the stream, (25) liberated at a specific time, (26) of steadfast *dharma*, (27) liberated by wisdom, (28) liberated both ways.

(E184-192; T85) Persons can be analyzed in eleven ways in relation to their (1) sense-organs, (2) group (i.e., various kinds of monks), (3) conduct (e.g., desirous, hating, deluded, proud), (4) vow (disciple, self-enlightened, Mahāyānist), (5) mode of progress, (6) path and result (stream-enterer, etc.), (7) application, (8) meditative attainment, (9) rearising, (10) time of release, (11) manner of release.

(E192-258; T86-91) What does one meditate on? Four kinds of supporting objects: (1) what is pervaded, (2) for the purification of conduct, (3) what is skilful, (4) for the purification of defilements.

The supporting object that is pervaded is of four kinds: (a) the image attended with conceptual constructions, which is the object of insight, (b) the image devoid of conceptual construction, which is the object of peace. (The image in either (a) or (b) is the reflected image, or thought, of the kinds of supporting objects (2)-(4) of the preceding paragraph); (c) the limits of actual entities of two sorts--the phenomenal limit of the entity and the noumenal limit of the entity; (d) the fulfilment of the requirement, the meditative object in fruitional stage, so that the meditator is free from depravity. (c) and (d) are the object of peace and insight combined.[468]

(2) The supporting objects for the purification of conduct are of five kinds: (a) foul objects, (b) loving kindness, (c) origination dependent on a thing, (d) analysis of the elements, (e) mindfulness of inspiration and expiration.

(3) The supporting objects for skill are of five kinds: (a) concerning the aggregates, (b) concerning elements, (c) concerning senses, (d) concerning dependent origination, (e) concerning abode or no abode.

(4) The supporting objects for purification of defilements are of two kinds: (a) grossness of lower realms and calmness of higher realms, (b) the four noble truths.

How to meditate on each kind of supporting object is explained.

(E258-348; T92-105) Four kinds of precepts: (1) nonerroneous, (2) successive, (3) traditional, (4) of attainment.

Three kinds of spiritual training: (1) concerning higher virtue, (2) concerning higher awareness, (3) concerning higher wisdom.

Ten kinds of factors for the adaptive knowledge of spiritual training: (1) prior cause, (2) adaptive teaching, (3) correct practice, (4) persevering respect, (5) intense interest, (6) basis for application of yogic power, (7) allayment of bodily and mental depravities, (8) constant reflection, (9) nondiscouragement, (10) lack of conceit.

Four kinds of breakdown of yoga--permanent, temporary, backsliding, wrong acquisition.

Four aspects of yoga--faith, interest, energy, method.

Four sorts of meditative attention: (1) careful, (2) interrupted, (3) uninterrupted and (4) effortless.

There follows discussion of a different set of four kinds of attention; of four signs of meditative objects and how they are to be treated; of the kinds of yogis (beginner, doer, and transcender of yoga); of the ways of cultivating yoga (cultivation of conceptual identification and cultivation of the thirty-seven limbs of enlightenment); of thirty-five kinds of bodies; of twenty kinds of awareness; of the establishment of mindfulness as antidote to the four delusions; of the four supernatural footings or concentrations (interest, energy, awareness and deliberation) and why they are called "supernatural footings"; of the five faculties (faith, energy, mindfulness, concentration and wisdom); of the good roots constituting aids to penetration; of the seven aids to enlightenment; and of a number of other such classifications.

## Section Three

(E351-388; T105-116) How the pupil should seek a teacher, and how the teacher should respond. First the would-be pupil should be questioned about his preparation and commitment, his lineage and his ability. Where one should meditate, where to sit, how to concentrate are discussed. There are nine kinds of peaceful concentration and four kinds of insight concentration. Insight concentration has three doors: associated with signs alone, associated with investigation, associated with reflection.

As well, insight concentration involves six ways of analysing what is to be meditated on into (1) the meanings of the terms used, (2) the internal or external entities to be meditated upon, (3) the marks--general and specific--by which the object is to be identified, (4) whether the object is good or bad, (5) the time of the object's occurrence, (6) the ways of construing the object in terms of (a) what it depends on or is depended on by, (b) its causal relations to other things, (c) how it is known, (d) what kind of factor it is.

The application of these six ways of analyzing to various sorts of objects of meditation follows, e.g., foul things, loving kindness, and other kinds of objects identified in Chapter 2 above.

(E388-398; T116-120) Nine kinds of "white" applications of concentration can be distinguished: (1) concordant, (2) repeated, (3) nondeviant, (4) energetic, (5) timely, (6) understanding, (7) discontented, (8) untroubled, (9) right. There are also nine opposed "black" kinds of application. "White" applications do not bind the practitioner, "black" ones do.

(E398-434; T120-124) Obstructions are removed by ascertainment of their essential natures, of their foundations, of their disadvantages and of their antidotes. There are four sorts of obstructions (*āvaraṇa*) so removed: distress, obstructions (*nivaraṇa*), thought that is only initial, and adherence to ego.

How to cultivate one's attention: by distressing one's awareness, by causing it to overflow, by tranquillizing it, and by purifying it. Examples are given, and the stages of such cultivation described, with appropriate quotations from canonical scripture.

## Section Four

(E437-470; T125-129) The yogi whose attention has been cultivated proceeds by two courses--worldly or supramundane. Followers of the worldly path are of four kinds: outsiders, those who have practised peacefulness with weak *dharma*, those who have practised peacefulness with keen *dharma* but whose good roots haven't yet matured, and Bodhisattvas who wish to delay enlightenment till a future life. Again, followers of the worldly course are of two kinds: ordinary folk and spiritual trainees. They seek nonattachment to sensual pleasures through the realms by gaining peace through practising meditation and being reborn again. Such beings range up to those nonattached in the realm of nothingness, or who have attained the five higher faculties.

This is further explained by reviewing the four trance states (of matter, etc.) and the four boundless states. It is explained how one accomplishes the five higher faculties and gains supernatural powers.

(E470-498; T130-132) As for the supramundane path, one who follows it, whether of cultivated attention or a meditator in the first or second trance states or in the boundless states, comes to realize the truth of frustration under four aspects--the impermanence of frustrations, their unsatisfactoriness, their emptiness and their lacking a self-nature. Next he comes to realize the truth of the origin of frustrations under four aspects--the cause of frustrations, their origin, their sources, and their conditions. Then he comes to realize the truth of the cessation of frustrations under four aspects-its being cessation, its peace, its excellence and its constituting deliverance. And he comes to realize the truth of the path under four aspects--its being a path, its logic, the understanding of it and its leading to liberation.

The truth of frustration is again analyzed into ten aspects--as involving change, destructibility, separation, closeness, factors, bondage by fetters, disagreeableness, unsuccessfulness, being without content and dependent.

Change is classified in fifteen weays, and again in eight ways, and discussed at length from various standpoints. The defilements are transitory and changeful, breeding disease and death; they are uncountable and decaying. They are not caused by God's magic.

(E499-503; T132-133) Having abandoned egoity one grasps the highest state of liberated objectless consciousness; one experiences the highest worldly factors. But the very highest awareness is not this awareness. Rather, it is the succeeding state of constructionfree perception gained by the nonreturner free from attachment, who has risen from the prior stages of stream-enterer and once-returner.

(E503-511; T133-134) What is the nature of spirituality, and how does one get it? Its nature is the attentive repetition of those good conditioned factors, the highest worldly factors. There are eight kinds of spiritual deeds, or eleven kinds of contemplation (of peace, of insight, of the worldly path, of the supramundane path, of weak, middling and intense contemplation, of the path of application, of the proximate path, of the liberating path, of the distinctive path).

Concentration at this level is called "diamond-like" (*vajropama*)--why? Because, like a diamond, this concentration is the best among the gems, it scratches everything else but is not scratched by anything else.

The noble state is the state of emptiness, signless, aimless, the attainment of cessation, abiding in loving kindness, compassion, joy and equanimity.

## CHAPTER FOURTEEN: *Pratyekabuddha*

(This brief Chapter has been edited by Alex Wayman.[469])

The Buddha who is self-enlightened is examined from five standpoints: his lineage, his path, his complete knowledge, his states, and his conduct.

## CHAPTER FIFTEEN: *Bodhisattvabhūmi*

Our summary of this the largest Chapter of the first Book of the *Yogācārabhūmi* is based on Nalinaksha Dutt's analysis.[470] Dutt's analysis is our "T", and the edition that follows it is "E". Some of the sections are translated and/or discussed elsewhere--where such are available they have been identified and used in preparing the following summary.

### Section One: Aids

#### Part One: Lineage[471]

E1-7; T8-9) There are ten kinds of factors constituting the Bodhisattva's path: his receptacle, his characteristic marks, his position (householder, monk), his inclination toward liberation, his state, his rebirth, his embracing others, the states of his spiritual advancement, his conduct and his ultimate end.

The "receptacle" is the Bodhisattva's own lineage, the arising of his awareness along with the factors pertaining to enlightenment; these lead him toward acts such as giving, morality, the six perfections and enlightenment.

There are two varieties of Bodhisattvas: those whose senses have beginninglessly comprehended the nature of factors, and those who have obtained this lineage through habitual practice of the good roots.

The main distinction between a disciple or self-enlightened being and a Bodhisattva is that the former two aim at the obstruction of defilements while the latter aims in addition at the removal of obstructions to the truth. Furthermore, a Bodhisattva has keener senses than a disciple or self-enlightened one, attains superior understanding, possesses more varied skills, and gains a better result. Bodhisattvas are especially competent at the six perfections.

A Bodhisattva may commit transgressions, for which he is reborn in lower states. But his suffering there is less severe than other hellish denizens experience, and he maintains the properties of his lineage there. Also, because he lacks proper instruction he may occasionally deviate from *dharma*.

## Part Two: The Awareness of Enlightenment

(E8-14; T9-11) The development of awareness of enlightenment is the first and most essential requirement of a person seeking recognition as a Bodhisattva, and after such recognition he is permitted to take up the career of a Bodhisattva. By "awareness of enlightenment" is meant (a) that a Bodhisattva firmly resolves to attain realization of the ultimate truth, and (b) that he dedicates his life and future lives to the service of others, helping as many persons as possible to attain enlightenment.

Awareness of enlightenment is explained from five standpoints: (a) its essential nature, (b) desire for it, (c) its having everything as supporting object, (d) its good qualities, and (e) its increase.

Enlightenment has been explained from four further standpoints: (a) admission into the path of a Bodhisattva, (b) its roots, (c) its effects, e.g., compassion, and (d) the basis it provides for spiritual exercises.

Awareness of enlightenment may lead to enlightenment without reverses or retrogression, or it may not. The kind that doesn't may be permanent or temporary.

There are four kinds of causes of the origin and development of the awareness of enlightenment:

(i) Four subsidiary conditions: (a) miracles shown by the Buddha, (b) the Buddha's teachings as recorded in the *Bodhisattvapiṭaka,* (c) his compassion for suffering beings, (d) the occasions for frustration that people experience.

(ii) Four basic causes: (a) inclusion in the lineage of Bodhisattva, (b) the teacher's loving kindness, (c) compassion, (d) courage to relieve the distress of all beings.

(iii) Four powers: (a) one's own powers, (b) the power of recruiting others as Bodhisattvas, (c) the power to visualize the Buddha, hear his words, associate with good persons and good deeds, (d) the power and desire to relieve distress.

## Part Three: Oneself and Others

(E15-24; T11-13) In this and the following four Parts the training of a Bodhisattva is outlined under ten headings:

(1) One's own purposes should not be pursued

exclusively. A Bodhisattva should develop his own spiritual improvement as a means to serve others and not just for his own pleasure or profit.

(2) The purposes of others likewise should not be pursued exclusively. Rather a Bodhisattva should seek his own spiritual improvement and not neglect it for the needs of others.

Giving, patience and compassion are examples of virtues that serve one's own purposes as well as those of others.

(3)-(4) One should, then, act in such a way as to produce what is fitting and satisfying for both oneself and others.

(5)-(6) The causes and results of a Bodhisattva's efforts affect (a) his actions and karmic results, (b) meritorious causes and results, viz. the five perfections of giving, morality, perseverance, energy and meditation, (c) the cause of knowledge and the resulting knowledge gained thereby. Both the causes and results are applied by a Bodhisattva to the good of others with a view to their gaining enlightenment. Hence a Bodhisattva should prefer to continue as a Bodhisattva and not become a Buddha, in order to render service to other beings.

(7)-(8) The results the Bodhisattva may expect to enjoy in his present life and in the lives to come.

(9)-(10) The accomplishments of ordinary folk in the realm of desire--the nature of one's experiences--are, however pure, the results of causes and not final. Three kinds of results are, however, final--the eradication of impurities, the experience of the merit gained by doing good deeds, and the attainment of liberation. These are achieved through practice of the eightfold path.

## Part Four: Reality[472]

(E25-36; T13-15) There are two ways of comprehending factors: as they are by themselves and as they are in their totality. And there are four ways of apprehending things: (1) as they are ordinarily understood, (2) as they are when understood through instruments of knowledge, (3) as purified from obstruction by defilements by disciples and self-enlightened beings whose contaminants have been destroyed--examples being knowledge of the four noble truths, of dependent origination and of no self and the aggregates, (4) as purified from obstructions by ignorance, by Bodhisattvas who understand the selflessness of factors, the indescribability of factors, that factors are only nominal designations, constructionfree, suchness, the nondual source.

The Bodhisattva, resolute about emptiness, remains in *saṃsāra* to thoroughly ripen the factors of realization for himself and others. Because of his resolve he does not spend his time thinking about momentariness, for if he did he would soon grow tired and achieve *parinirvāṇa.* But he is not frightened by liberation either; rather he stores up his equipment for it. He does not think about things too much, but sees all factors as the same and thus achieves the equanimity allowing him to realize by meditation the four sublime states, the five higher faculties and to understand ultimate reality.

How is the inexpressible nature of all factors to be understood? By understanding that every term intended to describe factors is nominal only, not essentially real and not nothing either. So both the view that nominal designations are real as well as the view that things don't exist at all are wrong. The latter, nihilist view denies designations as well as reality, and the Buddha termed nihilism a worse view even than realism. Emptiness should not be construed as nothingness; rather, a thing is "empty" in that it is not to be identified as having a nature answering to any description of it. That is what is meant by its having "suchness" (*tathatā*).

The indescribability of factors is attested in what the Buddha said. Canonical passages are quoted.

Because suchness is not understood eight sorts of conceptual constructions arise to create the insentient universe assumed to comprise them. The eight kinds of conceptual constructions or "ideas" are as follows: (1) the idea that things have essential natures, (2) the idea that there are particulars, (3) the idea that there are wholes, (4) the idea of ego, (5) the idea of "mine", (6) the idea that there are pleasant things, (7) the idea that there are unpleasant things, (8) the idea that there are things neither pleasant nor unpleasant. All these involve two aspects: the constructing and the object constructed. They are mutually caused and comprise a beginningless series.

Comprehension of conceptual constructions stems from four investigations and four kinds of detailed comprehension of specific factors. The four investigations concern a thing's names, its actuality, the designation of its essential nature, and the designation of its particularity. The four kinds of detailed comprehension are (1) the correct terms for a thing's nature, (2) the inexpressibility of a thing's actual nature, (3) the thing's lack of any essential nature, and (4) the thing's being perfected and so not really absent--or, to put it differently, that it is really without form and yet conventionally has form.

Now a Bodhisattva has detailed comprehension of the four above sorts; he understands the eight sorts of conceptual constructions and so is not subject to the kind of false construction of objects that breeds karma and *saṃsāra.* This cessation of discursive thought constitutes the Bodhisattva's Mahāyānic final liberation, accompanied as it is by complete mastery of supernatural powers such as the ability to magically create or transform himself into beings, as well as of staying in the world as long as he desires and leaving when he desires to.

Thus the Bodhisattva has five superior benefits: attainment of tranquil stations, clear knowledge and vision of all the branches of knowledge, not being wearied by his continuing *saṃsāra*, understanding of the speech of Buddhas, and undistracted devotion to Mahāyāna. He practises five kinds of actions in accord with these benefits.

## Part Five: Powers

(E40-54; T15-16) There are five kinds of powers that are gained by a Bodhisattva through his efforts:

1. Noble powers gained through control of one's meditations. There are six higher faculties: a number of supernatural powers (some thirty or more), knowledge of previous existences, divine ear, knowledge of one's future rebirths, knowledge of the thoughts of others, and knowledge of the removal of one's own contaminants.

2. The virtuous powers--what is gotten by mastering the six perfections of giving, morality, patience, energy, meditation and wisdom.

3. The special powers a Bodhisattva possesses in virtue of his having completed all but his last birth--mostly drawn from *sūtra*

passages.

4. The powers the Bodhisattva shares with disciples and self-enlightened ones.

5. The powers that distinguish a Bodhisattva from disciples and self-enlightened ones.

## Part Six: Maturation

(E15-21; T16-17) Five aspects of a Bodhisattva's development:

1. The nature required for maturation. A Bodhisattva possesses the seed for performing good deeds and he proceeds naturally to fulfill the duties prescribed for attaining enlightenment;

2. Disciples fall into four types: (1) disciples, (2) self-enlightened ones, (3) Bodhisattvas, (4) others trained by Buddhas.

3. Differences in progress towards maturation relate to (a) one's physique, influence and energy, (2) one's having good roots and avoiding bad ones, (3) one's learning and intelligence, (4) one's weak, middling or strong capacities.

4. Thirty-seven methods of development of maturation are distinguished.

5. The qualifications needed for someone to provide training are discussed under the headings of his resolve, the purity of his thought, his conduct, his determination and his progress towards concluson.

## Part Seven: Enlightenment

(E62-66; T17) Enlightenment is achieved through obstruction of the defilements as well as the contents of awareness. Such excellences of an enlightened person are explained. There can be only one *tathāgata* in each world (*lokadhātu*).

## Part Eight: Subsidiary Aspects of Lineage

(E67-69; T17-20) A Bodhisattva, in addition, (1) Has great resolve--firm faith in the Buddhist precepts.

(2) Masters various sorts of literature--the *Bodhisattvapiṭaka*, consisting of passages formed out of the Buddha's

sayings; the Hīnayāna literature; the literature on logic, etymology, medicine, various arts and crafts. "Logic" as understood by Asaṅga seems to pertain mainly to the analysis of causal conditions and their effects.

(3) Having mastered the literature the Bodhisattva should cultivate its teachings. Cultivation involves the application of peace (*śamatha*) and insight (*vipaśyanā*).

(4) He should understand the mental condition, intelligence and inclination of the person he proposes to instruct, and then choose the topics he concentrates on with these features in mind.

(5) He should encourage moral behavior in his pupils.

(6) He should cultivate the four methods of attaining popularity: (1) giving, (2) soft speech, (3) participation with others in community actions, (4) correcting the endeavors of others to worthwhile pursuits.

## Part Nine: Giving

(E80-94; T20-21) Nine aspects of giving are discussed: (1) the very nature of giving, (2) the range of possible gifts is unlimited, (3) the hardest to give away are the best gifts, (4) gifts to friends, relatives, employees, (5) gifts to saintly persons, (6) giving at any place or time, (7) gifts to the needy, (8) giving calculated to provide satisfaction in this life and hereafter, (9) gifts without self-interest.

These nine aspects are now applied in turn to:

## Part Ten: Morality (E95-129; T21)

## Part Eleven: Patience (E130-137; T21)

## Part Twelve: Energy (E138-142; T21)[473]

## Part Thirteen: Meditative Trance (E143-145; T21)

## Part Fourteen: Wisdom (E146-148; T21)

## Part Fifteen: Functions (E149-158; T21)

The four methods of attaining popularity (cf. Chapter 8, (6)) are discussed.

Part Sixteen: Respect, Services, Boundless States

(E149-170; T21-23) 1. Ten ways to worship the three jewels (the Buddha, the *dharma* and the order).

2. The services to be performed for "good company", i.e., one's teacher.

3. The four boundless states--of loving kindness, compassion, sympathy and equanimity--are called "boundless" because a Bodhisattva should extend his range of each to the whole universe without differentiation.

Part Seventeen: Limbs of Enlightenment

(E271-292; T23-28) This Chapter analyzes the process by which a Bodhisattva realizes the highest truth into sixteen stages:

1. Shame at improper conduct;.

2. Firm and steady suppression of impure types of awareness;

3. Lack of fatigue, nondistress;

4. Knowledge of Buddhist texts;

5. Understanding of frailties inherent in life, stemming from (a) the limited length of a lifetime, (b) human frailties, (c) impurities that can overcome one, (d) false views, (e) the evils of the age in which one lives;

6. Taking refuge in four methods: (a) following the teacher's understanding, not the literal meaning, (b) following logic, not authority, (c) following the basic meaning (*nītārtha*), not an interpretation (*neyārtha*), (d) following understanding attained by spiritual practice, not that gained merely by hearing and thinking;

7. Discrimination of factors, their meanings, the etymology of terms, their perspicuity in distinctions. One should apply discrimination to things, sense-organs and objects, the law of causation, and to the distinction between proper and improper situations;

8. Accumulation of merit and knowledge;

9. Application of the four methods of (6) to the thirty-seven limbs of enlightenment. The understanding of both Hīnayāna and Mahāyāna should be consulted;

10-11. Peace and insight, practised from both the conventional as well as the highest points of view;

12. Practising skilful methods by (a) study, (b) persuasion of others to do good deeds by transfer of merit, (c) elevating the understanding of people about the eight right methods, the middle way, the law of causation and the other basic Buddhist themes;

13. Citing or reciting texts in four ways: by memorizing after hearing one for the first time, by understanding its meaning, by uttering *mantras* to relieve the frustrations of others, by learning to persevere through mastering the *mantras*;

14. Taking the vows to develop the awareness of enlightenment, to get a good rebirth, to acquire good factors, to perform correct deeds, and the great vows of Buddhahood and *nirvāṇa*;

15. Concentration on emptiness, aimless concentration, signless meditation;

16. Recollection of *dharma* in the words of the Buddha.

### Part Eighteen: The Qualities of a Bodhisattva

(E163-203; T29-32) The duties of a Bodhisattva include extraordinary ones such as universal love and forbearance, ordinary duties such as foregoing liberation until others are liberated, viewing all others as equal, helping everyone, reciprocating the services of others, and a variety of other such services.

This is followed by a list of obligations of a Bodhisattva in groups such as: six predicted achievements, three conditions to be fulfilled, five indispensable conditions, five generally applicable conditions, various kinds of *dharma*, etc.

## Section Two

### Part One

(E206-210; T33-34) There are five characteristics of a Bodhisattva: sympathy, pleasing speech, energy, openhandedness, and the ability to explain the Buddha's deep meaning. Each of these is dealt with under five headings: its nature, its application, who has which characteristics, its effects and its place within the perfections. Sympathy is included in the perfection of meditation; pleasing speech in the perfections of morality and wisdom; energy included in the perfections of patience and wisdom; openhandedness included in the perfection of giving; and the ability to explain the Buddha's deep meaning falls within the perfections of meditation and wisdom.

### Part Two

(E211-214; T34) Four more characteristics of a Bodhisattva: he is steadfast, constant and faultless in his perfections; he is skilful in his tasks; he is helpful to others; his merit is transferred to other *tathāgatas*.

### Part Three

(E214-216; T35-38) A Bodhisattva is tender to all beings, mentally disposed to fifteen kinds of worthwhile actions, and capable of carrying them out.

### Part Four[474]

(E217-244; T35-38) This Part deals with twelve stages on the way to realization. (1) One is born into a lineage of Bodhisattvas (i.e., as a Mahāyānist). (2) He resolves to become a *tathāgata*. (3) He develops the pure intention to attain realization. (4) He begins to practise the moral precepts. (5) He practises meditation through the various stages up to the attainment of the higher faculties. (6) He completes the thirty-seven limbs of enlightenment. (7) He realizes the four truths and his misconceptions about ordinary things are removed. (8) He comprehends dependent origination, comes to understand the sameness of everything, comprehends emptiness, signlessness, aimlessness. (9) He rises above the stages of disciple and self-enlightened ones and completes the perfections without attachment to signs, but still experiences the results of those actions. (10) He appreciates the interdependence of all things, their indescribability and sameness, so that all misunderstandings are ended. (11) He teaches the *dharma* to others. (12) He becomes omniscient.

## Section Three: Accomplishment

### Part One

(E247-248; T39) The third Section summarizes the attainments, powers and functions of a Bodhisattva in the twelfth stage of the previous paragraph. This Part details five ways in which the Bodhisattva is reborn in order to provide service. (1) He may be reborn in roles where he can ward off famine, disease, wars, tyranny, etc. (2) He may be reborn to help others turn to better paths. (3) He may be reborn in a noble family, so that in that role he can provide more help to others. (4) He may be reborn in any of the stages. (5) He may be reborn as a King or minister to attain true enlightenment.

### Part Two

(E249-252; T40) The Bodhisattva relates to others by developing awareness of enlightenment and sympathy with everyone, as head of a household caring for his family, friends and servants, by guiding his fellows along the right path whatever their level of ability.

### Part Three.[475]

(E253-255; T40-41) The object of this Part is to show the relationship between the *bhūmis* of the 83.*Daśabhūmikaśāstra* and the stages discussed in Part Four of the previous Section.

### Part Four

(E256-258; T41-42) The conduct of a Bodhisattva is reviewed under headings that have already been discussed.

Part Five

(E259-264; T42) The object of this Chapter is to describe all the major and minor signs of a great man along with a description of the merits by which he acquires those signs.

Part Six

(E265-282; T42-46) Four kinds of purity of a Buddha: he can choose the plane of his last existence and his final time of departure, this awareness is purified and he has complete and altogether accurate knowledge.

Again, ten powers: knowledge of the difference between good and bad and their causes, of karmic maturations, of various meditations, both Hīnayāna and Mahāyāna, of others' senses of different realms, of others' intentions, of others' mental states, of the previous lives of all beings, of the time of death and birth of all beings, and of the destruction of impurities. These are explained again in terms of four aspects: their nature, differences, effectiveness in gaining liberation, and their being the same for all *tathāgatas*.

Other extraordinary powers attributed to Buddhas: freedom from fear, three kinds of mindfulness, the ability to confront various sorts of audiences, lack of any need to guard oneself from wrong moves, infinite compassion, appropriate actions because of infallible memory, freedom from all dispositions occasioned by traces, and omniscience.

## CHAPTERS SIXTEEN AND SEVENTEEN: *Sopādhika* and *Nirupādhika*

These Chapters are not available in Sanskrit.

## VOLUME TWO: *Viniścayasaṃgrahaṇī*

This and the remaining Volumes provide added discussions on the material in the first Volume, and this Volume is arranged in accordance with the sections of Volume One. Sections of Volume Two are studied by Lambert Schmithausen.[476] Schmithausen's discussions specially concern the *ālayavijñāna:* he treats various passages without attempting to order them consecutively.

BOOK ONE: *Pañcavijñānakāyamanobhūmiviniścaya*

CHAPTERS ONE AND TWO

(a) "Proof Portion"

This section is analyzed into five basic sorts by Schmithausen[477]. According to his account:

"Proofs (i) *upātta,* (vi) *kāyiko 'anubhavaḥ,* (vii) *acitte samāpatti* and (viii) *cyuti*. These proofs are all concerned with what one may call the 'somatic' aspect of *ālayavijñāna*: its function of appropriating the body at the moment of conception, of keeping it appropriated, as a whole and throughout life, even in unconscious absorption, of making its presence in the body felt by corporeal sensations even in the absence of tactile sense-perceptions, and of gradually abandoning the body at death."

"Proof (iv) *bīja*. This proof...is not concerned with the 'somatic' aspect of *ālayavijñāna* but with its function as the Seed (*bīja*) of ordinary forms of mind, based on the argument that the latter cannot be one another's Seed."

"Proofs (ii) *ādi* and (iii) *spaṣṭatva*. These two proofs do not prove the existence of *ālayavijñāna* but rather the fact that several *vijñānas* can arise simultaneously..."

"Proof (v) *karman*. This proof is...not of the existence of *ālayavijñāna* directly but rather of the simultaneity of several *vijñānas*...it does not, as proofs (ii) and (iii) do, prove the simultaneity of several *vijñānas* by referring to (allegedly) obvious cases in the sphere of *pravṛttivijñānas,* but does so rather by pointing out the simultaneity of experiential phenomena of which some--viz., one (at least largely) continuous perception of the surrounding world and of one's corporeal basis--most probably have to be directly referred to *ālayavijñāna*."

Another portion of this section, which is also found in Sthiramati's *Abhidharmasamuccayabhāṣya*, is edited and translated by Paul Griffiths.[478] We sumarize here that portion, substituting our translations of technical terms as usual where appropriate. Some lines of the passage are translated completely.

"Eight arguments demonstrate the existence of a store-consciousness (*ālayavijñāna*).

"1.The first argument appeals to the impossibility of appropriating a new body. It is divided into five sub-sections. Section (i) points out that an exhaustive categorization of the causes of the *pravṛttivijñāna* can be given by listing present or immediately preceding events, and that this leaves no place for causation by long past events. It is the *ālaya* which provides the locus for, and thus accounts for, this second kind of causation...Sections (ii) and (iii) state a fundamental presupposition of Buddhist theories about karma and causation; that the causal principle which brings about the maturation of karmic effect is in itself neutral. Since the six 'functioning consciousnesses' are not neutral in this way but consist in experience which has both affective and moral tone, Sthiramati argues that the *ālaya* must be postulated in order to allow for the maturation of karmic effect which in itself has no moral or affective tone...Sub-argument (iv) points out that the appropriation of a new physical body at the moment of a new birth would not be possible without a *vipākavijñāna*, a 'maturation consciousness' which can only be the *ālaya*. This is because the other six consciousnesses cannot appropriate the physical body as a whole since each of them has its own specific physical basis or locus (visual consciousness is located in or based on the eye and so forth). Each one of the six *pravṛttivijñānāni* therefore appropriates only its own specific physical basis. Something more is required to appropriate the whole of the physical body at once, and this, according to the argument, can only be the *ālaya*."

"2.The second argument is that without the *ālayavijñāna* there could not be simultaneous awarenesses of different things in one stream of consciousness. Since such simultaneous awareness happens there must be such a store-consciousness."

"3.Simultaneous awarenesses are required to explain how one can have a mental awareness of what one experiences visually, etc."

"4.Rather than the various kinds of sense-awareness mutually seeding each other, the store-consciousness acts as a receptacle for all seeds--for all future possibilities of action and sensation--even when these seeds have mutually incompatible qualities."

"5.Since each and every awareness involves at least four factors--a receptacle, a physical basis, a subjective aspect and an objective aspect, there must be a single locus where all are housed."

"6.To explain the fact that one experiences various things at once even when one is thinking correctly, meditating, etc., it is necessary to postulate a store-consciousness where all these experiences reside."

"7.Unless there is a store-consciousness the possibility of nonaware (*acitta*) consciousness could not arise, since one's stream would have left his body and he would be dead."

"8.Death, defined as the departure of consciousness from the body, requires there being a kind of consciousness which is contentless. The only consciousness that satisfies that description is the store-consciousness."

## BOOKS SIXTEEN AND SEVENTEEN: *Sopadhikā-* and *NIrupadhikā-Bhūmis*

The sections here dealt with are translated into Chinese by Hsüang-tsang (T.1579), by Paramārtha (T.1584), and in two other versions (T.1828-1829). Part of this section has been translated into German from the Tibetan by Lambert Schmithausen[479]. "T" references in the summary given here are to that German translation, and our summary is based on the summary Schmithausen provides on pp. 22-37, using Ronald Davidson's exposition of one section of it (from his dissertation, op. cit.).

### SECTION ONE

(T41-43) Question: Is one who has attained liberation with residues free from all defilements? Answer: Yes, he is.

Question: Is he free from all frustrations? Answer: He is free from all future frustrations, and from all accompanying mental frustrations, but he is not necessarily free from bodily existence

Question: If all perfected beings have attained control of their awareness, why do they remain embodied according to their appointed length of life (*āyuḥsaṃskāra*), since they are liberated and ready for *parinirvāṇa*? Answer: Some perfected beings are able to prolong their life, others are not and are liberated immediately.

(T43-53)[480] Objection: "If the senses of the Arhat remain unsuppressed and unchanged from the way they were before his enlightenment, just what is this revolution at the basis whereby there is no alteration in the basic pattern of causation? And if there is no revolution at the basis, then how does he possess the ability to turn back the defilements and enter the path when the states of "before" and "after" enlightenment are the same?

Answer: It is impossible to state definitely whether or not revolution at the basis is the same or different from the senses...Revolution at the basis is constituted by the purity of thusness; it is possessed of the lineage of thusness; it has the seed of thusness; finally, it has come into being from thusness. Since it is impossible to definitely state whether thusness is the same as or different from the senses, these conditions also apply to revolution at the basis. For example, suppose a butcher should kill a cow. Then, having taken out all the entrails, meat, bones, and ligaments, he should chop, beat, and slice them up. Finally, he wears the hide of the unfortunate beast as a garment. Now it should be understood that the cow is neither possessed nor nonpossessed of his hide. In the same way, the Arhat whose basis has been revolutionized has cut down all the fetters, the bonds, the proclivities, the afflictions, and the envelopers with the sword of wisdom. He cannot be said to have possession or nonpossession of the six senses which are like the hide of the cow for him.

Now the fundamental transformation which is associated with liberation with residues is connected with the six senses, while that associated with liberation without residues is disconnected from the senses. How is the latter possible? Since it is not developed from the causal nexus of the six senses but is generated through the cultivation on the path which has its objective support in thusness, it does not require either the presence or the absence of the senses. It cannot further transform or be spoiled. It should be understood to be existent, having the characteristics of unmanifoldness (*niṣprapañcatva*) and the purity of the factor element. Furthermore, both kinds of fundamental transformation can be said to exist because of its imperturbableness, and based on that imperturbableness there cannot be postulated either priority or posteriority. Certainly this *dharma* is not born, arisen, or stabilized. Like water it is clarity; like gold it is goodness; like the sky it is separated from clouds and haze; thus it may be said to exist. It is permanent since it is constituted by the purity of thusness. It is blissful but only by means of the satisfaction of the highest stage, not the bliss of feeling, since it is entirely separated from the defilements and their resultant suffering."

(T53-59) Revolution at the basis is eternal, since it constitutes purification of suchness. It is satisfying, since it goes beyond the frustrations born of the defilements, but not satisfying, since it involves feelings. One who attains liberation without remainder no longer experiences purposive distinctions.

Question: Isn't there a difference between a liberated Śrāvaka and a Tathāgata, since the former still has obstructions while the latter doesn't? Answer: There are two kinds of liberation with remainder: it may be either with or without obstructions. In the former all signs and depravities are completely blocked off and have ceased.

Question: So why isn't the perfected being (who is a Śrāvaka) a Buddha? Answer: Because he has not cultivated meditation and because a perfected being may not have the intention to elevate himself to liberation.

Question: Is remainderless liberation bodily or not? Answer: Neither, since to say it is not suggests it is something else, and in fact it is nothing!

Question: Does one in remainderless liberation attain mastery over his body, and is that his aim? Answer: Yes, he does attain mastery, but while the Tathāgata has that as his aim, the Śrāvaka doesn't.

A passage occurring later in this Volume has been translated by Davidson,[481] who calls it an "extraordinarily important section of the *Viniścayasaṃgrahaṇī*". Here are portions:

"It may be asked: what is the establishment of the reversal of the general defilements? Briefly, the underlying consciousness is the root of all of these defilements. In this way it is the root of the accomplishment of beings' conditioned existence since it generates the sensory organs, their physical bases, and the sensory consciousnesses. It is also the root of the accomplishment of the physical world since it generates that world...Thus it is the root of all the general difficulties."

"Now that underlying consciousness which has seized the seeds of the roots of goodness conducive to liberation and to penetration of the roots of goodness conducive to liberation and to penetration is not the cause of the origin of suffering...When these arise, the worldly roots of goodness, which are different from them, for the most part become clear light...(T)he underlying consciousness, which...is the root of all the general defilements, should be understood to be turned around by cultivating the wholesome qualities. Practice, for the sake of stabilizing the mind of the ordinary being or for the cultivation of the wholesome *dharmas*, is by means of mental application which focuses on the sensory consciousnesses. First one cultivates that for the sake of entering into the comprehension of the truths. If one does not obtain the eye which focuses on the truths which have not yet been seen, then he will be unable to comprehend the underlying consciousness which is the residence of all seeds...To comprehend the elemental realm of all elements is to comprehend also the underlying consciousness. All the various defilements are to been as collected there."..

"Since the underlying consciousness is the sphere for all that brings together the manifestations of the various formations, having collected, piled, assessed, and accumulated all of these into the underlying consciousness, because of service and meditation through the gnosis which focuses on thusness, the yogin transforms the fundament. Immediately after this fundamental transformation, it is said that the underlying consciousness is eliminated. Because it is eliminated, all the general defilements are also said to be eliminated. The fundament of that underlying consciousness is understood as changed by the antidotes and the enemies."

"The underlying consciousness is impermanent and appropriating. Fundamental transformation is permanent and nonappropriating, since it has been changed by the path focusing on thusness. The underlying consciousness is endowed with hindrances while fundamental transformation is permanently separated from them. The underlying consciousness is the cause for the operation of the defilements and not the cause of the operation of the path: fundamental transformation is the opposite of these and is the cause of stability but not of arising."

"Now immediately after the characteristic of eliminating the underlying consciousness, there is the elimination of both forms of appropriate and [the attainment of] the ability to place the body anywhere like a magical form. Since the cause of the arising of future suffering has been eliminated, there is the elimination of the appropriation [of a further body] arising in the future. Since there has been the elimination of all the general difficulties in this life, there is the elimination of all the subtle hindrances of the general defilements in this life. There being separation from all of these hindrances, there only remains those which are the conditions of life."

### VOLUME THREE: *Vastusaṃgrahaṇī*

### VOLUME FOUR: *Paryāyasaṃgraha*

### VOLUME FIVE: *Vivaraṇasaṃgrahaṇī*

Information on these three Volumes is to be found in Schmithausen, op. cit., by consulting the Index references to pages in the Chinese and Tibetan editions. Wayman renders a number of passages from these sections.[482]

## 167. ASAṄGA, **Āryadeśanāvikhyāpanaśāstra* and *Bhāṣya*[483]

"In the Chinese translation of Hsüan-tsang, the text consists of eleven chapters, which follow the *uddāna* found at the beginning of the verse text. The eleven chapter titles are: 1.*vastusaṃgraha*, 25 verses; 2.**viśuddhārthasaṃgraha*, 21 verses; 3.**kauśalasiddhi*, 25 verses; 4.**anityasiddhi*, 23 verses; 5.**duḥkhasiddhi*, 20 verses; 6.**śūnyatāsiddhi*, 23 verses; 7.**niḥsvabhāva*, 24 verses; 8.**abhisamayasiddhi*, 25 verses; 9.**yogasiddhi*, 4 verses; 10.**acintyasiddhi*, 10 verses; and 11.**viśiṣṭaviniścayasaṃgraha*, 47 verses."[484]

Section VII.19-21 of this text is translated in Davidson, op. cit., pp. 229-230.

## 168.ASAṄGA, *Abhidharmasamuccaya*

Summary by Paul J. Griffiths

*Editions*. A single incomplete manuscript of the Sanskrit original was discovered by Rahula Sankrtyayana in 1936 during his second journey into Tibet in search of Buddhist texts.[485] Thorough descriptions of this manuscript have been given by Prahlad Pradhan[486] and V.V.Gokhale[487] from which it emerges that about 40% of the text is preserved in this palm-leaf Magadhi manuscript. An edition of these fragments was published by V.V.Gokhale in 1947[488]. This is still the most careful and useful edition of the Sanskrit text. An edition/reconstruction of the entire text was published three years later by Prahlad Pradhan.[489] This was partly based on the sole manuscript, partly upon quotations from the text in Sthiramati's *Abhidharmasamuccayabhāṣya* and other texts extant in Sanskrit, but largely dependent upon reconstruction from the Tibetan and Chinese translations for the missing 60% of the text. Pradhan's edition/reconstruction is often helpful but must be used with extreme caution for those sections of the work which are not extant in Sanskrit.

*Translations*. (i) Tibetan: The entire work was translated into Tibetan by Jinamitra, Śīlendrabodhi and Ye Shes Sde (Tohoku #4049, D Sems-Tsam RI 44b1-120a7; Peking #5550, P Sems-Tsam LI 51a2-141b2). The translation is, as far as can be judged, largely faithful and accurate, and will be the primary reference in what follows for those sections which have no Sanskrit original. (ii) Chinese: There is a complete translation into Chinese by Hsuan Tsang (Taisho #1605, Vol. 31, 663a1-694b10) which, while it substantially follows the Sanskrit, contains some sections not present in the original. (iii) French: A complete French translation of this work, made by Walpola Rahula, was published in 1971[490] (174.2.8). This translation appears to be based exclusively upon Pradhan's edition/reconstruction, and therefore shares with that work some errors and dubious reconstructions.[491]

*Form and Influences*: The *Abhidharmasamuccaya* consists in a very concise series of definitions of key technical terms as these were understood by a leading scholastic thinker of Indian Yogācāra.

There are very few extended philosophical discussions since the text only occasionally extends itself beyond schematic outlines and brief definitions; a summary can be little more than a skeletal framework, a list of the headings and sub-headings by which Asaṅga organized his material. The major interest of the text lies in the fact that it is one of the few instances available to us of a Mahāyāna Abhidharma text; it therefore provides a systematic presentation of the major philosophical categories of Indian Buddhism as these were understood in one Mahāyāna school, one which gives some fascinating contrasts with this text's Theravāda and Vaibhāṣika analogues.[492]

The colophon of the Sanskrit manuscript of the *Abhidharmasamuccayabhāṣya* tells us that the *Abhidharmasamuccaya* consists of five chapters; the fivefold division is found also in the Tibetan translation, and will be used for this summary. The Chinese translation gives an eightfold division rather than a fivefold one, but this means only that Hsüan Tsang divides the first chapter of the Sanskrit text into four, which, added to the final four chapters, give eight chapters altogether. It is almost certain that the fivefold division was original.

The abbreviations used are: G = Gokhale's edition of the Sanskrit fragments; this reference is given first when the Sanskrit exists for the section under consideration.
P = the Peking edition of the Tibetan Tripiṭaka; reference are to folio and line of Volume LI of the Sems-Tsam section. D = the Derge edition of the Tibetan Tripiṭaka; references are to folio and line of Volume RI of the Sems-Tsam section. Pr = Pradhan's edition/reconstruction of the Sanskrit section. Not all sections will be commented on in the summary that follows, since the contents of the *Abhidharmasamuccaya* are often exhausted simply by giving a section-heading.

## A. COMPENDIUM OF CHARACTERISTICS

A1 Salutation (P51a3-5; D44b1-3; Pr1.2-5)

A2 Summary verse (P51a3-5; D44b1-3; Pr1.2-5)

A3 Enumeration of elements, aggregates and senses (P51a5-51b3; D44b3-7; Pr1.6-12)

A4 Why there are five aggregates, eighteen elements and twelve senses (P51b3-52a1; D44b7-45a5; Pr1.13-2.10)

A5 Characteristics of the aggregates, elements and senses (P52a1-53a1; D45a5-46a3; Pr2.11-3.11)

A6 Arrangement of aggregates, elements and senses (G15.1-19.22 (incomplete); P53a2-65a4; D46a3-56a5; Pr3.12-15.18)

A6.1 Arrangement of the aggregate of matter: classified according to the four great elements (earth, water, fire and air) and those things derived from them.

A6.2 Arrangement of the aggregate of feeling: classified according to the six senses which produce sensations (eye, ear, nose, tongue, body, mind), and according to the range of possible affective tones.

A6.3 Arrangement of the aggregate of conceptual identifications, classified according to the six senses from which they originate and according to the psycho-cosmic realms to which they pertain.

A6.4 Arrangement of the aggregate of conditioning factors: Asaṅga's definition of this group centers around the concept of volition and includes lists and definitions of the 53 Yogācārin accompanying factors, mental states ranging from volition itself to sustained thought. Special attention is given to the five kinds of view: the text briefly lists the five errors involved in belief in a self, and the twenty forms of wrong view concerning the self and the aggregates. There is also a complex subdivision of the concept of distraction according to its types.

Also included here are brief definitions of the twenty-three Yogācāra factors dissociated from awareness.

A6.5 Arrangement of the aggregate of consciousness. A more obvious Yogācāra thrust is apparent in the analysis of the aggregate of consciousness in which the key terms "awareness", "mind" and "consciousness" are distinguished and defined. Awareness is identified with the Yogācāra store-consciousness which holds all the karmic seeds produced by the actions of the other aggregates. The mind, in contrast, is identified with the supporting object of the store-consciousness, and is always more or less defiled, connected with incorrect ideas about personal identity. Finally, the term "consciousness" is identified simply as the standard six sense-consciousnesses.

A6.6 Arrangement of the elements: The list and definitions of the unconditioned elements, provided as part of the text's analysis of the element of factors, is greatly augmented when compared with those of the Vaibhāṣika and Theravāda schools. The Vaibhāṣikas recognize only three unconditioned elements and the Theravādins apply the term only to *nirvāṇa.* In this text we find eight unconditioned elements: (1) the true nature of good qualities, (2) the true nature of bad qualities, (3) the true nature of neutral qualities, (4) space, (5) uncalculated cessation, (6) calculated cessation, (7) the unchangeable, (8) the cessation of identification and perception.

A6.7 Arrangement of the senses. This section concludes with a discussion of some miscellaneous questions about the relationships between aggregates, elements and senses, and with quasi-etymological discussions of the meanings of the terms.

A7 Division of the aspects of the aggregates, elements and senses (G19.23-29.15 (incomplete); P64b4-82b5; D56a5-70a6; Pr15.19-32.20) In this lengthy section the aggregates, elements and senses are further analyzed using a threefold question-and-answer method. First, a category is stated - for example, the category of that which is dependently originated - and then three questions are asked: "What (among the aggregates, elements and senses) exists as dependently originated?" "How many (of the aggregates, elements and senses) exist as dependently originated?" "With what purpose does one examine (those aggregates, elements and senses) which exist as dependently originated?" The answer to the first question usually takes the form of a definition of the category under consideration; the answer to the second question consists of an enumeration of the aggregates, elements and senses which meet this definition; and the answer to the third question outlines the benefits gained from analyzing the aggregates, elements and senses by way of the category under consideration. Clearly, this is an open-ended method of analysis and the text applies some sixty categories in this manner before concluding that "the method of division using this approach is limitless." The list below outlines the categories applied in this manner.

A7.1 Real existence
A7.2 Existence as designation
A7.3 Nominal truth

A7.4 Highest truth

A7.5 Object of knowledge/distinct object of knowledge/transcendent object of knowledge

A7.6 Material/immaterial

A7.7 Visible/invisible

A7.8 Resistant/nonresistant

A7.9 Impure/pure

A7.10 Harmful/not harmful

A7.11 Fleshly/nonfleshly

A7.12 Based upon desire/based upon renunciation

A7.13 Conditioned/unconditioned

A7.14 Mundane/supramundane

A7.15 Originated/not originated: here twenty-four further subdivisions of ways of being originated are given.

A7.16 Grasper/grasped

A7.17 External/internal

A7.18 Defiled/undefiled

A7.19 Past/future/present

A7.20 Good/bad/neutral

A7.21 Connected with desire/connected with matter/connected with immateriality: here the text expounds the ten kinds of nonattachment.

A7.22 Training/nontraining/neither training nor nontraining

A7.23 To be abandoned by vision/to be abandoned by (meditative) development/not to be abandoned

A7.24 Dependently originated. The text here provides the usual twelvefold list of the elements comprising the cycle of dependent origination, and then further classifies them in a number of different ways, notable among them being the division into those factors which 'project' (*ākṣepāṅga* - namely, ignorance, conditioning factors and consciousness); those which are 'projected' (*ākṣiptāṅga* - namely name-and-form, the six senses, contact and sensation); those which 'produce' (*abhinirvartāṅga* - namely, thirst, grasping and becoming); and those which are 'produced' (*abhinivṛttāṅga*) - namely birth and old age/death.

The *Abhidharmasamuccaya* also provides here a version of the *catuṣkoṭi*, the tetralemma or four-cornered negation, relating to the twelvefold cycle of dependent origination: "(The cycle of dependent origination) does not arise from itself, nor from something else, nor from both (itself and something else), nor from its own action, from the action of something else, nor without cause."

A7.25 Condition: the text here applies the category of condition using the standard question-and-answer method; the standard fourfold system of conditions which is found also in the major *abhidharma* texts of other schools is also used here. The definition of the causal condition as "the storehouse consciousness and good proclivities" is interesting, showing once again the central causal importance of the storehouse consciousness in Yogācāra metaphysics.

A7.26 Homogeneous and homogeneous with that

A7.27 Grasped

A7.28 Senses

A7.29 Frustration that consists in frustration/frustration that consists in transformation/frustration that consists in being conditioned

A7.30 Possessing maturation

A7.31 Nourishment

A7.32 Inferior/superior

A7.33 Summary statement on the various methods of classifying the aggregates, elements and senses.

A8 An elevenfold analysis of the concept of inclusion (P82b5-84b2; D70a6-71b5; Pr32.5-33.16) Here we have an outline account of the different ways in which the aggregates, elements and senses can be grouped together.

A9 A sixfold analysis of the concept of connection (G29.16-26 (incomplete); P84b2-85b4; D71b5-72b4; Pr33.19-35.2)

A10 A threefold analysis of the concept of concomitance (G29.27-30; P85b4-86b3; D72b4-73a7; Pr35.2-22)

## B. ANALYSIS OF THE TRUTHS

B1 Four kinds of analysis (G30.17-18; P86b3-4; D73a7-73b1; Pr36.1-2) Here are listed the four kinds of analysis - of the truths, of doctrine, of obtaining and of debate - which will be analysed in the last four chapters of the text.

B2 The truth of frustration (G30.19-31.31 (incomplete); P86b4-

92b8; D83n1-78b1; Pr36.3-43.8) B2.1 The reference of the term "truth of frustration": The text states that the term refers to the entire universe, both animate and inanimate, insofar as this is produced by the defiled actions of sentient beings. The text gives in passing an outline of the standard Indian Buddhist cosmology, based upon the division between the sentient universe and insentient universe.

B2.2 Divisions of the concept of frustration: An eightfold division, a sixfold division, a threefold division, and, finally, a twofold division: suffering according to conventional truth and suffering according to highest truth.

B2.3 The defining characteristic of the concept of frustration: a list and definitions of the four general characteristics of frustration. The first is momentariness, which is further analyzed into twelve subdivisions, applying the concept to all aspects of the animate and inanimate world. The second is frustration itself. The third is emptiness, which is expounded in a manner quite different from that of the Madhyamaka thinkers: it is defined as perceiving the nonexistence of a particular thing in a particular location. Further, to perceive in this way is to perceive things as they really are. The example given of perceiving the nonexistence of a particular thing in a particular location is perceiving the nonexistence of a permanent self among the aggregates, elements and senses. Further, Asaṅga distinguishes three kinds of emptiness which relate to the three essential natures which are so central to Yogācāra thought. The three are: emptiness of essential nature, which is equated with constructed nature; emptiness which consists in nonexistence in any particular manner, which is equated with dependent existence; and finally, natural emptiness, which is equated with perfected nature. The fourth general characteristic of frustration is that of non-self.

B2.4 The nature of impermanence and momentariness

B2.5 The constituents of matter

B2.6 An eightfold classification of frustrations relating to various classes of beings who are born in different psycho-cosmic spheres.

B2.7 Death considered as an example of frustration: different types of death relating to various classes of individual are distinguished.

B3 The truth of origin (G32.1-9 (incomplete); P92b8-107b4; D78b1-90b2; Pr43.10-62.3)

B3.1 Definitions of the truth of origin. This consists in defilements and action dominated by passion, and is centrally concerned with the operation of thirst, the passionate and greedy desire for specific things.

B3.2 Defilements explained under ten headings:

B3.2.1 Enumeration: the standard six- and tenfold enumerations of defilement.

B3.2.2 Defining characteristic: defilement is defined as anything which disturbs the tranquillity of body or mind.

B3.2.3 Arising: defilements arise when the latent tendencies for them to do so are present, and an object with the capacity to engender them is at hand.

B3.2.4 Object: this section relates to the objects of specific defilements to the psycho-cosmic spheres in which practitioners find themselves.

B3.2.5 Connection; enumerates the possible combinations of different defilements.

B3.2.6 Synonyms: a lengthy exposition of the twenty-four major synonyms of the term "*kleśa*" and their different connotations.

B3.2.7 Obstructing activity; enumerates the obstructive functions of specific defilements.

B3.2.8 Realm: enumerates the psycho-cosmic realms in which each of the six (or ten) defilements operates.

B3.2.9 Group: divides the defilements into those which can be abandoned by vision and those which can be abandoned by meditative cultivation.

B3.2.10 Abandonment: discussion of the three kinds of abandonment of the defilements, that by analysis, by attention and by obtaining.

B3.3 Action dominated by defilement. The detailed analysis of defilements is then followed by an equally detailed analysis of action dominated by defilement and also of the types of action and their effects in general. There is no easily discernible scheme of organisation to this section: the treatment of karma begins with the standard definition of action as consisting in volition and that which occurs subsequent to volition, and then passes into a long series of *sūtra* quotations mentioning different classifications of action.

B4 The truth of cessation (P107b4-109b8; D90b2-92b1; Pr62.5-65.9) A brief analysis of the truth of cessation, considering it from twelve perspectives:

B4.1 According to defining characteristic,
B4.2 According to profundity,
B4.3 According to convention,
B4.4 According to ultimacy,
B4.5 According to incompleteness,
B4.6 According to completeness,
B4.7 According to absence of ornament,
B4.8 According to possession of ornament,
B4.9 According to possession of residue,
B4.10 According to absence of residue,
B4.11 According to supreme state,
B4.12 According to synonyms: this last section is by far the longest and contains a systematic analysis of all the major synonyms of "cessation" (*nirodha*), together with significant associated concepts.

B5 The truth of path (G32.10-34.20 (incomplete); P109b8-119b8; D92b1-100b7; Pr65.11-77.21) The *Abhidharmasamuccaya* uses the standard fivefold division of the path in order to expound the fourth truth.

B5.1 Definition and subdivisions of the path.

B5.2 The path of preparation, comprising the practice of morality, and with some preliminary meditative practises.

B5.3 The path of application, which comprises further preliminary meditational practices (especially the aids to penetration) and leads the practitioner to the highest stage of the mundane path.

B5.4 The path of vision, defined in characteristically Yogācāra terms as consisting in the realization of the similarity of subject and object, and as a knowledge which perceives objects without using conventional designations. The standard framework of eight patiences and eight knowledges is used to subdivide the path of vision.

B5.5 The path of cultivation:

B5.5.1 The mundane path of cultivation, defined

as the four mundane meditations and the four formless states. Each of these meditative states is in turn given detailed analysis. This part of the path has essentially to do with the development of altered states of consciousness of various kinds, and is seen as a preparation for the transcendent path.

B5.5.2 The transcendent path of cultivation, defined as the eight kinds of knowledge pertaining to the four truths (two for each truth) and the related concentrative states up to the third of the four immaterial states. Here, and in the following subdivisions of the path of cultivation, the text describes the re-presentation to the mind of the practitioner of the knowledge gained during the practice of the path of vision.

B5.5.3 The weak, powerful and intermediate paths, defined according to the types of passion that are abandoned by relative intensities of practice.

B5.5.4 The paths of application, immediate succession, liberation and distinction; further subdivisions of the path of cultivation.

B5.5.5 The methods of cultivating the path and the four antidotes.

B5.5.6 An elevenfold division of the path, including the thirty-seven qualities which aid enlightenment, each of which is given detailed analysis of its own.

B5.6 The final path, the conclusion of the meditative path, consisting essentially in the removal of all negative qualities in the mind of the practitioner and the attainment of final enlightenment.

B5.6.1 The twenty-four types of depravity removed by the final path.

B5.6.2 The concentration which is like a thunderbolt: an unshakeable condition of mental stability resulting from the destruction of negative mental qualities.

B5.6.3 The continuous revolution at the basis, a basic alteration in the cognitive and perceptual structures of the practitioner as a result of the practice of the path.

B5.6.4 The knowledge of destruction and the knowledge of nonarising, referring to the knowledge on the part of the practitioner that the cycle of karmic cause and effect has been broken.

B5.6.5 The qualities of the adept: a listing of the

ten qualities of the adept who has practised the path to its conclusion.

B5.7 Summary statement of the four modes of the path and the sixteen aspects of the four truths which comprise the framework of the entire path.

## C.ANALYSIS OF DHARMA[1]

C1 Divisions of the canonical literature (P119b8-121a5; D100b7-102a3; Pr78.1-80.4) The twelve types of canonical literature are set forth, defined, and related to the other standard three- and twofold divisions of the canon - into *sūtra, vinaya* and *abhidharma,* and into the scriptures belonging to the disciples and those belonging to the Bodhisattvas.

C2 *Dharma* considered as the object of mental activity (P121a6-122a6; D102a4-103a3; Pr80.4-81.14). A list of, and definitions of, a number of categories which illustrate and explain the ways in which *dharma,* and the texts which enshrine it, can become the object of the practitioner's thought:

C2.1 As an object capable of being pervaded,

C2.2 As an object productive of purification of conduct,

C2.3 As an object productive of skill, especially in the understanding and handling of key Buddhist doctrinal concepts,

C2.4 As an object productive of purification of passion.

C3 Reasons, methods and results of studying *dharma* (G34.21-29 (incomplete); P121a6-123b6; D103a3-104a7; Pr81.15-83.130).

C3.1 Four reasons for studying *dharma*

C3.2 Four methods of studying *dharma*

C3.3 Four types of exact knowledge of *dharma*

---

1.There is a substantial ambiguity throughout this section - as indeed throughout so much of Buddhist philosophical literature - in the meaning of the term "*dharma*". Most often it refers here to the texts through which the doctrine is expressed; but sometimes it refers to the doctrine as abstracted from any given text, and sometimes even to the nature of things, a category which abolishes the fact/value distinction. I have therefore left the term untranslated throughout the summary of this section.

C3.4 Five stages of spiritual practice belonging to one who studies *dharma* in a concentrated manner:

C3.4.1 *Dharma* considered as an aid. Here the stress is on intellectual understanding of *dharma* considered as textually-expressed doctrine.

C3.4.2 *Dharma* considered as a basis for application. Here the practitioner applies his faculty of attention to the intellectual understanding gained in the preceding stage.

C3.4.3 *Dharma* considered as a mirror. Here the practitioner attains a stage of concentration which, while based on intellectual understanding, reflects it signlessly.

C3.4.4 *Dharma* considered as radiance, the knowledge attained by the practitioner when he has passed beyond the duality of subject and object. Here everything is considered as awareness, a characteristic Yogācāra emphasis.

C3.4.5 *Dharma* considered as basis: the transformation of the basis.

C4 on the meaning of *vaipulya* (G35.1-4; P123b6-124a1; D104a7-104b2; Pr83.14-20). The exact sense of the term *vaipulya* remains obscure. It may simply be an inclusive term for all Buddhist scriptures, including the Mahāyāna *sūtras*. The *Abhidharmasamuccaya* devotes a great deal of discussion to it, and to the benefits of studying the literature denoted by it. As part of this discussion there is a long analysis of the scope and goals of the practice of the perfections.

C5 Twenty-eight wrong views of Mahāyāna doctrine (G35.5-14; P124a1-124b1; D104b2-105a2; Pr83.20-84.10)

C6 The implications and indirect intentions of doctrinal formulae (G35.15-24; P124b2-125a1; D195a2-7; Pr84.11-85.2). A list of the four types of indirect intention and the four types of purport, applying the hermeneutical models outlined therein to some specific doctrinal formulae. The general idea is that some doctrinal formulae contain indirect intentions and purport which are not *prima facie* obvious. These categories are an attempt to systematically describe some of the methods by which such purport and indirect intentions can be arrived at.

C7 Criteria for recognizing competence in meditative practice related to *dharma* (G35.25-32; P125a1-6; D105a7-105b3; Pr85.3-12)

## D. ANALYSIS OF OBTAINING

D1 Classification of individuals (G36.1-37.4 (incomplete); P125a36-130b8; D105b3-110b2; Pr 85.16-92.19). An exhaustive listing of the types of person to be found in the world.

D1.1 Sevenfold divsion according to conduct: those whose conduct is dominated by attachment, hatred, delusion, pride, conceptual thought, equilibrium, and dull passion.

D1.2 Threefold division according to deliverance. Those who belong to the disciples' vehicle, the self-enlighteneds' vehicle, and the great vehicle. Here we find the standard Mahāyāna polemic against those disciples who aim at only their own enlightenment and not that of all beings.

D1.3 Threefold division according to receptacle: those whose future births are not yet defined by their accumulation of spiritual attainments, those for whom there is only a limited number of births to come, and those who will have no more births.

D1.4 Twofold division according to application: those who follow confidence - which means that they rely on doctrine as taught by others - and those who follow doctrine, which means that they rely on doctrine as discovered by themselves.

D1.5 Twenty-sevenfold division according to result, ranging from one who is devoted to the practice of confidence to the noble person whose nature is unshakeable.

D1.6 Sixfold division according to realm: the ordinary man, the person undergoing training, the person beyond training, the Bodhisattva, the liberated-for-himself and the *tathāgata* - all discussed according to the psycho-cosmic realms they inhabit.

D1.7 Fivefold division according to career: five different types of Bodhisattva.

D2 Classification of realization (G37.5-38.21 (incomplete); P130b88-138a7; D110b2-117a6; Pr92.20-102.15). A systematic classification of the different types of realization.

D2.1 The ten kinds of realization: of doctrine, of meaning, of reality, subsequent realization, of the triple gem, of the absence of wandering, final realization, of disciples, of self-enlightened Buddhas, and of Bodhisattvas.

D2.2 The eleven differences between the realization of disciples and the Bodhisattvas and the ten differences between the result of their respective practices.

D2.3 The nineteen special qualities and their effects:

D2.3.1 Four boundless things: friendship, compassion, joy, equanimity, by means of which the practitioner rejects enmity, cultivates pity, amasses merit, and helps beings towards salvation.

D2.3.2 Eight liberations: a series of eight altered states of consciousness culminating in the complete cessation of conceptualization and sensation, by means of which the practitioner is able to dwell in supreme tranquillity.

D2.3.3 Eight spheres of mastery. Another series of eight altered states, by means of which the practitioner gains mastery over the methods learned and practised in the liberations.

D2.3.4 Ten all-inclusive senses, a series of ten meditational methods by way of which the practitioner perfects the liberations.

D2.3.5 Nonpassion, a state of peace in which the arising of passions is guarded against.

D2.3.6 Vow-knowledge, by means of which the practitioner learns to explain past, present and future and becomes highly esteemed in the world.

D2.3.7 Four discriminations relating to doctrine, meaning, grammar, and discourse, by means of which the practitioner is enabled to satisfy the minds of beings with teaching.

D2.3.8 Six higher faculties consisting in supernatural power, magical vision, telepathy, memory of previous births, knowledge of the birth and death of others, and knowledge of the destruction of passions. The practitioner uses these magical powers to attract others to an understanding of Buddhist doctrine.

D2.3.9 Major and minor characteristics: the distinguishing physical characteristics which belong to a Buddha by means of which he pleases beings.

D2.3.10 Four purities, consisting in purity of basis, of object, of mind and of knowledge, by mastery over which the practitioner is able to decide his future fate and can become a Buddha.

D2.3.11 Ten powers, not listed fully.

D2.3.12 Four confidences: concerning enlightenment, destruction of passions, hindrances and the path leading to deliverance. By means of these the practitioner overcomes heretics who disagree with him.

D2.3.13 Three foundations of mindfulness: not listed fully in this text. By means of these the practitioner attracts to himself a retinue.

D2.3.14 Three things which need not be guarded against, not fully listed in this text. By means of these the practitioner constantly exhorts and teaches the multitude.

D2.3.15 Nonloss: this consists in perfect memory, by means of which the practitioner is enabled to neither forget nor neglect the duties of a Buddha.

D2.3.16 Destruction of proclivities, the complete destruction in the past of a Buddha of all karmic effect, by means of which all his actions appear to others completely free of defilement.

D2.3.17 Great compassion, by means of which the practitioner surveys the world six times in each day and night.

D2.3.18 Eighteen qualities unique to a Buddha, not fully listed in this text. By means of these the practitioner, after becoming a Buddha, dominates all disciples and individual Buddhas.

D2.3.19 Knowledge of all aspects: omniscience, by means of which the doubts of all beings are destroyed.

D2.4 The progress of a Bodhisattva: Here the *Abhidharmasamuccaya* deals with some miscellaneous questions concerning the Bodhisattva's progress in spiritual practice, the differences between his practice and that of the disciples, and his development of skill in meditation.

D2.4.1 Skill in meditation concerning six kinds of knowables: error, the basis of error, the basis of the absence of error, error-and-non-error, non-error and the outflow of non-error.

D2.4.2 Skill in meditation concerning spiritual method of four kinds, consisting in skill in the methods of saving beings, in the development of Buddha-qualities, in the rapid attainment of superknowledge, and in the noninterruption of the path.

D2.4.3 Skill in meditation concerning discrimination of the unreal (*abhūtavikalpa*):[493] of ten kinds, basic discrimination, discrimination of an image, discrimination of the appearance of an image, discrimination of the transformation of an image, discrimination of the transformation of the appearance of an image, discrimination caused by someone else, incorrect discrimination, correct discrimination, discrimination consisting in attachment (to views), distracted discrimination. This last category is itself divided into ten subtypes. These categories are meant to describe the details of the mental process by which, in Yogācāra thought, the impression of an external world, a *lebenswelt*, is constructed.

D2.4.4 Skill in meditation concerning nondiscrimination: of three kinds, absence of discrimination consisting in contentment, in absence of error, and in absence of intellectual elaboration.

## E. ANALYSIS OF DEBATE

This section has to do with what are essentially hermeneutical questions: the proper principles to be used in the interpretation of texts and the appropriate methods to be used in deciding between opposed philosophical views.

E1 Definition and subdivisions (P138a8-138b1; D117a6-7; Pr102.18-20)

E2 Analysis of meaing (P138b1-138b6; D117a7-117b5; Pr102.21-103.8) in a sixfold division:

E2.1 The meaning of essential nature which has to do with the three natures of Yogācāra ontological theory.

E2.2 The meaning of cause, concerning the causes of arising, continuity, and accomplishment.

E2.3 The meaning of result, concerning the standard five results: of maturation, of outflow, of dominating result, of human action, of separation.

E2.4 The meaning of action, concerning the five actions of perception, of operation, of intention, of transformation, of obtaining.

E2.5 The meaning of bond, concerning the five types of union: collective, consequent, conjoined, circumstantial, transforming.

E2.6 The meaning of function, concerning five functions: that of characteristics, of position, of error, of non-error, of division.

E3 Analysis of explanation (P138b6-139a3; D117b5-118a1;

Pr103.9-15). The programmatic definition here is "that by means of which one explains the *sūtras*", thus a discussion of hermeneutical philosophy and commentarial methods.

E3.1 Sixfold division of the analysis of explanation without explaining the meanings of the terms used: the subject to be comprehended, the meaning to be comprehended, the approach to comprehension, the essential nature of comprehension, the result of comprehension, and the experience of that result.

E3.2 A fourteenfold listing of the means by which the explanation (of texts) can properly be achieved, essentially an explanation of commentarial methods. Once again, the terms are given no explanation.

E3.2.1 The grouping of explanation
E3.2.2 The grouping of subjects
E3.2.3 Major and minor factors
E3.2.4 Successive order
E3.2.5 Rejecting
E3.2.6 Transforming the letters
E3.2.7 Elimination and nonelimination
E3.2.8 Classification of persons
E3.2.9 Classification of divisions
E3.2.10 Methods
E3.2.11 Comprehension, etc.
E3.2.12 Force and gentleness
E3.2.13 Abstraction
E3.2.14 Endeavor

E4 Analysis of analytical demonstration (P139a3-4; D118a1-2; Pr103.16-18). Brief exposition of the method of commenting upon a text by relating its component parts one to another.

E5 Analysis of questions (P139a4-6; D118a2-4; Pr103.19-104.2). This method has to do with deciding issues of truth and falsity by refutation, proof, analysis, or explication.

E6 Analysis of grouping (P139a6-139b1; D118a4-6; Pr104.3-7). Ten topics according to which issues can be grouped, again without defining the terms used:

E6.1 According to the accomplishment of the task in hand
E6.2 According to entry (into the three vehicles)
E6.3 According to resolve
E6.4 According to reason

E6.5 According to debate
E6.6 According to penetration
E6.7 According to purity
E6.8 According to the diverse stages of endeavor
E6.9 According to effort and spontaneity
E6.10 According to the achievement of all goals.

E7 Analysis of argument (P139b1-141a1; D118a6-120a5; Pr104.7-106.18). A discussion of the possible types of argument, a discussion which at times clearly reflects public debate situations and at other times shades over into a comparatively undeveloped logical system. Here also the terms used are scarcely discussed.

E7.1 Argument: of six kinds, including argument itself, rumor, debate, reproach, approval, and instruction.

E7.2 Public argument: the context here is that of public debate; the text enumerates some of the settings in which such debates could occur.

E7.3 Basis of argument. In this section we are provided a brief summary of the technical terminology of logic current at the time.

E7.3.1 The object of proof, the theory to be established. The object of proof is divided into two kinds, the essential and specific.

E7.3.2 The method of proof is divided into eight kinds: thesis, reason, example, application, conclusion, direct perception, inference, and authoritative tradition. The first five are the major parts of a valid inferential schema; the latter three are the standard instruments of knowledge.

E7.4 Ornament of argument: this refers to a person skilled in the use of correct logic who argues well in public.

E7.5 Defeat in argument. Loss of an argument is said to occur in three ways: first, by abandoning the argument as a result of recognising the faults in one's own argument and the good qualities in one's opponent's; second, by an inappropriate diversion from the subject at hand; and third, by making a logical error.

E7.6 Escape from an argument: on the grounds of the opponent's incompetence, the inappropriateness of the audience or knowledge of one's own incapacity.

E7.7 Qualities greatly useful for argument, of which there are essentially three. First, thorough knowledge of one's own doctrine and that of one's adversaries; second, self-confidence in one's ability to perform in public; third, readiness with speech, the ability to think on one's feet. At this point the text also enumerates twelve reasons why, according to the *Mahāyānābhidharmasūtra*, a Bodhisattva possessed of all appropriate good qualities is no longer able to undertake debate with opponents. These twelve reasons consist essentially in the view that public debate based on the rules of logic - one of the major methods by which doctrinal disputes appear to have been carried on in Buddhist India - is not necessarily conducive either to finding truth or to attaining salvation, and may in fact be detrimental to both goals.

E8 Analysis of indirect intention (P141a1-141a8; D120a5-120b4; Pr106.18-107.14). An indirect intention is one obscured by the literal sense of the words expressing it, one which therefore requires the application of some more-or-less well defined hermeneutical method in order to make it manifest. The text quotes a number of *sūtra* extracts to illustrate this point, texts which are *prima facie* contrary to some fundamental Buddhist tenet, but which can be made to accord with it by using the appropriate interpretive method.

E9 The meaning of the title "*Abhidharmasamuccaya*" (P141a8-141b1; D120b4-6; Pr107.15-17). The work concludes thus: "Why is this work called '*Abhidharmasamuccaya*'? Because it is a collection made with comprehension; because it is a complete collection; because it is a perfect collection."

## 169.ASAṄGA, *Triśatikāyāḥ Prajñāpāramitā Kārikāsaptati*

The attribution of this commentary on the *Vajracchedikā* to Asaṅga is rather debatable; it is attributed to him by some subcommentators, to Vasubandhu by others. A commentary (see 191 below) on it is attributed to Vasubandhu. With no particular conviction, we shall treat the text here and the commentary under Vasubandhu below. See the introductory comments by Tucci on his edition/translation (our E and T) for speculation on these matters. Tucci himself seems unsure, though his last word (p. 18) decides in favor of Vasubandhu's authorship of both text and commentary. Conze,[494] on the other hand, has no doubt as to both being Asaṅga's, considering this commentary "a real masterpiece" and that it "shows how the different chapters (of the *Vajracchedikā*) are linked to one another".

The "*-saptati*", "seven", of the title apparently derives from the commentator Vasubandhu's division of the subject-matter covered in this text into seven topics (Tucci, p. 24).

The edition and translation that we use is the work of Giuseppe Tucci (*Minor Buddhist Texts*, Part I (Roma 1956; Japan 1978; Delhi 1986). The edition ("E") occupies pages 1-92; the translation ("T") pages 93-128. There is also an edition of the Sanskrit text.[495] Tucci uses a Sanskrit text of Nepalese origin that he says is rather the worse for wear, as well as a Chinese translation (T.1514) by I Ching.

1.(E54; T93)) The highest favor should be considered to the body and what it involves. The highest gratification will accrue should one neither give up what has been acquired nor what is yet to be acquired.

2.(E54; T93) The intention of helping others, resting in one's mind, is filled with positive characteristics. It is extensive, supreme, nonerroneous.

3.(E55; T94) The six perfections involve giving of good, fearlessness, and the *dharma*. This path, whether by one, two or three of these, is unlimited.

4.(E55; T94-95) No attachment to the existence of self, to reward, or to karmic maturation. Two things are to be avoided: failure to be generous and generosity wrongly motivated.

5.(E56; T95) Controlling awareness by keeping it free from the assumptions of signs of things and eliminating doubts.

6.(E56; T95-96) If it is supposed that success is something conditioned, it must be realized that it does not consist in acquiring any marks; rather, success is becoming a *tathāgata*, because of its being different from the three characteristic marks, being in fact the absence of these.

7.(E57; T96) The teaching of something deep, along with that of cause and effect involved in it, even in this cosmic age is not fruitless, since even now there are Bodhisattvas who have the three marks.

8.(E57; T97) Because of their devoted training and because of their attainment of goodness, those (Bodhisattvas) other than the

Buddha follow the precepts and possess merit.

9.(E58; T97) Since they have cut off any conceptual identification with persons or factors they possess wisdom. These identifications are of eight kinds because their objects are eight.

10.(E58; T97) There are four identifications of self--as stream of consciousness from an earlier existence, as something occurring now, as something living, and as something that has passed away.

11.(E59; T98) Identifications of factors are also four--because all factors don't exist, because absence exists, because there is nothing to be spoken about, and because we speak as if there were something to be spoken about.

12.(E59; T98-99) Identification of what actually exists occurs because of resolve, because of serenity, by grasping what is not spoken, and by grasping what is correctly indicated.

13.(E60; T99) These qualities are not inferred from their results, but the Buddhas identify their possessors' (the Bodhisattvas') vows and knowledge. This refutes those who ascribe such (to themselves) through desire for profit and honor.

14.(E60; T99) Attainment of *dharma* cannot be by resting in it nor by not conforming to it; like a raft it should be rejected (when one reaches the other shore). This is believed to be the proper interpretation of *dharma*.

15.(E61; T100) Neither Buddha nor *dharma* are sought as magical beings. Rather, what is taught is that (factors) are not grasped in either of two ways and are thus inexpressible, since it is not within the scope of definition.

16.(E61; T100-101) The grasping and teaching of that (*dharma*) is not useless, because it leads to acquisition of merit, merit because it is not the ground of enlightenment and because both (grasping and teaching) are enlightening.

17.(E62; T101) Merit is the summit, since it is the cause of attaining what is essential, because it leads to birth in another body, and because of the uniqueness of a Buddha's factors.

18.(E62; T102) Because it cannot be grasped it can't be spoken of, since one's own (karmic) fruits cannot be grasped. Because he is free from both obstructions, in Subhūti both are absent.

19.(E63; T102) (Śākyamuni) did not receive any instruction by words from the Buddha Dīpaṃkara. That shows that in his realization nothing was grasped or spoken of.

20.(E63; T102-103) One can't partake in the Buddha's field, since it is merely the outcome of the Buddha's awareness. Because of its unseparated and unique nature its arrangement is thought to be nonarrangement.

21.(E64; T103) Just as Sumeru cannot grasp itself as King of the mountains, so no Buddha can grasp himself as experiencing, since he is without contaminants and subject to conditions.

23-25.(E65-66; T104-106) The merit of *dharma* stands out from other merits because it makes two things worthy, because of the greatness of its outcome, because it is not the cause of defilements, because of the preferable frustrations that result from it, because its purposes are difficult to realize and are the highest purposes, because it is profound and deep, because it is superior to other *sūtras*, because its connections are great and pure.

26-27.(E66-67; T106-107) The difficult practice of the path is good because its merits are immeasurable. There is no frustration because of the absence of identifications of self or malice, because it is accompanied by satisfaction since, involving compassion, it does not involve frustration as its result.

28.(E67; T107) Because of this it takes strong effort to maintain the abandonment of awareness through the perfection of patience.

29.(E68; T108) Proper practice should be understood as the cause of the purposes of beings, but it should not be concluded that beings must therefore be admitted to be actual entities.

30.(E68; T108) A supposed actual entity is only the name of some aggregates. Through the departure of such identifications from the conquering one there is absence of them for the Buddhas who possess the vision of reality.

31.(E69; T109) The path does not depend on a result, but is nevertheless the cause of a result, because Buddhas tell the truth and that truth is fourfold.

32.(E69; T109) The thesis, the teachings of Hīnayāna, the teachings of Mahāyāna, and the teaching of all the grammatical forms.

33.(E70; T109-110) Since it is not about anything and is in agreement, the teaching is neither true nor false. The teaching behaves as an antidote to taking words in their literal meaning.

34.(E70; T110)[496] Though suchness is always everywhere, it cannot be realized by those who, on account of ignorance, have their mind reposing somewhere, but, on the contrary, it is realized by another whose mind, on account of knowledge, reposes nowhere.

35.(E71; T110) Ignorance is like darkness, while knowledge is like light. The antidote and its opposite respectively lead to realization and its opposite.

36.(E71; T110) Now it will be explained what kind of *dharma* is derived from which sort of practice and what are its karmic effects.

37.(E72; T111) The *dharma* is of three kinds: with respect to its phrasing, respecting understanding of it, and relating to spreading the word. Regarding its meaning, it is understood by oneself or another through hearing it and meditating on it.

38.(E72; T111) This behavior causes the spiritual ripeness of other creatures. So one kind of merit is superior to the other by the greatness of its actuality as well as by the longer time it takes.

39-41.(E73-74; T111-112) The following are the results of performance of *dharma*: not being accessible, isolation, being resorted to by great people, the difficulty of being understood, access to the highest realm, understanding the supreme *dharma*, ability to purify the place where the *dharma* was taught, the ability to clear away abstractions, the swift realization of the higher faculties, the ripeness of the accomplishments in various worlds.

42.(E74; T112-113) Thinking one is a Bodhisattva is called an obstruction to awareness. Awareness is unlocated.

44.(E75; T114) Factors are without any essential nature.

45.(E76; T114) By his having a body of factors (*dharmakāya*) the Buddha is like a person.

46.(E76; T114) This body is also a "great" body because of its great qualities. But the Buddha is said to be bodiless because he has no body.

47.(E77; T115) Wrong views include bad ideas about the ground of all factors, the notion that we can cause beings to be liberated, and the purification of fields.

48.(E77; T115) One who considers the factors of beings and Bodhisattvas as without self, whether he is noble or not, should be considered wise.

49.(E78; T115) Even though no factors are experienced by him, that doesn't mean the Buddha has no eyes, for his vision is fivefold and it sees erroneous things.

50.(E78; T115) Because those various erroneous manifestations are excluded from the establishment of mindfulness they are bound to be without basis--thus they are called erroneous.

51.(E79; T116) There is no erroneousness in merit, inasmuch as merit should be realized as the basis of knowledge. So an example of this sign of merit is given (in the *Vajracchedikāsūtra*).

52-53.(E79-80; T117) The fulfilment of the body of factors is not said to consist in secondary phrasing, nor should the accomplishment of one's marks be thought to be the absence of a body. But both these accomplishments, since they are not different from one's body of factors itself, should not be considered different from the *tathāgata* himself.

54.(E80; T117-118) Like the Buddha, his teaching can't be held to exist, since the teaching, not being different from a body of factors, has no essential nature of its own.

55.(E81; T118) It is not that there are none who have faith in the depth of what is taught or their teacher. They are not beings, nor are they nonbeings--but they are the nobles who are not (yet?) noble.

56-57.(E81-82; T119) In the body of factors there is no growth--there is a natural sameness of purity. Because no factor is defiled or involves a lower method, no factor is good.

58.(E82; T120) And so the teaching, being neutral, should not be thought of as unattainable. Therefore only this jewel of the *dharma* is superior to any other.

60.(E83; T120-121) Since beings are the same as the ground of all factors, none are liberated by the victorious ones, since factors along with names are not outside that ground.

61.(E84; T121) Belief in their being factors is like the fault of belief in a self. If someone who is to be liberated is admitted this should be considered to be the admission of something inadmissible.

62.(E84; T121-122) The *tathāgata* is not to be inferred from a material body since he is only a body of factors. A universal ruler cannot be considered a *tathāgata*.

63.(E85; T122) The body of factors is not gotten by the maturation of characteristic marks, for the method is different.

64.(E85; T122) Ordinary folk do not know the Buddha, since they only experience his form and hear his voice. The body of factors, which is suchness, goes beyond the field of consciousness.

65.(E86; T122-123) By following the Buddhist path, involving the belief that there are no real factors, etc., merit is not thereby destroyed, because one has arrived at the pure view.

66.(E86; T123) Since that merit does not mature into any result, acceptance of it does not lead to wrong grasping of it.

67-68.(E87; T123) The magical result of that merit is the action that Buddhas automatically accomplish. Their movement, etc. is accomplished by magical means, for a Buddha is always motionless. Their location in the ground of all factors is held to be neither identity with nor difference from it.

69.(E88; T124) The example of reducing the universe into atomic dust suggests the same point, showing how defilements should be destroyed in the way things are reduced to dust.

70.(E88; T124) The fact that matter is not caused by accumulation shows that there is not ultimate unity, and the fact that collectivity occurs shows that there is not ultimate diversity.

71.(E89; T125) Because the ordinary person only speaks in ordinary ways he understands all this in a different way. Attainment of enlightenment does not come through the absence of selves and factors, since both do not exist.

72.(E89; T125) Therefore both such a view and its rejection involve the construction of something pointless and nonexistent. Both are a subtle covering that is destroyed by knowledge.

73.(E90; T126) That covering should be eliminated by the twofold knowledge and by meditation on it.

74.(E90; T126) *Tathāgatas* do not say "I am a magical being"--so, since they do not speak of a self their teaching is correct.

75.(E91; T126-127) The *tathāgatas'* liberation is produced neither by conditions nor by something else. This can be understood by considering correct awareness in nine ways:

76.(E91; T127-128) As regards vision, signs, consciousness, support, body, experiences, what is past, what is present and what is future.

77.(E92; T128) Through understanding the activity of characterized experiences one obtains mastery over conditioning factors.

## 170. ASANGA, *Mahāyānasaṃgraha*

The Sanskrit text of this work is lost. There are Chinese translations by Buddhaśānta (T.1592), Paramārtha (T.1593), Dharmagupta (T.1596) and Hsüan-tsang (T.1594), as well as a Tibetan translation by Jinamitra, Śīlendrabodhi and Ye-śes-sde. Hsüan-tsang's and the Tibetan translation are provided in Étienne Lamotte,[497] whose French translation of Hsüan-tsang's version consitutes our "T". Lamotte has also translated the second Chapter into French,[498] indicated here as "T2".

Asaṅga's authorship of this work has been questioned.[499] It is one of the works ascribed to Maitreya, who seems to have been a fictional person. It is a seminal work in the development of Yogācāra philosophy. Since the philosophical weight of the work lies, however, in its first three Chapters, they are the only ones which will be summarized here. We provide translations of the titles of the remaining Chapters.[500]

### Summary by Stefan Anacker

### Introduction

1-2.(E1-6) The speech of the Buddha is marked by ten special qualities: (1) the support of that which can be known, (2) the characteristic marks of that which can be known, (3) entry into the characteristic marks of that which can be known, (4) the cause and effect of this entry, (5) the diverse cultivations involved in the cause and effect of this entry, (6) the higher virtue involved in these practices, (7) the higher awareness involved in these practices, (8) the higher wisdom involved in these practices, (9) the abandoning of adverse factors which is the result of these practices, (10) the knowledge which is the result of these practices.

3.(E7-9) The support of what can be known is the storehouse consciousness. The characteristics of what can be known are the three essential natures, viz., the constructed, dependent, and perfected. Entry into the characteristics of what can be known is the state of consciousness-only (*vijñaptimātratā*). The cause and effect of this entry comprises the six perfections. The diverse cultivations involved in the cause and effect of this entry are the ten stages. The

Bodhisattva's practice is higher virtue. Mahāyāna meditational concentrations are the higher awareness. Constructionfree knowledge is the higher wisdom. A *nirvāṇa* which takes its stand nowhere (*apratiṣṭhitanirvāṇa*) is the abandonment of adverse factors which is the result of these practices; and the three Buddha-bodies are the knowledge which is the result of these practices. These ten features form the ten subjects of the ten chapters of this treatise.

4.(E9-10) Since only the Mahāyāna treats these subjects, only the Mahāyāna can be considered the word of the Buddha.

5.(E10-11) These ten features follow a causal sequence: at first, Bodhisattvas realize dependent origination, then, to avoid the extremes of superimposition and denial, they know about the characteristics of factors dependently originated, then they penetrate these characteristics, then, based on the six perfections, they reach basic purification (*adhyāśrayaviśuddhi*), then they practise the perfections to an ultimate extent in the ten stages, then they fulfill the three spiritual trainings of the Bodhisattva, then they realize ultimate right enlightenment.

## CHAPTER ONE

1.(T12-13) Quotes a *sūtra*[501] as stating that the storehouse consciousness precedes temporal distinctions, is the common support of all factors, and makes possible all passages into other destinies and *nirvāṇa*.

2.(T13) The storehouse consciousness has all the seeds and settles (*ālīyate*) in all factors.

3.(T13-14) All factors are settled in the storehouse consciousness as its effect, and it itself settles in all factors as their cause.

4.(T14) This consciousness is also called the appropriating consciousness (*ādānavijñāna*). Quotes 136.*Saṃdhinirmocanasūtra* V.7 to this effect.

5.(T14-15) It is called thus because it appropriates the material organs and because it is the basis for the appropriation of a sense of identity in rebirths.

6.(T15-17) Though "*citta*", "*manas*", and "*vijñāna*" have been termed synonyms (all meaning awareness), there are two special senses of "*manas*": any sensory consciousness serving as the condition for an immediately subsequent mental consciousness (*manovijñāna*) is called "*manas*", but *manas* is also (in Asaṅga's new usage) a seventh type of consciousness, the defiled mind (*kliṣṭamanas*) which gives a false sense of self.

7.(T17-22) Question: How does one know that *manas* in the second sense exists?

Answer: Without it, there could be no uncompounded (*āveṇikī*) ignorance, i.e., a basic ignorance not yet associated with all the diverse defilements but standing as their basis. Besides, the mental consciousness must also have a simultaneous support, as do the sensory consciousnesses which have such supports in their material organs. Such a simultaneous support can only be the defiled mind. Also, the very etymology of *manas* has to do with "mine", which can be explained only by the *kliṣṭamanas*. Also, without it there would be no difference between the non-identifying trance and the cessation trance, for only the latter is free of defiled mind. Also, the sense of an existence of self is always existent in nonsaintly states: there must be some special consciousness to account for the persistence of this sense. This defiled mind is always defiled by the false view of self, pride of self, attachment to self, and ignorance, but is itself ethically neutral.

8.(T22-23) It is from the storehouse consciousness that all the other consciousnesses arise.

9.(T23) How can the storehouse consciousness be called "awareness" at all? Because it is accumulated by the proclivity-seeds.

10.(T23-26) Why is the storehouse consciousness not mentioned in the Hīnayāna? Because it is too subtle for it.

11.(T26-28) Besides, it *is* mentioned there under various synonyms--the root-consciousness of the Mahāsāṅghikas, etc. Asaṅga takes an *Ekottarāgama* (cf. *Aṅguttara* II, 131) passage and contorts it to indicate belief in the storehouse consciousness.

13.(T29-30) Considering the storehouse consciousness as being "themselves", sentient beings crave the annihilation of frustration. But at the same time, because they are linked to a false sense of "I", they in no way really want the annihilation of frustrating factors (since the sense of "I" is the basis of all these frustrations and yet sentient beings wish to continue to exist with an "I"). Even those sentient beings who have passed beyond attachment to pleasures, etc., are still attached to a sense of "I".

14.(T30-32) The storehouse consciousness is the generative cause of all experienced factors, as it colors them all. Furthermore, it is always present as the cause of all defiled factors. Finally, it is itself the result of traces.

15.(T33) What is meant by "trace"? A trace is a generative cause of an experienced factor which involves a simultaneous arising and perishing as far as this factor-sequence is concerned. For instance, sesame seeds are "impregnated" by their flower, but the seeds are the cause of the flower, too. The flower perishes, the seeds persist; the seeds perish, the flower arises. The same with awarenesses: the sensory awareness perishes, its impression persists; the impression fades, but colors future sensory awarenesses.

16.(T33-34) Is there then really a difference between the storehouse consciousness and the traces themselves? Actually, the storehouse consciousness is neither different nor nondifferent from the traces. But one says that the storehouse-consciousness stores the traces, because it has the power to engender defiled factors.

17.(T34-35) Storehouse consciousness and defiled factors are simultaneous reciprocal causes. How is this? An analogous case is a lamp, where the arising of the flame and the combustion of the wick are reciprocal and simultaneous. Thus, the storehouse consciousness is the cause of defiled factors, and the defiled factors are the cause of the storehouse consciousness.

18.(T36) How can a process leaving traces, which is itself nondiverse, give rise to diverse factors? This is like the case of a piece of clothing which has been treated at various places with different substances. Being put into a uniform dye, its colors appear as diverse when it is brought out of this uniform dye. (Processes like *batik* come to mind.) In the same way, the storehouse consciousness is impressed with various traces: at the moment of origination it is not diverse, but a multitude of diverse factors are manifested in the trace once originated.

19.(T36-37) In the Mahāyāna we speak of a subtle dependent origination. This is the dependent origination which has to do with the nature of things, which equals the storehouse consciousness.

20.(T37-38) It is those who are confused as to the storehouse consciousness who imagine the origin of phenomena in an essential nature, in previous retributory actions, in the transformations of a God, or in a self; or, they deny causality altogether. It is like blind men who are asked what an elephant is like--one touches the trunk and says an elephant is like a plough, another touches the tusks, and says an elephant is like a pestle, another touches the ears, and says an elephant is like a winnowing basket, etc. In the same way, people who do not have the whole picture of the storehouse consciousness imagine an own-being, retributory actions as creating phenomena, transformations of a God, etc.

21.(T38-39) The storehouse consciousness is a retributory consciousness which stores all the seeds.

25.(T44-46) Though the external seeds (sensory impressions) may not always arise, the internal seeds of the storehouse consciousness are always arising.

26.(T46) The other seven consciousnesses are called the evolving functioning consciousnesses (*pravṛttivijñāna*) and they relate to experience. (164.*Madhyāntavibhāga* is quoted as if a work by a different author.)

27.(T46-48) The evolving consciousness and storehouse consciousness are reciprocal conditions.

29.(T49) Defilement and purification are possible only with the existence of a substratum, thus the storehouse consciousness is demonstrated.

30.(T49-52) Because functioning consciousnesses are momentary, they cannot account for defilement and purification.

31.(T52) There would be no accounting for states where the functioning consciousnesses are absent (as in the attainment of cessation) if there were no storehouse consciousness.

32.(T52-53) Whenever a consciousness which is antidotal to the defilements arises, there could be no possibility for the future arising of defilements (which does occur) without there being a storehouse consciousness.

33-34.(T53-57) There would be no possibility for the carry-over of traces from one moment to the next, especially from one meditational sphere to another, without an underlying consciousness. There would also be no carry-over of proclivities from one birth to the next.

35.(T57-58) There could be no arising of material organs in an embryo without a consciousness preceding the arising of the seven functioning consciousnesses.

38.(T60-61) Though the carry-over of traces from one life to the next could be explained through a mental consciousness, in the case of the higher meditational states (where the mental consciousness is absent), if an organism dies in these states, there could be no possibility of the carry-over of proclivities into the next life if a storehouse consciousness did not exist.

40-42.(T61-63) This is also the case because a supramundane awareness destroys the series of other kinds of awarenesses.

43.(T63-64) Mundane purification would be impossible without the storehouse consciousness. Why? Those who have not yet abandoned the lusts of the realm of desire and have not yet attained an awareness belonging to the material realm make an effort, through a good awareness of the realm of desire, to free themselves from the lusts of the realm of desire. But this awareness of application belonging to the realm of desire could not arise or perish with a usual awareness of the realm of desire, so it can't be impressed by the latter, not can it be the seed of the latter. So it can only be a retributory consciousness which has all the seeds, and which continues as an uninterrupted series, which can be the causal condition of this awareness' entering the material realm, whereas the good awareness of effort belonging to the realm of desire can only be a dominant condition.

44.(T64-65)[502] In a similar way, supramundane purification would also be impossible without a storehouse consciousness. Why? For one thing, the Buddha has said "Words coming from another, and internal careful mental attentions, are the causes of right views". Words coming from another and internal careful mental attention impress either an auditory consciousness, a mental consciousness, or the two together. But during a careful mental attention, an auditory consciousness no longer arises, and the mental consciousness may still be distracted. When the awareness arises from careful mental attention the mental attention impressed by the former auditory consciousness has already perished. Thus it cannot be the seed for the awareness arising from careful mental attention. Furthermore, a worldly awareness associated with careful mental attention cannot arise with a supramundane awareness associated with right views. Nor can it be impressed by the former. Thus the former cannot be its seed. So supramundane alleviation is also impossible without a storehouse consciousness.

45.(T65-66) Objection: It seems that the same trouble arises if we assume the storehouse consciousness as the seed of a supramundane consciousness. The storehouse consciousness is endowed with all the seeds, and is the cause of affliction. How can it be the seed of an unafflicted awareness?

Answer: Because the storehouse consciousness does have *all* the seeds. The supramundane awareness arises from that seed which is a trace of a former auditory consciousness, and which is an outcome of the pure *dharmadhātu*.

46.(T66-67) Objection: Is this trace of an auditory consciousness identical with the storehouse consciousness, or is it something different? If it is identical, how can it be its seed? If it isn't identical, where is the locus of this seed-trace of an auditory consciousness?

Answer: Until complete enlightenment is reached this trace of an auditory consciousness stays in the storehouse consciousness. But it is not identical with the storehouse consciousness, since it is the seed or the antidote to the storehouse consciousness.[503]

50.(T71-72) In the attainment of cessation there is still an awareness--this awareness can only be the storehouse consciousness.

51.(T72) In the attainment of cessation, the functioning consciousness-streams are interrupted. Yet they are renewed after the attainment has ceased.

52.(T72-74) Certain people believe that the awareness in the attainment of cessation is a mental consciousness. But the object of a mental consciousness does not arise in the attainment of cessation, nor is the form of such a consciousness apparent in such a state. In fact, a mental consciousness always implies identifications and feelings, both of which are of course absent in the attainment of the cessation (of feelings and identifications).

53.(T74-75) Nor is it possible for any of the evolving consciousnesses to be separated from their accompanying mental factors.

55.(T77) Certain people claim that the uninterrupted production of the materiality-aggregate is the seed for the consciousnesses arising after the attainment of cessation. But in that case there could never be a descent from the immaterial realm to the realm of desire.

56.(T78) Defilement and purification would thus both be impossible without a storehouse consciousness.

57.(T78-80) If good mental attention were potentially impure, how could there ever be a revolution at the basis of such an awareness into a totally undefiled state? The antidotes cannot be the cause of such a revolutionizing, since an antidote is not equivalent to the severing of a defilement. If it were there would be no difference between cause and effect. If it is said that the revolutionizing of awareness is equivalent to the awareness' losing its seeds, this also won't do, since the awareness is already past by the time the revolutionizing occurs.

58-59.(T80-82) Characterizations of the storehouse consciousness in its various aspects: as proclivities to verbal activity, as proclivities to the view of self, as proclivities of all the constituent parts of the life-continuum, as projection of newly-arisen traces, as retribution, as cause of belief in a self held by the defiled mind, and a characteristic which is both similar in being the seed for the arising of that which is not consciously perceived and dissimilar in being the seed of that which is consciously perceived.

60.(T82-84) In these aspects, it is the cause of both the insentient universe and the seed of the individual conditions for consciousness. The storehouse consciousness in the latter aspect is destroyed by the Buddhist path, whereas the storehouse consciousness in the former aspect continues, but becomes the content of a totally cleared seeing, which may however continue to be different in its specific forms even from one yogi to the next.

61.(T84-86) The storehouse consciousness has both the characteristics of depravity and of complete tranquillity antidotal to such depravity--in its former aspect, it is the cause of defilements, in the latter it is the cause of good factors. The storehouse consciousness has the aspect of being consumed: thus a retribution finally ceases. It also has the aspect of being unconsumed, in the sense that new traces may arise. The storehouse consciousness, finally, is like a magical creation, like a mirage, like a dream, an optical illusion. It may further be either complete (in those of totally worldly awareness) or reduced (in those who have rejected worldly greeds). With disciples and Bodhisattvas it is partially destroyed; with nobles, self-enlightened ones and Buddhas it is exempt of all obstructions which are defilements.

62.(T86) Question: Why is the storehouse consciousness called unobstructed but ethically neutral? It is, after all, the cause of good and bad factors.

Answer: In being unobstructed but neutral, it opposes itself to neither the good nor the bad. If it were itself good, defilement would be impossible. If it were itself bad, purification would be impossible.

## CHAPTER TWO

1.(T87) The characteristic marks of what can be known are the dependent characteristic (*paratantralakṣaṇa*), the mental constructed characteristic (*parikalpita-lakṣaṇa*), and the perfected characteristic (*parinispannalakṣaṇa*).

2.(T7-89) The dependent is all the perceptual manifestations which have as their seed the storehouse consciousness: they include the perceptions of a body (=the five sense-organs), of a possessor of the body (=the defiled mind), of an enjoyer (the mental consciousness), all perception of number, the perception of locus, the perceptions which come through practical usage, the perception of a distinction between "self" and "others", and the perception of good and bad destinies, birth, and death. The first nine of these are the result of traces of verbal activity, the tenth is the result of traces of a view of a self, and the eleventh is the result of traces of all the constituent parts of existing. Cf. I, 58-59.

3.(T90) The mentally constructed is the appearance of an object when there is no object, but only perception.

4.(T90-91) The perfected is the absence of any characteristic of an object in the dependent.

5.(T92) Arrangement of the elements in II.2 as the internal sensory domains, the external sensory domains, and their corresponding consciousnesses.

6.(T92-93) Objection: Is there ever to be found a perception without a corresponding object?

Answer: Certainly, as in a dream.

Objection: But at emergence from a dream, it is recognized that the dream-perceptions had no corresponding objects. This, however, is not the case with other perceptions.

Answer: Yes it is, because those who are awakened by the knowledge of reality realize that all their perceptions are without a corresponding object.

7.(T93-96) Question: How can those who are not yet awakened in that sense know the existence of manifesting-only?

Answer: By scriptural authority, and by reasoning. In the 83.*Daśabhūmikasūtra* the Buddha has said that the triple world (i.e., the sphere of desire, the material sphere, and the immaterial sphere) is nothing but awareness. (Quotes further the 136.*Saṃdhinirmocanasūtra*.) And by reasoning one can determine that the blue sense-objects seen in meditation do not correspond to an external object, but are consciousness-only.

8.(T96-97) Furthermore, one may have perceptions in the form of memories of things long past--since those things no longer exist, it is clear that this is also consciousness-only .

9.(T97-98) Objection: This may be so for mental phenomena, but how can you say that the sensory domains of visibles, etc., and of the eye, etc., are nothing but perceptions?

Answer: By scriptural authority and by reasoning, as above.

Objection: But these domains form series which are clearly material.

Answer: It is this appearance of material series without there being really a material series which makes possible the perversion of considering the nonexistent existent. (Quotes 165.*Mahāyānasūtrālaṃkāra* XI.24 as if a work by a different author.)

11.(T99-101) Consciousness-only can be considered in three aspects: as unitary, in being consciousness-only; as dual, in being endowed with the appearances of perception and perceiver; as infinitely varied, because of the appearance of innumerable aspects.

12.(T101-103) Certain people believe that the first five consciousnesses do not exist, and that it is only the mental consciousness which takes these different aspects according to the sensory organ it is associated with. But the mental consciousness is never anything but a perception of a kind special to "itself"--it always has a double aspect: the appearance of an object only and the appearance of a conceptual construction. The perception of sensory organs is however different from this, since sensory characteristics are perceived.

13.(T103) All other perceptions are the perceptions of signs of the storehouse consciousness. The perception of a mental consciousness forms its perception of observation, which in turn makes the appearances of objects arise.

14.(T104-107) In regard to the same "object"-moment, different beings may have totally different perceptions. This demonstrates in itself that there is no "objective" object. Furthermore, the knowledge of Buddhas is a knowledge without objects--this again would be impossible if an "object" were something real.

15.(T107-108) If the dependent is consciousness-only, in what sense is it dependent? Because it arises from its own traces (seeds), it is dependent on conditions. And because, after it arises, it is unable to exist by itself even for a moment, it is dependent.

If the constructed is simply the appearance of a nonobject as object, in which way is it constructed? Because it lies at the origin of all the constructions of the mental consciousness, it is called constructed.

If the perfeced is the total absence of the constructed in the dependent, why is it called perfected? Because it is the object of a totally purified awareness, and the best of all good factors.

16.(T108-110) Construction is mental consciousness. The constructible is however the dependent. And the constructed nature is the aspect into which the dependent is constructed by the mental consciousness.

17.(T110) The three essential natures (dependent, constructed, perfected) are neither different nor identical. The dependent, for instance, is dependent from one point of view, constructed from another (as in this treatise!), and perfected from yet another. It is dependent in the sense that it depends upon another thing to arise--and that other thing depends upon it to arise. It is constructed as soon as it is a sign of a mental construction. It is perfected in the sense that it does not really exist at all in the way it is mentally constructed.

20.(T112-115) Ten kinds of mental construction may arise:

(1) the root construction, i.e., the store-consciousness;

(2) the construction of signs--this is the construction of the perceptions of visibles, etc.;

(3) the construction of the appearance of a sign, i.e., the notions of "visual consciousness", etc.;

(4) the construction which entails a modification of the "object"--as those resulting from old age, from a pleasurable sensation, a difference of time of year, etc.;

(5) the construction which is a modification of that which appears as an object, for instance, the modifications of perceptions

brought about by previous perceptions;

(6) construction which depends upon something other, i.e., the constructions following upon hearing something which is not the *dharma*, and the constructions following upon hearing the *dharma*;

(7) construction based on carelessness, e.g., the opinions of those completely removed from the Buddhist *dharma*;

(8) construction based on carefulness, e.g., the preliminary views of those following the *dharma*;

(9) constructions following from adherence to false views;

(10) constructions of distractions in the Bodhisattva-path.

21.(T115) The constructions of distractions in the Bodhisattva-path are: distraction as "nonbeing", distractions of "being", distractions on superimposition, distractions on denial, distractions on identities, distractions on differentiations, distractions on essential nature, distractions on specification, distractions involving interpreting an "object" according to its conventional name, distractions involving interpreting a name according to its "object".

22.(T115-118) The antidotes to these ten are found in 5.*Aṣṭasāhasrikāprajñā-pāramitā* XI.77. "The Bodhisattva, being really a Bodhisattva": this is the antidote to the distraction on "nonbeing". "Does not perceive a Bodhisattva": this is the antidote to the distraction of being. "Does not conceive of the name 'Bodhisattva', nor of any of the aggregates, etc.": this is the antidote to superimposition. "All this does not exist because of emptiness": this is the antidote to denial. "The emptiness of materiality is not materiality": this is the antidote to identity. "Outside of emptiness, there is no materiality": this is the antidote to differentiation. "Materiality is nothing but a name": this is the antidote to essential nature. "There is neither birth, nor cessation, nor defilement, nor purification": this is the antidote to specifications. "Names are artificial": this is the antidote to distractions involving interpreting according to names. "The Bodhisattva conceives of no names": this is the antidote to distractions involving interpreting a name according to an "object".

As an antidote to these ten distractions, the knowledge free from conceptual construction is taught in all the Prajñāpāramitāsūtras.

23.(T118) All of the three essential natures are really included in the dependent. If this is so, why aren't the three identical? Inasmuch as it is really dependent, the dependent is not simply mentally constructed, and it is not perfected, either. Inasmuch as it is mentally constructed, it isn't really dependent or perfected. Inasmuch as it is perfected, it isn't dependent and isn't constructed.

24.(T118-119) How can one know that the dependent which manifests itself as constructed is not really identical with the constructed? Before there is a name, a notion also doesn't exist.[504] (Quotes 165.*Mahāyānasūtrālaṃkāra* XIII.16 as if a work by another author.)

25.(T120) If the dependent does not exist as it appears, why isn't it entirely nonexistent? Without the dependent, the perfected cannot exist. And if the dependent and the perfected did not exist, there could be neither defilement nor purification.

26.(T120-122)[505] It is the mentally constructed which is really nonexistent. The dependent, on the other hand, is like a magic show, a mirage, a dream, a reflection, a flash, an echo, the moon in the water, a transformation, i.e., it is not existent as it appears, but it is not nonexistent. The perfected, finally, is emptiness, the ultimate purification, the factors conducive to enlightenment, and the teaching of the Mahāyāna.

27.(T122-124) The images used in relation to the interdependent answer questions such as the following: How can the nonexistent be perceived?

28.(T124-125) Why did the Buddha say in the *Brahmaparipṛcchāsūtra* that he sees neither *saṃsāra* nor *nirvāṇa*? Because the dependent is constructed sometimes and perfected sometimes. The Buddha had in mind the nondifferentiation of *saṃsāra* and *nirvāṇa*. The dependent in its constructed aspect = *saṃsāra*; the dependent in its perfected aspect = *nirvāṇa*.

29.(T125-126) The constructed in the dependent is defiled. The perfected in the dependent is purified. Thus the dependent itself can be either defiled or purified.

30.(T126-129) Question: The Buddha has said in the 133.*Laṅkāvatārasūtra* that all factors are eternal. But since factors are momentary, how could he say this? Answer: The dependent in its perfected aspect is eternal; the dependent in its constructed aspect is momentary. The same formula holds for other dualities: joy/frustration, welfare/lack of welfare, calm/noncalm, etc. Since factors are nonexistent and they arise in various ways (for example, the same sound-moment will appear different to each aggregate-complex in contact with it), there is neither a factor nor a non-factor. In a way they exist, in another they don't exist. (Quotes 165.*Mahāyānasūtrālaṃkāra* XI.50-51 as if a work by a different author.)

32.(T132-134) An exposition of the Mahāyāna must include the following points: the teaching of dependent origination, the teaching of the characteristics of the dependently originated, and the teaching of the meaning of received statements. The teaching of dependent origination comes in the statement that all factors have arisen from traces due to mental talk, and that the traces have also arisen from the factors. The teaching of the characteristics of the dependently originated is the teaching that the evolving consciousnesses have as their essential natures a perception endowed with a mental mark and an observation of this mark, and have as their characteristics the dependent as their support, the mentally constructed as their manner of appearance, and the perfected as underlying reality. For, in the dependent the constructed is really nonexistent, which is equivalent to saying that the perfected exists in the dependent.

33.(T134-143) Explanations of each of the received statements regarding the Buddha (i.e., "The Buddha has a pure intellect", "The Buddha penetrates the *dharma* without characteristics", etc.), in terms of preceding expositions in this treatise.

34.(T143-152) Bodhisattvas are characterized by the following factors: they have the high intention of doing good to all sentient beings, they introduce sentient beings to knowledge of everything, they know themselves perfectly, they have overcome all pride, their high intention is unswerving, they have a natural, unforced friendly love for all, the same awareness towards those friendly or inimical to them, and an infinite love (*prema*) for all beings, they express themselves in apt words and with a smiling face, their compassion has no limits, they are unfatigued by the burdens they have undertaken, their mental powers are indefatigable, they are insatiable to hear the *dharma*, they see their own faults and point out without anger the faults of others, they have the enlightenment-awareness constantly with them, they give without the notion of a reward, their ethical conduct does not depend on the condition of life they are in, their forbearance holds for everyone, their energy gathers all the roots of the beneficial, they practise meditations up to the imageless sphere without impediment, they are endowed with a wisdom which includes skill in means, their means are conformable to the four means of attracting others to the *dharma* respectfully, they live apart from the world and disdain its frivolities, they are not attracted to the Hīnayāna, they see the advantages of the Mahāyāna, they leave off bad friends and cultivate good friends, they perform all meditational practices, they do not abandon sentient beings in the good or bad destinies, their language is precise, they esteem the truth.

The Bodhisattvas' high intention of doing good to all sentient beings is comprised by sixteen acts: (1) acts of successive noninterrupted effort; (2) acts free from perversions, (3) acts undertaken even without another's asking them, (4) imperturbable acts, (5) acts without interest in reward, (6) bodily and verbal acts conforming to the high intentions, (7) acts equally efficacious for the unhappy, happy, and those who are neither, (8) courageous acts, (9) acts which can't be turned back, (10) acts conformable to skillful means, (11) acts putting aside that which is to be put aside, (12) acts with the reflection on the enlightenment-awareness always present, (13) acts in conformity with the six perfections and the four means of attracting others to the *dharma*; (4) acts of effort towards fufillment in supporting good people, hearing the *dharma*, living apart from the world, abandoning bad discriminations, and acts of high quality in mental attention, (5) fulfilled acts in purity of infinite practices, getting special powers, and high quality in understanding, (16) acts proceeding to the highest, i.e., qualities helping attract people to the *dharma*, advice and teaching given without hesitation, uniting material interest with the *dharma*, and awarenesses without defilement.

## CHAPTER THREE

1.(T153-154) Entry into the characteristics of that which can be known is through mental states impressed with the hearing of the *dharma*, which states are not to be confused with the store-consciousness.

2-3.(T154-156) Elaboration of this definition as having primarily to do with hearing Mahāyāna texts and entering into the path of the Bodhisattva.

4.(T156-157) Necessary in this process is fortifying the roots of the beneficial, in allowing the awareness of enlightenment to arise in three ways, in showing a continuous heedfulness directed at peace and insight.

5.(T157-159) The three ways the awareness of enlightenment arises: "Countless human beings in countless universes reach ultimate enlightenment in each moment"; "It's for this intention that sentient beings practise giving and the other perfections"; "Sentient beings with even limited beneficial actions arrive after death at the bodily perfections of their choice". The conclusion in all three cases is "if they can, so can I." (Quotes *165.Mahāyānasūtrālaṃkāra* X.11 as if a work by another author.)

6.(T159-160) The Bodhisattvas reject the mental attentions customary with disciples and self-enlightened Buddhas. They give up all doubts as to the Mahāyāna. They give up the idea of factors and selves. They abandon all discriminations to arrive at a constructionfree knowledge.

7.(E161-162) Description of the gradual entry of the Bodhisattva into understanding, starting with mental talk connected with hearing the Mahāyāna, then realizing that all words, objects, essential natures, and meaning of words are only nominal designations, then proceeding from this basis. Once it is realized that words, objects, essential natures and meaning of words are simply nominal designations because they have no objective character, the state of consciousness-only is reached.

8.(T162-164) Elaboration of this process, which involves unity (consciousness-only), duality (as sign and the observation of a sign), and multiplicity, since these two are manifested in limitless ways. Uses the image of the serpent and the rope, but in a more subtle way than is usual: Because it doesn't exist, the serpent seen in the rope is an illusion, but the rope itself, if one analyzes it according to its subtle aspects, is also an illusion since it can be perceived by different consciousnesses as being color, smell, taste, or tangible. In the same way, one finds out that word, object, essential nature, specifications, and essential nature and specifications together, are nonobjective, and one enters into the idea of consciousness-only. But then one must in turn reject the idea of consciousness-only itself.

9.(T164-165) Nominal designations are the constructed; consciousness-only is the dependent; abandonment of even the idea of consciousness-only is the perfected, constructionfree knowledge.

10.(T165-166) Factors, persons, religious statements, theses, brief expositions, more extended expositions, beings not yet purified, beings purified, conclusions, are all nothing but names.

11.(T166-167) Entry into consciousness-only is entry into the characteristics of the knowable. This is the first Bodhisattva-stage, the awareness of the sameness of all sentient beings, the path of vision.

12.(T167-169) Both a supramundane knowledge based on peace and higher vision, and a subsequently attained knowledge which is worldly inasmuch as it again makes use of concepts but only as means, enter into consciousness-only. This subsequently attained knowledge considers all phenomena arising from the storehouse consciousness as being like a magical creation.

13.(T169-170) In the course of entry into consciousness-only, the four aids to penetration arise.

14.(T171) Sustained practice of peace and higher vision is the spiritual path.

15.(T171-174) What difference is there between the full understanding of the disciples and that of Bodhisattvas? The full understanding of Bodhisattvas is different as to its object of consciousness: as to its support, because it is based on great preparations in merit and knowledge; as to its penetration, since it penetrates not only the selflessness of personality, but also the selflessness of factors; as to its *nirvāṇa,* since it involves only a *nirvāṇa* which is based nowhere (*apratiṣṭhitanirvāṇa*); as to its stages; as to its purification, since it suppresses not only the impressions of the obstruction which are defiling, but also the impressions of the obstructions of the knowable, and purifies the Buddha-fields; by being equally attentive to the aims of others as to "one's own"; by its birth, since it arises only in the Tathāgata-lineage; by its accomplishments, and by its results: the ten powers, the special Buddha-factors, etc.

16.(T174-175) (Quotes 165. *Mahāyānasūtrālaṃkāra* XIX, 47 as if a work by another author.) Since an "objective" object doesn't exist, the three essential natures (constructed, dependent, perfected) also don't exist.

17.(T175-176) (Quotes a lost *Yogācāravibhāga*) The meditationally concentrated Bodhisattva sees that all reflections are only mind. Rejecting all identifications of an object, he understands that only those identifications of his exist. He realizes that the object perceived does not exist, then he realizes that by this fact the subject apprehender also does not exist. And so he reaches a state of nonapprehenson.

18.(T176-179) (Quotes 165. *Mahāyānasūtrālaṃkāra* VI, 6-10 as if a work by a different author.)

(This Chapter of this treatise thus demonstrates that the final point of view, or nonpoint of view, of Yogācāra, at least as conceived at its origin, is neither the consciousness-theory (which is purely preliminary), nor the idea of the three essential natures (which is a way of outlining the process of defilement to purification), nor even the idea of consciousness-only which follows from a knowledge of the three essential natures, but a constructionfree knowledge where "subject" and "consciousness" are equally as absent as "object" and "the perceived." )

CHAPTER FOUR: Cause and Effect of Entry (T180-195)

CHAPTER FIVE: The Various Cultivations of the Cause and Effect (T196-211)

CHAPTER SIX: Spiritual Training in Higher Virtue (T212-217)

CHAPTER SEVEN: Training in Higher Awareness (T218-231)

CHAPTER EIGHT: Training in Higher Wisdom (T232-258)

CHAPTER NINE: Abandoning the Fruits of the Three (T259-265)

CHAPTER TEN: Knowledge of the Fruits (T266-345)

### 171. AUTHOR UNKNOWN, *Dharmadharmatāvibhāga*

The status of this text is discussed by Leslie Kawamura.[506] He finds that there are three texts in Tibetan, which he distinguishes as

Maitreya's prose text, Maitreya's *kārikā* text, and Vasubandhu's commentary text.[507] In all likelihood Maitreya was not an actual person, so we leave the question of authorship in this case open.[508] Kawamura discusses the sources of our knowledge of this text.

Stefan Anacker[509] has published a summary (our "T" below) of Vasubandhu's commentary (distinct from the summary provided later on as our #198) in which he summarizes as well some of the contents of our *Dharmadharmatāvibhāga*. We reproduce this minus the Sanskrit reconstructions of technical terms that he supplies.[510]

Summary by Stefan Anacker

(T27-28) "The provisional distinction is between *dharmas*, which have the characteristic of undergoing affliction, and *dharmatā*, which has the characteristic of alleviation. The characteristic of "*dharmas*", in contrast to *dharmatā*, is the construction of that which was not....*Dharmatā*, on the other hand, is the undifferentiated Suchness that lies behind all so-called objects apprehended, subjects apprehenders, things which can be designated and their designation."

(T29) "..The correct investigation of a "dharma" rests on six aspects: its characteristic, the proof of this characteristic, its severalness and non-separatedness, its locus, its commonness and uncommonness, and the understanding of the non-being of the appearances of the object apprehended and the subject apprehender..."

(T30) "...Another list for "the correct investigation of *dharmatā*", which also rests on six aspects: its characteristic, its support, its penetration, its contact, its memory and understanding its nature."

"Entry into revolution at the basis depends on ten aspects, and here we are introduced to a particularly impenetrable, on first sight at least, Maitreyanātha list: (1) its own-nature, (2) its domain, (3) the "persons" who undergo it, (4) its speciality, (5) its practice, (6) its basis, (7) its mental attention, (8) its use (9) its benefit, and (10) entry into it."

(T30) "...Another list...characterize(s) non-discriminatory knowledge, stating that it is the non-mental attention to discriminations, having passed beyond all discriminations, putting to rest all discriminations, being non-discriminatory simply by its nature, and that it can be apprehended simply by being noted."

## 172. AUTHOR UNKNOWN, *Abhisamayālaṃkāra*

Estimates of the source of this text vary widely. Warder[511] dates it to "about the middle of the 3rd century A.D.", while Conze[512] says it "may possibly belong to the 5th century, if we can believe Tāranātha's account". It is frequently claimed to be a work of "Maitreya", thus Asaṅga. It is a summary of 54.*Pañcaviṃśatiprajñāpāramitāsūtra,* which, in the words of Warder, "proceeds to set out the way, following the actual order of the *Sūtras,* as if these were arranged in such a systematic fashion."[513] This work has been edited a number of times, including the edition by Rama Sastri Tripathin in Bibliotheca Indo-Tibetica 2 (Varanasi 1977), our "E", and has been translated by Edward Conze, our "T".[514]

(E3) Two introductory verses of benediction.

(E3; T4) The purpose of this work is to explain the way to knowledge of all aspects. Remembering these *sūtras* one can satisfactorily understand the tenfold teaching concerning the *dharma.*

(E4-5; T4-7) There are eight perfections of wisdom (*prajñāpāramitā*) to be understood: (A) awareness of all the aspects, (B) awareness of all the paths, (C) complete awareness, (D) enlightenment concerning all the aspects, (E) attainment of the summit, (F) gradual attainment, (G) instantaneous attainment, (H) the *dharmakāya.*

(E5-6; T9-12) (A) *Awareness of All the Aspects.* (1) *The arising of awareness* is the desire for right enlightenment for others' sakes. (2) *Instructions* concerning the path, the truths, the three jewels of enlightenment, absence of attachment, persistence and acceptance of the path, awareness by five eyes, the qualities of the six higher faculties, the path of vision and the path of practice. Twenty kinds of disciples are identified: those with dull faculties, with keen faculties, who have achieved faith, who have achieved correct views, two kinds reborn again and again, those with one interval, those who are liberated during intermediate existence, those who are liberated as soon as they are reborn, doers, nondoers, those who have gone to the *akaniṣṭha* gods, three kinds of those who go by leaps, those who have gone to the highest sphere, who are satisfied in this life, who see with their bodies, and those self-enlightened.

(E6-8; T13-19) (3) *The aids to penetration*, viz., heat, summit, patience and the highest *dharma*, are classed into weak, medium or strong types depending on their objects, their aspects, their causes and accomplishments. These four also correspond to four sorts of conceptual construction. The aids to penetration are assisted by thoughtful attention, correct advice concerning lack of an essential nature, etc., and abandonment of attitudes contrary to these.

(4) *The aids to progress*. The lineage is the basis of six factors conducive to achievement, of antidotes, of abandoning, of overlooking the difference between (the last two), of wisdom involving compassion, of states not attained by disciples, of helpful activities, and of effortless awareness. Lineages are not correctly viewed as different, for the factor-element is not actually differentiated. But since the differences among factors are based on it the differentiation can be understood.

(5) *Supporting objects* comprise all factors. Good objects belong to either the worldly or the higher-worldly realm. The former have, and the latter lack, contaminants. Those without contaminants include both conditioned and unconditioned factors, as well as those shared with disciples and those confined to sages.

(E8-13; T19-29) (6) *The program* of self-existence involves three great qualities: trying to improve all beings, forsaking (false views) and achievement (of *nirvāṇa*).

(7) *Preparation* (lit. "putting on the armor") involves six times, six ways and the six perfections of giving, etc.

(8) *Setting out* to follow the Mahāyāna involves meditative trances and immaterial attainments, giving, etc., the path, loving kindness, etc., objectless awareness, the threefold purity, indication, six higher faculties and awareness of all the aspects.

(9) *Preparation of equipment*. The steps in the process of setting out include sympathy, the six perfections (giving, etc.), peace with vision and the path that combines them, skill in the method, awareness, merit, the path, mystical verses, the ten stages and the antidotes. The ten stages of moral perfection are described at length, and the antidotes are assigned to the path of vision or

practice.

(10) *Deliverance*, understood as (a) goal, (b) sameness, (c) the purpose of beings, (d) the absence of exertion, (e) free from extremes, (f) the mark of attainment, (g) the knowledge of all aspects, and (h) relating to the path.

(E14-18; T31-43) (B) *Awareness of All the Paths.* The *path of the disciples* involves the four noble truths and the aids to penetration. *The path of the self-enlightened*, who do not need instruction by others and who can bring something to another's mind without speaking, transcends the grasping of objects though not of their subject. In *the path of the Bodhisattva* there is the *path of vision*, involving the moments of patience and knowledge as understood relating to teachings of the four truths. There is also the *path of spiritual practice*, involving weak, medium or strong resolve for one's own and others' purposes. The process of transformation of merit into the cause of liberation is reviewed. It involves avoidance of contaminants and of perverted views, isolation, remembrance of the Buddha's virtues, a spiritual method, signlessness, attention to the Buddha's advice, transcendence of the world and attainment of great merit. Completion of the path is considered as to its essential nature, its excellence, its noninvolvement, its virtues, and how success is gained. The various forms of purity thus gained are reviewed.

(E19-21; T44-48) (C) *Complete Awareness* of the perfection of wisdom is not understood in *nirvāṇa*, in this world nor in between without application of skilful means. One needs to understand the emptiness of the aggregates, the factors, and the limbs of enlightenment such as giving. The antidotes to misconceptions about these include nonegoity, helping others to that, and the destruction of all attachment that occurs when all factors are understood to be of one nature.

There are ten kinds of things one who seeks understanding needs to reflect on: the aggregates, their impermanence, their being neither complete nor incomplete, the reversal of one's way of life since he is nonattached, immutability, nonagency, the difficulty of three aspects of training, consideration of the attainment of results, of unconditionedness, and of seven insightful analogies.

The path of vision is divided into sixteen ways of understanding the aggregates: as neither eternal nor noneternal, as beyond the extremes, as pure, as neither arisen nor ceased, as like space, as without pollution, as free from embracement, as essentially inexpressible, as incommunicable, as imperceptible, as absolutely pure, as free from frustration, as the destruction of calamity, as direct awareness of the fruit, as free from relation to signs, and as the nonproduction of any awareness and talk of entities.

(D) *Enlightenment Concerning All Aspects.* Aspects (*ākāra*) are topics in the understanding of entities, and are of three kinds briefly classed into 173 sorts. After listing the attributes of those worthy of studying these teachings, some twenty applications of the teachings are identified and the virtues, faults and features of the training explained.

These features are classified as kinds of awareness, the specific features of the training, the activity of that training, and its essential nature. Kinds of awareness are further divided as regarding omniscience, the paths, and the features comprised among them. Specific features of the training are classified under the four noble truths, and the style and nature of the training are described.

(E25-29; T64-76) The means to liberation are divided into five: faith in the Buddha, the *dharma* and the order, energy in giving, etc., mindfulness of the accomplishment of one's intentions, concentration, and wisdom which is the knowledge of all the factors in all their aspects.

The four aids to penetration are reviewed, and it is explained how to tell what has been accomplished at each of the stages of heat, summit, patience and highest *dharma*. A similar review is provided for the sixteen stages on the path of vision and the eight in the path of practice.

Since all factors are unreal like dream-objects the Bodhisattva understands that becoming and quiescence should not be distinguished; no traces are produced from this attitude of purity. Ten features of that awareness are listed.

(E30-36; T77-92) (E) *Attainment of the Summit.* One who attains the summit practises a yoga classified in twelve ways, the first of which is that one sees all factors as appearances in dream. One's growth is classified in sixteen ways. The *dharma* thus gained gives one stability of awareness, concentration.

This is now considered first according to the path of vision, then according to the path of practice. According to the path of vision the grasped (i.e., objects) are misunderstood as relating to activity and to withdrawal, each of these in nine ways. The grasper too is misunderstood, in nine ways each, as to his reality when viewed by ordinary folk and as to nominal reality when viewed by the noble ones. In fact both kinds of grasper are empty, falsely conceived, and one who knows the extinction of his impurities and that no future impurities will occur is called "enlightened". The path of practice is reviewed in a similar fashion.

(E37; T93) (F) *Gradual Attainment* involves giving, wisdom, memory of the Buddha, the *dharma* and the order, and the realization that no factors have an essential nature.

(E37; T94-95) (G) *Instantaneous Attainment*, the perfection of wisdom, occurs when at a single moment the understanding of the maturation of the karma of all remaining pure factors occurs, so that one realizes that all factors are absent like the objects of dreams, while not contrasting these dream-objects with the seeing of them.

(E38-44; T96-104) (H) *The Dharmakāya.* Reaching attainment one has the essential body of a sage, featuring twenty-one marks: the limbs of enlightenment, the boundless states, enlightenment, nine trances, ten meditative devices, eight kinds of senses of mastery, nonpassion, awareness of vows, the higher faculties, the discriminations, four kinds of completeness, ten controls, ten powers, four grounds for confidence, three kinds of establishment of mindfulness, three kinds of nonloss, an unbewildered nature, the uprooting of proclivities, great compassion for people, eighteen factors specific to a sage, and knowledge of all the aspects. The differences between the understandings of disciples, *jinas* and a Buddha are explained.

The enjoyment-body (*sambhogakāya*) of a sage features thirty-two features and eighty more additional signs, such as lines representing a wheel on hands or feet, webbed fingers and toes, golden skin, a tall body, blue eyes, deep voice, etc.

The magical body (*nirmāṇakāya*) of a Bodhisattva is the body in which he carries on doing good work until the end of the universe. Some twenty-seven ways in which such a Bodhisattva behaves in helping others are detailed.

(E44; T106) The eight topics (1-8 above) can be summed up under six, or even three, headings: the three kinds of awareness (A-C), the four stages which are the causes of enlightenment (D-G), and the result--the *dharmakāya* (H).

## VASUBANDHU

Perhaps no other figure in the history of Indian philosophy, with the possible exception of Śaṃkarācārya, has provided so much historical discussion as Vasubandhu. The author of what is recognized as the outstanding available summary of Abhidharma teachings, the 173. *Abhidharmakośa*, as well as of the exposition of the basic teachings of one of the major Mahāyāna schools, Yogācāra, in his 202. *Triṃśikā* and 203. *Viṃśatikā*, Vasubandhu is said to have been the younger brother of Asaṅga and subjected to severe criticism by Saṃghabhadra, both of whom, if these accounts are to be believed, lived during the fourth century. Despite this, estimates of Vasubandhu's date have ranged from the second to the sixth centuries, and there has been heated debate over whether the Abhidharma author was or was not identical to the Yogācārin.

Fortunately, however, we now have a plausible account of Vasubandhu's life and date provided us by Stefan Anacker. We do not suppose, of course, that given the amount of discussion generated that anyone's solution to the problems of Vasubandhu's date and authorship will be entirely convincing to all parties. However, rather than attempt to review all the arguments in the debate,[515] we have chosen here merely to provide in this introductory account excerpts from Anacker's attractive and well-documented description of Vasubandhu's life.[516]

"Vasubandhu was born in Puruṣapura, present-day Peshawar, in what was then the kingdom of Gāndhāra, around the year 316 A.D...His father was a Brāhmaṇa of the Kauśika *gotra,* and his mother was named Viriñcī. The couple already had a previous son, later called Asaṅga, and a third, nicknamed Viriñcivatsa, was to follow. Vasubandhu's father was a court priest."[517]

"...Vasubandhu was born one year after his older brother Asaṅga became a Buddhist monk...Vasubandhu...entered the Sarvāstivādin order, and was studying primarily the scholastic system of the Vaibhāṣikas...His main teacher seems to have been a certain Buddhamitra."

"In time, however, grave doubts about the validity and relevance of

Vaibhāṣika metaphysics began to arise in Vasubandhu. At this time, perhaps through the brilliant teacher Manoratha, he came into contact with the theories of the Sautrāntikas...Vasubandhu finally decided to go to Kashmir to investigate the Vaibhāṣika teachings more exactly."

"Bu-ston says that Vasubandhu in Kashmir entered the school of Saṅghabhadra. But it is unlikely that this intellectually acute and cantankerous individual assumed the professorship at that time, for, from what both Paramārtha and Hsüan-tsang tell us, Vasubandhu and Saṅghabhadra seem to have been about the same age. It is, however, more than likely that it was the school Saṅghabhadra was himself attending as a student, and this is in fact attested by P'u-k'uang. He says that the main master there was the teacher of Saṅghabhadra..."

"Vasubandhu studied in Kashmir for four years, probably from about 342 to 346. He was however no docile student, but rather in his increasing frustration with the over-intellectual and category-ridden dogmatics of the Kashmirian masters, frequently voiced his own refutations of many of their points. The master...disturbed by the obstreperous student...told Vasubandhu privately that he should return to Gāndhāra before his 'uncultured students', among whom one can well imagine the sharp-tongued Saṃghabhadra, found out and attempted to harm him..."

"Vasubandhu returned to Puruṣapura...Vasubandhu supported himself by lecturing on Buddhism before the general public...At the close of each day's lecture on the Vaibhāṣika system, Vasubandhu composed a verse which summed up his exposition for the day...So in time he composed over six hundred verses, which gave an extensive outline of the entire Vaibhāṣika system. These constitute the *Abhidharmakośa*...Vasubandhu sent it...to his old teachers in Kashmir, (who) exulted that Vasubandhu had come over to their side...They were disturbed only because Vasubandhu in his treatise so often used terms such as '*kila*' ('it is claimed') and '*ity āhuḥ*' ('so they say')."

"As a matter of fact, during this entire time, Vasubandhu was working on his real project, his autocommentary on the *Kośa*, which contains a thoroughgoing critique of Vaibhāṣika dogmatics from a Sautrāntika viewpoint...For the subsequent furious indignation of the orthodox Vaibhāṣikas, we need not rely on traditional accounts only; it is amply attested by the relentless invective employed by contemporary Vaibhāṣika writers such as Saṅghabhadra...Vasubandhu had thus at a fairly early age achieved a certain notoriety..."

"In the years directly following the composition of the *Kośa*, Vasubandhu seems to have spent much time in travelling from place to place. It is certain that he stayed for a time at Śākala, the modern Sialkot..."

"Around 350, Samudragupta completed his lightning-quick conquest of north India...It was, in all probability, subsequent to that event that Vasubandhu, as well as his teachers Buddhamitra and Manoratha, decided to move to Ayodhyā...Hsüan-tsang later saw the hall in Ayodhyā where Vasubandhu preached to 'kings and many eminent men'."

"Vasubandhu had, up to this time, but little regard for the Yogācāra treatises of his elder brother...Asaṅga heard about this attitude of his brother, and decided to attempt to open him up to the Mahāyāna. He sent two of his students with Mahāyāna texts to Vasubandhu..."

"Vasubandhu seems to have been quite overwhelmed by Mahāyāna literature...In view of the fact that they were the texts that converted him to Mahāyāna, Vasubandhu's commentaries on the *Akṣayamatinirdeśasūtra* and the *Daśabhūmika* may be his earliest Mahāyāna works. These were followed by a series of commentaries on other Mahāyāna *sūtras* and treatises..."

"Since the output of Vasubandhu's Mahāyāna works is prodigious...he could have been a very famous Mahāyāna master by the year 360, the approximate date in which Kumārajīva took instruction from Bandhudatta in Kucha. By this time, Vasubandhu could easily have written those works which Bandhudatta transmitted to his brilliant pupil..."

"The year 376 brings Candragupta II, Vikramāditya, to the throne of the Gupta Empire...Around the year 383, at his eighth birthday, the crown prince Govindagupta Bālāditya was placed by the Emperor under the tutelage of Vasubandhu. The Empress Dhruvadevī also went to Vasubandhu to receive instruction..."

"In his old age, Vasubandhu seems to have taken up the wandering life again. Some of his last works are known to have been written in Śākala and in Kauśāmbī. Kauśāmbī, for instance, is the place where he wrote his *Twenty* and *Thirty Verses*, and Hsüang-tsang saw the old brick tower there, near the ancient Saṅghārāma of Ghoṣira, where these famous expositions of Yogācāra were written."

"Around the year 391, the consecration of Govindagupta as "Young King" took place. He and his mother begged Vasubandhu to settle down in Ayodhyā and accept life-long royal support. Vasubandhu accepted the offer...The master was creative even at his advanced age, and more than a match for Vasurāta, the Young King's grammarian brother-in-law, in his favorite sport of debate...But...debate was to him mainly *upāya*: if it could lead to no one's interest in Mahāyāna, he would not engage in it. Thus, when Saṅghabhadra, who had written his two great treatises, one of which is a furious denunciation of the *Kośa Bhāṣya*, challenged Vasubandhu to defend the *Kośa*'s statements, and was invited to come to court and debate by the jealous Vasurāta, Vasubandhu told his pupils that he could see no good reason for such a debate, but diplomatically sent the official answer the Saṅghabhadra would indeed be hard to defeat....The debate never took place...Saṅghabhadra in fact died shortly after."

"Vasubandhu did not long survive Saṅghabhadra. In the eightieth year of his life, c. 396, he died..."

Over thirty works are attributed to Vasubandhu by tradition for which we have no special reason to doubt his authorship. A good many of these are commentaries on Mahāyāna *sūtras* and *śāstras*, most of them available now only in Chinese or Tibetan translations if at all. In keeping with the putative chronology provided by Anacker's account just provided, we shall place the Abhidharma works previous to those Mahāyāna *sūtras*, and the remaining, Yogācāra works at the end, with the *Trisvabhāvanirdeśa* last in keeping with Anacker's estimate.

## 173. VASUBANDHU, *Abhidharmakośa*

The *Kośa* was first known to modern readers in two Chinese translations, one by Paramārtha in the sixth century, the other by Hsüan-tsang in the seventh. There are also two Tibetan translations, one by Jinamitra and the other by Śrīkūṭarakṣita, dating from the ninth century. Rahula Sankrtyayana discovered the Sanskrit text at Ngor in Tibet in 1935 and made photocopies; these are the basis for more recent editions. Louis de la Vallee Poussin translated Hsüan-tsang's Chinese into French[518] and there are various partial translations.[519] In this summary "E" references are to the edition by Swami Dwarikadas Shastri,[520] whereas "T" references are to Leo M. Pruden's four-volume English translation of Poussin's French, op. cit., numbered consecutively.

## Summary by Stefan Anacker

### CHAPTER ONE: Realms

1. (E4; T56) Homage to the Buddha, who destroys all blindness.

2.(E11-13; T56) Abhidharma is defined as pure wisdom with accompaniments. It may also be used for impure wisdom or even for treatises which result in pure wisdom.

3.(E14; T57) The only way to lay to rest the defilements that cause worldly wandering is to investigate the factors, and it is for this investigation the Buddha taught Abhidharma.

4.(E16; T58) All conditioned factors except those of the path are contaminating because defilements adhere to them.

5.(E18-19; T59) The three unconditioned factors--space, calculated and uncalculated cessation--are noncontaminating.

6.(E20-22; T59-60) Calculated cessations are separate disjunctions. Uncalculated cessation is the complete end to arising.

7.(E25-26; T61) Conditioned factors can all be subsumed under the five aggregates. They are temporal, the objects of discourse, exist, and involve actual objects.

8.(E28-29; T62-63) Contaminating factors are grasping aggregates. They are harmful, being frustrating, originating, worldly, the topic of opinions, existent.

9.(E30; T63) Material form comprises the five sense-organs, five objects, and unmanifest form. The loci of the awarenesses of these are subtle matter, visual, etc.

10.(E32-35; T64-66) There are two (or twenty) material bases. Sounds are eightfold, tastes sixfold, smell fourfold, and tangibles are of eleven sorts.

11.(E38; T67) Unmanifest material form occurs in a series dependent on the great elements which is distracted or unaware.[1]

---

1.Unmanifest form is used to explain the karmic retribution of one who has instigated an action. Someone who prompts someone else to murder engenders an unmanifest form of karma as soon as he prompts; the unmanifest form "comes to maturity" when the other person actually commits the murder.

12.((E43; T68-69) The great material elements are earth, water, fire and wind. They function respectively as supporting, humidifying, heating and motion.

13.(E43; T69) As commonly used "earth", "water", "fire", and "wind" refer to colors and shapes.

14.(E47-48; T72) Feelings are experiencings. Conceptual identifications are the grasping of signs.

15.(E48-50; T73) The aggregates of feelings, identifications, and conditioning factors, together with unmanifest form and the unconditioned factors, belong to the sense-basis of factors (*dharmāyatana*), the realm of factors.

16.(E50; T74) Consciousness is the awareness of something manifesting (*prativijñapti*). It is the mental organ; it is seven elements, six consciousnesses plus mind.

17.(E51; T75) The term "mind" (*manas*) is used for any occurrence of the six types of consciousnesses which immediately afterwards gives rise to a mental-consciousness-moment. Eighteen sensory domains are enumerated to support there being just six types of consciousness.

18.(E54; T76) All conditioned factors are included in an aggregate, a sense-basis, or an element.

19.(E55; T75) Vaibhāṣika: Though the organs of sight, hearing, and smelling are double, they each count as only one sensory domain.

20.(E56-62; T77-80) On the etymology of "*skandha*", "*āyatana*" and "*dhātu*".

21.(E64; T81) Feelings and identifications are designated as separate aggregates because they are the causes of dispute, of *saṃsāra*, and because of order.

22.(E65-66; T81-83) The unconditioned can't be classified under "aggregates", since they aren't that sort of thing. The order in which the aggregates are listed reflects their relative grossness or subtlety, their defiling capacities, and their relative range in the four realms.

23.(E67-68; T84) The five sensory consciousnesses have objects which are simultaneously present. The arrangement of the sense-fields has to do with the range and rapidity of their functioning, the eye having a longer range and greater rapidity than the ear, the ear than the nose, etc.

24.(E69; T85) Only one sense-field is called a material basis because of its excellence and predominance. Only one sense-field is called a "basis of factors" because of what it includes.

25-26.(E70-72; T86-87) The rest of the large number of factors that the Buddha refers to fall among either the material or conditioning aggregate.

27.(E72-765; T87-88) Examples of how other factors can be classified as aggregates, senses and elements.

28.(E77-78; T88-89) The element of space is, according to some, light or dark. The consciousness element is contaminating, being the locus of birth.

29a-b.(E79-81; T89-92) Only one material element is visible. Ten material elements are resistant. Eight elements are neutral (those excluding matter and sound).

29cd-30.(E81-87; T92-93) The rest of the elements can be of three sorts, good, bad or neutral. All of the elements exist in the realm of desire; fourteen exist in the material realm (excluding smell, taste, the smell- and taste-awarenesses).

31.(E87; T95-96) In the material realm all the material sensory domains are absent. In that realm occur three elements--the mind element, the mental consciousness element, and the factor element. They can be contaminating or not.

32.(E88; T96-97) Five awareness elements involve initial and sustained thought. The mind, mental consciousness, and the factor elements involve three different combinations of initial and sustained thought. The rest of the elements involve no thought.

33.(E89-90; T97) The five awarenesses are constructionfree, not involving defining and memory. Those two kinds of construction affect any distracted mentality, be it wise or mnemonic.

34.(E90-91; T98) Seven elements of awareness plus one part of the factor-element have supporting objects. The seven plus the factor-element and sounds are never appropriated by a body. The remaining nine sensory domains are sometimes appropriated, sometimes not.

35.(E92-95; T99-101) Among the ten material elements, the tangible element consists, in part, of the great elements and in part of material form derived from these great elements. The remaining nine material elements are only derivative.

36.(E95-96; T102) Four elements can cut or be cut, burn or be burned, weigh or be weighed. There is disagreement about details.

37.(E97-99; T103-104) The five internal sense-bases are the result of karmic maturation and grow through nourishment. Sound is never the result of karmic maturation.

38.(E100-103; T105-106) Only one sensory domain grasps reality: the unconditioned (which is part of the sensory domain of mental cognizables), because only it is permanent.

39.(E104-107; T107-109) Twelve of the sensory elements are personal--the twelve excluding those six that are objects of consciousness.

The sensory element called "factor(-element)" is homogeneous. The remaining ones are partially homogeneous.

40.(E109-110; T112-114) Fifteen elements are abandoned in meditational concentration; the last thirteen are of three kinds. Undefiled and material factors are not abandoned by the path of vision.

41.(E112-114; T113-114) The term "view" (*dṛṣṭi*) is used for the visual organ as well as for eight views which form parts of the factor element. The five sensory consciousnesses are not views, as there is no judgment in them made after deliberation.

42.(E113-114; T114-115) Vaibhāṣika: It is the eye which sees visibles, not the visual consciousness. For when the visible is obstructed, or the eye, there is nothing seen.

43.(119-120; T119) Vaibhāṣika: The eye, ear, and mind perceive their objects without coming directly in touch with them. This is not the case with the other three organs of sense.

44.(E123-125; T122-125) The three organs starting with the olfactory grasp an object of equal size. The objects of the five sensory consciousnesses occur simultaneously with their consciousness, but the mental consciousness may have a past, present, or future object of consciousness.

45.(E126-127; T125) Since a consciousness depends both on the object and the organ, why is only the organ designated as its support? Because the consciousness changes according to the organ.

46.(E128-129; T127-128) There is no inferiority or superiority as regards different kinds of organs or consciousnesses in the same experiential sphere.

47.(E130-131; T128-129) Sometimes the mental consciousness of a psychophysical complex may be in a superior experiential sphere to the other consciousnesses--for instance, when it is meditationally concentrated.

48.(E131-132; T129-130) Everything perceived by the other consciousnesses is discerned by the mental consciousness. The unconditioned factors (I, 4-5) are eternal. There are twenty-two faculties, factors which have a predominance for the psychophysical complex. They are the faculties of the eye, ear, nose, tongue, tactile body, mind (meaning all six consciousnesses), femininity, masculinity, vitality, satisfaction, frustration, contentedness, irritation, equanimity, faith, energy, mindfulness, meditation, insight, coming to know what wasn't known, understanding, and perfect knowledge. (For the definitions of these see Chapter Two.)

## CHAPTER TWO: The Faculties

1.(E135-138; T153-155) Vaibhāṣika: Five faculties predominate in respect of four things, and four in respect to two; five and eight with regard to affliction and purification.

2.(E140; T155-156) The faculties which are sense-organs are really predominant in relation to the five sensory consciousnesses, and the faculty of mind (cf. I, 17) is predominant in regard to mental consciousness.

3.(E141; T156-157) Vitality, feelings and the five faculties beginning with faith are predominant in maintaining life, in afflictions and purifications.

4.(E141; T157) Coming to know what wasn't known, understanding and perfect knowledge predominate in respect to liberation.

5.(E142; T158) The faculties are the loci of awareness and what conceptualizes, maintains, afflicts, prepares and purifies them.

6.(E143; T159) Alternatively, there are fourteen (positive) faculties, comprising the loci of activity and the arising, maintenance and experiencing of those loci; the rest (negative) function similarly in regard to *nirvāṇa*.

7.(E145-146; T150-161) All the information regarding the faculties which is provided by II, 7-19, 30, 60-61 and IV, 8-127 may be diagrammed as follows:

Table I

(The following abbreviations are used:

A = internal

B = noncontaminating (potentially linked to proclivities)

C = noncontaminating (never linked to proclivities)

D = can be either good or potentially linked to proclivities or not liable to be linked to proclivities (e.g., when meditationally concentrated)

E = both in good and bad states, can be retribution for acts

F = retribution for a good act in a good state, for a bad act in a bad state

G = always retribution for a bad act when retribution at all

H = never retribution

I = always ethically neutral

J = always good

K = can be good, bad, or neutral, i.e., can belong to any ethical category

L = not retribution when good, bad, or unobstructed/neutral other than retribution

M = always retribution

N = always retribution for a good act when retribution at all.

Contaminated states are "bad", being frustrating, but are not necessarily "bad" in the sense of giving rise to further frustrations. Anything which comes about as a result of retribution is necessarily ethically neutral. Whatever arises from a conceptual construction is never ethically neutral, and whatever arises from interest is never retribution.)

| | |
|---|---|
| (1) Faculty of the Eye | ABFI |
| (2) Faculty of the Ear | ABFI |
| (3) Faculty of the Nose | ABFI |
| (4) Faculty of the Tongue | ABFI |
| (5) Faculty of the Tactile Body | ABFI |
| (6) Faculty of Mind | ADFI |
| (7) Faculty of Masculinity | ABFI |
| (8) Faculty of Femininity | ABFI |

| | |
|---|---|
| (9) Faculty of Vitality | BFMI |
| (10) Faculty of Satisfaction | KLN |
| (11) Faculty of Frustration | BGKL |
| (12) Faculty of Contentedness | KLN |
| (13) Faculty of Irritation | B (or H) |
| (14) Faculty of Equanimity | DKN |
| (15) Faculty of Faith | DHJ |
| (16) Faculty of Energy | DHJ |
| (17) Faculty of Mindfulness | DHJ |
| (18) Faculty of Meditation | DHJ |
| (19) Faculty of Insight | DHJ |
| (20) Coming to Know What is Not Yet Known | CHJ |
| (21) Faculty of Understanding | IHJ |
| (22) Faculty of Perfect Knowledge | IHJ |

The faculty of frustration is any disagreeable bodily feeling, and the faculty of satisfaction any agreeable one.

8.(E146-147; T161-162) The faculty of irritation is any disagreeable mental feeling, and contentedness is its opposite. Equanimity is neither agreeable nor disagreeable, and may be either bodily or mental.

For 9-19, cf. Table I

22.(E180-181; T185) In the material realm an "atom" (provided it is without sound or faculties) comprises eight substances, nine if the tactual organ is involved, ten if another organ is.

23.(E180-181; T185) Awarenesses and accompanying mental factors, meaning motivating dispositions, feelings, and cognitions, necessarily arise together. All conditioned factors arise with the characteristics of being general.

24.(E186-188; T189) The generally conditioning factors are feeling, volition, identification, interest, contact, intellection, memory, attention, resolve, and concentration.

25.(E177-191; T191) The good permeating factors are faith, heedfulness, tranquillity, equanimity, shame, modesty, absence of greed, understanding, noninjury, and energy.

26.(E191-194; T193-195) The defiled permeating factors are delusion, heedlessness, idleness, lack of confidence, lethargy, and agitation. Shamelessness and disregard are the bad permeating factors.

27.(E194; T196) The afflicting permeating factors are anger, vengefulness, craftiness, envy, spite, hypocrisy, selfishness, deceit, arrogance, and violence.

28.(E195; T197-198) Vaibhāṣika: Since initial and sustained thought coexist with every awareness in the realm of desire (see I, 30), every good nonmeditative awareness is accompanied by at least twenty-two accompanying mental factors.

29-30.(E197-198; T198-199) It is explained which accompanying mental factors go with bad awarenesses and which with neutral awarenesses.

31.(E199; T199) In the first meditational state the bad accompanying mental factors no longer exist, nor do regret nor sleepiness. In the state between the first and second meditational states, initial thought drops out. From the second meditational state on, sustained thought is dropped.

32.(E201-204; T200-202) Shame has to do with an emotion felt internally in regard to something done which is bad; modesty is an emotion felt in reference to the outer world.

33.(E204-207; T202-204) Vaibhāṣika: Initial and sustained thought are the grossness and subtlety of awareness.

What is the difference between pride (*māna*) and arrogance (*mada*)? Pride is an inflation of awareness. Arrogance is an exaltation and abolition of awareness in regard to "one's own" factors.

34.(E208-209; T205) "*Citta*", "*manas*", and "*vijñāna*" are synonyms (all meaning awareness).

35-36.(E209-211; T206-207) Vaibhāṣika: Among the motivating dispositions dissociated from awareness are possession, which makes for acquisition (see II, 23), and nonpossession, which makes for dissociation, loss of possession.

37-39.(E219-224; T212-215) More details about possession.

40.(E224-226; T215-217) Vaibhāṣika: The state of one who is separate from *dharma* is equivalent to nonpossession of the path.

41a.(E229; T221) Vaibhāṣika: Homogeneity within a lifetime is another kind of dissociated factor.

41b-42.(E233-236; T221-224) In nonideation trance the awareness and mental states cease; one practising it experiences only karmic maturation in the Bṛhatphala heaven. It presupposes entrance into the fourth meditative trance state by one desiring liberation. It is clear, and its karma is completely worked off in the next life. It is not attained by noble persons. It is experienced at one time.

43.(E236-238; T225-226) Cessation-trance is like the nonideation trance in several respects. However, cessation-trance constitutes the summit of existence, and the maturation of its karma is of two sorts or neutral. Nobles, not ordinary folk, can gain it by effort.

44.(E238-248; T226-233) Cessation-trance is obtained at enlightenment, not before. The two trances (nonideation and cessation) occur in the realm of desire and the material realm, but one's first cessation-trance must occur as a human.

45a.(E248-253; T233-238) Vitality is the life-force, the locus of heat and consciousness.

45b-46a.(E253-256; T240-247) Conditioned factors are characterized by birth, aging, duration and termination. Also by birth of birth, aging of aging, etc.

47-48.(E270-277; T250-254) Vaibhāṣika: The collection of words, collection of phrases, and collection of syllables are dissociated factors. They occur in living beings in the realm of desire and the material realm as outflows and neutral, as does also homogeneity.

48.(E277-279; T278-279) There are six kinds of causes: efficient cause, simultaneous cause, homogeneous cause, connected cause, pervasive cause, and retributory cause.

50.(E277-278; T255) All factors are efficient causes of everything except themselves. Simultaneous causes include the elements, awareness and its companions, marks and things marked--they are each others' effects.

51.(E283-284; T257-258) Companions of awareness include mental factors, the two restraints and their marks.

52.(E291-300; T262-268) Homogeneous causes are when cause and effect belong to similar group and state: thus good factors give rise to good factors, etc.

53.(E303-307; T269-272) Associated causes are only awarenesses and mental factors which have the same support.

54.(E308-310; T273-274) Pervasive causes are defiled factors, which arise in every instance of defiled states. Only good and bad factors susceptible to being linked with defilements are retributory causes.

55.(E316-317; T277-278) The unconditioned has neither a cause nor an effect.

56-60.(E327-340) T286-296) Discussion of which kinds of results accrue from the six kinds of causes, and when.

61.(E341-342; T296-297) There are four kinds of conditions.

62. (E342-349; T297-303) Except for the very last one, awarenesses and mental concomitants are the directly antecedent conditions.

63-64. (E350-3521; T304-306) There is always a plurality of causes and conditions making for the existence of any factor. Thus there is no unique cause like God. If there were a unique cause for all events, all events would occur at the same time.

65. (E355-356; T308-309) Causal relations among the great elements and derived factors.

66-72. (E357-372; T310-315) Classification of awarenesses and mental factors in the various realms, and which came before and after which.

73. (E372-376; T323-324) At conception in the womb, in meditation, in detachment, at the end of detachment, and upon developing the good roots, awarenesses arise which never arose before in the series.

## CHAPTER THREE: The World

1-3. (E379-383; T365-367) The realm of desire includes those in hells, ghosts, animals, humans and six kinds of gods--twenty states in all. The material realm is divided into four meditational states. The immaterial realm is not a state, but has four varieties as well. There the stream of awarenesses depends on homogeneity and vitality.

4. (E387-392; T371-374) In these three realms there are five courses: they are undefiled-neutral, comprise living beings, and exclude the intermediate state.

5. (E393; T374-377) Beings of the five sorts occupy seven states of consciousness: (1) where bodies and ideas are different; (2) where bodies differ but ideas are similar; (3) where ideas are different but they have similar bodies; (4) where both body and ideas are similar; (5) - (7) constituting the three immaterial kinds of beings.

6. (E396; T377) The remaining sorts of beings reduce consciousness.

7b-8. (E398-401; T378-380) Another classification of states of consciousness counts the four contaminating aggregates of the relevant spheres; (the fifth,) consciousness itself is not a state of consciousness.

9. (E402-403; T381) Human beings and animals are either born from an egg, born of moisture, born from the womb or are magical beings. Beings in hell or in the intermediate state, as well as gods, are

magical beings. Ghosts are either magical or womb-born.

10-12.(405-411; T384-387) The intermediate state is required, since a being cannot generate itself again if it were to cease. It can't be generated as a reflection (a mirror-image), since two things can't occupy the same place. Anyway, a reflection is not (part of) the stream, (that being) caused by something else (viz., the mirror).

*Sūtras* authoritative about the intermediate state are cited.

13-14.(E4129-424; T391-394) In the intermediate state one has the form he will have in his next birth. This form is seen by those occupying the same class and by those with the divine eye. One in the intermediate state has extraordinary strength and eats odors.

15.(E426-429; T394-397) The intermediate being, its mind perverted, goes to its place of rebirth because of sexual desire. Others go motivated by a place's smell or a desire for a place of residence, whereas hell-beings hang from their feet.

16-17.(E430; T397) Not all those in the womb are of perverted mind, but all those born from eggs are. *Cakravartins* enter the womb fully conscious, but do not remain or leave so. Self-enlightened *buddhas* remain fully conscious in the womb but do not leave it thus. A Buddha is always fully conscious.

18.(E432-433; T399) There is no self, only the aggregates. It is the aggregates which reincarnate in another existence, through the medium of an intermediary existence.

20-24.(E435-439; T401-404) Concerning the dependent origination formula: ignorance > conditioning factors > consciousness > psychophysical complex > six sense-fields > contact > feelings and identifications > craving > grasping > being > birth > aging and death. It can be interpreted in several ways: one can take ignorance and conditioning factors as referring to the anterior life, the next eight to the present life, and the rest to the life to come. On this interpretation "consciousness" is the consciousness at conception in the womb, and may stand for all the aggregates at conception. Contact first arises when the child is able to distinguish causes of frustration and satisfaction; "feelings" here refers to the feelings after sexual maturity, which are followed by cravings and graspings. "Being" refers to the conditions for the new rebirth.

25.(E440-441; T405) The reason for the teaching of dependent origination as relating to three lives is to remove misunderstandings.

27.(E443; T407) From a defilement another defilement may arise.

28b-29.(E463-464; T419-420) Ignorance is itself a distinct factor, the contrary of knowledge, as *amitra* (a "nonfriend") is an enemy (not just anyone other than one's friend). It is a separate fetter. Ignorance is not evil wisdom, for evil wisdom is a view, views are associated with ignorance, and ignorance is an affliction of wisdom (not of ignorance itself).

30-31.(E467-473; T422-426) Types of contact, which are produced by contiguity, are six in number. Five involve impingement. The sixth contact is of three sorts, (a) pure, involving knowledge, (b) defiled, involving ignorance, and (c) neither.

32ab.(E473; T426) Six feelings are caused by contact, five bodily and one mental.

32cd-35.(E479-485; T431-435) There are eighteen kinds of feelings, corresponding to the eighteen mental ponderings. All eighteen operate in the realm of desire, twelve in the material realm, and three in the immaterial realm.

37d-38c.(E491; T438-439) Among the four states of existence rearising is always defiled by the defilements of its stage of being. The other three can be good, bad or neutral.

38d-41.(E492-496; T439-444) On what is and what is not "food" in the three realms.

42-44.(E501-506; T447-451) Death and birth happen to mental awareness and involve equanimity. They don't occur during meditation, nor do they occur to one without awareness. The mind dies in that part of the body towards which it will proceed (the feet for hell, etc.).

45-93.(E506-544; T451-479) Cosmology. Description of our world, of hells, of the sun and moon, of heavens. The sizes and length of life of the inhabitants of these regions.

94-99.(E544-557; T481-489) Buddhas appear on earth when the age of men approximates 100 years a lifetime. Self-enlightened Buddhas appear at two different times. *Cakravartin* kings have a lifetime of 80,000 years or more. An eon terminates through war, sickness and hunger.

## CHAPTER FOUR: Karma

1.(E567-568; T551-552) Vasubandhu reduces all karma to volition and the bodily and vocal actions produced by volition.

2.(E568-569; T552) Bodily and vocal karma can be manifest or unmanifest. Manifest bodily karma determines configuration. There is no (acting in the sense of) movement, since all conditioned things are momentary, disappearing.

3.(E570-578; T552-560) Still, nothing disappears without a cause, so the cause of anything is also a destroyer.

Configuration is perceived by two. An atom has no configuration.

Vocal bodily action (on the other hand) is speech.

4ab.(E579; T560) *Sūtras* say that there are three kinds of material form, one of which is pure; that there is increase (of *dharma*); that one acts by giving order to others to act, etc.

4cd.(E590; T568) Unmanifest karma in the realm of desire is derived from past elements.

5-9.(E590-600; T569-575) Impure bodily and vocal actions in each realm arise with the great elements constituting their "agents" in that realm. Pure actions arise in the great elements of the "person" who produced them. Unmanifest actions are not appropriated; they bear fruit naturally in living beings alone. That fruit is never neutral, and occurs in the realms of desire and matter.

Manifest actions only occur in the first two realms (of desire and matter), but in the material realm the only such actions are movements of the great elements--the blowing of the wind, etc. Others say there are manifest actions in all four realms.

10-12.(E600-604; T576-579) Vaibhāṣika: That which originates something (*samutthāna*) is of two kinds; the inciting causal factor (*pravartaka*) called *hetusamutthāna* and the accompanying causal factor which originates in the same moment, called *tatkṣaṇasamutthāna*.

The kind of consciousness which is given up by seeing the four truths is an inciter only. The mental consciousness given up by meditation is both an inciter and an accompanying causal factor. The five sensory consciousnesses are inciting causal factors only.

That which arises from retribution arises spontaneously without any conditioning factors being necessary. Thus retribution is neither a primary nor an accompanying causal factor.

13-15.(E605-608; T580-583) There are three kinds of unmanifest karma: that involved in discipline, that not involved in discipline, and that which is neither. Disciplined action may be according to monastic discipline (*prātimokṣa*), that involving meditation, and that which is noncontaminating. Those practising monastic discipline may be of eight or (alternatively) four types, depending on whether men are classified with or separately from women. The four are: laymen, abstainers, monks and *bhikṣus*.

16.(E609-610; T309-310) Monastic discipline consists of following moral precepts, active good conduct, action, and restraint. According to the Sautrāntikas, but not according to the Vaibhāṣikas, it does not constitute a separate kind of entity.

17-31.(E610-627; T584-600) Which are those aspirants who possess which sort of manifest and unmanifest karma and for how long is explained.

32.(E628-630; T601) Someone who takes refuge in the Buddha, the *dharma* and the order is actually taking refuge in the special events which make for a Buddha, the events making up the action of the order, and *nirvāṇa*.

33.(E631; T603-604) Whereas the monk or nun takes on chastity, it is enough for laymen and laywomen if they renounce illicit love (see IV, 67).

34.(E632-635; T605) Among the bad vocal actions (see IV, 67) it is false speech which is the worst. Avoiding proclivities is enjoined upon the layman so that the other rules can be kept.

35-39.(E638-647; T607-614) More on moral matters.

40-44.(E646-651; T616-620) How one leaves a realm by either progressing or backsliding.

45-48.(E652-655; T621-624) Differentiation of good, bad and neutral actions and their three corresponding kinds of retributions.

In the realm of desire clean karma is merit. In the higher realms unchangeable action is good because its retribution can only take place in the realm in which the deed was done.

Clean karma breeds satisfaction in the first three meditative trances. In the fourth it breeds results that are neither satisfying nor frustrating. Bad karma breeds foul, frustrating feelings in the realm of desire.

Some say that neutral karma (that is neither satisfying nor frustrating) occurs below the fourth meditative state, because there is no maturation in the intermediate state (between the first two stages) and because karmic maturation of all three sorts (good, bad, neutral) can occur at the same time.

49-50.(E656-657; T624-625) There are five things that are called "feelings": feelings themselves, connections with things, supporting objects, maturations and experiencings of feelings. These feelings are determined or not determined. Determined feeling is that experienced in this very life.

51-52.(E658-660; T626-628) Some others say there are four (kinds of karma).

A noble person does not produce any karma experienceable in a later existence.

53.(E660-661; T628-629) One in the intermediate state in the realm of desire performs twenty-two kinds of actions that mature in the same existence.

54-55.(E661-662; T629-630) Determined feeling results from action involving intense defilements or intense serenity that has to do with certain fields, or from the murder of a father or mother.

56.(E663; T631) The effects of acts are immediately experienced by five sorts: one who has just left cessation-trance, one who has just left the nonpassionate trance, one who has just left the trance of loving kindness, one who has just left the path of vision, one who has become a noble person.

57-58.(E664-667; T632-634) Feelings that result from good actions free of initial thought are only mental. Feelings resulting from bad actions are only physical. Mental disorders--fear, hallucinations, irritation--are karmic results afflicting those in the realm of desire.

59-60.(E668-669; T635) About bad (black), good (white) and mixed (black-white) karma.

61-63.(E670-672; T636-637) The kinds of acts that destroy bad karma are twelve--four patiences and the first eight paths of nonattachment in the realm of desire. The thoughts of the ninth path are those that destroy mixed (black-white) karma. The thoughts that occur while practising meditative nonattachment destroy the good karma.

Others say that retributions of both bad and neutral karma occur in hell as well as in the realm of desire. Still others say that bad karma is that which can be abandoned by vision, whereas neutral karma can be abandoned by meditation.

64-65.(E672-674; T638-639) The adept's bodily, vocal and mental acts are the three sagely (*mauna*) things.

There are three bad practices that are not actions, and good practice is the opposite of these.

67.(E676; T641) Six courses of bad action can be unmanifest acts.

One bad act is always of two kinds, and the rest are of two kinds when one does them himself. Seven kinds of good actions are of two kinds; they are unmanifest only when occurring during meditation.

69.(E682; T646-647) Good actions, enumerated as the abandonments of the bad ones, arise from nondesire, nonhatred and lack of false views.

72.(E684; T648-649) Even someone who has been forced into the army should never kill.

73.(E685-687; T649-651) The "taking of life" enumerated refers to wilful killing, not accidental killing.

74.(E687-688; T651-652) Offenses of lust comprise intercourse with four kinds of women one should not consort with. False speech--lying--is addressing one who understands a meaning of the words used but where the speaker uses the words with a different intent.

75-78.(E689-695; T653-658) The rest of the six principal bad actions are discussed.

79-80.(E697-702; T659-663) The good roots are severed, among humans completely or gradually, by the view that they don't exist, the denial of causal relations. Both men and women may sever good roots or bad roots.

82-84.(E708-710; T666-668) Which courses of action are available in the different realms.

85.(E711-712; T669-670) Each course of action has retributional, outflowing, and dominant result. The retribution of murder is suffering, of outflows a short life; the dominant result is loss of energy.

86-94.(E713-720; T671-677) Details concerning the kinds and numbers of factors resulting from good, bad and neutral acts.

95.(E721-722; T677-678) But the retributional effect of an act can occur only in the same life, or in the next life: it cannot extend for two lives after the act. Even though they have a retribution, the highest meditational attainments don't project an action, because they don't coexist with conscious action. There are three kinds of obstructions: obstructions due to past actions, obstructions which are defilements, obstructions which are retributional.

96.(E722-724; T679-680) The obstructions due to actions are those coming primarily from the five grave offences: killing one's mother, killing one's father, killing a noble person, causing division in the order, and harming a Buddha. It is a graver offence to kill one's mother than it is to kill one's father.

98-102.(E725-729; T681-685) Causing divisions in the order is lying. One who causes such division falls to the *avīci* hell for an entire eon. More about such schisms.

103.(E730-732; T685-686) The same kind of gravity does not occur if a person kills his mother thinking it's someone else, or if he kills her accidentally.

106-107.(E734-735; T689-690) Other grave offences include defiling one's mother or a noble person, killing a Bodhisattva or an adept, stealing from the order, or destroying a *stūpa*.

108-112b.(E735-739; T690-694) The retributional effects of acts can be severed by the acquisition of perfect patience or forbearance, or by becoming a nonreturner (one who is never reborn among human beings, but may be reborn among gods), or by becoming a noble person.

One is a Bodhisattva when he performs actions that produce (some of) the (thirty-two) marks. Only males in Jambudvīpa have such marks, which arise from one hundred merits. The virtues of a Bodhisattva are described.

112c-127.(E739-755; T694-708) Giving, morality and meditation are meritorious acts separately and in combination. Whom to give to and what to give are indicated. Giving produces satisfying experience, morality produces heaven, meditation produces liberation.

## CHAPTER FIVE: Proclivities

1-2a.(E759-761; T767-768) Proclivities are the roots of existence. There are six: attachment, repugnance, pride, ignorance, views, and perplexity. Dividing attachment into attachment to sensual pleasure and attachment to existence there are seven.

2b-d.(E764-765; T771) There are two kinds of attachment to existence: attachment to existence in the material realm and attachment to existence in the immaterial realm (see I, 30).

3.(E765; T772) There are five kinds of false views: belief in a self, extreme beliefs, adherence to particular views, adherence to mere rule and ritual, and other false views.

4.(E765; T773) The four noble truths counteract these traces.

5.(E766-768; T773-774) Four proclivities are abandoned through meditation in the realm of desire, and (excepting repugnance) in the other three realms, so that there are ninety-eight proclivities in all.

8.(E773; T779) Insistence on God as cause of the world, etc., which arises from mistaken views about permanence and self, is abandoned through vision.

9.(E778-779; T781-782) There are four mistaken views falling into three of the five kinds of view. Identifications and awarenesses also can be erroneous.

10-11.(E782-785; T784-788) There are seven kinds of pride that are destroyed by vision and meditation. The enveloper of killing, etc. is destroyed by meditation, as well as the desire to leave off existing. Pride and foul regret, involving views, are never found in noble persons.

12-19.(E785-794; T788-798) On the pervasive proclivities, how they function, in which realm.

20-24.(E795-803; T798-805) Attachment, resistance and delusion are the bad roots. Three--craving, ignorance and intellection--are neutral roots. The other proclivities are not roots at all. The outsiders (*bāhyaka*) say four--craving, views, pride and delusion--are neutral.

Which are the questions that can be answered outright, which by making distinctions, which in relation to what, which involving complexity?

25-26.(E804-808; T806-810)[523] Vaibhāṣika: Future and past factors exist as well as present ones, because the Buddha taught it, because of two, because an object exists, because of result.

There are four kinds of Sarvāstivādins, depending on whether they teach difference in being, in definition, in state or mutually. The third view is best.

Temporal distinctions are established by their functioning.

28-31.(E819-823; T820-833) Is one who realizes the first truth (of frustration) released from previous frustrations altogether? No, since he is bound to them by the pervasive proclivities, and remains so through the fourth, immaterial stage.

32-33.(E828-829; T825-828) Doubt arises from delusion. It results in false views, and from false views arises the view of a fixed self in the body. From the view of a fixed self in the body arises adherence to mere rule and ritual; from this in turn arises adherence to particular views; from this arises attachment and pride; from that, aversion.

34.(E829-830; T828) The defilements arise when their proclivities have not been eradicated, or when an object liable to make them arise occurs, or from careless mental attention.

36.(E831; T830-831) Ignorance is the root.

37-40.(E832-835; T831-834) Likewise the floods and bonds, which include views, are proclivities, as well as the graspings, which include ignorance. These various classifications are interrelated.

42.(E838; T837) Envy and selfishness are particularly named because they arise from ignorance itself.

47-48a.(E844; T842) The envelopers are shamelessness, disregard, envy, selfishness, excitedness, regret, lethargy and sleepiness; anger and hypocrisy also.

48b-49.(E485; T843) From attachment arise shamelessness, excitedness and selfishness. From ignorance arise lethargy, sleepiness and disregard. From perplexity regret arises. From repugnance arise envy and anger.

50b-51a.(E486; T844) From attachment arise arrogance and deceit. From repugnance arise vengefulness and violence. From adherence to views arises spite. From views arises craftiness.

51b-52.(E847; T846-847) Shamelessness, disregard, lethargy, sleepiness and excitedness can be eradicated by seeing the truths and by meditation; the others can only be eradicated by meditation.

56.(E849-850; T849) Perplexity is associated with irritation. The others which are views, with the exception of false views and pride, are associated usually with satisfaction. All of them may be associated with indifference.

57.(E850; T849-850) Regret, envy, hypocrisy, violence, vengefulness and spite are always associated with frustration.

58.(E850-851; T850) Craftiness, deceit, hypocrisy and sleepiness may be associated with either satisfaction or frustration. Shamelessness, disregard, lethargy and excitedness can be associated with frustration, contentedness, satisfaction or irritation.

59-62.(E851-858; T851-857) Lethargy and sleepiness, and excitedness and regret, are two pairs that as pairs count as obstructions, since they oppose the same things.

Defilements are destroyed by comprehension, by destroying homogeneous defilements, by abandoning their objects.

63.(E860; T858-859) Destruction of homogeneous defilements takes place variously: by the arising of an antidote, by acquisition of results, or by perfection of the faculties.

64-70.(E861-870; T862-869) Discussion of the nine ascertainments and six results of patience, and how they are attained.

CHAPTER SIX: The Saints and the Path

1.(E871; T895) The path consists of two divisions: the path of vision, where false views are abandoned, and the path of meditation.

2.(E872; T896) On the four truths.

3.(E875; T899) Contaminating factors involve one or another of three kinds of frustration.

4.(E8898; T910) Awareness of a jar ends when the jar is broken; awareness of water ends when one analyzes it. Jug and water exist (only) conventionally. What is (highest) truth is different.

6.(E892; T913-914) Meditation succeeds when the practitioner is withdrawn from society and when his awarenesses are removed from bad mental applications.

7.(E893; T914-915) Insatiability has an antidote in contentment and in wishing for little. These are forms of absence of greed.

8cd.(E894; T916) Both the desire for an object and the ideas of "mine" and "I" are removed, either momentarily or definitively, in meditation.

9-11a.(E894-897; T916-919) Description of the meditational process by which one reduces one's body to its elements: skeletal system, etc.

12.(E898-899; T921-922) Description of the Buddhist breathing meditation.

13.(E901-902; T923-925) On breathing.

14-18.(E902-909; T925-932) Discussion of the four establishments of mindfulness focussed on the flow of the material elements of the body, on feelings, on awarenesses, and on factors, meaning here primarily conditioning factors.

19.(E911-912; T932-933) Relation of the meditational stages of the aids to penetration with the establishment of mindfulness.

20-24.(E914-921; T935-942) The four aids to penetration.

25-26.(E921-924; T942-946) Immediately after the aids to penetration the first moment of the path of vision occurs. It is called "the patience (necessary) for the knowledge of factors in frustration", whose content is frustration in the realm of desires. Immediately after it arises knowledge of factors which is frustration itself. Immediately after that occurs the subsequent patience (necessary) for the knowledge of factors in frustration. This, and the subsequent knowledges of factors in frustration relate to frustration of the material and immaterial realms. The same sequence of four patiences and knowledges occurs subsequently for the other noble truths.

27.(E925-928; T946-949) Thus in total there are sixteen awareness-moments on the path of vision.

29-32.(E933-936; T952-955) In the path of vision those who have mild faculties are faith-followers, those with keen faculties are factor-followers. Unless they have already conquered (the proclivities) by meditation they become candidates for stream-enterer-ship. Then, when they attain the ninth awareness-moment of the path of vision, they become candidates for the once-returner state, and thence candidates for the third state (of nonreturner) by abandoning that awareness. In the sixteenth moment they achieve the state for which they were candidates and become resolved in faith or in vision.

33-39.(E938-955; T956-971) Each of the four stages has nine levels, depending on whether it is weaker or stronger. Terms for those at certain points along the way: A stream-enterer-candidate who has not started to eliminate the proclivities conquered by meditation is "one who has seven more lives to live". When three or four levels of the first stage (the stage of desire) have been eliminated he is termed "going from family to family" (*kulaṃkula*). When five levels are eliminated he becomes a candidate for once-returner-ship (*sakṛdāgāmin*), and attains it on eliminating the sixth level. A "single-seeker" (*ekavīcika*) is one who has eliminated the seventh or eighth level.

There are seven kinds of nonreturners: (1) one who achieves liberation in the intermediate state, (2) one who achieves it as soon as he is reborn, (3) one who gains liberation through effort, (4) one who gets liberation without effort, (5) one who goes higher to the *akaniṣṭha* heaven or to the summit of existence, (6) one who goes to the immaterial state, and (7) one who is liberated in the present life. Nine kinds of nonreturners go to the material realm.

44.(E956-970; T980-981) The nonreturner is a candidate for perfected being until he destroys the eighth part of the summit of existence. The ninth part is diamond-like, involving knowledge of liberation.

45-49.(E971-977; T983-990) There are two kinds of spiritual path: mundane and supramundane. The learner detaches himself by the supramundane path from the world (at the summit of existence), from the other realms by either path.

50-57.(E978-990; T991-1003) Then, immovable, he is aware that he will not arise again, while retaining the insight of an adept. Then he is a true monk. Various classes of perfected beings are distinguished.

58.(E992; T1003) Who can regress from their genus and who from their realm.

63-64.(E1007-1011; T1016-1019) Noble persons can be of one of seven kinds, depending on their application, their faculties, their meditative attainment, their liberation, their being of two kinds. The adept achieving cessation is one liberated in both of the two ways; others are liberated through wisdom. A disciple is incomplete in meditative attainment, in faculties and in result.

67-79.(E1016-1032; T1023-1039) On the limbs of enlightenment.

## CHAPTER SEVEN: The Knowledges

(This Chapter relates primarily to the knowledges gained on the path of vision.)

1.(E1033-1035; T1087-1088) The patiences experienced on the path of vision are not knowledge.

2-4.(E1035-1036; T1088-1090) Awarenesses are contaminating or noncontaminating. Contaminating awareness is conventional. Noncontaminating awarenesses are either awarenesses of factors like frustrations, etc. or inferential awarenesses concerning them; together they constitute knowledge of destruction and of nonorigination.

5-6ab.(E1036-1038; T1090-1092) One can know others' awarenesses, though not those in a higher realm, nor the past and future, nor others' awareness of factors and inferences.

13.(E1057-1062; T1110-1117) There are sixteen aspects, and they constitute wisdom.

14.(E1062-1063; T1117-1118) Conventional knowledge may be either good, bad, or neutral. All the knowledges on the path of vision are good only.

15.(E1063-1064; T1119) Knowledge of others' awarenesses occurs only in the four meditational stages.

16.(E1064-1065; T1119-1120) It also involves necessarily knowledge of others' feelings, cognitions, and motivating dispositions.

33.(E1093-1095; T1143-1144) The great compassion of a Buddha differs from other compassion.

34.(E1096-1099; T1145) All Buddhas are equal as far as their body of essential teaching is concerned, and as far as their service to others, but they differ on less essential things: caste, duration of their lives, etc.

36-41.(E1100-1106; T1149-1156) Nonpassion is a conventional awareness of the fourth meditative sphere, produced by immovable (noble) humans, and helps block future defilements of others. So also are knowledge from vows and of factors and the discriminations of factors, objects, etymologies and perspicuities.

42-47.(E1106-1115; T1157-1167) The six higher faculties of a Buddha are supernatural powers: divine ear, knowing other' intentions and thoughts, memory of past lives, divine visual power, and the knowledge of the destruction of frustrations. They provide awareness of the path to liberation. Four are conventional awarenesses, five exist in one of the four trance states. They relate to their own or a lower sphere. The first three constitute the first establishment of mindfulness. All are good except the divine eye and ear which are neutral. Only the knowledge of the destruction of proclivities is found in the adept; knowledge of others' intentions and of past lives are said to belong there but in that relation do not constitute wisdom.

48-53.(E1115-1121; T1168-1176) Supernatural power is concentration, and enables one's mind to move rapidly and create magical beings. Magical beings can speak by their creator's speaking at another time and locating the speech in the magical body. He can even locate the speech after his death (though this is not accepted by some). Supernatural powers can also be exercised through *mantras*, through medicinal plants, or through karma.

## CHAPTER EIGHT: The Meditational Concentration

2.(E1129-1130; T1216-1220) The first meditational stage is accompanied by sustained thought, joy and satisfaction; these are successively abandoned in the other three states.

The immaterial meditational attainments are made up of the four aggregates excluding matter.

3.(E1137; T1225) There is no matter in the immaterial attainments. Matter arises from (karmically conditioned) awareness.

13.(E1150-1151; T1241) The consciousnesses in the higher stages of meditational concentration are all unobstructed and neutral.

14-23.(E1151-1163; T1243-1256) How and when the attainments are accomplished.

29-38.(E1170-1185; T1264-1280) The four boundless states and the eight liberations culminating in cessation trance.

39.(E1176; T1281) The *dharma* of the Buddha has two aspects: *āgama* (the teaching itself) and *adhigama* (the allies of enlightenment, cf. VI, 66) and their results.

## CHAPTER NINE: Refutation of the Self

(This Chapter, being in prose only, unlike the rest of the *Abhidharmakośa* which is in verse, seems to have been originally an independent treatise. It has as its aim the refutation of the self as found in Vaiśeṣika, etc., as well as of the "person" as found in the Vātsīputrīyas.)[522]

(E1189-1193; T1313-1315) How can we know that "self" is only a designation for a series of factors? There is no evidence of any sort for a "self" apart from the elements of constituting personality. The Vātsīputrīya admits a person (*pudgala*) which is neither totally identical with the aggregates nor totally different from them. Does this person exist as an entity (*dravyatas*) or only as a designation (*prajñaptitas*)? If the person is an entity, it has to be different from other aggregates, it has to be either produced by causes, which means it can't be lasting as the Vātsīputrīya claims, or be unconditioned, in which case it has no efficacy. Thus the person can't be an entity. But if it is only a designation, then we have no argument.

Vātsīputrīya: The person is neither an entity nor just a designation. It occurs in relation to the aggregates.

Vasubandhu: What do you mean? If you mean that the term "*pudgala*" arises only with the aggregates, then we have no argument.

(E1193-1195; T1315-1317) Vātsīputrīya: It is rather like the case of fire and the combustible material. Fire cannot exist apart from the material, and yet the two are not identical.

Vasubandhu: But what exactly is it that is being designated as "fire", as "combustible material"?

Vātsīputrīya: It is the series of the "combustible material" which is turned into ashes by the series "fire".

Vasubandhu: But the material must exist previously to the fire in order for the fire to arise. For your analogy to be exact, the person must thus arise after the aggregates, and be transitory as well.

Vātsīputrīya: No, because fire exists inherently in the combustible material. But since their characteristics are different--"fire" being that element in the combustible material which allows for its combustion--"fire"and "combustible material" are entities apart.

Vasubandhu: One can't claim that fire is the cause of the material, and any other clear relationship between them is also not established.

Vātsīputrīya: But there is a coexistence of fire and the material; thus fire has that material as its support.

Vasubandhu: This means that fire is different from the material, but that it doesn't exist unless the combustible material does. For your analogy to be exact, the person must be different from the aggregates, and yet exist only with the aggregates.

Vātsīputrīya: But in our analogy fire is not completely different from the material, since the material is also hot.

Vasubandhu: What is the nature of heat? If one defines the hot as being the element heat, i.e., fire, then the material is not itself fire. If one extends the adjective "hot" to include the material, then two different kinds of things are being defined by the same adjective.

Vātsīputrīya: Wood being burned is called both combustible material and fire.

Vasubandhu: What then is the sense of your statement that fire exists in relation to the material? From what you just said "fire" and "combustible material" are the same, and no relation can exist between them. Thus your analogy does not demonstrate a relationship between the person and the aggregates.

(E1195-1201; T1318-1322) Vātsīputrīya: The person is neither exactly the same as the aggregates nor completely different from them.

Vasubandhu: If the expression "*pudgala* (person)" is used only where the aggregates occur, it is nothing but the aggregates. If it is used in relation to an independent person, then why say it arises in relation to the aggregates?

Vātsīputrīya: When the aggregates exist, the person is perceived.

Vasubandhu: By which consciousness is it perceived?

Vātsīputrīya: By all six.

Vasubandhu: It is impossible to establish the existence of a perception of a person by the visual consciousness or any other consciousness.

(E1201-1204; T1322-1327) Canonical support for the nonexistence of the person.

(E1205-1206; T1327-1328) Vātsīputrīya: But there is also a *sūtra* which says "In the past, I had this form."

Vasubandhu: But the Buddha doesn't intend to say that there is a person which in the past had another form. This "I" is merely a metaphor for a psychophysical series. Similarly, one says "a current of water", even though this "current" really consists of a series of momentary events.

Vātsīputrīya: Then the Buddha is not omniscient. For one can't know all the aggregate-moments of all times. But one can know a person.

Vasubandhu: I don't believe the Buddha is omniscient in the way the Mahāsāṅghikas do. By the word "Buddha" I mean a certain psychophysical series which is associated with a particular power which allows any awareness arising in the series to completely know any particular object--this power in the series is called "omniscience".

(E1206-1207; T1328-1330) Vātsīputrīya: But there is a *sūtra* where the Buddha says "I will explain to you the burden, the taking of the burden, the depositing of the burden and the taker of the burden."

Vasubandhu: This *sūtra* does not establish the existence of a separate "taker". What it indicates is different phases in the psychophysical complex, as it itself explains.

(E1207-1214; T1330-1337) Examination of different *sūtra* passages where "person" is used metaphorically with the intention of reducing a questioner's confusion. Discussion of *sūtras* where the Buddha refuses to answer questions because whichever way he would answer would increase the questioner's confusion.

(E1214-1215; T1337-1338) Vātsīputrīya: If the person doesn't exist how can there be transmigration?

Vasubandhu: The term "transmigration" is a metaphor. Just as one says "the fire is spreading", new flames in reality arising at each moment, in the same way momentary events are arising which are related to each other as cause and effect, this series having different loci.

(E1215-1218; T1339-1342)[523] Vātsīputrīya: If there is no person, and only momentary events, how can there be memory of a long past event?

Vasubandhu: For memory to occur there must be a special

awareness directed at the object of memory which is connected with cognitions relating to the object or to objects similar to it, or to a resolution to remember.

Vātsīputrīya: But how can one awareness have perceived the object and another totally different awareness remember it later? Yajñadatta can't remember the object seen by Devadatta!

Vasubandhu: There is no connection between Yajñadatta and Devadatta--their awarenesses are not in a relation of cause and effect. However, the awareness which perceived an object and the awareness which later remembers it are related as cause and effect. The awareness which perceived is the cause of the awareness which remembers in the same way as a seed is the cause of a future fruit, through a transformation of the intermediary events of the series.

(E1219-1220; T1342-1344) It is said that Devadatta cognizes because the psychophysical complex which is termed "Devadatta" is the cause of a consciousness' arising. What is consciousness doing? Nothing. It arises coordinately (*sādṛśya*) with its object. Actually it does nothing in relation to the object, but it is said to perceive the object because it arises coordinately with it. This coordination consists of the fact that the consciousness has the aspect (*ākāra*) of the object. This is why the consciousness is said to perceive the object, even though the object is only one of its causes; the other causes, such as the sense-organ, are not related to the consciousness in the same sense that it takes its aspect. A factor gives rise to a succeeding factor which may have the same object--thus it is said to be an agent, because it is a cause. It is metaphorically said to perceive just as one says that an oil-lamp, or its flame, moves--in reality there are only successions of flame-moments. In the same way, "consciousness" is used as a term for a series of momentary awarenesses. When an awareness-moment occurs relatively to a new object it is said, metaphorically, that consciousness is perceiving its object.

(E1220-1222; T1344-1346) Sāṃkhya: If a succeeding consciousness arises from an anterior one, and not from a self, why is the succeeding consciousness not always similar to the previous one, and why don't the consciousnesses arise according to a fixed succession?

Vasubandhu: Everything is constantly transforming (see II, 45). And there is a certain order as to which awarenesses arise from which.

(E1222-1226; T1346-1348) The Vaiśeṣika claims that awarenesses arise from a self. But we can use the same arguments just used against us: Why is a succeeding awareness not the same as a previous one? Why don't awarenesses arise according to a fixed succession?

Vaiśeṣika: Because there is a great diversity in the contacts of the self and the internal organ.

Vasubandhu: Contact itself cannot be established. Your own definition of "contact" implies that two entities in contact are delimited and localized. Thus, following your theory, the self cannot be omnipresent as you claim. Following your theory, also, when the internal organ is directed towards a part of the body the self must also be so directed, and thus either it isn't devoid of action, as you claim it is, or it is not eternal, which you claim it to be. You can't claim that only a part of the self is conjoined with the internal organ, for according to you the self has no parts. And if there were an immutable contact between the self and the internal organ, how could one explain the diversity of awarenesses? This diversity is also inexplicable if the self is not diverse. If you say that this diversity results from the diversity of the contacts of the selves and internal organs, which diversity results from the diversity of traces, then why not say that the diversity of awarenesses results from the diversity of traces? The self is not necessary in that case. If you say that the self is the support of the traces and the internal organ, this cannot be literally true, since there can be no physical contact with an immaterial self. If you say that the self supports the traces in the same way that the earth supports smells, then you have come over to our position, for we claim that "earth" is nothing more than a designation for a collection of smells, etc.

Vaiśeṣika: If earth is nothing but smells, etc. how can one speak of "the earth's smell"?

Vasubandhu: In the same way that one can say "the statue's body". If the self produces awarenesses because of the variety of the traces, why doesn't it produce all awarenesses at the same time?

(E1226; T1348-1349) Vaiśeṣika: Because the strongest trace prohibits the weaker ones from producing their effects. The traces are not permanent and are subject to transformation.

Vasubandhu: But what is the self doing here? The awarenesses seem to be arising from the traces alone.

Vaiśeṣika: Traces, etc., are qualities: a quality must have a substance as its substratum. And the substratum of traces must be the self.

Vasubandhu: But the entire system of substances and qualities is not proven. We think that everything that exists is a "substance" or entity.

Vaiśeṣika: If there is no self, how can there be retribution for acts?

(E1226-1228; T1349-1352) Vasubandhu: The retribution of acts affects a psychophysical series. It is this series, or even just certain elements in it, which is considered a self, such as when it is said "I am black", etc. The self which you postulate has got nothing to do with blackness, and yet the word "I" is used in this case. In the same way, every instance of the use of the term "I" really refers to the psychophysical series, or certain elements within it.

Vaiśeṣika: When one says "I am black" this does not refer to the self but to the body which serves the self.

Vasubandhu: But all expressions of "I" and "self" are metaphorical.

Vaiśeṣika: If the notion of "self" is only in reference to elements of a psychophysical complex, how does one distinguish self and others?

Vasubandhu: Because there is no relation between those other psychophysical complexes and the notion. It is only the psychophysical complex which is in a causal relation to the notion which is designated by that term.

Vaiśeṣika: If there is no self, to what do you attribute the notion of an "I"?

Vasubandhu: The psychophysical complex itself, the experiences of which are interrelated.

Vaiśeṣika: Who is the agent or enjoyer?

Vasubandhu: What do these terms even mean?

Vaiśeṣika: The agent is one who has an independent power in relation to an action. The enjoyer is he who experiences the effects of an action.

Vasubandhu: These definitions are untenable. What does one mean by "Devadatta"? If one means a self, it is still undemonstrated. If one means a complex of aggregates, then Devadatta is an agent, but not an independent one. A bodily action depends on an awareness acting on the body, and this body and awareness themselves depend upon other causes and conditions, and in all this there is no one entity which could be designated as an independent agent. According to you, the self does not depend on causes and conditions, and it doesn't do anything, thus it can't be an agent, either. What one designates as an agent of an act is according to us the principal cause, among many causes, of the act.

(E1229-1232; T1352-1355) The series of causes and conditions for an action is as follows: A memory makes the desire to act arise, from this desire to act arises an initial thought, from this initial thought arises an effort, which gives rise to a motile element, which puts the body into "motion". Where is there any room for a self in this process?

Vaiśeṣika: Without a self, how can an action in the past, which has already ceased, bring about a future effect?

Vasubandhu: The effect does not arise from the action, which has ceased. The effect arises as the last moment of the transformation of a series which originated with the act. It is the same as a fruit "arising from a seed"--in fact, it arises from the transformation of a series which has its origin in the seed. By a "series" we mean material and psychological elements which succeed each other without interruption. Each one of the momentary elements is different: thus it is said that the series is transforming. The last moment of an evolution has a special efficacy to produce a special effect. There is a difference to be noted between the force of retribution and the outcome (see I, 37-38). When the force of retribution gives its effect, the force itself ceases, thus there is only one retribution for an act, but the force of flow, which is projected by homogeneous causes, continues to operate, and only ceases by virtue of a specific antidote. The force of retribution, on the other hand, is rather like the case where one dyes a lemon-flower red, and this gives rise to a transformation in the series flower-fruit which has the result that the center of the lemon arising from the flower will also be red. But the red seed in the center of this lemon, if it is itself planted, will not give rise to another lemon with a red center. In the same way, the retribution of an action does not give rise to another retribution. Only the Buddhas know exactly how the psychophysical series, impregnated by the volitions of past actions, transform to give a retributional effect. In no case is it necessary to assume a self or personality-entity.

### 174. VASUBANDHU, *Bhāṣya* on his *Abhidharmakośa*

Since it has been doubted by some scholars that the authors of the *Kośa* and this *Bhāṣya* are the same, we have separated the summaries of the two works. "E" and "T" references are to the same texts as for the previous (#173) summary.

## Summary by Stefan Anacker

### CHAPTER ONE

2.(E11-13; T56-57Z) The "accompaniments" of pure wisdom are the five pure aggregates.

5c.(E19; T59) Space does not obstruct, and is not displaced by material form.

6.(E20-2; T59-60) Calculated cessations involve disjunctions from contaminating factors gained by wisdom concerning the four noble truths. These disjunctions are "separate", since one does not achieve complete cessation by only one disjunction.

7.(E21-27; T61-62) Conditioned factors "ex-ist" since it is from and through them that one "ex-its" to *nirvāṇa*. They involve actual objects in the sense of being causally conditioned.

10.(E32-35; T64-66) The two material bases are color and shape. Color and shape may occur separately.

Sautrāntika: How can a single entity be both color and shape, if these are distinct things?

Answer: Because they're found in a single thing.

Sautrāntika: Then you should admit a "manifest form" as an additional type of material form.

The eleven tangibles are: the four great elements, smoothness, roughness, heaviness, lightness, cold, hunger and thirst.

11.(E38-39; T68) Unmanifest form is termed "material" because it is derived from the great elements.

13.(E44-47; T70-72) Vaibhāṣika: To be "material" is to be capable of being damaged.

Vasubandhu: Some say, however, that the characteristic of materiality is that it exercises a resistance which makes it impenetrable. But in that case, a single atom itself is not material, as it exercises no resistance.

Vaibhāṣika: But the single atom never exists in an isolated state, and in combination with other atoms does exercise resistance.

Vasubandhu: Material entities of the past and future can't really be material, as they exercise no resistance.

Vaibhāṣika: But they were exercising or will exercise it!

Vasubandhu: Unmanifest form can't be matter.

Vaibhāṣika: Yes it can. One moment of unmanifest form depends upon previous moments which are material, just as the shadow of a tree depends on the tree.

Vasubandhu: But unmanifest form isn't subject to transformations, and does not cease when the manifest form does. Thus the simile of shadow and tree doesn't apply.

Vaibhāṣika: But unmanifest form is material, because it depends upon the material elements of the body.

Vasubandhu: In that case, the five visual consciousnesses are also material.

Vaibhāṣika: No, because unmanifest form rests totally on the material elements, as a shadow does on a tree, whereas the consciousnesses do not rest utterly on their organs, which are only the causes of the arisings.

Vasubandhu: But according to your own thesis each of the atoms which make up a shadow depends upon the four great elements. Thus they don't depend on the tree.

Vaibhāṣika: A visual consciousness depends not only on the eye, which is material, but also on the mind, which isn't.

14.(E48-49; T72-73) Experiencings are frustrating, satisfying, or neither.

15.(E49-50; T72-74) Vaibhāṣika: Unmanifest material form and the three unconditioned factors are also included within the sense-basis of factors or the realm of factors.

16.(E50-51; T74) The six kinds of manifesting are visual, auditory, olfactory, gustatory, tactile and mental. The seven elements comprise the elements of visual, audial, olfactory, gustatory, tactual and mental consciousness plus the mental element. There is no "mind" distinct from these consciousnesses.

20.(E60-63; T79-80) Vasubandhu: If the meaning of "*skandha*" as "aggregate", i.e., a group, is to be taken literally, then aggregates are only nominal entities, since groups are not actual entities.

Vaibhāṣika: No, because the atom itself is an aggregate.

Vasubandhu: Then don't say that the *skandhas* are aggregates!

Vaibhāṣika: Every instance of matter, whether past, present or future, is called an "aggregate".

Vasubandhu: But nonetheless they have only a nominal existence, if they are mere groups. The material sense-fields cannot give rise to sensory consciousnesses unless they are groups, since the individual atoms are not perceived. Thus the sense-fields have only nominal existence. The teaching of the aggregates has been devised to counteract the view of a self.

21.(E64; T81) Disputes mainly concern desires involving feelings, and opinions involving identifications.

23.(E67-68; T84) A mental consciousness may have an object which is simultaneous, past or future, or simultaneous and past and future, or beyond time.

29.(E79-81; T89-92) There are three kinds of resistance: that of obstruction, that of the contact of a sense-organ with its content, and that of awareness accompanying mental factors with their contents. The difference between a "content" and a "supporting object" is that the content, or object of sense, is where the sensory organ carries out its function; the supporting object is what is grasped by awarenesses and mental factors. But why does one speak of a "resistance" inherent in contact with a sense-content? Because the organ cannot exercise its activity any farther than its sense-content. But when we speak of ten sensory domains exercising resistance, we are speaking of the resistance of obstruction only. Kumāralāta states that though a consciousness having a color as its content and the eye for its support may be impeded from arising by the interposition of another material body between the eye and the color, the mental consciousness and the domain of mentally cognizables cannot be impeded in the same way. For instance, if a feeling (a kind of cognizable) arises, nothing can stop the mental consciousness from perceiving it.

30.(E82-87; T92-95) Which of the material elements are good, which bad, which neutral? The five material organs plus smells, tastes, and touches are always karmically neutral. The seven mental elements of consciousness are good, bad or neutral according to the traces accompanying them. The factor element itself includes the traces and thus may be either good, bad or neutral. The elements of sight and sound are good or bad if they form part of a good or bad bodily or verbal action; in all other cases they too are neutral.

Tastes and smells do not occur in the material realm, which includes the first meditative trances.

Śrīlāta says that the organs of taste and smell do not function in those trances. However, we think that if tastes and smells are lacking there the organs of taste and smell should also be absent.

Vaibhāṣika: No, the organs of taste and smell must be there, but only because it makes a more elegant account.

31.(E87; T96) All material elements except the three mentioned (viz., mind, mental awareness, factor element) are always contaminating.

33.(E89-90; T97-98) Vaibhāṣika: There are three kinds of conceptual constructions: (1) essential, (2) defining and (3) mnemonic. The five awarenesses are essential but not defining or mnemonic. That is why the five sensory awarenesses, though involving initial and sustained thought, are still constructionfree.

34.(E91; T99) For instance, the visible is appropriated if it is an integral part of a sense-organ, but not if it is external.

35.(E92-95; T99-101) Bhadanta Buddhadeva claims that all sensory organs and their objects consist of the primary material elements only. No, says the Vaibhāṣika, the characteristics of the material elements (cf. I, 12) are perceived by the tactile consciousness only. The ten material elements are accumulations of atoms.

36.(E95-96; T102) The visibles, olfactories, gustatories and tangibles *can* cut, burn or weigh if they form what is conventionally called, e.g., an "axe". They can *be* cut, etc., when they form e.g. "wood". Cutting means making two series of material factors, or more, out of one. The organs can neither be cut nor can they cut. For instance, if one cuts all the limbs from a body, which is the sensory element underlying tactile sensations, the body will still feel tactually, and the cut limbs will no longer be sensory elements of touch. Sound does not cut, cannot be cut, and has no weight. According to some, that external material sensory elements excluding sound burn and have weight is a characteristic of one kind of secondary materiality only.

37.(E96-99; T103-105) Sounds may grow through nourishment, as vocal powers are diminished in a famished series. Which of the sensory domains are outflows? An "outflow" is where the result of a preceding factor closely resembles its cause--this is the case when one says that the same object is existing from one moment to the next, for actually it is a new factor entirely, but so similar to the preceding factor that the difference is not noticed. The five material internal sense-bases are outflows when they are also karmic results and grow through nourishment.

Objection: Sound may be the result of karmic maturation, because that pleasant voice called "sound of Brahmā" is the result of complete avoidance of harmful language.

Vaibhāṣika: This sound does not result immediately from the action of which you suppose it is the maturation; thus it is not the result of karmic maturation.

Objection: In that case, a bodily sensation could never be the result of karmic maturation, because it does not result immediately from an action, but rather from a change in the great elements resulting from the action.

Vaibhāṣika: But this sensation is never engendered by the desire to have the sensation, whereas sound may be engendered by the volition to make the sound.

38.(E101-103; T106-107) Whether acquisition of the visual organ and awareness occur together or separately depends, among other things, on what meditative trance state we are thinking of.

39.(E104-109; T109-111) Objection: How can one talk about what is "personal" when there is no self?

Answer: It is consciousness that is falsely called a "self". So the "personal" elements are awarenesses or supporting objects of awarenesses.

A sensory element is termed "homogeneous" (*sabhāga*) with a time when it functions, "partially homogeneous" (*tatsabhāga*) with a time when it doesn't function. The sensory element called "mental consciousness" is always homogeneous with the time when it is destined to arise, for it always has an object; thus it can be called "partially homogeneous" only when it doesn't arise completely. A visible element is homogeneous with a series which sees it, partially homogeneous with one which doesn't.

40ab.(E109-110; T111-112) The fifteen are ten material elements--organs and objects--and five elements of consciousness. The "last three" (of the eighteen elements)--the mental element, element of factors, and mental consciousness element--comprise three sorts of factors: (a) eighty-eight proclivities, abandoned by vision, (b) the rest of the proclivities, abandoned by meditation, and (c) the noncontaminating unconditioned factors, not to be abandoned.

Objection: Ordinariness, a neutral factor, as well as bad bodily or vocal karma, are classified by you as factors to be abandoned by meditation, whereas they are in fact abandoned by the path of vision.

41.(E110-113; T113-114) The "eight parts of the factor element" are the five false views, ordinary right view, the disciple's and the adept's view.

42.(E113-118; T114-118) Vijñānavādin: If the eye sees, then the eye of someone completely engrossed in a tactual or audial consciousness also sees.

Vaibhāṣika: Not every eye sees. But every homogeneous eye does.

Vijñānavādin: What sees is the visual consciousness.

Vaibhāṣika: No, because when an object is obstructed by a screen it isn't seen. The visual consciousness is not material, thus it exercises no resistance. Thus it should be able to penetrate a screen.

Vijñānavādin: No. The visual consciousness simply doesn't arise when the object is obstructed.

Vasubandhu: Does the eye perceive its object by entering into close proximity with it, as does the tongue? If not, why can't the eye see an obstructed object? And why does the eye see objects that are obstructed by glass, etc.? I say it is the visual consciousness which sees, but it needs light on the object for this seeing.

Vaibhāṣika: There is a *sūtra* which says that the eye sees.

Vasubandhu: What that *sūtra* means to say is that the visual consciousness sees through the locus of the visual organ. For there is also a *sūtra* which says that mind discerns factors, but a mental moment is already past by the time factors are cognized (cf. I, 17). It is really the mental consciousness which grasps factors. Another *sūtra* states clearly that the eye is the medium for seeing.

Vaibhāṣika: If the visual consciousness sees, what is it that discerns an object?

Vasubandhu: What is the difference between seeing and discerning an object? It is the same process designated in two different ways.

Vātsīputrīya: It is the visual consciousness which sees. If the eye sees, what exactly is the action of seeing which you attribute to the visual organ?

Vasubandhu: Your objection doesn't hold. For the distinction between agent and action can't be made.

Dharmaguptaka: It's the visual consciousness which sees, but since the eye is the support of this consciousness, one says that it sees.

Vaibhāṣika: In that case, one should also say that the eye cognizes, because it is the locus of visual consciousness.

Vasubandhu: No. In ordinary language one never says that a color is cognized; one says that it is seen. Even the *Vibhāṣā* itself admits that that which is "seen" is reached by the eye, but is experienced by the visual consciousness.

Sautrāntika: This discussion is vain. There is no organ which sees, nor an object which is seen, there is no action of seeing, and no agent who sees. There is nothing but the interplay of causes and effects. It is only metaphorically that one can talk about the eye seeing, consciousness discerning, etc.

43.(E118-122; T119-122) If some kind of proximity isn't necessary (as the Vaibhāṣika says) why is it that one can't see things very far away?

Vaibhāṣika: Some distance is necessary between the eye and a visible thing for sight to take place. For the eye doesn't see objects clearly that are laid directly on it.

Vasubandhu: The ear may hear sounds within itself: thus the same kind of distance from the object isn't necessary. What is even the meaning of "coming directly in touch with"?

Vaibhāṣika: It means that there is no object coming in between the object of sense and the organ. According to Bhadanta Dharmatrāta, it means that there is no interval between them, but this interpretation is erroneous, because atoms don't enter into direct contact with one another. If atoms touched completely, they would merge. If atoms touched partially, there would be parts to atoms, but atoms have no parts.

Vasubandhu: But if atoms don't touch each other, why does the aggregation of atoms not fall into pieces when it is struck?

Vaibhāṣika: Because the wind-element gives them cohesiveness. Aggregates of atoms do have parts, and thus touch.

Vasubandhu: Bhadanta Dharmatrāta is right. There is no contact between atoms. One merely says there is when there is nothing coming between them, and no interval between them. If atoms had an interval between them, the atoms could float into it, and they would no longer be separate. The reason two atoms do not merge even though there is no interval between them is that they exercise resistance. One cannot make a radical distinction between atoms and aggregates of atoms. Thus it is absurd to say that aggregates touch but individual atoms don't. If you admit any spatial division for atoms, then atoms have parts.

44.(E123-125; T122-125) For the organs of smell, taste and touch there must be the same number of atoms in the object as in the organ in order that the former be perceived. But for the organs of sight and hearing there is no such restriction: sometimes the object may be bigger, sometimes smaller than the organ.

The atoms of the visual organ are situated on the pupil of the eye, the atoms of the audial organ are within the oak-leaf-shaped configuration within the ear, the atoms of the olfactory organ are within the nostrils, and the atoms of the gustatory organ are on the upper surface of the tongue. The atoms of the visual, hearing, smelling and tasting organs can all occur simultaneously (cf. I, 39), but not all atoms of the tactile organ can occur simultaneously. Always more than one atom must occur simultaneously for perception to take place. Thus individual atoms can't be perceived.

Are the supporting objects for consciousnesses also their directly antecedent conditions? (A directly antecedent condition is any condition which helps give rise to a factor which is similar to it and which follows upon it immediately--cf. II, 62.) The eye is only the support for a visual consciousness, and not its directly antecedent condition, since it does not condition the nature of the consciousness. The mental factors which arise immediately previous to a consciousness-moment are always its directly antecedent conditions, since they not only help give rise to the consciousness-moment but color its very nature. As regards a mental consciousness, its supporting objects are always also its directly antecedent conditions, though again there are directly antecedent conditions which are not its supporting object, namely the mental factors still more antecedent.

45.(E123-126; T125-126) If the eye is feeble, the consciousness is too. The object, on the other hand, has no such direct effect on the consciousness.

48.(E132-133; T130-131) Everything perceived by the other consciousnesses is sorted and discerned by the mental consciousness. The unconditioned factors (I, 4-5) are eternal. There are twenty-two faculties, factors which have a predominance for the psychophysical complex. They are the faculties of the eye, ear, nose, tongue, tactile body, mind (meaning all six consciousnesses), femininity, masculinity, vitality, satisfaction, frustration, contentedness, irritation, equanimity, faith, energy, mindfulness, meditation, insight, coming to know what wasn't known, understanding, and perfect knowledge. (For definitions of these see Chapter Two.)

## CHAPTER TWO

1.(E135-139; T153-155) Vaibhāṣika: The five faculties of the eye, ear, nose, tongue, and tactile body are predominant in explaining four things: (1) the beauty of an organism, (2) its protection--since through them the harmful can be avoided, (3) the organism's ability to see and hear, and (4) its special sphere of activity: seeing visibles, hearing sounds, etc. The four faculties of masculinity, femininity, vitality and the mental faculty are predominant in the two areas of continuation of the species and in differentiation of living beings.

Objection: Even the individuals belonging to classes of gods who have no sexual organs can be differentiated. It is rather that the faculties of femininity and masculinity are predominant in the processes of thorough affliction and purification, since eunuchs and hermaphrodites can neither be totally subjected by mental afflictions, nor completely purified, nor can they attain attachment.

Vaibhāṣika: The faculty of vitality is predominant in relating together all the elements taking part in an organism, and for the prolongation of the series of these elements until death. The mental faculty is predominant in the process of rebirth and for control, since all factors are subject to consciousness. The five faculties which are feelings--those of satisfaction, frustration, contentedness, irritation and equanimity--are predominant in the processes of affliction and alleviation. The faculties of faith, energy, mindfulness, meditational concentration, insight, coming to know what wasn't known, understanding and perfect knowledge are predominant in complete alleviation.

Vasubandhu: It is not the organs of sense which are predominant in the protection of the organism, but the consciousness of sense! Similarly, the "special sphere of activity" belongs to consciousness.

2.(E140-141; T156) For instance, if the eye is dim, visual consciousness is indistinct. The faculties of masculinity and femininity really belong to the tactile body, but they are its part which are predominant for the organism's physical shape, types of gestures and wishes.

3.(E141; T157) The faculty of vitality is predominant for the prolongation of the organism's existence, but not in relating together all the elements taking part in the organism, as this takes place through mind, or the collection of six consciousnesses. On the rest of the faculties Vasubandhu has no disagreement with the Vaibhāṣikas.

4.(E141-142; T157-158) The last three faculties are predominant in the acquisition of liberation.

Objection: Why aren't other factors also faculties, such as the voice, the hands, the feet, etc.?

5.(E142-143; T158) Answer: Because in giving the list of faculties the Buddha wanted to highlight the supports of consciousness and that which prolongs, afflicts, and purifies them.

6.(E143-144; T159-160) On the other hand, the voice is not predominant in speech, as speech has to be learned. Hands and feet are not predominant in taking and moving, since "taking" and "moving" are really metaphors for something new arising in another locus immediately following upon something else (see Chapter Four), and snakes, etc., need neither hands nor feet to take or move. Similarly, the anus is not predominant for excretion, since heavy objects always fall in space, and it is the internal wind-element which really makes the excrement come out.

8.(E147; T162) Equanimity involves no conceptual construction, no differentiation, so it is not differentiated into mental physical.

10.(E151-168; T165-171) When a perfected being deliberately prolongs his life, the faculty of vitality involved can no longer be karmic retribution, because it is then the result of an impulse.

How can one say that the faculty of irritation is never retribution? A *sūtra* says that a feeling experienced as irritation may be retributory.

Vaibhāṣika: But the *sūtra* doesn't mean to say that the irritation is the result of an action: it means only that the action is accompanied by a feeling of irritation.

Vasubandhu: The same *sūtra* speaks of feelings experienced as contentedness and indifference. To be consistent, you must interpret these expressions in the same way.

Vaibhāṣika: The same difficulty doesn't arise. The *sūtra* may be interpreted as saying that contentedness and indifference are retributions in certain cases, or that the action is accompanied by contentedness or indifference.

Vasubandhu: But there is no logical ground for saying that irritation is never retribution.

Vaibhāṣika: Irritation is always caused by conceptual construction, when one thinks about what one fears or doesn't like. Being the result of conceptual construction, it isn't retribution.

Vasubandhu: The same must hold for contentedness, which consequently can't be retribution, either.

Vaibhāṣika: If you say that irritation is retribution, then when someone has committed a grave offence and feels regret, this is tantamount to saying that the retribution occurs immediately after the act, because regret is a kind of irritation. But we do not admit immediate retributions.

Vasubandhu: But you do admit that contentedness is retribution, and yet this may occur immediately after a good act.

Vaibhāṣika: People detached from any desires do not have the faculty of irritation, but they do have faculties which are retributional; thus the faculty of irritation is not retribution.

Vasubandhu: But such people cannot have contentedness, which *is* retribution, either. They do have a contentedness which comes from meditation, but this is good and thus isn't retribution.

Vaibhāṣika: They have contentedness, whether retribution or not.

17-21.(E171-179; T179-184) Objection: Since (see Table I in the summary of the *Kośa*) only nine faculties are always ethically neutral features of a perfected being, why does the *Jñānaprasthāna* say that eleven are?

Answer: That passage is speaking of one who is able to gain perfection--he may experience satisfaction or contentedness as well as equanimity, e.g., after backsliding. However, one cannot have more than one at any time.

Further details about the faculties possessed in the different realms, and which go along with which.

22.(E181-185; T185-188) Do conditioned factors arise independently, or do they sometimes arise necessarily together?

Vaibhāṣika: Sometimes they must arise together. For instance, a molecule (*saṃghātaparamāṇu*) must consist of at least eight actual entities: one atom of each of the great material elements (cf. I, 12), and four atoms of derived materiality, corresponding to the visible, smell, taste and tactile. The molecules making up the simplest sentient beings must consist of at least nine atoms, the eight mentioned above plus an atom of the sense of touch.

Vasubandhu: If every molecule contains atoms of each of the four great elements, why is it that solidity is perceived only in some material agglomerations, heat only in some others, etc.?

Vaibhāṣika: What is perceived is the element which is the most intense.

Vasubandhu: How do you know that a molecule has elements which aren't perceived?

Vaibhāṣika: But they are in evidence anyway. Solid things may become liquid, such as when iron is melted. Thus iron contains the liquid element "water". The element of fire exists in water, as it is colder or warmer.

Vasubandhu: How can you maintain that air contains color? If each molecule contains at least one atom of the visible, then air should have color.

Vaibhāṣika: This is a matter of faith, not of inference. Or else, one can say that color exists in air because the air carries odors, and odor is never dissociated from color.

Vasubandhu: You say that a molecule must have at least eight atoms, which you sometimes call "substances" (*dravya*). Do you mean actual substances, which have an essential nature, or do you mean sense-fields, which have only distinctive general characteristics? In the first case, the minimum number of atoms given is too small, because the molecule must contain also a shape-atom, since several atoms are aggregated. It must also contain the derived materiality called "tactile", etc. In the second case, the proposed number of atoms is too large, because the great material elements are part of the tactile sense-field, and thus the molecule consists only of four entities: the visible, smell, taste, and the tactile.

Vaibhāṣika: In our usage "*dravya*" may mean both a substance in the strict sense and a sense-field. Among the eight *dravyas* of the molecule there are four real *dravyas*, the four great elements, and four sense-fields, which are four kinds of derived materiality supported by the great elements.

Vasubandhu: If each of the atoms of derived materiality is supported by four atoms of the great elements, then the molecule has twenty atoms or *dravyas*. Besides, your usage of the term "*dravya*" is ambiguous and capricious.

23.(E186; T188-189) Vaibhāṣika: The conditioned factors constituting sentient beings always arise with possession, a connector-factor linking them together.

Vasubandhu: The accompanying mental factors may be divided into the following groups: generally permeating factors, those arising with every awareness; good permeating factors, those arising with every good awareness; defiled permeating factors, those arising with every bad awareness; and limitedly defiled permeating factors, those arising with secondary afflictions.

24.(E187; T190) Among the generally permeating factors, "contact" means the contiguity of organ, object of consciousness, and consciousness.

28.(E194-195; T196) Some other accompanying mental factors are indeterminate: they can be associated with a good, bad or neutral awareness. They are regret, sleepiness, initial and sustained thought (see I, 32).

31.(E200; T199) Arrogance may exist in all three realms of existence.

33.(E204-207;T202-204) Vasubandhu: How can initial and sustained thought be associated with the same moment of awareness? The *Vibhāṣā* compares sustained thought to cold water, initial thought to the heat of the sun, and the awareness with clarified butter which is floating on the cold water. Because of the water and the sun, the clarified butter is neither too liquid nor too compact. In the same way, initial and sustained thought may be associated with the same awareness: initial thought makes the awareness not too subtle, and sustained thought makes it not too gross.

But, for the simile to be exact, initial and sustained thought are not the grossness and subtlety of awareness, but the causes of grossness and subtlety of awareness. Besides, "grossness" and "subtlety" are relative. For instance, the awareness of the first meditational state is subtle in relation to an awareness of the realm of desires, but gross in relation to an awareness of the second meditational state. And if initial and sustained thought are grossness and subtlety of awareness respectively, then they would continue to exist even up to the next to the last of the highest immaterial meditations. But in fact they both cease after the second meditational state. Besides, it is not logical that "grossness" and "subtlety" can establish a specific difference. According to the Sautrāntikas, initial and sustained thoughts are not separable events but the collection of awarenesses and mental factors which make for speech and inner discursiveness.

Vaibhāṣika: But what is the objection to having a subtle and gross factor coexist with one awareness?

Vasubandhu: There is no objection if the two factors are specifically different--for example, if there is a gross feeling and a subtle awareness coexisting. But if one is speaking of two states of one kind, then it is a contradiction to speak of them as being subtle and gross simultaneously.

Vaibhāṣika: But there is a specific difference between initial and sustained thought. This difference is difficult to indicate, but it is manifested by the feebleness or strength of an awareness.

Sautrāntika: Feebleness and strength do not demonstrate the presence of two factors which are specifically different; for each specifically different factor, there may be feebleness or strength.

Vasubandhu: Initial and sustained thought do not coexist with the same awareness. They exist successively.

35-36.(E211-218; T207-213) Vasubandhu: How can you demonstrate the existence of possession? Such a thing can neither be directly perceived, nor can it be inferred from its efficacy.

Vaibhāṣika: Possession does have efficacy, for it is the cause of the arising of events.

Vasubandhu: This reply will get you in trouble. You say that one can possess the two kinds of cessation (see I, 4-5), yet these are unconditioned, and hence don't arise. And as for conditioned factors, there can't be possession if they haven't yet arisen, nor can there be any for factors which have been abandoned by a change of realm of existence (see I, 30). So how can the first arise, and how can the second have arisen?

Vaibhāṣika: The arising of these factors is caused by a possession which is simultaneous with them.

Vasubandhu: If all factors arise because of possession, then there is no role for birth (*jāti*) nor for the birth of birth, events which don't pertain to sentient beings wouldn't arise (since possession exists only in psychophysical complexes), and there would be no difference in degree of the afflictions "possessed" by one in the realm of desires. If you say that these differences arise from causes other than possession, we will simply maintain that these other causes are the sole causes, and ignore possession.

Sarvāstivādin: Possession is not the cause of the arising of factors, but it is the cause of their particular states. If you suppose there is no possession, what difference is there between a noble person, in the moment in which he has a worldly awareness, and an ordinary person? For us, the difference lies in the fact that the noble one, even when he has a worldly awareness, is still connected by possession to undefiled consciousness, while for those at (b), the summit, one practising the cessation-trance has hardly any consciousness at all.

12d.(E411-419; T387-391) Vibhajyavādin: There are three ways of being liberated while in the intermediate state: (1) as soon as one arrives there (*dhātugata*), (2) while ideas of material things are still operative (*saṃjñāgata*), (3) while thoughts are occurring (*vitarkagata*).

13-14.(E419-426; T391-394) Objection: If the one in the intermediate state has the form of his next birth, then if an embryo dies in the womb of a dog and is replaced by the intermediate state of one going to burn in hell, the dog's womb will get burned!

Answer: Intermediate state "bodies" are neither visible nor tangible.

An intermediate being is the size of a five-year-old but has fully developed organs and, for modesty's sake, is clothed.

There is no intermediate existence in the immaterial realm.

How long does an intermediate existence last? Different opinions: no fixed time; seven days; seven weeks; for various periods depending on circumstances.

15.(E427-429; T395-396) The intermediate being sees, through its divine eye, its parents copulating, and because of its own desire for the parent of the opposite sex hates the other parent as a rival and seeks sexual satisfaction. Thus, arriving at the place of copulation the intermediate being enters the semen and blood of its parents and ceases to exist (as intermediate) as its aggregates harden.

The question arises: where do the organs, etc. of the new body come from? Two answers are possible: (1) they come from the intermediate being's organs, (2) organs arise from actions that create new elements, like leaf-worms. These descriptions apply to those born from eggs and from the womb. "Others", i.e., moisture-born ones, "go motivated by a place's smell or", in the case of magical beings, "from a desire for a place of residence." How can one desire residence in hell? Through confusion--being cold, one seeks a hot place!

24.(E439-440; T404-405) But one can also interpret the entire twelvefold dependent origination formula as taking place in a single moment, when the factor-complex is linked with defilements: there is ignorance there, conditioning factors in the form of a volition-moment, there is a consciousness-moment, there are the other aggregates accompanying this moment, there are the organs in relation to the psychophysical complex, there is contact, a feeling, a cognition-

definition of one who is separate from *dharma*?

Vaibhāṣika: All three.

Vasubandhu: In that case the Buddha, because he doesn't have all three kinds of patience, would become one separate from *dharma*.

Vaibhāṣika: But we intend a nonpossession of patience which isn't accompanied by possession.

Vasubandhu: Why bring up these totally hypothetical entities? According to Sautrāntikas the state of being separate from *dharma* is simply a series where the factors of the path have not arisen.

Vaibhāṣika: Nonpossession ceases with the arising of possession, or by a change of experiential sphere (cf. I, 30).

Vasubandhu: When one exchanges experiential spheres there is nonpossession of the nonpossession of the new sphere. But can there be such a thing? Doesn't this lead to infinite regress?

Vaibhāṣika: No, because one has a possession by possession of possession, and that possession of possession by the same possession.

Vasubandhu: When a good factor arises in a series three factors must co-arise: the good factor, its possession, and the possession of that possession. In the next moment, six factors co-arise: the possession of the good factor, the possession of the possession of the previous moment, the possession of that possession, and three possessions of possessions for the three possessions. In this way, possessions will keep increasing from moment to moment. It's very fortunate that they're immaterial, otherwise there'd be no room for them!

41a.(E232; T221) Vasubandhu: There is no special factor called "homogeneity within a lifetime". Such a postulate reeks of Vaiśeṣika. The homogeneity of factors in an organism can be explained in other ways.

41b-42.(E233-236; T221-224) Nonideation stops awareness and the arising of factors. One who does not conceptually identify in this way remains so for a long time, and dies immediately in heaven, being born again later in the realm of desire.

There are said to be two meditational attainments, the nonideation trance and the cessation trance. Noble persons do not place any value on the nonideation trance. Ordinary people do not value it either, and so do not reap its reward. "It is experienced at one time", i.e., in the present alone.

43.(E236-238; T225-26) "Two sorts or neutral", i.e., its karmic maturing takes place either in the next life or later at the summit of existence, or else it is unnecessary in the case of one who achieves *parinirvāṇa* in this life.

44.(E238-248; T226-233) Although the "Western masters" (Sautrāntikas?) believe the Buddha first attained cessation-trance as an adept and subsequently became liberated, the Vaibhāṣikas deny this, holding that a Buddha needs only thirty-four moments as adept (sixteen moments of realization of the noble truths and eighteen moments abandoning the defilements), with awareness of destruction (of defilements) constituting the final step in which one abandons the summit of existence.

"One's first cessation-trance must occur as a human", for a human can fall from it. Other schools' opinions about backsliding are reviewed.

In the two meditational attainments the series of awarenesses is interrupted for quite some time. When there is emergence from the trance, how is it that awareness again arises, since the series has been interrupted?

Vaibhāṣika: There is no difficulty for us, because past factors exist (see V, 25). Thus the awareness which entered into the attainment is the directly antecedent condition (cf. I, 44) for the awareness which emerges from the attainment.

Some Sautrāntikas say that the awareness which emerges comes from the body fitted out with its faculties, not from a previous awareness. Bhadanta Vasumitra, in his treatise *Paripṛcchā*, says that there is a subtle awareness existing during cessation which is the cause of the awareness on emerging. Ghoṣaka, however, argues that all awarenesses must be accompanied by the generally permeating factors (see II, 24). And since the generally permeating factors include feelings, identifications, and volition, the presence of awareness is required and cessation would be impossible.

Bhadanta Vasumitra: A *sūtra* says that feelings give rise to desires, and yet this isn't the case for perfected beings, for example. So not all contacts involve feelings.

Ghoṣaka: But the *sūtra* clearly says that it is feelings arisen from a contact accompanied by ignorance that give rise to desires, but contacts invariably give rise to feelings.

Bhadanta Vasumitra: If there is no awareness in the meditative attainment, how can one even call it an "attainment"?

Ghoṣaka: It is designated that way because the great elements have reached an equilibrium which is counteractive to the arising of awarenesses.

Vasubandhu: Should these meditative attainments be considered to be existing in themselves as actual entities, or only as designations for awarenesses not arising in the series?

Ghoṣaka: They are entities because they prohibit awarenesses from arising.

Vasubandhu: But it isn't the meditative attainment which prohibits them from arising; it's the awareness which enters the attainment that prohibits further awarenesses from arising.

Ghoṣaka: If the attainment is not an entity, how can it be considered a conditioned factor?

Vasubandhu: It is designated as a conditioned factor because it has a beginning and end. But really there is no such factor as "attainment of cessation".

45a.(E248-255; T233-239) Vasubandhu: Where is the life-force located?

Vaibhāṣika: In heat and consciousness.

Vasubandhu: If these three factors are located in each other and continue to exist in series, how do they ever end? Which of the three ceases first?

Vaibhāṣika: Vitality is located in karma; when karma ceases vitality does too.

Vasubandhu: Then why don't you say that heat and consciousness are located in karma and dispense with vitality?

Vaibhāṣika: That which is located in karma is by necessity karmic maturation. If consciousness were supported by karma alone, then all life states would be maturations, which isn't the case.

Vasubandhu: So you say that karma supports the bodily heat and the consciousness. You still don't need a separate vitality.

Vaibhāṣika: It is necessary, because in the immaterial realm there is no heat.

Vasubandhu: Consciousness in the immaterial realm could be supported by karma.

Vaibhāṣika: You are twisting your own thesis. Before, you said that consciousness is supported by heat, and now you say it's supported by karma.

Vasubandhu: I don't deny that there's something like vitality, only

I don't think it's a separate kind of entity. It is just a force in past acts which allows the aggregates to renew themselves in a series.

The *Prajñaptiśāstra* lists four kinds of death: (1) by maturation of the karma from the present life; (2) by maturation of experiencings; (3) by both (1) and (2); (4) by not avoiding calamities. To these should be added (5) death by abandoning the life-faculty.

Citing the *Jñānaprasthāna* as authority it is explained that if one is in the realm of desire and not in either nonideation or cessation trance then the life-faculty ends when one's body ends. If one is in either of those trances or in a higher realm, life goes on for its allotted length.

An extended discussion concerns precisely which beings--gods, those in hell or the intermediate state, etc.--are destined to live out their allotted time, and which can be terminated by external forces or by themselves.

46bd.(E256-269; T240-249) Birth, duration, etc., are not entities apart. There are three instruments of knowledge: perception, inference, and reliable authority. By none of the three can these characteristics be established as entities apart.

Vaibhāṣika: But there is a *sūtra* which says that arising can be discerned.

Vasubandhu: You are just like the fools who think that a series of factors forms a self. What the *sūtra* wants to say is that the members of the series are conditioned, i.e., arisen by dependent origination. A series begins, a series continues, a series evolves, and a series ceases. One may say that in each moment these characteristics exist, but only if one knows that they're not separate entities. For each factor arises after having not existed, it exists for a moment, transforms in this moment, and ceases.

Vaibhāṣika: But some factors have no duration or transformation--some just have arising and ceasing. According to you, arising is the factor itself when it exists after not having existed. There is thus no difference between characteristic and characterized.

Vasubandhu: So what? The horns of a cow aren't something different from the cow. If for every adjective which can be imputed to an event or collection of events you posit an entity to explain it, then there must be an entity underlying "one", "two", "large", "small", etc. and you will, like the Vaiśeṣikas, be asserting an entire series of special entities like their number, extension, individuality, etc. Sure, one says "the birth of a color", but this doesn't mean that "birth" and "color" are two separate entities. One can also say "the torso of a body": this doesn't mean that the torso is an entity separate from the body.

Vaibhāṣika: With the entity birth we can easily explain why the unconditioned factors don't arise.

Vasubandhu: I say that conditioned factors arise because they exist having not existed. But the unconditioned is eternal, so how could it arise?

47.(E271-276; T251-254) Vasubandhu: Aren't all three collections speech (*vāc*), and consequently sound (*śabda*), and thus belong among the material aggregates, not conditioning factors?

Vaibhāṣika: If they were only sound there would be no way to distinguish meaningless from meaningful sounds.

Vasubandhu: When I say "speech" I don't mean just sound, but sounds which human beings have agreed to mean certain things. But once this agreement has been made, the vocal sound itself gives rise to an understanding of the meaning. So there is no necessity for a special entity "word".

Vaibhāṣika: We say that vocal sound produces a word, which is something separate.

Vasubandhu: But it is absurd to assume that vocal sound produces an entity "word", for the vocal sounds making up a word don't all exist at the same time. The sounds are heard successively, and if the "word" is an entity it can't be produced by parts.

Vaibhāṣika: The case is analogous to that of unmanifest karma (see I, 11). It is the last moment of a manifest bodily or verbal action which produces unmanifest karma, but this last moment depends on the previous moments of the action.

Vasubandhu: If the last moment of sound produces the word, then it would suffice to hear the last moment of vocal sound in order to understand the word. If you say that the syllables bring about a word, the same objection holds as before, because the syllables are produced successively. I hold that it is the syllables which ultimately exist, and that the word is a composite of syllables, with no more unity than a row of ants or a series of awarenesses.

50.(E280-283; T256) Though one can call all causes "efficient causes", the term is more specifically used for a generative cause. Thus the eye and color are efficient causes of visual consciousness.

51.(E283-291; T257-262) The "two restraints" are meditative trance and pure restraint.

Vaibhāṣika: Simultaneous causes are factors related as cause and effect which coexist in the same moment, such as an awareness and its accompanying mental factors.

Sautrāntika: No such thing as a simultaneous cause can exist, because a cause must precede its effect.

Sarvāstivādin: A light arises at the same time as its luster, and yet the light is the cause of the luster.

Sautrāntika: The light and its luster are both effects of a complex of anterior causes: the oil, the wick, etc.

Sarvāstivādin: The relation of cause and effect is demonstrated by the existence or nonexistence of that which is called an effect in relation to the existence or nonexistence of that which is called cause. Where A isn't, B isn't--thus A is the cause, B the effect.

Sautrāntika: How can simultaneous factors stand in a cause-effect relation?

Sarvāstivādin: Just as three sticks may stand because they support each other, so awarenesses and mental factors support each other.

Sautrāntika: But anterior causes have gone into this result of three sticks supporting each other. And besides, there are other causes here too, such as the earth, a string, etc.

52.(E292-302; T262-269) An example of a homogeneous cause is the first stage of an embryo's existence, which is the cause of the later stages.

The question whether a later factor can be the cause of an earlier one is discussed, citing *Jñānaprasthāna* both for and against. Vasubandhu's answer is "no".

54.(E310-316; T274-277) Neutral factors are not retributive causes, because a retribution is caused only by a factor which is conjoined with craving. Factors which are never linked to defilements can only be karmically neutral. (Note the distinction between that which is intrinsically good--the factors which are never linked to defilements--and those which are karmically good--the good potentially linked with defilements.)

55.(E319-327; T278-286) How can an unconditioned factor be an efficient cause? Because it does not obstruct the occurrence of any fact, although, being timeless, it cannot produce a result.

Sautrāntika: An unconditioned factor can't be a cause at all.

Sarvāstivādin: Then how can it be the supporting object of the awareness of it?

Sautrāntika: The "unconditioned factors" are merely absences. Space is just the absence of tangibles, calculated cessation the nonarising of future proclivities, uncalculated cessation the absence of any future factors at all arising. Other definitions are reviewed.

Sarvāstivādin: If unconditioned factors don't exist how can a *sūtra* say, e.g., that detachment is the best of all the factors, since detachment (=cessation) doesn't exist?

Sautrāntika: Before, e.g., a sound occurs we speak of its prior absence; afterwards we speak of its posterior absence. To speak thus does not imply that the absence of sound exists; likewise for the absences which are the unconditioned factors.

The rest of this lengthy discussion turns on the interpretation of *sūtras*.

61.(E342; T296) The four are causal, directly antecedent, supporting, and dominant causes.

62.(E342; T297) There is discussion here of how many mental concomitants accompany the awarenesses that make up a series of factors, and of whether factors of a certain sort can only be a directly antecedent condition of another of that type or not.

The dissociated conditioning factors and material factors are not directly antecedent conditions. Nor can future factors be so, despite passages in scripture that appear to imply it.

63-64.(E352-355; T306-308) Theist: Factors arise in succession because of the desire of God that one factor arise now, another later.

Vasubandhu: If that is so, then they don't arise from a single cause, but from the desires, which are plural. Since God is supposed to be nonmultiple, His desires should be so too, and thus there can only be simultaneous generation of everything.

Theist: The desires of God are not simultaneous, because He takes notice of other causes.

Vasubandhu: Then God is not the unique cause of all things. And the causes He regards depend upon other causes, *ad infinitum*.

Theist: Well, let's admit that the series of causes has no beginning.

Vasubandhu: In that case, the world has no beginning, and this is contrary to your thesis.

Theist: But God wants things to arise successively.

Vasubandhu: What advantages does God get from making things?

Theist: It's for His own satisfaction.

Vasubandhu: If He needs to do something for His own satisfaction, then He isn't really sovereign. And besides, to think that God takes satisfaction in all the suffering of the world, what kind of a God is this? If you admit any other causes at all, you can't claim that God is the unique cause. Maybe to avoid denying causes which are obvious, and to avoid claiming that God is active now, which isn't apparent, the theist will say that the work of God is His first creation. But then, since God is eternal, His creation will be eternal too. All theories of a unique cause, whether called "God" or "*puruṣa*" or "*pradhāna*", are nonsense.

## CHAPTER THREE

3.(E383-384; T366-367) The four immaterial varieties are the bases of space, consciousness, nothingness and neither-identification-nor-nonidentification.

Whereas the awarenesses of material beings depend on matter, the streams of awareness of the immaterial realm depend on homogeneity and vitality. But what do those two depend on? On each other, say the Ābhidharmikas, but we Sautrāntikas say they need no support other than themselves.

4.(E387-393; T371-374) The first four courses (of hell-dwellers, ghosts, animals and humans) and some of the fifth (gods) are in the realm of desire; the rest of the gods are in the other two realms.

"Undefiled-neutral", i.e., those in the five courses are karmically conditioned.

Another view is that the five courses are undefiled and good. But the Vaibhāṣikas say all five realms are undefiled-neutral, although some say they involve only karmically-produced factors, while others say that some factors are the result of growth.

5.(E393-396; T374-377) Specifically, (1) humans and some gods of the first stage have differing bodies and ideas, (2) comprises Brahmā and his associates, (3) contains the Ābhāsvara gods, the highest gods of the second stage, who are sometimes satisfied and sometimes experience neither satisfaction nor frustration, (4) are the Śubhakṛtsna gods, who experience only satisfaction, (5) are those who meditate on endless space, (6) those who meditate on endless consciousness, and (7) those who meditate on nothingness.

6a.(E397-398; T377-378) "The remaining sorts of beings" include (a) those in the first three courses (hell, ghosts, animals) and (b) those at the summit of the fourth stage. For those in (a) experience limits consciousness, while for those at (b), the summit, one practising the cessation-trance has hardly any consciousness at all.

12d.(E411-419;T387-391) Vibhajyavādin: There are three ways of being liberated while in the intermediate state: (1) as soon as one arrives there (*dhātugata*), (2) while ideas of material things are still operative (*saṃjñāgata*), (3) while thoughts are occurring (*vitarkagata*).

13-14.(E419-426; T391-394) Objection: If the one in the intermediate state has the form of his next birth, then if an embryo dies in the womb of a dog and is replaced by the intermediate state of one going to burn in hell, the dog's womb will get burned!

Answer: Intermediate state "bodies" are neither visible nor tangible.

An intermediate being is the size of a five-year-old but has fully developed organs and, for modesty's sake, is clothed.

There is no intermediate existence in the immaterial realm.

How long does an intermediate existence last? Different opinions: no fixed time; seven days; seven weeks; for various periods depending on circumstances.

15.(E427-429; T395-396) The intermediate being sees, through its divine eye, its parents copulating, and because of its own desire for the parent of the opposite sex hates the other parent as a rival and seeks sexual satisfaction. Thus, arriving at the place of copulation the intermediate being enters the semen and blood of its parents and ceases to exist (as intermediate) as its aggregates harden.

The question arises: where do the organs, etc. of the new body come from? Two answers are possible: (1) they come from the intermediate being's organs, (2) organs arise from actions that create new elements, like leaf-worms. These descriptions apply to those born from eggs and from the womb. "Others", i.e., moisture-born ones, "go motivated by a place's smell or", in the case of magical beings, "from a desire for a place of residence." How can one desire residence in hell? Through confusion--being cold, one seeks a hot place!

24.(E439-440; T404-405) But one can also interpret the entire twelvefold dependent origination formula as taking place in a single moment, when the factor-complex is linked with defilements: there is ignorance there, conditioning factors in the form of a volition-moment, there is a consciousness-moment, there are the other aggregates accompanying this moment, there are the organs in relation to the psychophysical complex, there is contact, a feeling, a cognition-moment, craving, grasping, rigidification of being, the arising of all these events (which is a kind of birth), their maturity (old age), and their cessation (death).

25.(E441; T406) The "misunderstandings" arise from questions such as "Did I exist in the past?", "Will I exist in the future", "Where are we?".

26.(E442-443; T406-407) Ignorance, craving, and grasping are defilements; conditioning factors and being are action. (This latter classification rests on the fact that mental action, the basic kind of action entailing retribution for Vasubandhu, is volition, the most important of the conditioning factors and the basis of being-again or rigidification of being.

27.(E443-449; T407-410) Defilements breed defilements, as when grasping arises from craving. The basic members of dependent origination (i.e., those which are neither affliction nor action) give rise to other basic members, as when the psychophysical complex arises from consciousness during conception in the womb. They may also result in defilements, as when feelings give rise to cravings. Actions arise from defilements, as when ignorance gives rise to conditioning factors. And from action, the basic members may arise, as when conditioning factors give rise to consciousness.

Vaibhāṣika: There is no infinite regress because ignorance itself also has a cause, unreasoned attention. It is not specifically mentioned in the formula because it is the same as grasping.

Vasubandhu: How do you know this? It may be associated with grasping, but also with ignorance and craving.

Vaibhāṣika: A careful examination brings the following results: with perfected beings, feeling is not the cause of craving, since only defiled feeling causes craving. That is, the kind of feelings that give rise to cravings is a contact accompanied by ignorance, and this is what one may call unreasoned attention.

Vasubandhu: Some, such as the Mahīśāsakas, assert that dependent origination is an unconditioned factor. If one means by this that it's always by reason of ignorance that conditioning factors arise, etc., and thus dependent origination is in a sense eternal, this is true. But if one means that there is a special entity "dependent origination", then it isn't.

28a.(E449-463; T410-419) A number of grammatical arguments here.

Various explanations are offered as to why the Buddha provides different definitions of dependent origination. Different interpretations of dependent origination are distinguished.

30b.(E469-470; T422-424) What is "contact"? The Sautrāntikas say that it's simply the meeting of sense-organ, object and consciousness. The Sarvāstivādins say that it's a special entity associated with awareness, different from the meeting of the three. Śrīlāta says that contact is the organ/object/consciousness which are related as cause and effect. How does the Sarvāstivādin explain the *sūtra* which clearly defines "contact" as the meeting together of the three?

32ab.(E473-479; T427-433) Does a contact precede the feeling it produces, or is it simultaneous with it?

Vaibhāṣika: They are simultaneous causes of each other.

Sautrāntika: Then they must be reciprocal causes of each other, and that is wrong.

Vaibhāṣika: There is no fault. Causes sometimes precede their effects but are sometimes simultaneous with them.

Śrīlāta: The contact must precede the feeling. First there are organ and object, next there is contact, which is the coming together of three things: organ, object and consciousness. Following that arises the feeling.

Vaibhāṣika: Then in the second moment there is consciousness but no feeling--how can that be?

Śrīlāta: The consciousness in the second moment is caused by an earlier contact.

Vaibhāṣika: Then a feeling produced by visual contact would be produced by an earlier auditory contact, for example. That is impossible.

Śrīlāta: No. The consciousness of color is not contact but produces a feeling at *t*, while the consciousness of sound is contact but does not produce feeling at *t*.

Vaibhāṣika: This contradicts the rule that *all* the generally permeating factors (including sensations, feelings, etc.) are associated with *every* awareness.

Śrīlāta: We do not recognize the authority for that "rule". Or, if you please, we have a different theory of "generally permeating factors". According to our (Sautrāntika) theory, although the ten factors of consciousness, feelings, etc., occur in all the *kinds* of stages there are, it is not that *every* awareness includes each and every one of those factors.

32cd.(E479-482; T431-433) There are six contented mental ponderings, six irritated ones, and six of equanimity. Each group has six since they relate to the five kinds of sense-objects and to factors as the sixth.

What does "mental pondering" (*manopavicāra*) mean? The Vaibhāṣikas say that the mind supports the contentment, irritation and equanimity with which sense-objects are grasped. Another opinion is that these eighteen cause the mind to reconsider sense-objects, etc.

Objects are not satisfying, irritating, etc. by nature, but may be satisfying for one person, irritating to another, etc. But all mental ponderings are impure.

37d-38c.(E491; T438-439) The "four states of existence" are intermediate existence, rearising, living and dying.

98.(E554-555; T487-488) The *Kośa*'s theory of "social contract": Originally, when rice was first used by human beings as food, it was gathered not cultivated, and one cut it once in the morning for the morning meal, once again in the evening for the evening meal. But one person, who was too lazy to want to do both cuttings, cut a lot at a morning cutting and saved some for his evening meal. Others imitated him. With this storing of food arose the idea of "mine". The rice which was cut repeatedly ceased to grow. So efforts had to be made to make the rice grow--this was the beginning of agriculture. They divided the fields among themselves. But the stronger began to take away the fields of the weaker--this was the beginning of stealing. To prevent stealing, they held a meeting and gave a sixth of their produce to an outstanding man, who was told to guard the fields. The term "*kṣatriya*" to denote the warrior-ruler class is derived from "*kṣetrapa*". The first *kṣetrapa*, Mahāsamata, made his office hereditary: this was the beginning of dynasties. Later there were many thieves and highway-robbers. The *kṣetrapa*, or king as we call him now, punished them with the sword. Others said "We didn't do anything wrong"--this was the beginning of lying.

99.(E556-557; T489) An eon ends when life expectancy is only ten years.

100.(E557-563; T491-494) Vasubandhu's arguments against the Vaiśeṣika conception of composite whole:

(1) When the organ of the visual or tactile consciousness is in contact with one thread, the cloth is not perceived. If the composite

whole "cloth" exists in each thread, it would have to be perceived even if only one of its threads is.

(2) If the Vaiśeṣika says that the composite whole does not exist within each of its parts, how will it be demonstrated that it is anything but the collection of these parts?

(3) If the Vaiśeṣika says that the composite whole does exist within each of its parts, but that perception of one thread does not result in the perception of cloth because the perception of cloth presupposes contact of the organ with several of the parts, then if one sees the border of a cloth one would see the whole cloth.

(4) If the Vaiśeṣika says that the perception of the composite whole depends upon the perception of its central and other portions, one would never see a composite whole, because one can never see its central- and end-parts simultaneously.

(5) If the Vaiśeṣika says that these parts are perceived in succession, then the perception of cloth does not differ from the perception of a "circle" that results from hurling a torch in full arc. Objects of consciousness of such perceptions cannot be real entities in any way.

(6) When threads of different colors come together to form a cloth, how can the cloth be considered an entity? According to Vaiśeṣika, qualities like color must pervade their substances totally. Thus one substance can have only one quality of a type. So what does one do with a cloth of many colors? Unlike the Vaiśeṣika atomic theory, which needs the composite whole because atoms are absolutely imperceptible, the Vaibhāṣikas state that atoms in aggregation are perceived.

## CHAPTER FOUR

1.(E568; T552) The Vaibhāṣikas assume bodily and verbal karma also, which constitute manifest and unmanifest karma (see I, 11).

2.(E569-570; T553-554) Vātsīputrīya: If things are momentary, what is the cause of their destruction?

Vasubandhu: There is no special cause of destruction, because destruction is an absence and absences need no causes. If things were not arising and ceasing all the time, nothing could ever change at all. If you say that there is no more weighty means of cognition than direct perception, and that we can *see* wood being destroyed by fire, so that in this case a cause of destruction is directly perceived, we must investigate the phenomenon of combustion. Actually, we do not directly perceive the destruction of the wood: all we perceive is that we don't see the wood after its prolonged contact with fire. To say that the fire is the cause of the destruction of wood rests upon an inference, and what's more, an inference which isn't foolproof. It is equally possible to say that wood-moments are perishing incessantly of themselves, and arise again incessantly except when they come in relation with fire. You admit that the destruction of a flame occurs by itself. Even in the case when a gust of wind puts out a flame, you don't say it's the wind that is the cause of the flame's destruction; you say that the flame has ceased to renew "itself"--or rather the flame-series has ceased, because of "its" relation with wind. The same for a hand covering a bell: the hand simply impedes the renewal of the continuation of the sound-series, which would in any case cease by itself.

3.(E570-578; T554-560) If destruction needed a special cause, as arising does, then there would be no case of destruction without a cause. But you admit that awarenesses, flames, and sounds perish without a special cause. If one says that the destruction of wood takes place because of fire, then one has to admit that the generative cause of something can at the same time cause its cause destruction. For example, in the process of dyeing, the color of the object being dyed is changing from moment to moment. Thus the first with the dye-stuffs is both the cause of one color's arising and the cause of another's destruction, and subsequent moments of the fire-series are causes of the next color's destruction and another one's arising, etc. But it is impossible that the same kind of thing be both the generative cause and the cause of destruction of another kind of thing. I conclude that things cease because they are by nature momentary, and the other factors are catalysts only for the nonremoval of the series. Everything being momentary, no movement of the same thing is possible.

As to the Vaibhāṣika theory that manifest bodily karma is a shape (the changing shapes of what is conventionally called "a hand moving", "lips moving", etc.), shape as a separate entity can't be demonstrated either. The visible can in fact be reduced totally to color. When there is color in one direction in great quantity, one calls it "long". When it is seen in small quantity one calls it "short". When it spreads in four directions one calls it "quadrangular" (*caturasraka*). When it is equal in every direction from the center one calls it a "circle".

What is termed "shape" is really perceived by two different kinds of organs. One can tell that something is "long" by the eyes, one can also do so by the organ of touch.

Vaibhāṣika: But the tactual organs don't directly perceive shape: they only construe it from arrangements of the soft, hard, etc.

Vasubandhu: In the same way, shape isn't directly seen by the eye, but construed from arrangements of color.

Vaibhāṣika: When we get the idea of a shape from touch, it's not that touch directly perceives it--rather we remember the shape that we saw and tell by touch that the tactile sensation corresponds. Just as when we see the color of a fire we remember its heat, or when we smell the fragrance of a flower we remember its color.

Vasubandhu: In this case, there is a strict correlation; fire is always hot, etc. But there is no tactile sensation which is invariably associated with a shape. In a variegated tapestry one sees various shapes. In the same part of it one can construe two or three different ones. Thus there are various kinds of visibles in one place, following your theory, and this is impossible.

Vaibhāṣika: If shape isn't distinct from color, then the shape of one thing couldn't differ from another's when their colors are the same.

Vasubandhu: No. "Long" refers to real things arranged in a certain way, just as ants may form lines or circles.

Vaibhāṣika: When an object is far away one can see its shape before its color.

Vasubandhu: Actually, one sees its color, but mainly indistinctly.

Vaibhāṣika: Well, what *is* manifest karma to you, then?

Vasubandhu: I admit that manifest karma is shape, but I deny that shape is a special sort of entity.

Vaibhāṣika: But there must be a real entity underlying manifest karma.

Vasubandhu: A bodily action is actually a thought which puts the body into activity.

Vaibhāṣika: But a *sūtra* clearly states that there are two kinds of karmic results: volition and the action after volition. How can you distinguish these?

Vasubandhu: There are two kinds of volition. One is preparatory, the next is the thought "which raises a hand", etc.

Vaibhāṣika: In that case, you're actually denying manifest karma as an entity.

Vasubandhu: True.

Vaibhāṣika: If there is no manifest action, unmanifest karma can't exist either, as it always depends on the manifest sort.

Vasubandhu: The goodness or badness of a long-past decision brought into effect by others rests on the volition involved in that decision and its traces in the series. Thus, the concept of "unmanifest karma" isn't necessary.

4ab.(E579-590; T560-568) If you say that the *sūtras* mention a kind of materiality which exercises no resistance, and that this must refer to unmanifest karma, I reply that someone in meditation may see a skeleton, etc., and yet this materiality occupies no locus and exercises no resistance. If you say that there is a *sūtra* which says there is a materiality not liable to connection with proclivities this may also refer to such meditationally-seen materiality. If you say that there is a *sūtra* which says that merit increases, this phenomenon can as well be explained as volition. If you say there is no way to make the instigator of a murder responsible for the act if there is no unmanifest karma, I say that the thought of the instigator is bad in itself and carries its retribution by a transformation of "his" series.

Vaibhāṣika: Why this preference for a "transformation of a series"?

Vasubandhu: Actually, both the theory of unmanifest karma and the theory of transformation of the series are difficult to demonstrate. But it is easier to see how a volition transforms a mental series than how a certain material factor suddenly arises which has nothing to do with the awarenesses of the instigator. If you say that without unmanifest karma there is no violation of the *prātimokṣa* rules when a monk who has committed misdeeds does not admit them, the badness of this violation can be explained by me by his decision to stay silent.

4cd.(E590; T568) As soon as one performs an action those great elements constitute a set of unmanifest karma, which set then generates the set in the next moment, and so on, and thus karma is stored up for later retribution.

8b.(E597; T573) Actions are good or bad depending on the factors involved. Factors are good or bad (1) from the highest standpoint (e.g., liberation is absolutely good), (2) in terms of their intrinsic nature (e.g., medicine), (3) through their association with good or bad things (a particular medical treatment), (4) because of the goodness or badness of their cause (e.g., cow's milk).

10.(E600; T576) For instance, someone may have the intention to go to the village (inciting causal factor), but he may die at the next moment so no accompanying causal factor ever occurs.

The kind of consciousness which is given up by seeing the four truths is an inciter only. The mental consciousness given up by meditation is both an inciter and an accompanying causal factor. The five sensory consciousnesses are inciters only.

That which arises from retribution arises spontaneously, without any conditioning factors being necessary. Thus retribution is neither an inciter nor an accompanying causal factor.

12.(E603-605; T579-580) According to you, is manifest karma good, bad or neutral according to the character of its inciter or of its accompanying causal factors?

Vaibhāṣika: What is the point of this question?

Vasubandhu: The view of a self in the body and views regarding the impermanence and permanence of the elements constituting personality are, according to you, inciters (see IV, 11). They are always obstructed but neutral (i.e., they are liable to be connected with afflictions, but are karmically neutral). If the manifestation which follows upon these views has the same karmic nature as they do, it has to be unobstructed but neutral too. And according to you, a retribution-causing action which is unobstructed but neutral in the realm of desires does not exist. Or otherwise you must abandon your first thesis in IV, 11. As regards the view that manifest actions follow the karmic nature of their accompanying causal factors, the manifest action of a person undergoing monastic discipline could not be good in that case, if his awarenesses at the time are bad or neutral.

Vaibhāṣika: The unmanifest karma has the same karmic nature as its inciter when it is an awareness susceptible to abandonment by meditation. It is not of the same nature as its inciter when it is an awareness susceptible to abandonment by right views, for example the awareness that the self exists, because in that case there is, in between the inciter and the manifest karma, another inciter, an awareness susceptible to abandonment by meditation, turned outwardly, accompanied by the initial and/or sustained thought (see II, 33) which results in the view of a self. The first primary causal factor is neutral, the second is bad, the manifest karma is bad. From an inciter susceptible to abandonment by right view there arises another inciter susceptible to abandonment by meditation and which is good, bad, or neutral; from this second inciter arises manifest karma which is of the same nature.

Vasubandhu: But if manifest karma is not good, bad or neutral according to its secondary causal factors, then your theory--that views are inciters, that they generate manifest karma, that an awareness susceptible to abandonment by right views doesn't engender a manifest karma, and that there is no manifest karma in the realm of desires which is obstructed by the neutral--becomes unintelligible.

50.(E657; T625) "In this life, etc.": in this life, the next life, or one still later.

Others say that karmic retribution that has begun to be experienced in one life can continue to be so in a later life. Others, the Vaibhāṣikas, disagree.

51-52.(E558-560; T626-628) "Some others", viz., the Dārṣṭāntikas, who classify karma into (1) karma whose time of maturation is determined but whose kind of maturation is not; (2) karma whose kind of maturation is determined but whose time is not; (3) karma whose time and kind of maturation are determined; (4) karma whose time and kind of maturation are not determined.

There is no bad action in the three higher realms. Good actions in hell produce good or neutral karmic results in later existences, but not in hell itself, for there is no good retribution in hell.

54.(E661; T630) All actions other than those mentioned are not determined.

65.(E673; T639) The three bad practices that are not actions are covetousness, malice and false view.

Dārṣṭāntika: No, they are mental acts (citing textual authority).

Vaibhāṣika: But *sūtras* tell us that defilements are not actions (re-explaining the authoritative text cited).

67.(E676-677; T641-642) The principal six bad actions are the taking of life, stealing, offences of lust--as when one steals another's wife, or ravishes a young girl--false speech, slander, harsh or unconsidered speech.

Vaibhāṣika: If one has someone else do such an act it constitutes his unmanifest karma, except for offences of lust, which must always be committed by the agent and so are always manifest actions.

Vasubandhu: The entire Vaibhāṣika concept of manifest and unmanifest karma has already been rejected. It is the volitions to do these acts which are bad, as well as the volition which sets the body or voice into activity to perform them.

"One bad action always of two kinds" is adultery, since one must do it in person.

68.(E677-780; T642-646) The taking of life means the taking of animal as well as of human life. Even to willfully kill the smallest animal is a bad action, and carries a karmic retribution. In fact, it is even wrong to cut the leaves off a tree, or to trample down green plants so that they're destroyed. There are different motives for the taking of life: because of desire; for the sake of robbery; just for the "fun" of it; for the sake of defending oneself or others; because of hatred; because of false views, such as when a kind man thinks he has to have criminals executed, when the Persians think their old people should be killed, or when one says that one should kill snakes, scorpions, etc., or when one is convinced there is no future life or no retribution for killing. Stealing may also come about through desire, or through hatred, or from false views (such as when a king thinks criminals' possessions can be taken away). Offences of lust may of course usually take place through desire, but also through hate and through false views, such as when the Persians have sexual intercourse with their mothers. False speech may also arise from the same three causes.

73.(E685-687; T650-651) Objection: How can there be murder, since aggregates are momentary?

Reply: Taking away the life of an aggregate-series is murder.

According to the Jains, even nonintentional killing is murder. By analogy, even touching someone else's wife without her consent constitutes a case of adultery. And the Jain teachers are themselves guilty, because they preach terrible austerities.

74.(E687-688; T651-653) "Four kinds of women"--intercourse with (1) those one shouldn't consort with (mother, daughter, another's wife), (2) one's wife in an improper way, (3) in an unsuitable place or (4) time.

There are different views about the case of intercourse with someone mistaken for someone else.

79-80.(E697-702; T659-663) Only humans can sever good roots, not animals, not gods, etc., and indeed only *some* humans, though opinions differ as to which.

81.(E703-708; T664-666) There is retribution for each intended action. If someone has committed a murder he may be reborn as a human being, but his life will be either short or miserable.

82-84.(E708-710; T666-668) E.g., killing doesn't occur in hell, nor do stealing or adultery or lying. Gods don't kill one another (though perhaps they can cut off each others' heads, etc.), but they can kill those in other realms.

85.(E710-712; T669-670) E.g., the retributional result of bad action is a hellish existence. The outflowing result will lead to a short life; the dominant result of killing is reduction of life's force. Three results are rehearsed for each of the ten courses of bad action.

95.(E721-722; T677-678) But the retributional effect of an act can occur only in the same life, or in the next life: it cannot extend for two lives after the act. Even though they have a retribution, the highest meditational attainments don't project an action, because they don't coexist with conscious action. There are three kinds of obstructions: obstructions due to past actions, obstructions which are defilements, obstructions which are retributional.

96.(E722; T679) The obstructions due to actions are those coming primarily from the five grave offences: killing one's mother, killing one's father, killing a noble person, causing divisions in the order, and harming a Buddha. It is a graver offence to kill one's mother than it is to kill one's father.

97.(E724-725; T680-681) The five grave offences can't be committed by eunuchs, etc., and a human born of demons does not offend in killing his parents.

103.(E730-732;T685-686) The same kind of gravity does not occur as in full-fledged cases if a person kills his mother thinking it's someone else, or if he kills her accidentally.

105.(E732-734; T688-689) The action which has the greatest good retribution is that mental action which allows entry into the highest meditational attainment.

107cd.(E735; T690) The retributional effects of acts can be severed by the acquisition of perfect patience or forbearance, or by becoming a nonreturner or by becoming a noble person.

## CHAPTER FIVE

1-2a.(E760-764; T767-771) It is because of the proclivities which have arisen in series that karma is accumulated for future retribution. Since to the Vaibhāṣika past and future factors don't change in 644 fundamental nature, he can regard the traces and the defilements themselves as identical. For the Sautrāntika, however, they are truly seeds of défilement, i.e., proclivities.

Objection: What does the expression "attachment to sensual pleasure" mean? If one says that attachment to sensual pleasure is itself a trace, this contradicts the *sūtra* which makes a distinction between attachment to sensual pleasure and its trace. If one interprets "attachment to sensual pleasure" to mean the trace laid down by attachment to sensual pleasure, then it would have to be for the Vaibhāṣika a possession, and would therefore be a conditioning factor dissociated from awareness. But this is in contradiction to the Abhidharma, which says that attachment to sensual pleasure can be accompanied by the three kinds of feelings (see I, 4), for a conditioning factor dissociated from awareness cannot be accompanied by feelings.

Vaibhāṣika: The expression should be taken in the first sense. In the *sūtra*, "trace" also includes all the defilement's consequences. Besides, the traces cannot be dissociated from awareness, because they defile and so hinder awarenesses.

Sautrāntika: The expression should be taken in the second sense. But a trace is neither associated with an awareness nor dissociated from an awareness, because a trace is not an entity. A trace is simply a defilement-series in a nonmanifest state. It is a seed (*bīja*). And by "seed" we mean a certain capacity or power (*śakti*) to produce this defilement again, which has arisen from a past occurrence of the same kind of defilement.

4.(E765-766; T773) All proclivities can be abandoned by the truth of frustration. Extreme beliefs can be abandoned by the truth of the origin of frustration and the truth of the cessation of frustration.

5.(E766-768; T773-774) Attachment, repugnance, ignorance and pride can be abandoned by meditation. Other false views can be abandoned by all four noble truths, and so can attachment to views and perplexity. Adherence to rule and ritual can be abandoned by the truth of frustration and the truth of the path. Some people claim that a non-Buddhist can't abandon the traces which are counteracted by a knowledge of the truths. But yet these people may meditate, and be separate from the traces of the realm of desire.

There are thirty-six proclivities in the realm of desire (twelve views, four perplexities, five attachments, five repugnances, five ignorances, and five prides), and thirty-one in each of the material and immaterial realms; thus the total of ninety-eight.

6.(E769-772; T774-776) Of the ninety-eight proclivities eighty-eight are destroyed by vision when calmed through patience; the other ten are destroyed by meditation.

Can non-Buddhists destroy proclivities by vision? There are texts that speak of non-Buddhists detached from all views. But how can that be--they have not destroyed the views of the realm of desire?

Vaibhāṣika: They lose that detachment when they accept a view.

7.(E772-773; T777-778) The five views explained (cf. V, 3 above). "Extreme beliefs" are beliefs in persistence or in nihilism. Although all five views listed in V, 3 are false, those classified as "false views" in the list are those that are the worst, e.g., denying the four truths. "Adherence to views" is to consider wrong views as right ones. And "adherence to mere rule and ritual" covers all sorts of false beliefs about causes and effects as well as about what is and is not the path.

8.(E773-775; T778-780) The belief that suicide or asceticism is noble has nothing to do with the view of the permanence of the self. So how can one say that it is abandoned by the knowledge of the truth of frustration? It is rather the knowledge of the truth of the origin of frustration which makes for its abandonment.

Vaibhāṣika: But this belief is an error concerning frustration.

Vasubandhu: But it is equally an error concerning the path.

There are four perverted views (meaning views which invariably give rise to frustration). They are: considering what is impermanent as permanent, what is frustrating as satisfying, what is impure are pure, what isn't self as self.

9.(E778-780; T780-784) For the Sautrāntika, but not for the Vaibhāṣika, the reversal relating to "self" also includes the belief in "mine", "my".

10-11.(E782-785; T784-788) The seven kinds of pride are basic pride, greater pride, the pride that is more than pride, the pride of thinking "I am", conceit, the pride of deficiency, and false pride. Basic pride is any inflation of awareness which thinks "I am superior" or "I am equal" relative respectively to an inferior or an equal. Greater pride is thinking "I am superior" or "I am equal" in relation respectively to an equal or a superior. The pride of thinking "I am" is when the aggregates are taken as a self. Conceit is thinking one has attainments when one doesn't. The pride of deficiency is thinking one is only a little bit inferior to one vastly superior. False pride is thinking one has qualities one doesn't have. The *Jñānaprasthāna*, however, says that all of the following views are pride: "I am better", "I am equal", "I am worse", "Somebody else is better than me", "Somebody else is equal to me", "Somebody else is worse than me", "Somebody else isn't better than me", "Somebody else isn't equal to me", "Somebody else isn't worse than me".

12.(E782; T788) There are eleven pervasive proclivities.

25-26.(E803-808; T806-810) Vaibhāṣika: The proof of the existence of past and future as well as present lies in the fact that consciousness is the result of "two", its organ and its content. A mental consciousness, for instance, arises in regard to a content only when this object is already past, because it belongs to a previous moment. A factor can only arise with an existing object as content. If past and future factors did not exist, then there would be factors without objects. If the past did not exist, how could good and bad actions give their retribution? For when the retribution arises the actions are past.

Explanations of the existence of past and future: (1) Bhadanta Dharmatrāta: The manner of being of a factor in the three times differs, but the factor itself does not differ. Example: a golden vase which one makes into something else golden--its shape is altered but not its color. (2) Ghoṣaka: When a factor is past, it has the characteristic of a past event; but it is not disconnected from the characteristics of future and present factors. And so on for the rest. Example: A man attached to one woman isn't unattached to other women. (3) Bhadanta Vasumitra: Factors in the three times differ by their condition, not by their nature. Example: A bead in an abacus signifies "one" in the one-place, "ten" in the ten-place, etc. (4) Buddhadeva: The three times differ by relative otherness. That is, a factor is called present, future, or past in relation to what precedes and what follows. Example: The same woman is a daughter and a mother. To the *Vibhāṣā*, Bhadanta Dharmatrāta's view is untenable because it is the same as Sāṃkhya's. Ghoṣaka's is untenable because factors in the three times are not distinguished. Buddhadeva's is untenable because the three times would exist at the same time, a past event, for instance, being both previous to and successive to other things would be both previous and subsequent, a moment could be both past and future, etc. Thus, says the *Vibhāṣā*, the theory of Bhadanta Vasumitra is to be accepted.

Vasubandhu: If the past and the future exist, then why call them "past" and "future"?

Vaibhāṣika: When the factor exercises its function it is present. When it does not exercise its function it is future. When it has exercised its function and its function has stopped, then it is past.

Vasubandhu: But a nonsimultaneous eye does not exercise its efficacy (see I, 39). Does this mean it isn't present? If you say that its function is to give and receive an effect, then homogeneous causes (see II, 59), which give their effect when past, are present when past.

27.(E808-819; T810-820) If a factor exists always, why doesn't it always exercise its function? If its functioning ceases, why not the factor itself?

Vaibhāṣika: A conditioned factor which hasn't yet arisen is called future; one having arisen but not having been destroyed is present; one which has been destroyed is past.

Vasubandhu: If they all exist, how can they be not yet arisen or already destroyed?

Vaibhāṣika: Because the essential nature of a factor continues to exist.

Vasubandhu: How can you even talk about anything arising at all if everything exists all the time?

Vaibhāṣika: But there is a *sūtra* which says that past and future actions exist.

Vasubandhu: The past is that which existed, the future is that which will exist. In this sense, they exist, but they don't exist in the way the present does.

Vaibhāṣika: But I didn't say they exist as the present does! They exist in the manner of past and future.

Vasubandhu: In the *sūtra* the word "exists" is used in the same sense as when one says "there is (exists) nonexistence of the flame before it arises", etc.

Vaibhāṣika: But there is a *sūtra* which clearly says that past actions exist.

Vasubandhu: That only means that past actions have exercised a function the results of which carry on into the present. Anyway, there is another *sūtra* which says that the eye which arises came from nowhere, and the eye which ceases disappears.

Vaibhāṣika: The expression "it exists after it was nonexistent" means only that after being nonexistent in the present it became existent in the present.

Vasubandhu: What does *that* mean? In this example the eye doesn't differ from present time. (In the *Vibhāṣā* time is explained as a conditioned event's arising and ceasing.) As to the argument that the past and future exist because consciousness arises as the result of past and future events, are these events really generative conditions of the consciousness, or only conditions inasmuch as they're its supporting objects? A future event, which may arise in a thousand years or may never arise, may of course be an object of consciousness (as an anticipation, for instance), but it is difficult to see how it can be the generative condition of a present factor.

Vaibhāṣika: If past and future factors don't exist, how can they be objects of consciousness?

Vasubandhu: Something which does not exist can be an object of consciousness, such as when there is consciousness of fantasies.

Vaibhāṣika: If that which does not exist can be an object of consciousness, a thirteenth sense could be an object of consciousness too. (Remember there are only twelve sense-fields, see I, 14).

Vasubandhu: What is the object of consciousness relating to the statement you have just made? If you say that "thirteenth sense" is only a name and no existent entity, then you have just admitted that an object of consciousness need not exist. What is the object of consciousness which relates to the consciousness of the prior absence of a certain sound?

Vaibhāṣika: The object of consciousness is the sound itself and not its prior absence.

Vasubandhu: But if a future sound, for which there is no prior absence, exists, why does one have the idea that it doesn't exist?

Vaibhāṣika: It doesn't exist as a present factor, thus one has the idea that it doesn't exist.

Vasubandhu: But you are claiming that it is the same factor which is past, present, and future! Or if you say that there is a difference between the future sound and the present one, and that the judgment "it doesn't exist" relates to the first, then this is tantamount to saying that the present one exists after not having existed.

Vaibhāṣika: If the nonexistent could be an object of consciousness, how is it that the future Buddha in his last life said that it's impossible for him to perceive anything which doesn't exist?

Vasubandhu: In the context, he was contrasting himself with other religious teachers who claim a nonexistent enlightenment for themselves. Besides, if everything that is thought is real, there is no place for any investigation into things, and the future Buddha of this passage is not different from the other religious teachers. Again, the Buddha speaks of knowing what exists as what exists, and what doesn't exist as what doesn't exist.

Vaibhāṣika: But if past and future factors do not exist, past acts could have no effects.

Vasubandhu: In a retributory process the effect of an act doesn't occur immediately after the act. It occurs through a special transformation in the series where the act, i.e., the volition, previously arose. If you assert that past and future factors exist, you are then forced to say that their effects always exist too; thus what effect can an action bring about?

Vaibhāṣika: But if past and future factors don't exist, how can one be bound by a past or future defilement?

Vasubandhu: One is bound to the past defilement because of the existence of its traces in the present; one is bound to a future defilement by the existence of a trace which helps give rise to a future defilement.

32.(E828; T826) Delusion is the same as ignorance. The doubt intended in the passage of the *Kośa* is principally doubt as regards the four noble truths.

34.(E829-830; T828) The fundamental causes of defilements are traces; objects are causes as sensory contents, and careless mental attention is cause as application.

36.(E831; T830-831) Ignorance is the "root" of all the defilements and their traces; one can speak of it as a "contaminant" inasmuch as it is an evil influence.

41.(E836; T835) The fetters are attraction, repugnance, pride, ignorance, views, adherence to views, rules, etc., perplexity, envy and selfishness.

48a.(E844; T842) Anger and hypocrisy are added by the Vaibhāṣikas.

52-54.(E846-848; T845-847) Lethargy, excitedness and sleepiness can be bad or neutral in the realm of desire. The rest of the envelopers are always bad, while the afflictions are neutral there. Deceit and craftiness occur in the material realm as well as the realm of desire. Except for pride and sleepiness, which are eliminated by practice, all the defilements are eliminated by correct view.

55.(E848-849; T847-848) Attachment is associated with the faculties of satisfaction and contentedness, repugnance is associated with the faculties of frustration and depression, and ignorance may be associated with any feeling. False views are associated with frustrations concerning those of good actions and with satisfaction concerning those of bad actions.

59bd.(E852; T851-852) The two pairs constitute obstructions to perceptual identification in the first case, to peace in the second. In any case, all the defilements count as obstructions.

63.(E860; T859) "An antidote" such as the path of liberation: "acquisition of results", i.e., the result of stream-enterer, etc.

64.(E861; T860) Ascertainments are of two kinds--those constituting knowledge and those constituting abandoning. There are nine of them: three for the realm of desire, three for the material realm, three for the two higher realms taken together, and the destruction of the proclivities in each of three realms. The six results of patience are the first six ascertainments.

## CHAPTER SIX

1.(E871; T895) The path of meditation may be either mundane or supramundane; the path of vision is always supramundane.

3.(E871-889; T899-910) As regards the four noble truths, which are the objects of the path of vision, how can it be said, for instance, that all conditioned factors liable to be connected with distress are frustrating only? For in fact they may be linked with satisfaction, etc.

Vaibhāṣika: There are three states of frustration. The first is the state of frustration itself, the second is the state of frustration inherent in conditioned factors, and the third is the state of frustration inherent in transformation. Thus, even the conditioned factors associated with satisfaction are frustrating, because this satisfaction is transitory, and thus they are frustrating by the state of frustration inherent in transformation.

Vasubandhu: But why aren't they perceived as frustrating in themselves?

Vaibhāṣika: It's just like the case of an eyelash, which is not felt in the palm of the hand but which causes pain when it is put in the eye. In the same way, ignorant people do not see that conditioned factors associated with pleasure are really frustrating, but noble ones do.

Vasubandu: But the path itself is conditioned. Thus it is frustrating, too.

Vaibhāṣika: No, for the definition of "frustration" is that it be contrary, whereas this is not the case for the path.

Vasubandhu: Why is only frustration spoken of as one of the truths, when there is also satisfaction?

Vaibhāṣika: Because there is so much more frustration than satisfaction. In the same way one calls a pile of lentils with which there may be mixed some beans "a pile of lentils".

Vasubandhu: But how can one regard as frustrating feelings which are experienced as satisfying?

Vaibhāṣika: Because they are impermanent, and this impermanence leads to frustration.

Vasubandhu: This is confusing two aspects in conditioned factors. Impermanence and frustration are not the same.

Vaibhāṣika: But there is a *sūtra* which says that all feelings are conjoined with frustration. And there is also an argument by reasoning: The causes of satisfaction may themselves give rise to frustration. Thus drink or food, when ingested excessively, do so. Since it is illogical that the same thing be the cause of two contrary results, one must conclude that even when the result is perceived as satisfying there is really some frustration there. What is sometimes perceived as satisfying may be only the remedy or the transformation of a frustration. For instance, someone carrying a heavy burden may put this burden on the other shoulder, and thus feel some pleasure, but really this is only a transformation of frustration.

Vasubandhu: Satisfaction does exist in itself. If your criterion for frustration is that someone perceives it as such, in the same way our criterion for satisfaction is that someone perceives it as such. No sensation which is in itself desirable becomes in itself undesirable. If noble persons don't like satisfaction, it's not because of its nature itself, but because of its effect of making one lose good qualities. If satisfaction were undesirable in itself, who would ever be attached to it? As to the *sūtra* cited, the Buddha clearly states there that he is speaking of the frustration coming from the transformation and impermanence of satisfaction, and not of the state of frustration itself. If all feelings were frustrating, they would never have been categorized as triple by the Buddha. You claim that all satisfaction is accompanied by some frustration, but this cannot empirically be seen to be the case.

To say that satisfaction means only less frustration is also not possible, because the satisfaction felt in the first three meditational states would then be "less frustration", and then this satisfaction fades in the fourth meditational state. This would be then "more frustration"! As for your argument that the causes of satisfaction can be causes of frustration, it is inexactly put. For there are not any absolute causes of satisfaction and frustration. It depends on the state of the perceiver. But if the state of the perceiver is uniform, a cause of satisfaction is always a cause of satisfaction and never a cause of frustration. As for your argument about transferring a burden to another shoulder, this is really satisfaction, because relief, and cannot in any way be interpreted as a transformation of frustration.

4.(E890; T910-911) Though four noble truths have been spoken of by the Buddha, he also speaks of the "two truths", the conventional and highest or ultimate truth. Conventional truths arise when things have not been completely analyzed, such as when one speaks of a pot as a pot, water as "water", etc. Ultimate truth is where one analyzes all the constituent parts of some "thing" to such an extent that the very notion of the "thing" disappears. The conventional is a kind of truth because a person is not lying when he calls a pot a pot, and as far as conventional designations are concerned, he is using them properly. But further analysis will show that no pot really exists as an entity.

5.(E890-891; T912-913) There are three phases in the seeing of the four noble truths. First, one studies them from other sources, then contemplates what one has studied, and finally one engages in real meditation. This corresponds to the three kinds of insight: insight through study, insight through reflection, and insight through meditation.

12.(E898-899; T921-922) In meditation on breathing one is conscious of how many inhalations and exhalations are made, how the air enters and leaves the lungs, how the air currents enter parts of the body; the breath is analyzed into material elements, etc.

20-24.(E914-921; T935-942) The aids to penetration are heat, summit, patience and supreme factors.

As a woman one may acquire the highest worldly factors and be reborn as a man; thus there is uncalculated cessation of femininity.

The aids to penetration are lost at death by those other than noble ones; noble persons lose them when they quit this earth either at death or by moving to another realm. Specifics provided about their acquisition, loss or retention by nobles and by those who transmigrate.

More details about the expectancies of a transmigrator, a self-enlightened one, a Bodhisattva.

27.(E925-928; T947-949) Debate on the question of whether there can be full understanding, a notion which is rejected by Vasubandhu as being incompatible with the idea of progressive path of vision.

34ab.(E940-944; T959-962) Objection: "One who has seven more lives to live" actually will be reborn twenty-eight more times--seven as a human, seven in the intermediate states, seven as gods and seven more in intermediate states

Vaibhāṣika: But twenty-eight is four groups of seven, and there is no eighth type of rebirth in the same realm.

Vasubandhu: Yes there is: the one who attains the summit of existence is reborn eight times in the same realm.

Vaibhāṣika: The reference is only to rebirths in the realm of desire.

One who becomes a stream-enterer as a human will be reborn among humans to attain liberation; one who attains it as a god will be liberated as a god.

Why can't a stream-enterer backslide? Because he does not do things that would produce rebirth, since his good roots and purity preclude it.

39.(E953-955; T970-971) Three kinds of nonreturners who go to the material realm are those who achieve liberation in the intermediate state, those who achieve liberation on rebirth, and those who "go higher." Each is of three sorts depending on how long it takes them to gain liberation.

44.(E966-970; T981-982) All traces of defilements are finally removed with the diamond-like meditational concentration. This type of concentration may occur on the path of vision, in any of the meditational states, or in any of the immaterial meditation attainments. The diamond-like meditational concentration occurring at the last of the immaterial meditational attainments, i.e., the attainment of the cessation of awareness and feelings, results in the practitioner becoming an adept (*aśaikṣa*, literally "one who has nothing further to learn"), or noble person. According to the Vaibhāṣikas, but not according to the Sautrāntikas, one may backslide from the state of being a noble person.

58-60b.(E996-1006, T1006-1012) Why one can't backslide from the perfected state explained, citing scripture and giving arguments.

There are three kinds of backsliding: from what is attained, from what is not yet attained, and from experiencing. The Buddha experiences only the first; the immovable perfected ones only the first two; perfected beings experience all three. But one who has fallen away cannot die, and does not misbehave.

63-64.(E1007-1011; T1016-1019) Seven kinds of noble persons: (1) faith-followers, (2) factor-followers, (3) resolved in faith, (4) of attained views, (5) eye-witnesses, (6) liberated by wisdom, (7) liberated both ways.

## CHAPTER SEVEN

1.(E1033-1035; T1087-1088) The patiences are not knowledge because at the moment of their existence doubts still exist. But it is the very patiences themselves which make the doubts cease.

11.(E1054-1055; T1107) When one knows the awareness of another one does not know it as the other knows it; one isn't aware of its content, but only knows that the other's awareness is contaminated. One knows, that is, the specific characteristic of its content but not its general properties; one knows mental but not material factors; one knows present factors but not past or future ones. One knows these in meditation, not by ordinary vision.

12.(E1055-1057; T1108-1109) (Cf. also VI, 67) Enlightenment is knowledge of the cessation of factors as well as the non-(further)-arising of factors. When one knows "Frustration is fully known by me, the origin of frustration has been abandoned by me, the cessation of frustration has been realized by me, the path has been cultivated by me", this is knowledge of cessation. When one knows "Frustration is fully known by me and doesn't have to be known by me again", etc., "the path has been cultivated by me and doesn't have to be cultivated again", this is the knowledge of non-(further)arising (VII, 7). These knowledges may be regarded as both ultimate and conventional, because the subsequent judgments relating to "me" can be only conventional.

13.(E1057-1062; T1110-1117) The knowledges on the path of vision have the following aspects as objects: for the truth of frustration impermanence, frustration, emptiness, and absence of self; for the truth of the origination of frustration, causes as past seed, originating (proximate) cause, successive causes as forming a series, conditions as the collection of co-factors; for the truth of the cessation of frustration, cessation of defiled aggregates, calm because of the annihilation of greed, hostility, and confusion, exalted because free of all trouble, and related to liberation; for the truth of the path, the path itself, logic (for the path is based on logical means and in itself contains means), mode of progress, and leading to liberation. These aspects constitute wisdom. They relate to both subject and object. Awarenesses and accompanying mental factors are subject and object; all other factors, whether conditioned or unconditioned, are only objects.

28.(E1083-1085; T1136-1137) The powers of a Buddha include special knowledges. These are: the power of knowing what is possible and what impossible, the power of knowing the retributions for acts, the power of meditations, deliverances, concentrations and special attainments, the power of knowing others' faculties, the power of knowing others' various dispositions, the force of knowing paths that go everywhere (into all the life-destinies), the power of the knowledge of former lives and their loci, the power of knowing the death and rebirth of beings, the power of knowing how to destroy all distress.

32.(E1090-1093; T1141-1143) The special grounds of the confidence of a Buddha rest on these knowledges. The three special establishments of mindfulness of a Buddha are his indifference to whether his hearers accept, don't accept, or partially do and partially don't accept his teachings.

33.(E1093-1095; T1143-1144) The Buddha's great compassion is impartial, extends to all sentient beings, is produced after great preparation, is grounded in the noble truths, has not the slightest admixture of hostility.

43.(E1109-1110; T1159-1160) The four higher faculties that are conventional awarenesses are divine eye, divine ear, memory of past lives and knowledge of supernatural powers.

Why don't the "five" (excluding knowledge of destruction of proclivities) exist in the immaterial realm? The first three have material things as contents, knowledge of others' minds involves material colors and shape, and the memory of past lives pertains to the realm of desire.

## CHAPTER EIGHT

1.(E1126-1128; T1216-1218) The Sautrāntika objects that if

meditational concentration is to be defined as "one-pointed awareness" then it is awareness itself, and not a special kind of entity as the Vaibhāṣikas claim.

Vaibhāṣika: No, meditational concentration is a special kind of factor by which awarenesse become concentrated. The concentrated awarenesses themselves are not meditational concentration.

Vasubandhu: Since awarenesses are momentary, all of them, whether meditationally concentrated or not, have only one object. You may say that meditational concentration makes it so that the second awareness is not distracted from the object of the first awareness. But in that case, meditational concentration is doing nothing as far as the first awareness is concerned, and yet you consider the first awareness to be associated with meditational concentration. Also, you have defined meditational concentration as a generally permeating factor (cf. II, 24), a factor occurring with every awareness. Thus all awarenesses must be meditationally concentrated.

Vaibhāṣika: No, because in nonmeditational states the meditational concentration occurring with an awareness is not very strong.

Vasubandhu: For the Sautrāntika, meditational concentration is the meditationally concentrated awarenesses themselves and nothing else.

2.(E1130-1131; T1219-1220) In the second meditational stage there is no more thought; the third meditational state has no more joy; and the fourth finally discards satisfaction for a pure equanimity.

3.(E1131; T1220) Some schools say there is some matter in the immaterial attainments; they are called "immaterial" because they are less material than other factors. Vasubandhu rejects this claim, arguing that it contradicts various theses propounded elsewhere, is illogical, and that alleged textual authority for it is based on misunderstandings.

9.(E1143-1147; T1231-1236) Vaibhāṣika: The satisfaction existing in the meditational states is not bodily pleasure but a mental state arising from tranquillity.

Dārṣṭāntika objection: The satisfaction of the meditational states is bodily, for all satisfaction has a bodily aspect. The idea that "satisfaction" stands for an aspect of tranquillity is untenable, for in that case, since tranquillity increases, satisfaction should increase too. The Vaibhāṣika also wishes to subsume all "joy" under the faculty of satisfaction.

We, however, maintain that there is joy which is not simply satisfaction.

24. (E1163; T1256) Three special meditational attainments may be named the meditational concentration on emptiness, on the signless, and on the wishless.

25cd. (E1165; T1259) There are futher succeeding meditational concentrations which focus on the emptiness of emptiness, the signlessness of the signless, and the wishlessness of the wishless.

29. (E1170; T1264) From meditational concentration arise the four boundless states: loving kindness, compassion, sympathy and equanimity. They are called "boundless" because they can be applied to innumerable sentient beings, their merit is boundless.

## 175. VASUBANDHU, *Pratītyasamutpādavyākhyā* on *Pratītyasamutpādavibhaṅganirdeśa*

The work is available in Tibetan, and a small portion of it exists in Sanskrit.[524] This portion has been edited by Giuseppe Tucci,[525] comprising sections of the discussions of ignorance, feeling, thirst, grasping and existence among the twelve components of the Buddhist chain. Two sections--on *saṃskāra* and on *vijñāna*--have been edited and translated in Muroji (see note 524), who also provides a helpful brief summary of the entire work in French and a summary of the two sections he deals with.

## 176. VAŚUBANDHU, *Aparāmitāyuḥsūtropadeśa*[526]

Summary by K. Timura

"This work consists of two parts, viz., the verse and the prose...The verse part contains twenty-four verses, each of which has four lines. In this part Vasubandhu expresses at first his undivided devotion to Amitābha...The next twenty-one verses describe the adornment of the Pure Land. In the last verse Vasubandhu confesses his aspiration to be born in the Pure Land with others.

"In the prose part, Vasubandhu interprets the verses and explains the 'Five spiritual Gates', viz., the Gate of Worship, the Gate of Praise, the Gate of Aspiration, the Gate of Perception and the Gate of Merit Transference. The Gate of Worship means bodily action and the Gate of Praise moral action. The Gate of Aspiration is solely and exclusively the aspiration to be born in the Pure Land. The Gate of Perception which is taught in detail will be explained below. The last, the Gate of Merit Transference, is the accomplishment of the compassionate heart in transferring merit to all beings in suffering.

"In the Gate of Perception, the three kinds of adornments, may be perceived. These are the 17 kinds of adornments of the Buddha Land, the 8 kinds of adornments of Amitābha and the 4 kinds of adornments of the bodhisattvas in the Pure Land. Thus, the three kinds of adornment are further divided into twenty-nine. But all these can be condensed into one word, i.e., *dharma,* which means 'purity'. By the word "purity" is meant the true wisdom and non-created *dharmakāya.*"

"This is the most important doctrine of the Pure Land. All adornments of the Pure Land are condensed into one *dharma,* namely, *tathatā...*"

## 177. VASUBANDHU, *Buddhānusmṛtiṭīkā*[527]

## 178. VASUBANDHU, *Bhadracaryāpraṇidhānaṭīkā*[528]

## 179. VASUBANDHU, Commentary on a *Caturdharmakasūtra*[529]

## 180. VASUBANDHU, *Vyākhyāna* on the *Ṣaṇmukhī*[530]

Summary by Stefan Anacker

This is a commentary on work number 56 above. The material is considered under six headings: (1) the realization of insight (*prajñā*), (2) the purification coming from the force of compassion, (3) the hindrances to "one's own" series (*saṃtāna*), (4) knowing well the hindrances of others, (5) the accumulation of all that is necessary for enlightenment, (6) its result: correct knowledge and *tathatā.*

Other topics treated here are (1) supporting all sentient beings in times of suffering and of pleasure, (2) removal of the obstructions of "oneself" and "others", (3) acquiring of merit, (4-5) accomplishing both "one's own" and "others'" aims, (6) the efforts needed so that others may achieve their aims.

But this is all done in six brief headings only. The first and second have been taught in view of maturing sentient beings, by not abandoning them in either suffering or pleasurable states. The fifth has to do with maturing them in all that is necessary enlightenment. The third and the fourth have to do with removing obstructions "to oneself". The sixth has to do with the enlightenment body, and its extraordinary result, that one can stay in *saṃsāra* without any limits and stand by to accomplish others' aims.

In the first part, we can see four aspects: the knowledge of the selflessness of factors, lack of agitation at sentient beings with perverted views or at the sufferings of *saṃsāra*, and recognizing the defilements of sentient beings. This work also succinctly deals with the perfections. It is through these kinds of vows and contemplations which are included in this work that knowledge and all the other Buddha's factors can be obtained, because they are the cause of them. Practice and knowledge of the Mahāyāna is by necessity neither in *saṃsāra* nor in *nirvāṇa*. The reason for wanting to obtain this practice and knowledge is explained in part 2.

Thus we see that six efforts are being described here, which are taken up for the nonabandonment of sentient beings.

### 181. VASUBANDHU, *Daśabhūmikasūtravyākhyā*[531]

### 182. VASUBANDHU, *Dharmacakrapravartanasūtra*[532]

### 183. VASUBANDHU, *Gāthāsaṃgrahaśāstrārtha*[533]

### 184. VASUBANDHU, *Gayāśīrṣasūtraśāstrārtha*[534]

### 185. VASUBANDHU, *Mahāyānaśatadharmaprakāśamukhaśāstra*[535]

### 186. VASUBANDHU, *Nirvāṇasūtrapūrvabhūtotpannabhūtaśāstra*[536]

### 187. VASUBANDHU, Commentary on a *Prajñāpāramitāsūtra*[537]

### 188. VASUBANDHU, Commentary on *Ratnacūḍāmaṇisūtra*[538]

### 189. VASUBANDHU, Commentary on the *Śrīmālāsiṃhanādasūtra*[539]

### 190. VASUBANDHU, *Saddharmapuṇḍarīkopadeśa*[540]

## 191. VASUBANDHU, *Sukhāvatīvyūhopadeśa*[541]

### Summary by Minoru Kiyota

Minoru Kiyota has translated this text: this summary is taken from his article,[542] which also contains a translation ("T").

"The *Upadeśa* is one of the important Pure Land texts in the Sino-Japanese pure Land tradition. It neatly organizes ideas which are described in a less structured manner in the 29.*Larger Sukhāvatī-vyūha-sūtra.*"

"The *Upadeśa* consists of two parts, the verses and the prose. The former summarizes the central theme of the text; the latter analyzes and interprets that theme...(T)his paper establishes ten arbitrary topic headings. Each topic is an elaboration of the preceding one."

"1.(T278) Vow...After years of spiritual practice, accumulating insight at each stage of practice, Bodhisattva Dharmākara...finally becomes Buddha Amitāyus. At each stage he makes a vow. The eighteenth stipulates as follows: 'Even when I am able to attain Buddhahood, if sentient beings of the ten quarters, with sincerity and faith, desire to be born in my land by practising up to ten thoughts (i.e., chanting the name of Buddha Amitāyus) and are not born there, I will not accept supreme enlightenment."

"2.(T278-279) Faith. Birth in Pure Land is realized through faith. This section describes that faith in terms of the five items of mindfulness (*anusmṛti*). They are: 1. Worship. 2. Praise. 3. Vow. 4. Meditation. 5. Transferring Merits...Worship and praise (which the *Upadeśa* identifies with *śamatha*, i.e., mental calm) parallel the practices of body and speech, respectively; vow and meditation (which the *Upadeśa* identifies as *vipaśyanā*, i.e., insight derived from *śamatha*) parallel the practice of mind-perfection. The four...are prerequisites to the final practice, the transferring of merits."

3.(T279-285) "Objects of Faith...They are described in terms of twenty-nine merits: seventeen merits of Buddha-land, eight merits of Buddha Amitāyus, and four merits of the bodhisattvas."

4.(T285-286) "One *Dharma*. One Dharma means Pure Land: One means universal. Dharma refers to the twenty-nine merits and hence embraces *dharmakāya* (Pure Land), *sambhogakāya* (Buddha Amitāyus), and *nirmāṇakāya* (the *bodhisattvas*)...One-Dharma faith...enables all beings of the world to be transformed into the beings of Pure Land, the representation of the unconditioned realm (*asaṃskṛta-dharma-kāya*). Transformation, however, requires skillful means."

5.(T286-287) "Skillful means...The practices of Dharmākara represent the *Sukhāvatī-vyūha-sūtra*'s version of transforming *prajñā* (perfect wisdom) to *jñāna* (nondiscriminative wisdom)...th(is) transformation is described as skillful means....*prajñā* is insight into One Dharma, the 'short' (twenty-nine merits distilled into an essence) version; *jñāna* is insight into the ways and means to deal with the world of sentient beings, the 'long' (the distilled expanded into twenty-nine merits) version. Hence, *prajñā* and *jñāna* are not two distinct entities, nor is Pure Land a distinct realm existing outside the world of sentient beings."

6.(T287) "The Three Teachings to Eliminate the Three Errors. Improvising skillful means--the transferring of merits--is a means of eliminating obstacles which hinder the realization of enlightenment...The rationale underlying this theory is that action (karma) produces latent or habit seeds (*avijñapti-bīja*) and habit seeds in turn shape future action. The unwholesome habits are greed, idleness, and self-conceit. They are referred to as the three errors..."

7.(T287-288) "Three Pure States of Mind. The *bodhisattvas* who have eliminated the three errors realize the three pure states of mind. They are: 1. Pure mind which seeks the undefiled (i.e., the absence of greed), 2. Pure mind which brings peace to all beings, 3. Pure mind which enables universal salvation..."

8..(T288) "The Conventional and the Supreme...The understanding of conventional truth needs insight into supreme truth in order to deal effectively and unpervertedly with the problems of sentient beings...Skillful means, the external expression of compassion, is dependent on the feedback between the conventional and the supreme."

9.(T288-289) "Perfection of All Things Vowed. The vow of Bodhisattva Dharmākara is to save all beings, a matter that is realized by the Pure Land practitioner by observing the five items of mindfulness. A reexamination of the five items now follows..."

10.(T289-290) "The Practices to Benefit Others. Practices here...are the products of the practices of the five items of mindfulness. The five are: 1.Nearing Pure Land by worshipping Amitāyus (product of worship), 2.Joining the congregation which praises Amitāyus (product of praise), 3.Entering Amitāyus' domain by vowing to be born in his Pure Land (product of vow), 4.Entering his palace (product of meditation), 5.Entering the garden of *saṃsāra* and enjoying the work of enlightening others (product of transferring merits)."

## 192. VASUBANDHU, Commentary on Asaṅga's *Vajracchedikābhāṣya*[543]

## 193. VASUBANDHU, *Viśeṣacintībrahmaparipṛcchāśāstra*[544]

## 194. VASUBANDHU, *Vyākhyāyukti* or *Sūtravyākhyāyuktyupadeśa*[545]

## 195. VASUBANDHU, *Vādavidhi*

The *Vādavidhi* does not survive as an integral text in any language, but it has been frequently quoted in Dignāga's *Pramāṇasamuccayaṭīkā*. All available fragments of the *Vādavidhi* quoted in those texts have been arranged in the edition of Erich Frauwallner.[546] "T" references here are to the translation by Stefan Anacker.[547]

### Summary by Stefan Anacker

This is the only work on logic by Vasubandhu which has to any extent survived. It is apparently the earliest of the logical treatises Vasubandhu wrote. It contains one of the earliest definitions of pervasion (*vyāpti*) as "invariable concomitance" (*avinābhāva*), reduces the earlier five-membered inference schema to one with three members, insists on the statement of invariable concomitance being included in the inference-schema, and reduces the twenty-four kinds of futile rejoinder of *Nyāyasūtra* V.1.1 ff. to three kinds of flaws. Many innovations previously ascribed to Dignāga can thus be found in this text, and the treatise may in fact be regarded as marking the dawn of Indian formal logic.

The stock example of an inference-schema most discussed here is the following:

Hypothesis: Sounds of speech are not eternal.

Reason: Because of their state of arising immediately upon an effort.

Statement of Invariable Concomitance: For whatever is in a state of arising immediately upon an effort does not have eternality.

Example: Just as a pot and unlike space.

1.[548](T38) The *pakṣa (p)* is defined as the object (*artha*) one wishes to investigate.

2-3.(T38) The characteristic of a hypothesis is the statement of a *sādhya (s),* i.e., something one wishes to demonstrate. A factor-possessor (*dharmin*) must be shown to have demonstrability through a factor (*dharma*) which is directly manifest.

4.(E38-39) The reason is the indication of the invariable concomitance of the *s* with the *hetu* (*h*). There is really no reason unless there is an indication of an invariable concomitance.

5.(T39) The example (i.e., the third member or *dṛṣṭānta*) should include not only parallel cases (pot, space), but also a statement of invariable concomitance.

6-7.(T39) There are three general types of fallacious reasons (*hetvābhāsa*): (1) an *h* which is not demonstrated; (2) an *h* which is not sufficiently certain; and (3) an *h* which is self-contradictory. Examples are: (1) "Sounds of speech are eternal, because they are perceived by the eye, (2) "Sounds of speech are eternal, because they are without a body", (3) A Vaiśeṣika says "Sounds of speech are not eternal, because they are perceived through the senses"; a Sāṃkhya says "The effect is contained in the cause, because it comes to be through the cause" (i.e., inconsistency with one's own unstated theses is not an extralogical ground for rejecting an argument in Vasubandhu's method).

8.(T39-40) If the example is undemonstrated, it counts as type (1) also. Example: "Sounds of speech are eternal, because of their nontangibility, like a cognition, not like a pot."

9.(E40) Perception is consciousness which arises only on account of the (sense-) content after which it is designated. Examples: Awarenesses of visibles, awarenesses of pleasure. This definition excludes false awarenesses such as the awareness of shell as silver, because this awareness is designated as a "silver-cognition", but does not arise because of silver but because of shell. This definition also excludes conventional awarenesses like an awareness of a pot. Pots themselves cannot give rise to an awareness, because of their conventionality and their thus not being causal. "Pots" are only juxtapositions of visibles, etc., which are interpreted as pots. (According to the provisional theory of Vasubandhu, what are normally perceived as entities are in no way really entities: "pot" is a mere conventional expression for a dependent complex with no unifying entity involved.) Inferential awareness is also excluded from perception by this definition, because such an awareness arises, for instance, through the awareness of smoke and the memory of its invariable concomitance with fire, and not through the fire itself. That through which exclusively the awareness arises, and does not exist unless it arises, is called a "content" in this passage.

10.(T40) "Invariable concomitance" means that one object cannot exist unless the other one does. Example: smoke is invariably concomitant with fire. Inferential knowledge can be described as an observation of the *h* (here, *liṅga*) and the memory of its invariable concomitance with that which is to be inferred. The *h* itself must be directly known: otherwise, there is no inference.

11.(T41) Definition of the three types of fallacious reasons given in 6-7. They may be termed (1) unreal (*asamyak*), (2) undermined (*viparīta*) and (3) contradictory (*savirodha*). "Unreal" or "incorrect" is where the object does not exist in the manner the hypothesis states it does. "Undermined" is where the argument is formulated without a true reason. "Contradictory" is where the reason cannot coexist with the hypothesis.

12-13.(T41) The types of fallacies in arguments which are enumerated in *Nyāyasūtra* V.1.1 ff. can all be reduced to one or another of the three types.

14.(T41-43) Reduction of the *Nyāyasūtra*'s (V.1.3-4) futile rejoinder "proceeding from extension and reduction" (*utkarṣāpakarṣasama*) to an undermined argument.

Example: if the reason demonstrates that the *s* is associated with a certain factor, then it is not different from the *s*, like the water of a stream which has entered the ocean. But if the *s* is already obtained, what purpose can the reason have?

Reply: A reason is a causal factor for an awareness, not a material cause.

16.(T43-44) Reduction of the *Nyāyasūtra*'s (V.1.27) futile rejoinder "based on direct apprehension" (*upalabdhisama*) to an "undermined" type.

Example: "The argument for sounds of speechs' noneternality

through their state-of-arising-immediately-upon-an-effort is not valid, because in the case of a flash of lightning, noneternality is demonstrated by direct perception, but there is no state-of-arising-immediately-upon-an-effort involved.

Reply: We are not claiming that something can be noneternal because of a state-of-arising-immediately-upon-an-effort only.

17. (E44-45) Reduction of the futile rejoinder "based on nonutterance" (*anuktisama*)[1] to the undermined type.

Example: "Since the reason does not exist prior to its apprehension and utterance, it follows that the *s* also does not exist. Thus, since sounds of speech are said to be noneternal because they have arisen due to an effort, it follows that, because the reason does not exist prior to its utterance, the sound is not yet noneternal. Thus it must be eternal prior to the utterance of the reason. But once it is eternal, how can it become noneternal?"

Reply: A reason brings about the arising of an awareness, not a cessation. This pseudo-argument however attempts to uphold that a reason brings about a cessation. Thus it is undermined.

18. (T45) Reduction of the *Nyāyasūtra*'s (V.1.37) futile rejoinder "based on a difference in effect" (*kāryasama*) to the "undermined" type.

Example: "A pot is noneternal because of being an effect of a different sort, so how does it apply to sounds of speech?"

Reply: Every effect is noneternal, so the pot's being a different sort of effect is irrelevant.

19. (T45) The unreal fallacious reason includes futile rejoinders based on unwarranted overextension of principles (*atiprasaṅgasama*) (cf. *Nyāyasūtra* V.1.9-10) and on mere presumption (cf. *Nyāyasūtra* V.1.21).

20. (T435) Example of a futile rejoinder based on overextension of principle: "What is your justification for saying that the pot itself is noneternal?" Reply: It can be directly perceived that the arising of a pot occurs. Thus this argument is wrong.

21. (T46) Example of a futile rejoinder based on mere presumption: In reply to the argument that a self does not exist, because it cannot be apprehended, just like the son of a barren woman, this type of futile

1. Not found in the *Nyāyasūtra* but similar to is *anutpattisama* (NS V.1.12); see also section 23 of the present text, below.

rejoinder might arise as follows: "Then it becomes self-evident that everything which is directly perceived must exist. But there are objects which, though directly perceived, do not exist, such as the wheel of fire".

Reply: We are not assuming that there is existence for everything which can be directly perceived. But that which is not directly perceived, and cannot be inferred, does not exist.

22.(T46) The "contradictory" includes futile rejoinders based on nonarising (*anutpattisama*)(cf. *Nyāyasūtra* V.1.12), on eternality (*nityasama*)(cf. *Nyāyasūtra* V.1.32), etc.

23.(T46-47) Example of a futile rejoinder based on nonarising: "If sounds of speech are noneternal, because they have arisen due to an effort, then prior to its arising it has not arisen due to an effort, and hence is eternal."

Reply: Before its arising the sound does not exist. To maintain that it does not exist and is eternal is a contradiction. For the adversary is saying "Since before the arising of the sound its state-of-arising-immediately-upon-an-effort does not exist, it follows that it has not arisen due to an effort, and thus is eternal, because of its state-of-not-arising-immediately-upon-an-effort". But there is no certainty that something is eternal because of its state-of-not-arising-immediately-upon-an-effort. Because some things are eternal, like space, some are noneternal, such as flashes of lightning, and others don't exist, such as a sky-flower.

24.(T47) Example of a futile rejoinder based on eternality: "Sounds of speech are eternal, because they are eternally connected with noneternality, and its unchanging nature is thus eternal."

Reply: This is a contradiction, because something noneternal is being called "eternal".

## 196. VASUBANDHU, *Pañcaskandhaprakaraṇa*

The Sanskrit text does not survive. There are various editions, reconstructions and translations; cf. Potter, *Bibliography*. Third Edition, op. cit., p. 174.

Summary by Stefan Anacker

The work seems on the surface to be another one of the many definitional treatises which have been written in Abhidharma since its inception. But it is at the same time a critique of a particular Abhidharma system. It has been called "a free reworking of Asaṅga's *Abhidharmasamuccaya*", and this seems to be the case, as the Abhidharma entity-list is identical to that of that work, and many of the definitions, though much more concise than those of Asaṅga, are essentially identical. The treatise, though mainly an Abhidharma work, was written when Vasubandhu was a Mahāyānist, as the Yogācāra store-consciousness is introduced.

The Abhidharma list of factors defined and criticized here seems most akin to that of the Mahīśāsikas, as it supposes a great number of unconditioned factors. It is true that the *Pañcaskandhaka* discusses only four of these, whereas the original Mahīśāsika list seems to have had nine.[549]

The topic is the five aggregates which make up a "person".

(1) Matter consists of the four great elements and everything which is derived from them. The elements are enumerated and defined as in *Abhidharmakośa* I, 12. What is derived from them are the sense-organs of the eye, ear, nose, tongue, tactile body, and visibles, sounds, smells, tastes, tactile sensations, and unmanifest karma (see *Abhidharmakośa* I, 11; IV, 3-4). The definition of unmanifest karma has been changed from that of the *Kośa* I, 11.[1] The new definition: Unmanifest karma is karma which has arisen from manifest action or meditational concentration: it is invisible and exercises no resistance.

(2) Feelings, defined as of three kinds: satisfying, frustrating, and that which is neither. "Satisfying" is defined as whatever there arises a desire to be connected with again, once it has stopped; "frustrating" as whatever there arises a desire to be separated from, once it has arisen.

(3) Identification, defined as the grasping of signs in a sense-object.

(4) Conditioning factors. The following list is presented:

Those occurring in every awareness (i.e., pervasive): contact, attention and thinking.

---

1.Perhaps as a result of Saṅghabhadra's criticisms of the *Kośa*'s definition in his *Abhidharmasamayapradīpikā*.

Those occurring only with certain contents: interest, resolve, mindfulness, concentration and wisdom.

Good: faith, shame, modesty, absence of greed, lack of hostility, lack of hatred, energy, tranquillity, heedfulness, equanimity, kindness.

Defilements: attachment, repugnance, pride, ignorance, views and perplexity.

Afflictions: anger, vengefulness, hypocrisy, spite, envy, selfishness, deceit, craftiness, arrogance, violence, shamelessness, disregard, lethargy, excitedness, lack of confidence, sloth, heedlessness, forgetfulness, distraction, noncomprehension.

Either afflicting or good: regret, sleepiness, initial thought, sustained thought.

Most interesting among the definitions of these terms are that of "hypocrisy" as "unwillingness to recognize one's own faults"; of "initial thought" as "a discourse of inquiry by the mind, a certain kind of volition and discernment, which can be characterized as an indistinct state of awareness"; of "sustained thought" as "a discourse of examination by the mind, which can be characterized as a distinct state of awareness".

Dissociated conditioning factors: Though Vasubandhu gives the list of these "factors", he considers them pure designations (*prajñapti*) for situations in matter, awarenesses, and accompanying mental factors. They are thus rejected as true entities. They are enumerated as possession (see *Abhidharmakośa* II, 23, 25-26), described by Vasubandhu as being a mere designation for "seeds" (*bīja*--see explanation at 197.*Karmasiddhiprakaraṇa* 20), capacities, approachments or adjustments; nonidentifying awareness, described by Vasubandhu as a cessation of awarenesses and associated factors coming about through attention dispensing with cognitions about to arise, where former cognitions do not exist; the attainment of the cessation trance, a similar situation in awareness coming after the other immaterial attainments have been practised; a nonidentifying kind of awareness similarly described as the cessation of awarenesses and accompanying factors; life-force, described by Vasubandhu as being any continuity of conditioning factors projected by past action within events taking part in an organism; homogeneity-force, defined as interdependence of bodily parts; birth, defined as any arising of a stream of conditioning factors which has not already arisen, as regards any collection of factors taking part in an organism; old age, duration and extinction, all similarly defined as changes in streams of factors occurring "in" an organism; the collection of words, defined as the expressions for the essential natures of factors; the collection of phrases, defined as expressions for the particularities of factors; the collection of syllables, defined as the actual sounds through which the other two are disclosed; and ordinariness, defined as the nonattainment of good factors.

(5)[550] Consciousness, defined as the manifestation of a supporting object. But not only are the usual six types of perception (visual, audial, olfactory, gustatory, tactual and mental) enumerated, but also the store-consciousness and ego-consciousness (*manas*, here used in Asaṅga's new sense of the term). Vasubandhu admits that the store-consciousness' objects are undiscerned, but within his definition of it gives reasons for assuming its existence: it joins an assemblage pertaining to an organism into a felt relationship, and continues as a series of factors; it is the consciousness which exists in the attainment of cessation of feelings and perceptions; it is the state of evolvement into another aspect once there has been a perception dependent upon any supporting object; it is the state of awareness' arising again even after the stream of awarenesses has been severed; it is entry into transmigration. The ego-consciousness is defined as being merely one of the contents of the store-consciousness, which content gives rise to the sense of self. It is eliminated in the Buddhist path. Vasubandhu asks why the "aggregates" are designated in this way. He says that it is through their collectivity, i.e., various kinds of matter, etc. being heaped up together, that "time", "series", "aspects", "developments" and "sense-objects" seem to occur.

In the discussion of the senses which follows, the most important innovation of Vasubandhu is in the discussion of the unconditioned factors, which are considered by the Mahīśāsikas (?) as being part of the sense-field of mentally cognizables. The list of these unconditioned factors is: space, uncalculated cessation, calculated cessation, and suchness. Vasubandhu eliminates these as special kinds of "factors": space is only any interval separating materialities; uncalculated cessation is a nonseparation of the cessation of mental factors without antidotes to defilements entering in; calculated cessation is a similar nonseparation of cessation of mental factors where antidotes to defilements are operative; and suchness is the inherent nature of all factors, the selflessness of events. (In other words, the only inherent nature in all factors is that they have none!)

Interesting in the light of Dignāga's and post-Dignāgan discussions of discriminative and nondiscriminative judgments is Vasubandhu's statement that all of the sensory domains of the sensory consciousness, mental consciousness, and mentally cognizables involves conceptual constructions (*savikalpaka*).

## 197. VASUBANDHU, *Karmasiddhiprakaraṇa*

The Sanskrit text does not survive, but early translations into Chinese and Tibetan do; thus all editions are editions of translations.

The work has been edited and translated into French from Tibetan (Tohoku 113) by Étienne Làmotte, and thence into English by Leo M. Pruden.[551] It is also translated by Stefan Anacker,[552] which is our "T".

### Summary by Stefan Anacker

This work attempts to explain karmic retribution, psychic continuity, etc. by introducing the Yogācāra concept of "storehouse consciousness" (*ālayavijñāna*). Like the *Abhidharmakośa*, it directs itself also against many Vaibhāṣika and Vātsīputrīya/Sammitīya theories.[553]

1-2.(T93-94) Statement of the Vaibhāṣika definition of the three kinds of acts (bodily, verbal, and mental): Acts committed by the body are bodily acts, speech itself is verbal action, and these two kinds of acts together constitute manifest and unmanifest karma (see *Abhidharmakośa* I, 10-11; IV, 1-3). "Manifest bodily karma" is defined by the Vaibhāṣika as a shape (see *Kośa* I, 10; IV, 2-3) which has arisen from an awareness which has a content referring to it (the shape). It is assumed by the Vaibhāṣika to belong to the sense-field of material factors.

3.(T94-95) Vasubandhu: Is shape a special kind of atom (see *Kośa* II, 22), some special aggregation of atoms, or some single entity pervading the aggregations of color-atoms? If it is a special kind of atom, "long", "short", etc., it would have to be comprised separately in each part of the aggregate to which it belongs, just as color is. If it is a special aggregation of atoms, why can't it be just a special aggregation of color-atoms? If it is a single entity, it would have to be perceived separately in each part of the aggregation, because it would have to be in all of the parts at one time. Otherwise, if it had parts, it could not be a single entity. This last view is also invalid because the Vaibhāṣika must hold the sense-fields to be aggregations of atoms, and because it is identical to the Vaiśeṣika doctrine of wholes.[1]

4.(T95) "Shape" is really only color. When color appears in one direction in great quantity, it's called "long"; in small quantity, "short"; equal in each of four sides, "square"; if there is an equal distance everywhere from the center to the circumference, "circular"; if there is a greater quantity of color at its central portion, "convex", a smaller quantity, "concave"; going along in one direction, "even", going in various directions, "uneven". If shape were a separate kind of entity, which the Vaibhāṣikas claim, various shapes couldn't be situated within one locus, just as various colors can't. (Cf. *Kośa* IV, 2-3).

5.(T95-96) Vaibhāṣika: How can one discern something's shape at a long distance, then, and not discern its color? (Cf. *Kośa* IV, 3)

Vasubandhu: How can one discern the shape of a group before one discerns the shapes of its members? Actually, when something's color isn't clearly discerned, its shape isn't either. (Cf. *Kośa* IV, 3)

6.(T96) Sammitīya:[2] Manifest karma is a movement which has arisen from an awareness which has its object as content.

7-8.(T96-99) Vasubandhu proceeds to show that the concept of movement, or the progression of the same thing to another locus, cannot be demonstrated. The argument is identical to that of *Kośa* IV, 2: the nonperception of subtle differences between the thing at locus A and the "same thing" at locus B does not mean that there are no differences, causes of destruction for the thing at locus A not being necessary because of the inherent momentariness of everything. This

---

1.Vasubandhu had already criticized this theory in *Abhidharmakośa* III, 100.

2.The identification of opponents are taken from Sumatiśīla's commentary. Only the "Sauryodayika" of 11-13 is mentioned by Vasubandhu. The "Theravādin" of 35 ("the Tāmraparṇīyas") are however given by Vasubandhu himself.

constitutes a refutation of the Sammitīya theory of combustion. Some new examples are adduced: though no special characteristics can be ascertained for different flames burning tall grass, this doesn't mean that they aren't all different. Assuming the necessity of a cause of destruction leads to an infinite regress.

9.(T199) Sammitīya: The thing at locus B is the same as the thing previously at locus A because there is no cause for anything new arising.

Vasubandhu: But the preceding thing at locus A could be the cause of the thing at locus B. This is like the case where an awareness arises from another awareness, or curds arise from milk, etc. (These are examples of what the Vaibhāṣika calls "homogeneous causes" (see *Kośa* II, 52).

10.(T99-100) If a thing is stable, it can have no movement. And if it is not stable, it can also have no movement (because movement is defined as "the progression of the *same* thing to another locus). Motion cannot be demonstrated, though it is true that it cannot always be demonstrated that the thing at locus B is clearly different, either.

11.(T100-101) Sauryodayika:[1] There is a special kind of factor that makes something new arise in locus B immediately after another thing at locus A. This is called "motion", though really there is no progression of the same thing.

Vasubandhu: Such a special entity can in no way be perceived or deduced. It is through the motile gaseous element (see *Kośa* I, 12) that something arises at another locus immediately subsequent to something else at locus A.

12-13.(T101-102) Sauryodayika: Are you defining "manifest karma" as the motile element?

Vasubandhu: No, because the motile element can be neither good nor bad, and "manifest action" refers only to acts with a karmic retribution. For the same reason, several other alternatives raised by the Sauryodayika (the body itself is manifest karma, color which arises from a special awareness is manifest karma, etc.) are also rejected by Vasubandhu.

Since there is no kind of entity under which "manifest karma" can

---

1.Sauryodayikas were followers of 67.Kumāralāta, one of whose works was titled *Sūryodaya*.

be subsumed, the concept of "manifest karma" itself must be rejected.

14.(T102) Arguments against the Vaibhāṣika concept of "unmanifest karma", which are similar to those in *Kośa* IV, 3-4). Additional elaboration of the example of a monk who doesn't confess his misdeeds during the recital of the *prātimokṣa* rules: the monk has incurred the retribution for a bad act by remaining silent, and yet there has been no good or bad "manifest action" which would by necessity according to the Vaibhāṣika precede an unmanifest action.

15-17.(T103-104) How can bodily and vocal actions give the result of a retribution when they are long past? The Vaibhāṣika explains it by the existence of the past and the future. Vasubandhu thus next argues against this Vaibhāṣika theory. These arguments are akin to those in *Kośa* V, 27, with some added subtleties. If the Vaibhāṣika claims that an action becomes "past" because it no longer exercises its full efficacy of projecting an effect, it must be asked why it ceases to do so. The Vaibhāṣika replies that the act no longer projects an effect because it has already completed projecting it, just as what has arisen does not arise again. (The Vaibhāṣika vocabulary employed here involves some technicalities.) An act "projects" (*ākṣip*) an effect as long as it is present, but it "gives" its retributional effect when it is already past. The "projection" of an effect includes, for instance, it being directly perceivable by one or more kinds of sensory consciousnesses, which can occur only for present events.

Vasubandhu: Why can't a past act project another effect similar to the one it did when it was present? How does it project an effect at all?

Vaibhāṣika: It prepares a consciousness for the possibility of perceiving it.

Vasubandhu: There are some factors which never project an effect, for instance, the last state of one who has overcome all frustration. If your theory is to hold, this last state is never present, and thus can never become past, either. If an act ceases to project its effect as soon as it becomes past, but yet continues to exercise some kind of force, the problem is to determine this force, as well as the final giving of a retributional effect. The idea of an existing past and future event must be rejected.

18.(T104-105) Opponent: In that case, the retributional force of an act must lie in a special factor dissociated from awareness which is associated with good and bad bodily and verbal acts. This theory is in fact accepted by the Mahāsāṃghikas, who call it "accumulation", and by the Sammitīyas, who call it "the imperishable".

19. (T105) Vasubandhu: But the question of what accounts for the goodness or badness of an action is only part of a broader problem of psychic continuity. Since "accumulation" or "the imperishable" occur only for good or bad actions, it cannot explain a memory which comes from a totally karmically indeterminate act such as studying a text. If there is a special kind of entity which makes a memory arise, there is the problem as to which moment produces this entity. Is it the moment of the initial perception of the object which is later remembered, the moment in which the memory arises, or yet some other moment? None of these alternatives can explain the phenomenon. In the attainment of the cessation of feelings and identifications, the awareness-series is interrupted. Yet after a while the awareness-series resumes with all the memories of those past awarenesses before the series was suspended by the attainment. How is this to be explained? Can one really have recourse to "a special kind of entity" in these cases? When a lemon flower is dyed red, there is no special entity which can account for its fruit also being red long after the flower has perished. (Cf. *Kośa* II, 44)

20. (T105) Rather it is the entire series from flower to fruit that has been penetrated by the dye. In the same way, a special force (*śaktiviśeṣa*) is produced within the awareness-series by a decision, and a retributional effect arises through a transformation of the series which has been altered by this decision.

21. (T105-106) This explanation may also help in understanding memory. A perception of an object transforms the awareness-series to which it belongs, and this transformation is the conditional ground for a future memory. But the problem of the continuity of consciousness before and after noncognitional trance states still remains.

22. (T106) Some Sautrāntikas attempt to explain this continuity in the same way: The awareness-series is transformed by its decisions and memories, and this transformed series retakes its course after the meditative trance ceases.

Vasubandhu: But *how* does it "retake its course"?

Sautrāntika: The awareness which attains the trance is the directly antecedent condition (see *Kośa* I, 44) for the awareness-series which emerges after the attainment.

Vasubandhu: But the awareness that attains the trance has elapsed long before the trance ceases. So how can it be a directly antecedent condition? We have already rejected the notion of an effect being brought about by that which is completely past.

23.(T106-107) Some other Sautrāntikas say that the seeds of the awareness-series (see *Kośa* II, 35-36) rest upon the material organs during the trance.

Vasubandhu: But an awareness cannot arise where the material organs do not function so as to give rise to an awareness!

24.(T107) Opponent: The flaw lies within the theory that these trance states are without awareness. Bhadanta Vasumitra, in his *Paripṛcchā*, says there *is* a kind of awareness within the attainment of the cessation of feelings and identifications (cf. *Kośa* I, 16).

25.(T107-108) Vasubandhu: What kind of an awareness is this?

Opponent: It could be a mental consciousness (cf. *Kośa* I, 16).

Vasubandhu: But a *sūtra* clearly says that a mental consciousness can arise only dependent upon *manas* (meaning a case of any consciousness of any of the six types--cf. *Kośa* I, 16-17--as well as a mentally cognizable factor, and at the same time there must be feelings, identifications, and thoughts.

Opponent: Though there is a *sūtra* which says that craving is conditioned by feelings, yet not all feelings are conditions of craving. So in the same way, the contact of consciousness with its object is not always a condition for feelings.

Vasubandhu: But there are *sūtras* which clearly distinguish which feelings give rise to craving, whereas contacts have nowhere been distinguished. (Cf. *Kośa* II, 44)

26.(T108-109) Sautrāntika: The attainment of the cessation of feelings and identifications is a state where there exists a mental consciousness without the force to enter into contact with mentally cognizables, and thus powerless to help give rise to feelings and identifications.

Vasubandhu: To which ethical category does this mental consciousness belong? Is it good, or defiled, or neutral?

27.(T109) If it is good, how can it be so without being connected with the good roots: lack of greed, lack of hatred and lack of delusion? When these good roots occur there must of necessity be contact, feelings and identifications as well. (Conditioning factors must depend upon decisions to be good.) The "lack of greed" occurring in trance is not lack of greed as a good root, because no choice can arise there, due to the absence of contact with a specific object. In the absence of such choice, and in the absence of consciously-motivated good roots, there can be no good awareness.

Sautrāntika: What if it were good because it is the result of a directly antecedent condition which is good?

Vasubandhu: Even if it were such a result this would not guarantee its being good itself. Immediately subsequent to something good there may arise an awareness which is bad. If good roots exist for a good awareness directly preceding the trance, it is difficult to see why these should suddenly vanish within the trance. Whatever awareness exists in the trance can also clearly not be bad. The trance can be called "good" only in the same way that final cessation is (i.e., it is really karmically indeterminate--since nothing results from it--and is good only in the sense of being a good goal). Similarly, it cannot be defiled, because there can be no defilement without contact with an object, and such contact presupposes feelings and identifications. If it is unobstructed-neutral, is it the result of retribution, or is it related to bodily postures, to artistic activity, or to magical creations?[1]

28.(T109-110) Since one of the purposes of meditation is to sever defiled awarenesses which are retributional, all mental retributional consciousnesses will be severed by trance. Any retributional awareness which involves traces of the past is in fact removed in trance.

29.(E110-111) The awareness in the trance can clearly not be related to bodily postures either, since an awareness related to bodily posture has as its content the particular posture intended, and this cannot occur without awarenesses.

As the other two types of unobstructed-neutral mental consciousness cannot occur in the meditational trance for similar reasons, it cannot be that the awareness in the trance state is a mental consciousness.

---

1.Only these four types of awareness are traditionally regarded as unobstructed but neutral by the *Vibhāśā*-inspired philosophers. Anything born of retribution is by necessity neutral, and awarenesses concerned with artistic or professional activity, and with postures of the body such as sitting, lying, etc., are of course also karmically indeterminate and unobstructed. The fourth category of awareness refers to any awareness which produces fantasies, which beholds a magical creation, or which deals with afterimages in meditation. Cf. *Kośa* II, 71-72.

30.(T111-112) Instead, it must be assumed that there is a special kind of retributory consciousness. This consciousness has all the seeds coloring future perceptions, continues in a stream, takes on various forms because of various retributory causes, and is not severed until *nirvāṇa*. Both the theoreticians who say that the trance state is without awareness and those who say that it involves awareness are right, for all other kinds of awareness are severed in trance.

31.(T112) There are two kinds of awareness: one accumulates seeds; the second is variegated on account of having various contents.

32.(T112-113) The trance state impairs the emergence of the effects of the seeds to a conscious level. But this impairment gradually becomes weaker and weaker, in the same way as there is a gradual diminution of boiling water, or in the velocity of a projected arrow. During the time of the trance, the retributory consciousness continues to operate and transform, so that once the impairing force has stopped, all the other consciousnesses renew themselves with the seeds of perceptions of the past. The retributory consciousness is only the seeds themselves. They change and are influenced by the good and bad events arising in the series of the other consciousnesses with which they are connected, and thus bring about retributional effects. This kind of retributory or appropriating consciousness (*ādānavijñāna*) is mentioned in the Mahāyāna 136.*Saṃdhinirmocanasūtra.*[1]

33.(T113) It is called "appropriating consciousness" because it appropriates a body at the time of rebirth. Because it is the support of the seeds of all experienced events, it is also called the "store-consciousness" (*ālayavijñāna*).

34.(T113-114) By what other consciousness could a body be appropriated? If there is no store-consciousness, where do the residues of defilements abide when the defilements themselves have been removed? Why doesn't an organism just die when it has reached the highest meditational states where all the other kinds of consciousness are severed? Homogeneity-force and life-force, which are used by Vaibhāṣikas to explain this, are not really entities, because they are only metaphors for the similarity and perpetuation of retributor-aggregates. (Cf. *Kośa* II, 41, 45)

---

1.This is the first hint we have that Vasubandhu is a Mahāyānist at the time of the writing of this treatise.

35.(T114) The Theravādins accept such a special consciousness which they call "the consciousness which is the requisite for existence" (*bhavāgravijñāna*).[554] The Mahāsāṃghikas also accept it. They call it the "root consciousness" (*mūlavijñāna*).

36.(T114) Opponent: What is the content of this consciousness?

Vasubandhu: Its content is undiscerned.

Opponent: How can it be a consciousness then?

Vasubandhu: Anyone who claims that there is consciousness in trance faces the same problem.

Opponent: To which aggregate does it belong?

Vasubandhu: To the aggregate of consciousness.

37.(T114-115) Opponent: The aggregate of consciousness has been defined in *sūtras* as being only the six types of consciousness (see *Kośa* I, 16).

Vasubandhu: The intent there was to speak only of the consciousnesses which are easily delimited, in order not to confuse learners. Some learners might confuse the store-consciousness with a self.

Opponent: And why would they do *that*?

Vasubandhu: Because the store-consciousness is without fundamental changes.

38.(T115) Opponent: Then there will be two consciousness-series simultaneously.

Vasubandhu: So what?

Opponent: A body which has two consciousness-series must be regarded as two sentient beings.

Vasubandhu: No, because the two series are related. The store-consciousness stores traces from the other consciousnesses; these in turn color all future consciousnesses.

39.(T115-116) Opponent: Aren't you ignoring the difference between a seed and the series which has the seed?

Vasubandhu: Sometimes there is no difference.

40.(T116-117) Opponent: Why not just accept a self?

Vasubandhu: What do you mean by a "self"? If a self is only a series of factors which transform themselves constantly through conditions, then it is the same as the store-consciousness. But if you claim a self which is single and devoid of transformations, then you can't explain how it can be influenced by past traces. It is the traces which make the consciousness-series continue in certain grooves. If there is nothing which undergoes transformation, then no trace is possible. So how can memories, recognitions, passions, etc., arise from an immutable entity? If the arising of a consciousness is subject to the self, why does it arise gradually, as there are no transformations within the self?

41.(T117) But in the same way, the Vaibhāṣika definition of the three kinds of acts (cf. 1-2) must also be rejected. For it is thinking which causes transformations in a consciousness-series.

42.(T117) Bodily and vocal actions were taught in order to make beings avoid the performance of bad actions. The Jains claim that only bodily actions have retribution, and it was to refute this claim that three types of action were spoken of.

43.(T118) The body is a special collection of great material elements and materiality derived from the great elements (see *Kośa* I, 12), a corporeal mass connected with sense-faculties. Action is volition. Thus, bodily action is a volition directed toward the body.

44.(T118) A body exists only as an accumulation of factors.

45. (T118) An act is prepared behavior.

46.(T118-119) A volition which sets the body into agitation is called "a bodily act". There are three kinds of volitions: those which prepare, those which decide, and those which set into agitation. It is always the volition which carries a retributory result.

47.(T119) Though *sūtras* distinguish "volition" and "the act committed after having willed", the latter is really the volition which sets into agitation.

48.(T119) Vocal action is a volition which brings about speech, i.e., those special vocal emissions which communicate meanings.

49.(T120) Opponent: If bodily action is only volition, how can there be either restraint or lack of restraint in those who are of distracted awareness or without the six kinds of awareness, as there can be no volition in these states?

Vasubandhu: The traces left by volitions have not been suppressed in these states, thus restraint or lack of restraint may exist there.

50.(T120) Only actions connected with a conscious effort are discussed here, because only these have a retributory effect. The simple performances of the eye, etc., have no such effect. An "action connected with an effort" is anything which motivates a consciousness-series.

## 198. VASUBANDHU, *Vṛtti* on Asaṅga's *Dharmadharmatāvibhāga*

The entire Sanskrit text of this work has now been found, but aside from one Sanskrit fragment published at the end of Levi's (and consequently Bagchi's) edition of the 165.*Mahāyānasūtrālaṃkāra*[555] it is not yet available. The Tibetan translations, in both its Derge (sDe-dge) and Peking editions, were collated and edited by Jōshō Nozawa in *Yamaguchi hakukshi hanreki kinen Indogaku Bukkyōgaku ronsō* (Kyoto, 1955), pp. 19-45. This is our "T". The Tibetan translators are Majana Paṇḍita and Blo-ldan-ses-rab.

In view of its importance this is a work that has remained strangely neglected. Since the time Stefan Anacker prepared this summary he has published a paper in which the work is summarized: "An unravelling of the *Dharma-dharmatā-vibhāga-vṛtti* of Vasubandhu", Asiatische Studien/Études Bouddhiques 46.1, 1992, 26-36, which should be consulted for further details on the contents of this work.

Summary by Stefan Anacker

(T20) The "distinction" (*vibhāga*) referred to in the title is that between factors (*dharma*), which have the characteristic of affliction, and the true nature of factors (*dharmatā*), which has the characteristic of purification.

The question arises whether the two can be definitely distinguished. It is, after all, nothing but the aggregates, senses, etc., which may be subsumed under either of these two broader categories.

Nonetheless a distinction between factors and the true nature of factors can be made in regard to the aggregates, etc.

(T21) A factor is the construction of what was not (*abhūtaparikalpa*), which always involves the construction of a duality. In fact, whenever there is the conception of "an object apprehended", a duality is implied: e.g., "visible" implies visual consciousness as well.

(T22) All conception of "essential nature" and differentiation is construction of what was not. The construction of what was not may be described as the appearance of that which doesn't exist as existing. That which does not exist may appear to exist, and will only be discerned as nonexistent with careful mental attention. All factors constructed by the construction of that which is not will be seen to be illusion. And such is the characteristic of all factors.

The characteristic of the true nature of factors, on the other hand, is the undifferentiated suchness (*aviśeṣatathatā*) which lies behind all so-called objects apprehended, subjects apprehending, things which can be designated and their designation. For example, there is no difference between that which can be designated and its designation.

(T23) It is the illusion which arises because of the appearance of the nonexistent as existent which is the cause of affliction, or rather it is the subsequent insistence on holding fast to such illusions which is the cause of affliction.

Objection: How can there be the appearance of the nonexistent as existent?

Reply: As in the case of an elephant seen in a magic show. It is the construction of that which was not which makes the nonexistent appear as existent, and this appearance of the nonexistent as existent is the defining characteristic of illusion. Accordingly, without the appearance of the nonexistent as existent, there could be no illusion, and without illusion, there could be no freedom from illusion.

(T24) There could be no affliction, either, since illusion is the cause of affliction. And if there is no affliction, there could be no purification either. Because anterior to purification there must be affliction. Without affliction, liberation would take place without any effort, and this is contradicted by direct perception.

(T25) Factors and the true nature of factors must be regarded as being neither the same (for the reasons given above) nor different, for in the latter case the aggregate-series' realizing purification would never be possible. Factors and the true nature of factors can be differentiated because the nonexistent and the existent can be differentiated, but the existent and the nonexistent really cannot be differentiated, because the true nature of factors is only realized when there are no factors, and when objects apprehended, etc., are not differentiated.

The correct investigation of a factor rests on six aspects: (A1) a factor's characteristic mark, (A2) the proof of that mark, (A3) a factor's separatedness and nonseparatedness, (A4) a factor's locus or occasion for arising, (A5) that which a factor has in common with other factors, and which it doesn't, (A6) understanding the absence of the appearances (*pratibhāsa*) of object apprehended and subject apprehending.

(A1) The characteristic marks of factors are always talked about in a manner which is an unreal construction, in which the nonexistent appears as existent. (A2) The proof of this is that without the nonexisting appearing as existent, there could logically not be illusion or lack of illusion, and neither affliction nor purification. (A3) "Separatedness" and "nonseparatedness" relate to existence and nonexistence, distinction and nondistinction; thus a factor is existent as perceived, is nonexistent because of being a construction, is distinct as it appears, is nondistinct as nonexistent.

(T26) (A4) "Locus" relates to the environment, i.e., *saṃsāra*. (A5) "That which it has in common with other factors" relates to its birth, its practical activity, its utility (*upakāra*) or detriment (*apakāra*), its being a good quality or a flaw. "That which it does not have in common with other factors" relates to the nature of its basis, i.e., the store-consciousness, the nature of its evolving consciousnesses (*pravṛttivijñāna*) which make it appear, and its karmic effect as good, bad and neutral.

(T27) This is said because the origin of each factor lies in a different store-consciousness-series or in a different moment of "the same" store-consciousness-series, and its becoming manifest depends always on a particular evolving consciousness-moment not shared by other factors. Its karmic effect is also peculiar to it alone.

(A6) "Understanding the nonbeing of appearances of object apprehended and subject apprehending" means realizing that the "external" arises because of perceptions ("manifesting": *vijñapti*), and that perceptions arise differently in regard to the same moment for different consciousness-series, and thus can't relate to an "objective" object.

(T28) Perceptions may be divided into trance perceptions and the ordinary ones. The ordinary kind includes all perceptions where an object apprehended appears through construction, and where this serves as an object of sense for one awareness but not for another. Trance perception relates to perceptions of images in meditational concentration which are not shared by other consciousness-moments. Again, we see by these examples the nonexistence of an "objective" object shared in one moment by all consciousness-series present. If the "object apprehended" has no existence, the "subject apprehending" has no existence either.

(T29) In a perfected state, neither object apprehended or subject apprehender appear.

The correct investigation of the true nature of factors rests on six aspects: (B1) its characteristic, (B2) its locus, (B3) its penetration, (B4) its contact, (B5) its recollection, and (B6) understanding its nature.

(B1) The characteristic of the true nature of factors is suchness, where there is no differentiation of object apprehended, subject apprehending, that which can be designated, and its designations.

(B2) The locus of the true nature of factors is the material factors making up the aggregates. It is they which undergo affliction and purification.

(T30) (B3) The penetration of the true nature of factors is all of the factors in the path of application comprised by mental attention on all methods (in all aspects) in Mahāyāna *sūtras*: hearing, contemplating, practicing.

(B4) The "contact" of the true nature of factors: In the path of vision right vision is attained, that is, it is experienced by direct perception.

(B5) Recollection of the true nature of factors is the memory of the experience of the path of vision which leads to the allies of enlightenment, i.e., the path of cultivation. The path of cultivation begins immediately after the path of vision, and it is the memory of its fulfilled penetration which impels all the allies of enlightenment, i.e., the elimination of the roots of all afflictions.

(T31) (B6) The understanding of the true nature of factors: that, because the roots of all afflictions can be eliminated in the path of cultivation, suchness is without afflictions, and signless suchness is all there is. This is realized in a revolution at the basis (*āśrayaparāvṛtti*).

The correct investigation of "revolution at the basis" rests on ten aspects: (C1) its essential nature, (C2) its actuality, (C3) the persons (*pudgala*) who realize it, (C4) its special quality, (C5) its use, (C6) its locus, (C7) its mental attention, (C8) its application, (C9) its benefit (*anuśaṃsā*), (C10) its correct investigation (*praveśa*).

(C1) The essential nature of revolution at the basis: flawless suchness, which has only adventitious flaws. Suchness is not manifested because of adventitious flaws, but they are manifest in a realization of suchness.

(C2) The actuality of revolution at the basis: (1) a revolution through the suchness of the perceptions relating to the common environment, (2) a revolution through the suchness of the *dharmadhātu* in the *sūtras,* (3) a revolution they do not hold in common.

(C3) The persons who realize revolution at the basis: The first two of the revolutions mentioned immediately above occur only to Bodhisattvas, i.e., only Bodhisattvas are interested in a "revolution" of the common environment, e.g, that not only themselves, but all sentient beings may be liberated; and only Bodhisattvas know of the *dharmadhātu* mentioned in the Mahāyāna *sūtras.* The third occurs also with Śrāvakas and Pratyekabuddhas as well as with Bodhisattvas, and refers to a revolution undergone by the "individual" alone.

(C4) The special quality of revolution at the basis: (1) its special quality of purifying the Buddha-fields of Buddhas and Bodhisattvas, which includes the ability to teach the stainless knowledge of suchness to others, (2) its special quality of seizing the nature of awareness: this occurs in a knowledge of all aspects, (3) the special quality of realizing the higher faculties, etc., for the sake of all beings. These three relate to the *dharma-, sambhoga-* and *nirmāṇa-kāyas* respectively.

(C5) The use of revolution at the basis: (1) it fulfills former vows of the Bodhisattva; (2) it displays the Mahāyāna teachings, (3) it is of use in the ten stages.

(C6) The locus of revolution at the basis is constructionfree awareness. How can constructionfree awareness be entered? In six ways: through its supporting object, through the abandoning of all signs, through its right use, through its characteristic, through its benefit, and through its complete comprehension.

(T34-35) (C7) The basis for constructionfree awareness is the Mahāyāna teachings, resolve in them, gaining certainty, and accumulating all preparations (*sambhāraparipūri*). Through the abandoning of all signs, even the subtlest of signs will be lacking.

(C8) The right use of constructionfree awareness is the apprehension of consciousness-only (*vijñaptimātropalambha*), i.e., the nonapprehension of any object, thus the nonapprehension of consciousness-only itself in the absence of any object, and the nonapprehension of both objects and consciousness-only. The characteristic of constructionfree awareness is that it is based on the true nature of factors, that it is free from duality, and that it is ineffable (*nirabhilāpya*). Furthermore, because it is based on none of the sense-fields, it is unbased (*apratiṣṭhita*). For it is not an object of sense. It has no appearances, and has none of the appearances of materiality and the other aggregates. Because it has no perception, it is nonperception. All factors, through their appearances, become like space, (T36-38) for the mental marks of all sense-objects are absent. The benefit of constructionfree awareness has four aspects: it gains the *dharmakāya*, it dwells in the highest bliss, it has power over the teachings, it has preeminence in advising others.

Complete constructionfree awareness has four aspects: (1) comprehension of antidotes, (2) comprehension of characteristic marks, (3) comprehension of its special qualities, and (4) comprehension of its action. Comprehension of antidotes is equivalent to constructionfree awareness because it is the antidote to all ideas of personality, transformation, separatedness, denial of the existent, taking the nonexistent for the existent. An apprehension of a nonexistent separatedness comes, for instance, when there is an insistence upon separating factors from their true nature, for actually factors and the true nature of factors are not separate. The comprehension of its characteristic marks has to do with its nonmental attention to signs, its passing beyond all signs, the inner peace of signs, its having no discriminations by its essential nature, and seizing the meaning of its special characteristic. These are the categories of the Maitreyanātha/Asaṅga text, to which Vasubandhu, however, objects.

Objection: If constructionfree awareness were simply a nonmental attention to constructions, then little children would have this awareness. If constructionfree awareness were simply a case of passing beyond all constructions, then it would be attained already at the second of the four meditational stages, because it is entirely without initial or sustained thought. If constructionfree awareness were simply a putting to rest of all constructions, then states of sleep, intoxication and fainting would be included in this knowledge. If constructionfree awareness were defined simply by its basic nature of having no constructions, then the aggregate of matter would be constructionfree awareness, since it does not discriminate. If constructionfree awareness were simply the seizing of its special characteristic, then by being mentally attentive to the fact that there is constructionfree awareness it would be attained. In fact, Vasubandhu concludes, constructionfree awareness is free from all these characteristics. Thus, for him, the complete knowledge of the characteristic of constructionfree awareness is a complete knowledge of the fact that constructionfree awareness has no characteristics.

The comprehension of the special qualities of constructionfree awareness are: no discrimination, unlimited, its being unbased anywhere, its permanence, and its supremacy. As far as its special quality of no discrimination is concerned, disciples and self-enlightened ones do not reach this, since they always have discriminations of qualities and flaws in *saṃsāra*. They are always trying to determine in terms of the four noble truths, and are thus not with its unlimited character, either. They are basing themselves on liberation, and thus are not unbased. They do not realize its permanence, since they seek it in a *nirvāṇa* where there are no factors. They are not involved in supremacy, since the highest state is that of a Buddha, which only Mahāyānists strive for.

By considering the opposites of these propositions the special qualities of constructionfree awareness can be known. For in constructionfree awareness there is no consideration of *nirvāṇa* and *saṃsāra*, good qualities or flaws. It is not limited, because it reaches the limits of the knowable. It is unbased, because it is based on neither *nirvāṇa* nor *saṃsāra*.

(T39) It is permanent, because through it a *nirvāṇa* without a remainder (*nirupādhiśeṣanirvāṇa*) is attained. It is supreme in its action, because it removes discriminations; because it brings about the supreme benefit, the elimination of obstructions (cf. 200.*Madhyāntavibhāgabhāṣya* II), because it allows one to enter the subsequently attained knowledge which again makes use of discriminations, but only for purposes of method and without attachment to them; because it clears the Buddha-field; because it matures sentient beings; and because it grants the knowledge of all aspects. Vasubandhu makes further comments: it involves the elimination of all obstructions because it overcomes even past proclivities. He glosses "subsequently attained knowledge" as knowing all knowables in all aspects with a previous constructionfree awareness, even though the subsequently attained knowledge is again with objects.

(T40) Constructionfree awareness removes mental proclivities of the past.

It can first be understood that the mental construction of nonexistent objects is a case of perception-only; afterwards, through this apprehension, the nonapprehension of all objects is attained, through perception-only. Once this nonapprehension of all objects is reached, the nonapprehension of consciousness-only is reached, because it is illogical that there be "perception" without an object to be perceived.

(T41) Similarly, once the nondistinguishing of object apprehended and subject apprehender is reached, it can be understood that dualities in general do not exist. Thus, if there is mental attention to these sequences, constructionfree knowledge itself can be reached. In this way, there is the nonapprehension of even the factors accepted in Buddhism: aggregates, etc. In fact, the definition of constructionfree awareness is the nonapprehension of any mental signs.

The application of revolution at the basis: The first "practice" in the practice of interest in Mahāyānic resolve; this is followed by the practice of discrimination in the path of vision, the practice of cultivation in the path of cultivation (see 194.*Madhyāntavibhāgabhāṣya* IV), and the completely skilled practice, where constructionfree awareness comes spontaneously and there is no longer anything to be consciously done.

(T42) (C9) There are four kinds of apprehensions of flaws which come when there is no revolution at the basis. One apprehension of a flaw comes when it is considered that there is no basis for nonentry into afflictions: Without revolution of a basis, afflicted states could never enter the true nature of factors. Just as there must be a basis for entry into afflictions, there must by necessity be a basis for nonentry into afflictions. It is thus that impure consciousnesses have a basis, and their antidotes also have a basis. The second apprehension of a flaw is that there is no basis for entry into a path, for instance, when it is assumed that personality necessarily belongs to *saṃsāra*. But it is the aggregates which give rise to the idea of a personality, and it is also they that constitute the basis of personality in *nirvāṇa*.

(T43) Some people conclude from this that awareness is itself suchness, but this doesn't hold, because of the arising of adverse factors (*vipakṣa*) and of antidotes (*pratipakṣa*). The basis of adverse factors, i.e., awareness, cannot be the same as the basis of the antidotes, because they are mutually exclusive, just as cold and heat are.

The third and fourth apprehensions of flaws are not especially commented on by Vasubandhu. They are: assuming that there is no basis for the conception of a personality in *nirvāṇa*--i.e., that there is nothing lying behind such an erroneous conception, and that there is no basis for the conceptions of the excellences of the three kinds of enlightenment (i.e., though these conceptions are false, there is something which lies behind them, and it is a flaw to deny this). In sum, there *is* a basis for revolution, and by realizing the opposite of these apprehensions of flaws, the four kinds of qualities in the true nature of factors are known.

(C10) Examples of construction of what is not and of factors: magical creations, dreams, mirages, a city of Gandharvas, a reflection in a mirror, the moon in the water. In all these cases, an object is apprehended which does not exist. And so it is for all factors.

(T44) Revolution at the basis takes place without any factors or any conception of factors--thus it is that these similes are used for so-called factors. The similes for "revolution at the basis": space, gold, and water, which are pure by nature. Space may be obstructed by fog, and be utterly cleared from it the next moment. In the same way, emptiness is obscured by adventitious flaws, but cleared from them in one moment. In the same way, gold may be found in a mine vein mixed together with dirt, but the dirt was only "adventitiously" connected with the gold, and may be totally removed from it. In the same way, water in a stream may be connected with particles of earth, and may be cleared from them without the arising of anything new--in fact it was clear from the beginning. In this way the basic luminousness of revolution at the basis can be exemplified.

(T45) It is when the appearance of adventitious obstructions is removed that they no longer appear. That which appears to be separated from them is the true nature of factors, but since it was there from the beginning, there is no "arising" or "appearance" of it, properly speaking. This is true because a revolution at the basis may take place at any moment. By giving the examples of gold and water one can see that this state of affairs is endowed with a positive parallel example. Clothes being washed from adventitious flaws can also serve as an example.

## 199. VASUBANDHU, *Bhāṣya* on Asaṅga's *Mahāyānasūtrālaṃkāra*

Summary by Stefan Anacker

This excellent and subtle commentary seems to be an earlier work of Vasubandhu's than the 200.*Madhyāntavibhāgabhāṣya.* For instance, some of the more radical statements of Maitreyanātha/Asaṅga are interpreted in such a manner that indicates that Vasubandhu probably didn't quite know what to do with them. There is a tendency to see "path philosophy" in passages which are clearly not "path philosophy" at all. Thus it is quite different from the *Madhyāntavibhāgabhāṣya*, which may be said to be more radical than the Maitreyanātha/Asaṅga text itself!

"ET" refers to the edition and translation by Surekha Vijaya Limaye in Bibliotheca Indo-Buddhica Series No. 94, Delhi 1992.

## CHAPTER ONE

4.(Et4-5) There are three kinds of special excellences to the *dharma*: it is like a medicine, as it removes the obstructions; it is the cause of psychic power, as it leads to the higher faculties of meditation; and it is the cause of the enjoyment of the noble knowledge.

7.(ET5-7) Mahāyāna is defined as antidotes to the defilements coming through being based on constructionfree awareness.

8.(ET7-8) Explains this as "the effortless development of knowledge in Buddhas".

9.(ET8-9) Hīnayāna does not include the idea of service to others, nor the idea that one can become a Buddha, nor method (*upāya*, skillful means).

10.(ET9-10) Hīnayāna strives for one's own *nirvāṇa* in a short time, but to Mahāyāna this is an error.

12.(ET11-12) Ways by which one can tell that the *dharma* is not an object of *tarka*.

(1) *Tarka* has as its object truths which cannot be directly perceived.

(2) *Tarka* is impermanent in form, as arguments change according to the requisites of different times.

(3) *Tarka* does not penetrate all knowable objects of consciousness.

(4) *Tarka* concerns conventional truth only and not the highest truths.

(5) *Tarka* is a difficult topic, whereas Mahāyāna is always without difficulties, as the 53.*Śatasāhasrikāprajñāpāramitā* and other *sūtras* teach.

## CHAPTER THREE

8.(ET37-38) The Bodhisattva risks dangers for a long time. She or he quickly releases others from them, and is aware of even the smallest frustrations which have arisen for them. With an agitated spirit, full of compassion, she or he matures the sentient beings she or he meets.

## CHAPTER FOUR

1.(ET42-43) The great enthusiasm in Mahāyāna is glossed as the deep and difficult concern to make antidotes arise for a long time.

8.(ET46-47) The arising of the awareness of enlightenment is ultimately connected with rejoicing at the joy of others.

9.(ET46-47) The sameness of awareness towards all phenomena arises with the knowledge of the selflessness of all factors. The sameness of awareness towards sentient beings arises with a knowledge of the sameness of "self" and "others". The sameness of awareness towards what sentient beings do arises from the knowledge that they all desire the end of frustration as much as "oneself" does. The sameness of awareness towards Buddhahood comes with the knowledge of the nondifference between "oneself" and the *dharmadhātu*. The knowledge of clearing the Buddha-fields is equivalent to the knowledge of spiritual method.

23.(ET54) Vasubandhu explains "unmindful of one's own body": one can be unmindful of one's own body and life for the sake of others.

24-25.(ET55-56) By seeing all factors as a magical creation, the Bodhisattva doesn't fear defilements at the time of accomplishment. By seeing them all as unsubstantial as a scarecrow, he does not fear frustration in adverse time, because the awareness of enlightenment is devoid of fear.

26.(ET56) Vasubandhu sees this verse as counteracting the fear of frustration,

27.(ET57) and sees this one as counteracting indifference towards others.

## CHAPTER FIVE

4-5.(ET61-62) There are thirteen different activities for the sake of others: (1) advice, (2) instructing, (3) winning over others through supernatural powers, (4) bringing others to the *dharma* through making them understand the teachings, (5) keeping them in the *dharma* by severing their doubts, (6) maturing them in the good, (7) specific instructions for steadiness in awareness, i.e., meditational concentration,[556] (8) deliverance through wisdom, (9) full knowledge through the higher faculties, etc., (10) birth in the *tathāgatakula*, (11) prediction of full enlightenment, (12) consecration on the tenth stage, and (13) the knowledge of *tathāgatas*. All these are seen as activities for the sake of others.

## CHAPTER SIX

1.(ET68-69) Ultimate truth is a nondual object. This nonduality is revealed in five aspects: It does not exist because of the characteristic marks of the constructed and dependent; it doesn't fail to exist because of the characteristic marks of the perfected. But by this fact there is still nonbeing for the perfected, except when being one with the constructed and dependent. Yet it does not exist in a different way, because of the nonbeing in it of any otherness between the two. It neither arises nor ceases, because of the nonconditionedness of the *dharmadhātu*. It neither diminishes nor increases, because in it there is the cessation of the alternatives of defilement and purification. It is not purified, because it is undefiled by nature. Nor is it not unpurified, because of the removal of adventitious defilements.

2.(ET69-70) Even the view of self itself does not have the characteristics of a self. Nor does the self undergo any frustrated state according to those who believe in it. Thus the view of self, being itself linked with frustration, is devoid of the characteristics of "self" as constructed. The five aggregates, however, evolve because of the power of depravity through defilements. The unchanging characteristic of self, or its being always in a blissful state, is thus not demonstrated. Since the view of self is a delusion the idea that there is liberation is also a delusion, since there is nobody to be liberated.

3-4.(ET70-71) As long as people rely on the view of self which is only delusion, they don't see the frustrating nature of motivating dispositions. For this frustrating nature may go unnoticed. But once noticed through an experience of frustration it can be seen that there is frustration for the frustrated one. But since there is no self, it is not right to speak of a frustrated one. For everything consists only of factors, because of the selflessness of personality. And yet it does not consist of factors, because of the selflessness of factors. People could observe by direct perception that such and such factors arise through such and such conditions. How is it that people don't see dependent origination which manifestly exists, and instead search after a self which doesn't exist?

6-9.(ET72-74) Explains these verses as to a successive path: (1) When preparations are fulfilled, and one's cultivation is based on meditational concentration, one realizes that all events are only mental talk. (2) Realizing that all this is only mental talk, one realizes that it is only awareness which makes factors appear. (3) Then seeing the *dharmadhātu* by direct perception one is freed from any characteristics of duality, thus also from the idea of object and subject. This takes place on the path of vision. Once it is realized that there is no supporting object apart from consciousness, one understands the nonexistence of awareness-only itself, because of the nonexistence of the subject. (4) Through the power of constructionfree knowledge, taking as its basis the dependent (and not the constructed), the Bodhisattva works for the removal of defilements in the spiritual path.

## CHAPTER NINE

1-3.(ET103-104) The state of knowledge of everything in all aspects is equivalent to Buddhahood.

4-5.(ET104-105) All factors are Buddhahood, because there are no divisions in suchness. And there is not a single factor in Buddhahood. It is only from the constructed point of view that there are good and bad factors.

12.(ET109-110) This verse relates to the seeds of adverse factors, and shows how a revolution at the basis occurs through the completion of the antidotes through attainment of a path based on supramundane (constructionfree) knowledge, and on the path based on the succeeding mundane and supramundane knowledge (where factors are again seen separately, but only for purposes of spiritual method).

24.(ET116) Buddhahood can't be called a being, because of the selflessness of self and factors. Nor can it be called a nonbeing, because of the being of the *tathāgata*-characteristics.

60.(ET135) Briefly explains the three Buddha-bodies: *dharmakāya*

= revolution at the basis; *sambhogakāya* = body of Buddha which appears in the *maṇḍalas*; *nirmāṇakāya* = bodily manifestations Buddhas take on for the sake of sentient beings.

77.(ET143-144) It is not so much the three different vehicles which are intended here, Vasubandhu says. It's rather that there are limitless Buddha-lineages. One Buddha does not become enlightened in the same way as any other will.

Objection: But in that case all preparations for merit and knowledge are useless, if they are not applicable to other Bodhisattvas.

Reply: They are applicable, but in spite of this there is no one Buddha to liberate all sentient beings. And yet there is no Buddhahood which is not established in some Buddha! There can be no Buddha without the preparations, and without relying on some already enlightened Buddha, but for this very reason one Buddha is not logical.

## CHAPTER ELEVEN

1.(ET159-161) The *Tripiṭaka* consists of *sūtra*, *vinaya*, and *abhidharma*. But, according to whether they relate to Hīnayāna or Mahāyāna, it can be divided into two sections only: *Śrāvakapiṭaka* and *Bodhisattvapiṭaka*. In either case, the term "*piṭaka*" is used because they are compilations or abridgements of all objects which are to be known. The *Sūtrapiṭaka* gives the basis of the teaching, *Vinaya* relates to antidotes to the two extremes (lust for life and desire for death), and *Abhidharma* relates to skill in determining the exact meanings of terms used in the *dharma*. The *Tripiṭaka* first changes proclivities, then brings knowledge, then calm, then penetration. Through hearing it, new proclivities are started; by reflecting on it, knowledge arises. By cultivating the measures recommended in it, calm is reached. And by insight penetration is gained. The dualities inherent in the *Tripiṭaka* relate to the division between object and subject inherent in language. But suchness is realized when object and subject are seen as undivided.

6-7.(ET164-166) True understanding of the *dharma* depends on three higher faculties. In the faculty which consists of hearing the *dharma*, the understanding which is gained is still framed in mental talk, i.e., the constructed. In the faculty which consists in reflecting upon the *dharma*, there is the fixing of the mind on what one has heard, and this is still framed in mental talk. The faculty which consists of cultivation involves putting into practice all that which has been understood by reflecting upon the *dharma.*

8-12.(ET166-171) Further elaborations of this sequence.

13.(ET171-172) Reality is always separate from dualities because the constructed, with its divisions of objects and subjects, does not exist in any way. Based on this illusion, the dependent further constructs it. The perfected, however, is ineffable and without illusion. The first is to be comprehended, the second is to be abandoned inasmuch as it constructs, and the third is to be cleared from adventitious flaws, though it is clear by nature.

15.(ET173-174) The wood which the magician has before him in a magic show while he is uttering the *mantra* to make it appear differently is like the dependent as constructing. The elephant which appears where the wood really is, is like the constructed.

20.(ET176) Since the illusions of the constructed are not being, they are nonbeing. But its appearance is being, i.e., the illusion itself has being. Thus there is no distinction between "being" and "nonbeing". For the phenomenon which can be designated as "the being of the appearance" is the same as that which can be called "the nonbeing of the elephant." So the nonbeing of the elephant is the same as the being of the illusion.

23.(ET177-178) The warding off of false superimposition and denial which is sought by Hīnayāna assumes that when the nonbeing of a nonbeing is understood, it is no longer falsely superimposed on experience, and that when the being of a being is understood, it is no longer falsely denied. But when it is known that there is no difference between being and nonbeing, one is not alarmed by any "being", and one does not seek *nirvāṇa* in the manner of the Hīnayāna.

25-26.(ET177-178) Duality is constructed through the illusion of an object apprehended, such as a magically-created elephant. When this illusion is no longer seen, both object apprehended and subject apprehender are seen to be nonexistent, and there is no longer any duality which is apprehended.

27.(ET179-180) Both the illusions and that which serve as their antidotes are existent and nonexistent, like a magical creation. Why is this? They are existent because of being in that way through the construction of what was not. They are nonexistent because of the appearance of object apprehended and subject apprehender, which are nonexistent. Thus, since both being and nonbeing are indistinguishable, they are both existent and nonexistent, like a magical creation.

28.(ET180) The same thing applies to all stages in Buddhist practice--establishments of mindfulness, etc.

29.(ET181) Antidotal phenomena are themselves illusory, also, but are effective in removing those other illusions which are the defilements.

31.(ET183) A construction of what was not is a construction which is not in conformity with supramundane knowledge. It is being until the aids to penetration, then it is neither being nor nonbeing. Suchness and supramundane knowledge are without constructions. The subsequently attained knowledge is neither construction nor absence of construction (since constructions are used as method but are not clung to).

35.(ET186) The "coloring" of experience relates to the intrusion of attachments, aversions, etc.

37.(ET187) Vasubandhu amends the *Mahāyānasūtrālaṃkāra* by stating that this awareness which makes a characterized thing appear is both consciousness and materiality. By "views" Vasubandhu further adds, not only views but all accompanying mental factors are intended.

38.(ET187-188) In speaking of "characteristics" one can always further subdivide, by reason of the three essential natures. For instance, three characteristics can be determined in the constructed, the sign of the cognition of an object arising because of talk, the proclivities of this talk, and the appearance of this object because of the proclivities.

40.(ET189) There are three kinds of appearances: the appearance of words, the appearance of objects of sense and understanding, and the appearance of material forms or bodies. These three kinds of appearances figure in the "internal" appearances, which are mind, taking up of "objects", and construction. "Mind" in this connection is equivalent to the seventh, ego-forming consciousness or defiled mind. The taking up of "objects" is equivalent to the five sensory consciousnesses. But their discrimination takes place because of the sixth consciousness, mental consciousness. The true characteristic of an "object apprehended" is the first three kinds of appearances (appearance of words, objects, and material forms); the true characteristic of a "subject apprehender" is the second of the three kinds of appearances (above). All of them constitute the construction of what was not, i.e., the dependent as constructing.

41.(ET190) The characteristic of the perfected, suchness, is nonbeing because it is the nonbeing of the constructed, and it is being because of the being of this nonbeing. Thus "being" and "nonbeing" are unseparate. It is noncalmed because of adventitious defilements; it is calmed because it is clear by nature. It is nondiscrimination and nondiscriminatory.

44-46.(ET192-194) It is through a revolution of the seeds that there is a revolution of consciousness. A revolution of consciousness arises when there is a nonappearance of words, objects of sense and understanding, and material forms. As a result of this nonappearance, there is the nonappearance of mind, taking up of objects, and discrimination. Four kinds of mastery result: lack of discriminations, lack of motivating dispositions, clearing the Buddha-field, and knowledge. These appear in full strength at different moments in the Bodhisattva path.

47.(ET194-195) "Lack of self" in factors refers to the nonbeing of a constructed personality, and to the nonbeing of constructed events. It is not that persons and factors don't exist in any way. Actually, there is consciousness-only, which is the same as the act of apprehension. Ultimate liberation is where consciousness-only becomes manifest, and there is the nonapprehension of "persons" and "factors".

## CHAPTER THIRTEEN

11.(ET250) The Buddha is quoted in a *sūtra* as saying that he is not speaking of deliverance from passion except through passion, from hatred except through hatred, from confusion except through confusion. Because, Vasubandhu comments, there is no event which is separate from the *dharmadhātu*, because of the nonbeing of a factor separate from *dharmatā*.

13.(ET251) If passions, etc., are taken up with carefulness, one may be liberated from them by completely knowing them.

20-23.(ET254-256) The Bodhisattva has affection for all sentient beings.

## CHAPTER FOURTEEN

14.(ET261-262) Includes a detailed description of the different phases in meditational concentration.

## CHAPTER SIXTEEN

16.(ET294-300) Elaborate description of the fivefold practice of the perfections: (1) based on limitations, as in spiritual method; (2) based on retribution--as when there is proclivity towards giving because one has given in the past; (3) being based on the Bodhisattva-vows; (4) being based on wisdom; (5) being based on mental attention. Vasubandhu emphasizes also the extensiveness and persistence of Mahāyāna compassion. All kinds of helping others are grouped under the perfection of giving. Rejoicing at the joy of others is seen as the basis for the perfection of moral precepts.

30.(ET309) There is a sevenfold attachment possible: (1) attachment to enjoyments, (2) attachment to procrastinations, (3) attachment to satisfying only one's own requirements, (4) attachment to partiality, (5) attachment to reward, (6) attachment to karmic retribution, and (7) attachment to adverse factors. Only these attachments form an obstacle to the Mahāyāna.

## CHAPTER SEVENTEEN

33-66.(ET358-377) Affection is the characteristic of Mahāyāna, which the loveless unaffectionate disciples and self-enlightened Buddhas lack. This affection is linked to compassion.

## CHAPTER EIGHTEEN

82-83.(ET425-430) Arguments for momentariness. It is illogical that conditioned factors function without momentariness. Functioning, by its very definition, means the cessation of one state in favor of another. This also implies causality, as the preceding state conditions the next. As the cause must precede its effect, and as differences are perceptible from one moment to the next, a different thing arises in each moment. A sequence of causes is assumed because it is not logical that the thing cease by the same cause which made it arise. Why? Because there is a contradiction between arising and ceasing, and the causes of two contradictory results cannot be one, as in the case of shade and light, cold and heat. The momentariness of all phenomena can be seen by direct perception, if there is mental attention. If a conditioned factor, once arisen, were to remain stable for a certain time, it would have to do so either of itself or because of some power which makes it remain stable. Now it is illogical that it have this capacity of itself, because later it does not remain stable of itself! As far as a power which makes it remain stable is concerned, such a power cannot be determined, because it cannot be apprehended.

Objection: Even without such a power, the stability of a conditioned event is logical, because of there not being a cause for its destruction. It ceases only when the cause of its destruction is obtained, just as darkness is destroyed by fire.

Answer: This is also illogical, because such a cause of destruction does not exist. It is really that the darkness-series is no longer perceived, and not that the darkness itself has been destroyed, because it will reappear again once the fire is removed. And when water is being boiled it decreases gradually through its contact with fire, until finally at the end it is no longer there. But this nonbeing didn't come about through a simple contact with fire (i.e., if fire were the cause of destruction of the water, the water would have to be destroyed immediately upon its contact with fire.)[557]

Nor is the stability of things once arisen logical. The Buddha stated impermanence to be one of the characteristics of conditioned things. Now a characteristic, in order to truly be one, must have exclusivity. Thus, if a conditioned factor were not to be destroyed immediately upon arising, there would be a certain time period in which it wouldn't be impermanent--thus the exclusivity of the impermanence-characteristic would become absurd. Now it may be argued that if a conditioned factor arises in each moment, not having existed before, that this would be commonly recognized. But this argument is also not valid, because of the subtlety of the dissimilarity from moment A to moment B, which may make the difference in the two events imperceptible. That conditioned factors arise and perish in every moment proves that the "series", perceived often as one thing, does eventually cease, even without there being any special feature in the moment of cessation to distinguish it from the previous moment. In other words, if things were not changing all the time, it is difficult to see why they would ever change at all.

Transformation means the state of becoming something else, and this must begin already in moment A, otherwise it could never manifestly occur in moment B.

In the case of mental phenomena, such as awarenesses, they can be directly observed to be momentary. And all conditioned events are the result of awareness. How is this known? It is through awareness that all conditioned factors are known, for in a state of fainting, they are not perceived. Thus they, as phenomena, are the result of awareness. Awareness is also sovereign over the conditioned factors because, as the Buddha says, it is through awarenesses that the living world is led along. It is also through awareness that internal conditioned factors can be totally transformed, as in the case of yogis.

If awarenesses are momentary, their results (other conditioned factors) must also be momentary, because it is not logical that a momentary cause have a nonmomentary result.

85-88.(ET431-436) Comments here include arguments against the notion of motion,[558] but with a Madhyamaka twist: If there is such a phenomenon as motion, Vasubandhu says, does it exist when the conditioned factor has already arisen, or when it has not arisen? If it is when it has already arisen, then, because of the lapse of time it would take for it to move, it couldn't move, because it has no stability. But if it had stability it couldn't move either. If it exists when it hasn't yet arisen, then, since it hasn't arisen yet, it is nonexistent, and thus can't move either.

89-91.(ET436-441) Focuses on the momentariness of the four great material elements. Water is in a state of constant flux, and evaporates all the time. This transformation must be accepted as taking place in each moment, because there is an absence of any particular cause which would give rise to evaporation at a particular time only. Wind is inconstant by its nature, and is constantly increasing and decreasing. In combination with other elements, earth is also constantly changing. Fire is manifestly different in each moment.

A flame along with its fuel cannot be demonstrated as existing when the flame or fuel has not yet arisen. Nor can a flame persist when the fuel is already burnt. (This again is an argument with a Madhyamaka twist!)

Objection: When the fuel is already burnt, one cannot speak of it as "fuel" at all.

Reply: Nonetheless, the momentariness of a flame is demonstrated in the same way as the momentariness of sounds. The momentariness of sounds can be directly perceived by their gradual diminution. A gradual diminution is impossible without momentariness.

Objection: But how do you know that *all* conditioned factors are momentary? Not everything is perceived to be different from one moment to the next.

Reply: Even you admit that a flame is momentary, and yet it may appear to be unchanging, as in an oil-lamp. Following your argument, why don't you admit that the flame in an oil-lamp is nonmomentary, too? There are two kinds of differences: differences of essential nature and differences through development. The flame of an oil-lamp may be unchanging in its essential nature, and yet is different in each moment of development.

Objection: That's all right for a flame, but if everything is momentary, even when a chariot is standing still, it would move, thus there would be no difference between it when stationary and moving.

Reply: What appears to be stable to the eye may still be constantly changing, if exact perceptions are taken into account. For instance, in a burning oil-lamp, the wick is contantly being diminished, though this will not be visible in each moment to the eye. It is only because of an uninterrupted series of similar moments that the momentariness of given conditioned events is not recognized. And thus the perverted view arises that "it" is the same thing from one moment to the next. If this were not so, there could not be the perversion of taking the noneternal for the eternal, and in its absence, there could not be mental defilement, and in the absence of mental defilement, there could never be purification either. Thus the momentariness of all conditioned factors is demonstrated.

92-103.(ET441-452) Vasubandhu gives a long passage to demonstrate that "person" is only a designation and should never be perceived as an entity. Furthermore, it has no efficacy of its own which would distinguish it from the sensory domains. Also, the idea of a fixed personality is always linked with defilements to be eliminated in the path.

## CHAPTER NINETEEN

4.(ET456-457) Absence of desires is unsurprising in the context of giving, compassion is unsurprising in the context of ethics and forbearance, the ultimate cultivation of antidotes is unsurprising in the context of vigor.

47.(ET476-477) An investigation of a name is an investigation of the adventitiousness of the name in relation to the 'thing' it expresses. An investigation of a thing is an investigation of the adventitiousness of the thing in relation to the word that expresses it.
Investigations using the conceptions of essential nature and specific characteristics are investigations based only on conceptions, e.g., conceptions of essential nature, specific characteristic, etc.

## CHAPTERS TWENTY AND TWENTY-ONE

10-14.(E502-504) It is in the first stage that emptiness, i.e., the selflessness of persons and factors, is realized. In the second, the lasting karmic effects of action are realized. In the third, meditations are cultivated. In the fourth, by cultivating the aids to enlightenment to a great extent, a transformation of *saṃsāra* is achieved. In the fifth, while being based on the four noble truths, one matures as many sentient beings through various treatises and works of art. In the sixth, one understands dependent origination completely, and guards against the rising of defilements. In the seventh, while understanding the unity of the diverse formulations of the path, one practises the one path, which is signless. In the eighth, one completely purifies the Buddha-field by achieving the lack of motivating dispositions and the signless. In the ninth, one perfects the ability to mature sentient beings by mastering the particular knowledges. In the tenth, one realizes perfect clarity through meditational concentration and the *dhāraṇīs*. In the eleventh, one attains the abandonment of all obstructions to the knowable. (As often, Vasubandhu interprets Maitreyanātha verses in reference to a successive path, where it is not clear that this was Maitreyanātha's original intention.)

15-21.(ET504-508) are again explained as relating to a successive path.

24.(ET509) The stage where Mahāyānic resolve is cultivated is not perfected, the rest are perfected, but of these seven are perfected and unperfected, the rest are perfected.[559]

43.(ET521) Compassion is the desire to see sentient beings separated from frustrations; rejoicing at the joy of others is the desire to see sentient beings unseparated from joy.

58. (ET532) Vasubandhu gives the three Buddha-bodies as *svābhāvika*, *sāṃbhogika*, and *nairmāṇika*. He says that they represent

the knowledge of everything that can be known in all aspects and that this has the effect of cutting away all beings' doubts. (Again a change, as the verse speaks of "desires", not "doubts".)

60.(ET533-534) Perfectly clear suchness is the ultimate truth, and equals the perfected. It is the essential nature of Buddhas. It is the cause of deliverance in each Bodḥisattva-stage. It is the ultimate fruition to be attained by sentient beings. It has the action of delivering all sentient beings. Its practice means becoming joined to indestructible and unequalled qualities.

61.(ET534) One is seen in the world through the magical body, one is seen in the *maṇḍalas* through the enjoyment body, and one is unseen through the *dharma* body.

## 200. VASUBANDHU, *Bhāṣya* on Asaṅga's *Madhyāntavibhāga*

Summary by Stefan Anacker

This is one of the several commentaries Vasubandhu wrote on works by Maitreyanātha/Asaṅga.[560] It is a striking example of what can be called Yogācāra Śūnyavāda: it delimits a path and uses the theory of the store-consciousness and of the three natures, and at the same time the only fundamental reality for it is emptiness (*śūnyatā*).

"E" references are to the edition by Gadjin M. Nagao[561]. "T" refers to the translation by Stefan Anacker.[562]

### CHAPTER ONE[563]

1. (E17; T211-212) The construction of what was not (*abhūtaparikalpa*) exists. It is the construction of object apprehended and subject apprehender (*grāhyagrāhakavikalpa*). But when this construction vanishes, then there is only emptiness. "Emptiness" can in fact be defined as the separation of the construction of what was not from the (apprehended) being of object apprehended and subject apprehender. Fundamentally, only emptiness exists in the construction of what was not, and the construction of what was not exists in emptiness.

2.(E18; T212) Everything can be designated as neither empty nor nonempty. Both emptiness and the construction of what was not can render everything nonempty--emptiness because it is "itself" the flow of all factors, the construction of what was not because it constructs the flow into discrete entities. But everything *is* empty because there is the appearance of separate objects and subjects in the latter case, which constructions are seen to be empty. The nonexistence of duality is emptiness.[564]

3.(E18-19; T212-213) How do the dualities which come from the construction of what was not first arise? It is because of the existence of visibles, etc. that the appearance of objects separate from consciousness arises; it is because of the five sense-faculties in "one's own" and "others" series of psychophysical events that the appearance of sentient beings arises. The appearance of self or ego arises only with a defiled mind.[565] It is the six consciousnesses themselves which make the appearance of manifestations arise. But there is no real object for consciousness, because there is no fixed aspect to the appearances of objects and sentient beings, and because of the false state of appearances of the appearances of self and perceptions.[566] In these four ways there is absence of objects, of sense-faculties, of mind, and of the six consciousnesses which cognize. But in their absence, the subject apprehender, fundamental consciousness, is also nonexistent.

4.(E19; T213) The construction of what was not does not exist as it appears. Yet it is not totally nonexistent, because so much confusion *does* arise! Also, liberation is sought in the destruction of the construction of what was not--thus it can't be just nonexistent.

5.(E19; T213) Even though this is only a construction of what was not, there is the possibility of speaking of three essential natures--three different kinds of reality. The constructed nature is an "object of sense and understanding." The capacity for this construction lies in the dependent nature. The nonexistence of object apprehended and subject apprehender is the perfected nature

6.(E20; T214) There is a characteristic within the construction of what was not which allows it to penetrate its own nonexistent character. There is no more apprehension of objects of sense or understanding when there is the apprehension that everything is only manifestation. But a nonapprehension of consciousness-only comes about dependent upon this nonapprehension of objects. In this way, the nonexistent character of object apprehended and subject apprehender can be seen.

7.(E20; T214) So these "apprehensions" just mentioned are really nonapprehensions, because there is nothing to be apprehended.

8.(E20; T214-215) Awarenesses and accompanying factors are different divisions in the construction of what was not. "Observing an object" is awareness; "observing" in terms of special qualities are the accompanying factors.[567]

9.(E20-21; T215) The construction of what was not may also be divided into two according to its functioning: there is the storehouse-consciousness, the conditioned ground for all other consciousnesses, on the one hand, and then there are the functioning consciousnesses (*pravṛttivijñāna*) which relate to experience on the other.

10-11a.(E21; T215-216) All of the limbs of dependent origination are the construction of what was not's characteristic of involving afflictions.

11b.(E22; T216-217) Among the limbs of dependent origination, the afflictions proper are ignorance, craving and clinging; motivating dispositions and being (which depends on volition) are the afflictions which are karmic action; and the afflictions which come about by birth itself are the remaining limbs of dependent origination. The causal limbs are those of action and affliction; the resultant ones are the rest.

12-13.(E22-23; T217-218) Emptiness is the nonexistence of duality and the being of this nonbeing. Thus it can be called neither being nor nonbeing. It is neither the same nor different from the construction of what was not. If it were different, the nature of a factor would be different from the factor itself, since emptiness is the nature of the construction of what was not. But they cannot be totally the same either, because if they were, there could be no alleviating knowledge.

14.(E23; T218) Suchness, the reality-limit, the signless, the highest, and the *dharmadhātu*, are all synonyms for emptiness.

16.(E24; T218-219) Emptiness may be either afflicted or alleviated. But it is adventitious flaws that make it afflicted. Fundamentally it is clear, just as the fundamentally clear nature of water is not changed by its becoming turbid, the nature of gold is not changed by its being hidden in the earth, and space is not changed by disturbances in space.

17.(E25; T219) Sixteen kinds of emptiness can be spoken of: the emptiness of the personal, the emptiness of external, the emptiness of personal and external, the great emptiness, the emptiness of emptiness, the emptiness of highest truth, the emptiness of the conditioned, the emptiness of the unconditioned, the extended emptiness, the emptiness of "inferior" and "superior", the emptiness of nature, the emptiness of characteristic marks, the emptiness of all factors, the emptiness of nonbeing, and the emptiness of the essential nature of nonbeing. These can be known in brief as the emptiness of the personal, the emptiness of whatever is experienced, the emptiness of the body--the body being the seat of both personal and external, the emptiness of the insentient universe--this is the emptiness referred to as "the great emptiness", the emptiness of the emptiness through which it is seen that all is empty, and the emptiness of any object of understanding which may be resorted to.

18-19.(E25-26; T219-220) The only reasons Bodhisattvas resort to an object of understanding is to aid other beings and to gain Buddha-knowledge.

20.(E26; T2200 The nonbeing of persons and factors is emptiness, and it is also the existing being (*sadbhāva*) of this nonbeing. This is said so that the superimposition of "persons" and "factors", as well as the denial (*apavāda*) of emptiness, can be removed.

22.(E27; T221-222) Constructions, dismay, idleness and perplexity are brought to rest by understanding emptiness.

## CHAPTER TWO

1.(E28; T222) There are two kinds of obstructions, the obstructions which are defilements and the obstructions of the knowable. The first kind is the only type accepted by the Hīnayāna, but the Mahāyāna accepts both kinds as being obstructions. Aside from these, there are the "excessive" obstructions of those who act with attachment, hostility, or confusion, the "equal" obstruction which is that of "those who make everything alike" and are governed by apathy, and the obstruction of completely accepting or abandoning *saṃsāra*, which is again an obstruction peculiar to Mahāyānists.

2.(E28-29; T222-223) The obstructions which are defilements are equivalent to the fetters: attraction, which is an obstruction to agitation (agitation is desirable in Mahāyāna if it is of the kind that urges people to be active in the alleviation of frustration); repugnance, which is an obstruction to equanimity; pride, which leads to the view of self; ignorance, which is an obstacle to knowledge about external objects; holding fast to views, which is an obstruction to the knowledge of the truth of cessation of frustration, because of the anxieties caused by false views; addiction to moral precepts and vows, which is an obstruction to the truth of the path; perplexity, which is an obstruction to the knowledge of the qualities of Buddha, *dharma* and the order; envy, which is an obstruction to satisfaction in others' attainments; and selfishness, which is an obstruction to the knowledge of satisfaction with little.

3-10a.(E29-31; T223-225) The obstructions of the knowable, which are obstructions specifically to the activist path of the Mahāyāna, are lack of means to rouse "oneself" from inactivity, lack of complete use of "one's" sense-fields, careless activity, nonproduction of good, lack of mental attention to what lies around one, failure to make the necessary preparation, separation from people in the same spiritual lineage, distress and agitation of awareness, lack of opportunity to practise the Mahāyāna, being forced to live with people who are counteractive to the practice of Mahāyāna, natural susceptibility to harm, lack of control, lack of maturation of insight, attachment to becoming something particular, longing for enjoyment, muddle-headedness, lack of confidence, lack of faith, deliberating on things according to words only, lack of reverence for the *dharma*, respect for gain, lack of compassion, casting away what's been learned regarding the *dharma*, being ill-versed in the *dharma*, and lack of engagement in meditation. These are, by threes, obstructions to the welfare of others, to enlightenment, to lack of confusion, to the lack of obstructions, to the ability to evolve, to fearlessness, to lack of selfishness, and to control.

10b.(E31-33; T225-227) There are ten kinds of causes. There is a cause as one thing's being the direct condition for the arising of another, such as when the eye gives rise to a visual consciousness. There is a cause as one thing's maintaining another, such as the food's maintaining sentient beings. There is a cause as one thing's providing a support for others, as the inhabited world does for sentient beings. There is a cause as one thing's manifesting another, as the action of looking causes the visible. There is a cause as one thing's transforming another, as fire does to that which is being cooked. There is a cause as one thing's disjoining another--this is the relation of a cutting instrument to that which is being cut. There is a cause as one thing's evolving another gradually, such as the action of a goldsmith, who makes bracelets out of masses of gold. There is a cause as one thing's giving rise to the idea of another, such as the perception of smoke giving rise to the idea of fire. There is a cause as one thing's making for the deduction of another, such as a justification in an inference-schema does for a thesis. There is a cause as one thing's leading to the attainment of another, such as the path leading to *nirvāṇa*.

Thus, an obstruction to the arising of alleviation is an obstruction to welfare of others; an obstruction to the maintenance of alleviation is an obstruction to enlightenment; an obstruction to the sustension of alleviation is an obstruction to the full taking up of *saṃsāra*; an obstruction to manifesting it to others is an obstruction to insight; an obstruction to transformation is an obstruction to lack of confusion; an obstruction to becoming disjoined from obstructions are all the obstructions themselves; an obstruction to alleviation's gradually evolving is an obstruction to awareness' ability to evolve towards enlightenment; an obstruction giving rise to the idea of Mahāyāna is an obstruction to fearlessness, because this idea does not arise where there is any fear; an obstruction to causing the idea of Mahāyāna to arise in others is an obstruction to lack of selfishness; an obstruction to its attainment is an obstruction to control.

It is because of the desire to obtain enlightenment that the good roots are first made to arise. This means that the first awareness of enlightenment (*bodhicitta*) is necessary for the good in a Mahāyāna sense. Once there is some potency in the good roots, perversions, meaning such mental habits as lead invariably to frustration, can be removed. After perversions are removed in the path of vision, all obstructions are eradicated in the spiritual path.

11.(E33; T228) Further obstructions to particular parts of practice are: lack of skill in regarding the meditational object, which is an obstruction to the establishments of mindfulness;[568] sloth, an obstruction to the right exertions; slackness and excitedness, two obstructions to concentration since they obstruct the faculties of interest, energy, awareness, and deliberation; noncultivation of the aids to liberation (faith in the basic direction of Mahāyāna practice, energy, mindfulness, meditational concentration, and insight) is an obstruction to the limbs of enlightenment; faulty views are an obstruction because they obstruct the path of vision. To the limbs of the path, essentially the path of meditation, natural susceptibility to harm (depravity, etc.) is an obstruction.

12-13.(E34; T228-229) Enumeration of obstructions to the perfections (see V,6).

14-16.(E234-36; T229-230) Obstructions to the stages in the career of a Bodhisattva: to the first stage, anything which obstructs the knowledge of the similarity of "self" and "others"; to the second, anything which obstructs the undertaking of special practices for the removal of defilements; to the third, any obstruction to courage; to the fourth, any obstruction of grasping; to the fifth, any obstruction to the similarity of motivation in all the stages; to the sixth the idea of defilement and alleviation itself is an obstruction, because in this stage it should be realized that no factor can be defiled or alleviated since no moment-event has any fixed nature or can be said to really arise at all; to the seventh, preoccupation with misleading diversities in the *sūtras* is an obstruction; to the eight, any belief in "inferior" or "superior" is an obstruction. Four potencies arise in the last two states: potency in the absence of discriminations, achieved in the eighth stage; potency in total alleviation of one's "Buddha-field", also attained in the same stage; potency in the particular knowledges needed for sustaining this alleviating action in the ninth stage; and potency of action, which is the state of being able to do actions for the sake of sentient beings through various transformations of will in the tenth or Buddha-stage.

17.(E36; T231) All of these obstructions may be enumerated in brief as the obstructions which are defilements (II, 2) and the obstructions of the knowable (all obstructions enumerated from II, 3 to II, 16).

## CHAPTER THREE

1-2.(E38; T231-232) Enumeration of the different kinds of reality (*tattva*) to be discussed in this chapter.[569]

3.(E38; T232) A basic kind of reality may be signalled, but this again is no unified reality, but is rather the three kinds of reality called "the constructed", "the dependent", and "the perfected". (See also I, 5)

The constructed is always really nonexistent, "and thus there is reality in the constructed, because of its unreversedness."[1] The

1.This extremely difficult passage seems to be a kind of a joke: The constructed does not change, because it is nonexistent, so it cannot be "reversed" or defiled by frustration-inducing mental habits. The nonexistent has a reality if it is so constructed. It is ultimately nonexistent in the sense that it can be utterly removed. But as long as it isn't, it has an effect, and thus has reality.

dependent is existent, but not in a real way, since there is a state of confusion in its appearance as long as the transformation to the perfected has not been made. The perfected is both existent and nonexistent. The perfected is existent as it is the removal of the "nonexistent" constructed, but by the same token it is nonexistent, since it is simply the nonexistence of the constructed. When the fulfilled is realized, "the perfected" is nonexistent, since the notion of "perfected" is constructed.

4.(E38; T232) Each of these three kinds of realities may be related to a special realization, which may be called "the reality of the characteristic marks" (*lakṣaṇa-tattva*). When it is realized that there is a false superimposition and denial involved in assuming "persons" and "factors", this relates to the constructed. When it is similarly realized for the assumption of "objects apprehended" and "subjects apprehending", this relates to the dependent. When it is realized that there is a false superimposition and denial involved in assuming anything's being or nonbeing, this relates to the perfected.

5-6a.(E38-39; T233) The existence of impermanence, etc., is the constructed, dependent, and perfected, is an antidote to perverted views of permanence, etc., and thus the reality of impermanence, etc. is called "the reality of nonperversion". The constructed is impermanent because it is objects of sense and understanding which are seen to be nonexistent. The dependent is impermanent because it is objects of sense and understanding which are fluxional. And the perfected is impermanent because it goes through the phases of defilement and alleviation.

6b.(E39; T233-234) Frustration exists in each of the three kinds of reality, also: the constructed is associated with that grasping that comes through intentness upon views concerning "persons" and "factors"; the dependent is associated with frustration because of the basic characteristics of the world itself, and the perfected is associated with frustration because of voluntary connection with frustration.

7a.(E39-40; T234) Emptiness exists in each of the three also. The constructed is empty because it is not finally existent. The dependent is empty because it is not as it is constructed and yet is not totally nonexistent. And the perfected has the nature of emptiness itself. Thus,

---

But as long as it isn't, it has an effect, and thus has reality.

the emptiness of the constructed is its nonexistence; the emptiness of the dependent is the nonbeing of any definite thing; and the emptiness of the perfected is its fundamental nature.

7b-8.(E40; T234-235) Selflessness exists in each of the three: the constructed because it has no characteristic mark, the dependent because it has a characteristic mark apart from the constructed, the perfected because it is selflessness by nature.

The truth of the origination of frustration exists in all three also: by means of the proclivities which cause insistence on the constructed; actions causing frustration are dependent; and the nonseparation of suchness from the obstructions is the origination of frustration in the perfected.

9a.(E40; T235-236) The truth of the cessation of suffering exists in all three: nonarising by nature in the constructed; nonarising of object apprehended and subject apprehender as things apart in the dependent; and the process from affliction to alleviation in the perfected.

9b-10a.(E41; T236) The truth of the path leading to the cessation of frustration exists in all three also: in the comprehension of the constructed; in the comprehension and abandoning of the dependent as constructed; in the comprehension, acquisition and direct realization of the perfected.

10b.(E41; T236) Conventional truth may belong to any of the three kinds of reality, because of the conventionality of designations, which relates to the constructed, the conventionality of perceptual understanding, which relates to the dependent, and the conventionality of words used in religious practice, which relates to the perfected.

10c.(E41; T236) The highest truth relates only to the perfected.

11b.(E41-420 T237) The perfected can be called both conditioned and unconditioned: unconditioned because it consummates a lack of transformation back into what was before; conditioned as all the things comprised in the path, which are perfected in the sense that they consummated a lack of the reverse.

12.(E42; T237-238) There are two kinds of reality which are commonly called "accepted reality" (*prasiddhatattva*). There is that accepted by the world at large, which is due only to the constructed--where, regarding a range of events, there is a certain sameness of views among all worldly people because their intellects have adapted themselves through acquaintance with certain conventional symbols. Then there is that accepted by right reasoning, which is whatever is established by logical rules which depend on the three instruments of knowledge: perception, inference, reliance on reliable authority.

13.(E42-43; T238-239) There are three kinds of comprising reality: that through apprehending objects of sense of five varieties and the discrimination of their sensory characteristics, which occurs through the dependent; that through naming, which occurs through the constructed; that through suchness and right knowledge, which occurs through the perfected.

14.(E43-44; T239) The reality of positive activity is the constructed and dependent. From it there evolves intentness and becoming disturbed. The clearing through the perception of characteristics comes about through the perfected.

15-16a.(E44; T239-240) The reality of skill is an antidote to fixed views, for instance, skill in the concept of the aggregates, which serves as an antidote to the view of a self. There is a view of a self whenever there is the idea of one entity underlying a living being, a oneness comprising it, one cause, one experiencer, one doer, one in control of all its movements, one possessor, one entity lasting through time, one substratum for defilement and alleviation, one entity in meditational concentration, or one entity that is either bound or liberated. These views can be removed by observing the grasping involved in this supposed "oneness", "causeness", "experiencerness", "doerness", "independent", "possessorness", "being afflicted or cleared", "being in concentration", "being bound or being freed".

16b.(E44; T240) The aggregates belong to all three kinds of reality. The concept of any aggregate is a construction, and thus belongs to constructed reality. But this construction rests on a discrimination, which belongs to the dependent. And when the aggregate in this sense takes part in realization, it belongs to the perfected.

17a.(E45; T240-241) The aggregates can be known in three different ways. Every present materiality-moment is distinct from each past and future one, and each simultaneously-occurring materiality-moment is different from all the rest. On the other hand, in a given moment all the aggregates may be interreacting to such an extent that it is impossible to clearly divide them from one another. But again, one may distinguish them by their separate characteristics.

17b.(E45; T241) It is the sensory realms of eyes, ears, nose, tongue, sensate body, and consciousness which are the objects of sense and understanding giving rise to the traces making for the concept of a "subject apprehender". Similarly, the sensory domains of visibles, sounds, smells, tastes, tactile sensations, and mentally cognizables, leave traces in the series, and this gives rise to the concept of "objects apprehended" which exist outside the consciousness-series. It is the traces of the visual, etc. consciousnesses themselves which make for the concept of "apprehension". All three are the result of traces, and the distinction between them is empty.

18a.(E45; T241) The six internal sense-fields are the doors to felt experiences; the six external sense-fields are doors to the experience of distinguishing objects of sense and understanding.

18b.(E45; T241-242) Dependent origination, another concept used in the reality of skills, has as its aim non-superimposition and nondenial as regards cause, effect and activity. A superimposition arises, for instance, when a self is assumed; a denial occurs when it is claimed that nothing like causality takes place at all.

20a.(E46-47; T242-243) The concept of the faculties also can serve in the reality of skills, as it also can counteract the idea of a unified self. They are explained here in a manner identical to Vasubandhu's emendation of Vaibhāṣika explanations at 173. *Abhidharmakośa* II, 1-4.

20b.(E47; T243) The concept of time can also be used in the reality of skills. The completed efficacy of both cause and effect is referred to as "something in past time." If neither the efficacy of the cause or effect has been completed, it is called "something in future time." And if the efficacy of the cause has been completed, but the efficacy of the effect has not, it is called "something in present time".

21.(E47; T243-244) As regards the four noble truths, which are also part of the "reality of skills": the truth of frustration is equivalent to feelings when it has preparatory ensnaring signs constricting it, and the rest of the truths have correspondingly to do with the arising of such ensnaring factors and their removal.

22a.(E48; T244) The three "vehicles" (*yāna*) of Buddhism, another concept used in the reality of skills, can be defined as follows: If through hearing from others about the so-called flaws of *saṃsāra* and merits of *nirvāṇa*, and emancipation from *saṃsāra* is striven for, this is the vehicle of the disciples. If nothing is heard from others regarding these flaws and merits, but emancipation from *saṃsāra* is sought "by oneself", this is the vehicle of the self-enlightened Buddhas. If a knowledge free from discriminations arises by itself, and through this knowledge there is emancipation, this is the Great Vehicle (*mahāyāna*).

22b.(E48-49; T244-246) As regards the concepts of "conditioned" and "unconditioned", which are also used in the reality of skills, it can be known that all the consciousnesses, including the store-consciousness, all environmental factors, all experienced objects, all apprehensions, discriminations, and designations, all are conditioned. The unconditioned is everything that goes into a putting to rest of all these, which is equivalent to suchness and the path leading to cessation.

The compact meaning of realities: One may summarize all these realities as being basically of two kinds: mirror-reality (*ādarśatattva*), and the reality of that which is seen in the mirror (*dṛśyatattva*). Mirror-reality is the primary three-fold reality (constructed, dependent, perfected); the realities seen in the mirror are: the reality seen in the absence of pride of self, the reality seen in antidotes to perversions, the reality seen in the vehicle of the disciples, the reality seen in the Great Vehicle, the realities seen in the flaws of others; theories brought to light through logical investigation, the realities seen while revealing the Great Vehicle to others, the reality seen when one penetrates what can be known in all its aspects, the reality seen in revealing suchness, and the realities seen in penetrating the motives lying behind the different manners of grasping after "self".

## CHAPTER FOUR

1.(E50; T246) The cultivation of antidotes to the obstructions is the practice of the allies of enlightenment (see *Kośa* VI, 66). Among them, the establishments of mindfulness (see *Kośa* VI, 14-18) can be related to the four noble truths, since depravity is a characteristic of the body, the cause of cravings is feelings, and disappearance of any fear of the cessation of self occurs when it is realized that "self" is only awarenesses, and it is through understanding conditioning factors that it is known which factors afflict and which alleviate.

2.(E50; T246-247) The right exertions follow on the establishment of mindfulness, and have to do with energy in the removal of bad factors, and in the engendering of good factors.

3.(E251; T247) The practice of the bases of supernatural power follows upon that of the right exertions, and these bases are essentially skill in meditation.

4.(E51; T247) The main flaws in meditational practice are sloth, forgetting instructions, slackness, excitedness, lack of motivating factors when slackness and excitedness are to be eliminated, and the presence of motivating factors which too definitely channel the flow of meditation once slackness and excitedness have been eliminated.

6.(E52; T248-249) The five faculties (faith, vigor, mindfulness, meditational concentration, and insight) arise after the bases of supernatural power. Faith is sovereign in zest for further practice, vigor is sovereign in the application of practice, mindfulness is sovereign for nonloss of the meditational object, meditational concentration is sovereign for the non-gliding-about of awareness, and insight is sovereign for the discernment of factors.

7.(E53; T249) When these faculties are powerful, they are called "the powers" (*bala*). The faculties are enumerated as they are because each is the cause of the next.

8.(E53-54; T249-250) The limbs of enlightenment are the different factors contributing to enlightenment on the path of vision (see 173.*Abhidharmakośa* VI, 25-26). The limb which is the basis of enlightenment is mindfulness, the limb which is enlightenment by nature is insight or the discernment of factors, the limb which delivers from afflicting characteristics is vigor, the limb which is of good effects to others is joy, the limbs which cause absence of affliction are tranquility, meditational concentration, and equanimity.

9a.(E54; T250) The initial cause of absence of affliction is tranquillity, as it works against those afflictions caused by susceptibility to harm. The support for absence of affliction is meditational concentration, and by nature, absence of affliction is equanimity.

12. (E55; T251-252) The establishments of mindfulness are not the same for followers of the Hīnayāna and Mahāyāna. The Hīnayānists concentrate only on their own bodies, etc., and they do it for nonattachment. The Mahāyānists are attentive to the bodies, etc., of both themselves and others, and do it neither for attachment nor for nonattachment.

14.(E56; T252-253) The stages of the Bodhisattva result in complete enlightenment. The three "Buddha-bodies", sometimes mystically explained, are interpreted quite simply by Vasubandhu as follows: the situation of attaining enlightenment is the body of factors, the situation of being of good effect to others is the enjoyment-body, and the situation of completing beneficial actions is the magical body.

15-18.(E56-59; T253-256) The quest for enlightenment is a gradual process, going through the stages of disciples and adepts.

## CHAPTER FIVE

1.(E60; T256) The supremacy of the Mahāyāna lies in its path, its supporting objects, and its full realization.

3.(E61; T257-258) The practice of Mahāyāna is distinguished by its strength, persistence, development, indestructibility, continuity, lack of trouble, embracing of others, beginning undertakings, obtaining merit, steady flow, and fulfilment.

6-7.(E62-63; T258-259) The perfections are giving, defined as all favoring of others; moral precepts, defined as the nonharming of others; patience, defined as the pardoning of all harm done by others; energy, defined as actively increasing the good qualities of meditation, wisdom, skill in means, and resolve in bringing enlightenment to others; power, defined as the twin strengths of calculation and cultivation of antidotes; and knowledge needed for liberating others.

11.(E64; T260-2610 Practice "after-*dharma*" involves actions which may have to be taken immediately after emerging from meditation. Distraction may arise then, because of the nature of things, because of the renewed impinging of the external, because of mental signs, because of susceptibility to harm, because of mental attention. Relishing the meditational state, slackness and excitedness are examples of distraction due to the internal; deliberate intention in meditation is an example of distraction due to mental signs; mental attention linked with a sense of "I" is distraction due to susceptibility to harm, as it is through the force of susceptibility to harm that the pride of thinking "I exist" arises.

13-14.(E65; T262) In connection with a so-called object, it may be thought: "Such and such is its name!": such a statement has meaning only because of past familiarity, but is meaningless being based on error.

15.(E65-66; T262) A lack of perversion in regard to an "object" arises when it is observed that the "object" does not exist as it appears, since it appears with the duality of object and subject. This lack of perversion is avoidance of the idea of the object's existence, because of the absence of object apprehended and subject apprehender, and also avoidance of the idea of the object's absence, because of its erroneous appearance.

16.(E66; T262) It is mental attention towards talk which is the basis for the discrimination between object apprehended and subject apprehender.

17.(E66; T262-263) In what way can an object be said to exist, in what way not to exist? The object is to be regarded like a magical creation. A magical creation does not exist with the true being of elephant, etc., produced in the spectator's visual field in a magic show, and yet it doesn't not exist, because of the existence of the illusion itself. In this way, there can be a removal of the very concepts of "being" and "nonbeing".

18.(E67; T263) Everything, from visibles seen by the eyes to cognizables grasped by the mind, is only names.

19.(E67; T263) Not a single factor is found without the absence of self. Therefore, emptiness is the universal characteristic of all factors. (In other words, the universal characteristic of all factors is that they have no characteristic!)

20.(E67; T263-264) Nonclarity in emptiness is only the nonabandonment of perverted mental attention.

22.(E68-69; T264-265) Because there are neither persons nor factors, there can be neither afflictions nor alleviations for them. So there is no detriment and no excellence. So how can there be fear? How can there be pride?

The Ten Thunderous Words (*vajrapadāni*): The existence of the perfected, the nonexistence of the constructed, the dependent being the locus of both, its likeness to a magical creation, lack of discriminations, luminousness of nature, affliction and alleviation, their likeness to space, lack of detriment, and lack of excellence.

Objection: If the constructed does not exist, why is it apprehended? If it does exist, luminousness of nature is not logical.

Answer: That which is magically created does not exist, and yet is apprehended.

Objection: If there is luminousness of nature, how can there be afflictions?

Answer: Space, which is perfectly pure by nature, may yet be disturbed.

Objection: If the afflictions of limitless beings have been brought to rest with the arising of limitless Buddhas, why has there been no eradication of *saṃsāra?*

Answer: There is no detriment in *saṃsāra,* and no excellence in *nirvāṇa.*

23-26.(E70-73; T266-270) The practice of the avoidance of extremes: To say that there is a difference between materiality, etc., and the self, is an extreme, and to say that there is an identity between them is also an extreme. To avoid these extremes there is the middle path, where there is no consideration of "self" or of "humanity". To say that there is no life-force except the body is another view. The extreme of the Jains is to say that this materiality is eternal; the extreme of the Hīnayāna Buddhists is to say that it is not eternal. To avoid these extremes there is the middle path, which regards it as neither eternal nor noneternal. If it is said "There is a self", this is the extreme of superimposing a fixed personality; if one says "All is without a self", this is the extreme of denial. To avoid these extremes there is a middle path free from discriminations, which neither maintains nor denies "self". To say "A consciousness-moment just existed" is an extreme of superimposition; to say that it didn't exist is an extreme of denial. To avoid these extremes there is a middle path, where there is no awareness, volition, mind, or consciousness. To assume bad factors is an extreme; to assume antidotes is an extreme. To avoid these extremes, there is a middle path, which has nothing to do with dualities. It is an extreme to say that factors continue to exist; it is an extreme to say that they cease to exist. Any duality of ignorance and wisdom is equally an extreme. To avoid it, there is the middle path, which says that ignorance and wisdom are not separate, because of the nonbeing of the notions of ignorance, wisdom, objects apprehended, apprehenders, etc.

Practically, the antidote to views, attachment, hostility and confusion are the emptiness in knowledge, the signlessness of knowledge, and aimlessness in knowledge. To unafflicted and afflicted motivating dispositions the antidote is the lack of motivating dispositions in knowledge; to the afflictions of birth, the antidote is the lack of arising in knowledge, and lack of essential nature in knowledge. But all this can be said only by way of expedience, because there are no afflictions or alleviations by nature, and assuming dualities of this kind is an extreme. An avoidance of extremes comes by not making factors empty by calling them "empty", and yet seeing all factors as empty.

Discriminations in regard to being and nonbeing are extreme. A discrimination in regard to nonbeing is, for instance, one as follows: the person must exist because it is through its destruction that emptiness, an absence of self, exists. To avoid this extreme: Emptiness doesn't occur because of the destruction of person, rather, emptiness is already empty, by the emptiness of the extremes of assuming "anything previous", the emptiness of the extreme of assuming "anything subsequent", and the emptiness of the present.

A discrimination as to "something to be abandoned" is an extreme because of the fear that arises with such conceptions. For avoiding this extreme, there is the example of space (see comments on Ten Thunderbolt Words, above). A discrimination of "something to be feared" is an extreme. For avoiding it, there is the example of the painter.[570]

A discrimination of "objects apprehended" or "subject apprehender" is an extreme. To avoid it, there is the example of the magician (see V, 17). With the knowledge of manifesting-only, there is no separate object. But with the knowledge that there is no object, there is no "manifesting-only".

A discrimination of "rightness" or "wrongness" is an extreme. For all investigations are investigations of what is already past, hence no longer existent. For avoiding this extreme, there is the example of two sticks of wood. Just as from the friction of two sticks of wood a fire suddenly arises and burns up the two sticks, just so an examination of how factors were, which has no rightness, makes that which has the characteristic of rightness, i.e., the faculty of insight, arise. And when it has arisen, it causes the same investigation to disappear. For there is no rightness without an investigation of what already was, which has the characteristic of wrongness.

A discrimination of "practice" and "non-practice" is an extreme. For there is no practice leading to enlightenment or non-practice not leading to enlightenment. To avoid this extreme there is the example of the oil-lamp.[571]

A discrimination of nonarising or simultaneity is an extreme.[572] To avoid this extreme there is the second example of the oil-lamp.[573]

29-30.(E74-77; T271) Not remaining tranquil in the state of

complete nonobstruction is one of the full realizations of activist Mahāyāna. Others rest in the skills in aiding others, fulfillment of the perfections, being non-based in either *saṃsāra* or *nirvāṇa*.

This treatise is so named because it separates the Middle Path from extremes, explains the Middle and extremes, and the ways of avoiding extremes.

## 201. VASUBANDHU, *Bhāṣya* on Asaṅga's *Mahāyānasaṃgraha*

Summary by Stefan Anacker

The Sanskrit original does not exist. Of old translations, there are the following: (1) Tibetan, by Jinamitra, Śīlendrabodhi, Yes-śes-sde: Peking. Tokyo Tibetan Tripiṭaka volumes 112-113; (2) Chinese, by Hsüan-tsang, Taishō 1597. No modern translations or summaries (except the following one, which is incomplete) exist, though occasionally Lamotte quotes from it.[574] Most often, though, Lamotte refers to the *Upanibandha* of Asvabhāva.

### INTRODUCTION

1.Vasubandhu begins his commentary with a discussion of canonical Buddhist literature in general. This is similar to his comments in 198.*Mahāyānasūtrālaṃkārabhāṣya* XI, 1-3: *Sūtra*, *vinaya*, and *abhidharma* form the three *piṭakas*, but one can also speak of two *piṭakas* only, the *Śrāvakapiṭaka* (Hīnayāna) and the *Bodhisattvapiṭaka* (Mahāyāna). What is the necessity for their being three *piṭakas*? The *Sūtrapiṭaka* is an antidote to perplexity, as it always gives a precise meaning. The *Vinaya* is an antidote to questions regarding the two extremes to be avoided (the two extremes are desire for life and desire for death), as it gives remedies for excessive attachment to pleasures, while at the same time permitting pleasures which are not offences. The *Abhidharma* is an antidote to self-concocted theories, because it illuminates the unreversed (*aviparīta*) characteristics of factors. The *Sūtrapiṭaka* teaches the three trainings: higher virtue, higher awareness through meditational concentration, and higher wisdom. The *Vinaya* puts into effect the first two, while the *Abhidharma* puts into effect the third. The *Sūtra* presents theses, the *Vinaya* completes the sense of these theses, and the *Abhidharma* settles disputes raised by these theses. By hearing the *tripiṭaka*, new proclivities are set into motion in consciousness; by reflecting on its meaning, calm is cultivated, and by penetrating its meaning, insight is reached. Bodhisattvas reach omniscience in this way; disciples destroy their propensities to contaminants in this way. The *Sūtras* always tell where a sermon was given, deal with both conventional and highest truths, and introduce the concept of aggregates, dependent origination, and meditations. The *Abhidharma* systematically shows a path to liberation and gives definitions of each factor raised in the *Sūtras*. The *Vinaya* has as its aim the recognition of offences and their censure, confession, etc.

2.(1) The "support of that which can be known": "What can be known" are defiled and purified factors, the three essential natures. "Support" = cause = the store-house-consciousness. (2) "Characteristics of that which can be known" are the three essential natures. (3) "Entry into the characteristics of that which can be known" involves the method for understanding these characteristics, i.e., consciousness-only. (7) "Higher awareness involved in these practices" is meditational concentration.

3.Constructionfree knowledge is different for Bodhisattvas and disciples. For disciples it means not making fundamental mistakes, such as taking that which is impermanent for the permanent, the nonexistent for the existent, etc. For Bodhisattvas, it means not to have any conception whatever.

4.These ten subjects, if properly understood, deny neither *saṃsāra* nor *nirvāṇa*.

5.Considering the construction of what was not as existent is "superimposition". Denying the perfected is "denial". After realizing consciousness-only, Bodhisattvas cultivate the six perfections, then, in the ten stages, they cultivate them to an ultimate extent. They do this for innumerable lives. In this they differ from disciples, who liberate themselves after only three lives. During the concluding part of the cultivation of the stages they fulfill the three trainings completely. Finally, they reach *nirvāṇa*, in the sense of complete enlightenment.

## CHAPTER ONE

1."Support", that is, cause, because the storehouse-consciousness is the place of origin of all factors. How is the storehouse-consciousness the cause of *nirvāṇa*? Because there must be a state of defilement before there can be a state of purification.

2.In order to show that the storehouse-consciousness is also the place of origin of ethically neutral factors it is stated that the storehouse-consciousness has *all* the seeds.

3."All factors are settled in the storehouse-consciousness" means all factors function in the storehouse-consciousness. "Settles in all factors" means the storehouse-consciousness develops in all factors.

4.Two kinds of appropriations can be distinguished: the appropriation of material organs and the appropriation of signs, names, discriminations, and ensuing manifoldness which are based on the seeds of the storehouse-consciousness and which grow and increase there. The storehouse-consciousness collects also all the traces of visibles, sounds, smells, tastes, tangibles, and mentally cognizables, and on account of these traces the six consciousnesses relating to these objects of sense continue.

5.A visual consciousness arises dependent on a visible and the eye, together with the storehouse-consciousness.[575]

6.Whether it arises from two kinds of sensory consciousnesses, or from three, from four, or from five all together, the resulting mental consciousness-moment is always one. But innumerable discriminations and notions may follow from this mental consciousness. It is as one disturbance in water causing innumerable waves to arise, or one mirror reflecting innumerable images. But those who have realized ultimate truth see no basis for holding to different essential natures, see no appropriating consciousness, see no storehouse-consciousness, see no accumulation of traces, see no awarenesses, see no eye, see no visible, see no visual consciousnesses, or any other consciousnesses or their organs or objects, see no mind, see no factors, see no mental consciousness. Only those who do not observe any of these factors can be called skilled in ultimate truth.

The storehouse-consciousness could never be mistaken for a self for this reason, and also because innumerable transformations arise in and from it all the time, as waves arise in disturbed water.

7.Defilements in general are impossible without a temporarily existing defiled mind, thus antidotes to them would also be illogical in such a case. A mental consciousness cannot be considered the source of the basic defilement of assuming a self, since a mental consciousness may produce the antidotes to this conception. But this defiled mind may be entirely eliminated from the consciousness-series.

8.It is the traces of the storehouse-consciousness that cause all consciousness, and all phenomena in general, to arise.

15."Seed" is essentially a metaphor for a special power (*śaktiviśeṣa*) within the "consciousness-series" which leads to the series' own transformation, and which is the result of a trace. It is because of the arising of these special powers that the storehouse-consciousness is called the cause of defiled, good, and neutral factors, because the storehouse-consciousness constitutes the seeds.

Retribution is also to be explained as the development of seeds left by former good and bad decisions.

29-30.Vasubandhu states here that the storehouse-consciousness is also a series of factors, but each moment leaves a trace in the next. But these traces themselves imply a store-consciousness, for all theories of traces that dispense with a store-consciousness are untenable. Some maintain that the awarenesses taint each other mutually. No, Vasubandhu replies, because there is no contact between different awarenesses, because these awarenesses are serially momentary. Furthermore, each of them has its own special support, object, and mental attention, and manifest themselves in totally different aspects. The Dārṣṭāntikas maintain that the previous awareness-moment taints the succeeding factor, but, Vasubandhu replies, these two factors are never simultaneous. No previous factor taints the next. Two factors which are not simultaneous can of course not be in contact. Some say that because these awarenesses are all of the same kind, they can taint each other. No, Vasubandhu says, because, for instance, all sensory organs are of the same kind in being sentient materiality, but this does not mean that an auditory factor can taint a visual one.

Only a Vaibhāṣika could consistently maintain that an already past factor can influence a present one! That a factor arises with its retributional force already intact is also untenable, since the attachment due to a visual impression does not arise simultaneously with the visual awareness factor but rather after it. Vasubandhu shows, through similar arguments regarding the nonpossibility of causality between a past factor and a present one, how the storehouse-consciousness is necessary for any explanation of traces, defilement, and purification. It might be asked whether, within a strict theory of momentariness, the storehouse-consciousness can itself account for tainting or retribution, since it also consists of factors, and if a previous factor cannot taint the next, the same problem seems to remain. But, as Asaṅga has said in *Mahāyānasaṃgraha* I, 17, the awareness-moment and the storing of a seed in the storehouse-consciousness are simultaneous. The storehouse-consciousness being the series of traces, once the seed is deposited, the trace-series (also changing moment to moment) continues in the storehouse-consciousness. The arguments given here against the awarenesses tainting each other are still valid, because they cannot taint each other due to the lack of possibility of contact between them, because each of them has a separate support, object, and mental attention. Nor can two awarenesses of the same kind--even mental awarenesses--arise in the same moment, so contact between two mental awareness factors is also ruled out.

31.Elaboration of the argument: Awareness at birth is already afflicted with all of the defilements of its sphere of existence (realm of desire, say), yet the previous life may have been in the immaterial realm. In other words, the first awareness of a new life in the realm of desire is already tainted with the defilements arising from defilements of the past, even when the directly antecedent life was of the immaterial realm. For an entire life, then, these defilement-series had to remain latent, and this is possible only with the existence of a storehouse-consciousness.

32.When an awareness-factor antidotal to defilements arises, all the worldly awareness-factors, i.e., of the six awarenesses, are eliminated. Yet the seeds of their traces must remain, because the same kind of defilements may arise again at a future moment with all the associations they had in the past. The seeds of these defilement-traces cannot lie in the awareness-factor antidotal to defilements, since it is free of them by definition. Yet a defiled awareness-factor with the associations of past defilements may arise after such an awareness antidotal to the defilements, or at least after a series of awareness-factors antidotal to such defilements. Thus these traces, which by necessity imply a consciousness associated with them, can only be in the storehouse-consciousness during the duration of the series of awarenesses antidotal to the defilements.

33-34.There is no possibility of the arising of defilements linked with an awareness due to motivating dispositions without a store-consciousness.

35. In the embryo, the six functioning awarenesses could not appropriate the material organs, because each of these awarenesses

presupposes its material organ for its functioning. This shows that it cannot be awarenesses that appropriate all the material organs together. Furthermore, these awarenesses are extremely unstable, and disappear under one aspect after a moment, thus they could never be the awarenesses which gradually appropriate the material organs in an embryo.

38.Saying that the series of traces of one life cannot transfer into another life is tantamount to saying that the conditions for the defiled awareness which arises at birth with associations from a past life would be impossible.

40.Though a supramundane awareness destroys the series of other kinds of awarenesses, yet defiled awarenesses may arise again: without a storehouse-consciousness, there would be no seed for such awarenesses.

50.The consciousness which is in the attainment of cessation can only be the store-consciousness, as only it can be exempt of identifications and feelings. The awareness which enters into the attainment still has feelings and identifications, and as it ceases before the attainment of cessation arises, it cannot account for psychic continuity. Besides, any other consciousnesses (besides the storehouse-consciousness) must have an object of consciousness.[576]

52-54.The good roots in the attainment of cessation are not the good roots in the usual karmic sense, since the good roots which are themselves karmically good can arise only with contact with an object of consciousness, and there is no contact without feelings and identifications. Obviously, these good roots cannot be bad, either.

A mental awareness is also impossible without contact, thus is also impossible as the consciousness in the attainment of cessation. Besides, would it be good, bad, or karmically neutral? The problems with assuming its goodness or badness have already been discussed. If it is neutral, is it related to bodily postures, related to artistic activity, related to magical creations, or the result of retribution? (Only these four categories of mental awareness are accepted as karmically indeterminate by the *Vibhāṣā* and all who inspire themselves with the *Vibhāṣā*.) Obviously none of the three first alternatives is possible, since in the attainment of cessation there can be no object of awareness relating to any of these. The only category of neutral awarenesses which remains is that of "consciousnesses which are the result of retribution". But only the storehouse-consciousness can be neutral in this sense.[577]

55.Turns the argument around to state that a *nirvāṇa* without remainder of a noble one would be impossible in the case that an uninterrupted materiality-aggregate-series accounts for the attainment of cessation, since neither the materiality-series nor the awareness-series could in that case ever be severed.

57.Explains in detail the passage, underlining especially that an antidote is the cause of the severance of a defilement.

59.The storehouse-consciousness is the object of consciousness for the view of the self which is held by the defiled mind.

62.From the good further good arises, from the bad further bad. Thus if the storehouse-consciousness were not unobstructed-neutral there would never be an end to *saṃsāra*.

## CHAPTER TWO[578]

2."Perceptions of a body", i.e., the five sense-organs. "Possessor of the body", i.e., the defiled mind. "An enjoyer", i.e., the mental consciousness.

3.Defines the "constructed" as follows: "Whenever there is the appearance of a truth corresponding to an object which really does not exist."

The delimitation of strictly divided objects of sense is a function of the constructed only. For in ultimate truth these distinctions are empty. This can be directly perceived in meditational states. This also explains why the memory of a past event never fully corresponds to the past event, and why it always arises with different nuances. The existence of totally mentally constructed contents of consciousness, which have no reference to an existing external object, is also demonstrated by memories, since the object they supposedly refer to is long past, and thus cannot be their object of consciousness in the present.

9.Defilements arise precisely because the nonexistent has been taken for the existent, as, for example, a satisfaction anticipated which cannot be attained, or a view which does not correspond to any reality. Both of these phenomena would be impossible unless the mental consciousness had the capacity to construct another "reality" which is not identical with existent interdependent reality.

12.This is also why all six types of awareness are considered to be part of the mental sense-field. But in order to coordinate these awarenesses and give them a continuity, there must also be a storehouse-consciousness. There could be no liberation at all if there were no abandonment of perverted views, and an abandonment of perversions is not possible unless there have been perversions previously to be abandoned.

16.The constructed is that which is constructed by the mental consciousness only. Vasubandhu qualifies the constructed as having "the essential nature of having no essential nature".

20-22.On constructions of distractions in the Bodhisattva-path, Vasubandhu says the antidote to these is the *prajñāpāramitā*. All differentiations considered in such distractions are annihilated by the realization of emptiness, i.e., by constructionfree knowledge.

24.If the constructed essential nature is the manner in which the dependent appears, how can it be ascertained that it has no nature? If the dependent and the constructed were identical, even without a name, there would be attachment to a notion. But as a matter of fact, the notion of "pot" does not exist unless the name "pot" already exists. Now it may be said that the name "pot" is equivalent to the characteristic of a pot. But there is no one characteristic for a pot, while the name "pot" is single! This name and notion (the latter resting on characteristics seen, touched, etc.) cannot be the same. But it could be argued that it is the name which is dependent, and the object which is constructed. But in that case, through the dependent power of a name, the object would be constructed as one thing, and never as many. That is, one name would always equal one object, and one name could never be used for objects with different appearances. It may be argued that the characteristics of the name and the object are totally identical. But in that case, when there are different names for the same object, the objects themselves would have to be different, too. Furthermore, one name may have different meanings, and this is also impossible given the identity of name and notion. Ambiguity in language would be impossible if one name = one notion.

Two problems arise in distinguising the constructed from the dependent. The first: "How can a factor which does not exist be apprehended?" (The constructed does not exist, since the perfected is the dependent without the constructed, so how is it that it constantly appears?) Reply: It is as in the case of a magical illusion, where an elephant is seen where no elephant exists. The second: "How can there be unpurified defilements?" (Defilements are constructed. If the constructed does not exist, defilements cannot exist either.) Reply: It is as in the case of space, which is perfectly pure by nature, but which is said to be disturbed by fog, etc. When the fog disappears, it is said that space has been cleared, but actually space was totally clear from the beginning. It is the same for all factors. They are pure by nature, but when adventitious obstructions are removed, it is said that they are purified.

25.Why is it said that without the dependent the perfected cannot exist, and if the dependent and the perfected do not exist, there can be neither defilement nor purification? Because without defilements (the dependent) there cannot be purification (the perfected).[579]

27.The images are those given by Asaṅga in II, 26. If it is asked, "How can the nonexistent be a sense-object?", the answer is: Just as a magical creation is a sense-object. If it is asked, "If awareness and accompanying factors have no objects, how can they arise?", the answer is: Just as in a mirage, when there is no water, water is seen. If it is asked, "In the absence of objects, how can there be satisfying and frustrating experiences?", the answer is: Just as in a dream there may be satisfying and frustrating experiences. If it is asked, "In the absence of any object, how can good and bad actions produce a satisfying or frustrating karmic result?", the answer is: Just as a reflection is seen with various colors, when actually it does not have various colors. If it is asked, "How, in the absence of objects, can diverse awarenesses arise?", the answer is: Just as various flashes may arise in the play of shadows, which are seen even though they correspond to nothing. If it is asked, "How can there be practical dealings with a variety of things without any objects existing?", the answer is: Just as an echo is not an independent sound, and yet is heard as one, just so vain ways of speaking may be heard but yet correspond to nothing. If it is asked, "Without objects, how can there be images seen in meditation?', the answer is: Just as a moon is seen in the water when there is no moon there. If it is asked, "Without objects, how can Bodhisattvas take on births at will for the sake of sentient beings?", the answer is: Just as a transformation is not real in itself, but results in something perceived as different.

There is also another reason for these eight images. The image of a magical creation serves to contradict the idea that the six internal sense-fields exist. The image of the mirage serves to contradict the idea that an insentient universe exists. The image of the dream serves to contradict the idea that karmic results of bodily action truly exist. The image of an echo serves to contradict the idea that karmic results of vocal action truly exist. The image of the flash serves to contradict the idea that karmic results of nonmeditative mental actions exist. The image of the moon in the water serves to contradict the idea that the karmic results of meditative mental action exist. The image of a transformation serves to contradict the idea that karmic results due to hearing the *dharma* truly exist.

28-29.Vasubandhu states that the Buddha could make the statement quoted by Asaṅga because there is no difference between *nirvāṇa* and *saṃsāra*, and because "*nirvāṇa*" and "*saṃsāra*" are totally mentally constructed concepts. Without one, the other cannot be conceived. One can say that the constructed is the defiled and the perfected the purified, but the dependent partakes of both. It is just like a vein of gold in a gold mine, where the gold and dirt are mixed. The process of separating the gold from the dirt by fire is like the separation of the perfected from the defiled by constructionfree knowledge.

30.Because factors are nonexistent, there are no factors, but because factors appear with various aspects, there are not no factors. So, since there are neither factors nor the absence of factors, there is the nonduality of factor and absence of factor. On the one hand factors don't exist, i.e., in their essential nature; on the other hand they do exist because they are manifest. Thus they are both existent and nonexistent. The dependent partakes of both these aspects: thus one can say that it too is both existent and nonexistent. Factors do not exist as they appear, and yet they do not not exist, because of their appearance. Why is it said that factors have no essential nature? Because they don't exist of themselves, but arise dependent on conditions; because once they have ceased, they can never arise again; because they don't last but a moment--these three reasons are accepted in Hīnayāna also. But then there are the two other reasons accepted only by Mahāyāna: Because they are not such as they are believed to be, and because they do not exist with their constructed nature as expressed in words. Since factors have no essential nature it follows that they cannot arise at all. For that which has no essential nature cannot arise, and that which does not arise cannot cease, and that which neither arises nor ceases is calm from the beginning and liberated by nature. These various conclusions arise gradually, i.e., each following one dependent on the preceding one.

## CHAPTER THREE

1.Merit and knowledge are the two main aspects of the Bodhisattva-path. In the initial acquiring of merit, the strengths of the root-cause (enlightenment), of good friends, of mental attention and one's introduction to *dharma* are important. By "strength in mental attention", resolve in Mahāyāna is meant. Once this resolve has arisen, the increasing of the good roots in the Mahāyāna sense may begin.

3.First, an interest in Mahāyāna may be aroused through mental discourses with initial and subsequent discursive thought. But finally this interest will take the practitioner beyond mental discourse, and beyond mental application and discursive thought.

6.The mental attention of Bodhisattvas which is not shared by disciples and self-enlightened ones is: Regarding phenomena as magical creations, dreams, etc., factors neither arise nor perish, because they have no essential nature; thus there is no attachment to any factors, and no more adhesion to any names, words, or doctrines.

7.Four investigations and four right comprehensions enter into this process: First one investigates the fact that the essential natures and specifications attributed to names and factors are only designations, because there is no object which exists. Then, one knows rightly that all this is absolutely nonexistent. At the moment of discovery there is an investigation; once the investigation is completed, the fourfold right comprehension is attained. The four investigations are seeing that name is only a mental fiction (*prapañca*), seeing that "object" is only a mental fiction, seeing that the own-being attributed to name and object is mental fiction, seeing that the differentiations attributed to name and object are mental fictions. These result in the four comprehensions: knowing that name is a mental fiction, etc. Investigation means right sustained thought, right knowledge, the nonapprehension of any object.

10.The awareness of sameness towards all sentient beings means that one considers all sentient beings equal to oneself, and one desires the ending of all their frustrations as much as one desires the end of one's own frustrations.

13.Meditation, after the first state, means in itself already a knowledge without objects, and from this comes the knowledge of the selflessness of all factors. Vasubandhu states clearly that the store-consciousness is not only the cause of traces of defiled factors, but also of the factors of complete purification.

14.Supramundane knowledge is constructionfree knowledge. But the knowledge directly subsequent to this knowledge without constructions is again a knowledge of determinations. It cannot be called worldly, because it is impregnated by the impressions of constructionfree knowledge. It cannot be called supramundane, because it again uses concepts.

15-17.There is a total identity between the so-called apprehender (*ālambaka*) and that which is apprehended (*ālambya*). Everything is thus included in emptiness.

There is no possibility of any supporting object without something being constructed. Thus, when the nonbeing of objects is realized, it is realized that no constructible object exists, and so that not even the act of apprehension exists.

## 202. VASUBANDHU, *Triṃśikākārikā*

Summary by Stefan Anacker

This famous work expands classical Abhidharma consciousness-theories into the Yogācāra consciousness-theory and, more importantly, into the idea of three "essential natures" (*svabhāva*) in reality. Combined with 203.*Viṃśatikā* the pair is known as *Vijñaptimātratāsiddhi*. Both works have been edited and translated many times.

("ET" references here are to K.N. Chatterjee[580])

1.(ET27-29) "Self" and "factors" are both metaphors and develop in many different ways. All these take place in the transformation of consciousness only.

2.(ET30) The kinds of maturation of mind are the store-consciousness, the thinking consciousness (i.e., the mind), and the maturations (as six sensory consciousnesses). The store or maturational consciousness has all the "seeds" of experience.

3.(ET31-32) Though it is not fully conscious, it is always connected with subliminal contacts, mental attentions, feelings, identifications and volitions.

4.(ET46-49) Its feelings are equanimous: it is unobstructed and ethically neutral.

5.(ET49-50) Its devolvement takes place in a perfected being (i.e., the removal of consciousness from the hold of traces is possible).

Dependent on this store-consciousness, and having it as its object of consciousness, is mind, the ego-sense,

6.(ET53-54) which is always connected with the view of self, self-delusion and self-affection.

7.(ET55-57) But it is also totally removable, as it doesn't exist in the state of perfection, the cessation-trance, or in the supramundane path.

8.(ET59) The third transformation is to the six kinds of sense-objects, which can be either good, bad, or neutral.

9.(ET60) They are always connected with the pervasive things: contacts, mental attentions, feelings, identifications, and volitions. Sometimes they are connected with good factors associated with awareness, with defilements, and with afflictions.

11-14.(ET61-80) The enumeration of these accompanying mental factors is exactly the same as in 196.*Pañcaskandhaka*

15.(ET96) These consciousnesses may all arise together, or not.

16.(ET99) A mental consciousness follows on instances of other consciousnesses except in the nonidentifying consciousnesses, the attainment of cessation, in torpor, fainting, or in a state without awareness.

17.(ET102) This transformation of consciousness is a conceptual construction, and as such does not really exist--so everything is consciousness-only. (All discriminations are emptied in the perfected state.)

18.(ET105) The storehouse-consciousness is only all the seeds.

19.(ET107) Proclivities cause other maturations of seeds to occur, when the former maturation has been exhausted.

20.(ET116) Whatever is discriminated is just a constructed essential nature and doesn't really exist.

21.(ET117-118) The dependent is what underlies these constructions, and the perfected is the dependent's being separated from the constructed.

22.(ET119-121) Thus the dependent and the perfected are neither exactly the same nor different.

23.(ET122) The three kinds of essential nature (constructed, dependent, and perfected) are brought up only because of a three-fold absence of essential nature.

24.(ET123) The constructed is without essential nature through its character itself; the dependent is without essential nature because of its nonindependence; and the perfected *is* the absence of essential nature.

25.(ET123-125) The perfected is the highest; it is suchness, consciousness-only.

26.(ET126) As long as manifestation-only is not realized, the proclivities of dual apprehension won't come to an end.

27.(ET128) This is even true for the consciousness that "All is consciousness-only", because this also involves an awareness and an attempt to make something stand still.

28.(ET129) When consciousness does not apprehend any object of consciousness, it's in consciousness-only.

29.(ET130) But accordingly this state is also without awareness (since if no object is apprehended there is no consciousness, either): it is supramundane knowledge, revolution at the basis, and the ending of depravity.

30.(ET131) It is the *dharmadhātu* and the *dharmakāya* of the Buddha.

## 203. VASUBANDHU, *Viṃśatikā* and *Vṛtti* thereon

Summary by Stefan Anacker

"E" references are to the edition by Sylvain Levi.[581] "T" references are to the translation by Stefan Anacker.[582] There are numerous other editions and translations.

This is a famous work, but as often misinterpreted as not. It has been used as authoritative source for contradictory opinions none of which are in the text itself.

1.(E1-2; T161) All this is consciousness-only (*vijñaptimātra*), just as there may be the seeing of nonexistent nets of hair by someone suffering from an optical disorder.

2.(E1-2; T161-162) Objection: Why in that case do manifestations of certain kinds of visibles arise only in certain places, and not everywhere, and only at certain times, and not all the time? Why is it that these manifestations arise for all moment-series that are in the same place, and not just for some of them? The hair, etc., seen by someone suffering from an optical disorder does not perform the functions of hair, etc., whereas it is not the case that other hair, etc., don't perform them.

3.(E2; T162) Reply: It is as in a dream. In a dream, even without there being an external object, certain things appear only in certain places and times. And all ghosts will see the same things, even though others won't see them.

4.(E2; T162-163) An activity may be performed in a dream, such as when a man has a sexual dream and semen is released. In hellish exepriences all the criteria mentioned by the opponent are manifested, and yet there are no external objects corresponding to these experiences. Those having hellish experiences see hell-guardians, etc., though these guardians are really nonexistent.

Opponent: What do you mean, they're nonexistent?

Reply: Because they are illogical. The guardians would have been experiencing hellish frustrations themselves, if they were real.

Opponent: But there are animals in a heaven-state.

5.(E4-5; T164) Reply: Yes, but they are there experiencing retribution for past actions bringing pleasure to their environment, whereas the hell-guardians don't experience hellish frustration themselves.

6.(E4; T164) Opponent: Maybe special material elements arise, which are interpreted by the one in the hell-state as hell-guardians.

Reply: It is more logical merely to assume a transformation of awareness.

7.(E5; T164-165) Since traces arising from actions are different from the action's results and yet are not material, why do you say that the retributions resulting therefrom are something material and not merely awarenesses?

8.(E5; T165) Opponent: If there were no external objects of consciousness, sensings of color, etc., would not have been spoken of by the Buddha.

Reply: The Buddha spoke of these sensings only to instruct those being introduced to *dharma,* just as he spoke of magical beings (*upapādukasattva*),[583] which do not really exist.

9.(E5-6; T165-166) A "sensing of color" is where manifestation of something seemingly visible arises from its appropriate seed.

10.(E6; T166-167) Through consciousness-only one can understand the selflessness of the person, because it can be seen that there is not any one seer, etc. And through it one can also understand the selflessness of factors, because one understands that consciousness-only makes appearances of visibles, etc., arise, but that there is no experienced factor with the characteristic marks of visibles, etc.

Opponent: But if there isn't any factor in any way whatsoever, then consciousness-only also isn't.

Reply: But it's not that there isn't any factor in any way whatsoever. It's rather that the constructed "selves" of factors do not exist. Vasubandhu leaves the possibility open for an ineffable self (*anabhilāpyātman*), which is the scope of Buddhas. Besides, consciousness-only must itself be self-dissolving, otherwise consciousness-only would be a real object.

11.(E6-7; T167) An object can be neither one thing nor several things. If it were a unity, it would have to be like the composite whole constructed by the Vaiśeṣikas. It cannot be plural, either, because atoms can't be apprehended singly .

12.(E7; T167-168) An atom, in fact, can't be demonstrated either, because by the simultaneous contact with, say, six elements the atom comes to have six parts, and is thus no longer an atom. If it is maintained that the locus of each single atom is the locus of all six elements, then the molecule would be only one atom, because of the mutual exclusion of occupants of a locus.

Vaibhāṣika: It's only when atoms are in a molecular state that they can join together.

13.(E7; T168) Reply: But atoms can't join together to form molecules unless they have parts which contact each other. And if they have parts they're not atoms.

14.(E7-8; T168-169) Even the division of directional dimensions which is necessary to assuming the contact of atoms becomes impossible, because what has such divisions is no unity. It is useless to speak of molecular contact if individual atoms can't come into contact.

15.(E8; T169-170) The unity of objects is obviously absurd, because there could be no simultaneously grasping one thing and failing to grasp another, and there would be no reason for subtle water-creatures not to see things.

Since visibles cannot be reduced to atoms, they are not real sense-fields, and thus consciousness-only is demonstrated.

16.(E8-9; T171-172) There are three instruments of knowledge (perception, inference, appeal to reliable authority). Of these, perception is the most weighty. But since there is no external object there is no perception. When a perceptual awareness arises in the form of "I perceive it" the object is already not seen, because of momentariness. Thus that awareness is not a perception.

17.(E9; T171-172) Opponent: Nothing which hasn't been experienced by other awarenesses is remembered by the mental consciousness, so perception still occurs in this way.

Reply: The remembering of an experienced object isn't demonstrated either. Perceptions arise without an external object, and memories arise from these perceptions.

Opponent: If, even when one is awake, perception has objects which don't exist, as in a dream, then people would understand their nonexistence as obvious.

Reply: No, because people who are asleep don't know that the visual objects they see are only a dream. In the same way, people realize the nonexistence of external objects only upon gaining constructionfree supramundane knowledge, a clear, subsequently-attained knowledge.

18.(E9; T172-173) Opponent: How can there be any certainty in that case?

Reply: One awareness influences the next, and it is only the consistency of these influences which allow for "certainty".

Opponent: Why is there not an equal retribution for bad volitions in a dream?

Reply: Because awareness is affected by sleepiness in a dream.

19.(E9-10; T173) Opponent: In that case, there can be no bodily or vocal action.

Reply: Even death may result from the special perceptions of another, as when a seer destroys through his mental power.

20.(E10; T172-174) If this were not so, why would mental harm have been called a great offence?

21.(E10-11; T174) Opponent: Do those who know the awarenesses of others really know them, then?

Reply: Yes, they do, but their knowledge is not like their knowledge of an object. It is in fact the removal of the idea of "object" and "subject" which makes such empathic perception, and the knowledge of

Buddhas, possible (i.e., the appearance of an "object" always implies the presence of an appearance which is abandoned in these two kinds of awareness). Thus these "knowledges" are really "nonknowledges", because a specific object is not known within them.

22.(E11; T175) Consciousness-only cannot be discussed in all its aspects, because it is beyond the scope of awareness, and is known entirely only by Buddhas.

## 204. VASUBANDHU, *Trisvabhāvanirdeśa*

Summary by Stefan Anacker

This may be Vasubandhu's last work. It seems as if the conclusion of the *Viṃśatikā* and the *Triṃśikā* lead to the insights of this text. But it is nonetheless a startling one, inasmuch as the distinctions between the three natures are subtly undermined, whereas at the same time their successive development is maintained. It is a work fundamentally Śūnyavādin in inspiration, though the Ābhidharmika's interest in psychological processes is maintained.

"E" references are to the edition by Louis de la Vallée Poussin.[584] "T" references are to Stefan Anacker's translation.[585]

1-2.(E154; T291) That which appears is the dependent, "how it appears" is the constructed. The former develops subject to conditions; the latter is construction-only.

3.(E143; T291) The perfected is the constant absence of "how it appears" in that which appears.

4.(E154; T291) What appears? A construction of what was not. How does it appear? Through dualities. But nonduality is the perfected.

5.(E154; T291) What is a construction of what was not? An awareness by which the dependent becomes constructed, in such a way that the object which it constructs cannot be completely found in that way.

6.(E154; T291) This awareness may be either the store-consciousness or the functioning consciousness of seven kinds (i.e., the six sensory awareness and the mind or ego-sense).

7.(E154; T292) The store-consciousness is called "*citta*" because it becomes accumulated (*citatvāt*); functioning consciousnesses are "*citta*" because they evolve various (*citra*) aspects.

8.(E154; T292) The construction of what was not is of three kinds: maturational, having signs, and flashing appearances.

9.(E154; T292) Maturational is the storehouse-consciousness: the others are the functioning consciousnesses, because they always function as cognitions of "seen" and "seeing" ("heard" and "hearing", etc.).

10-11.(E154; T292) The constructed is perceived as existent, but it is nonbeing; thus it has both an existent and nonexistent character.

12.('E154; T292) The dependent exists, but not as it appears, so it also has an existent and nonexistent character.

13.(E155; T292) The perfected exists because of nonduality, and is only the nonbeing of "two", so it also has an existent and nonexistent character.

14.(E155; T292-293) Because the constructed always involves at least the duality of object apprehended and subject apprehender, and because this duality is nonexistent, the constructed consists of duality-and-unity.

15.(E155; T293) Because the dependent appears with there being a duality, but this duality is only construction, the dependent also consists of duality-and-unity.

16.(E155; T293) Because the perfected is the essential nature of the two beings, and because it is the one essential nature of nonduality, the perfected also consists of duality-and-unity.

17.(E155; T293) The afflictions-together[586] are constructed and dependent. Purification is the perfected.

18.(E155; T293) Because the constructed is the essential nature of a nonexistent duality, and because the perfected is the essential nature of the nonbeing of that duality, the constructed and the perfected are indistinguishable.

19.(E155; T293) Because the perfected is the essential nature of nonduality, and because the constructed is the essential nature of the nonbeing of duality, the perfected and the constructed are indistinguishable.

20.(E155; T293) Because the dependent is nonexistent as it appears, and the perfected is the essential nature of this nonexistence, the perfected and the dependent are indistinguishable.

21.(E155; T293-294) Because the perfected is the essential nature of a nonexistent duality, and the dependent has not essential nature as it appears, the dependent and the perfected are indistinguishable.

22.(E155; T293) But there is a difference in the occurrence of their arising.

23.(E155; T294) The constructed constitutes practical affairs, and that which engages in practical affairs is the dependent. The perfected is the severance of the dependent from practical affairs.

24.(E155; T293) First there is the dependent, and only then can construction-only, nonexistent duality, arise. Only after the processes of construction can their devolvement, i.e., the perfected, arise.

25.(E155; T294) Thus the perfected is said to both exist and not exist. (It exists inasmuch as it is the dependent without the constructed; it does not exist inasmuch as it is the nonbeing of any duality.)

26.(E156; T294) These three essential natures are ungraspable, because of the constructed's simple nonbeing, the dependent's nonbeing in the manner in which it appears, and the perfected being the essential nature of that nonbeing.

27.(E156; T294) A magical creation produced by *mantras* may appear like an elephant, but this is only an appearance, and there is no elephant there at all.

28.(E156; T294) The constructed is like the elephant, the dependent is like its appearance, and the perfected is like the nonbeing of the elephant there.

29.(E156; T294) The construction of what was not appears in the same way, because of duality. There is no duality there at all: there is only the appearance of duality there.

30.(E156; T294) The storehouse-consciousness is like the *mantra* which sets the magical creation going, suchness is like the pieces of wood the magician has in front of him and which he makes appear like an elephant, construction is like the elephant's appearance, and duality is like the elephant itself.[587]

31-32.(E156; T295) In a true penetration of this phenomenon, there is, simultaneously, the ascertainment of the constructed (which leads to its dissolving), the abandoning of the dependent as constructing, and the realization of the perfected. The ascertainment of the constructed is its nonapprehension, the abandonment of the dependent as constructing is its nonappearance, and the realization of the perfected is its signless apprehension.

33.(E156; T295) With the nonapprehension of duality the appearance of duality vanishes, and with this disappearance the perfected is understood.

34.(E156; T295) It's just as when the apprehension of the elephant, its appearance's disappearance, and the apprehension of the wood take place simultaneously.

35.(E156; T295) Because there are contradictory views in relation to the same moment, because of the intellect's seeing without a true object, because of the different development of the three kinds of knowledge (constructed, dependent, and perfected, cf. 22-25), and because, without all this, the attainment of liberation would come without effort,

36.(E156; T295) there is the nonapprehension of the knowable, because it is awareness-only, and through this nonapprehension of a knowable object there is the nonapprehension of awareness itself. (Without the apprehension of a knowable object there is no awareness either.[588])

37.(E156; T295) Through the nonapprehension of any duality, there is the apprehension of the *dharmadhātu*, and through this, the apprehension of psychic mastery.

38.(E157; T295-296) With psychic mastery attained, and through perfecting both one's own and others' aims, the enlightenment which has no higher is attained.

## 205. VASUBANDHU, *Bodhicittotpādasūtra(śāstra)*

Summary by Bhadanta Santi Bhiksu

This work, which as translated into Chinese by Kumārajīva in the fifth century (Nanjio 1218), is ascribed to Vasubandhu, though no one seems very convinced by the ascription. It has been reconstructed into Sanskrit by Bhadanta Santi Bhiksu,[589] with an English introduction from which we provide excerpts.

"This treatise contains twelve chapters...the first deals with "*adhyeṣaṇā*" after propounding the greatness of *Bodhicittotpāda*, an inspiration to cultivate *Bodhicitta*. The title of the second chapter is *Bodhicittotpāda*, in which a reference to the helpful means of

*Bodhicittotpāda* has been made. The third chapter is called *Praṇidhāna,* in which aspirations (*praṇidhāna*) for the attainment of Bodhi have been described. From chapters four to nine *Dāna, Śīla, Kṣānti, Vīrya, Dhyāna* and *Prajñāpāramitās* respectively have been expounded. In chapters ten and eleven, *Śūnyavāda* has been treated. The whole of the eleventh chapter appears to be some Sūtra...The first and the twelfth chapters also appear to be part of Sūtras..." (p. ii)

"Ācārya Vasubandhu...explains *Bodhicitta* with the help of similes and inferences: 'In the beginning when the great ocean manifests itself, it should be known that it is the store of all kinds of jewels, ordinary, medium and the best; valuable invaluable 'wishing stones' (*cintāmaṇi*) and the like; because these precious stones are found in the oceans. The *Cittotpāda* of Bodhisattva is also like this. When, in the beginning, *Bodhicitta* is born, then, it should be known that it is the store from which originate gods, men, *Śrāvakas, pratyekabuddhas,* Bodhisattvas, all *kuśaladharmas,* all moral actions, meditation and Prajñā (1, 5).'" (p. v)

"How to cultivate *Bodhicitta* and why? This question has been answered in the first, second and the third chapters. Just as this earth provides shelter to all creation irrespective of their good or bad nature, so also *Bodhicitta* provides refuge to all beings (1, 6). Just as the world of living beings knows no end, so also there is no end to the cultivation of *Bodhicitta* (I, 7).. .." (p. vii)

"How is *Bodhicitta* cultivated?...In the second chapter, (some basic) causes from which the *Bodhicitta* springs forth are enumerated. Here, it should be borne in mind that the meaning of *Bodhicittotpatti* according to the Mahāyāna school is simply the awakening of the dormant Bodhicitta. Except in the case of the few lowliest sinners, the *Bodhicitta* does remain latent in all beings in its unconscious state. When the *Bodhicitta* is awakened due to the cultivation of its causes and essentials, the individual no more remains an ordinary individual. He becomes Bodhisattva. What the Bodhisattva aspires [to] has been treated in the third chapter. Among his aspirations, the principal one is that he may sacrifice his wealth and body for the sake of other beings..." (p. viii)

"*Bodhi* is attained through six *pāramitās*. The Ācārya has described the *pāramitā* in a very graphic manner. First the Bodhisattva practises the *pāramitā* of *dāna* and gives up every thing that belongs to him. This is *sarvadāna,* sacrifice...(4.6). Sarvadāna implies that a donor believes that there is nothing which he cannot give, and such a *dāna* only is the perfection of *dāna-pāramitā...*" (p. ix)

"While describing the *pāramitā* of conduct (*śīlapāramitā*) it has been remarked that the conduct of a Bodhisatva is extra-ordinary conduct. It can neither be compared with the conduct of an *Arhat* nor with that of a *Pratyekabuddha.* On account of its extra-ordinary nature, the practice of such a conduct is called the practice of good (*kuśala* or *sādhu*) conduct; because by means of such a conduct it makes all the beings gainers (5.8)." (p. ix)

"So far about the development of conduct of a Bodhisattva. The preliminary conduct is a fear of even the most insignificant sin (5.1). The practice for the conduct of a Bodhisattva is for the well-being of all living beings. He never aspires as a fruit of the practice of conduct to live himself in a better world (5.10). While describing the *pāramitā* of forgiveness, the unparalleled ideal of a Bodhisattva, it has been said that if anybody indulges in abuses or violence he should be forgiven as a madman. For self-consolation it should be taken as the result of one's actions in a previous birth (6.67). Describing the *pāramitā* of *vīrya*, it has been said that the preliminary stage of *vīrya* of a Bodhisattva is that which never retreats from its aim. But in its developed form, *vīrya* is boundless. Very mysterious things have been told about the *pāramitā* of meditation. Only Yogins can understand them. But meditation has a use for the common beings also. While practising meditation a Bodhisattva wandering in the world is not attached to it. Thus by meditation his mind becomes calm and steady. (8.9) Even this much good resulting from meditation is not negligible. For a mystic, meditation is the means for attaining all kinds of divine powers. From it are produced 'divine ear' and 'divine eye', with which we can hear sounds far off and also can perceive things far off. By the divine powers we can also know the thoughts in others' minds, recollect past lives and can perform many more wonders (8.10)." (pp. ix-x)

## SAṄGHABHADRA

In the introductory comments on Vasubandhu (p. 339 above) the name of Vasubandhu's rival Saṅghabhadra appears. The account given there provides Stefan Anacker's reconstruction of Vasubandhu's life from the traditional stories reported by Hsüang-tsang, Paramārtha and

Bu-ston. In fact, however, the three accounts differ in many respects. Collett Cox remarks: "All three versions agree that Saṅghabhadra was a native of Kāśmīra while Vasubandhu was not, that both Vasubandhu and Saṅghabhadra were knowledgeable in Abhidharma, that Vasubandhu composed a work, which was, at least in part, critical of the *Vibhāṣā*, and that Saṅghabhadra wrote a refutation of Vasubandhu's work."[590]

"Though the primary object of Saṅghabhadra's criticism in the **Nyāyānusāra* is Vasubandhu's *Abhidharmakośabhāṣya*, others such as the Dārṣṭāntika or Sautrāntika master, Sthavira, figure significantly among his opponents. Thus, the **Nyāyānusāra* is not simply a refutation of the *Abhidharmakośabhāṣya*, but rather is a broad-based attempt to defend Kāśmīra Sarvāstivāda-Vaibhāṣika doctrine against the objections of all opponents. Though Saṅghabhadra's interpretations are generally consistent with the Sarvāstivāda-Vaibhāṣika positions in response to them, Saṅghabhadra's treatment of the conditioned forces dissociated from thought offers several key examples of his innovations...In methods of argumentation also, Saṅghabhadra's **Nyāyānusāra*, though influenced by the *Abhidharmakośabhāṣya*, represents a distinct advance over previous Abhidharma texts. For these reasons, Saṅghabhadra's works mark a turning point in the development of Sarvāstivāda-Vaibhāṣika thought; as a result, Saṅghabhadra is credited as the inaugurator of the so-called 'neo-Vaibhāṣika' period."[591]

## 206.SAṄGHABHADRA, Nyāyānusāra

This vast work is not available in Sanskrit or Tibetan. Only Hsüang-tsang's translation is extant. Some of the original Sanskrit has been preserved in citations in Sthiramati's, Pūrṇavardhana's and Yaśomitra's commentaries and in Kamalaśīla's *Tattvasaṃgrahapañjikā*. The title *Nyāyānusāra is a reconstruction. The work is three times the length of Vasubandhu's *Abhidharmakośabhāṣya*.

There is no complete translation into any Western language. It has been translated into Japanese by Chizan Anakuma in Kik. Bidombu, volumes 27-30. Louis de la Vallée Poussin has rendered a few passages into French, and some other passages have been translated into English by various writers (indicated in footnotes to certain sections below). The most extensive inroads to date on this material comes in Collett Cox's dissertation.[592]

The work is an extended commentary on and critique of 174.Vasubandhu's *Abhidharmakośabhāṣya.* The summary provided here has been numbered in keeping with our summary of the *Kośa* earlier in this Volume, the numbers of which correspond to those of Vasubandhu's *sūtras.* Only the first two Chapters are summarized here.

"E" references are to the Chinese text (T. 1562), translated by Hsüan-tsang. "C" references are to the Cox translation cited above.

Summary by Collett Cox

## CHAPTER ONE

1.(E329a) Those who write treatises inevitably belong to a particular school. Vasubandhu begins his treatise with praises of the Buddha as the founder of his school, and thereby distinguishes him from false teachers.

2.(E329a) "Abhidharma" means pure wisdom, that is, noncontaminating investigation of factors. When one has seen the characteristics of all factors through this pure wisdom, one is no longer deluded. Abhidharma also includes those noncontaminating awarenesses, accompanying mental factors, and dissociated factors that occur with wisdom.

3.(E329c) Apart from this investigation of factors there is no method of extinguishing defilements through which frustration is produced and the world is led through the cycle of rebirth. Despite Vasubandhu's skepticism, the Abhidharma definitely represents the teaching of the Buddha himself. Granted, sectarian differences are evident in the Abhidharma collections belonging to different schools, but this is true also of the collection of discourses, which no Buddhist would deny is the teaching of the Buddha.

4-6.(E330c) In general, factors are of two types: those that are contaminating and those that are noncontaminating. All conditioned factors, with the exception of those classified under the fourth noble truth of the path, are contaminating because defilements adhere to them. These defilements, such as the view of belief in the existence of self, are "contaminating" because they cause defiled states of mind to flow forth. These contaminating and conditioned factors are also referred to as the five grasping aggregates. Quotations from scripture and arguments can be offered (1) to establish the character of factors that are contaminating or noncontaminating, and (2) to disprove the Dārṣṭāntika thesis that insentient material form and the body of a practitioner of the noble path are both noncontaminating.

Noncontaminating factors include those classified under the truth of the path, that is, the five aggregates that are without defilements as well as the three unconditioned factors. These three are (1) space, whose nature is nonobstruction because it neither obstructs material form nor is obstructed by it; (2) cessation calculatedly sought through contemplation of the four noble truths, the nature of which is disjunction from a defilement attained through a particular type of wisdom, each defilement to be eradicated being abandoned through a separate cessation; (3) cessation uncalculatedly sought through the obstruction of the arising of future factors by which they remain forever in the future. For example, when occupied with one sense object, perceptual consciousness of other present sense objects is obstructed; those sense objects pass away without their corresponding perceptual consciousness ever arising.

7.(E332c) Conditioned factors are defined as the five aggregates of material form, feeling, identification, traces, and perceptual consciousness. They are also defined as the time periods, the foundations of discourse, and so on. These factors are conditioned because they arise due to a collocation of conditions. Future factors that have not yet arisen, and even those that will not arise, can still be said to be conditioned because they are of the same category as those present or past factors that have already arisen. Factors can also be classified in terms of twelve sense bases, including the six sense organs and their six corresponding objects, or in terms of eighteen elements, including the six sense organs, the six objects, and their six corresponding types of perceptual consciousness.

8.(E333a) Contaminating conditioned factors are defined as the five grasping aggregates because they are both produced by grasping and produce grasping. The contaminating factors are also defined as frustration, the origin of frustration, and so on.

9.(E333b) The material aggregate includes the five externally directed sense-organs, their five respective objects, and unmanifest form. This unmanifest form, though classified within the material aggregate, is perceived only by the mind and, therefore, is included in the mental sense basis. The five externally directed sense-organs are composed of a subtle type of matter.

10. (E333c) Material form, the object of the visual sense-organ, is of two varieties--color and shape--with twelve varieties of color and eight of shape. Though both color and shape can be observed in most varieties of material form, this does not mean that one entity has two essential natures; rather, both color and shape have material form as their essential nature.

Vasubandhu in the *Abhidharmakośa* enumerates eight varieties of sound, including pleasant and unpleasant varieties of the following four types: those that are caused by the four great elements that are either appropriated by sentient beings or unappropriated, and those that are indicative of sentient beings or not. However, the first two categories of the appropriated and unappropriated encompass all varieties of sound.

There are six varieties of flavors and four varieties of odors.

Tangibles are of eleven varieties: the four great elements and seven derivative forms of matter including smoothness, roughness, heaviness, lightness, cold, hunger, and thirst. Each of these derivative types of material form results from a predominance of one of the four fundamental material elements.

11. (E335a) Vasubandhu defines unmanifest form as that series of good or bad factors which is dependent upon the four great elements, found even in those beings whose successive thoughts are of a different moral quality, or in those who are temporarily without thought. However, unmanifest form should not be defined as a series. It is that material form which lacks resistance, which is morally determined as good or bad, and is found even in thoughts of differing moral quality, or in those who have passed beyond thought.

12. (E335c) Space is not one of the four great material elements because it is singular and permanent, has no capability of injuring or benefiting, and has no effect. The four great elements are never separated from one another; the presence of each can be inferred from the observation of their respective activities of supporting, cohesion, ripening, and expansion. Apart from these activities, the four fundamental material elements have solidity, liquidity, heat, and motion respectively as their essential nature.

13. (E336c) Earth, water, and fire, as popularly conceived, are

actually simply visible material form, that is, the object of visual perception, and not the great elements themselves. Wind, however, as popularly conceived is, at times, merely the visual object, and, at times, the great element itself. The world at large recognizes only those things that exist as nominally true and not things, such as the four great elements, that exist as actual entities. Therefore, common parlance does not reflect the true analysis of the composition of experience.

14a-b.(E337b) These five externally directed sense-organs and their corresponding objects, which are included in the material aggregate, also constitute ten of the twelve sense spheres and ten of the eighteen elements. The material aggregate is defined as that which can be damaged, is a cause of feelings of frustration, is liable to alteration, and offers physical resistance.

Objection: In that case a single atom, of which all material form is composed, would not be material because it, by itself, offers no resistance.

Answer: Atoms are always found in an aggregate, which can then offer resistance. Others suggest that even a single atom, though incapable of producing consciousness alone, still offers resistance. Even though past and future material form, as well as form that will not ever arise, offer no resistance, they can still be referred to as "material form" because they are of the same category as present material form.

Objection: How can unmanifest form offer resistance, and if it cannot, why is it classified as material form?

Answer: It does not offer resistance, but it is still classified as material form. Some have suggested that unmanifest form is given the name "material form" because it arises from manifest material form, specifically, corporeal and verbal actions, which offer resistance. This explanation is unacceptable, because in that case those types of unmanifest material form that arise in accordance with mental action and are not produced from manifest material form would not be classified as material form. We propose that unmanifest material form is classified as "material form" because its locus, or the four great elements upon which it is based, offer resistance.

Objection: Unmanifest form should not be classified as "material" form simply because its locus is material form. In that case, since the loci of the five externally directed types of perceptual consciousness are the material sense organs, perceptual consciousness also should be material.

Answer: Perceptual consciousness cannot be used as a counterexample because there are types of perceptual consciousness, specifically, ordinary mental perceptual consciousness and mental perceptual consciousness in dreams and in the immaterial realm, that do not have a material sense organ as their locus. By contrast, there is no unmanifest material form not based on the four great elements.

14c-15.(E338c) The feeling aggregate is experience produced through sensory contact. The three kinds of feelings (satisfying, frustrating and neutral) each exist as distinct, actual entities. Feelings can also be classified as of two types: (1) appropriative feeling, which is able to experience the object upon which it is supported, and (2) feeling proper, which is able to experience the sense contact to which it conforms. The second variety is described as feeling "proper" because this function of experiencing contact is not shared by any other mental concomitant and therefore is easier to recognize. Feelings can also be divided into six varieties depending upon the type of sense contact through which they are produced.

The conceptual identification aggregate is the grasping of marks, that is, the grasping of all supporting objects according to their particular characteristics. Like feelings, identifications are of either three or six varieties.

The conditioning aggregate includes all conditioning factors--those associated with thought and those dissociated from both thought and material form--except for those included in the other four aggregates.

Objection (by the Dārṣṭāntika teacher Śrīlāta): All conditioning factors are merely varieties of thinking.

Answer: This interpretation is not justified. The aggregate of conditioning factors is often represented by thinking because thinking is the essence of action, is predominant in the development of the effects of action, and therefore is the primary factor among the conditioning aggregates. However, the conditioning aggregate as a whole karmically prepares other conditioned and contaminating factors.

Śrīlāta: "Karmically developing conditioning factors" means that thought creates conditioning factors that were originally nonexistent.

Answer: We Abhidharma masters maintain that factors in their essential nature exist as actual entities. Only nominal entities can be said to exist after being originally nonexistent. "Developing" means projecting the production of an effect: though the effect already exists in its essential nature as an actual entity, its activity can be projected and then produced.

These three aggregates of feelings, identifications and conditioning factors, together with unmanifest material form and the three unconditioned factors, constitute the sense basis of factors and the realm of factors.

16. (E342a) The aggregate of perceptual consciousness is apprehension of the general characteristic of a perceptual object. For example, visual perceptual consciousness, though presented with varieties of material form, grasps only visible color-shape, and as such does not apprehend its specific characteristics. Each of the six types of perceptual consciousness grasps only its particular kinds of objects.

Within the classification according to sense bases, these aggregates of perceptual consciousness correspond to the mental sense-basis, and within the classification according to the elements, to the seven elements consisting of the six varieties of perceptual consciousness and the mind. The mind element is that variety of perceptual consciousness which is immediately past and which constitutes the locus of the arising of the present moment of perceptual consciousness.

17. (E342b) The arising of any variety of perceptual consciousness depends upon both a supporting object and a locus; for example, in the case of visual perceptual consciousness, the supporting object is a colored shape and the basis is the visual sense-organ. Though the mental element is, in its nature, simply one of the six varieties of perceptual consciousness that has just become past, it is included as a separate element in the classification of eighteen elements in order to provide a locus for present mental perceptual consciousness. This past consciousness acts as the directly antecedent condition for the arising of present perceptual consciousness.

18. (E342c) In these systems of classification, the aggregates include all conditioned factors; the grasping aggregates include all contaminating and unconditioned factors; and the sense bases and elements include all factors. But all factors can also be included in three components, one taken from each of the three classification systems: the material form aggregate, the mental sense basis, and the factor element. The inclusion of a particular factor in any category is determined by a similarity of essential nature, and not by the presence

of certain conditions. Therefore, the classifications apply regardless of the temporal status of a particular factor.

19. (E343b) Though such factors as the eyes, ears, and so on occur in pairs, they have the nature of one element because their category, the sense-content upon which they depend, and the perceptual consciousness that they produce are the same. Though Vasubandhu suggests that they occur in pairs for the sake of beauty, what the world considers beautiful actually has functional superiority.

20. (E343b) Each of the five aggregates is a group or an agglomeration of all varieties of material form, feelings, and so on. A sense basis is an entrance because it prepares a way for the arrival of awareness and accompanying mental factors. An element is a genus (*gotra*). Though these elements also are foundations from which thought and thought concomitants are produced, in order to avoid confusion with the sense bases it is best to understand the elements as a category of those factors having the same nature.

Objection: If aggregates are groups they cannot, in themselves, exist as actual entities because groups exist only nominally.

Answer: The genitive determinative compound defining the aggregates, sense bases, and elements in the verse indicates that they are to be identified with the entity that serves as the locus of the group and so on, and not with the group itself; the group has no reality apart from its locus. Similarly, as the scriptures state, there is no reality of self apart from the aggregates of which it is composed. Though actually unlimited, the aggregates are designated as five as an aid to disciples in their practice. The fact that each of the five aggregates contains many components of the same general nature precludes the belief in the existence of a composite entity, equivalent to the aggregate as a whole. The term "aggregate" can also be used to refer to each factor as it arises, or to several instances of a factor of a given category in different states, for example in the future, present, or past.

These three classification systems of aggregates, sense bases, and elements are appropriate to disciples in each of the three levels of delusion, three levels of ability, and three levels of preference for a particular style of teaching.

Śrīlāta: The classification of factors into aggregates is presented in order to clarify the makeup of composite entities. The classification into sense bases indicates the distinction between the object and the organ, and the classification into elements indicates the distinctions among the various types of perceptual consciousness according to the organ and object by which they are produced.

Response: This interpretation leads to confusion in the case of the classification of the sense bases. Since all factors can be the object of mental perceptual consciousness, and therefore, according to your interpretation, should be included in the realm of actors, the other eleven categories are superfluous.

Śrīlāta: Indeed, all factors can be included in the one category of the realm of factors, the objects of mental perceptual consciousness; the other eleven sense bases represent simply varieties within that one category.

Answer: This interpretation contradicts the scripture, which clearly states that there are twelve distinct sense bases. Further, though all factors can be the object of mental perceptual consciousness, these twelve sense bases are established in order to clearly distinguish, by mutual contrast, the activity of the organ bases from that of their corresponding objects, and the activities of the five externally directed organs and their corresponding objects from one another. For example, the visual sense organ perceives only visible material form, and though visible material form is also a possible object for mental perceptual consciousness, it is not an object for any of the other four externally directed types of perceptual consciousness.

22.(E345a) Unconditioned factors cannot be included in any one of the aggregates, nor do they constitute their own sixth aggregate since there are no varieties of unconditioned factors which can then be grouped together by a similarity of essential nature to form an aggregate. Further unconditioned factors are not the basis of mistaken views like the contaminating grasping aggregates, nor are they expedient means for eradicating defilements like the uncontaminating aggregates. Others suggest that, because the unconditioned factors are equivalent to the inactivity of the aggregates, they cannot themselves be aggregates. The inactivity of the aggregates results from the termination of the false imagination of self because the aggregates, in every case, serve as the basis for the imagination of self. The sense bases and elements, however, do not necessarily give rise to the idea of self. Therefore, the unconditioned factors can be included within the factor basis of the twelve sense bases, or the factor element of the eighteen elements.

The order of the five aggregates is determined according to a number of different criteria: for example, their relative grossness; their progression in the production of defilement; by analogy with the example of a bowl, food, and so on; by their predominance in the three realms; or by the order in which they operate in one's progress along the path.

23.(E345c) The order in which the six sense organs are listed--the eyes, ears, nose, tongue, body, and mind--can be explained by the following reasoning. The operation of the first five sense organs occurs only with regard to a given present object and necessarily arises before the operation of the mind with regard to the same object. Within these five, the first two, the eyes and ears, function at a distance because the object is not directly contacted; further, the eyes function at a greater distance than the ears. The next three, the nose, tongue, and body, are arranged in the order of the clarity of their functioning. Finally, the order of all six sense organs is determined by their position on the body, from the eyes at the top to the major portion of the body below; the mind is not located in any one place.

Objection: If the five externally directed organs function first with regard to a given external object, and only then mental perceptual consciousness arises with regard to the same object, how is grasping an external object possible in a dream?

Answer: Several explanations of perception in a dream can be offered. For example, some suggest that one remembers, through mental perceptual consciousness, objects perceived previously by the five externally directed types of perceptual consciousness. Others suggest that mental perceptual consciousness in a dream actually perceives material form or other objects. In general, the five externally directed organs precede the sixth, mental organ in their operation because the perceptual consciousness they and their corresponding object produce becomes the equivalent contiguous condition, or the mental organ, for the arising of the succeeding mental perceptual consciousness. However, there are certain exceptions: for example, perception in dreaming and meditation.

24.(E346b) Though ten of the twelve sense bases have the nature of material form and all sense bases may be objects of mental perceptual consciousness, they are differentiated in order to enable disciples to distinguish their characteristics, that is, to distinguish those that *are* contents and those that are organs, i.e., *have* contents. The visible material sense basis is predominant among all varieties of material form because it is visible and has resistance. Therefore, the name of the general category of material form, "*rūpa*", is also given to this subcategory, visible material form. Though the sense basis of factors includes many different types of factors, including the factor of cessation through realization or *nirvāṇa,* their character as factors enables them to be placed in the same category.

25-27.(E346c) Other phenomena referred to as aggregates, sense bases, or elements are to be included in the appropriate categories among the aggregate, sense basis, or element classifications according to their own specific characteristic. For example, the scripture mentions the 80,000 factor aggregates of which the Buddha's teaching is composed. If the essential nature of the teaching is considered to be speech, these factor aggregates should be included in the aggregate of material form. If, however, the essential nature of the teaching is considered to be name, they should be included in the dispositions aggregate. ("Name" (*nāma*) is classed as a force dissociated from both thought and material form, which force is included within the dispositions aggregate.) These 80,000 factor aggregates, have been interpreted in various ways, as the content of a specific text by that name, or as the discourse on each of the topics of the teachng, but actually they are antidotes to the 80,000 types of defiled behavior.

28.(E347a.23) One other list of elements mentioned in the scripture includes the six elements of earth, water, fire, wind, space, and perceptual consciousness. This list indicates those components that serve as the basis of one lifetime from the moment of conception to death.

Śrīlāta: The space element referred to here is identical with the unconditioned factor, space.

Answer: This opinion is to be rejected. The space element in this list of six is to be included in the material form aggregate and is not an unconditioned factor. The unconditioned factor, space, and the space aggregate both exist as distinct actual entities. The perceptual consciousness element referred to in this list of six, which serves as the basis of the lifetime of sentient beings, includes only contaminating perceptual consciousness.

29-30a. (E348a) The eighteen elements mentioned previously are to be analysed from various perspectives, such as their visibility, resistance, moral quality or the realms to which they are connected. Resistance can be of three kinds: (1) resistance of a sense-organ, or of awareness or mental concomitants, or of any other factor having a content with regard to that content. (2) Resistance of awareness and mental concomitants with regard to their own supporting objects. A "content" is that place where the sense-organ carries out its function, while the supporting object is that which is grasped by awareness and mental factors, allowing them to arise. This contact between the sense-organ, awareness or awareness concomitants and the content or supporting object is referred to as "resistance" because the sense organs, awareness and so on cannot operate with regard to anything else. (3) Resistance by obstruction, or the prevention of the arising of one mass of material form by another in a single place. The ten material elements have this type of resistance.

Among these ten material elements eight, excluding visible matter and sound, are morally neutral, that is, they cannot be determined as good or bad because their nature is unclear. "Good" refers to that which counteracts evil or leads to wisdom. Visible matter includes bodily gestures and sound includes speech, both of which may also be morally good or bad depending upon whether they are associated with a good or bad moment of thought. The seven mental elements are good or bad depending upon whether they are associated with the bad dispositions of greed, hatred, delusion and so on, or the good dispositions of absence of greed and so on. Otherwise, they are neutral. The element of factors, that is, the object of mental perceptual consciousness, is good or bad depending upon whether or not it is associated with or arises from good or bad dispositions. Uncalculated cessation, included in the factor element, is also good. All other factors are neutral.

Objection: The group of the five externally directed types of perceptual consciousness are nonconceptual and only perceive their object for one moment. Therefore, they must be morally neutral.

Answer: Even if they were nonconceptual they would not necessarily be morally neutral. For example, concentrated states of mental perceptual consciousness are nonconceptual and yet good. In any case, these five externally directed types of perceptual consciousness are associated with initial and sustained thought. Among the three varieties of conceptual awareness (see 1.33), these five types of perceptual consciousness involve construction in its essential nature alone. Finally, even if they only grasp the general characteristic of their object for one moment, they can still be associated with good or bad associated mental factors for that moment, and therefore, can be good or bad.

30b-31b.(E349b) Concerning the realm to which these eighteen elements are connected, all eighteen are connected to the realm of desire; fourteen, the eighteen minus odor and flavor and their corresponding perceptual consciousnesses, are connected to the material realm. These four are absent because they have no function other than to stimulate desire for food, and beings in the material realm have abandoned desire for food. However, the olfactory and gustatory organs are found in the material realm because they also serve the functions of beautifying the body and of speech.

In the immaterial realm only the last three elements including the mind element, mental awareness element, and their objects, the factors, occur because beings there have abandoned desire for material form. Therefore, the five external objects and the five externally directed sense-organs, together with their corresponding types of perceptual consciousness, are absent.

31c-d.(E349c) The three (mind, mental awareness, and factor elements) are noncontaminating if they pertain to the fourth noble truth of the path or are associated with the three unconditioned factors; otherwise, they are contaminating.

32.(E350a) Concerning the association of these eighteen elements with initial and sustained thought, the five externally directed types of perceptual consciousness are always associated with both initial and sustained thought because these types of perceptual consciousness arise only in regions where both occur, that is, the realm of desire and the first trance state in the material realm. The mental awareness element, the mind element, and that part of the factor element associated with thought, except for initial and sustained thought themselves, are associated with both initial and sustained thought in the realm of desire and the first trance state in the material realm. They are associated with initial thought alone in the interval between the first and second trance states, and with neither in the higher trance states. Initial and sustained thought are always associated with one another in the realm of desire and the first trance state of the material realm.

33.(E350b) Even though the five externally directed types of perceptual consciousness are associated with initial and sustained thought, they are said to be nonconceptual because they do not involve conceptual construction through discrimination or through recollection. Rather, they involve only conceptual construction in its essential nature, which is merely initial thought. Mental perceptual consciousness involves all three types of conceptual construction. Construction through discrimination refers to distracted wisdom associated with mental perceptual consciousness that discriminates the supporting object in this way or that. It does not occur in states of concentration. Construction through recollection refers to memory associated with distracted or concentrated mental perceptual consciousness. Conceptual construction occurs only in the immediate apprehension of an object and not before or after an object has been apprehended.

34. (E350b) Concerning whether or not these eighteen elements are "appropriated", i.e., have supporting objects, the six elements of perceptual consciousness, the mind element, and those mental concomitants included within the factor element have supporting objects.

Śrīlāta: Neither the supporting object nor the locus that give rise to the five externally directed types of perceptual consciousness exist, in themselves, as actual entities. The atoms of which they are composed only carry out their function as composite objects, not individually, and composite objects only exist as notional designations. Therefore, the sense bases, which are composite objects, exist only as nominal designations; the elements alone exist as actual entities.

Answer: The five types of perceptual consciousness do indeed have an object that exists as an actual entity; that is precisely the individual atoms collected together. Individual atoms are visible to the visual sense organ, but they cannot be cognized individually. In any case, atoms are always found collected together, and as such are both visible and capable of being cognized. Further, since the five types of externally directed perceptual consciousness lack conceptual constructions they cannot take a fully sufficient set of causal conditions as their content. A set of conditions is not a distinct factor, and therefore cannot be the content of sensory contact. It is grasped only by conceptual constructions, and hence is the object of mental perceptual consciousness alone. Finally, since no distinction in terms of essential nature can be drawn between those factors classified among the elements and those classified among the sense bases, one cannot consistently maintain that the sense bases are mere composite objects, and hence nominal, while the elements are actual entities.

The externally directed sense organs are appropriated if presently functioning and not if past or future. The four external objects, excluding sound, are appropriated if presently perceived, and not if past or future, or if present and not perceived. Some claim that presently perceived sound should also be appropriated. The term "appropriated" refers to those material elements that are taken by awareness and accompanying mental factors as their support, and to which awareness and accompanying factors conform in terms of benefit and injury.

35.(E352b) Śrīlāta: The tangible element consists only of the great elements because this so-called derivative material form is merely a distinctive arrangement of these four great elements. Since the eye is able to recognize smoothness and so on, derivative material form does not exist apart from the four great elements.

Answer: How does this prove that these types of derivative material form are not different from the great material elements? The eye does not perceive the great elements themselves, but only the derivative material form called "*rūpa*". In any case, since the activities of smoothness and so on belonging to derivative material form are recognized as distinct from the activities hardness and so on belonging to the four great elements, derivative material form and the four great elements must be admitted to exist separately. Further, even if we admit that smoothness is recognized through a particular arrangement of great elements, this smoothness must have a locus, and that locus is none other than the derivative material form, smoothness. Like all types of perceptual consciousness, tactile perceptual consciousness depends upon an actually existent entity and not a nominal designation. Smoothness must therefore be actually real and not nominal.

Śrīlāta: Further, lightness and heaviness, two other varieties of derivative material form, are established simply by mutual comparison and do not exist as actual entities.

Answer: Though one thing may be light or heavy with respect to two different things, it is not light and heavy with regard to the same thing. Therefore, though the description of a thing may vary relative to other things, its nature as light or heavy is without alteration. Varying description does not constitute a reason for the unreality of the quality described.

Śrīlāta: Coldness, another type of derivative form, is simply a small degree of or the absence of the fundamental element fire.

Answer: This is not acceptable because injury resulting from cold is alleviated by increasing the degree of heat. If cold were merely a small degree of heat, it would make sense to alleviate a small burn with more heat. Also, the mere absence of heat is a form of nonexistence, and nonexistence cannot be cognized and cannot have activity such as that exerted by cold. Further, since the fire element, as one of the four fundamental elements, is present in all material form, nothing could become cold; the existence and nonexistence of the same quality, in this case heat, cannot be simultaneously maintained in the same entity.

Śrīlāta: Hunger and thirst have the mental factor called "interest" as their nature and therefore do not exist as actual entities.

Answer: Interest is one of the ten concomitants of awareness always present in moments of thought, and yet hunger and thirst are not always present. Therefore, hunger and thirst must be distinct from interest.

Śrīlāta: All types of derivative form are nothing other than the four great elements.

Answer: In that case, all material sensory objects would have the same characteristics of hardness and so on that define the four great elements, and the sensory range of all externally directed sense-organs would be identical. Furthermore, the sense-organs and their objects would have the same inherent characteristic of hardness and so on, and would not be capable of being distinguished from one another.

Only the ten material elements, including the five sense-organs and their objects, are referred to as collected because they consist of conglomerations of atoms. Unmanifest form does not consist of such conglomerations.

36.(E357c.26) Concerning the activities of cutting, burning, and weighing, of these eighteen elements, the four sensory objects of material form, odor, flavor, and the tangible are cut, can cut, are burned and weigh.

Objection: How can conditioned factors that are momentary by nature cut and be cut?

Answer: The stream of successively arising factors or atoms is divided, giving rise to a separate stream. Sense-organs cannot be divided in this way, such that a second functioning organ is produced;

nor can they cut because they are composed of a subtle material form that is transparent. Sound is excluded because its stream is discontinuous. There is disagreement among masters as to what burns and has weight. Some say that the fundamental material element of fire alone burns, and heaviness, among the seven types of derived material form, has weight; others say that these four sense objects burn and have weight.

37.(E358a) Concerning the manner of arising, status as an actual entity, and momentariness of these eighteen elements, the five personal sense bases are said to be results of karmic maturation or through accumulation. Though they are also the result of outflow, as when a past eye acts as the cause of the present eye, they are never the result of outflow alone. The term "*vipākaja*", "result of karmic maturation", is interpreted in various ways: an effect is produced by maturing apart from the cause; or, it is produced from a cause of maturation, that is, a past action.

Accumulation is growth resulting from food, sleep, and so on. The stream of the effects of accumulation protects the stream of the effects of maturation, and there are no effects of maturation apart from accumulation. There are, however, effects of accumulation apart from those of maturation.

Sound is not an effect of maturation, because it is discontinuous and arises in accord with one's wish at any given time. It is, however, the result of outflow and of accumulation.

The seven mental elements and the factor element are effects of maturation and effects of outflow, from homogeneous or pervasive causes. They are not the effects of accumulation because, unlike material form, they do not consist of collections of atoms, and therefore cannot be accumulated.

The four remaining elements--visible material form, odors, flavors, and tangibles--are effects of maturation, accumulation, and outflow.

Some suggest that the factor element alone exists as an actual entity because it contains the unconditioned factors. That mind, factor element, and mental awareness which occur with the first moment of noncontaminating thought, that is, the first moment of the noble path, are said to be momentary; they are not the result of outflow produced by prior homogeneous causes because they are the first uncontaminating factors to arise within the life-stream of contaminating factors.

Others suggest that all factors exist as actual entities and all factors, with the exception of the unconditioned factors, are momentary.

39.(E360b) Concerning which of these eighteen elements are internal or external, twelve elements, including the six types of perceptual consciousness and their six corresponding organ-bases, are internal, while the six objects are external. There exists no self by which the "internal" can be determined. However, Vasubandhu suggests that since awareness serves as the basis for the sense of self, it can be referred to figuratively as the internal "self", and those factors that serve as its basis, that is, the sense bases, should be internal.

This interpretation is unacceptable because there would inevitably be confusion concerning whether or not certain factors act as the basis of thought. For example, how can present or future moments of perceptual consciousness possibly act as the basis of a present moment of perceptual consciousness, and thereby be considered internal? Or, why aren't thought concomitants, the objects of thought that are simultaneous with and share the same effect as thought, considered internal? Instead, the "self" should be figuratively understood as referring to that which always operates with complete self-mastery with regard to its own object; thereby, the thought concomitants would be excluded from what is "self" and internal.

Śrīlāta: Even though all factors including thoughts are to be included in the factor element as objects of mental perceptual consciousness, a distinction can still be drawn between internal and external as follows. That which serves as the locus for the six types of perceptual consciousness is internal, and that which serves as their supporting object is external. A sense organ can then be either internal or external depending upon whether it is the locus for the arising of perceptual consciousness or its supporting object.

Response: This interpretation is to be rejected. One should not assume that simply because mental perceptual consciousness is capable of taking any factor as its supporting object, all factors are to be included in the factor element. Further, we would also accept that the loci of perceptual consciousness are referred to as internal, and their supporting objects are external. However, the sense organs should not be considered to be at times internal and at times external depending on their role as locus or supporting object. The immediately prior moment of perceptual consciousness and the other sense organs are characterized by their nature as loci of perceptual consciousness in all three time periods even though they can also function as supporting objects. Therefore, they should always be classed as internal. Those factors that can never be the loci of perceptual consciousness are then external.

The eighteen elements can also be classed as homogeneous or partially homogeneous. Those elements that have carried out their own activity, are carrying it out, or will carry it out together are called homogeneous because they share their function, depend for their functioning upon the functioning of others, or share the same contact. For example, when the eye and the object function as the conditions for the arising of visual perceptual consciousness, these three elements are homogeneous. The elements that do not carry out their activity are partially homogeneous because they are of the same category as those elements that do function. That is to say, they have the same specific characteristic, or are classed as the same sensory basis or element, and so on. The factor element is only homogeneous because there is no factor with regard to which mental perceptual consciousness has not arisen, is not arising, or will not arise. Mental perceptual consciousness is always homogeneous unless it does not arise; in that case, it is partially homogeneous. The organs are determined to be homogeneous or partially homogeneous only with regard to the life-stream in which they function. Therefore, if they are homogeneous with regard to a particular life-stream, they are exclusively homogeneous. The same object, however, can be homogeneous to one who perceives it, and partially homogeneous to one who does not.

40.(E362b) Concerning the method by which these eighteen elements are abandoned:

Those elements that are not defiled, or that are not produced from the mental organ, or that are material form, whether defiled or undefiled, are to be abandoned by the path of cultivation and by the path of vision. Further, those elements that are uncontaminating are not to be abandoned. Therefore, fifteen elements--the ten elements of material form and the five externally directed types of perceptual consciousness--are to be abandoned by cultivation. Within the last three elements--the mind, mental perceptual consciousness, and the factor element--some are to be abandoned by the path of vision, some by the path of cultivation, and some are not to be abandoned.

41-42.(E363c) Concerning which of these elements are

characterized as view, only two among all factors have view as their essential nature: among factors having material form, the visual sense-organ alone is view because it illumines visual matter, it opposes darkness, and its activity is acute; among factors lacking material form, internally directed wisdom that is acute with respect to reflection upon the features of the mental object, and judges it, has view. This wisdom is of eight types: including the five defiled views, beginning with the view that the self is identified with the body, and the three types of correct views, including the worldly correct view, the correct view of the disciple, and the correct view of the adept. These eight types of view represent stages in the cultivation of purity and clarity of insight into an object; the purity or clarity does not then reside in the object, but rather in the view itself.

Only the wisdom associated with mental perceptual consciousness consists of both reflection upon and judgment of an object; therefore, the wisdom associated with the other five types of perceptual consciousness does not have view.

Objection: If this were so, the visual sense-organ also should not have view because it lacks judgment.

Answer: As we have explained, the visual sense-organ has view or sees because it illumines material form, and so on.

Objection: If the organ itself perceives, then all objects would be perceived at one time by their corresponding organs.

Answer: Only the homogeneous eye, that is, the eye that functions together with visual perceptual consciousness, sees, and not all eyes in all three time periods.

Objection: In that case, it is visual perceptual consciousness and not the eye that sees.

Answer: No, since visual perceptual consciousness cannot see apart from the eye, perceptual consciousness merely serves as the support for the predominant activity of vision, which is unique to the eye. Further, since all six types of perceptual consciousness have the same nature, if visual perceptual consciousness had the capability of sight, all six types of perceptual consciousness would have the same capability. Only the sense organ loci are capable of distinguishing the various types of perceptual consciousness. Further, if visual perceptual consciousness were capable of sight, one should be able to see even when one is blind or asleep.

Other masters claim that if visual perceptual consciousness were capable of sight, obstructed objects should be seen; perceptual consciousness has no resistance, and therefore should not be obstructed by physical objects. To this Vasubandhu responds simply that since visual perceptual consciousness does not arise with respect to an obstructed object, it cannot be expected to see. However, as has been shown, even if visual perceptual consciousness were to arise, one cannot claim that visual perceptual consciousness alone among the six varieties of perceptual consciousness sees. Further, Vasubandhu gives no reason why visual perceptual consciousness cannot arise with regard to an obstructed object. If he claims that visual perceptual consciousness sees colored shapes, since it is without physical resistance, it should arise even with regard to an obstructed object. Or, if he claims that visual perceptual consciousness cognizes colored shapes, and such cognition does not arise with respect to obstructed objects, this assumes that visual cognition proceeds in accordance with the same object as the visual organ--a position that implies that the visual organ sees. Further, visual perceptual consciousness arises with respect to objects obstructed by other transparent objects. The nonobstruction of light by transparent objects cannot account for the arising of visual perceptual consciousness because nocturnal animals are capable of seeing even in darkness; we cannot assume that the same darkness prevents sight in the case of human beings and allows it in the case of animals.

For those who accept the theory that the eye sees, the eye is incapable of seeing an obstructed object because that eye has resistance. Since visual perceptual consciousness proceeds in accordance with the same object as its locus, the eye, it cannot cognize obstructed objects. Vasubandhu maintains that visibility of an object obstructed by something transparent is due to the ability of light to pass through to the object. I (Saṃghabhadra), however, claim that the visibility or invisibility of an obstructed object depends upon the degree of resistance offered by the atomic structure of the obstruction.

The visual organ has two activities: (1) it acts as a door, or as the locus for the emerging of aspects within awareness and accompanying mental factors with regard to the object. (2) It is able to grasp the object, that is, it sees colored shapes. Now we maintain that visual perceptual consciousness supports the eye and enables it to see because the eye cannot see apart from visual perceptual consciousness. However, visual perceptual consciousness itself does not see because, if it did, all types of perceptual consciousness, which are not different in nature from one another, should be able to see. The difference in the perceptual activity of seeing, hearing and so on can only be accounted for by the distinctions among the various organs.

Dārṣṭāntika: The distinctions among the sense organ, perceptual consciousness, and the object are merely figurative; sight is simply a phenomenon that occurs as a result of causal process.

Answer: This interpretation fails to take into account the specific characteristic and activity of individual factors by which factors are distinguished from one another and their causal interaction is determined. The Buddha advises only that we not pursue and become attached to the universal characteristic or to the gross activities that are employed conventionally in describing composite objects. However, to deny the actual specific characteristic and activity of factors that are the highest reality is to blur the distinction between the highest reality and what is only conventionally real. Finally, causal interaction can only be maintained as long as the specific characteristic and activity of distinct factors is maintained.

43ab.(E368a) Both eyes can be said to see material form at the same time because the object appears clearer when both eyes are open. If the eyes saw in succession, there would be no difference between the clarity of an object seen with two eyes or one.

Śrīlāta: The two eyes give rise to their activity successively. Perceptual consciousness produced by two eyes is clearer than that produced by one alone because the two successive moments of the visual organ exchange their activity producing a clearer perceptual consciousness.

Answer: Whether one or two eyes are open in any given moment, only one moment of visual perceptual consciousness is produced. However, if two eyes, both open, acted successively, they would produce two distinct moments of visual perceptual consciousness. Finally, since awareness and accompanying mental factors, which include all varieties of perceptual consciousness, cannot be established in a particular place, the two spatially distinct sense-organs do not produce two spatially distinct instances of visual perceptual consciousness.

43cd.(E370a) Concerning whether or not the various sense-organs touch their respective objects: If we understand "touch" to mean that the capability of the sense organ reaches the object, all sense-organs "touch" their objects. However, if we understand "touch" to mean that atoms of the organ and the object are found without an interval between them, the following points should be made. The eye does not touch its object because both close and distant objects can be seen at the same time, it can see objects obstructed by other transparent objects, and it cannot see objects with which it comes into direct contact, like eye ointment. Further, the eye can produce doubtful or erroneous visual perceptual consciousness; if it touched its object, all visual perceptual consciousnesses would be certain. The ear also does not touch its object because distinctions of direction, distance, and clarity are noticed in the perception of sounds. The mind does not touch its object because it does not apprehend connected factors that are simultaneous with it. Further, the mind is not material form, and therefore cannot touch or be touched.

Objection: If these organs do not touch their objects, what prevents any of these organs from apprehending, at all times and in all places, all such untouched objects?

Answer: These organs are like a magnet or a mirror. Even though they do not touch their objects, at any given time they only operate with regard to some objects, and not all.

Concerning the inability of the eye to grasp objects in the dark, the Dārṣṭāntikas propose that it is due to the absence of light, which is a necessary condition assisting in the arising of visual perceptual consciousness. However, I propose that an object is not seen in the dark due to the obstruction of darkness, which can then be counteracted by light; darkness and light exist as two distinct and actual entities.

The nose, the tongue, and the body are said to touch their objects. "Touching" here cannot mean direct contact between atoms because if atoms came into contact with their entire extent, they would merge completely, and if they only came into partial contact these atoms, which are by definition, partless, would have parts. Therefore, to "touch" means that atoms of the organ and the object arises in close proximity to one another.

Some maintain that though atoms do not come into contact with one another, they form composite objects that can have contact. However, since the composite object does not exist apart from the atoms, if the composite object comes into contact, the atoms must also.

Śrīlāta: There must be material contact; otherwise, atoms would not hold together and there would be no composite objects. This composite object cannot simply be held together by the air element.

Answer: On the contrary, a composite object consists simply of atoms arranged in close proximity that hold together due to the force of the air element. Similarly, injury and benefit are to be explained not through direct contact, but rather through mutual proximity.

One master proposes that atoms do not contact one another; instead, the idea of contact arises when there is no interval between atoms. This proposal can be accepted as long as a clear distinction is drawn between "having no interval" and "contact". "Having no interval" means that the atoms of the four fundamental elements arise in close proximity; it does not mean that atoms have contact and hence, parts. Nor does it mean that they have no resistance and hence abide in the same place.

44. (E373c.18) For the three sense-organs that touch their objects, the number of atoms apprehended in the object can be no greater than the number of atoms in the sense-organ. For the visual and auditory sense-organs, the object may be either larger than, equivalent to, or smaller than the sense-organ. Since the mind is without material form, its size cannot be discussed.

Since the atoms in these five externally directed organs cannot be seen, their arrangement is difficult to determine, but because they have resistance, and therefore occupy a particular place, they are arranged. The atoms of the visual organ are found in the pupil covered with a transparent shield, or according to others, are themselves transparent and arranged in a lump on the front of the material eyeball. The atoms of the auditory organ are found in the cavity of the ear, the atoms of the olfactory organ within the nostrils, the atoms of the gustatory organ on the surface of the tongue, and those of the tactile organ all over the body.

The atoms of the visual, auditory, olfactory, and gustatory organs can be all homogeneous, all partially homogeneous, or both. However, the atoms of the tactile organ can never all be homogeneous (see 1.39).

Since the five externally directed types of perceptual consciousness take only collections of atoms as their locus and supporting object, one atom of the sense-organ or object will not give rise to perceptual consciousness.

Concerning the time period during which the locus and supporting object of any given moment of perceptual consciousness occur, the mental organ, or the basis of mental perceptual consciousness, is any of the six varieties of perceptual consciousness that has immediately passed away; there, it is past. This past locus is also the equivalent contiguous condition for the arising of present mental perceptual consciousness. However, the immediately preceding accompanying mental factors, which are also equivalent contiguous conditions for present mental perceptual consciousness, are not its locus. The five externally directed types of perceptual consciousness each have two loci: the immediately preceding mental organ, and the present corresponding sense-organ of the eye, and so on. The immediately preceding mental organ is both the equivalent contiguous condition and the locus for these five externally directed types of perceptual consciousness. However, their respective sense-organs are only their loci and not their equivalent contiguous conditions because these sense-organs are simultaneous with them and are not thought concomitants.

Whereas mental perceptual consciousness takes objects from all three time periods as its supporting object, the supporting objects of the five externally directed types of perceptual consciousness are only present temporally. The sense-organs specific to the five externally directed types of perceptual consciousness operate only with regard to present objects, and perceptual consciousness must operate with regard to the same object as its locus.

Some claim that the five externally directed types of perceptual consciousness operate only with regard to past objects, which exist only as nominal designations, and not as actual entities. However, this position results in several faults: (1) As nominal designations these past objects could become the object only of constructionfilled thought. Since the five externally directed types of perceptual consciousness are constructionfree in the sense that they lack two of the three varieties of discursive thought, how could they then take nominal designations as their objects? (2) Present perceptual consciousness should take all past objects as its supporting object because no distinction can be made between objects of the immediately preceding moment or remote past. (3) If you claim that an object serves as the supporting object of perceptual consciousness, you should claim that future perceptual consciousness, which is on the point of arising, takes a present object. (4) The three sense-organs of the nose, the tongue and the skin would not touch their objects since past objects are distant. (5) If all objects are only past, direct perception becomes impossible.

45.(E375a) The sense-organs and not the supporting objects are referred to as the loci of perceptual consciousness because changes in the quality of the sense-organ produce similar changes in the quality of its corresponding perceptual consciousness. Changes in the object produce no such changes in the quality of perception.

Objection: Since changes in the body result in changes in the quality of mental perceptual consciousness, the body also should be the locus of mental perceptual consciousness.

Answer: Changes in the body produce changes in its corresponding tactile perceptual consciousness. When this tactile perceptual consciousness becomes past, it acts as the mental organ (or locus), and as the equivalent contiguous condition for the arising of present mental perceptual consciousness. This present mental perceptual consciousness can then be indirectly affected by changes in the body.

Perceptual consciousness is named according to its corresponding organ and not its corresponding object because consciousness changes in accord with the organ and not the object, and because whereas the object may be shared by the perceptual consciousness of many people, the organ is unique to each one. Though the arising of perceptual consciousness depends upon many causes and conditions, the organ and the object are designated as the locus and supporting object because they are essential for its arising in each and every case.

46-47.(E375c) Concerning the stage to which the body, eye, visual color-shape and visual perceptual consciousness belong: for one born at a particular state, in general, the eye is never of a stage lower than the body. Color-shape and visual perceptual consciousness are never of a higher stage than the eye. Color-shape may be of a higher, lower, or the same stage as visual perceptual consciousness, and color-shape and visual perceptual consciousness may be of a higher, lower, or the same stage as the body. The same holds for the ear. For the nose, tongue and the body, all belong to the same stage, but in some cases tactile perceptual consciousness may be of a lower stage. The mental organ may belong to a higher, lower, or the same stage as its corresponding perceptual consciousness, object, and body.

48.(E377a) Concerning the medium of perception for each of the eighteen elements, the five external sense objects are perceived by their corresponding perceptual consciousness and by mental perceptual consciousness. All other elements are perceived only by mental perceptual consciousness. Concerning which of the elements are permanent, only the three unconditioned factors, included as one part of the factor element, are permanent. Concerning those elements that are controlling faculties, the five sense organs, the seven mental elements, part of the tactile organ element, and part of the factor element are controlling faculties. The tactile organ element includes the masculine and feminine faculties, and the seven mental elements constitute the mental faculty. Those controlling faculties included within the factor element are the five feeling faculties of satisfaction, frustration, contentedness, irritation and equanimity; the five faculties of faith, energy, mindfulness, meditation and insight; the controlling faculty of vitality; and the three faculties of coming to know what is as yet unknown, understanding, and perfect knowledge.

## CHAPTER TWO

1.(E377b) These elements listed in the previous verse are enumerated as controlling faculties because they are dominant or have supreme self-mastery with regard to a certain state. Though all factors have their own dominant activity, these twenty-two are exceptionally powerful, and therefore are listed separately.

The five sense organs have control over beauty, protection, the clarity of perceptual consciousness and its associated thoughts, and the particular sensory activity of each organ. The feminine and masculine faculties control the primary distinctions among sentient beings according to gender and differences of secondary characteristics. According to others, the masculine and feminine faculties control the possibility of complete affliction and purification of defilement since eunuchs are not capable of either. Vitality controls the connection to the psycho-physical complex from one lifetime to the next, and the support of that homogeneous character in one lifetime (see 2.42). The mental faculty controls the connection to the first moment of the next existence, and it controls all factors since all factors come under the mastery of the mind. The five feeling faculties and the five faculties beginning with faith control affliction and purification since they respectively produce and remove defilements.

2-4.(E377c) Those, like Vasubandhu, who claim that perceptual consciousness and not the sense organ sees, object to this explanation of the activity of the sense organ faculties, claiming that perceptual consciousness has the function of protection and of the particular sensory activities. They claim that the functions exerted by the controlling factors should be explained differently. However, these explanations as offered by these verses of the *Abhidharmakośa* either contradict doctrine or merely repeat the explanations of Verse 1.

5.(E379a) Other factors that have certain areas of control, such as ideas, or defilements, of *nirvāṇa*, of the five organs of action proposed by the Sāṃkhya school, are not controlling faculties because only those factors that support, differentiate, afflict, prepare to purify, and purify perceptual consciousness are referred to as controlling faculties.

6.(E379c) Others suggest that fourteen of these twenty-two controlling faculties are the loci, the origin, the continuation, and feeling of *saṃsāra*; the remaining eight have the same functions with regard to *nirvāṇa*.

7-9.(E379c) Concerning the nature of these controlling faculties, satisfaction and frustration characterize corporeal feelings, that is, those associated with the five externally directed types of perceptual consciousness, while contentedness and irritation characterize mental feelings, or those associated with the sixth type of mental perceptual consciousness. Equanimity is neither agreeable nor disagreeable and is not designated as corporeal or mental because it is not produced through discursive thought.

The three uncontaminating controlling faculties--coming to know what is not yet known, understanding, and perfect knowledge--each consist of these nine other faculties: the mental organ, satisfaction, contentedness, equanimity, and the five faculties beginning with faith, which belong to the path of vision, the path of cultivation, and the path beyond training respectively.

Like all factors, these controlling faculties can be classified according to a number of different perspectives. Concerning those that are contaminating or noncontaminating, the last three faculties, coming to know and so on, are noncontaminating. The seven material faculties, vitality, and the two disagreeable feelings are contaminating, and the remaining nine faculties can be either contaminating or noncontaminating.

10a-c.(E380c) Concerning those faculties that are the result of maturation, vitality is only the result of maturation.

Objection: Vitality that results from the practice of meditation cannot be the result of the maturation of past actions.

Vasubandhu: This vitality is merely the momentum of the period of abiding of the fundamental elements of which the material basis and the sense organs are composed. In meditation, that momentum produced from past action is exchanged for a momentum produced by the power of meditation.

Answer: This interpretation is to be rejected. Instead, the vitality resulting from meditation is a result of the practice of meditation itself, or of the transformation of the effects of certain prior acts, from maturation having the effect of enjoyment to maturation having the effect of vitality.

Irritation and the last eight controlling faculties--the five beginning with faith and the three noncontaminating faculties--are never the result of maturation because they are morally determinate as good or bad; results of maturation are always morally neutral. The seven material faculties are results of maturation except when they are the result of accumulation. The mental faculties and the four feeling faculties, excluding irritation, are the result of maturation except when they are morally good or bad or arise in association with the three indeterminate factors, the modes of proper deportment, skill in the arts, and magical creations.

10c-11a.(E381a) Concerning those faculties that produce a matured effect, only irritation always has a matured effect. Those faculties that are neutral and those that are noncontaminating never have a matured effect. Among the remaining ten faculties, including the mental faculty, the four feelings with the exception of irritation, and the five beginning with faith, those that are good or bad and are contaminating have a matured effect; those that are neutral or are noncontaminating do not have a matured effect.

11b-d.(E381b) Concerning their moral quality, the last eight faculties are only good. Irritation is either good or bad. The mental faculty and the other four feeling faculties are good, bad or neutral. The first eight faculties including the five sense-organs, the masculine and feminine faculties, and vitality are only indeterminate.

12.(E381b) Concerning the realm to which the various faculties are connected, nineteen are connected to the realm of desire: that is, all with the exception of the last three noncontaminating faculties. Fifteen of these nineteen are connected to the material realm: that is, excluding the masculine and feminine faculties, irritation and frustration. Eight of these fifteen are connected to the immaterial realm: that is, excluding the five material faculties, satisfaction, and contentedness.

13.(381c) Concerning the method by which they are abandoned, those that are contaminating are to be abandoned by the path of vision or the path of cultivation, and those that are noncontaminating are not to be abandoned. Even those noncontaminating faculties that are not to be abandoned by either path can be said to be abandoned upon attaining *nirvāṇa* without remainder. Those faculties that are defiled, are mental, or are produced by the six types of perceptual consciousness are to be abandoned by the path of vision. Those that are material or are undefiled are to be abandoned by the path of cultivation. The mental faculty, satisfaction, contentment and equanimity may be abandoned by the path of vision, by the path of cultivation, or are not to be abandoned. Frustration is to be abandoned by the path of vision or cultivation. The seven material faculties, vitality, and frustration are to be abandoned only by the path of cultivation. The five faculties of faith and so on are to be abandoned by the path of cultivation or are not to be abandoned. The three noncontaminating faculties are not to be abandoned.

14.(E381c) Concerning those faculties that are first acquired at the moment of conception, only those that are the result of maturation (see 2.10a-c) can be so considered. In the case of beings born from an egg, the womb, or by moisture in the realm of desire, only the tactile faculty (i.e., the body) and vitality are acquired first. In the case of beings born by spontaneous generation, for whom there is no growth, six, seven, or eight faculties are acquired first at conception: that is, the five sense organs and vitality, and possibly the masculine or feminine faculties, or both. Beings born in the material realm attain six faculties: that is, the five sense organs and vitality. Those born in the immaterial realm acquire only one faculty: vitality. From this it is clear that vitality exists as an actual entity: otherwise, there would be nothing upon which birth in the immaterial realm could depend.

15-16b.(E382a) Concerning the faculties that cease at the moment of death, for beings in the immaterial realm, whose thoughts are defiled or neutral, vitality, the mental faculty, and equanimity cease at the last moment. In order to explain death in the immaterial realm, vitality must be accepted, since in the immaterial realm there is no other effect of maturation whose termination will result in death. In the material realm vitality, the mental faculty, and equanimity together with the five material sense-organs cease at the moment of death. In the case of sudden death in the realm of desire, there are ten, nine, or eight faculties that cease at the last moment, including the previous eight and one or two gender faculties. In the case of gradual death in the realm of desire there are four faculties that cease at the moment of death: the tactile organ, vitality, the mental organ and equanimity. For those beings whose thought is good at the moment of death, the five faculties beginning with faith should be added to the previous cases.

16c-17b.(E382b) Concerning the faculties characterizing one who attains any of the four fruits of the path, the first fruit of the stream-enterer and the last fruit of the perfected being are attained through nine faculties; the mental faculty, equanimity, the five faculties beginning with faith, and the two uncontaminating faculties, coming to know and perfected knowledge. The second fruit, the once returner, and the third fruit of the nonreturner are attained through seven, eight, or nine faculties depending upon the path through which they are attained.

17d-19.(E382c) When certain faculties are present, others are also necessarily present. For example, anyone accompanied by vitality, the mental faculty, or equanimity is necessarily accompanied by all three. Or, anyone accompanied by one of the five sense organs is necessarily accompanied by these first three and the tactile organ.

20.(E383b) The minimum number of faculties possessed by any being is eight; that is, for example, in the case of one in the realm of desire who lacks the good roots the eight include vitality, the mental faculty, the tactile organ, and the five feeling faculties. An ordinary being born in the immaterial realm also has only eight: equanimity, vitality, the mental faculty, and the five faculties beginning with faith.

21.(E383b) The maximum number of faculties is nineteen: (1) a hermaphrodite lacks the three noncontaminating faculties, or (2) one in the learner's path lacks one of the sexual faculties, the last faculty of perfected knowledge, and if still in the path of vision, the faculty of understanding, or if still in the path of cultivation, the faculty of coming to know.

22.(E383c) Now, all conditioned factors arise from both previous and simultaneous causes and conditions. The simultaneous arising of various conditioned factors will be presented in order to refute erroneous theories of causation. For example, some maintain that conditioned factors arise only from previous causes, or that they arise from only one cause, or that they arise from their own essential nature, or that they arise spontaneously without a cause.

First, concerning the simultaneous arising of factors that are material form, in the realm of desire, a molecule of material form consists of eight actual entities that arise together: that is, the four great elements and the four derived elements, which are the four sense spheres of visible color-form, odor, flavor, and the tangible. A molecule of animated material form also has at least nine actual entities including one atom of the tactile organ. If sound is present, the number is raised to ten or eleven respectively. Molecules in the realm of form lack odor and flavor, but otherwise are the same as those in the realm of desire.

An atom is the finest particle of material form having resistance, which is not capable of further analysis either by another particle of material form or by the intellect. Such atoms are never found separately, but rather are always collected in molecules.

The term "actual entity" (*dravya*) is used here both in the strict sense of a distinct actual entity characterized by its own specific characteristic, for example, the four great elements, and in the broader sense of a category characterized by a certain general characteristic, for example, the four sense fields of visible material form, and so on.

23a-b.(384a) Concerning the simultaneous arising of those factors that are not material form, awareness and accompanying mental factors necessarily arise simultaneously, and all conditioned factors necessarily arise simultaneously with the four conditioning characteristics (see 2.45-46). Those factors indicative of sentient beings also necessarily arise simultaneously with their possession (see 2.36).

The factors in the first of the five groups indicated in the text ("generally permeating") are called "*mahābhūmika*" because they are "great" (*mahā*), or found in all moments of thought of their category, and they originate from or are contained within the stage (*bhūmi*), that is, awareness.

24.(E384a) Śrīlāta: There are actually only three, and not ten factors that accompany every awareness: that is, feelings, identifications, and thinkings. Contact is, according to scripture, nothing more than the composite of the locus, supporting object, and perceptual consciousness; contact does not exist as a distinct actual entity.

Answer: This scriptural passage presents the conditions for the arising of contact, and not its particular inherent characteristic. In any case, since Śrīlāta's school does not accept simultaneous arising and mutual causality, he should not suggest that the three simultaneous factors, the locus, object, and perceptual consciousness, are mutually cause and effect, and that their assemblage is provisionally referred to as contact. Contact, like all mental factors, cannot be discerned independently, but it can be known to exist through its activity; that is, it acts as the cause of feeling.

Similarly, Śrīlāta's attempts to refute the existence of other mental factors by reducing them to capabilities of thought itself are futile. The existence of these mental factors is established by their activity. Further, Śrīlāta should explain how he justifies the existence of only the first three mental factors--feelings, identifications, and thinkings--apart from awareness. For these reasons, these ten generally permeating accompanying factors should be accepted as distinct factors that exist as actual entities apart from thought.

27.(E392a) The first ten accompanying factors listed in the text are found in afflicted awarenesses. They are associated with that ignorance which arises through mental perceptual consciousness and is to be abandoned through the path of cultivation. In addition to these mental factors there are others that are undetermined and may be associated with thought of any moral quality: they include regret, sleepiness, pride, initial and sustained thought and so on. All these mental factors exist as actual entities.

28-30.(E392a) Five types of awareness are distinguished according to their moral quality: (1) good, (2) bad and characterized by ignorance alone, (3) bad and characterized by other defilements, (4) neutral and obstructed due to association with false views, and (5) neutral and not obstructed. Concerning those accompanying factors that necessarily arise with moments of awareness of these five types, in the realm of desire good awareness is associated with at least twenty-two mental factors: the ten generally permeating factors, the ten good permeating factors, initial and sustained thought. Good awareness may also be associated with regret. Bad awareness independent of all defilements except ignorance is associated with at least twenty mental factors: the ten generally permeating mental factors, the six defiled permeating factors, the two bad factors (lust and hatred), and the two neutral ones (initial and sustained thought). A bad awareness, when associated with one of the four defilements of attachment and so on, or with one of the secondary defilements, or with regret, is associated with twenty-one mental factors. An unobstructed neutral awareness is associated with at least eighteen: the ten generally permeating factors, the six defiled permeating factors, and the two neutral factors. Unobstructed neutral awareness is associated with the fewest number of factors--twelve, including the ten generally permeating factors and the two neutral factors. Sleepiness may appear in any thought.

32.(E393a) Certain mental factors require further clarification. Shamelessness and disregard can be distinguished from one another in various ways: shamelessness is lack of respect for good qualities, or for those who possess them, while disregard means lack of remorse with regard to manifest vices. Or, shamelessness is lack of aversion to one's own defilements, while disregard is lack of aversion to evil conduct. Or, shamelessness leads to displaying vices alone, while disregard leads to displaying vices in public. Or, shamelessness is not reconsidering the cause of one's actions, while disregard is not reconsidering its effects. Faith is affection that is not defiled, that is to say, it is not attachment.

33.(E393c) Objection: Initial and sustained thought are not actual entities different from awareness, but are merely varieties of awareness itself. Further, even if they are different from awareness, since they are mutually contradictory they should not be present in the same moment of thought.

Answer: This interpretation is not correct. Initial and sustained thought are indeed actual entities distinct from thought. Even though they are present in one moment of thought, their activities predominate at different times. For example, in a gross moment of thought because the activity of initial thought predominates, the activity of sustained thought is difficult to discern; both do not predominate in the same moment. Others claim that initial thought acts as the gross obstruction of thought preventing the attainment of the intermediate state between the first and second trance states. Sustained thought acts as the subtle obstruction of awareness preventing the attainment of the second trance state. Since their activities are distinct, they must exist as actual entities. The upper trance states do not have initial and sustained thought and no difference of grossness or subtleness; therefore, they are said to be of one flavor.

Pride is asserting one's superiority over others due to an inflated estimation of one's own thoughts, while conceit is attachment to one's own qualities, which causes exhaustion. That is to say, due to the exhaustion caused by arrogant thoughts attached to themselves, one withdraws from the pursuit of good factors.

34.(E394c) The difference in terminology between *citta, manas* and *vijñāna* has been explained from a number of perspectives. For example, *citta* collects together *(cinoti), manas* considers (*manute*), and *vijñāna* cognizes (*vijānāti*). Or, the three terms are used in the element, sense basis, and aggregate classifications respectively.

Accompanying mental factors and awarenesses are said to share a locus, that is, they are based on one of the six sense organs; share a supporting object, that is, one of the objects becomes their supporting object; share an aspect, that is, they have the same features in grasping supporting objects and are connected because they are equivalent and simultaneous. This equivalence of awareness and mental factors is fivefold: of locus, supporting object, features, time of arising and passing away, and substantial nature. "Equivalence of substantial nature" means that only one awareness and one instance of each category of mental factors can be produced in any given moment.

Śrīlāta: There is only awareness. There are no separate mental factors because even if, for example, awareness and a mental factor were simultaneous, a distinction between them on the basis of aspects is not possible. How can you justify your claim that aspects reside in mental factors and not in awareness? Further, numerous scriptural passages demonstrate that these supposedly associated mental factors are not distinct from awareness.

Answer: Since awareness and mental factors share the same content, arise and pass away simultaneously, and share the same moral quality, their distinction in essential nature is difficult to discern. I, however, distinguish them as follows: perceptual consciousness apprehends the nature of its object in general; mental factors grasp the various particular characteristics of the object. The existence of awareness and mental factors as distinct actual entities can also be proven through numerous scriptural passages. The scripture clearly states that the three mental factors of feelings, identifications, and thinkings arise simultaneously with contact, which is produced through the collocation of the sense-organ, the supporting object, and perceptual consciousness. Since perceptual consciousness or awareness and the mental factor of feelings and so on are mentioned separately, they must refer to two distinct actual entities. Further, it cannot be maintained that awareness in the form of perceptual consciousness first apprehends the essential nature of the object and then, in the next moment, another awareness in the form of an identification grasps its particular characteristics. In this subsequent moment the object has already passed away. How could identification grasp its particular characteristics? As the scriptural passage indicates, the mental factor of identification arises simultaneously with awareness or perceptual consciousness, not subsequent to it. If these mental factors were of the nature of awareness itself, more than one perceptual consciousness would arise within one moment--a conclusion that cannot be accepted. Though mental factors share the same time of arising and passing away, the locus, supporting object, and form with awareness itself, they have their own particular activities. Therefore, they can be known to exist as distinct actual entities.

35-36a.(E396c) There are also factors among the conditioning factors dissociated from awareness and material form that necessarily arise simultaneously with other factors. There are fourteen such dissociated forces: possession, nonpossession, homogeneity, nonidentification, the nonidentification trance, the cessation trance, vitality, the four conditioning characteristics, duration, aging and termination, the collections of words, of phrases, and of syllables. These dissociated forces are conditioned, but are not awarenesses, mental factors, or material form.

36b-d.(E397-399) Possession (*prāpti*) is of two types: (1) the possession of that which has never been attained, which is called acquisition, and (2) the possession of that which has already been attained, which is called accompaniment. Similarly nonpossession is of two types: (1) the nonpossession of that which has never been attained, and (2) the nonpossession of that which has been attained and lost. Among conditioned factors, one has possession and nonpossession only of those factors that fall within one's own life-stream. Among the unconditioned factors, one has possession and nonpossession only of the two cessations, and not of space.

Vasubandhu: How do we know that possession exists as a distinct entity?

Answer: Scriptural passages can be cited that refer to possession. We can thereby infer that it exists as a distinct actual entity.

Vasubandhu: It is unjustified to posit the existence of possession because its essential nature cannot be perceived, as in the face of form or sound, and its activity cannot be inferred, as in the case of the eyes or ears.

Answer: Possession does indeed have activity, namely, it prevents the loss of factors that have been obtained and it is the marker for the knowledge that this belongs to that.

Vasubandhu: These activities are performed by seeds within the corporeal basis. When the seed-nature of a given factor is not damaged, or when one has mastery with regard to the arising of a factor, one can be said to have accompaniment of that factor. Nonpossession refers to the opposite case. For example when the seeds of good factors are damaged, or one does not have mastery with regard to their arising, or when the seeds of bad or neutral factors have been eradicated by the path, or when there is no effort which can produce their present operation, one is said to have nonpossession of them.

Answer: What is this that is given the name "seed"?

Vasubandhu: Seeds are name and form, or the five aggregates, that have the capability, either remotely or directly, to produce their own effect; this capability becomes effective as a distinctive characteristic in the transformation of the life-stream. This "transformation of the life-stream" is the change in the stream of conditioned factors having the nature of cause and effect. This "distinctive characteristic" is the capability to produce an effect immediately. That is to say, a particular capability, referred to as a seed, arises in a succeeding awareness, distinguished by the distinctive characteristic of that preceding moment of thought. Future effects originate through this distinctive characteristic in the transformation of the life-stream. For example, even within a good awareness there lies a bad capability, or seed, projected by a previous bad awareness: this seed will produce its bad effect either remotely or directly.

Answer: Is this seed an entity separate from the momentary awareness in which it is found?

Vasubandhu: It is not entirely separate.

Answer: This seed, whether good or bad, should then produce the same effect as the awareness in which it is found. However, factors of differing moral quality must be distinct entities. Therefore, the seed and the awareness in which it is found must be distinct.

Next, how would the preceding awareness and the particular capability within the succeeding awareness function as cause and effect?

Vasubandhu: It is the nature of factors to function as cause and effect: that is to say, from the preceding awareness the succeeding capability is produced; if there were no preceding awareness the succeeding capability would not arise. This principle defines a cause and effect relation.

Answer: Since Vasubandhu rejects the existence of factors in the past and future, when the preceding awareness exists the succeeding seed does not yet exist. When the succeeding seed is produced, the preceding awareness has already passed away. A causal relation cannot be established between an existent and nonexistent entity.

Therefore, this theory of seeds proposed by the Dārṣṭāntika should be rejected. Likewise, all such theories of subsidiary elements, traces, capabilities, growth, or nondisappearance, which are simply other names for seeds, are rejected.

37-39b.(E398c) The character of possession generally agrees with the character of the factor to which it applies. For example, good, bad, and neutral factors are acquired by good, bad, and neutral possession respectively. Or, factors belonging to one of the three realms are acquired by possession belonging to that realm. However, good and bad factors belonging to any of the three time periods each have possessions belonging to any of the three time periods.

39c-40.(E399a) The character of nonpossession, however, generally does not depend upon the character of the factor to which it applies. For example, the moral quality of all nonpossessions is unobstructed and neutral, regardless of the moral quality of the factor to which it applies. Or, factors belonging to any of the three realms may have a nonpossession belonging to any of the three realms. Past and future factors may have a nonpossession belonging to any of the three time periods. However, since the possession and nonpossession of the same factor cannot operate simultaneously, a present factor, whose possession is, by definition, in operation, has only past and future nonpossession.

There is no noncontaminating nonpossession. Accordingly, the nonpossession of noncontaminating factors that constitute the noble path is not noncontaminating in itself. The nonpossession of noncontaminating factors is defined in the scripture as the nature of an ordinary person. If this nonpossession of noncontaminating factors were, itself, a noncontaminating factor, this nature of an ordinary person would also be noncontaminating.

Vasubandhu: This "nature of an ordinary person" is not an actual entity, but rather refers simply to a life-stream of the corporeal basis that has not yet produced the noble factors of the path.

Answer: Since Vasubandhu accepts the existence of present factors alone, the term "stream" can have no meaning for him. Further, when this "nature of an ordinary person" is discarded and one becomes a noble one through the arising of the first noncontaminating factor, one's stream of the corporeal basis is still characterized by factors such as the sense-organs and so on that are of the same nature as those of an ordinary person. How then can this "nature of an ordinary person" be defined as the stream of factors comprising the corporeal basis?

Objection: If it is claimed that there exists a "nature of an ordinary person" apart from the corporeal basis of an ordinary person, then there should also be a "jar-nature" that exists apart from the material components of the jar.

Answer: In the case of the jar one cannot discard this supposed "jar-nature" without breaking the material jar. However, in the case of an ordinary person, when the first noncontaminating factor arises, one discards the nature of an ordinary person even though the corporeal basis is as it was previously. Therefore, the example of the jar is not pertinent.

Objection: This "nature of an ordinary person" should be defined as the possession of ordinary or contaminating factors and not the nonpossession of noble, noncontaminating factors.

Answer: If these ordinary factors belonged to ordinary persons alone and were possessed by ordinary persons everywhere, they could be considered to be the nature of an ordinary person. However, neither of these conditions can be fulfilled: certain noble ones possess ordinary factors, such as vitality, and certain ordinary factors, such as an evil rebirth, are not possessed by ordinary persons everywhere.

Objection: The homogeneous character of ordinary persons fulfills these two conditions, and should therefore be the nature of an ordinary person.

Answer: This homogeneous character simply causes the mutual similarity of the body, appearance, and so on, of sentient beings in a particular group. The nature of an ordinary person acts as the cause of those contaminating factors belonging to an ordinary person, which prevent the acquisition of noncontaminating factors.

Objection: These contaminating factors are produced by previous action and defilements; what activity would this nature of an ordinary person have in producing them?

Answer: Certain factors are capable of causing other factors only in dependence upon still other factors. For example, even though the sense organs are produced from previous actions and defilements, they also depend for their operation upon the four great material elements. Therefore, contaminating factors can be said to depend upon the nature of an ordinary person in addition to previous action and defilements.

By these arguments, this "nature of an ordinary person" is unequivocally established.

The nonpossession of a particular factor is discarded when one acquires that factor, or when one passes to another stage. Specifically, a nonpossession is discarded by abandoning the possession of that nonpossession, and by producing the nonpossession of that prior nonpossession. There is no fault of infinite regress in this theory of possessions and nonpossessions because a given factor arises together with two other factors: its possession and the possession of that possession (*prāptiprāpti*). Since possession and the possession of that possession establish one another, there is no fault of infinite regress. In the case of nonpossession, infinite regress is avoided because the nonpossession of the nonpossession of a particular factor never arises together with its nonpossession.

41a.(E400a) Homogeneity is the uniformity or mutual similarity among sentient beings. It is the cause of the mutual similarity of body, appearance, the faculties, modes of activity, types of sustenance, or aspirations of beings born in a certain destiny, and so on. These similarities among beings in one group and distinctions from beings of other groups cannot be caused by previous action alone.

Homogeneity is found only among sentient beings, not among insentient objects like plants. There are innumerable varieties of homogeneity in accordance with distinctions in realm, destiny, type of birth, stage, body and so on. Further, there is homogeneity of factors belonging to sentient beings in accordance with the aggregate or element classifications, and so on.

The homogeneity of a particular category of sentient beings is discarded when one enters a state contradictory to it. For example, the homogeneity of the state of an ordinary person is discarded when one first attains a noncontaminating factor and becomes a noble one.

Vasubandhu: Since homogeneity has no material form, it cannot be known by direct perception. How then can its activity of determining categories of things be known?

Answer: Its activity can be observed in any grouping of similar factors belonging to sentient beings.

Vasubandhu: Why do you not allow that there is homogeneity also of insentient objects?

Answer: Insentient objects are without mutual similarity in modes of activity and aspirations. Further, homogeneity is caused by actions in a previous life, or zealous effort in the present life. Plants neither exert activity nor have aspirations and therefore cannot be said to have a common lot.

Vasubandhu: Since a common lot enables the cognition of mutual similarity among distinct entities, and the various types of common lot are distinguished from one another, there must then also be a general category of homogeneity enabling the concept of homogeneity in general.

Answer: Homogeneity does not act as the cause of the cognition of mutual similarity; this cognition is derived from the observation of particular instances. No further "homogeneity" is required to support this general concept. Rather, homogeneity acts as the cause that produces similar categories of things.

Śrīlāta: This homogeneity is identical to the category of universals proposed by the Vaiśeṣika school.

Answer: If the Vaiśeṣika school maintained that this "universal" is not singular, is momentary, and is distinct from the object to which it applies, we could accept their opinion with no major objection.

41b-d.(E400c) Nonideation is that cessation of awareness and associated factors attained by those reborn among the gods who are without ideation; these gods are found in the fourth trance state in the realm of form. This factor, "nonideation", is exclusively the karmically matured effect of the nonideation trance. The other conditioned factors of these beings without ideation are the effect of both the nonideation trance and the fourth trance state, or the fourth trance state alone. Even though those born among the gods without ideation have awareness before entering and after emerging from the nonideation trance, this factor of nonideation obstructs the arising of future thought and thought concomitants for a long period of time. Sentient beings fall from this region of gods without ideation through the arising of ideation, which occurs when the force of the life-span produced by the previously cultivated nonideation trance has been exhausted. They are then reborn in the realm of desire due to their past action.

42.(E401a) The nonideation trance, like nonideation, is a distinct actual entity that obstructs the arising of awareness and associated factor. It arises for those who are detached from the desires of the third level of trance in the material realm. "Trance" means either accomplishing (*āpatti*) correctly (*sama*), or else bringing awarenesses or the four great material elements into a state of equable (*samatā*) operation. Though all awarenesses and mental factors are extinguished, this trance is referred to simply as the nonideation trance because one produces it through aversion specifically to ideation. The state of nonideation is mistakenly considered by ordinary persons and non-Buddhists to be the true liberation, and the nonideation trance is considered to be the path of deliverance. Therefore it is not to be practised by those noble ones on the true path. This nonideation trance acts as a cause of karmic maturation, and its effects, including rebirth in the state of nonideation, are received in the next lifetime.

43.(E401b) The cessation trance is a distinct actual entity that obstructs the arising of awareness and mental factors. It arises after one has abandoned desires in the basis of nothingness, which is the third meditative base in the immaterial realm. It then arises in the fourth base of neither-ideation-nor-nonideation, which is the summit of existence. This cessation trance is produced merely with an intention to abide tranquilly, and not to seek deliverance. Further, it can only arise after one abandons all defilements that are to be abandoned by the path of vision. Therefore, it is to be produced by noble ones practising the path, and not ordinary persons. It acts as the cause of maturation of the four aggregates within the summit of existence, which may be received in the next lifetime, the third lifetime, or not at all. If after one has given rise to this trance in a lower state one then enters *nirvāṇa* without being reborn in the summit of existence, its effects are not received. This cessation trance is attained only through application and not by mere detachment. However, even though a Bodhisattva attains cessation trance he does not, in the practice of the noble path, actually enter it prior to attaining enlightenment. A Bodhisattva attains enlightenment in thirty-four consecutive moments of practice, which cannot be interrupted by a moment of a dissimilar category. Therefore, this process of noncontaminating moments of the path cannot be interrupted by a contaminating moment of this equipoise.

44c-d.(E402b) These two types of trance without awareness will occur to one supported by a corporeal basis in either the realm of desire or the material realm. One who has been reborn in the immaterial realm cannot enter the cessation trance because there is no corporeal basis to support the trance in that realm. Vitality necessarily proceeds in dependence upon either material form or awareness. If one who had been reborn in the immaterial realm were to enter the cessation trance, neither material form nor awareness would be present and vitality would be abandoned.

Objection: If all awarenesses and mental factors are extinguished in this cessation trance, why is it also referred to as the trance involving only the cessation of identification and feelings?

Answer: One produces this trance by opposition specifically to those two because they are capable of forming the basis of wrong views and desires.

Dārṣṭāntika: In this cessation trance one only extinguishes identifications and feelings, not all awarenesses. Four reasons can be given for this: (1) there are no sentient beings who are completely without awareness; (2) there must be a distinction between this cessation trance and death; (3) scriptural passages state that perceptual consciousness is not separated from the body; and (4) one's life-force, warmth, and perceptual consciousness are never separated from one another.

Answer: This interpretation is unreasonable because no awarenesses and mental factors occur without identifications and feelings. As the scripture states: "Visual perceptual consciousness arises in dependence upon the eye and material form. Contact results from the collocation of these three factors. Feelings, identifications and volitions arise together with contact." Therefore, feelings and identifications necessarily arise when there is perceptual consciousness. The successive model would contradict the definitions of "awareness" and "associated mental factor" (see 2.34).

Now in response to the four reasons offered by the Dārṣṭāntika, first, the existence of sentient beings without awareness is verified by scriptural references. Second, those who have entered cessation trance are not dead because they still have vitality. Sentient beings may lack material form, as in the immaterial realm, or they may lack awareness, as in these states of trance without awareness. Third, these scriptural passages state that awareness is not separated from the body simply because awareness will be produced again in the body that serves as the corporeal basis after emerging from this trance. Fourth, the life-force, warmth, and perceptual consciousness are indeed separated from one another only in certain cases. For example, in the immaterial realm there is no warmth; similarly in the states of trance without awareness there is no perceptual consciousness.

The duration of the cessation trance is determined by the extent of its force, which depends upon the degree of application through which it is produced. The moment of thought just prior to the trance acts as the directly antecedent condition for the arising of thought upon emerging from it.

Vasubandhu: This cessation trance has no activity, and therefore is not an actual entity. Awareness is obstructed not by the cessation trance itself, but by awareness in the moment just prior to entering this trance. This awareness arises opposed to other moments of awareness, and it brings about a corporeal basis opposed to the arising of other moments of awareness. This mere nonproceeding of awarenesses is then provisionally referred to as trance. This nominally designated trance can be included among conditioned factors because it does not exist either before entering or after emerging from it. Since the corporeal basis and awareness contain each others' seeds, awareness arises upon emerging from this trance from seeds of awareness within the corporeal basis.

Answer: Why then does perceptual consciousness not always arise merely from these seeds within the corporeal basis? Further, what would prevent the simultaneous arising of more than one perceptual consciousness, one supported by seeds in the corporeal basis, and the other supported by the previous moment of perceptual consciousness?

It is unreasonable to assume that, in ordinary circumstances, perceptual consciousness arises on the basis of a prior moment of perceptual consciousness, but upon emerging from the cessation trance it arises from the corporeal basis. Further, if the seeds of the directly antecedent awareness lie in the corporeal basis, suppressing the seeds of other awarenesses during trance, what cause enables these other seeds to produce awareness after emerging from trance? Then, in ordinary states also thought should be produced from these seeds within the body. Further, even if this trance is merely nominal, it can only exist if supported by an actual entity. What would this actually existing basis be other than this distinct factor, the cessation trance? Further, if this trance were merely the nonproceeding of moments of awareness, it would have nonexistence as its nature, and it should not then be included among conditioned factors. Therefore, it should be clear that the moment of awareness immediately prior to trance is not capable of obstructing other awarenesses. There must then be another separate factor with this capability, namely, the cessation trance.

45a-b.(E404b) Vitality is life-force, which serves as the support of warmth and perceptual consciousness, and enables the continuance of the life-stream of sentient beings. This life-force is supported by previous action and proceeds uninterrupted for the period of one lifetime.

Vasubandhu: This life-force does not exist as an actual entity; it is merely the momentum of the period of continued successive arising of the corporeal basis and six sense-organs, which is determined in accordance with the force of previous actions.

Answer: When, for example, one is reborn in the immaterial realm, the five externally directed sense-organs are absent, or when one enters a state without thought, the sixth mental sense-organ is not produced, or when one produces a moment of awareness of differing moral quality, the momentum of the continued successive arising of the corporeal basis and six sense organs is interrupted. In these cases there is no momentum of a continued successive arising of the corporeal basis. To what then would the life-force or vitality refer?

The life-force is projected by action in a previous life and proceeds in dependence upon homogeneity in the present life. Death may result from the exhaustion of the force of those actions that have vitality as their matured effect; or from the exhaustion of those meritorious actions that have property as their matured effect; or from the exhaustion of both; or from unfavorable circumstances. For those sentient beings in the realm of desire who do not enter the two trance states without awareness, their life-force proceeds in dependence upon their life-stream. There is then the possibility of obstruction of the life-force; when their corporeal basis is damaged, their vitality is also damaged. There is then, for sentient beings in the first category, the possibility of untimely death. For all other sentient beings, the life-force continues in its successive arising having arisen once, without obstruction.

45c.(E405c) The four conditioning characteristics indicate the conditioned nature of all conditioned factors. They include birth, duration, aging, and termination. Birth acts as the predominant cause of the nonobstruction of the production of conditioned factors; it draws out the conditioned factors from the remote future, enabling their immediate production. Duration acts as the predominant cause of the nonobstruction of the present activity of conditioned factors through which they draw out their own effect. Aging is the cause of the fact that previous moments differ from later ones. Termination acts as the predominant cause of the destruction of the activity of conditioned factors.

46a-b.(E406a) Objection: Since these four characteristics are themselves conditioned factors, they should each have four additional conditioning characteristics of birth, and so on. Would there not then be a fault of infinite regress?

Answer: There are also four secondary characteristics, the birth of birth, duration of duration, and so on, each of which carries out its function on its own respective characteristic. That is to say, each of the primary characteristics carry out their functions on eight factors: the four secondary characteristics, the other three primary characteristics, and the factor which they all characterize. However, no factor can function with regard to itself. Therefore the secondary characteristics carry out their function on only one factor, their respective primary characteristic. There is, then, no fault of infinite regress. These nine factors, comprising the four primary conditioning characteristics, the four secondary conditioning characteristics and the characterized conditioned factor arise and pass away together.

Vasubandhu: There is no instrument of knowledge, whether direct perception, inference, or scriptural authority, through which the existence of these characteristics as actual entities can be proved.

Answer: Is there then some instrument of knowledge through which their existence as nominally true can be proved? If Vasubandhu denies both their actual and nominal existence, they must be absolutely nonexistent because there is no third form of existence. The nominal existence of these characteristics cannot be proved for the following reasons: (1) unlike a jar, they cannot be directly perceived; (2) no scriptural passage asserts their nominal existence; and (3) if their nominal existence were proved by inference, their actual existence could also be proved by inference. In any case, the existence of these conditioned characteristics as actual entities is proven by scriptural authority: as the scripture states, "There are three conditioning characteristics of conditioned factors; their arising, passing away, and change in continuance also can be known." This passage, by repeating the word "conditioned", clearly indicates that the conditioning characteristics actually exist apart from the conditioned factor that they characterize.

Vasubandhu: This passage simply indicates that the series of conditioned factors is conditioned or dependently originated. These conditioning characteristics as applied to one moment cannot be cognized. Therefore, they must apply to the conditioning of the stream as a whole, and not to a single moment. The purpose of this passage is to undermine any belief in a permanent self. The beginning of the stream is birth, its extinction is termination, the proceeding of the stream is continuance, and the distinction between former and later moments in the stream is senescence.

Answer: This single birth and termination of an individual life-stream is commonly recognized, and yet belief in a lasting self is still prevalent. Therefore, the purpose of this passage must be to make known the birth and termination of each moment within the stream, and thereby undermine any false belief in a self. This scriptural passage is presented precisely because these conditioning characteristics as applied to each moment cannot be directly perceived. These conditioning characteristics can, however, be known through subtle discriminative intellect that examines the uninterrupted succession of moments within a given stream.

Vasubandhu: In the previous scriptural passage the repeated word "conditioned" merely indicates that the nature of conditioned factors is conditioned; it does not indicate the separate actual existence of these characteristics from the factor characterized.

Answer: Vasubandhu contradicts his own position. Since he maintains that conditioned factors do not exist in the future, when they are about to be produced, birth must indicate not only the production, but also the existence of such conditioned factors. Vasubandhu maintains that birth is merely the fact of a conditioned factor acquiring its own nature; birth must also then indicate that a given factor exists.

Next, what is this stream to which Vasubandhu refers?

Vasubandhu: This stream exists only provisionally; mutually similar moments are interconnected through a relation of cause and effect in which conditioned factors proceed in succession without termination.

Answer: In that case, it is not reasonable to apply birth to the stream as a whole since the conditioned factors of which the stream consists do not arise at the same time. Duration cannot be applied to the stream of conditioned factors as a whole since these numerous moments of conditioned factors never abide at the same time. If "aging" merely refers provisionally to the change between former and later moments in the stream, a cause for this apparent change must be found. Granted, at times this change can be explained through the activity of external conditions; but there are cases in which apparent change occurs without a corresponding change in external conditions. In this case, an internal cause of change must be found. Finally, if termination is merely the extinction of the stream, it must take the nonexistence of conditioned factors as its nature. And since conditioned factors are often said to be impermanent, or have this termination as their nature, they must all be nonexistent by nature.

Vasubandhu: If these conditioning characteristics are not assumed to exist as actual entities, they could be interpreted as belonging to conditioned factors in each moment. Birth would refer to the fact that a factor exists, not having existed, and termination to the fact that having existed it no longer exists. Duration would be the connection between previous and later moments, and aging the change in that connection.

Answer: Through this admission Vasubandhu falls prey to the same criticism he levels against us. That is to say, one factor in one moment is produced, abides, decays, and is destroyed. Since it is not admitted that these four characteristics are actual entities distinct from the factor that they characterize, their functions must then be mere aspects of that characterized factor. Then what would prevent this single factor from undergoing all four of its aspects at once? In any case, distinctions in the capability of one factor in one moment are impossible. Only if one allows that the conditioning characteristics of birth and so on exist as actual entities, distinct from the factor that they characterize, can this fault be avoided. In this case, the distinct capabilities of production and so on are attributed to distinct factors and not to the characterized factor itself.

Conditioned factors can be said to exist in several different states. In the past and future, they exist as essential nature, which may or may not be associated with capability. In the present, they exist as essential nature that is necessarily associated with a function. This function refers to the predominant capability of a factor in projecting its own effect. "Capability" refers to the subordinate capability of assisting factors of a different category in the projection of their effect. These four conditioning characteristics function as capabilities that assist the characterized factor in the projection of its effect. Furthermore, they do not exert their capabilities in the same states. The characteristic of birth exerts its capability when both it and the characterized factor are still future, leading the characterized factor toward the state of having already been produced. The other three characteristics exert their capability when they and the characterized factor are present.

Vasubandhu: Don't these three characteristics then exert their capabilities at one time?

Answer: These three characteristics exert their capability separately, giving the characterized factor three distinct points of dependence.

Vasubandhu: If birth performs its activity when it is future, it should be referred to as present, and not future. Further, when it has arisen, since it has already functioned, it should be referred to as past. How can you define the present moment as that time when a factor functions and yet claim that birth functions when it is future?

Answer: Fool! You do not understand the difference between function and capability. The efficacy of these four characteristics has nothing to do with functioning. For example, a present eye in the dark does not function in assisting visual perceptual consciousness to arise; nonetheless, its function of projecting its own effect, or acting as the homogeneous cause in the arising of a subsequent eye, is performed. Similarly, these four characteristics exert only capability in assisting the characterized factor to arise. Therefore, birth may exert this capability when it is still future.

Vasubandhu: Even if birth, duration and termination are accepted, aging can in no way be applied to one moment. Since aging is defined as change or the distinction between former and later moments, if this is applied to one factor we must admit that this factor, within one moment, becomes something other than itself.

Answer: Aging refers to the degeneration of the present function of the characterized factor, but not of the factor's essential nature. When a future factor, already existing as essential nature, encounters the power of previously produced or simultaneous conditions, its distinctive activity arises, and that factor becomes present. This produced functioning is able to project its effect through the assistance of continuance, and this projection of its effect degenerates through the assistance of aging.

Vasubandhu: If the function of a factor undergoes change, the factor itself must also change in essential nature.

Answer: As you maintain in your theory of seeds, these seeds or traces and the moment of thought in which they are found can neither be said to be identical nor completely different. The same is true of the function or capability and essential nature of conditioned factors. Further, since we maintain that a factor exists as essential nature in the past and future, when the present functioning of a factor ceases the factor merely abandons the present; the factor, however, still exists as essential nature. Therefore, a function may degenerate without a corresponding degeneration of essential nature. For you, Vasubandhu, who claims that a factor exists for one present moment only and does not admit aging within that moment, how is change in any sense possible?

Finally, aging can also be understood as that cause in each moment which produces degeneration in the subsequent state of the effect; in this way every moment in a stream of conditioned factors causes a later moment to change.

46c-d.(E411a) Vasubandhu: If birth in its future state produces an existent factor, since this productive cause and that which is to be produced are always provided, why are future factors not all produced together?

Answer: Birth alone, apart from a complete collocation of other causes and conditions, is not capable of producing a factor that is to be produced.

Vasubandhu: In that case we observe only the productive capability of these other causes and conditions, and not that of this characteristic of birth.

Answer: If you maintain that a mere collocation of causes and conditions produces the effect, with no cause as predominant, then the effect should be produced even if one cause or condition is lacking. Further, even though the efficacy of a particular cause is not observed, we cannot deny that this cause is effective. For example, the four great material elements serve as causes in the production of the visual sense-organ even though their efficacy is not observed. Further, you suggest karmic seeds of action as causes for transformations in the life-stream, and also claim that these seeds produce their effects through the assistance of other conditions. Why then do you reject this characteristic of birth simply because it avails itself of various other conditions?

Śrīlāta: Conditioned factors are without continuance because if they were to abide for even the shortest period of time why would they not then abide for a much longer period?

Answer: If conditioned factors did not abide for even the shortest period of one moment, they would be absolutely nonexistent. You, Śrīlāta, maintain that conditioned factors are destroyed immediately after they have acquired their nature. Must they not then abide while they are acquiring this nature? This is precisely the time when continuance enables that conditioned factor to exert its activity and project its effect. We also would not claim that its activity abides after this moment.

Śrīlāta: If the characteristic of impermanence exists apart from the conditioned factors that are impermanent, why is there not also a characteristic of frustration apart from the fact of frustrations?

Answer: You have confused the conditioning characteristic of termination under discussion here with the nature of all conditioned factors as impermanent. Conditioned factors are by their very nature impermanent, but they are destroyed with the characteristic of termination as the cause. Even you would admit that conditioned factors, which are impermanent by nature, are produced due to certain causes. Why then do you deny that they also have a cause of destruction?

Śrīlāta: Causation is necessarily successive; the productive cause precedes its effect. If destruction were also caused, a succession of the destructive cause and its subsequent effect would be required. The momentariness of all conditioned factors would thereby be violated.

Answer: Productive causes can either precede or be simultaneous with their effect. Similarly, the cause of destruction can be simultaneous with its effect. As the scriptures state, "everything has a cause"; therefore, destruction must also have a cause.

47ab.(E412c) "Collection of words" refers to the collection of identifications. Identifications grasp a factor through conceptual construction, and names, issued from syllables, correspond to these ideas. Names are manifested by sound and are then able to manifest the object. They are commonly established specifications that indicate both the intention of the speaker and the essential nature of the object that is known. "Collection of phrases" refers to the collection of sentences. A sentence is an explication, which brings the desired meaning to completion. Phrases are able to explicate, from both a cursory and detailed perspective, the object-referent in terms of its distinctive characteristics. "Collection of syllables" is the collection of phonemes such as *a, ā,* or *ka, kha* and so on. Syllables cause an utterance to be remembered by the speaker after the sound has passed away, maintaining this utterance without doubt, and allowing it to be transmitted to another. Both name and phrase have their origin in syllables.

Question: Are objects called forth directly by uttering their names?

Answer: Obviously not, for uttering the name "fire" does not burn the tongue, and so on.

Question: Then how is one's understanding of any word not a misunderstanding?

Answer: The relationship between words or ideas and the objects referred to is established provisionally by consensus at the beginning of each world cycle. These words are then handed down and used conventionally. Others suggest that utterances refer to the object indirectly because speech issues forth a word, and a word manifests the object. There exists no factor that is without a name. If there were, that factor would not be known. How then could it be said to exist?

Vasubandhu: Word, phrase and syllable have speech as their essential nature, and therefore should be included among factors of material form, not among those factors that are dissociated from material form and thought.

Answer: Numerous scriptural passages indicate that these three, word, phrase, and syllable, are distinct from sound. Logical arguments may also be offered. One may hear sound and not understand the phoneme, as when one does not understand the object-referent to which the sound refers. Or, one may understand the phoneme without hearing the sound, as when one reads lips. Or, one can understand the name of an object-referent through odor, and so on. Therefore, word must be distinct from sound. Sound,. phoneme, word and the object exist separately in successive dependence. The distinctions within intelligible sound depend upon phonemes, and these phonemes combine in a particular order to produce name. This name alone is able to manifest the object.

Vasubandhu: Speech is not mere sound, but rather only articulated sound that refers to object. Since a word only manifests the object through speech, why imagine that the word exists distinct from speech?

Answer: Certain phonemes are established in common with regard to certain objects. Words that specify the object are then evolved from these phonemes. When speakers are about to speak, they must first reflect upon these specifying words in order to understand the object indicated in their own speech, or in that of others. Therefore, the object can only be indicated through this succession from sound to word; each component has a distinct function in the process, and therefore exists.

Vasubandhu: If we assume that syllables actually exist, words and phrases are only collections of these syllables; they would not exist as distinct actual entities. Further, a name can consist of a single phoneme. What would the difference between a word and a phoneme be in this case?

Answer: This interpretation is untenable because there is no one moment in which the syllables of a name operate simultaneously. In the case of a word consisting of a single phoneme, this phoneme alone is without meaning; it acquires meaning only when it serves as the condition for the arising of a word. Further, if sound or speech alone were able to specify an object, any grouping of articulated sounds should specify the object; or, a particular grouping of sounds should have the ability to specify an object without being established by prior common consensus.

Vasubandhu: Indeed, the various syllables of which a word consists cannot be uttered in one moment, and a single factor cannot be produced part by part. How then would the string of syllables of which a word consists be able to produce it? If you respond that the last syllable of a word, which depends upon the previous syllables, produces a word, that last syllable alone should be sufficient to produce the word.

Answer: Since you reject the existence of past factors, how, in your view, could a string of syllables constitute one word? Further, how could you establish any relation of successive dependence among the syllables since you deny the existence of factors in the past or future? In that case, one would be as unable to understand a word upon hearing the last syllable as one was when hearing the first. Precisely because we accept the existence of past and future factors, a word can be produced by last syllable in dependence upon the previous ones.

Śrīlāta: People speak without recognizing these sets of words, phrases, and syllables as factors dissociated from thought. Why then should we assume that they exist?

Answer: Certainly, we cannot conclude that simply because common understanding does not include awareness of the subtle dynamics of communication and of the actual relation of speech, word and object, these components do not exist! One must engage in careful consideration of the distinctive characteristics of factors in order to understand their true functioning.

47cd.(E415c-416a) The words, etc. are connected to the realm of desire and the material realm. Some, claiming that word and so on depend upon speech, suggest that words can be found only through the first trance state in the material realm, above which speech is not found. Others claim that because a word is dependent only upon the existence of a body, which occurs throughout the material realm, words also can be found throughout that realm. Collections of words, etc., are indicative of sentient beings because words accompany the person manifesting the object and not the object itself. The collections of words, etc. are morally only neutral; when one utters the word for a good factor that word is not itself good.

The other forces dissociated from thought can also be discriminated from various perspectives; for example, the realm to which they are connected, their nature as an effect, moral quality, their status as indicative of sentient beings, and so on.

49.(E416b) The six kinds of causes are listed according to the extent of their inclusiveness. The efficient cause includes all factors, the simultaneous cause includes all conditioned factors, and the remaining causes each include a portion of conditioned factors. Though there is no extant scriptural passage that attests to these six causes as a group, numerous passages refer to each type of cause individually. These six types of causes can be divided into two groups: those that arise prior to their effects, including the homogeneous cause, the pervasive cause, and the cause of maturation; and those that arise simultaneously with their effects, including the simultaneous cause and the associated cause. The efficient cause can arise either prior to or simultaneously with its effect.

50a.(417a) Efficient causes are of two types: (1) those that act as causes of another factor simply because they do not obstruct its arising, and (2) those that act as productive causes of another factor. Any factor can function as a nonobstructing cause of all other factors with the exception of itself. This is due to the fact that a factor is always an obstruction to itself, no entity is self-caused, and no entity functions with regard to itself, just as a sword does not cut itself and so on.

Objection: Something that is capable of obstructing the arising of another and yet does not obstruct can be a nonobstructing cause. But how can something that is not capable of obstructing be a nonobstructing cause?

Answer: Since all factors are mutually dependent, all have the power of obstruction. Further, in its capacity as a nonobstructing cause, a factor that does not have the power of obstructing is not different from one that has such power but is not obstructing.

A factor of any of the three time periods of past, present and future can be efficient cause for factors of the other two time periods, but only those factors that are simultaneous with or subsequent to an efficient cause can be its effect. Conditioned factors can be causes of other conditioned factors and can be caused by both conditioned and unconditioned factors. Unconditioned factors, however, are not caused and therefore are neither caused by one another nor by conditioned factors.

Factors acting as simultaneous causes include the four great elements, the four conditioning characteristics and the factors they characterize, and thought and those factors that accompany thought. However, in addition to these simultaneous causes that function as mutual causes and therefore are also mutual effects, factors that arise together and share a common effect are also simultaneous causes.

These factors that function as simultaneous causes must be of different categories.

51.(E418a) Those factors that accompany thought include thought concomitants, the two restraints, and the conditioning characteristics of awareness, mental factors, and the two restraints. A factor's status as accompanying thought is determined by ten criteria including whether or not this factor is produced at the same time or in the same time period as a moment of thought, whether or not it shares the same effect, and whether or not it is of the same moral quality.

Objection: How is there a cause and effect relation among simultaneously arising factors? When factors are about to be produced, since they are not yet produced, they do not yet exist. At this time, how is it possible to speak of one factor that is able to produce and one that is produced? Further, since according to the definition of causal relations, when the cause exists the effect exists. If future factors are said to be able to produce, their effects should be produced at all times. Further, if simultaneous causes were mutually cause and effect, there would be no way to determine which of two simultaneously produced factors is the cause and which is the effect. Finally , this simultaneous production of the cause with its effect is not attested by common examples and is contrary to accepted definitions of cause and effect.

Answer: The definition of causal relations is twofold according to scripture: (1) "When A exists, B exists; when A does not exist, B does not exist." This refers to simultaneous causation. (2) "From the production of A, B is produced: when A is not produced, B will not be produced." This refers to successive causation.

Objection: Then there can be no simultaneous causation, because a factor that causes a simultaneously arising factor must act when both it and its effect are in the future, and future factors do not exist.

Answer: Though the present functioning of a future factor has not yet arisen, it still can be said to exist as an actual entity, and can also manifest causal capability. It can then be that which is able to produce and is produced. However, since this capability of production itself depends upon other requisite conditions, these future factors do not produce their effects at all points in the future, but rather just when they are on the point of arising.

Śrīlāta: This twofold definition of causal relations refers only to successive causal relations among streams, and not to simultaneous and successive causal relations among individual momentary factors.

Answer: Since for Śrīlāta "existence" is identical with "production", this twofold definition would be redundant even if applied to streams. Further, since for Śrīlāta past and future factors do not exist, if only successive causation is admitted, when the cause exists the effect does not yet exist and when the effect exists the cause has already passed away. Therefore, no causation at all would be possible. Further, not all simultaneously produced factors serve as simultaneous causes, but rather only those that are mutually causes and effects, or those that share an effect, or those that are able to produce another simultaneously arising factor. Abhidharma masters do not designate the specific cause and effect among factors that are mutually cause and effect; instead, all factors in a sufficient condition are mutually cause and effect. Finally, there are indeed attested examples of causation among simultaneously produced factors, such as a lamp and its light. One cannot claim that they arise successively, nor that they arise simultaneously simply because they are produced by one prior cause. Some factors produced by the same prior cause do not arise simultaneously, and other factors arise simultaneously as a result of different prior causes. Still others do indeed arise simultaneously due to the same prior causes. Therefore, the necessary simultaneous arising of two factors cannot be explained through an identity of prior causes. Other examples of simultaneous causation include the first arising of a noncontaminating moment of thought and its simultaneous causes, and the arising of an externally directed moment of perceptual consciousness on the basis of its simultaneous organ and object.

Therefore, we must reject Śrīlāta's claim that simultaneously produced causes, and specifically the simultaneous causes under discussion here, are impossible. Future factors that are just about to arise do have the capability of acting as causes in the simultaneous production of other factors.

52-53b.(E422a.9) Homogeneous causes act to produce similar factors either immediately or remotely. "Similar" means of the same moral quality, the same category in terms of method of abandonment, and the same stage.

The Dārṣṭāntikas claim that material form cannot act as a homogeneous cause because material form is produced and accumulated through the assistance of sufficient conditions; but this is to be rejected.

The causal relation involving homogeneous causes is sequential and the homogeneous cause is always produced prior to its effect. Past factors can be homogeneous causes of present and future factors, and present factors can be homogeneous causes of future factors. Future factors cannot be homogeneous causes with respect to other future factors because there is no sequential ordering among them.

Objection: Future factors that have become free of obstructions and are just on the point of being produced are prior to those that are not yet to be produced. Why then are they not able to function as homogeneous causes?

Answer: Sequential ordering among factors is determined by their state, and a factor's state is determined by whether or not it has performed its function, i.e., has projected its own effect; this occurs only when a factor is in the present time period. Since future factors have not yet performed their function there can be no sequential ordering among them and they cannot be homogeneous causes.

Though contaminating factors can only be homogeneous causes for factors of the same state, factors of the path that are noncontaminating can be homogeneous causes for another factor of an equal or superior stage of the path.

Unlike causes of karmic maturation, homogeneous causes do not necessarily give, or complete the production of, their effects. For example, a perfected being may attain *nirvāṇa* without receiving the effect of previous homogeneous causes. All causes function in a two stage process: first, they project or take their effect, and then they produce or give their effect. No cause may produce its effect without having first projected it; but some causes, like the homogeneous cause, may project their effects without then producing it.

Unlike the directly antecedent condition, homogeneous causes may produce their effect immediately, remotely, or not at all.

53c-d.(E425b) Connected causes include only awarenesses and mental factors. All connected causes are simultaneous causes, but there are simultaneous causes that are not connected causes (i.e., the two restraints and the conditioning characteristics). Like simultaneous causes, connected causes have the same effect and are simultaneous, but they share a fivefold equivalence (see 2.34) not necessarily shared by simultaneous causes.

54a-b.(E426a) Pervasive causes are prior proclivities that serve as causes of later defiled factors of the same stage. Their effect may be either of the same or a different category of abandonment. The power of pervasive causes exceeds that of homogeneous causes because pervasive causes are able to effect factors of a category of abandonment different from their own.

54c-d.(E426c) Causes of karmic maturation are contaminating factors that function causally by differentiating sentient beings according to their past actions. Only good and bad factors can act as causes of maturation. Noncontaminating factors cannot act as causes of maturation because they are not characterized by craving, and because they are not connected to any realm. Morally neutral factors are not causes of maturation because they are weak. These causes of maturation are of two types: projecting action, which determines the general character of any given lifetime, and completing action, which determines its specific character.

The effect of a cause of maturation is not simultaneous, nor does it follow immediately; the cause of maturation requires a successive stream for the production of its effect.

There are thus endless varieties of causes and one actual entity may act as a cause in different ways. Further, no cause acts alone, or is itself sufficient in the production of its effect. Thus we must examine each situation, in any given moment, to determine the way in which a particular entity acts as a cause.

55a-b.(E428b) Concerning the time period of these various causes, past and present factors may function as pervasive or homogeneous causes, while factors of all three time periods may function as connected or simultaneous causes or as causes of maturation. Conditioned factors of the three time periods may function as comprehensive causes. Unconditioned factors, which act as comprehensive causes, are not connected to any time period.

55c-d.(E428c) All conditioned factors are effects. The unconditioned factor, calculated cessation, is also an effect, that is, the effect of disconnection. Though this unconditioned factor is a cause and an effect, it does not have a cause nor an effect.

Objection: If this unconditioned factor is an effect it must have a cause.

Answer: The noble path is the cause of attaining this disconnection; therefore, disconnection is not an effect that is produced, but rather an effect that is attained. The path acts as the homogeneous or simultaneous cause for the production of the possession of this disconnection, but this possession produced by these three causes is not the desired end of the noble path; the end is this disconnection, or the unconditioned factor itself, which is attained through this possession.

Objection: If the unconditioned factors are comprehensive causes, why are they without an effect?

Answer: Unconditioned factors act as comprehensive causes only in the sense of nonobstructing, and not in the sense of producing. Present and past conditioned factors have the twofold capability of taking and giving their effects; future and unconditioned factors lack this twofold capability; therefore they are said not to have an effect. The unconditioned may also serve as the supporting object of mental perceptual consciousness, but in that case, it is not a productive cause.

Vasubandhu (adopting the Sautrāntika position): Since, unlike material form, unconditioned factors are not distinct entities, they do not actually exist. These unconditioned factors are mere absences. For example, space is the mere absence of the tangible; the concept of space is produced with regard to the absence of material form.

Answer: Space exists as a distinct actual entity that acts to support wind and is manifested by light. The existence of space can be inferred from these activities. Its characteristic is the nonobstruction of others, and nonobstruction by others. Further, precisely because space can serve as the supporting object in the production of the concept "space", it can be said to exist as an actual entity. Cognition is not produced without an existent supporting object.

Vasubandhu (as a Sautrāntika): The unconditioned factor, uncalculated cessation or *nirvāṇa,* is merely the cessation of seeds of proclivities brought about through the power of realization such that they will never arise again. By cultivating the antidotes to these proclivities one develops a personal physical and psychic basis that is opposed to their arising. This cessation is then a mere absence of these proclivities and their seeds; it is not an existent entity in itself.

Answer: Calculated cessation does exist as an actual entity constituting the abandonment of all defilements of a particular category in all three time periods. Through the practice of the noble path, one first severs one's possession of a particular category of defilements; then one acquires possession of the cessation, or disconnection from, this category of defilements. Therefore, one acquires possession of this cessation for each particular category of defilements that are to be abandoned.

Vasubandhu (as a Sautrāntika): Uncalculated cessation is a mere deficiency or absence of conditions necessary for the arising of a particular factor.

Answer: A mere absence is not capable of preventing the arising of a factor. Rather, uncalculated cessation must be a distinct factor attained due to a deficiency of conditions, which then itself prevents a factor from ever arising.

56-58.(E435c) These six types of causes produce four types of effects as follows: effects of karmic maturation are produced by the cause of maturation. These effects of maturation are the products of previous action and are limited to those factors indicating sentient beings. The cause of maturation must be either virtuous or unvirtuous, and its effect is always morally neutral.

Effects of outflow are always similar to their causes in moral quality and often in essential nature. They are produced by either the homogeneous cause or the pervasive cause.

An effect of service is an effect produced through the power of another. In its specific sense, this effect is produced by simultaneous and associated causes. In its broader sense, this effect can be produced in the same moment as its cause, in the immediately succeeding moment, temporally separated from its cause, or may not be produced. This last category refers to the cessation through realization or *nirvāṇa* which, though not produced, is attained through the power of the path.

The dominant effect is produced by the comprehensive cause. Since all factors may act as comprehensive causes, as nonobstructing causes in the arising of any factor other than itself, any conditioned factor may be the dominant effect of all other conditioned factors. However, a given factor cannot be the sovereign effect of those factors that arose prior to it; an effect never precedes its cause.

The effect of disconnection, which is identical to the cessation through realization, *nirvāṇa*, is not attained through a cause of production. Therefore, it is not attained through the activity of any of the six causes.

59.(E437c) These six causes function causally in two stages. The first is that of taking or projecting the effect, through which the cause draws out a future factor preparing it for its production. This "taking" occurs only when a cause is itself in the present time period; this present activity alone is referred to as that cause's function. The second stage is that of giving or producing the effect, through which the cause gives the effect power enabling it to arise. This "giving" may occur when the cause is in the present or past time period and is referred to as a cause's capability. This second stage of "giving" the effect cannot occur without the first stage of "taking" the effect.

All six causes take or draw out their effects only when they themselves are in the present time period. The simultaneous and associated causes also give or produce their effect only when they are in the present time period. The homogeneous and pervasive causes give their effect when they are present or past. If the effect of the comprehensive cause is produced by it, this effect is given when the comprehensive cause is present or past. The cause of maturation gives its effect only when it is in the past time period.

60-61c.(E438b.26) No factor is produced by one cause alone. The number of causes that produce any given factor is determined by that factor's essential nature as thought, material form, or dissociated from thought and material form, its moral quality, and so on. Further, though certain categories of factors may not function as certain types of causes, all classes of factors, with the exception of unconditioned factors, may function causally in more than one way. Unconditioned factors can only be comprehensive causes.

61c-62d.(E440a) Causal relations can also be described in terms of four kinds of conditions. The first of these four, the causal condition, includes five of the previously listed six causes with the exception of the comprehensive cause. These conditions only include conditioned factors; since unconditioned factors can also serve as comprehensive causes, they are excluded from the four conditions. Even though conditioned factors exist in their essential nature in the three time periods, the arising of their activity is dependent upon the power of conditions, among which the causal condition, which is equivalent to the previously listed five causes, is predominant.

Śrīlāta: This causal condition should not be interpreted in terms of five distinct types of causation; rather, all causes are simply the subsidiary element, which acts as the cause in the reciprocal and successive conditioning process referred to as the life-stream of sentient beings. For example, even though evil qualities may be manifest in any given moment, there are latent roots of virtue which have not yet been severed from which other virtuous qualities may arise. These latent roots of virtue are the subsidiary element; it is an element permeated by factors of various types.

Answer: This "subsidiary element" is simply another name for the seed, whose existence we have already refuted (see 2.36). Causal interaction can only be explained through the activity of these five causes, which are equivalent to the causal condition. Each of these five causes functions in different circumstances, which should be clearly distinguished; the differences among them should not be obliterated by equating them with a general "subsidiary element".

The second of the four conditions, the directly antecedent condition, includes all present awarenesses and associated mental factors, with the exception of the last moment of awareness before a perfected being attains *nirvāṇa.* These awarenesses and accompanying factors condition the arising of subsequent equivalent awarenesses or accompanying factors. "Equivalent" refer to factors of the same general category, such as feelings, ideas, and so on, and does not exclude a conditioning relationship between morally different accompanying factors of the same category. However, since the causal efficacy of the directly antecedent condition operates only successively, it does exclude the possibility of two equivalent accompanying factors arising in the same moment. "Contiguous" indicates that no factor of the same general category can arise between this condition and its effect. Therefore, the stream of awarenesses and accompanying factors may be interrupted by forces dissociated from awareness, as in the case of meditative states without awareness. Even in this case, awareness and accompanying factors immediately prior to the state without awareness can function as directly antecedent conditions in the arising of subsequent awarenesses and accompanying factors (see 2.42-43). Material form cannot act as a directly antecedent condition because more than one material factor of any given category arises in one moment in the life-stream of sentient beings.

The third of the four conditions, the supporting object condition, provides support for the production of perceptual consciousness and accompanying factors. All factors may serve as a supporting condition since no factor exists other than those that support perceptual consciousnesses. The five externally directed types of perceptual consciousness are supported by five corresponding supporting objects that are present and simultaneous with perceptual consciousness; the sixth type of mental perceptual consciousness may be supported by any factor in any time period.

Śrīlāta: The external objects corresponding to the five externally directed types of perceptual consciousness cannot be their supporting object conditions, because this supporting object cannot be simultaneous with the perceptual consciousness that it produces. Mental perceptual consciousness would also be incapable of being supported by a present object. Instead, mental perceptual consciousness takes the previous objects of the five externally directed types of perceptual consciousness as its supporting object. Since this prior supporting object has already passed away, it no longer exists; nonetheless, it still may serve as a supporting object for perceptual consciousness. However, the cause for the arising of a present moment of perceptual consciousness is the prior moment of perceptual consciousness within the same stream; this causal relation between a prior and successive moment is one of reciprocal succession within the same stream.

Answer: Since Śrīlāta does not allow that the supporting objects of the five externally directed types of perceptual consciousness are simultaneous with their corresponding perceptual consciousness, mental perceptual consciousness cannot depend upon the supporting object of a prior moment of the five externally directed types of perceptual consciousness. Further, it is absurd to claim that even though this past object does not exist it can still serve as the supporting object for present mental perceptual consciousness; perceptual consciousness can only be supported by an existent object. Indeed, since the Dārṣṭāntikas accept the existence only of present factors and reject those of the past and future, one cannot speak of reciprocal succession. How can there be a causal relation between a nonexistent past factor and an existent present one? Therefore, supporting objects of perceptual consciousness must exist, and those of the five externally directed types of perceptual consciousness are simultaneous with their corresponding perceptual consciousness.

The last of the four conditions, the dominant condition, is identical to the nonobstructing variety of comprehensive cause. This condition is named "dominant" because it both includes and effects the greatest number of factors; all factors can act as the dominant condition in the production of all factors other than itself.

Even though causes and conditions do not differ in their essential nature in general, they can be distinguished as follows: causes are only able to produce, that is, project or take their own effect, while conditions nourish, assist, or support the arising of the effect of another factor. Therefore, the arising of any factor will have at least one cause and many conditions. When the four conditions are compared to the five causes, the directly antecedent condition and the supporting object condition cannot be identified with any of the five causes.

63.(E450a) Vasubandhu suggests that the simultaneous and associated causes and the supporting object condition perform their function with regard to present factors that are about to pass away. He also claims that homogeneous and pervasive causes, causes of maturation, and the equivalent contiguous condition function with regard to future factors that are about to be produced. Vasubandhu, however, has confused a factor's functioning, which only occurs in the present and only refers to that factor's projecting its own effect, with its capability, which occurs in all three time periods and may assist in the arising of the effect of another factor. This confusion of functioning and capability is particularly obvious in the case of causes of maturation. A cause of maturation acts to produce its effect, which is just about to be produced, when it is long past. This causal activity cannot, then, be its present functioning. Therefore, causal efficacy is not limited to present functioning, but also includes capability. Further, causal efficacy is not limited to production, but includes the activities of supporting and so on.

64.(E457a) All conditioned factors are produced from a number of causes and conditions. For example, awareness and mental factors are produced from the four conditions; the two balanced states without awareness are produced from three conditions; and the other forces dissociated from awareness and material form are produced from two conditions. All conditioned factors are produced from such causes and conditions; there is none that arises from one cause, whether this single cause be a God, the self, or a primal source. If conditioned factors arose from a single cause, all factors would arise simultaneously and not in sequence because that single cause would always be present. What other factor would prevent this simultaneous arising of all conditioned factors? If you say that the sequential arising of factors results from the successive desires of this God, or single cause, then these factors arise from multiple desires and not from a single cause. In any case how would this singular God have multiple desires? If you say that God's desire produces the sequential arising of conditioned factors through the activity of other causes, these other causes would in turn depend on others *ad infinitum*. If you accept this, responding that these other causes have no beginning, then you have accepted the Buddhist position. Further, there is no advantage for God to cause these conditioned factors. If you say that it is merely for God's own satisfaction, then God would not be God in the true sense of the term because his satisfaction depends upon this creation. Further, what kind of God would create frustration? If one accepts God as the unique cause, one denies causes that are apparent in ordinary experience. If one says that God works through these ordinary causes, we reply that the activity of God is not apparent and need not be inferred; therefore, it cannot be assumed to exist. All such theories of production from one cause are thereby rejected.

65.(E452a) The four great elements act as homogeneous and simultaneous causes in the arising of other great elements. They act as causes of derived material form in five ways: production, dependence, support, maintenance, and growth.These are all forms of the comprehensive cause; the five other types of causal activities are absent in the causal relation between the fundamental elements and derived material form. Derived material form acts as the simultaneous and homogeneous causes, and as the cause of maturation of other derived material form.

66-71b.(E453a-464) Causal relations among moments of awareness must be discussed in terms of the twelve types of awareness. In the material realm there are four types of awareness: good, bad, obscured neutral, and unobscured neutral. In both the material and immaterial realms there are three, excluding bad awarenesses. Therefore, there are ten varieties of contaminating awareness within these three realms. There are only two types of uncontaminating awareness: those of disciples and adepts. Causal relations among these twelve types of awareness are determined by those types of awareness that may follow others.

These twelve categories of awareness may be expanded to twenty as follows: (1) by dividing good awareness in each realm into two types--acquired at birth, and acquired through effort; (2) by dividing unobstructed neutral awareness of the realm of desire into four types--those that are the matured effects, those associated with the modes of proper deportment, those associated with skill in the arts, and those associated with magical creations; (3) by dividing those of the material realm into three types, including the four previous types with the exception of those associated with skill in the arts. Again, causal relations among these twelve types of awareness are determined by those types that may follow others.

73.(E465b) The arising of each of these twelve or twenty types of thought entails also the possession of certain other categories of thought that may be produced if certain other requisite conditions are present.

## 207. SAṄGHABHADRA, *Abhidharmasamayapradīpikā*

This work is about one-third the size of 206.*Nyāyānusāra*, and also follows Vasubandhu's 173.*Abhidharmakośa*'s verses, but lacks the extended critique of the views of Vasubandhu and Śrīlāta, etc. Collett Cox suggests that it "can be understood as Saṅghabhadra's own exposition of what he considers to be orthodox Kāśmīra Sarvāstivāda-Vaibhāṣika doctrine."[593]

The title is a reconstruction suggested by Unrai Wogihara. It is available in a Chinese translation by Hsüan-tsang (T.1563), made in 651-652. No translation into Western languages is available. There is a Japanese translation by Hayashi Goho in KIK.Bidambara, vols. 23-24.

Collet Cox comments: "(T)he **Nyāyānusāra* and the **Abhidharmasamayapradīpikā* differ in their approach. In both texts, Saṅghabhadra follows Vasubandhu's *Abhidharmakośakārikā*, adopting its verses with minimal emendations. However, the **Nyāyānusāra* is almost three times longer than the *Abhidharmakośabhāṣya* and contains lengthy refutations of doctrinal interpretations offered by Vasubandhu and others whether or not they are cited in Vasubandhu's text. By contrast, the **Abhidharmasamayapradīpikā* omits these explicit refutations and, thus, can be understood as Saṅghabhadra's own exposition of what he considers to be orthodox Kāśmīra Sarvāstivāda-Vaibhāṣika doctrine."[594]

## ENDNOTES

**1.** Alex Wayman studies a few passages where lists of views are found. Cf. Wayman, "The twenty reifying views", in *Studies in Pāli and Buddhism. J. Kashyap Memorial Volume* (1979), pp. 375-380.
**2.** For a review and critique of those who take some of these views see J.W.de Jong, "The problem of the Absolute in the Mādhyamika", Journal of Indian Philosophy 2.1, 1972, 1-6, and "Emptiness", Journal of Indian Philosophy 2.1, 1972, 7-15.
**3.** Cf. 34.*Vigrahavyāvarttanī.*
**4.** Cf. A.K.Warder, "Is Nāgārjuna a Mahāyānist?", in Mervyn Sprung (ed.), *The Problem of Two Truths in Buddhism and Vedānta* (D. Reidel: Dordrecht 1973), 78-88.
**5.** There have been a few attempts to show Nāgārjuna dealing with non-Buddhist views.
**6.** Gregory Schopen, "The inscription on the Kuṣān image of Amitābha and the character of the early Mahāyāna in India", Journal of the International Association of Buddhist Studies 10.2, 1987, p. 117.
**7.** Ibid., p. 118.
**8.** Gregory Schopen, "The generalization of an old yogic attainment in medieval Mahāyāna Sūtra literature: some notes on *jātismara*", Journal of the International Association of Buddhist Studies p. 132.
**9.** Schopen, ibid., 132-133.
**10.** Schopen, "The inscription on the Kuṣān image" (see note 6), p. 109.
**11.** Ibid., p. 125.
**12.** Ibid., p. 125.
**13.** E. Zürcher, "A new look at the earliest Chinese Buddhist texts", in *From Benares to Beijing: Essays on Buddhism and Chinese Religion* (ed. Koichi Shinohara and Gregory Schopen)(Oakville, Ontario 1991), 277-304.
**14.** Nancy Schuster in her unpublished dissertation (University of Toronto 1976) assigns the authorship of a *Maitreyaparipṛcchā* (T. 348) to An Shih-kao; the work constitutes #41 of the Ratnakūṭa collecton. This work does not appear in Zürcher's list.
**15.** Zürcher, op. cit., pp. 282-283.
**16.** Pp. 93-95.
**17.** E.g., T.W.Rhys Davids, "Schools of Buddhist belief", Journal of the Royal Asiatic Society 1892, 1-38; Nalinaksha Dutt, "Introduction to the evolution of the schools of Buddhism", Journal of the Department of Letters, University of Calcutta 3, 1920, 247-266 and "The Buddhist sects: a survey", in D.R.Bhandarkar et al., eds., *B.C.Law Volume* One, Calcutta 1945, 282-292; Étienne Lamotte, *Histoire du Bouddhisme Indien* (Louvain

1958), translated into English by Sarah Boin, Louvain 1988, p. 518; Edward Conze, *Buddhist Thought in India* (London 1962).
18. Étienne Lamotte, *Histoire du Bouddhisme Indien*, ibid., English translation, p. 518.
19. Ibid., p. 519.
20. Ibid., p. 521.
21. Bareau, *Les Sectes Bouddhiques...*pp. 36-37.
22. Drawn from Bareau, ibid., pp. 36-38. Added information along these lines is available there.
23. These seventy-two views are set forth in Bareau, ibid., pp. 89-98.
24. Bareau, ibid., p. 112.
25. K.R.Norman, *Pāli Literature* (Wiesbaden 1983), pp. 1-7.
26. For an account of what is known of these *Aṭṭhakathās*' history cf. K.R.Norman, ibid., pp. 118-120. For an extended attempt to organize the quotations and references in Buddhaghoṣa's writing to these *Aṭṭhakathās* consult Friedgard Lottermoser's published dissertation *Quoted Verse Passages in the Works of Buddhaghosa: Contributions Towards the Study of the Lost Sīhaḷaṭṭhakathā Literature* (Göttingen 1982).
27. Ho-Li-Pa-Mo Ch'uan, quoted in the Ch'u-San-Ts'ang-Chi-Chi, 11, Taisho vol. LV, pp. 78b-79b.
28. For a summary of some of these cf. James P. McDermott, "Karma and rebirth in early Buddhism", in Wendy Doniger O'Flaherty (ed.), *Karma and Rebirth in Classical Indian Traditions* (Berkeley, California: University of California Press), pp. 165-192, on which the account given here is largely based.
29. On the intermediate state see Alex Wayman, "The intermediate-state dispute in Buddhism" in *Buddhist Studies in Honor of I.B.Horner* (ed. L. Cousins, A.Kunst and K.R.Norman) (Riedel: Dordrecht 1974); Y. Krishan, "Buddhism and belief in *ātmā*", Journal of the International Academy of Buddhist Studies 7.2, 1984, 117-132; Donald W. Mitchell, "Karma in Buddhist thought" in S.S.Rama Rao Pappu (ed.), *The Dimensions of Karma* (Delhi 1987), 66-93.
30. Cf. Kyodo Yamada, "On the idea of '*avijñapti-karma*' in Abhidharma Buddhism", Journal of Indian and Buddhist Studies 10.1, 1962, 51-55.
31. Shanta Ratnayaka, "Metapsychology of the Abhidharma", Journal of the Indian Academy of Buddhist Studies 4.2, 1981, 76-90..
32. Collett Cox, *Disputed Dharmas. Early Buddhist Theories on Existence* (Tokyo 1995)., pp. 69-70. I have replaced Cox's term "defilement", by which she translates *anuśaya*, by the translation of that word used in our present volume, "proclivity", in order to avoid confusion.
33. For further discussion of these matters cf. Cox, ibid., pp. 70-74.
34. For an extensive discussion of this section cf. Cox, ibid., pp. 82-90.
35. Cox, ibid., p. 83.

**36.** Akira Hirakawa, *A History of Indian Buddhism From Śākyamuni to Early Mahāyāna* (tr. Paul Groner), Asian Studies at Hawaii No. 36 (Honolulu, Hawaii: University of Hawaii Press, 1990), pp. 306-309.
**37.** Cf. Ria Kloppenborg, *The Paccekabuddha. A Buddhist Ascetic* (Leiden 1974) for the basis for these remarks and a survey of the literature relevant to the self-enlightened.
**38.** *Majjhima Nikāya* 112.
**39.** E.J.Thomas, "*Nirvāṇa* and *parinirvāṇa*", in *India Antiqua* (Leiden 1947), pp. 294 ff.
**40.** Peter Masefield, "The *Nibbāna-parinibbāna* controversy", Religion 9, 1979, 215-230.
**41.** Kenneth R. Norman, "Mistaken ideas about *nibbāna*" in Tadeusz Skorupski and Ulrich Pagel, eds., *The Buddhist Forum, Volume III* (School of Oriental and African Studies, University of London: London 1994), pp. 216-217.
**42.** Paul Harrison, "Who gets to ride in the great vehicle? Self-image and identity among the followers of the early Mahāyāna", Journal of the International Association of Buddhist Studies 10.1, 1987, 67-90.
**43.** Or *āśraya-parivṛtti*; both forms are found. Cf. Ronald Mark Davidson's 1985 doctoral dissertation at the University of California at Berkeley, unpublished, on Buddhist Systems of Transformation: *Āśraya-parivṛtti/-parāvṛtti* Among the Yogācāra, pp. 151-155, for a discussion of the terminology.
**44.** Davidson, ibid., pp. 160 ff.
**45.** Cf. Davidson, ibid., pp. 150-151.
**46.** This paragraph is based on Davidson, ibid., pp. 183-184, for which see appropriate references.
**47.** Paul J. Griffiths, *On Being Mindless: Buddhist Meditation and the Mind-Body Problem* (LaSalle, Ill., 1986), pp. 49-50.
**48.** A. Charlene McDermott, "Asaṅga's defense of *ālayavijñāna*. Of catless grins and sundry related matters", Journal of Indian Philosophy 2, 1973, 167-174.
**49.** Hugh B. Urban and Paul J. Griffiths, "What else remains in *śūnyatā*? An investigation of terms for mental imagery in the Madhyāntavibhāga-corpus", Journal of the International Association of Buddhist Studies 17.1, 1994, 1-25.
**50.** Gadjin M. Nagao, "What remains in *śūnyatā*: a Yogācāra interpretation of emptiness" in Minoru Kiyota (ed.), *Mahāyāna Buddhist Meditation: Theory and Practice* (Honolulu: University of Hawaii Press, 1978).
**51.** Urban and Griffiths, op. cit., p. 1.
**52.** Ibid., p. 19.
**53.** Ibid., p. 20.
**54.** This paragraph is based on Noriaki Hakamaya, "The realm of

enlightenment in Vijñaptimātratā: the formulation of the four kinds of pure *dharmas*", translated by John Keenan, Journal of the International Association of Buddhist Studies 3.2, 1980, 22-26

55. Cf. Griffiths, *On Being Mindless*, op. cit., pp. 86-91 for an excellent discussion of this point.

56. Griffiths, ibid., p. 18.

57. Ibid., pp. 18-29.,

58. Griffiths, ibid., pp. 64-65.

59. Griffiths, ibid., pp. 71-72.

60. Griffiths, ibid., p. 73.

61. Paul Griffiths analyzes eight such arguments, found for example in Asaṅga's *Yogācārabhūmi*. Cf. Griffiths, ibid., pp. 96-104.

62. Cf. Brian Galloway, "A Yogācāra analysis of the mind, based on the Vijñāna section of Vasubandhu's Pañcaskandhaprakaraṇa with Guṇaprabhā's commentary", Journal of the International Association of Buddhist Studies 3.2, 1980, 7-20. Cf. as well Paul Williams, "Some aspects of language and construction in the Madhyamaka", Journal of Indian Philosophy 8, 1980, 1-45

63. Cf. Aruna Haldar, "*Saṃjñā skandha* or perception formation/composition", Journal of the Bihar and Orissa Research Society 44, 1958, 37-42.

64. Memory in Buddhism has received extended attention in the book *In the Mirror of Memory* edited by Janet Gyatso (State University of New York Press: Albany, N.Y. 1992). See especially Collett Cox's article dealing with the treatment of this concept in Sarvāstivāda, the *Mahāvibhāṣā*, Vasubandhu and Saṅghabhadra, and Paul Griffiths' article concerning its treatment in Yogācāra.

65. We adopt the standard translation of *kleśa*, but with misgivings. Stefan Anacker remarks, "...'*kleśa*' has never meant, either in Sanskrit or for any people in direct contact with Indian masters, "defilement", as it is usually translated. The Sanskrit root '*kliś*' means 'to be afflicted, to be tormented, to suffer', and a *kleśa* is accordingly 'an affliction, pain, anguish, suffering" (Anacker, *Seven Works of Vasubandhu* (Motilal Banarsidass: Delhi 1984), 146-147). Since the translation is "standard", we have stuck with it despite Anacker; the term "affliction" is standardly used (and we follow this usage) to translate a different Sanskrit term in Buddhist studies, viz., "*upakleśa*".

66. See the discussion in Anacker, ibid., pp. 147-148.

67. Cf. Nathan Katz, "Does the 'cessation of the world' entail the cessation of emotions? The psychology of the *arahant*", Pali Buddhist Review 4, 1979, 53-65.

68. Collett Cox, *Disputed Dharmas...*, op. cit., p. 10. The remainder of the present section is based on Cox's book.

69. This section is based on Cox, ibid., 53-58.

**70-**. For the various solutions to this problem that were proposed in Abhidharma literature see Cox, ibid., 53-68.
**71**. Cox, ibid., pp. 65-66.
**72**. Hirakawa, op. cit., p. 276.
**73**. Hirakawa, op. cit. For example, a *Bodhisattvapiṭaka* appears as a portion of the *Ratnakūṭa* collection (T.310 (12) and T. 316, as well as Toh. 56).
**74**. Hirakawa, op. cit., p. 276
**75**. As indicated in Hirakawa, ibid., p. 276.
**76**. Jacques May, "On Mādhyamika philosophy", Journal of Indian Philosophy 6, 1978, 233-234.
**77**. Chinese *Tao-hsing pan-jo ching* is T. (=Taisho) 224, the earliest translation is by Lokakṣema, who translated over twenty Mahāyāna works between 147 and 186 A.D. This is the earliest of some seven Chinese renditions (T. 225-228 and 220.4-5) stemming from different periods. These seven translations are discussed extensively in Lewis R. Lancaster, "The oldest Mahāyāna Sūtra: its significance for the study of Buddhist development", The Eastern Buddhist n.s. 8.1, 1975, 30-41. It is also extant in Sanskrit manuscripts found in Nepal. This Sanskrit text is edited by Rajendralal Mitra in Bibliotheca Indica 110, 1888, reprinted in the edition by Unrai Wogihara published from Tokyo in 1932-35, and (with revisions) in P.L.Vaidya's revised edition from Darbhanga 1960. A complete English translation of this text by Edward Conze can be found in Bibliotheca Indica 284, Calcutta 1958, reprinted in Bolinas, California 1973, 1975. For details on these and other materials consult Conze, *The Prajñāpāramitā Literature* (Mouton: The Hague, 1960; Second Edition revised and enlarged, The Reiyukai: Tokyo, 1978.)

Some chapters of the work have been translated into Western languages in various places. See K.H.Potter (ed.), *Bibliography of Indian Philosophies*, Third Revised Edition (Motilal Banarsidass: Delhi 1995, pp. 72-73.
**78**. Hirakawa, op. cit., 248-249.
**79**. A. K. Warder, *Indian Buddhism* (Motilal Banarsidass: Delhi 1970), p. 367.
**80**. Robert F. Olson, "Whitehead, Mādhyamika, and the Prajñāpāramitā", Philosophy East and West 25, 1975, pp. 453-457.
**81**. Zürcher, op. cit., pp. 397-298, provides a list of sixteen titles in Chinese that correspond to sixteen different Taisho translations made by An Shikao (active ca. 150-170 A.D.), and also gives a brief description of the contents of each. Our numbers 5-14 are taken from this list, choosing the ten texts which, given Zürcher's description, seem to contain philosophical content.
**82**. Émile Zürcher, *The Buddhist Conquest of China* (Second edition, Leiden 1972), p. 34.

83. Zürcher, ibid., p. 33.
84. T.31, 1 chuan.
85. T.32, 1 chuan.
86. T.36, 1 chuan.
87. T.57, 1 chuan.
88. T.98, 1 chuan.
89. T.112, 1 chuan.
90. T.602, 2 chuan.
91. T.603, 1 chuan.
92. T605, 1 chuan.
93. Chinese *A-she-shih-wang cing* (T.626). There are four Chinese (T.626-629) and one Tibetan version, ranging in date from Lokakṣema's Chinese translation in 196 A.D. to as late as 1000. The Sanskrit text is lost. Cf. Paul Harrison, "Who gets to ride...", op. cit., pp. 67-90. In another place Harrison discusses some passages from the Tibetan translations, and remarks on "the doctrinal richness of (it)...as well as the presence in it of apparent Yogācāra tendencies" (Paul Harrison, "Is the *dharma-kāya* the real 'phantom body' of the Buddha?", Journal of the International Association of Buddhist Studies 15, 1992, 44-93).
94. This work is extant in five Chinese (including T.310 (43), 350-352) and one Tibetan (Toh. 87) version. Fragments of the Sanskrit are known. The oldest Chinese translation (T.350) is attributed to Lokakṣema. Most of the versions have been translated into German and/or English. Cf. Harrison, "Who gets to ride...", ibid., p. 70; Bhikkhu Pasadika, "Biographical remarks bearing on the Kāśyapaparivarta", Buddhist Studies Review 8, 1991, 59-70. Hirakawa feels that "early versions of the *Ratnakūṭa*" (of which this work is one of the oldest sections) "must have existed by the first century C.E." (Hirakawa, op. cit., p. 251).

The 45th section of this work constitutes T.310 (45) and Toh. 89, titled *Akṣayamatiparipṛcchā*. It is translated in Garma C. C. Chang, *A Treasury of Mahāyāna Sūtras. Selections from the Mahāratnakūṭa Sūtra* (Pennsylvania State Press: University Park, Penna., 1983), pp. 415-424.
95. Chinese *A-ch'u-fo-kuo ching* (T.310 (6)), translated into Chinese by Lokakṣema, as well as a Tibetan version from the ninth century; cf. Harrison, "Who gets to ride...", op. cit., p. 71. Another Chinese translation dates from 335 or so, and a third from the eighth century. For full references cf. Buddhist Text Information 40, 1984, 3-5. A French translation of Book I, Chapters 1-3 is available in Jean Dantinne, *La Splendeur de l'Inébranlable (Akṣobhavyūha)*(Louvain-la-Neuve 1983). There is an English translation of most of this work in Chang, *Treasury...*, op. cit. pp. 315-338.
96. Chinese *Tun-chen-t'o-lo-ching*. There are two Chinese translations (T.624 and 625) and one Tibetan version. The oldest is by Lokakṣema.

The Sanskrit is lost. The Tibetan text has been edited by Paul Harrison in *Druma-kinnara-rāja-paripṛcchā-sūtra. A Critical Edition of the Tibetan Text (Recension A) Based on Eight Editions of the Kanjur and the Dunhuang Manuscript Fragment* (Tokyo 1992).

**97.** Harrison, ibid., pp. xv-xvi.

**98.** This work is T.807. There is one Tibetan translation by Jinamitra, Dānaśīla and Ye ses sde from the beginning of the ninth century. Paul Harrison (in "Sanskrit fragments of a Lokottaravādin tradition", *Indological and Buddhist Studies. Volume in Honour of Professor J.W.de Jong on his Sixtieth Birthday* (Canberra 1982), pp. 211-234) reports the Chinese title as *Fo shuo nei zang bai bao jing*, which he renders as *Sūtra of the Hundred Gems of the Inner Treasury as Expounded by the Buddha.* Our summary is taken from p. 212 of Harrison's article.

**99.** In Chinese *Pan-chou san-mei ching* (T.416-419) and in Tibetan. The oldest Chinese translation is Lokakṣema's. The Sanskrit text is lost, except for the portion (T.418) published as *Bhadrapālasūtra* by A.F.R.Hoernlé in *Manuscript Remains of Buddhist Literature found in East Turkestan* (Oxford 1916; Amsterdam 1970), pp. 88-93, 410-411. The Tibetan version is edited in Paul Harrison, *The Tibetan Text of the Pratyutpanna-Buddha Sanmukhāvasthita-Samādhi-Sūtra* (Studia Philologica Buddhica Monograph Series 1) (Tokyo 1978) and translated in Paul Harrison, *The Samādhi of Direct Encounter with the Buddhas of the Present* (Studia Philologica Buddhica 5) (Tokyo 1990). There is also a Mongolian version and Japanese translations of T. 417 and T. 418. Harrison is publishing an English translation of T. 418 in the forthcoming English translation of the Chinese Tripiṭaka, Bukkyo Dendo Kyokai, Tokyo.

**100.** T. 280. "There are two other Chinese versions (T.278, T.279), and one Tibetan version, the *Sangs-rgyas phal-po-che zhes-bya-ba shin-tu rgyas-pa chen-po'i mdo.* The material corresponding to (this text) occurs in Chap. XII...and Chap. XIV...(of the *Avataṃśaka Sūtra).* For an English translation of the entire *Avataṃśakasūtra* see Thomas Cleary, tr., *The Flower Ornament Scripture: A Translation of the Avataṃśaka Sūtra*, Vol. I (Shambala, Boulder 1984)." (Quoted from Harrison, "Who gets to ride...", pp. 69-70.

**101.** T. 458. The Sanskrit title is unknown. This is the only version.

**102.** The Sanskrit text is lost. Lokakṣema is credited with having translated this *sūtra* into Chinese in 186 A.D., followed by other such translations during the third century (cf. Étienne Lamotte, tr., *La Concentration de la Marche Héroique*, Melanges Chinois et Bouddhique 13, 1965, pp. 66-97). The earliest version available to us is the Chinese translation by Kumārajīva (T. 642) at the beginning of the fifth century. This is translated into French by Lamotte, ibid., pp. 117-275. Portions of a Tibetan edition are translated into English in Thubten Ḳalsang Rinpoche and Bhikkhu

Pasadika, *Excerpts from the Sūraṅgama Samādhi Sūtra* (Dharamsala 1970).

Various later versions are the bases of translations by Ernst Leumann, *Zur nordarischen-sprache und Literatur* (Strassburt 1912); Dwight Goddard (ed.), *A Buddhist Bible* (Thetford, Vt. 1932; New York 1935-37, 1952; Boston 1990), and R.E.Emmerick, *The Khotanese Sūraṅgamasamādhisūtra* (London 1970). The last renders a Khotanese fragment which may predate Kumārajīva. There is also an English translation by Charles Luk (London 19660.

**103**. George Teschner, "Mind and body in the Sūraṅgama Sūtra", Journal of Indian Philosophy 9, 1981, 77-83. The selections are from pp. 78-81.

**104**. T. 109, it was translated by An Shih-kao between 125-220 according to Stanislaw Schayer, "Notes and queries on Buddhism", Rocznik Orientalisticzny 11, 1935, 206-213.

**105**. According to Nancy Schuster (op. cit.) this is T. 348, translated by An Shih-kao in 150-180 A.D. It constitutes #41 of the Ratnakūṭa collection, translated by Bodhiruci. There is also a Tibetan translation, P780.42. The work does not appear, at least under this title, in Zürcher's list of An Shih-kao's works.

**106**. Chinese *Fa-ching ching*. There are four Chinese translations: T. 310 (19), T. 322-323 and T.1521 (three more are said to have been lost). T322 was translated by An Gen (or, according to Hirakawa, op. cit., pp. 251, 275, by An Hsuan and Yen Fo-t'iao) around 180 A.D. Three Chinese translations are translated into English by Nancy Schuster in her doctoral dissertation from the University of Toronto 1976.

Paul Harrison attributes the translation T.322 to An Xuan and Yan Fpts around 180 A.D. He also cites a Tibetan version that has been translated into Japanese by Hajime Sakurabe in *Daijo button 9* (Tokyo 1974), pp. 231-335 (Harrison, "Who gets to ride...", op. cit., p. 72).

**107**. Schuster, ibid., p. 27.

**108**. Schuster, ibid., pp. 37-38.

**109**. T. 630. The translation is attributed to Zhi Yao of the late second century.

**110**. Zürcher, op. cit., p. 299.

**111**. There are two *Sukhāvativyūhas*. Though they appear not to have been translated into Chinese until the middle of the third century A.D., Gregory Schopen dates the larger (Chinese *Wu-liang-shou ching*, T. 360) to the same period as the 45. *Samādhirājasūtra*, viz., the second century A.D. The larger (Chinese T.310 (5), T360-364; Tibetan P760.5; and several more translations, now apparently lost) has been translated into English several times; cf. Hajime Nakamura, *Indian Buddhism* (Japan 1980; Motilal Banarsidass: Delhi, 1987), pp. 203-206 for bibliography. One of the lost commentaries is said to have been by Lokakṣema.

Perhaps the most available of the many translations is by E.B.Cowell in *Buddhist Mahāyāna Texts*, Volume Two (Sacred Books of the East 49, 1894; Delhi 1965, 1968, 1972, 1975; New York 1969, etc.), p. 1-85. A somewhat more truncated rendition can be found in Chang, Treasury, op. cit., 339-360. Numbered sections in our summary correspond to those in Cowell's translation.

**112**. Chinese *A-mi-t'o ching*, this is T. 366-367 and Toh. 115. Hirakawa, op.cit., pp. 286-287 thinks this, the smaller, may have been earlier than our 29. Both works have been available for many years in Max Müller's translation (Journal of the Royal Asiatic Society n.s. 12, 1880, 168-186). There are many other translations; cf. *Bibliography of Indian Philosophies*, Volume Three Revised, op. cit., #45 for references.

**113**. Sanskrit Recension A (the manuscript in the Asiatic Society of Bengal, Calcutta) is edited in A. Yuyama, *Rgs (Sanskrit Recension A)*(Cambridge 1976). The date of this manuscript is 1174 A.D. The Sanskrit and Tibetan Recensions B are edited by Obermiller (Bibliotheca Buddhica 29, 1937) from a Chinese blockprint. For complete information about these sources see Yuyama, ibid., pp. xxiii-liii.

**114**. Edward Conze (tr.), *The Perfection of Wisdom in 8,000 Lines and Its Verse Summary* (Bolinas 1973), 1-73.

**115**. Cf. p. x of Conze, ibid.

**116**. Edward Conze, "The Calcutta manuscript of the Ratnaguṇasaṃcayagāthā", Indo-Iranian Journal 4, 1960, 37-58; 5, 1961, 1-18.

**117**. A portion of the *(Buddha)Avataṃśakasūtra*. The Sanskrit text is edited by D.T. Suzuki and Hokei Idzumi in four volumes, Kyoto 1934-36, and reprinted Tokyo 1949. The entire *Avataṃśaka*sūtra is translated by Thomas Cleary as *The Flower Ornament Scripture* (Boulder, Colo. 1984 et passim.).

The *Bhadracaryāpraṇidhāna* (T.278 (31), T279, T.293.40, T.296; Toh. 1095; Toh. 4377, a chapter of the *Gaṇḍavyūha*, has been translated into English a good many times. See *Bibliography of Indian Philosophies*, Third Edition, Volume I, pp. 84-85, for detailed information on texts, translations and analyses. The summary provided here draws from Warder, op. cit., pp. 423-430.

**118**. For a development of some of the themes so briefly indicated in this quote from Warder see Luis O. Gomez, "The Bodhisattva as wonder-worker", in Lewis Lancaster (ed.), *Prajñāpāramitā and Related Systems*. Studies in Honor of Edward Conze (Berkeley Buddhist Series 1. 1977, pp. 221-261, which contains a translation of a section of the text.

**119**. Chr. Lindtner, *Nagarjuniana. Studies in the Writings and Philosophy of Nāgārjuna*. Indiske Studier 4. (Akademisk Forlag: Copenhagen, 1982), referred to hereafter as Nagarjuniana.

**120**. Nalinaksha Dutt, *Buddhist Sects in India* (Calcutta 1970), p. 277.

Consult P.S.Sastri, "Nāgārjuna and Āryadeva", Indian Historical Quarterly 31, 1955, 193-202 for an extensive review of the evidence regarding Nāgārjuna's domicile.

**121.** On the relations between the arguments of Gautama and Nāgārjuna see Johannes Bronkhorst, "Nāgārjuna and the Naiyāyikas", Journal of Indian Philosophy 13, 1985, 107-132.

**122.** The time and location of scholarship concerning this work has been unusually piecemeal, growing largely by editions and translations of selected chapters with commentarial assistance, an appropriate procedure given the difficulty of understanding the text without commentarial help. There are numerous complete editions of verses, and English translations of the entire work by Frederick Streng, *Emptiness: A Study in Religious Meaning* (Nashville, Tenn. 1967); Kenneth K. Inada, *Nāgārjuna: A Translation of his Mūlamadhyamakakārikā* (Tokyo 1970); David J. Kalupahana, *Nāgārjuna. The Philosophy of the Middle Way* (Albany, N.Y., 1986); by Ram Chandra Pandeya in *Nāgārjuna's Philosophy of No-Identity* (Delhi 1991); by Jay L. Garfield, *The Fundamental Wisdom of the Middle Way: Nāgārjuna's* Mūlamadhyamaka-kārikā (Oxford University Press: Oxford, New York 1995). Summaries of the complete work exist in Satischandra Vidyabhusana, *History of Indian Logic* (Calcutta 1921; Delhi 1971); David Seyfort Ruegg, *The Literature of the Madhyamaka School of Philosophy in India* (Wiesbaden 1981); and S.M. Shah, *The Dialectic of Knowledge and Reality in Indian Philosophy: Kundakunda, Nāgārjuna, Śaṃkara* (Delhi 1986), pp. 73-83. A guide to selected English translations of specific passages in specific chapters, frequently with explanatory discussion, is provided in the following footnotes for each Chapter of the work.

**123.** See I 1; II 1, 21; IV 6, 8, 9; V 8; VI 4; VII 34; IX 5; X 10, 11, 16; XI 1; XIII 1, 8; XIV 5-7; XV 1, 2, 10; XXI 6, 12; XXII 12, 15, 16; XXIII 1; XXIV 8-10.

**124.** Complete translations of this Chapter in English in Th. Stcherbatsky, *Conception of Buddhist Nirvāṇa* (Leningrad 1927; The Hague 1965; Varanasi 1968; Delhi 1972, etc.); Swami Vimuktananda in Prabuddha Bharata 44, 1939; Heramba N. Chatterjee, *Mūla-Madhyamaka-Kārikā of Nāgārjuna*. Chapters I-V. Part I (Firma K.L. Mukhopadhyay: Calcutta 1957; Paul M. Williams in The Middle Way 52, 1977, 72ff. Studies of verses 1-2 in Gadjin M. Nagao, "From Mādhyamika to Yogācāra, an analysis of MMK 24.18 and MV 1.1-2", Journal of the International Association of Buddhist Studies 2.1, 1979, 29-43; of verse 1 in Yamakami Sogen, *Systems of Buddhist Thought* (Calcutta 1912; Varanasi 1970); of verses 1-3 and 12 in Richard Robinson, *Early Mādhyamika in India and China* (U. of Wisconsin Press: Madison 1967); *Lucid Exposition of the Middle Way* (tr. Mervyn Sprung et al.)(Routledge and Kegan Paul: London 1979); verse 6 in Claus

Oetke, "On the non-formal aspects of the proofs of the Madhyamakakārikās", *Panels of the 7th World Sanskrit Conference, Leiden, Aug. 23-29, 1987. Volume 2: Earliest Buddhism and Madhyamaka* (ed. D.S. Ruegg and L. Schmithausen)(Leiden 1990); verses 24-40 in Alex Wayman, "Contributions to the Mādhyamika school of Buddhism", Journal of the American Oriental Society 89, 1969, 141-152.

**125.** Complete translations of this Chapter in Vidyabhusana, op. cit., Vimuktananda, op. cit.; H.N. Chatterjee, op. cit.; Kamaleswar Bhattacharya, "Nāgārjuna's arguments against motion", Journal of the International Association of Buddhist Studies 8.1, 1985, 7-16; Brian Galloway, "Notes on Nāgārjuna and Zeno on motion", Journal of the International Association of Buddhist Studies 10.2, 1987, 80-87; K.V. Apte, "Going? You cannot go! An exposition of Nāgārjuna's Madhyamakakārikā, Chapter II", Journal of Shivaji University 4, 1971, 43-60; Alex Wayman, "The gait (*gati*) and the path (*mārga*)--reflections on the horizontal", Journal of the American Oriental Society 105, 1985, 579-588; Sprung et al., op. cit. Translations of 1, 8, 15, 24 and 25 in Robinson, op. cit.; of 1-6 in Kamaleshwar Bhattacharya, "The grammatical basis of Nāgārjuna's arguments: some further considerations", Indologica Taurinensia 8-9, 1980-81, 35-44; of 22 and 23 in Oetke, op. cit. Studies in T.R.V.Murti, "Nāgārjuna's refutation of motion and rest", Philosophical Quarterly 9, 1933-34, 191-200; Kamaleswar Bhattacharya, "A reconsideration of Nāgārjuna's arguments against motion", Visva-Bharati Annals n.s. 2-3, 1990, 1-13.

**126.** Complete translation of this Chapter in Sprung et al., op. cit.; Vidyabhusana, op. cit.; H.N. Chatterjee, op. cit.; William Longstreet Ames, Bhāvaviveka's Prajñāpradīpa: Six Chapters. Ph.D.Thesis, University of Washington 1986. Translations of specific verses: 6-8 in Robinson, op. cit.; 2 in David J. Kalupahana, *The Principles of Buddhist Psychology* (SUNY Press: Albany, N.Y. 1987). Summarized in Apte, "Perception is impossible: an exposition of Nāgārjuna's Madhyamakakārikā Ch. III", Journal of the Asiatic Society of Bombay 49-50, 1974-76, 1-14.

**127.** Entire Chapter summarized in Sprung et al., op. cit.; H.N. Chatterjee, op. cit.; Ames, op. cit. Specific verses: 3 in Robinson, op.cit., 7-9 in K. Bhattacharya, "A note on the interpretation of the term *sādhyasama* in Mādhyamika texts", Journal of Indian Philosophy 2, 1974, 225-230.

**128.** Complete translations in Nathan Katz, "Nāgārjuna and Wittgenstein on error", in A.K. Narain (ed.), *Studies in History of Buddhism* (Delhi 1980); Sprung et al., op. cit.; Vidyabhusana, op. cit.; H.N. Chatterjee, op. cit. Translation of verses 1-7 in Robinson, op. cit.

**129.** Complete translations in Sprung et al., op. cit.; H.N. Chatterjee, op. cit. Verse 5 translated in Robinson, op. cit.

**130.** Chapter summarized in H.N. Chatterjee, op. cit., part 2 (Calcutta 1962); Vidyabhusana, op. cit.; Verses 1, 3, 20, 23, 29, 30, 33, 34 translated in Robinson, op. cit.; verses 2 and 17 in Oetke, op. cit.; 4 in Eli Franco, "Mahāyāna Buddhism--an unfortunate misunderstanding? Review of David J. Kalupahana's *Nāgārjuna: The Philosophy of the Middle Way*", Berliner Indologische Studien 4-5, 1989, 39-48; verses 33 and 34 in Richard King, "*Śūnyatā* and *ajāti*: absolutism and the philosophies of Nāgārjuna and Gauḍapāda", Journal of Indian Philosophy 18, 1989, 385-406.

**131.** Complete translation in Sprung et al., op. cit.; Vidyabhusana, op. cit.; H.N. Chatterjee, part 2, op. cit. Verse 7 translated in Robinson, op. cit.

**132.** Entire Chapter translated in Sprung et al., op. cit.; Vidyabhusana, op. cit.; H.N. Chatterjee, part 2, op. cit.

**133.** Complete translation in Sprung et al., op. cit.; Vidyabhusana, op. cit. Verses 1, 11 and 15 translated in Robinson, op. cit.; verses 7 and 11 in Oetke, p. cit.

**134.** Complete translation in Vidyabhusana, op. cit. Verses 1-7 translated in Katz, "Nāgārjuna and Wittgenstein...", op. cit.

**135.** Complete translation in Vidyabhusana, op. cit.

**136.** Complete translation in Sprung et al., op. cit.; Oetke, op. cit. Sections 3, 4, 7, 8 translated in Robinson, op. cit..

**137.** Verse 7 translated in Robinson, op. cit.

**138.** Chapter translated in Sprung et al, op. cit. as well as in Anviksiki 6.3-4, 1973, 147-155; also in Williams, op. cit. Stanzas 1-3, 5, 8-9 translated in Robinson, op. cit.; 4-6 in King, op. cit.; 6 in Wayman, "Contributions to the Mādhyamika school...", op. cit. and in Diana Ames, "Nāgārjuna's concept of *śūnyatā*", The Pacific World 3, 1987, 15-23.

**139.** Chapter translated in W. Ames thesis, op. cit. Verses 2 and 9 translated in D.Ames, op. cit.; verses 4, 6-10 translated in Robinson, op. cit.

**140.** Stanza 8 translated in Indra Gupta, "An enquiry into 'real'--the Mādhyamika way", Journal of the Department of Buddhist Studies, South Delhi University 11.1, 1987, 97-103. Stanza 33 translated in Christian Lindtner, "The Laṅkāvatāra in early Indian Madhyamaka literature", Asiatische Studien 46.1, 1992, 244-279.

**141.** Chapter translated in Sprung et al., op. cit.; Peter Della Santina, "The treatment of the self (*ātman*) in Madhyamaka philosophy", Journal of the Department of Buddhism, Delhi University 3, 1976, 8-11; Williams, op. cit. Verses 4 and 5 translated in King, op. cit.; 4, 5, and 7 in Streng, op. cit.; 5-7 and 9 in I. Gupta, op. cit.; 5 in D. Ames, op. cit.; 7, 8 and 10 in Robinson, op. cit.; 7 in Douglas A. Fox, "Nāgārjuna and Śaṃkara", Aligarh Journal of Oriental Studies 5, 1988, 127-130; 7 in Franco, op.cit.; 12 in Lindtner, op. cit.

**142.** Complete translations in K.V. Apte, "Where is the time: an exposition of Madhyamakakārikā XIX", Journal of Shivaji University 7, 1974, 49-54;

Sprung et al., op. cit.; in J.G.Arapura, *Hermeneutical Essays on Vedānta Topics* (Delhi 1986). Partially translated in Shoson Miyamoto, "Time and eternity in Buddhism", Journal of Indian and Buddhist Studies 7.2, 1959, 3-18. Verses 1-6 translated in Robinson, op.cit.; verses 1-4 translated in Oetke, op. cit.

**143**. Verses 1, 2, 5-7, 10, 15-20 translated in Robinson, op. cit.

**144**. Verses 1-6 translated in Oetke, op. cit.; verses 4, 14 and 21 in Robinson, op. cit.; 11 in Lindtner, op. cit.

**145**. Chapter translated in Alex Wayman, "The Tathāgata chapter of Nāgārjuna's Mūla-madhyamaka-kārikā", Philosophy East and West 38, 1988, 47-57; Sprung et al., op. cit.; Williams, op. cit. Verses 1-2, 4, 11, 12, 14, 16 in Sogen, op. cit.; verses 7-11, 16 in Streng, op. cit.; 11 in King, op. cit.; 11 and 16 in Robinson, op. cit.

**146**. Chapter translated in Willliam L. Ames, "The soteriological purpose of Nāgārjuna's philosophy: a study of Chapter 23 of the Mūla-madhyamaka-kārikās", Journal of the International Association of Buddhist Studies 11.2, 1988, 7-20; Sprung et al., op.cit.; Verse 1 translated by I. Gupta, op. cit.; verses 2, 5, 8 and 9 translated in Robinson, op. cit.

**147**. Chapter translated in Robert F. Olson, "Whitehead, Mādhyamika and the Prajñāpāramitā", Philosophy East and West 25, 1975, 449-464; Sprung et al., op. cit.; Williams, op. cit. Verses 7, 10 and 11 translated in I. Gupta, op. cit.; verse 7 in Lindtner, op. cit.; verses 8-10, 14, 18-19, 36-37, 40 in Streng, op. cit.; verses 8-10, 18 in King, op. cit.; verses 8-11, 18, 21-25, 40 in Robinson, op. cit.; verses 8-10, 14, 16, 19 in Sogen, op. cit.; verse 18 in Nagao, op. cit.; 18 in N. Aiyaswami Sastri, "*Śūnyatā* and its significance in Buddhism: Bulletin of Tibetology 12, 1975, 5-18; verse 18 in I T'ao-t'ien, "An attempt to examine the inner logical connections of the dialectical development from the Buddhist traditional doctrine of the *satya*-in-duplication being transmitted and maintained by Nāgārjuna to the T'ien-t'ai Buddhist doctrine of the *satya*-in-triplication being created and advocated by Chih-I on the inquiring about the 18th verse in Ch. 24, entitled Viewing the Four Noble Truths, of Nāgārjuna's Madhyamaka-Śāstra" (summary), Transactions of the International Congress of Orientalists in Japan 11, 1956, 49-50; verses 18-19 in Yensho Kanakura, *Hindu-Buddhist Thought in India* (tr. S. Iida and N. Donner)(Yokohama 1980); in Wayman, "Contributions to the Mādhyamika school...", op. cit.

**148**. Chapter translated in Sprung et al., op.cit.; Stcherbatsky, op. cit.; Williams, op. cit. Verses 1-2, 4, 7, 11, 15 translated in Arthur Herman, "Skepticism and Mādhyamika: how not to think about things", Philosophica 15-16, 1986-87, 139-161; verses 3, 5 translated in Lindtner, op. cit.; verses 3, 24 translated in Rita Gupta, "Mādhyamika dialectics: search for truth and soteriological analysis", Vishwabharati Journal of Philosophy 21.2, 1985, 83-89; verses 17-18 in Robinson, op. cit.; verse 19 in Sogen, op. cit.;

verse 19 in King, op. cit.

149. Chapter translated in W. Ames' doctoral dissertation, op. cit. Verse 11 translated in Robinson, op. cit. The authenticity of this Chapter is discussed in Tilmann Vetter, "On the authenticity of the Ratnāvalī", Asiatische Studien 46.1, 1992, 497-499.

150. Summarized in Nalinaksha Dutt, "The Brahmajala Sutta (in the light of Nāgārjuna's exposition)", Indian Historical Quarterly 8, 1932, 706-746. Verses 3, 6, 7, 9, 11, 15, 22-25 translated in Robinson, op. cit. Verse 7 translated in D. Ames, op. cit. The authenticity of this Chapter is discussed by Tilmann Vetter, op.. cit., 497-499.

151. Cf. Lindtner, op. cit., p. 70.

152. Translations in Giuseppe Tucci, *Pre-Diṅnāga Buddhist Texts on Logic*. Gaekwads Oriental Series 49, 1929; Kamaleswar Bhattacharya in Journal of Indian Philosophy 1, 1971, 217-261 (reprinted Delhi 1978). Summarized by Satkari Mookerjee in Nava-Nalanda-Mahavira Research Publications I (Nalanda 1957) and in Ruegg, op. cit., pp. 21-23.

153. Cf. E.H. Johnston and A. Kunst in Melanges Chinois et Bouddhiques 9, 1951, 99-152.

154. Cf. Lindtner, op. cit., note 74.

155. Kamaleswar Bhattacharya, "A note on...*sādhyasama*...", op. cit., p. 8.

156. Kamaleswar Bhattacharya, "Some notes on the Vigrahavyāvarttanī", Journal of Indian Philosophy 5, 1978, 237-242.

157. In the Introduction to Johnston and Kunst's edition, op.cit.

158. Giuseppe Tucci, "A Sanskrit biography of the *siddha*s and some questions connected with Nāgārjuna", Journal of the Asiatic Society of Bengal 26, 1930, 125-160; reprinted in Giuseppe Tucci, *Opera Minore* (Roma 1971-72), pp. 229-244.

159. Kamaleshwar Bhattacharya, "A note on...*sādhyasama*...", op. cit..

160. Lindtner, op. cit., p. 71, note 10.

161. This verse and the next, with verses 33-34, are studied in R.K. Sharma, *Studies in Indology. Prof. Rasik Vihari Joshi Felicitation Volume* (ed. A. Kumar et al.)(New Delhi 1988-89).

162. Verses 36-39 are rendered into quantificational logic by Shohei Ichimura in *Buddhist-Christian Dialogue* (ed. Paul O. Ingram)(Honolulu 1986), 95-114.

163. Cf. *Nyāyasūtra* II.1.19 and Kamaleswar Bhattacharya, "On the relationship between Nāgārjuna's *Vigrahavyāvarttanī* and the *Nyāyasūtras*", Journal of Indo-European Studies 5, 1979, 265-273.

164. In addition, the work is translated in Pandeya and Manju, *Nāgārjuna's Philosophy of No-Identity* (Delhi 1991) and summarized in Ruegg, op. cit., 20-21.

165. Tibetan editions of the *Vaidalyaprakaraṇa* and its *Prakaraṇa* constitute Toh. 5226 and Toh. 5230 respectively. Both are printed in Yuichi

Kajiyama's edition (Miscellania Indologica Kiotensia 6-7, 1965, 129-155 and in Sempa Dorje's edition (Varanasi 1974). Kajiyama, p. 130, reports that "S. Yamaguchi first published an exposition of the text in 1927 and later incorporated the work into his book, *Chūkan Bukkyō Ronkō*, pp. 113-166." Kajiyama also points out that Th. Stcherbatsky was mistaken in identifying this text with the (lost) *Pramāṇavihethana* (also called *Pramāṇavidhvaṃsana*)(cf. Kajiyama, ibid., 129-130).

166. Michael Hahn, *Nāgārjuna's Ratnāvalī*. Volume One: The Basic Texts (Sanskrit, Tibetan, Chinese). Indica et Tibetica, Band 1 (Bonn 1982), pp. 1-34.

167. Tilmann Vetter, "On the authenticity of the Ratnāvalī", Asiatische Studien 46.1, 1992, 492-506.

168. Giuseppe Tucci, "The Ratnāvalī of Nāgārjuna", Journal of the Royal Asiatic Society 1934, 307-325; 1936, 237, 423. Partly reprinted in Giuseppe Tucci, *Opera Minore* (Roma, 1971-72), 321-336. The 100 verses edited by Tucci have been reprinted in P.L. Vaidya's Appendix to *Madhyamakaśāstra* (Buddhist Sanskrit Texts 10)(Darbhanga 1960), pp. 299-310, and in Heramba Chatterjee Sastri, *The Philosophy* of *Nāgārjuna as Contained in the Ratnāvalī* (Calcutta 1977), 83-100. These editions have since been superseded by Hahn's (cf. footnote 166, above).

169. This Nāgārjuna's authorship of the present text has been controverted by Carmen Dragonetti, "The Pratītyasamutpādahṛdayakārikā and the Pratītyasamutpādahṛdayavyākhyāna of Śuddhamati", Wiener Zeitschrift fur die Kunde Sudasiens 22, 1978, 87-94 and "Some notes on the Pratītyasamutpādahṛdayakārikā and the Pratītyasamutpāda-hṛdayavyākhyāna attributed to Nāgārjuna", Journal of the Department of Buddhist Studies, South Delhi University 6, 1979, 70-73, with a reply by Christian Lindtner in Praci-Jyoti: Digest of Indological Studies 26, 1982, 167ff.

170. Sieglinde Dietz, "The author of the Suhṛllekha" in E. Steinkellner and H. Täuscher (eds.), *Contributions on Tibetan and Buddhist Religion and Philosophy*. Wiener Studien zur Tibetologie und Buddhismuskunde, Heft 11. Proceedings of the Csoma de Koros Symposium held at Velm-Vienna, Austria, 13-19 September 1981. Volume 2 (Wien 1983), pp. 59-72.

171. Lindtner, op. cit., pp. 218-224.

172. Bharat Singh Upadhyaya in B.V. Bapat (ed.), *2500 Years of Buddhism* (Delhi 1959), pp. 218-224.

173. Lindtner, op. cit., p. 225.

174. In Giuseppe Tucci, *Minor Buddhist Texts* (Roma 1956, 1958; Japan 1978; Delhi 1986), pp. 193-208.

175. Cf. Journal of Indian Philosophy 13, 1985, 1-54.

176. This set of terms, first coined by Democritus, reflects a way of thinking common to Greek and Indian philosophers in general. The latter

spoke of the two *bodies* (*kāya*) of the Bhagavat in terms conceived as a cosmic *mahāpuruṣa*. So the two kinds of cosmos provides the classical Greek counterpart to two bodies and two truths in ancient India.

177. Here, as elsewhere, Nāgārjuna alludes to the *Laṅkāvatārasūtra*. Cf. C. Lindtner in Asiatische Studien XLVI.1, 1992, 244-279.

178. Like *lokavyavahāra, lokasaṃvyavahāra*, a common synonym of *saṃvṛtisatya.*

179. A Chinese translation by An Shih-kao, who flourished in the second century A.D., is recorded in the catalogues. The earliest redaction of the text is in two fragments of a Chinese translation dating from 420-479.

This is a *vaipulya* or extensive text with a vast history. It evidently underwent sizable expansion and revision as it found its way to various parts of Asia. There is no sure way of telling which portions are the earlier.

The complete Sanskrit text, discovered in Gilgit, is edited by Nalinaksha Dutt in *Gilgit Manuscripts* 2.1-3 and by P.L. Vaidya, Buddhist Sanskrit Texts 2 (Darbhanga 1961). There is no complete translation. Footnotes to Chapters in the following summary give details of editions and translations of specific chapters. The titles of sections are taken from Luis O. Gomez and Jonathan A. Silk, *Studies in the Literature of the Great Vehicle* (Ann Arbor 1989).

180. Cf. Konstantin Regamey, *Three Chapters from the Samādhirājasūtra* (in Polish) (Warsaw 1938), reprinted by Motilal Banarsidass, Delhi 1994, p. 10.

181. Nalinaksha Dutt, op. cit., p. iii.

182. Vaidya, op. cit.

183. Gomez and Silk, op. cit.

184. Rajendralal Mitra, *The Sanskrit Buddhist Literature of Nepal* (Calcutta 1882).

185. Edited by Sheiren Matsunami in Taisho Daigaku Kenkyu Kiyo (Tokyo) 60, 1975. Translated into English in Gomez/Silk, op. cit.

186. Edited in Matsunami, ibid., and translated in Gomez/Silk, op. cit.

187. Edited in Matsunami, ibid., and translated in Gomez/Silk, op. cit.

188. Edited in Matsunami, ibid., and in Nepali in John Rockwell, Jr.'s 1980 M.A. Thesis at The Naropa Institute, Boulder, Colorado. French translation by Jean Filliozat, "La mort volontaire par le feu et la tradition bouddhique indienne", Journal Asiatique 251, 1963.

189. Edited in Matsunami, ibid. Translated from Nepali by Rockwell, ibid.

190. Edited in Matsunami, ibid. Edited and translated in Regamey, op.cit.

191. Edited in Rockwell, op. cit. Edited and translated in Christopher Cuppers, *The IXth Chapter of the Samādhirājasūtra* (Stuttgart 1990).

192. Edited in Tibetan and translated in Mark Tatz' M.A. Thesis at the University of Washington 1972 titled Revelation in Mādhyamika Buddhism.

193. Partially edited by Sarat Chandra Das and Hari Mohan Vidyabhusana

(Calcutta 1896; Shanghai 1940).
**194.** Edited in Das and Vidyabhusana, ibid.
**195.** Partly edited in Russian by G. Bongard-Levin, "A new fragment of the Sanskrit Samādhirājasūtra from Central Asia", *Sanskrit and Indian Culture* (Moscow 1979), pp. 62-72, with English summary on p. 252.
**196.** Edited and translated in Regamey, op. cit.
**197.** Translated in Regamey, op. cit.
**198.** Most of this Chapter is translated into French in Filliozat, op. cit.
**199.** Most of this Chapter is translated into German by Friedrich Weller, "Der arme Heinrich in Indien", Orientalistischer Literaturzeitung 68, 1973, 437-448.
**200.** T.474-476, translated into Chinese by Shi Ken in 252, and by others earlier, though their translations are lost. Ètienne Lamotte, in *L'Enseignement de Vimalakīrti* (Louvain 1962; translated by Sara Boin as *The Teaching of Vimalakīrti*, Pali Text Society, Translation Series 1976; also Sacred Books of the Buddhists 32, 1976), gives a thorough review of available information about the various translations into Chinese, Japanese, Tibetan and Sogdian of this work, as well as a concordance, together with analysis. Nakamura, op. cit., p. 224, reviewing the literature, states that this *sūtra* "was already existent as early as prior to 200 or 150 A.D.", citing Japanese authorities. To Lamotte's and Nakamura's bibliographical information should be added the following: Richard B. Mather, "Vimalakīrti and gentry Buddhism", History of Religions 8, 1968, 60-73; Edward Hamlin, "Magical *upāya* in the Vimalakīrtinirdeśa", Journal of the International Association of Buddhist Studies 11.1, 1988, 89-122. There are numerous partial translations. An alternative summary to that by A.K. Warder, quoted here, is by Charles Luk (Berkeley 1972).
**201.** See Warder, op. cit., pp. 397-399.
**202.** Noble Ross Reat, *The Śālistamba Sūtra* (Motilal Banarsidass: Delhi 1993).
**203.** Reat, ibid., p. 4.
**204.** Reat, ibid., pp. 15-16, gives a thorough review of the literature on this text. Since this work is absent from the Bibliography volume of the Encyclopedia of Indian Philosophies we give here the major references: L. de la Vallee Poussin, *Théorie des douze causes* (London 1913), containing a reconstructed Sanskrit text and a Tibetan text; N. Aiyaswami Sastri, *Ārya Śālistamba Sūtra* (Theosophical Society: Adyar 1950), with Tibetan text and reconstruction of the Sanskrit, reprinted in *Mahāyāna-Sūtra-Saṃgraha* (ed. P.L. Vaidya), Buddhist Sanskrit Texts 17 (Darbhanga 1961); V.V.Gokhale's version found in the same volume of Buddhist Sanskrit Texts.
**205.** Cf. Tom Tillemans, *Materials for the Study of Āryadeva, Dharmapāla and Candrakīrti* (Wien 1990), pp. 5-7.

206. See Vidhusekhara Bhattacharya, "Āryadeva", Indian Historical Quarterly 9, 1933, 978 and P.S. Sastri in Indian Historical Quarterly 31, 1955, 193-202.
207. This work has been edited and translated by Karen Lang in Indiske Studier 7 (Copenhagen 1986), and partly edited in H.P. Shastri, Memoires of the Asiatic Society of Bengal 3.8, 1914, 449-514 and by Bhagchandra Jain Bhaskar (Nagpur 1971). Summaries are to be found in Lang, ibid., pp. 16-21, and in Ruegg, op. cit., pp. 51-53. For relations between passages in this work and texts such as *Sūtrasamuccaya*, *Bodhicittavivaraṇa*, *Bhavasaṃkrāntisūtra*, *Triṃśikā*, et. cf. Lindtner, "The Laṅkāvatāra...", op. cit., Excursi 1-6.
208. Studied in Karen C. Lang, "Āryadeva and Candrakīrti on the *dharma* of kings", Asiatische Studien 46.1, 1992, 232-243.
209. Edited and translated by V. Bhattacharya in Proceedings of the All-India Oriental Conference 4, 1928, 831-871.
210. Edited and translated into French by P.L. Vaidya, *Études sur Āryadeva et son Catuśśataka* (Paris 1923). Edited by Vidhusekhara Bhattacharya at Visvabharati Studies 2.2, 1931.
211. Edited and translated into French in Vaidya, ibid. Translated into French by Jacques May, (1) "Āryadeva et Candrakīrti sur le permanence", *Indianisme et Bouddhisme offerts à Msgr. Étienne Lamotte*. Publications de l'Institut Orientaliste du Louvain 23 (Louvain-la-Neuve 1980), pp. 215-232; (2) Bulletin de l'Ecole Francaise d'Extreme-Orient 69, 1981, 75-96; (3) Asiatische Studien 35.2, 1981, 57-66; (4) *Études de Lettres*, Revue de la Faculte des Lettres de l'Universite de Lausann 19982, n.s. 3, 45-76; (5) "Āryadeva V" in *Shinpi Shiso ronshu/Studies of Mysticism in Honour of the 1150th Anniversary of Kobo Daishi's Nirvāṇam*. Acta Indologica 6: Naritesan Shinshoji 1984, 115-144. Edited in V. Bhattacharya, Visvabharati Studies 2.2, 1931.
212. The close relation of this verse to 138.*Laṅkāvatāraśūtra* 3.70 is discussed in Lindtner, "The Laṅkāvatārasūtra...", op. cit., pp. 256-258.
213. Edited and translated into French in Vaidya, *Études*..., op. cit. Edited by V. Bhattacharya, Visvabharati Studies 1931.
214. Edited and translated into French in Vaidya, *Études*..., op. cit. Edited in V. Bhattacharya, ibid. Outlined by Ichigo Ogawa in Annual Report of Researches of the Otani University 29, 1976, pp. 6-8.
215. Edited and translated into French in Vaidya, *Études*..., op. cit. Edited by V. Bhattacharya, Visvabharati Studies 1931. Edited and translated into French in Tom J. F. Tillemans, *Materials for the Study of Āryadeva, Dharmapāla and Candrakīrti*. Wiener Studien zur Tibetologie und Buddhismuskunde, heft 24.1 (Wien 1990).
216. Edited and translated into French in Vaidya, *Études*..., op. cit. Edited in V. Bhattacharya, ibid. Edited and translated in Tillemans, ibid.

**217**. Edited and translated into French in Vaidya, *Études...*, op. cit. Edited in V. Bhattacharya, ibid.
**218**. Edited and translated into French in Vaidya, *Études...*, op. cit. Edited in V. Bhattacharya, ibid.
**219**. Edited and translated into French in Vaidya, *Études...*, op. cit. Edited in V. Bhattacharya, ibid.
**220**. Tucci in Pre-Dinnaga Buddhist Texts, op. cit., p. 14.
**221**. Ibid., pp. xii-xiv. Robinson, op. cit., pp. 210-211, translated Seng Chao's preface.
**222**. See Lang, *Catuḥśataka*, op. cit., pp. 10-14.
**223**. Editions can be found at Peking 5234 Tsa f. 157a, Tohoku 3234 Tsa 138b, and with commentary at Taisho 1572, volumes 30, pp. 250b-252c; Peking 5235, vol. 95, Tsa ff. 157a-165b; Tohoku 3835 Tsa 138b-146b. A Japanese translation by R. Hadani appears in Kokuyaku Issaikyo, Chugan-bu, vol. 3, Tokyo 1976, pp. 1-19.
**224**. This is Taisho 291. It was translated into Chinese around 300 by Dharmarakṣa.
**225**. The Chinese translation, T. 1551, was made by Narendrayaśas together with others in 563. Cf. Charles Willemen, *The Essence of Metaphysics. Abhidharmahṛdaya* (Bruxelles 1975), pp. xiv-xv, for information about the translator.
**226**. Willemen, ibid., p. xiv.
**227**. Willemen, ibid., p. xiii.
**228**. Cf. Edward Conze, *The Prajñāpāramitā Literature* (The Hague 1960), pp. 31-33. The first fourteen chapters are published in three volumes in Sanskrit by Pratap Chandra Ghosha, Bibliotheca Indica 115, 1888-1895. Sections of the Tibetan text are provided by M. Lalou (cf. Conze, ibid., p. 31). Chapter 9 is translated into French by Sylvain Levi in "Ysa", *Mémorial Sylvain Lévi* (Paris 1937).
**229**. Conze, ibid., p. 10.
**230**. Conze, ibid., p. 32.
**231**. Conze, ibid.
**232**. Conze, ibid.
**233**. Cf. Conze, ibid., pp. 34-35. The work is translated in Conze, *The Large Sūtra...*, op. cit.
**234**. Edited and translated by Conze, ibid. Portions are also edited by Bidyabinod, Memoirs of the Architectural Survey of India 32, 1927, and by Sten Konow, "Central Asian fragments of the Aṣṭādaśasāha-srikāprajñāpāramitāsūtra and of an unidentified text", Memoirs of the Architectural Survey of India 69, 1942. See also Conze, "Preliminary note on the Prajñāpāramitā manuscript", Journal of the Royal Asiatic Society 1950, 32-36.

**235**. T. 1360; Toh. 141, 526, 916. It is edited in Sanskrit, Tibetan and Chinese and translated by K. Mimaki in *Report of the Japanese Association for Tibetan Studies* 23, 1977. Mimaki has also published the Introduction to his edition/translation at Journal of Indian and Buddhist Studies 25.2, 1977, 29-36.

**236**. T. 169 and 171, translated into Chinese by Shi Ken (250 A.D.)

**237**. T. 533, translated into Chinese by Shi Ken (250).

**238**. T. 559-561; Toh. 171. Partially translated into French by Leon Feer, *Fragments extraits du Kandjour* (Annales du Musee Guimet 5, 1883).

**239**. T. 713-715, translated into Chinese by Shi Ken (250).

**240**. T. 597, translated into Chinese by Shi Ken in 250.

**241**. T. 1356-1359. Earliest translation into Chinese by Shi Ken in 260.

**242**. T. 632-634, translated into Chinese by Shi Ken in 250.

**243**. T. 808-809, translated into Chinese by Shi Ken in 250

**244**. T. 692-694. The earliest Chinese translation is by an anonymous translator dated between A.D. 25 and 220.

**245**. Earliest translation into Chinese by Haku En or Po-yen of the Wei dynasty in 258. T. 310, number 27 of the Mahāratnakūṭa collection, is Bodhirūci's Chinese version, translated into English in Chang, *Treasury*, op. cit. pp. 243-255. Another Chinese translation is T. 329, and into Tibetan there is P760.27.

**246**. Edited by Christian Lindtner (Bern 1984).

**247**. Cf. Mātṛceṭa's *Sugatapañcatriṃśatstotra* in praise of the thirty-five Buddhas.

**248**. The numerous hymns to the Buddha in early Mahāyāna from the hands of teachers such as Nāgārjuna and Mātṛceta testify to the human need of *bhakti*, the need to have and worship a "strong leader" (as opposed to some silly "star") who teaches *and* practises for all to see a *dharma* that basically consists of *ahiṃsā* and *śūnyatā*, i.e., yoga in a practical and in a theoretical sense, who has, as it were, two bodies. The same pattern is, *mutatis mutandis*, to be found in Jainism and in the Krishnaism of the *Bhagavadgītā*. Mahāyāna Buddhism, therefore, should be seen as but a specific form of an early pan-Indian religious movement with ancient Aryan roots. (CL)

**249**. Ruegg summarizes this work, op. cit., p. 55.

**250**. Ruegg, op. cit., p. 54, note 54.

**251**. Ruegg, op. cit., pp. 55-56. The text is edited by Wogihara and Tsushida from Tokyo (1934-35, 1958) and by R. Hikata, *Suvikrāntivikrāntivikramī-Paripṛcchā-Prajñāpāramitā-Sūtra* (Fukuoka 1958), pp. 1-2. It is translated by Edward Conze in *Buddhist Texts through the Ages* (Oxford 1954), pp. 147-149. Cf. Conze, *The Prajñāpāramitā Literature*, op. cit., pp. 94-95 for added information.

**252**. Quoted from Ruegg, op. cit., p. 55.

**253.** *bhavena*, "really, truly" or "resolutely, devotedly, affectionately."
**254.** Jean Przyluski, "Sautrāntika et Dārṣṭāntika", Rocznik Orientalistyczny 8, 1932, 14-14-24.
**255.** J. Kato, "Kumāralāta et Śrīlāta" in *Indianisme et Bouddhism. Mélanges offerts à Msgr. Étienne Lamotte*. Publications de l'Institute Orientliaste de Louvain 23 (Louvain-la-Neuve 1980), pp. 197-213.
**256.** Cf. Przyluski, op. cit., as well as Przyluski, "Dārṣṭāntika, Sautrāntika and Sarvāstivāda", Indian Historical Quarterly 16, 1940, 246-252.
**257.** This fragment was edited by H. Lüders in Asia Major 1926. However, the ascription is controversial; cf. Kato, op. cit. and Sylvain Lèvi, "La Dṛṣṭāntapaṇkti et son auteur", Journal Asiatique (juillet-septembre) 1927, 95-126, as well as Lévi, "Encore Aśvaghoṣa", Journal Asiatique (october-décembre) 1928, 193-216, Jean Przyluski, "Aśvaghoṣa et la Kalpanāmaṇḍitikā", Bulletins de la Classe des Lettres et des sciences morales et politiques, Academie Royale de Belgique, 5th series, Tome XVI, 1930, and Przyluski, "Sautrāntika et Dārṣṭāntika...", op. cit.
**258.** Part 12 of the Mahāsaṃnipāta collection. Translated into Chinese by Dharmarakṣa as T. 403. It also exists in Tibetan, Tohoku 175. It has been translated by Jens Braarvig, *Akṣayamatinirdeśa*, Volume II (Oslo 1993), pp. 1-591. Two discussions pertaining to it are Alex Wayman, "The *samādhi* lists of the Akṣayamatinirdeśa-sūtra", Acta Orientalia (Budapest) 34, 1980, 305-318, and Leslie S. Kawamura, "The Akṣayamatinirdeśasūtra and Mi pham's mKhas 'jug" in E. Steinkellner and H. Täuscher (eds.), *Contributions on Tibetan and Buddhist Religion and Philosophy*. Wiener Studien zur Tibetologie und Buddhismuskunde, Heft 11, Volume 2 (Wien 1983), pp. 131-146. The summary provided here is excerpted from the latter article.
**259.** Kawamura provides the Tibetan terms and textual pagination, which we omit. We also use Kawamura's own translations here rather than those adopted in the Volume elsewhere.
**260.** T. 118-120, translated into Chinese by Dharmarakṣa around 300 A.D. According to Nakamura, op. cit., p. 23, this work is quoted in the 138.*Laṅkāvatārasūtra*.
**261.** The earliest translation of this work into Chinese is by Dharmarakṣa around 300 A.D. Buddhaśānta's Chinese translation, T. 310 (32), is translated in Chang, *Treasury*, op. cit., pp. 115-133.
**262.** Translated into Chinese by An Hokin in 300.
**263.** T. 427-428 and T. 430-431. T. 427 is a translation by Dharmarakṣa around 300.
**264.** T. 425 was translated into Chinese by Dharmarakṣa in about 300. The work has been translated by Sten Konow in *Śaka Versions of the Bhadrakalpikasūtra* (Oslọ 1929).
**265.** Nakamura, op. cit., p. 178.
**266.** T. 310 (21) and T. 324. The latter is a Chinese translation by

Dharmarakṣa (300). It has been translated twice, by Constantin Regamey, *The Bhadramāyākāravyākaraṇa* (Warsaw 1938) and in Chang, *Treasury*, op. cit., pp. 115-133.

**267**. Regamey, ibid., pp. 3, 9.

**268**. T. 810, translated into Chinese by Dharmarakṣa in 300.

**269**. T. 534-536. T. 534 is a Chinese translation by Dharmarakṣa.

**270**. T. 378, translated by Dharmarakṣa, and T. 379, a later translation. Cf. Ratna Handurakande at Encyclopedia of Buddhism 3.4, 1977, 715-716, who gives a generous summary of T. 379.

**271**. Chinese *Shih-ti ching* (T. 287 (22), 279 (26), 285-286, and in Tibetan in portions of Toh. 44. A portion of the *Avataṃśakasūtra*, this work is available in Sanskrit and edited by Ryuko Kondo (Tokyo 1936; Kyoto 1983). An older edition by Johannes Rahder (Le Museon 39, 1926, 125-252) is available as revised by P.L. Vaidya (Buddhist Sanskrit Texts 7, Darbhanga 1967). It has been translated into English (including the quotations in our summary) by Megumu Honda in "Annotated translation of the Daśabhūmikā Sūtra (revised by Johannes Rahder)" in D. Sinor (ed.), *Studies in South, East and Central Asia (presented to Prof. Raghu Vira)*(New Delhi 1968), 115-276.

**272**. These ten stages are also described in Hirakawa, op. cit., pp. 307-308.

**273**. Hirakawa, op. cit., p. 281.

**274**. T. 435 translated into Chinese by Dharmarakṣa in 300.

**275**. #12 of the *Ratnakūṭa* collection (T. 310), also translated into Chinese by Dharmarakṣa around 300. The work is translated into German by Huebotter in Mitteilungen der Deutschen Gesellschaft fur Natur- und Volkerkunde Ostasien 36 (Tokyo 1932), Teil C. 26 pp.

**276**. T. 813-814 and Toh. 207. The first of these is a translation into Chinese by Dharmamitra (266-313). Nakamura, op. cit., p. 231, says this text is quoted in the *Laṅkāvatārasūtra*.

**277**. Nakamura, op. cit., p. 171

**278**. T. 345, translated into Chinese by Dharmarakṣa around 300.

**279**. T. 245-246. Summarized in Conze, *The Prajñāpāramitā Literature*, op. cit., pp. 75-77 and in M. W. de Visser, *Ancient Buddhism in Japan* (1928-35), I, 116-189.

**280**. T. 481-482 (Chinese) and Toh. 174 (Tibetan). T 481 is a Chinese translation by Dharmarakṣa.

**281**. T. 477-479. The first of these is a translation into Chinese by Dharmarakṣa (265-318). According to Nakamura, op. cit., p. 285, this is "a continuation of the 'Spotless Fame Sūtra'", i.e., of 46.*Vimalakīrtinirdeśasūtra*.

**282**. T. 297 (3); T 399.

**283**. Another of Dharmarakṣa's (265-318) Chinese translations, this is T. 349. Cf. Nakamura, op. cit., p. 180, notes 43-46 for references. An alternative title is *Maitreyabodhisattvasūtra*.

**284**. Translated into Chinese by Dharmarakṣa (265-318) and others later, this is the fifteenth section of the Ratnakūṭa collection (T. 310). Cf. the partial translation by Étienne Lamotte in T'oung Pao 48, 1960, 20-23. A later Chinese translation by Śikṣānanda (685-699) is the basis for the portion translated in Chang, *Treasury*, op. cit., pp. 164-188.

**285**. T. 817, translated into Chinese by Dharmarakṣa (300). In Tibetan, Toh. 96.

**286**. T. 589, translated into Chinese by Dharmarakṣa (300).

**287**. Translated into Chinese as T. 112 by Hōkō around 300.

**288**. T. 460, translated into Chinese by Dharmarakṣa (300).

**289**. T. 61-63, the first of which is a translation into Chinese by Dharmarakṣa (300).

**290**. T. 433, Chinese translation by Dharmarakṣa (300).

**291**. #47 of the Ratnakūṭa collection. Also in Tibetan, Toh. 91. The Ratnakūṭa translation is the work of Dharmarakṣa (300).

**292**. T. 433, Chinese translation by Dharmarakṣa (300).

**293**. T. 461, by Dharmarakṣa (300), T. 362 and Toh. 118.

**294**. T. 263, the earliest of several Chinese translations, was made by Dharmarakṣa in 286 A.D.--at that time the work had 26 chapters. The standard Chinese translation, though, is by Kumārajīva (T. 262) in 405-46. T.265 is another Chinese translation, and a Tibetan translation is found in Toh. 113. For a thorough review of the textual history of the work see Hirakawa, op. cit., pp. 282-286. For an exhaustive résumé of the literature on this work one should consult Nakamura, op. cit., pp. 183-188. Portions of the work are translated in a variety of collections; see *Bibliography*, Volume One of the *Encyclopedia of Indian Philosophies* (ed. K.H. Potter), Third Edition 1995, #103 for these and for references to secondary materials.

**295**. Translated into Chinese by Dharmarakṣa (300) in T. 598. Other translations into Chinese (T. 599, T. 601) and into Tibetan (Toh. 153-155). Chapter 14 is translated in Diana Paul, *Women in Buddhism* (Berkeley 1979). pp. 235-298.

**296**. #10 of the Ratnakūṭa collection. Translated into Chinese by Dharmarakṣa in 200 (T. 315). Also translated into Tibetan (Toh. 54). Translated into English in Chang, *Treasury*, pp. 134-147.

**297**. Translated into Chinese as T. 381 by Dharmarakṣa (300).

**298**. Translated into Chinese as T. 274 by Dharmarakṣa (300).

**299**. Chinese translations are T. 310 (37) and T. 343-344. Tibetan translation, Toh. 47.

**300**. This is #48 of the Ratnakūṭa collection. According to Alex and Hideko Wayman, *The Lion's Roar of Queen Śrīmālā* (New York 1974), p. 5, where the work is translated, it was composed in the Āndhra region in the third century. Only a few sentences have survived in Sanskrit. The earliest Chinese translation appears to be by Dharmakṣema around 420. This *sūtra*, however, is obviously known to the author of the *Laṅkāvatārasūtra*, who seems to have lived during the fourth century.

The present summary by the Waymans is taken from their translation, pp. 21-23.

Alex Wayman, "The Mahāsāṃghika and the Tathāgatagarbha (Buddhist doctrinal history, study 1)", Journal of the International Association of Buddhist Studies 1.1, 1978, 35-50, traces the beginnings of the Tathāgatagarbha doctrine to this text, and argues that it represents Mahāsāṃghika leanings. He also explicitly argues for the location of our text's source in Āndhra district.

**301.** T. 567 is a translation by Dharmarakṣa (300).

**302.** T. 562 is a translation into Chinese by Dharmarakṣa (300).

**303.** T. 310 (30), Ts. 334-346. Translated into Chinese by Dharmarakṣa (300). There are translations of this *sūtra* in Paul, op. cit., pp. 292-301 and in Chang, *Treasury*, op. cit., pp. 41-70.

**304.** #36 of the Ratnakūṭa collection (T. 310), translated into Chinese by Dharmarakṣa (300).

**305.** #4 of the Ratnakūṭa collecton (T. 310), translated into Chinese by Dharmarakṣa (300).

**306.** Also known as *Tathāgataguṇajñānacintyaviṣayavaranirdeśasūtra*. T. 310 (3) and T. 312, and in Tibetan Toh. 47. Portions are translated in various places; See K.H. Potter (ed.), *Encyclopedia of Indian Philosophies: Bibliography*, Third Edition, op. cit., #114 on p. 134.

**307.** Also known as *Tathāgatamahākaruṇanirdeśasūtra*, #1 of the Mahāsaṃnipāta collection (T. 397). Also T. 398, translated into Chinese by Dharmarakṣa in 300. David Seyfort Ruegg reports that this text is mentioned in the *Mahānirvāṇasūtra* and in the *Mahābherisūtra* and is therefore prior to the *Laṅkāvatārasūtra*.

**308.** #29 of the Ratnakūṭa collection (T. 310). Translated into Chinese by Hōkō in 300 (T. 332). Another Chinese translation is T. 333. It is translated into English in Paul, *Women in Buddhism*, op. cit., pp. 27-50.

**309.** #38 of the Ratnakūṭa collection (T. 310). Translated into Chinese by Dharmarakṣa in 300 (T. 345). Tibetan translations at Toh. 82 and 261. Translation of the Ratnakūṭa version in Chang, *Treasury*, pp. 427-465.

**310.** T. 513, translated into Chinese by Dharmarakṣa in 300.

**311.** Translated from Bodhiruci's version (T. 310 (20)) in Chang, *Treasury*, pp. 129-162. This text is translated as Toh. 64 into Tibetan.

**312.** #38 of the Ratnakūṭa collection (T. 310). Translated into Chinese by Haku Hosso in 300 (T. 330). Also translated into Chinese as T. 331 and into Tibetan as Toh. 72.

**313.** T. 310 (33), T. 338-339 and Toh. 77. T. 338 is a translation by

Dharmarakṣa, T. 310 (33) is a translation by Nieh Tao-chen of the Western Chin. This last is translated Chang, *Treasury*, pp. 73-97.

**314**. T. 585-587 and Toh. 160. T. 585 is a Chinese translation by Dharmarakṣa (300).

**315**. Cf. P.V. Bapat in Annals of the Bhandarkar Oriental Institute 15.3-4, 1935; in Indian Culture 1.3, 1935, 455-459 and 3, 1937, 743-746.

**316**. Fragments of this are edited in H. Hoffmann, *Bruchstücke des Atānātikasūtra aus den Zentral Asiatisch Sanskrit Kanon der Buddhisten* (Leipzig 1939).

**317**. This text constitutes T. 1646 (Nanjio 1274), translated by Kumārajīva into Chinese in 412 A.D.

**318**. Volume One (Baroda 1975) contains the edition, Volume Two (Baroda 1978) the translation.

**319**. This section provides a *mātṛkā* for each of the four noble truths. They are set out in K. 68-76, where Katsura discusses Harivarman's use of *mātṛkās* here and elsewhere in the text.

**320**. 20 pairs, 5 triples, 9 quadruples, 1 quintuple, 8 sextuples, 1 septuple, 1 octuple, 1 nontuple, 1 decatuple, 1 dodecatuple. Cf. K.66-68.

**321**. This entire section is translated in K.33-38 as "Document I".

**322**. Katsura (K, p. 42) lists those who believe in the intermediate state as the Pūrvaśailas, Vātsīputrīyas, Sammitīyas, Sarvāstivādins, and perhaps the Dārṣṭāntika-Sautrāntikas, and those who oppose it as the Mahāsāṃghikas, Mahīśāsakas, Dharmaguptakas and Theravādins.

**323**. There are the Āndhakas, Vātsīputrīyas, Sammitīyas, Bhadrayaṇīyas and Sarvāstivādins, according to K., p. 43.

**324**. There are the Mahāsāṃghikas, Mahīśāsakas, Theravādins and Dharmaguptakas, according to K, p. 43.

**325**. Pūrvaśailas, Vātsīputrīyas, Sammitīyas, Bhadrayāṇīyas and Sarvāstivādins, according to K, p. 43.

**326**. The Mahāsāṃghikas, Mahīśāsakas, Theravādins and Dārṣṭāntika-Sautrāntikas, according to K, p. 43.

**327**. Mahāsāṃghikas, Āndhakas and Dharmaguptakas, according to K, pp. 43-44.

**328**. Say the Sarvāstivādins along with Harivarman; cf. K, p. 43.

**329**. Sarvāstivādins and Theravādins, along with Harivarman (K., p. 44). Katsura notes, however, that Harivarman's "notion of *anuśayas*...is significantly different from (that) of the Sarvāstivādins and Theravādins and he does not accept *caitasikas* as an independent category apart from *citta*, nor association between *citta* and *caitasikas*."

**330**. The view of the Mahāsāṃghikas, Vātsīputrīyas, Sammitīyas, Dārṣṭāntika-Sautrāntikas, Mahīśāsakas and Dharmaguptakas, says Katsura (K., p. 44).

**331**. The view in question is that of the Mahīśāsikas. Cf. K., p. 45.

332. This section is translated in K., pp. 116-118.
333. Much of this section is translated in K., pp. 120-124.
334. 60-64 are translated in large part in K., pp. 134-138.
335. According to K., in the following argument Harivarman takes the side of Buddhadeva, the Dārṣṭāntika-Sautrāntikas and the Andhakas against that of the Sarvāstivādins and Theravādins.
336. Sections 65-67 are translated on pp. 139-143 of K.
337. 68-72 are translated in K., pp. 145-149.
338. 73-74 translated in K., pp. 152-153.
339. 75-76 are translated in K., pp. 155-157.
340. This paragraph summarizes a section that is translated in K., pp. 171-173.
341. See C.D. Priestley, "Emptiness in the Satyasiddhi", Journal of Indian Philosophy 1, 1970-71, 30-39 for summary and discussion of this Book.
342. This section is translated in K., p. 160.
343. The following three paragraphs summarize a section that is translated in K., pp. 175-178.
344. This paragraph is also summarized in K., pp. 179-181.
345. This section is translated in K., pp. 192-193.
346. Partly translated into French by Louis de la Vallee Poussin in Melanges chinois et bouddhiques 5, 1931, pp. 203-204.
347. This section is translated into French by Louis de la Vallee Poussin in Melanges chinois et bouddhiques 5, 1936-37, 204-215.
348. This is #26 of the Ratnakūṭa collection, translated anonymously into Chinese between 265-316 A.D. Other Chinese translations are T. 895 and T. 896.
349. Translated into Chinese anonymously between 265-317 as T. 79-81.
350. Translated into Chinese by Dharmarakṣa in 300, according to Nakamura, op. cit., p. 192.
351. According to Paul Pelliot "the 12th or the last, and undoubtedly, the oldest chapter of the *Fo-chouo-ta-kouan-ting-chen-tchou-king* (Nanjio 167) was translated by Śrīmitra between 317 and 322 A.D." from Chinese (cf. Paul Pelliot, "Le Bhaiṣajyaguru", Bulletin de l'Ecole Francais d'Extreme-Orient 3, 1903, 33-37). Translations are to be found at T. 449-451, T. 1331 (12) and Toh. 503-504. A thorough discussion of it is provided in Volume 1 of Nalinaksha Dutt's *Gilgit Manuscripts*, op. cit., pp. 48-57, with the text edited on pp. 1-32 of the Sanskrit materials. It has been translated several times (cf. Potter, *Bibliography*, op. cit.). The summary provided here is taken from Paul Pelliot's French summary referred to above, as rendered by Dutt, ibid., pp. 51 ff with emendations and additions. The work has been translated in Raoul Birnbaum, *The Healing Buddha* (Boulder, Colo. 1979) and S. Sen, "Two medical texts in Chinese translations", Visva-Bharati Annals 1, 1945, 70-95.

**352.** According to John Keenan ("Original purity and the focus of early Yogācāra", Journal of the International Association of Buddhist Scholars 5.2, 1982, 7-18), who translates a few passages, the work "is extant only in fragments quoted in other texts. These have been collected in Yuki Reimon, *Yuishikiron yori mitaru yuishiki shisōshi* (Tokyo 1935), pp. 240-250. Six quotations appear in Asaṅga's *Mahāyānasaṃgraha-śāstra*, one in his *Abhidharmasamuccaya*, and one in K'uei-chi's *Weishih erh shih lun shu-chi*. The text is clearly before Asaṅga." (ibid., footnote 17, p. 17).

**353.** This work has been edited twice (by Nishio Kyoo, *The Buddhabhūmisūtra and the Buddhabhūmivyākhyāna* (Nagoya 1939), and by John Keenan in his doctoral dissertation of 1980 at the University of Wisconsin. The summary below is provided in Keenan's "Pure Land systematics in India: the Buddhabhūmisūtra and the *trikāya* doctrine", The Pacific World 3, 1987, 29-35. In his article Keenan argues that this *sūtra* antedates the *Saṃdhinirmocanasūtra* (our #136 below), for which he says it was the source.

**354.** Of this translation there is a very old manuscript (Stein 996 - Giles 4335) found in Tun-huang, dated year 3 of T'ai-ho of the Northern Wei (i.e., 479 A.D.). It is the oldest Tun-huang manuscript and covers the end of the third chapter. There is a Japanese translation by Watanabe U. and Mizuno K. in KIK, Bidon-bu, Vols. XX and XXI, and a study of the second chapter by F. Watanabe in Gatare Dhammapala et al., eds., *Buddhist Studies in honour of Hammalavai Saddhatissa* (Nugagoda, Sri Lanka 1984).

**355.** A Chinese translation is T. 1555. The work has been reconstructed into Sanskrit with Vasubandhu's commentary by N. Aiyasvami Sastri (Visvabharati Annals 10, 1951, 1-54). Louis de la Vallee Poussin notes that Vasubandhu cites a Vasumitra (different from the master of the *Mahāvibhāṣā*) whom Vasubandhu terms a Sautrāntika. However, Poussin finds no Sautrāntika leanings in this work. Cf. Poussin's French translation of Vasubandhu's *Abhidharmakośa* and *Bhāṣya* (Paris 1923-31; English translation by Leo Pruden, Berkeley 1988-1990), Volume 6, xliii-xlv.

**356.** There are two Chinese versions, T. 762, translated by Fa-hsien in 982-1000, and T. 763, translated by Chin-tsun-chi around 1113. These "differ enormously", according to N.H. Samtani in his edition of this work at Tibetan Sanskrit Works Series 13, (Patna 1971), p. 33. In addition, there are several manuscripts from Tibet and Nepal, used by Samtani in preparing his edition. The text is referred to by Yaśomitra (8th century). The translation by Ms. A. Ferrari (Atti della Reale Accademia d'Italie. Memoire. Classe di Scienze morali et storiche. Series VII, fasc. 13, Roma 1944, pp. 535-625) is of only a fragment of the text.

**357.** For bibliography cf. K.H.Potter (ed.), *Bibliography*. Third Edition, op. cit., #135 on pp. 142-143.

358. Lambert Schmithausen, *Ālayavijñāna. On the Origins and the Early Development of the Central Concept of Yogācāra Philosophy.* Studia Philologica Buddhica IVa-b, in two volumes (Tokyo 1987), Part One, p. 12; also cf. Stanley Weinstein, "The *ālayavijñāna* in early Yogācāra Buddhism: a comparison of its meaning in the Saṃdhinirmocanasūtra and the Vijñaptimātratāsiddhi of Dharmapāla", Kokusai Toho Gakusha Kaigikiyo 3, 1959, 46-58, where sizable sections of the text are translated.
359. The translation of this passage is taken from Paul J. Griffiths et al., *The Realm of Awakening* (New York 1989), pp. 5-6.
360. The *Akutobhayā* is edited by Max Walleser (Materialen zur Kunde des Buddhismus 2, 1923), reconstructed by R.C. Pandeya (Delhi 1988-89), and translated into German by Max Walleser (Die Mittlere Lehre des Nāgārjuna nach der Chinesischen Version übertragen, (Heidelberg 1912).
361. The *Prajñāpradīpaṭīkā* (Peking no. 5259) of Avalokitavrata lists eight major commentaries on the *Mūlamadhyamakakārikās*, beginning with Nāgārjuna's own (fol. 85a; no title is mentioned). The colophon of the *Akutobhayā* itself contains an identical list. The *Bodhimārgadīpapañjikā* (Peking no. 5344) of Dīpaṃkaraśrījñāna specifically refers to the *Akutobhayā* as Nāgārjuna's commentary (fol. 324b).
362. According to Akira Saito, "Buddhapālita in the history of Mādhyamika philosophy", Transactions of the International Journal of Oriental Studies 31, 1986, 106-107) these may be taken as an indication that Buddhapālita and the author of the *Akutobhayā* were working from slight variations in the text of the Sanskrit *kārikās* in each of these five instances. They are listed on p. xvii by Saito as the following locations in Buddhapālita's *Madhyamakakārikā-Vṛtti*: I.8ab; VII.16ab; VII.17cd; VII. 28; and XI.1ab. Several later Tibetan scholars claimed that the *Akutobhayā* did indeed differ from the other commentaries on doctrinal and philosophical issues, but such claims do not seem to be entirely justified on the basis of present evidence.
363. This lengthy work is available in "three Chinese translations, two Tibetan translations (both from the Chinese, one being merely a partial summarization, i.e., a *hṛdaya* of the full-length version), and two modern Sanskrit editions largely derived from a relatively recent Nepalese Mss." (George Crevoshay, "Some traces of Vedic divinities in the Laṅkāvatārasūtra" in T.N. Dharmadhikari (ed.), *Golden Jubilee Volume, Vaidika Saṃśodhana Maṇḍala* (Poona 1982), p. 39). Consult the many citations listed in the *Bibliography*, Volume One of the *Encyclopedia of Indian Philosophies*, Third Edition, #137 (pp. 143-145).
364. Christian Lindtner, "The Laṅkāvatāra...", op. cit., pp. 245 ff.
365. Schmithausen, *Ālayavijñāna...*, Volume 2, op. cit., note 102 on pp. 263-264.
366. Daisetz Teitaro Suzuki, *Studies in the Laṅkāvatāra Sūtra* (London

1930, 1957), pp. 4-15.
**367**. Suzuki, ibid., pp. 15-37.
**368**. Jikido Takasaki, "Analysis of the Laṅkāvatāra. In search of its original form", *Indianism et Bouddisme offerts à Msgr. Étienne Lamotte.* Publication de l'Institut Orientaliste du Louvain 23 (Louvain-de-Neuve 1980), pp. 339-345.
**369**. Jikido Takasaki, "Sources of the Laṅkāvatāra and its position in Mahāyāna Buddhism", *Indological and Buddhist Studies.* Volume in Honour of Professor J. W. de Jong on his Sixtieth Birthday (Canberra 1982), p. 565.
**370**. Darbhanga 1963.
**371**. Translated by Daisez Teitaro Suzuki, *The Laṅkāvatāra Sūtra* (London 1932).
**372**. Edward Hamlin, "Discourse in the Laṅkāvatāra Sūtra", Journal of Indian Philosophy 11, 1983, 267-313.
**373**. Suzuki, *Studies in the Laṅkāvatāra Sūtra*, op. cit.
**374**. This introductory Chapter is translated in S 65-85 and summarized in H 270-275, including translations of one or two passages. Suzuki says it "appears in all the *Laṅkāvatāra* texts except Guṇabhadra...(and) is...no doubt a later addition" (S 65).
**375**. H, p. 270.
**376**. Translated and discussed in H, pp. 290-291.
**377**. On the classification into eight kinds of *vijñāna* see H, pp. 279-281, as well as Gishin Tokiwa, "*Svacittamātra*, the basic standpoint of the Laṅkāvatāra Sūtra", Journal of Indian and Buddhist Studies 26.1, 1977, 34-39.
**378**. This section is studied, and excerpts translated, in H, pp. 282-286.
**379**. Translated and discussed in H, pp. 288-289.
**380**. Translated and discussed in H, p. 291.
**381**. Translated and discussed in H, p. 309.
**382**. This sentence and the previous one, which relate directly to the distinction in question, do not appear in T but are found in E. T on this passage is rather confusing, as there is apparently a difference between the Chinese and Sanskrit texts at this point.
**383**. The text is apparently garbled here; it is unclear what is the eighth theory.
**384**. Concerning these five see Akira Suganuma, "The five *dharmas* in the Laṅkāvatārasūtra", Journal of Indian and Buddhist Studies 15.2, 1967, 32-39.
**385**. A goodly number of these verses are translated in S.
**386**. This is T. 86.
**387**. This is T. 125.
**388**. This is T. 155.

**389**. T. 653.

**390**. In Chinese, T. 397 (15) and in Tibetan, Toh. 27. Parts of Chapters 17-19 are translated into French by Sylvain Levi, "Notes chinoises sur l'Inde, IV" in Bulletin de l'Ecole Francaise d'Extreme-Orient 5, 1905, 262-284. A few pages are translated in A.F.R. Hoernle, *Manuscript Remains of Buddhist Literature found in East Turkestan*. Two volumes (Oxford 1916; Amsterdam 1970).

**391**. T.464-467 and Toh. 109.

**392**. T. 657.

**393**. T. 982-988. This work is edited by Shuyo Takubo (Tokyo 1972).

**394**. T. 454-455 and T. 457.

**395**. T. 310 (12), T. 316 and Toh. 56.

**396**. T. 1465.

**397**. T. 650-652 and Toh. 180.

**398**. T. 1137-1140. Edited in H.W. Bailey, *Khotanese Buddhist Texts*. Cambridge Oriental Series 3 (London 1951). Portions edited in G. Bongard-Levin, *Studies in Ancient India and Central Asia*. Soviet Indology Series 17 (Calcutta 1971), pp. 247-256.

**399**. This work, in Chinese as T. 310 (24) and T. 325-326, in Tibetan as Toh. 68, has been translated into French in Pierre Python, *Vinayaviniścayasūtra. Enquete d'Upāli pour un Exegése de la Discipline* (Paris 1973), into English in Chang, *Treasury*, pp. 262-278.

**400**. T. 420-421.

**401**. T. 1521, available in Chinese only. Opinions differ about whether Ṇāgārjuna, the author of the works #s 33-44, is also the author of this text. Lindtner (*Nāgārjuniana*, op. cit., p. 14) thinks "there are several reasons to render it likely that it is authentic: The very early Chinese evidence; quotations from the *Bodhisambhāra*;...*Daśabhūmika-sūtra* is known to have been used by Nāgārjuna elsewhere". Ruegg, *The Literature of the Madhyamaka School...*, op. cit., p. 29, note 67, reports that "the authorshp of this work has been questioned by A. Hirakawa", but confirmed by R. Hikata

Chapter Nine, which deals with "The Path of Easy Practice" as well as with classifications of various and sundry Buddhas and Bodhisattvas, is reconstructed into Sanskrit by Hisao Inagaki, "The path of easy practice", Ryukokudaigaku Ronsho 422, 1983, 38-55. Inagaki has also translated Chapter Five, titled "Retrogression and Non-retrogression", in his "The easy method of entering the stage of non-retrogression", The Pacific World n.s. 3, 1987, pp. 24-28.

**402**. Nakamura, op. cit., p. 241.

**403**. Edited and translated many times; cf. Potter, *Bibliography*: Third Edition #160.1 for references.

**404**. Edward Conze, *The Short Prajñāpāramitā Texts* (London 1974) pp.

142-143.
**405**. Probably the most recited, studied and revered of all the Prajñāpāramitāsūtras, it is usually rendered (improperly, Edward Conze argued) as the "Diamond" or better "Diamond-cutter" *sūtra*. Bibliographical materials are provided in Potter (ed.), *Bibliography:* Third Edition.#161.1.
**406**. Conze's edition and translation (Serie Orientalia Roma 13, 1957), pp. 10-11.
**407**. Prabal Kumar Sen, "Śrīlāta: a pre-Vasubandhu philosopher", Journal of the Department of Philosophy, University of Calcutta 1, 1983-83, 119-131.
**408**. J. Przyluski, "Sautrāntika et Dārṣṭāntika", op. cit., 14-24.
**409**. Two versions of the same text are extant only in Chinese, constituting T. 1505 and T. 1506. The name of the author of T. 1505 is given as Kind-hien; its translator as Kumārabuddhi, who made the translation in 382: the Chinese of its title is *Ssu A-han-mou tch'ao-kiai.* As to T. 1506, its Chinese name is said to be *San-fa-tou louen*, it is fifteen pages long; its translator is Gautama Saṃghadeva, who made it in 391. Translations come down to us in Sanskrit palmleaf found in Turfan (present-day Xinjiang). This information, with the spellings, is provided in Leon Hurvitz, "The road to Buddhist salvation as described by Vasubhadra", Journal of the American Oriental Series 87, 1967, 434-486.

Both versions have been translated into English by Eric Grinstead in a book, unpublished to our knowledge, scheduled to be titled *Buddhism by Threes*. Grinstead tells us in his Introduction to the forthcoming book that "there is a close relation between" T. 1505 "and the later (and much larger) (*Abhidharma*)*Kośa*". The present summary is prepared by us on the basis of a manuscript of Grinstead's translation. An opening Preface in T. 1505 tells us the date surrounding the preparation of that Chinese translation at Ye in Turfan in 382 A.D., and that the entire project of translation, of which this is one part of three, took eight years.
**410**. Thich Thein Chau, "The literature of the Pudgalavādins", Journal of the International Association for Buddhist Studies 7.2, 1984, p. 8, however, argues that this is not a Sammitīya text.
**411**. T. 1649.32.464a.27. See the comments by K. Venkataramanan in Visvabharati Annals 5, 1953, p. 174 and pp. 218-219, note 24.
**412**. K. Venkataramanan's English translation of the Chinese text, ibid., should be used with considerable caution. Venkataramanan himself admits his own tentativeness at several places, and much of his translation makes little sense. In his defence, however, the Chinese of this treatise is often problematic. The text itself seems occasionally corrupt and the edition provided in the Taisho canon is plagued by atrocious punctuation and absurd sectional divisions.

Part of this text is reviewed in N.N. Dutt and K.D. Bajpai,

*Development of Buddhism in Uttar Pradesh* (Lucknow 1956), pp. 302-307.
413. Discussed in Venkataramanan, "Did the Buddha deny the self?", Proceedings of the Indian Philosophical Congress 30, 1955, 221-228.
414. See discussion in Venkataramanan's translation, op. cit., pp. 219 note 24, 221-222 note 34.
415. As Venkataramanan has noted, ibid., p. 223 note 26.
416. The text of the Sammitīya rebuttal to positions four and five is corrupt. This section of the text (465b.10-13) has been wrongly placed under the refutation of the fifth proposition, and it is moved here, following Venkataramanan's emendation; see Venkataramanan's translation, ibid., pp. 178 and 223 note 42.
417. T. 618.
418. This is #44 of T. 310 in Chinese, Toh. 88 in Tibetan. It is translated in Chang, *Treasury*, op. cit., pp. 280-311.
419. See Robinson, *Early Mādhyamika...*, op. cit., pp. 32-33.
420. Ruegg, op. cit., pp. 27-28.
421. Lindtner, *Nagarjuniana*, op. cit., pp. 11-12, footnote 13.
422. Hsueh-Li Chang, "Nāgārjuna's approach to the problem of the existence of God", Religious Studies 12, 1976, 207-216.
423. Visvabharati Annals 6, 1954, 165-231.
424. Robinson, op. cit., pp. 208-209.
425. Similar to *Madhyamakakārikās* 1.12, 15.4, 1.1-4, according to Robinson, ibid., p. 32.
426. = *Madhyamakakārikā* I.9, according to Robinson, ibid.
427. = *Śūnyatāsaptati* 19, according to Robinson, ibid.
428. = *Madhyamakakārikā* 13.3 according to Robinson, ibid.
429. = *Madhyamakakārikā* 12.1 according to Robinson, ibid.
430. See *Madhyamakakārikā* 11.2, advises Robinson, ibid.
431. See *Madhyamakakārikās* 7.15 and 2.1, advises Robinson, ibid.
432. Ronald Davidson's unpublished doctoral dissertation, University of California at Berkeley 1985, pp. 133-134.
433. Stefan Anacker, *Seven Works of Vasubandhu, the Buddhist Psychological Doctor* (Delhi 1984), pp. 211-273.
434. Ronald M. Davidson writes in his as-yet unpublished Ph.D. dissertation (Berkeley 1985): "In the MSABh [i.e., the *Mahāyānasūtrālaṃkāra-Bhāṣya* ascribed to Vasubandhu]...the name of the author of the MSA is given as Vyavadātasamayabodhisattva. Demieville has shown that Yogācāras (meditation masters) who were associated with the cultus of Maitreya have received the posthumous epithet of Bodhisattva. It is entirely likely that this was the case here and Vyavadātasamaya was a monk in northern India similarly involved in the Maitreya cult. I take Vyavadātasamaya to be the compiler of all the verses of the received text and the author of the later ones" (p. 133).

The work is standardly ascribed to Asaṅga. However, Davidson notes that Asaṅga "refers to it (the *Mahāyānasūtrālaṃkāra)* in the *Viniścayasaṃgrahaṇī* [section of the *Yogācārabhūmi*] as an example of a well-constructed *śāstra*, but he gives no author's name" (Davidson, ibid., p. 134).

**435**. This simile may "reflect" the difference between the true *dharma*, which is ineffable, and its faint "reflection" which is the words of the *dharma*.

**436**. Perhaps the designation "*jalpamātra*" rather than "*vijñaptimātra*" for the school would have made its intentions more evident!

**437**. IX.11-14 translated in Davidson, ibid.., pp. 263-264.

**438**. IX.41-48 are translated in Davidson, ibid., pp. 266-270.

**439**. IX.70-75 are translated in Davidson, ibid., pp. 315-318.

**440**. XI.15-19 are translated in Davidson, ibid., p. 232.

**441**. XI.39-45 translated in Davidson, ibid., pp. 249-250.

**442**. XIX.41-54 translated in Davidson, ibid., pp. 249-250.

**443**. Alex Wayman goes into greater detail on this at pp. 25-29 of his *Analysis of the Śrāvakabhūmi Manuscript*, University of California Publications in Classical Philology 17 (Berkeley 1961).

**444**. Lambert Schmithausen, *Ālayavijñāna...*, op. cit.

**445**. For a critical review of Schmithausen's work cf. the review of it by Paul J. Griffiths in Journal of the International Association of Buddhist Studies 12.1, 1989, 170-177. A work by a student of Schmithausen, unavailable to us at the time of writing, is H.S. Sakume, *Die Āśrayaparivṛtti-théorie in der Yogācārabhūmi*, Two Volumes (Stuttgart 1990), reviewed by Eli Franco in Indo-Iranian Journal 36, 1993, pp. 343-349, who extends this type of study of the present work to other topics.

**446**. Schmithausen, op. cit., pp. 110ff. discusses this passage.

**447**. Line 2 of page 23 in Schmithausen, ibid., Volume 2, note 844 on pp. 429-431.

**448**. Sections of this are discussed in various passages and footnotes in Schmithausen, ibid. See the references on his p. 668 to various lines in this section.

**449**. This section is freely translated by Esho Mikogami, "A refutation of the Sāṃkhya theory in the Yogācārabhūmi", Philosophy East and West 19, 1969, 443-448.

**450**. Lines 13-15 of E129 are translated by Schmithausen, op. cit., p. 132. The section is restored into Sanskrit by Vidhusekhara Bhattacharya in his "Ātmavāda as in the Yogācārabhūmi of Ācārya Asaṅga", *Dr. Kunhan Raja Presentation Volume* (Madras 1946), pp. 27-37.

**451**. This section is translated in George Chemparathy, "Two early Buddhist refutations of the existence of *īśvara* as the creator of the universe", Wiener Zeitschrift fur die Kunde des Sud- und Ostasien 12-13,

1968-69, 129-138.

452. Schmithausen, *Ālayavijñāna...*, op. cit., p. 135 contains a translation of p. 192, lines 6-9 of E192.

453. Alex Wayman in Journal of Indian and Buddhist Studies 8.1, 1960, pp. 379ff. Reprinted in Alex Wayman, *Buddhist Insight* (ed. George Elder)(Delhi 1984), pp. 327-332.

454. Schmithausen, op. cit., p. 18.

455. Schmithausen's translations of technical terms have been replaced by the translations standard for the present Volume.

456. Wayman in Journal of Indian and Buddhist Studies 8.1, op. cit.

457. Schmithausen, op. cit., pp. 221-222.

458. Schmithausen, ibid., p.669.

459. Wayman, *Buddhist Insight*, op. cit., p. 354.

460. Schmithausen, op. cit., footnotes, pp. 228-241.

461. Schmithausen, ibid., footnotes 1420-1426.

462. This summation is based on Schmithausen's translation of what he calls "a difficult line". See his notes in Schmithausen, ibid., pp. 538-543.

463. This section has not been translated into Sanskrit so far.

464. This Chapter is not available in Sanskrit.

465. Wayman, *Analysis of the Śrāvakabhūmi Manuscript*, op. cit.

466. In Tibetan Sanskrit Works Series 17, 1973.

467. The last section, on food, is translated in Wayman, *Analysis...*, p. 139.

468. This paragraph is taken from Wayman, ibid., p. 86, with replacement of his translations of technical terms by ours.

469. Journal of Indian and Buddhist Studies 8.1, 1960, pp. 379ff., reprinted in Wayman, *Buddhist Insight*, pp. 327-332.

470. Nalinaksha Dutt's edition of *Bodhisattvabhūmi* (Pataliputra 1966, 1978), pp. 8-46.

471. Gustav Roth provides an improved Sanskrit text and English translation of the first few lines in his "Observations on the first chapter of Asaṅga's Bodhisattvabhūmi", Indologia Taurinensia 3-4, 1975-76, 403-412.

472. This Chapter has been translated in Janice Willis, *On Knowing Reality.The Tattvārtha Chapter of Asaṅga's Bodhisattvabhūmi* (New York 1979). Our summary draws on her translation as well as E and T.

473. This Chapter is translated into French by Paul Demieville, "Le chapitre de la Bodhisattvabhūmi sur la perfection du *dhyāna*", Rocznik Orientalistyczny 21, 1957, 109-128, reprinted in Paul Demieville, *Chois d'Études bouddhiques (1969-1970)*(Leiden 1973), pp. 304-319.

474. This Chapter is translated into French by Johannes Rahder in Acta Orientalia (Copenhagen) 4, 1926, 214-256.

475. This Chapter is translated into French by Johannes Rahder, ibid.

476. Schmithausen, op. cit.

477. Ibid., pp. 194-196.

**478**. Paul J. Griffiths, *On Being Mindless...*, op. cit., pp. 130-137.
**479**. Lambert Schmithausen, *Der Nirvāṇa-Abschnitt in der Viniścaya-saṃgrahaṇī der Yogācārabhūmi*. Osterreichische Akademie der Wissenschaftern. Veroffentlichungen der Kommission fur Sprache und Kulturen Sudasiens 8, 1969, pp. 41-71.
**480**. Quoted passages are from Davidson's thesis, op.cit., pp. 186-188, except that we have substituted the translations of technical terms used in this Volume for Davidson's translations.
**481**. Davidson, ibid., pp. 205-207.
**482**. Alex Wayman, "Nescience and insight according to Asaṅga's Yogācārabhūmi", *Buddhist Studies in Honour of Walpola Rahula* (ed. S. Balasoriya et al.) (London 1980), pp. 251-266. Reprinted in Alex Wayman, *Buddhist Insight*, op. cit., pp. 193-214.
**483**. T. 1602 and T. 1603. There is no Tibetan translation. T. 1617 is a commentary by Paramārtha title **Triniḥsvabhāvaśāstra*, which is a commentary on the seventh chapter of the present work. Schmithausen, in footnote 99 (pp. 261-262) of Part II of his *Ālayavijñāna* (op. cit.) provides a wealth of information on the evidence pertaining to it. The work is referred to as **Prakaraṇāryaśāsanaśāstra* by Demieville; another suggestion of the real title is *Śāsanodbhāvanā*, and still others have been suggested. Schmithausen gives evidence to show that it is certainly subsequent to the *Yogācārabhūmi*, but probably prior to the "Maitreya" works.
**484**. Ronald M. Davidson, Ph.D. dissertation, op. cit., note 28 on p. 147.
**485**. Rahul Sankrtyayana, "Second search of Sanskrit palm-leaf mss. in Tibet", Journal of the Bihar and Orissa Research Society 33, 1937, 1-57.
**486**. P. Pradhan, "Ms. of Asaṅga's Abhidharmasamuccaya", Indian Historical Quarterly 24, 1948, 87-93.
**487**. V.V. Gokhale, "A rare manuscript of Asaṅga's Abhidharmasamuccaya", Harvard Journal of Asiatic Studies 11, 1948, 207-213.
**488**. V.V. Gokhale, "Fragments from the Abhidharmasamuccaya of Asaṅga", Journal of the Royal Asiatic Society of Great Britain and Ireland, Bombay Branch 23, 1947, 13-38.
**489**. As Visva-Bharati Studies 12, 1950.
**490**. Walpola Rahula, *Le Compendium de la superdoctrine (philosophie) (Abhidharma-samuccaya d'Asaṅga)*. Bulletin de l'École Francaise d'Extreme-Orient 78 (Paris 1971).
**491**. Walpola Rahula in fact says that he made use of the Tibetan and Chinese translations as well as Pradhan's Sanskrit edition/reconstruction (p. xx), but there is scant evidence to support this claim (T'oung Pao 1973, pp. 339-346, and Lambert Schmithausen's "Zu Walpola Rahula"s Überstezung von Asaṅga's Abhidharma-samuccaya", Wiener Zeitschrift für die Kunde des Sudasien 20, 1976, pp. 111-122) and must, like the edition/reconstruction upon which it is based, be used with extreme care.

**492**. The text has close links with another major work at least parts of which may come from Asaṅga: the 166.*Yogācārabhūmi*. Also, many of its definitions are reproduced in Sthiramati's *Triṃśikābhāṣya*. There is only one Indian commentary extant in Sanskrit, the *Abhidharmasamuccayabhāṣya*.

**493**. The Sanskrit here is not quite certain. Pradhan reconstructs *abhūta-parikalpa* 102.2 and makes no comment. This is certainly the usual Sanskrit form, but the Tibetan reads *yang dag pa ma yin pa'i rnam par rtog pa* (P137b6/D116b5-6) which should probably be reconstructed as *abhūta-vikalpa*, less common though this form is. Matters are complicated by the fact the the *Abhidharmasamuccayabhāṣya* seems to have read *abhūta-parikalpa*, judging from both the extant Sanskrit (137.8) and the Tibetan translation (*yang dag pa ma yin pa'i kun tu rtog pa* (101b7). It's noteworthy that, as far as I can see, the Tibetan translations of both the *Abhidharmasamuccaya* and the *Bhāṣya* consistently use *rnam par rtog pa* for *vikalpa* and *kun tu rtog pa* for *parikalpa* elsewhere, which seems to strengthen the supposition that the Tibetan translators were reading *abhūta-vikalpa* here. Following the *lectio difficile*, then, I give *abhūta-vikalpa* here, though with some hesitation. (PG)

**494**. Edward Conze, The Prajñāpāramitā Literature, op. cit., p. 96.

**495**. Edited, with the *Vajracchedikāprajñāpāramitāsūtra*, by Lal Mani Joshi and Samdhong Rinpoche (Sarnath 1978).

**496**. Summary based on Tucci's translation of the Chinese--the Sanskrit is missing.

**497**. Etienne Lamotte, *La Somme du Grand Véhicule*. Two volumes (Louvain 1938-39).

**498**. Lamotte, "L'*ālayavijñāna* (le réceptacle) dans le Mahāyānasaṃgraha Chap. II)", Melanges Chinois et Bouddhiques 3, 1939, 169-255.

**499**. Ronald Davidson discusses at some length the evidence for and against ascribing this work to Asaṅga. He notes that the *Mahāyānasaṃgraha* cites the *Mahāyānasūtrālaṃkāra*, the *Madhyāntavibhāga*, and the *Bodhisattvabhūmi* section of the *Yogācārabhūmi*, and that this pattern of quoting contrasts noticeably with the followed in, e.g., the *Yogācārabhūmi* itself, which does not quote the *Mahāyānasūtrālaṃkāra* at all and only mentions it once. Davidson points out, further, that "many of the categories standard to Asaṅga's previous works have been altered", giving examples. However, he concludes that "while it is obvious that there was a model and methodology shift from the *Yogācārabhūmi* and allied works, it is equally obvious that there exists some degree of continuity" (Davidson, op. cit., pp. 136-137).

**500**. It will be seen below that a number of quoted passages from other works attributed to Asaṅga are identified by the summarizer as "quoted as if a work by a different author". Though this may be taken to signify that the present work is not a work of Asaṅga's that is not the only possible explanation. Another may be that someone after Asaṅga inserted these references without recognizing that they were by the same author, or through murky language failing to make it clear. Still, we have cited this work as the last among those attributable to Asaṅga as a way of taking note of the frequent references of this sort.

**501.** The *Abhidharmasūtra*, which is not extant, and which according to some scholars never existed but is an invention of Asaṅga's!

**502.** I.44-49 is translated in Davidson, ibid.

**503.** Contrary to the opinion of Sthiramati expressed in the *Triṃśikābhāṣya*, the storehouse consciousness is conceived by Asaṅga primarily as the cause of affliction.

**504.** Name = constructed, notion = dependent. The dependent notion arises successive to the name and the name is anterior to any notion.

**505.** This section is translated in Noriaki Hakamaya, "The realm of enlightenment in *vijñaptimātratā*: the formulation of the four kinds of pure *dharmas*", Journal of the International Association of Buddhist Studies 3.2, 1980, 21-41.

**506.** Leslie S. Kawamura, "The Dharmadharmatā-vibhāga, Journal of Indian and Buddhist Studies 32.2, 1984, pp. 10-17.

**507.** Respectively, these are in D.T. Suzuki's *Tibetan Tripiṭaka, Peking Edition* (Kyoto/Tokyo 1958), all in Volume 128, No. 5524, pp. 22-24; no. 5523, 21-22; and no. 5529, 133-138.

**508.** Davidson, op. cit., p. 134, comments: "That the DhDhV...was evidently unknown to Hsüan-tsang, Dharmapāla, or Sthiramati, in no way indicates that the DhDhV is not by the same author (i.e. Vasubandhu) as the other commentaries on the "Maitreya" texts. In fact, the DhDhV may have been deliberately ignored by these writers because it doesn't fit into their conception of Yogācāra. Not into Sthiramati's, because the existent and the nonexistent cannot be differentiated, and not into Dharmapāla's and Hsüan-tsang's, because the primordial nature of *vijñāna* is denied. The original 'five works of Maitreya' also included a *Yoga-vibhāga*, which no language has preserved. This may indicate that this text was too radical even for the Tibetans! (who were after all at the time under the influence of Śāntarakṣita and Kamalaśīla)." (Anacker, private communication).

**509.** Stefan Anacker, "An unraveling of the Dharma-dharmatā-vibhāga-vṛtti of Vasubandhu", Asiatische Studien 46.1, 1992, pp. 26-36.

**510.** A portion reconstructed into Sanskrit, together with the Tibetan translation of the rest, is provided in Davidson, op. cit., pp. 289-293 and footnotes thereon.

**511.** Warder, op. cit., p. 407.

**512.** Conze, *The Prajñāpāramitā Literature*, op. cit., p. 37.

**513.** Warder, op. cit., p. 408.

514. Serie Orientale Roma 6, 1954. There are also other summaries than ours, by Edward Conze, "Maitreya's Abhisamayālaṃkāra", Sino-Indian Studies 5, 1957, 21-36, and by Warder, *Indian Buddhism*, op. cit., pp. 407-413, and an extended analysis by Ernst Obermiller, *Analysis of the Abhisamayālaṃkāra*. Three volumes (London 1933-39, also Calcutta Oriental Series 27, 1933-36). See also Conze's discussion in *the Prajñāpāramitā Literature*, op. cit., pp. 103-107. Our summary here attempts to minimize the complexities involved in the relationship with other texts.

515. For representative literature cf. Potter, *Bibliogrraphy*, Third Edition, op. cit., under #175.24.

516. Excerpted from Stefan Anacker, *Seven Works of Vasubandhu*, op. cit., pp. 11-23.

517. The account is slightly different in the Tibetan sources. Cf. Anacker, ibid., p. 11.

518. Edited and translated into French by Louis de la Vallee Poussin. Seven volumes (Paris 1923-31). Translation revised by Etienne Lamotte in six volumes, Melanges chinois et bouddhiques 16, 1971. This has been translated into English by Leo M. Pruden in four volumes (Berkeley, Calif. 1988-1990).

519. See Potter, *Bibliography*, Third Edition, op. cit., #175.1.

520. Edited, with Yaśomitra's *Sphuṭārtha*, by Dwarikadas Sastri (Varanasi 1970, 1981)

521. Sections 25-27 are freely translated in Th. Stcherbatsky, *The Central Conception Buddhism and the Meaning of the Word Dharma*. Royal Asiatic Society Publication Fund 7 (Calcutta 1923, 1926; Dellhi 1970), pp. 62-77.

522. In addition to "T", this section has been translated by Th. Stcherbatsky in *Soul Theory of the Buddhists*, Bulletin de l'Academie des Sciences de URSS 1919; reprinted Delhi 1970.

523. This section is summarized in Padmanabh S. Jaini, "*Smṛti* in the Abhidharma literature and the development of Buddhist accounts of memory of the past", in Janet Gyatso (ed.), *In the Mirror of Memory* (Albany, N.Y., 1992), pp. 49-51.

524. Cf. Yoshihito G. Muroji, *Vasubandhu's Interpretation des Pratītyasamutpāda* (Wiesbaden 1993) for references to these editions as well as to Japanese translations and discussions of portions of the text.

525. Giuseppe Tucci, "A fragment from the Pratītyasamutpāda of Vasubandhu", Journal of the Royal Asiatic Society 1930, pp. 611-623.

526. Ascribed to Vasubandhu by Bu-Ston. See Marek Mejor, *Vasubandhu's Abhidharmakośa and the Commentaries preserved in the Tanjur* (Stuttgart 1991), p. 9. The sections of the summary in quotations are from the article by K. Timura on this work in *Encyclopedia of Buddhism* (ed. G.P.Malalasekara et al.)(Colombo) 2.1, pp. 21-22. This work was translated

into Chinese by Bodhiruci in ca. 530. It constitutes T. 1524.

**527**. Available in Chinese (T. 3987) and Tibetan translation; cf. Mejor, op. cit., p. 9. This work is also ascribed to Vasubandhu by Bu-ston; ibid., p. 9.

**528**. According to Mejor, ibid., p. 11, this work is ascribed to Vasubandhu by Susumu Yamaguchi.

**529**. Mejor, ibid., p. 9, says Bu-ston ascribes this commentary to Vasubandhu.

**530**. The text exists in several Tibetan and Chinese versions. The present summary is made using Peking/Tokyo Tibetan Tripiṭaka, volume 104, pages 34 and 35.

**531**. T. 3993, also available in Tibetan. See Mejor, ibid., pp. 9-11. This was translated into Chinese by Bodhiruci around 508-511. A general survey of the contents of the seventh *bhūmi* is provided by Johannes Rahder, op. cit., reprinted from his doctoral dissertation, Leuven 1926.

**532**. T. 1533, ascribed by Japanese scholars to Vasubandhu. See Nakamura, op.cit., p. 272, notes 32, and Mejor, ibid., p. 10.

**533**. T. 4103, also preserved in Tibetan. See Mejor, ibid., p. 9. Mejor also reports that this work "shows a direct dependence on the *Abhidharmakośa*", citing A. Schiefner, "Über Vasubandhu's Gāthāsaṃgraha", Melanges Asiatiques VIII (1876-1881), pp. 559-593.

**534**. Ascribed to Vasubandhu by Bu-ston. Cf. Mejor, ibid., p. 9.

**535**. Cited in Mejor's (ibid., p. 11) list of works ascribed to Vasubandhu by Susumu Yamaguchi.

**536**. T. 1527-1529 and Nanjio 1206-1210 = 2207, 209, ascribed to Vasubandhu in Paramārtha's *Life of Vasubandhu*, probably written in ca. 565.

**537**. T. 1511, 1513 and Nanjio 1168 and 1231. Also ascribed to Vasubandhu by Bu-ston. Cf. Mejor, ibid., pp. 8-9.

**538**. Cf. Nakamura, op. cit., p. 272, note 30.

**539**. Mentioned as a work of Vasubandhu's by Paramārtha, *Life of Vasubandhu*.

**540**. T. 1519-1520 and Nanjio 1232-1233. Cf. Mejor, op. cit., pp. 8-10.

**541**. T. 1524, translated around 529 by Bodhiruci. An important text in Japan; see Nakamura, op. cit., p. 271, note 28 for references to Japanese translations and studies. Paul Williams, *Mahāyāna Buddhism: The Doctrinal Foundations* (London 1989), p. 257, doubts that this is a work of Vasubandhu's.

**542**. Minoru Kiyota, "Buddhist devotional meditation: a study of the Sukhāvatī-vyūhopadeśa", in Minoru Kiyota (ed.), *Mahāyāna Buddhist Meditation: Theory and Practice* (Honolulu 1978), pp. 293-323.

**543**. There are several commentaries on the *kārikās* on the *Vajracchedikā* extant in Chinese and Tibetan. Giusppe Tucci (*Minor Buddhist Texts*, op. cit.) attempts to unravel the question of their authorship without great success. He argues that the work T. 1510 = Tohoku 3816, translated by Dharmagupta and summarized above as our #169, is the prose commentary that Asaṅga wrote on his own verses, and that Vasubandhu probably wrote the commentary (on that?) translated by Bodhiruci and again by I Ching which constitutes T. 1511 and T. 1513 respectively. Finally, he gives an analysis of T. 1510, ascribing it (confusingly) to Vasubandhu. Frauwallner ascribes a commentary on the *Vajra* to Vasubandhu "the elder". At the moment it is difficult to say much that is definitive about all this.

544. T. 1532 = Nanjio 1193, ascribed to Vasubandhu by Susumu Yamaguchi. See Mejor, op. cit., p. 10, note 29.

545. T. 4061 = Tohoku 649. The alternative reconstruction of the title is Hajime Nakamura's, who remarks that it "teaches how to interpret and explain the content of a *sūtra*" (Nakamura, op. cit., p. 271).

546. Erich Frauwallner, "Vasubandhu's Vādavidhi", Wiener Zeitschrift fur die Kunde des Sud- und Ostasien 1, 1957, 104-134.

547. Anacker, *Seven Works of Vasubandhu*, op. cit., pp. 29-48.

548. The numbering corresponds to the enumeration of the fragments in Frauwallner, "Vasubandhu's Vādavidhi", op. cit. This enumeration is also followed in "T".

549. See Andre Bareau, *Les sectes bouddhiques...*, op. cit., pp. 180-189.

550. This section is translated by Brian Galloway, "A Yogācāra analysis of the mind, based on the Vijñāna section of Vasubandhu's Pañcaskandhaprakaraṇa with Guṇaprabha's commentary", Journal of the International Association of Buddhist Scholars 3.2, 1980, pp. 7-20.

551. French at Melanges chinois et bouddhiques 4, 1935-6, pp. 151-288; English from Berkeley, California 1988.

552. Anacker, *Seven Works of Vasubandhu*, op. cit., pp. 83-156.

553. Attention is also drawn to explanatory articles by G. Morichini, "The spiritual struggle of Vasubandhu and his Karmasiddhiprakaraṇa", East and West 6.1, 1955, 1-33 and Stefan Anacker, "Vasubandhu's Karmasiddhiprakaraṇa and the problem of the highest meditations", Philosophy East and West 22, 1972, pp. 247-258.

554. Cf. *Paṭṭhāna* I.1.3.365, etc.

555. Paris 1907, 1911; Darbhanga 1970.

556. "Steadiness in awareness" is defined as meditational concentration at *Madhyānta-vibhāgabhāṣya* IV, 3.

557. This is similar to the argument on wood and fire in *Abhidharmakośa* IV, 2-3 and in *Karmasiddhi* 8. The more one studies the works of Vasubandhu, the less likely the theory of two Vasubandhus enunciated by Frauwallner appears to be valid.

558. Again very akin to the passages cited in footnote 554.

559. In this case Vasubandhu's interpretation actually does violence to the

verse; the verse clearly states that *all* the stages are unperfected, unperfected and perfected, and perfected.

**560.** It should be noted that Vasubandhu in this work distinguishes the "author", Maitreyanātha, from "the expounder of the text to us and others".

**561.** Tokyo 1964.

**562.** *Seven Works of Vasubandhu*, op. cit., pp. 211-273.

**563.** We shall follow Nagao's practice and that of the Anacker translation in numbering the verses of the *Madhyāntavibhāga* starting with the second *kārikā* of the text. In reading the present summary as a commentary on the summary of 164.*Madhyāntavibhāga*, the commentary numbering thus corresponds to the "T" numbering of the earlier summary.

**564.** If one simply said "Everything is empty", this would be characterizing everything by a single characteristic, which would be a construction of that which was not; if one simply says "It is nonempty", that would be denying the possibility of emptying out all constructions from the flow.

**565.** This term is being used in Asaṅga's new sense of a witness consciousness connected with the illusion of self.

**566.** The appearances are false because a self does not exist, and because the perceptions appear with divisions which do not exist.

**567.** See *Abhidharmakośa* II, 23.

**568.** See *Abhidharmakośa* VI, 14-18, and the present work IV, 12b.

**569.** Characteristically, there is no "reality" in this work, only "realities" from different viewpoints.

**570.** The example is that of the painter who himself paints the painting of a demon, and then becomes frightened by what he has himself painted.

**571.** Just as an oil-lamp, as soon as it is lit, causes darkness to disappear, just so knowledge can suddenly arise in a consciousness-stream and cause all non-knowledge to disappear. Because this knowledge is non-discriminatory, it has nothing to do with any effort. So there is not really "anything to be done", any practice.

**572.** The discrimination arises, for instance, when it is said "The antidotes aren't arising the way they should", or "Afflictions have sure been going on for a long time!"

**573.** The example goes as follows: There may be a house where nobody has lit an oil-lamp for a thousand years. And then suddenly somebody comes there and lights one. In the same way, there may be affliction-series which have lasted thousands of years which disappear in one moment of insight.

**574.** Etienne Lamotte, *La Somme du Grand Véhicule*, op. cit.

**575.** This statement of Vasubandhu's seems to imply the possibility of external stimuli for the sensory consciousness.

**576.** The same arguments are found at *Karmasiddhi* 27.

**577.** Similar argument in *Karmasiddhi* 28, except that there, even the possiblity of a retributional awareness in the usual sense is ruled out.

578. This Chapter is translated into French in Etienne Lamotte, "L'*ālayavijñāna*...dans le Mahāyānasaṃgraha", op. cit.

579. This seems to be in contradiction to the comments on II, 24, but it is a contradiction frequently met in Yogācāra texts--at *Madhyāntavibhāga-bhāṣya* I, 4 it is said that defilement and purification cannot be denied, but in V of the same text it is clearly stated that defilement does not really exist.

580. Krishnanath Chatterjee's translation of *Triṃśikā* with Sthiramati's *Bhāṣya*, Anviksa 3.1, 1968 - 6, 1972. Reprinted in K.N. Chatterjee, *Vasubandhu's Vijñapti-mātratā-siddhi* (Varanasi 1980), 33-133.

581. (Paris 1925; reprinted Tokyo, n.d.)

582. Anacker, *Seven Works of Vasubandhu*, op. cit., pp. 181-190, 422-423.

583. These magical beings, Anacker tells us, "are those that arise all at once, with all their organs neither lacking nor deficient. They do not have to undergo embryonic stages or any other development. Traditionally, gods, hell-beings, and the intermediate existences between one full life-'series' and the next (the *bardo* of...*The Tibetan Book of the Dead*) are considered to be" such beings. (Cf. T, p. 176, footnotes 7-8).

584. Melanges chinois et bouddhiques 2, 1932-33, pp. 147-161.

585. Anacker, *Seven Works of Vasubandhu*, op. cit., pp. 287-298, 464-466.

586. Cf. *Madhyāntavibhāgabhāṣya* I, 10-11a.

587. The store-consciousness of "seeds" of residual impressions is like the *mantra* which makes the magical creation arise, because it is only by power of traces that dualities appear to arise. The constructing of dualities is like the appearance of the apparitional elephant in the magic show. The dualities which are held to are like the elephant, or the belief in the elephant's existence. What underlies it, nondual suchness or emptiness, is like the wood the magician has before him.

588. Cf. *Madhyāntavibhāgabhāṣya* I, 6-7.

589. Visvabharati Annals 2, 1949.

590. Collett Cox, *Disputed Dharmas*, op. cit., p. 53.

591. Ibid., p. 56.

592. Cox, ibid.

593. Cox, ibid., p. 54.

594. Cox,ibid., p. 54.

# GLOSSARY-INDEX

The following Index attempts to provide a guide to references to names, titles and topics. It also indicates which Sanskrit words are likely to be translated by which English expressions, and vice-versa. Page references in bold face indicate the primary citation of the work.

# ENCYCLOPEDIA OF INDIAN PHILOSOPHIES (27 Vols.)

## General Editor *Karl H. Potter*

The aim of this series is to present the contents of different streams of Indian Philosophical texts to make more and more people aware about Indian Philosophical thought, citing experts on the points that seem debatable. So far, **thirteen** volumes have been brought out.

**Vol. I: Bibliography (Sections I and II)** indicates the scope of the project and provides a list of sources which will be surveyed in the subsequent volumes, as well as provides a guide to secondary literature for further study of Indian Philosophy.

**Vol. II: Indian Metaphysics and Epistemology** provides a detailed résumé of current knowledge about the classical Indian philosophical system of Nyāya-Vaiśeṣika in its earlier stages. It covers the literature from the beginning, i.e., the *sūtra* of Gautama and Kaṇāda up to the time of Gaṅgeśa (about 1350 A.D.). Herein are included summaries of the major works of the school.

**Vol. III: Advaita Vedānta (Part I)** summarizes early Advaita Vedānta upto Śaṅkara's pupils. An introduction introduces to the concepts utilized by Gauḍapāda, Śaṅkarācārya and Maṇḍanamiśra in expounding and defending the Advaita views. This is followed by summaries of all the authentic works of these authors together with those of Sureśvara and Padmapāda.

**Vol. IV: Sāṁkhya** includes lengthy introduction (by G. J. Larson) which discusses the history of the system and its philosophical contours overall. The remainder of the volume includes summaries in English of all extant Sanskrit texts of the Sāṁkhya system.

**Vol. V: The Philosophy of the Grammarians** summarizes the main sources concentrating on the philosophical ideas contained therein. An exhaustive bibliography of original and secondary writings on the philosophy of grammar is also appended.

**Vol. VI: Indian Philosophical Analysis** takes up the history of Nyāya-Vaiśeṣika where Volume Two left off, i.e., from Gaṅgeśa to Raghunātha Śiromaṇi, in the 14th century. It also reconstructs the development of Nyāya-Vaiśeṣika through the next two centuries.

**Vol. VII: Abhidharma Buddhism to 150 A.D.** summarizes as the gist of Buddhist philosophical teachings, termed Abhidharma, from the first texts that developed after the Buddha. All the texts summarized here originated in a period from no earlier than 350 B.C. through no later than 150 A.D.

**Vol. VIII: Buddhist Philosophy from 100 to 350 A.D.** limits itself to chronologically summarize texts of philosophical interest with all its polemics well expounded in a context where defence of one view among alternatives is appropriate.

**Vol. IX: Buddhist Philosophy from 350 to 600 A.D.** The most important author treated here is clearly Dignaga, who is almost entirely responsible for turning Indian Buddhism toward an exhaustive analysis of epistemic considerations and in particular of inferential reasoning. Among other authors whose works are summarized here include Yogacara commentators, Buddapalita and Bhavya.

**Vol. X: Jain Philosophy (Part-1)** explores the basic questions and their possible answers regarding the position which lead to evident problems in assessing any of the philosophical thesis broached by a Jain.

**Vol. XI: Advaita Vedānta from 800 to 1200 A.D.** takes up the history of that movement from where Volume Three of this Encyclopedia left off, and covers the literature from Vācaspati Miśra in the tenth century to Citsukha in the thirteenth.

**Vol. XII: Yoga** volume traces the intellectual history of Pātañjala Yoga philosophy from the early centuries of the Common Era through the twentieth century and provides a systematic discussion of the philosophy of classical Yoga. Altogether the volume contains summaries and or notations for some seventy-five Sanskrit texts.

**Vol. XIII : Nyāya-Vaiśeṣika philosophy from 1515 to 1660 A.D. (2010)** resumes the history of Nyāya-Vaiśeṣika from Volume Six of the series and brought up to the time of Gadādhara (ca. 1660). This is the period of the great sub-commentators (Jagadīśa, Mathurānātha, Gadādhara) on Raghunātha Śiromaṇi's *Tattvacintāmaṇididhiti*, the culmination of some of the most intricate philosophical analysis the world has ever known.